Collins EUROPE
ESSENTIAL ROAD

Published by Collins
An imprint of HarperCollins Publishers
Westerhill Road
Bishopbriggs
Glasgow G64 2QT
www.harpercollins.co.uk

First published 2004

New edition 2019

© HarperCollins Publishers Ltd 2019
Maps © Collins Bartholomew Ltd 2019

Collins® is a registered trademark of HarperCollins Publishers Ltd

A catalogue record for this book is available from the British Library

ISBN 978-0-00-831975-5

10 9 8 7 6 5 4 3 2 1

Printed by RR Donnelley APS Co Ltd, China

All mapping in this atlas is generated from Collins Bartholomew digital databases. Collins Bartholomew, the UK's leading independent geographical information supplier, can provide a digital, custom, and premium mapping service to a variety of markets.
For further information:
Tel: +44 (0)141 306 3752
e-mail: collinsbartholomew@harpercollins.co.uk
or visit our website at: www.collinsbartholomew.com

If you would like to comment on any aspect of this book, please contact us at the above address or online.
e-mail: collinsmaps@harpercollins.co.uk

 facebook.com/collinsref @collins_ref

Contents

Map symbols

Road maps	Carte routière	Strassenkarten
E55 Euro route number	Route européenne	Europastrasse
A13 Motorway	Autoroute	Autobahn
Motorway – toll	Autoroute à péage	Gebührenpflichtige Autobahn
Motorway – toll (vignette)	Autoroute à péage (vignette)	Gebührenpflichtige Autobahn (Vignette)
37 Motorway junction – full access	Echangeur d'autoroute avec accès libre	Autobahnauffahrt mit vollem Zugang
12 Motorway junction – restricted access	Echangeur d'autoroute avec accès limité	Autobahnauffahrt mit beschränktem Zugang
Motorway services	Aire de service sur autoroute	Autobahnservicestelle
309 Main road – dual carriageway	Route principale à chaussées séparées	Hauptstrasse – Zweispurig
Main road – single carriageway	Route principale à une seule chaussée	Hauptstrasse – Einspurig
516 Secondary road – dual carriageway	Route secondaire à chaussées séparées	Zweispurige Nebenstrasse
Secondary road – single carriageway	Route secondaire à seule chaussée	Einspurige Nebenstrasse
Other road	Autre route	Andere Strasse
Motorway tunnel	Autoroute tunnel	Autobahntunnel
Main road tunnel	Route principale tunnel	Hauptstrassetunnel
Motorway/road under construction	Autoroute/route en construction	Autobahn/Strasse im Bau
Road toll	Route à péage	Gebührenpflichtige Strasse
Distance marker / Distances in kilometres / Distances in miles (UK only)	Marquage des distances / Distances en kilomètres / Distances en miles (GB)	Distanz-Markierung / Distanzen in Kilometern / Distanzen in Meilen (GB)
Steep hill	Colline abrupte	Steile Strasse
2587 Mountain pass (height in metres)	Col (Altitude en mètres)	Pass (Höhe in Metern)
Scenic route	Parcours pittoresque	Landschaftlich schöne Strecke
International airport	Aéroport international	Internationaler Flughafen
Car transport by rail	Transport des autos par voie ferrée	Autotransport per Bahn
Railway	Chemin de fer	Eisenbahn
Tunnel	Tunnel	Tunnel
Funicular railway	Funiculaire	Seilbahn
Rotterdam Car ferry	Bac pour autos	Autofähre
2587 Summit (height in metres)	Sommet (Altitude en mètres)	Berg (Höhe in Metern)
Volcano	Volcan	Vulkan
Canal	Canal	Kanal
International boundary	Frontière d'Etat	Landesgrenze
Disputed International boundary	Frontière litigieuse	Umstrittene Staatsgrenze
Disputed Territory boundary	Frontière territoriale contestée	Umstrittene Gebietsgrenze
GB Country abbreviation	Abréviation du pays	Regionsgrenze
Urban area	Zone urbaine	Stadtgebiet
28 Adjoining page indicator	Indication de la page contigüe	Randhinweis auf Folgekarte
National Park	Parc national	Nationalpark

1:1 000 000

1 centimetre to 10 kilometres   0 10 20 30 40 50 60 70 80 km   1 inch to 16 miles
0 10 20 30 40 50 miles

City maps and plans	Plans de ville	Stadtpläne
★ Place of interest	Site d'intérêt	Sehenswerter Ort
Railway station	Gare	Bahnhof
Parkland	Espace vert	Parkland
Woodland	Espace boisé	Waldland
General place of interest	Site d'intérêt général	Sehenswerter Ort
Academic/Municipal building	Établissement scolaire/installations municipales	Akademisches/Öffentliches Gebäude
Place of worship	Lieu de culte	Andachtsstätte
Transport location	Infrastructure de transport	Verkehrsanbindung

Places of interest

	English	Français	Deutsch
🏛	Museum and Art Gallery	Musée / Gallerie d'art	Museum / Kunstgalerie
	Castle	Château	Burg / Schloss
	Historic building	Monument historique	historisches Gebäude
	Historic site	Site historique	historische Stätte
	Monument	Monument	Denkmal
	Religious site	Site religieux	religiöse Stätte
	Aquarium / Sea life centre	Aquarium / Parc Marin	Aquarium
	Arboretum	Arboretum	Arboretum, Baumschule
	Botanic garden (National)	Jardin botanique national	botanischer Garten
	Natural place of interest (other site)	Réserve naturelle	landschaftlich interessanter Ort
	Zoo / Safari park / Wildlife park	Parc Safari / Réserve sauvage / Zoo	Safaripark / Wildreservat / Zoo
★	Other site	Autres sites	Touristenattraktion
	Theme park	Parc à thème	Freizeitpark
	World Heritage site	Patrimoine Mondial	Weltkulturerbe
	Athletics stadium (International)	Stade international d'athlétisme	internationales Leichtathletik Stadion
⚽	Football stadium (Major)	Stade de football	Fußballstadion
	Golf course (International)	Parcours de golf international	internationaler Golfplatz
	Grand Prix circuit (Formula 1) / Motor racing venue / MotoGP circuit	Circuit auto-moto	Autodrom
	Rugby ground (International - Six Nations)	Stade de rugby	internationales Rugbystadion
	International sports venue	Autre manifestation sportive	internationale Sportanlage
	Tennis venue	Court de tennis	Tennis
Valcotos ⊛	Winter sports resort	Sports d'hiver	Wintersport

Country identifiers

A	Austria	Autriche	Österreich	I	Italy	Italie	Italien
AL	Albania	Albanie	Albanien	IRL	Ireland	Irlande	Irland
AND	Andorra	Andorre	Andorra	IS	Iceland	Islande	Island
B	Belgium	Belgique	Belgien	L	Luxembourg	Luxembourg	Luxemburg
BG	Bulgaria	Bulgarie	Bulgarien	LT	Lithuania	Lituanie	Litauen
BIH	Bosnia and Herzegovina	Bosnie-et-Herzégovine	Bosnien und Herzegowina	LV	Latvia	Lettonie	Lettland
BY	Belarus	Bélarus	Belarus	M	Malta	Malte	Malta
CH	Switzerland	Suisse	Schweiz	MA	Morocco	Maroc	Marokko
CY	Cyprus	Chypre	Zypern	MC	Monaco	Monaco	Monaco
CZ	Czechia (Czech Republic)	République tchèque	Tschechische Republik	MD	Moldova	Moldavie	Moldawien
D	Germany	Allemagne	Deutschland	MNE	Montenegro	Monténégro	Montenegro
DK	Denmark	Danemark	Dänemark	N	Norway	Norvège	Norwegen
DZ	Algeria	Algérie	Algerien	NL	Netherlands	Pays-Bas	Niederlande
E	Spain	Espagne	Spanien	NMK	North Macedonia	Macédoine du Nord	Nordmazedonien
EST	Estonia	Estonie	Estland	P	Portugal	Portugal	Portugal
F	France	France	Frankreich	PL	Poland	Pologne	Polen
FIN	Finland	Finlande	Finnland	RKS	Kosovo	Kosovo	Kosovo
FL	Liechtenstein	Liechtenstein	Liechtenstein	RO	Romania	Roumanie	Rumänien
FO	Faroe Islands	Iles Féroé	Färöer-Inseln	RSM	San Marino	Saint-Marin	San Marino
GB	United Kingdom GB & NI	Grande-Bretagne	Grossbritannien	RUS	Russia	Russie	Russland
GBA	Alderney	Alderney	Alderney	S	Sweden	Suède	Schweden
GBG	Guernsey	Guernsey	Guernsey	SK	Slovakia	République slovaque	Slowakei
GBJ	Jersey	Jersey	Jersey	SLO	Slovenia	Slovénie	Slowenien
GBM	Isle of Man	île de Man	Insel Man	SRB	Serbia	Sérbie	Serbien
GBZ	Gibraltar	Gibraltar	Gibraltar	TN	Tunisia	Tunisie	Tunisien
GR	Greece	Grèce	Griechenland	TR	Turkey	Turquie	Türkei
H	Hungary	Hongrie	Ungarn	UA	Ukraine	Ukraine	Ukraine
HR	Croatia	Croatie	Kroatien				

International road signs and travel web links

Informative signs

 Motorway
 Motorway
 End of motorway
 Lane for slow vehicles
 'Semi motorway'
End of 'Semi motorway'
European route number

Priority road
End of priority road
Priority over oncoming vehicles
One way street
One way street
No through road
Hospital
Parking
Pedestrian crossing
Subway or bridge for pedestrians

First aid post
Information
Hotel / Motel
Restaurant
Mechanical help
Filling station
Telephone
Camping site
Caravan site
Youth hostel

Warning signs

Right bend
Left bend
Double bend
Roundabout
Intersection with non-priority road
Traffic merges from left
Traffic merges from right
Road narrows

Road narrows at left
Road narrows at right
Give way
Slippery road
Uneven road
Steep hill – descent
Tunnel
Opening bridge
Road works
Loose chippings

Level crossing with barrier
Level crossing without barrier
Tram
'Count down' posts
'Danger' level crossing
Low flying aircraft
Falling rocks
Cross wind
Quayside or river bank
Two-way traffic

Traffic signals ahead
Pedestrians
Children
Animals
Wild animals
Other dangers
Width of carriageway
Beginning of regulation
Repetition sign
End of regulation

Regulative signs

End of all restrictions
Halt sign
Customs
No stopping ("clearway")
No parking/waiting
Priority to oncoming vehicles
Use of horns prohibited
Roundabout

Direction to be followed
Pass this side
Minimum speed limit
End of minimum speed limit
Cycle path
Footpath
Riders only
All vehicles prohibited
No entry for all vehicles
No right turn

No u-turns
No entry for motor cars
No entry for all motor vehicles
Lorries prohibited
Buses and coaches prohibited
No trailers
Motorcycles prohibited
Mopeds prohibited
Cycles prohibited
No entry for pedestrians

No overtaking
End of no overtaking
No overtaking for lorries
End of no overtaking for lorries
Laden weight limit
Axle weight limit
Width limit
Height limit
Maximum speed limit
End of speed limit

Travel & route planning

Driving information	www.drive-alive.co.uk
The AA	www.theaa.com
The RAC	www.rac.co.uk
ViaMichelin	www.viamichelin.com
Bing Maps	www.bing.com/mapspreview
Motorail information	www.seat61.com/Motorail
Ferry information	www.aferry.com
Eurotunnel information	www.eurotunnel.com/uk/home/

General information

UK Foreign & Commonwealth Office	www.gov.uk/government/organisations/foreign-commonwealth-office
Country profiles	www.cia.gov/library/publications/resources/the-world-factbook/index.html
World Heritage sites	whc.unesco.org/en/list
World time	wwp.greenwichmeantime.com
Weather information	www.metoffice.gov.uk

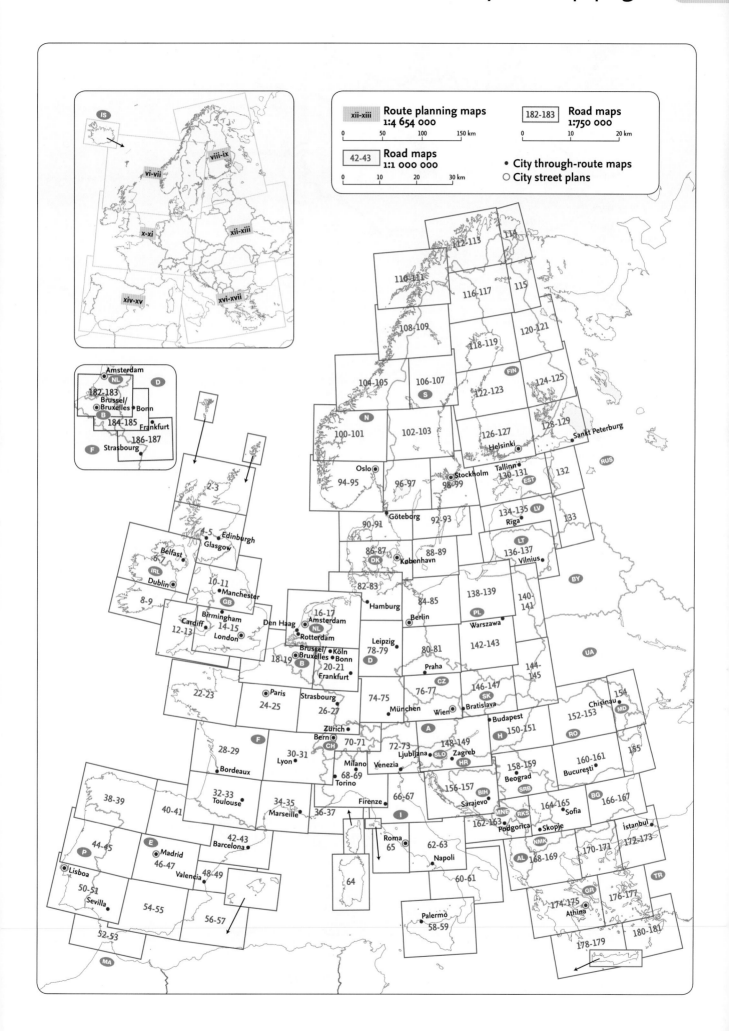

Route planning maps xii-xiii 1:4 654 000
0   50   100   150 km

Road maps 42-43 1:1 000 000
0   10   20   30 km

Road maps 182-183 1:750 000
0   10   20 km

• City through-route maps
○ City street plans

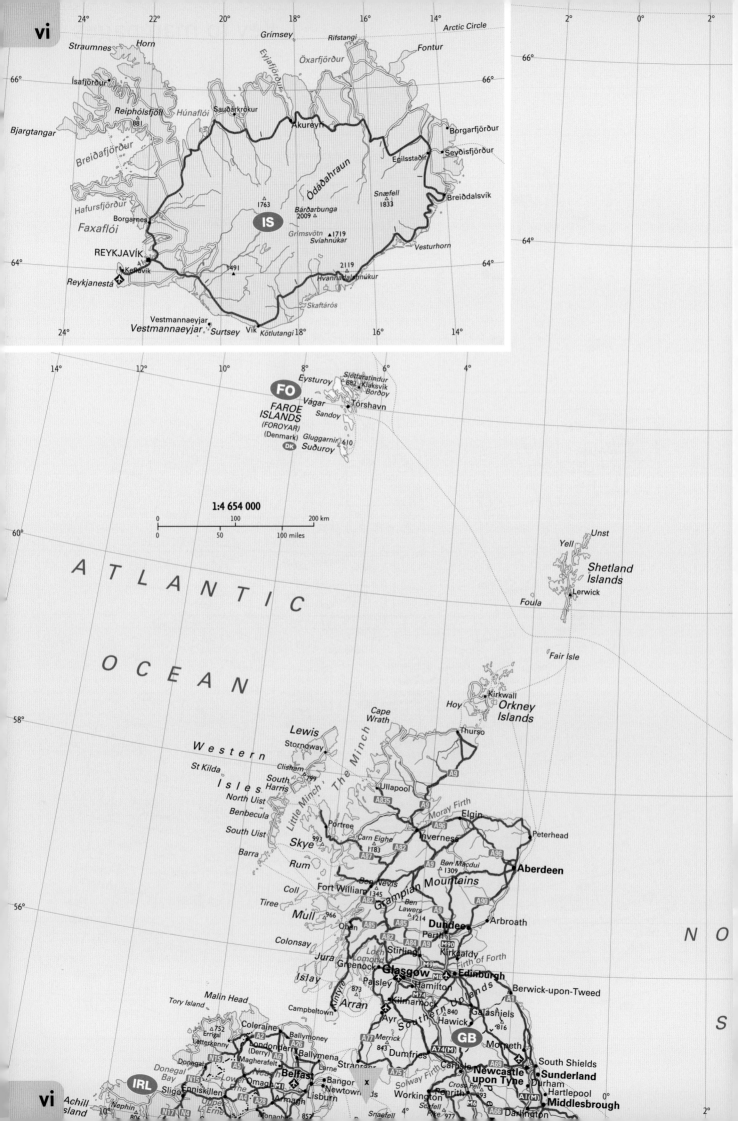

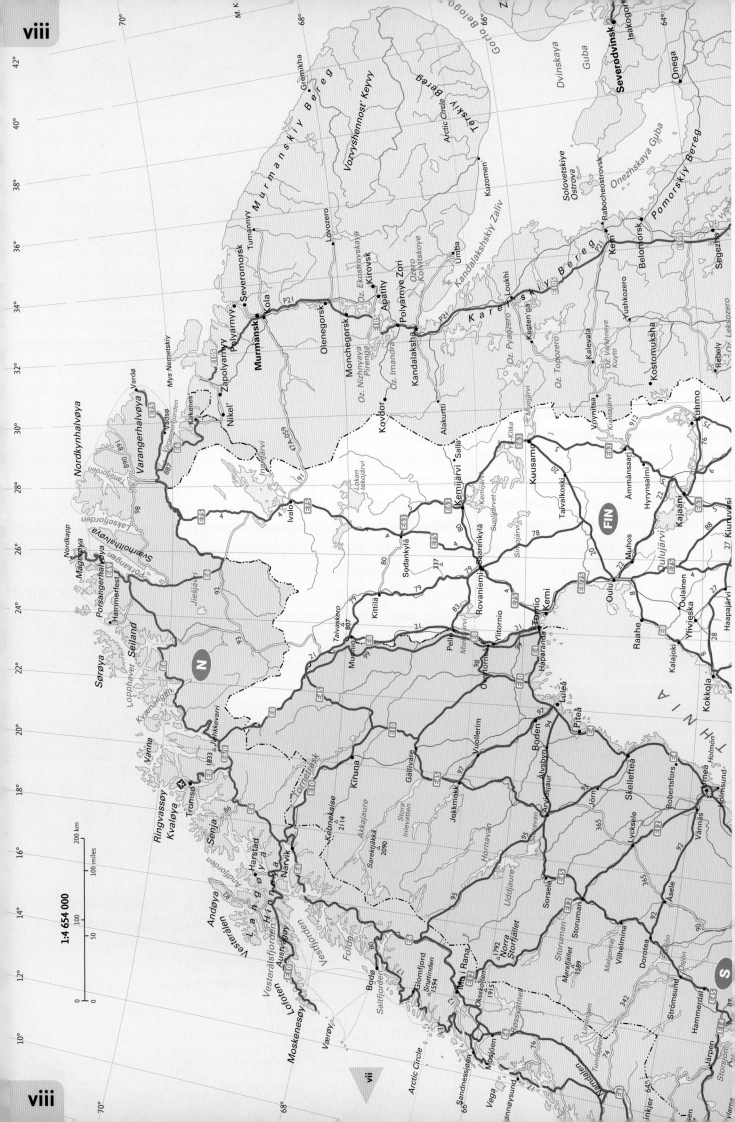

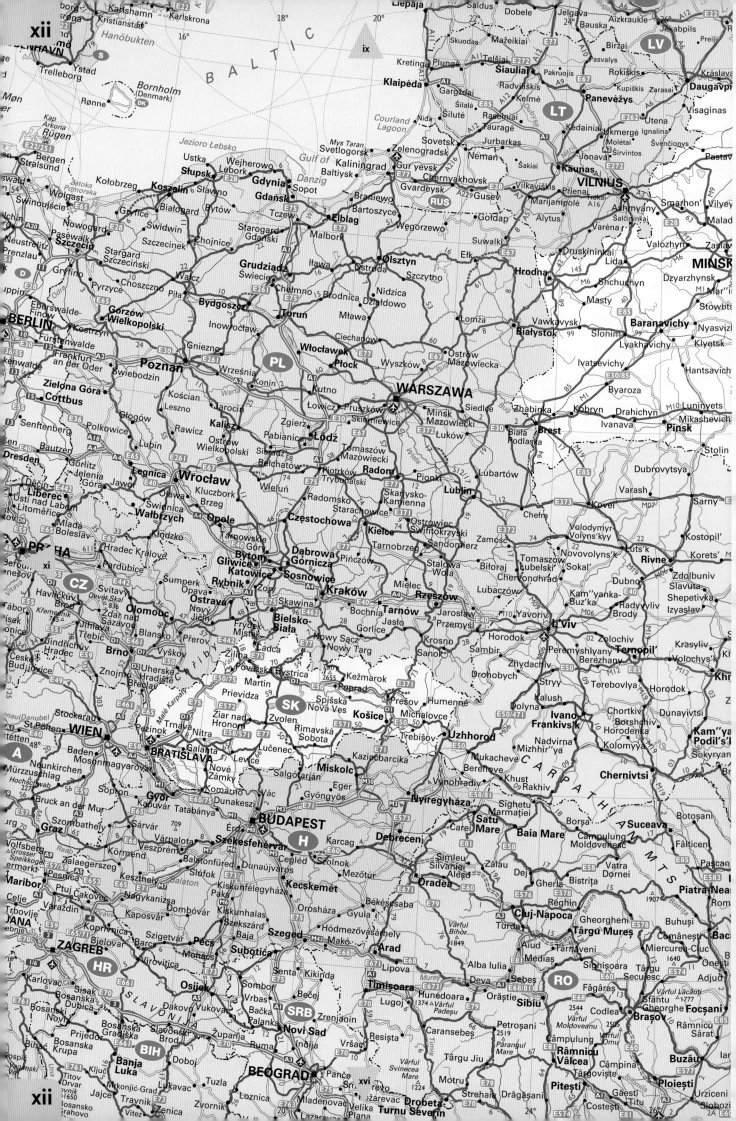

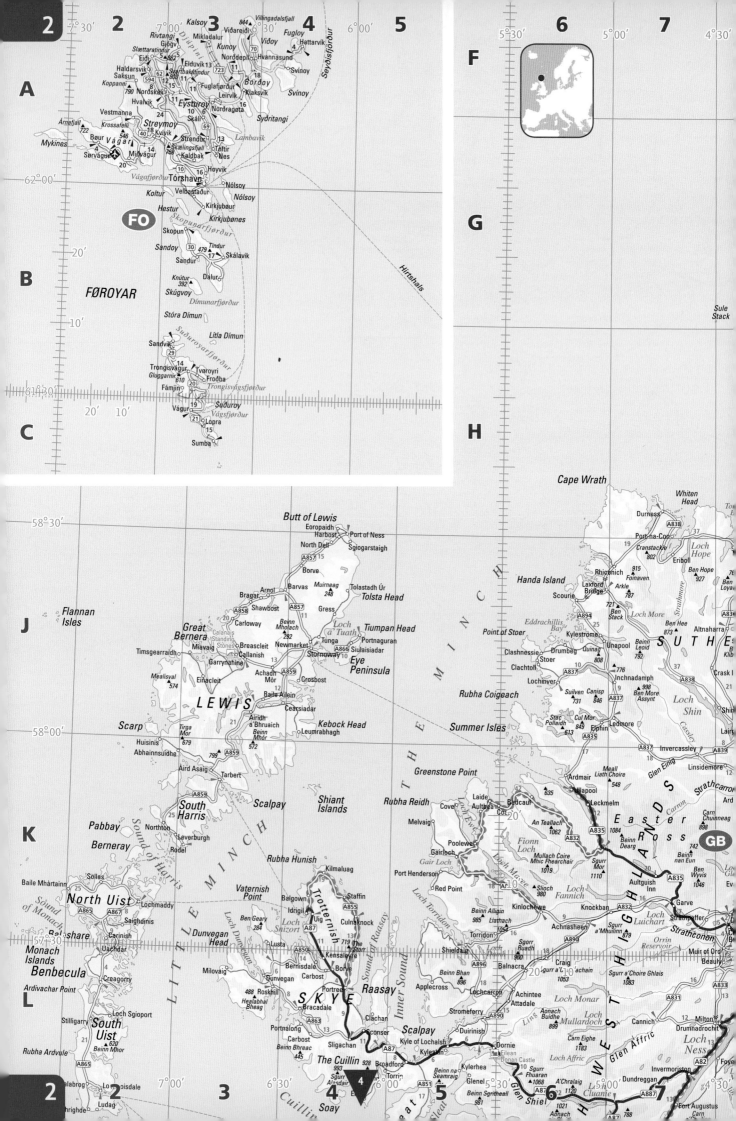

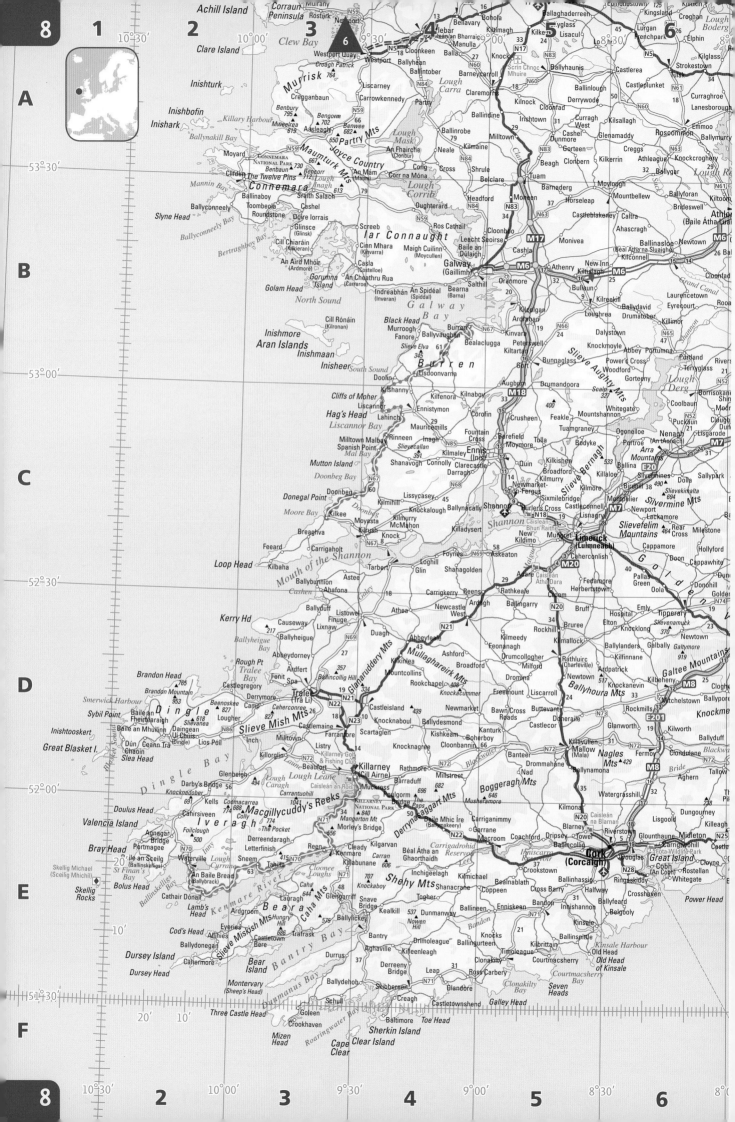

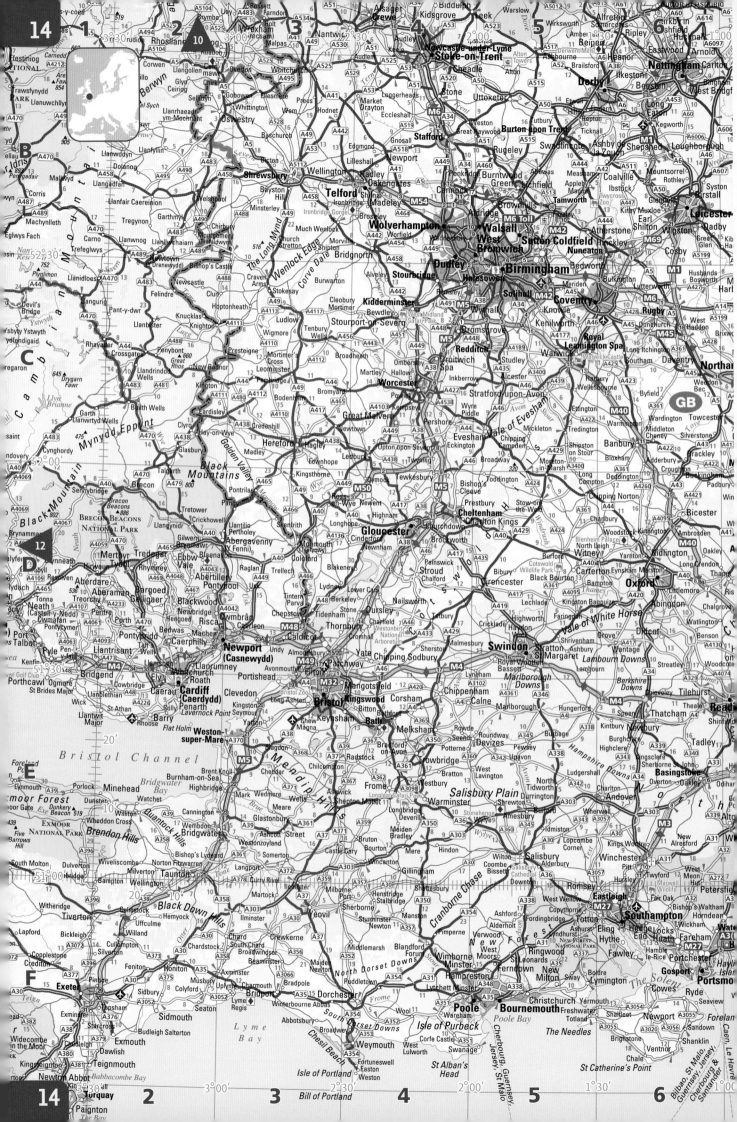

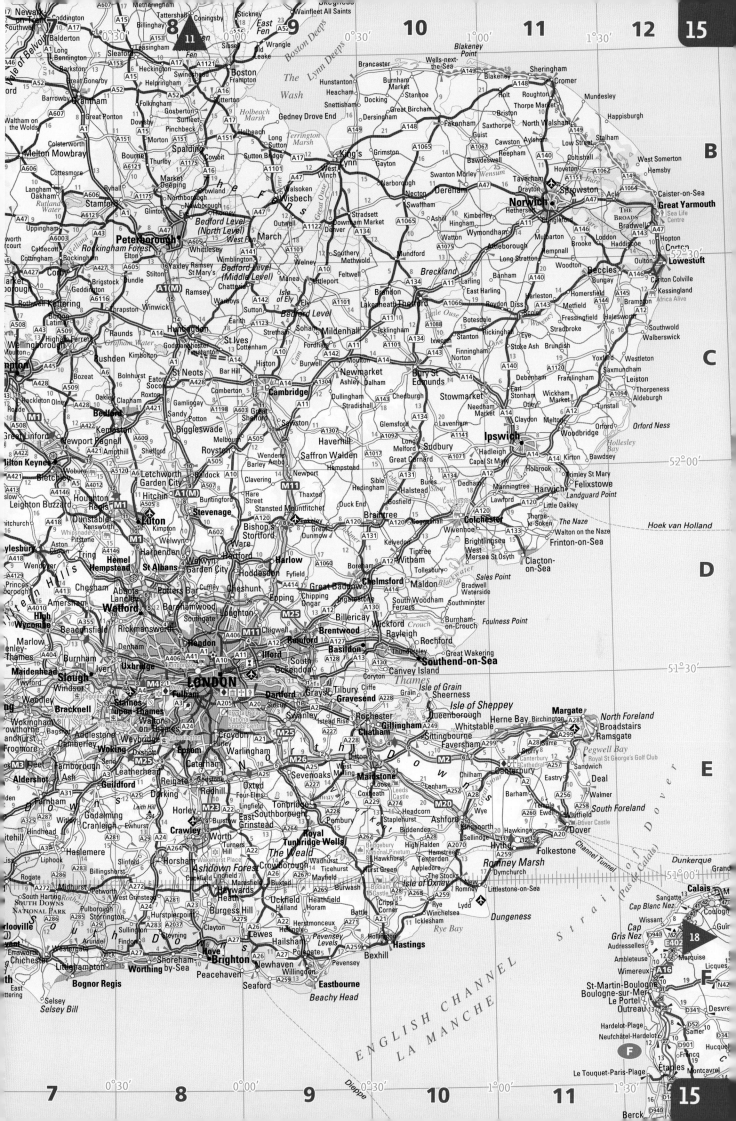

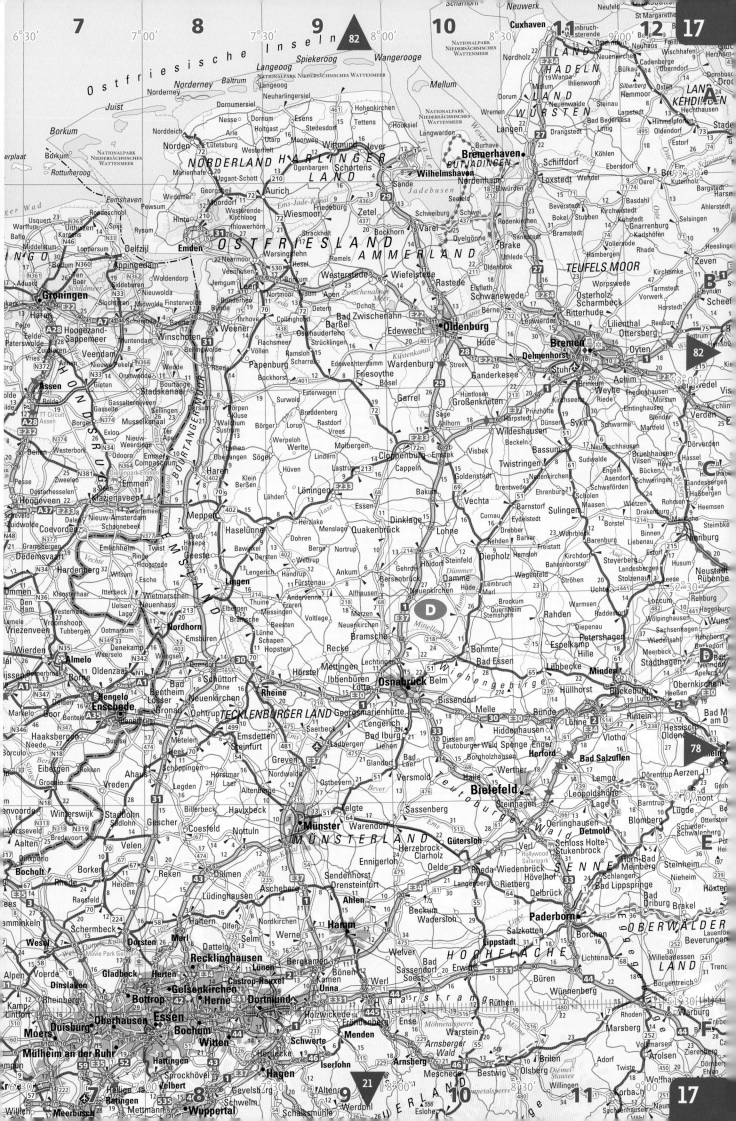

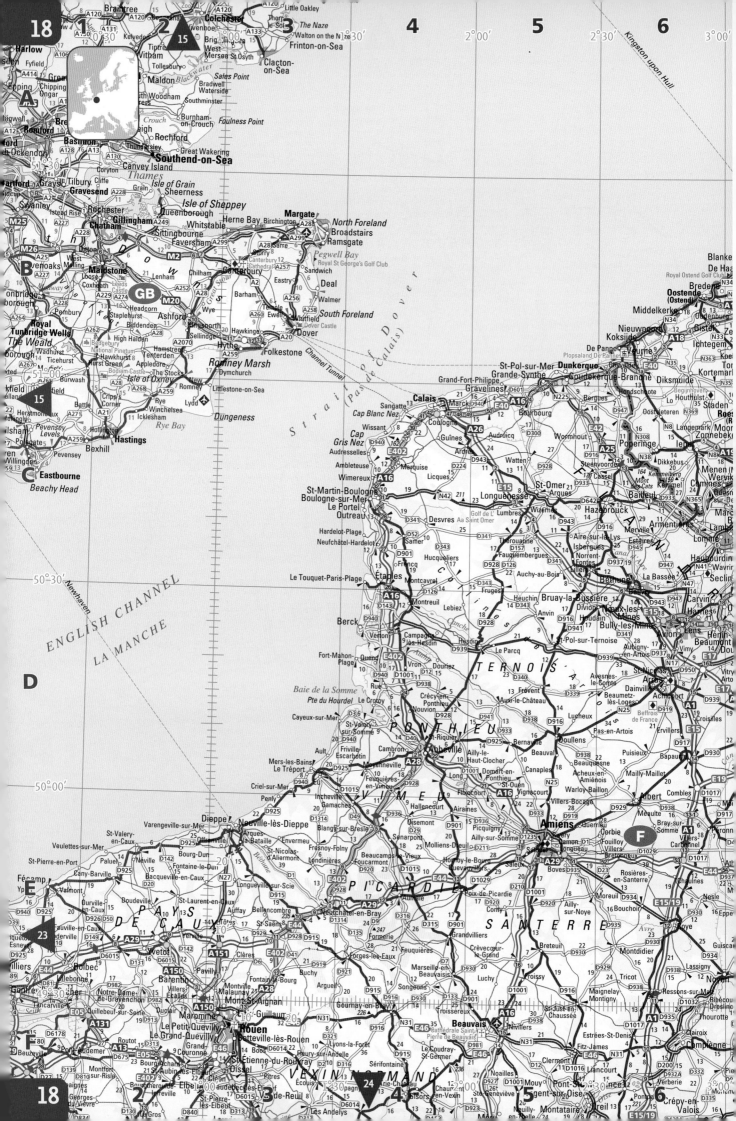

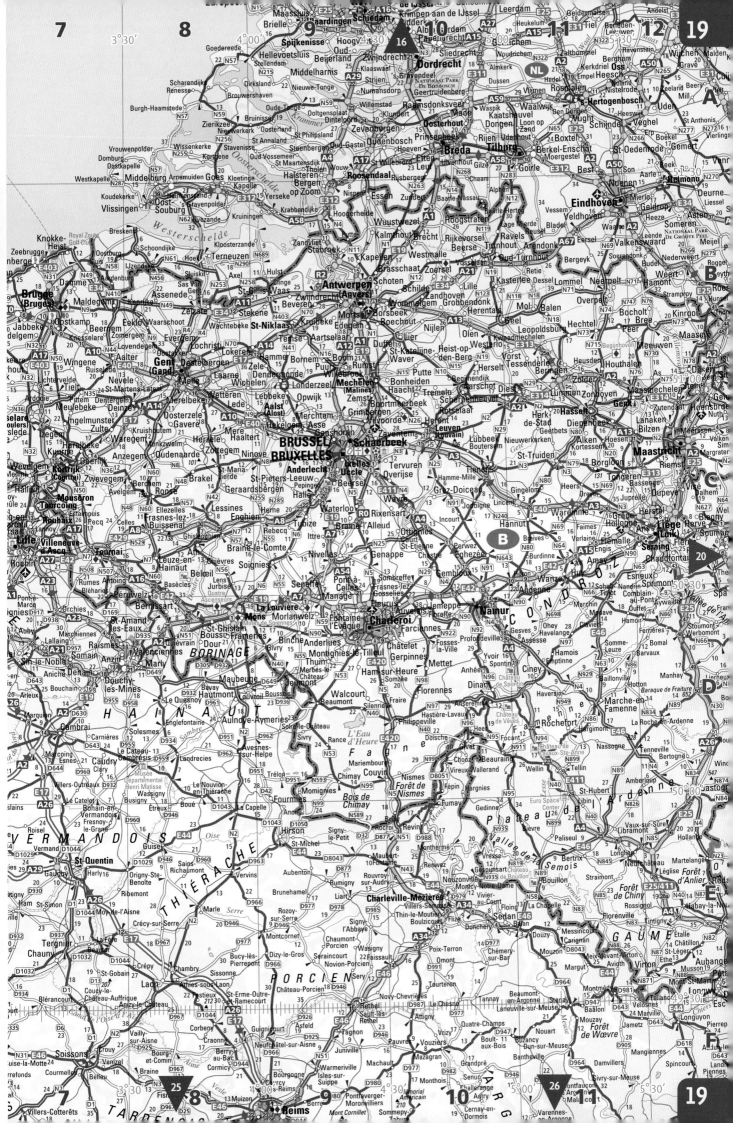

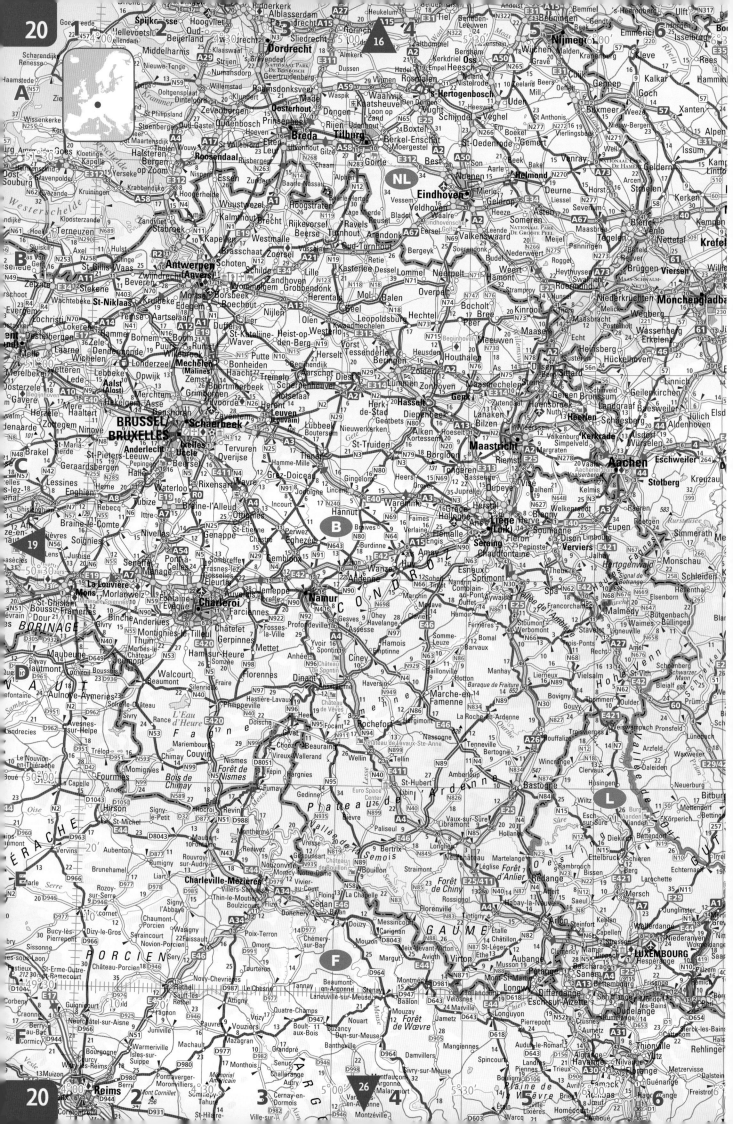

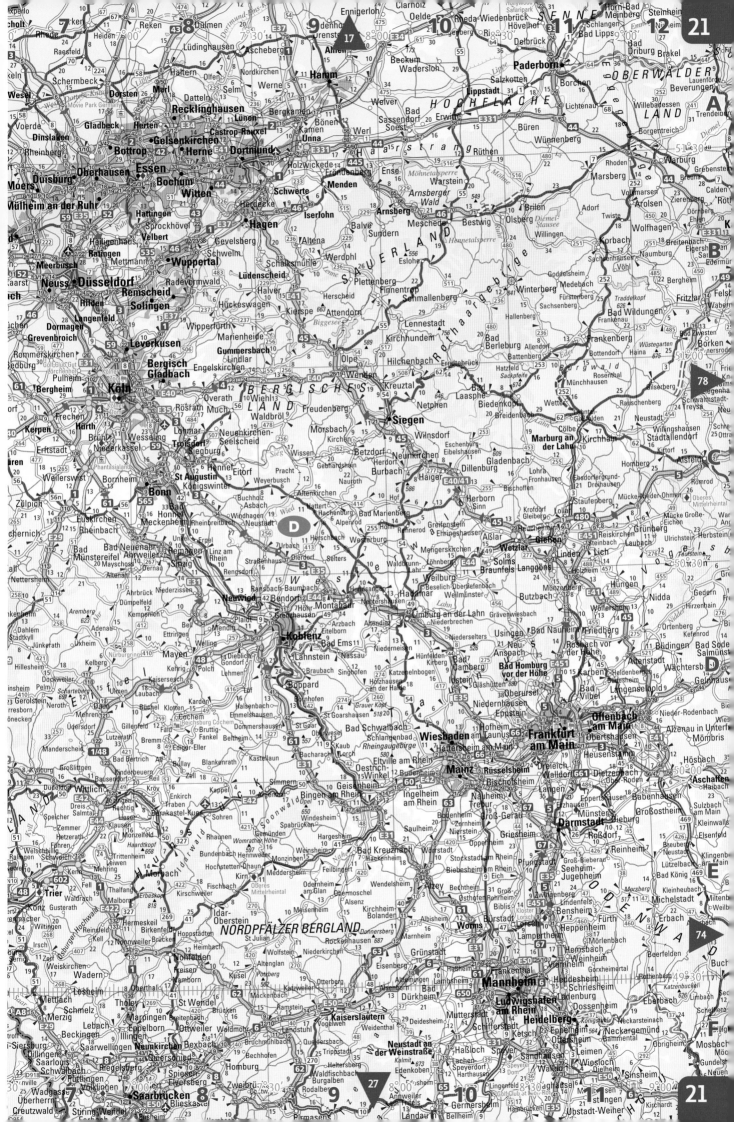

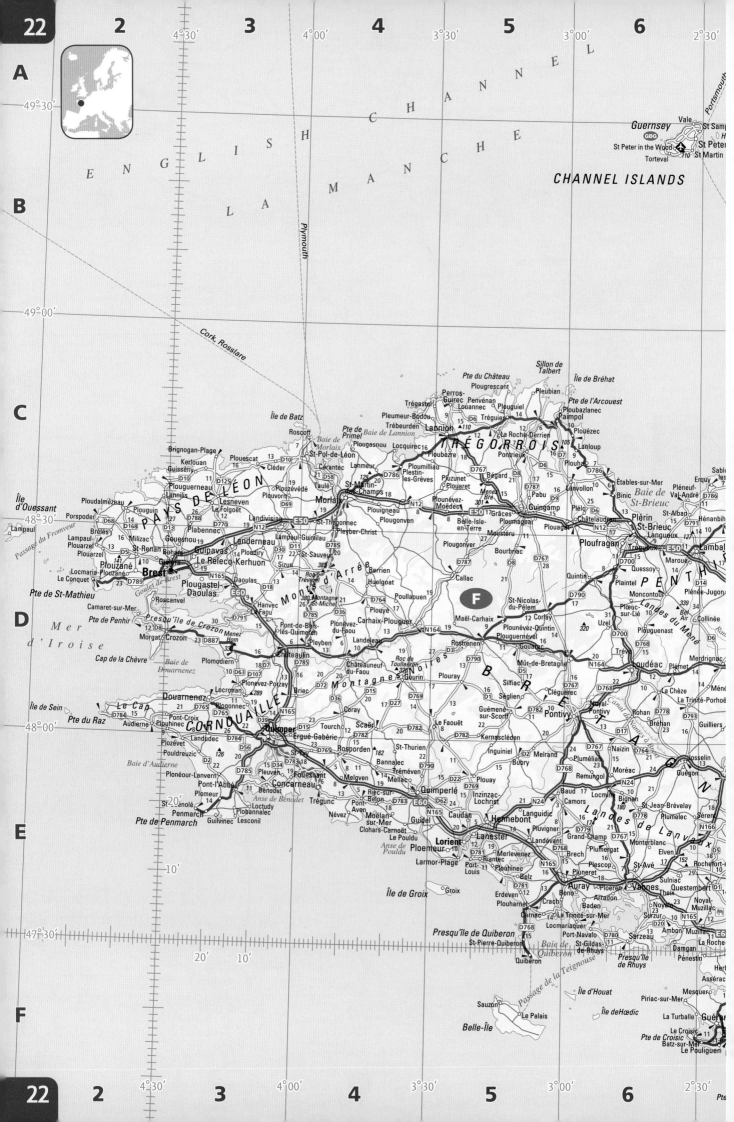

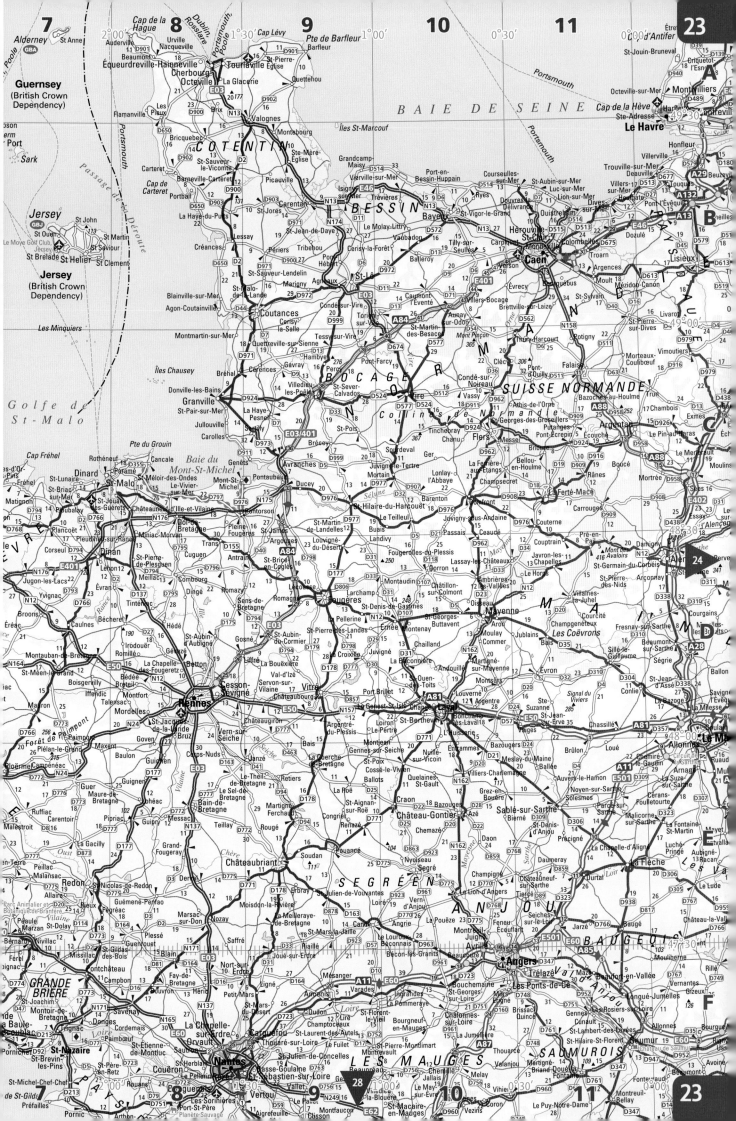

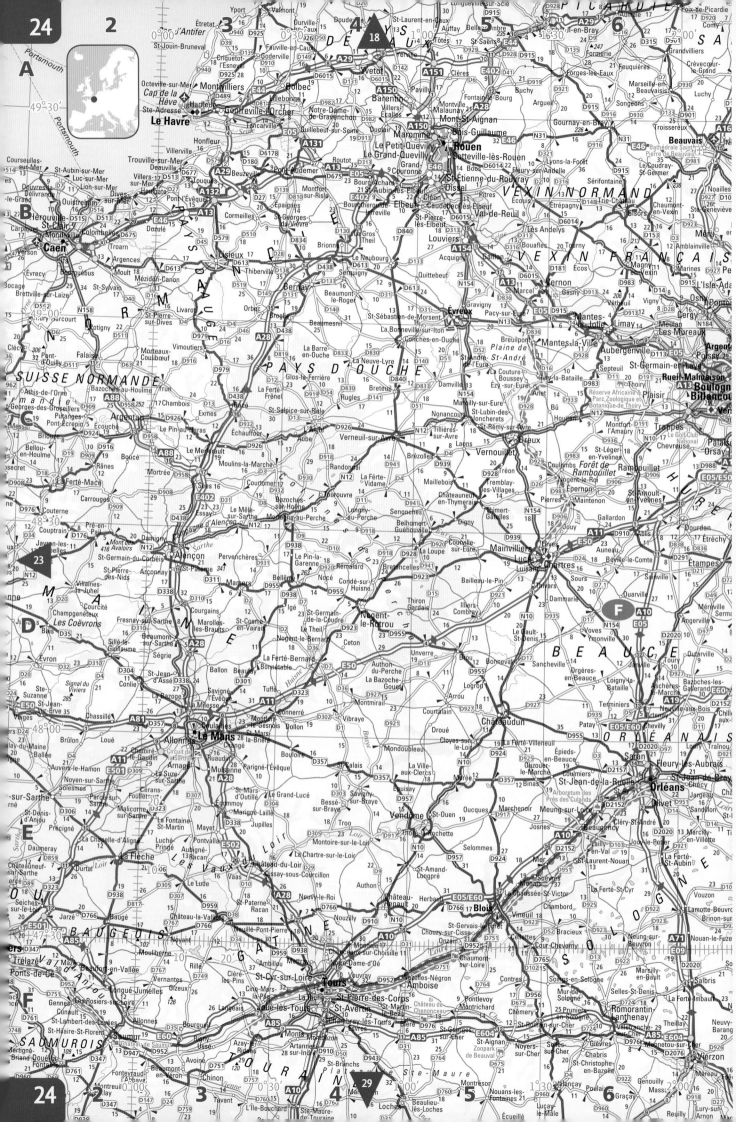

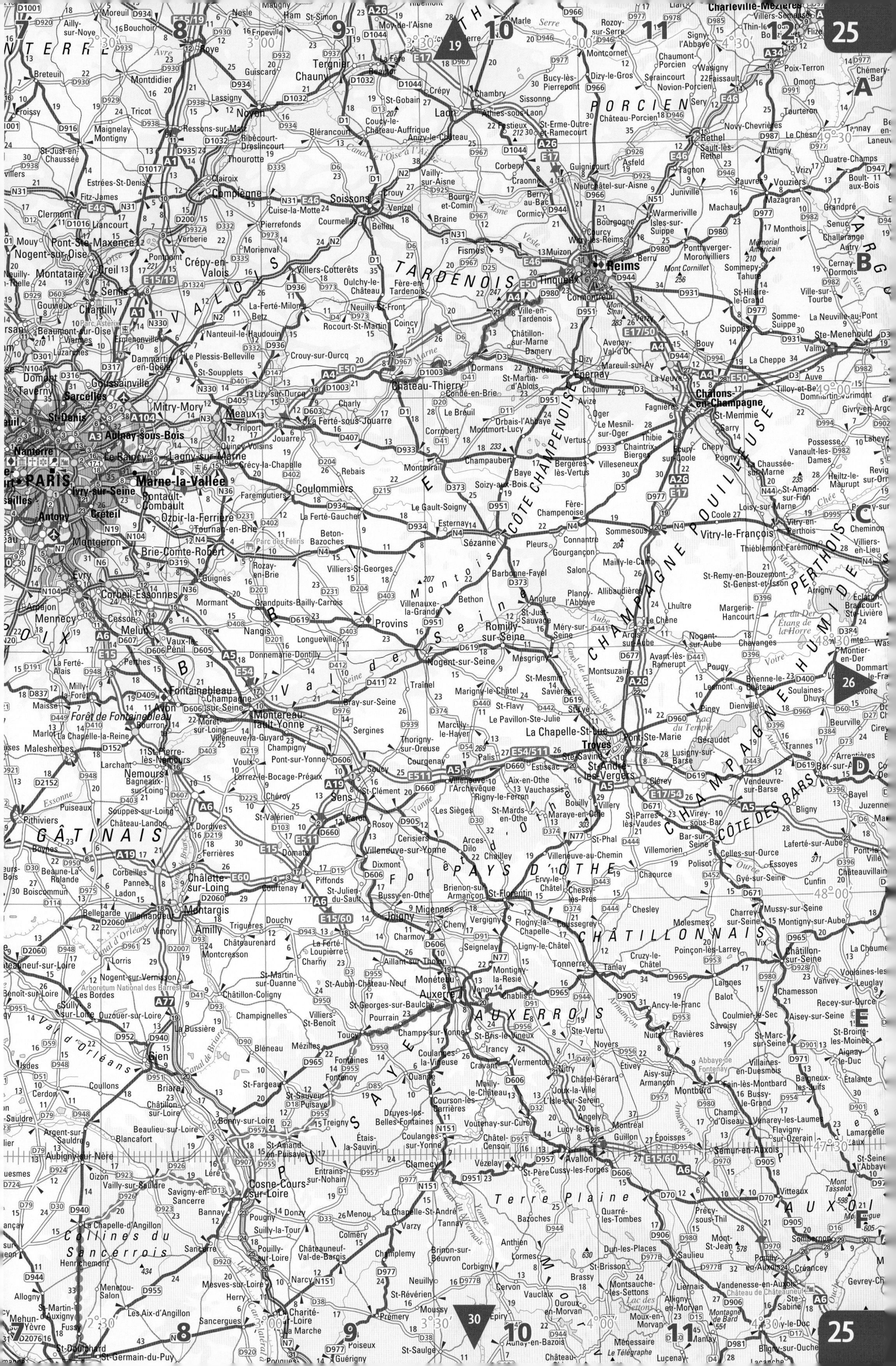

PARIS
Nanterre
St-Denis
Sarcelles
Aulnay-sous-Bois
Marne-la-Vallée
Ivry-sur-Seine
Créteil
Antony
Évry
Corbeil-Essonnes
Melun
Fontainebleau
Nemours
Montargis
Gien
Cosne-Cours-sur-Loire
La Charité-sur-Loire
Pithiviers
Meaux
Coulommiers
Provins
Nogent-sur-Seine
Montereau-Fault-Yonne
Sens
Joigny
Auxerre
Avallon
Clamecy
Vézelay
Saulieu
Semur-en-Auxois
Montbard
Tonnerre
Châtillon-sur-Seine
Bar-sur-Seine
Troyes
Romilly-sur-Seine
Sézanne
Épernay
Reims
Châlons-en-Champagne
Vitry-le-François
St-Dizier
Château-Thierry
Soissons
Laon
Compiègne
Noyon
Chauny
Creil
Senlis
Chantilly
Crépy-en-Valois
Villers-Cotterêts
Rethel
Vouziers
Ste-Menehould
Charleville-Mézières
VALOIS
TARDENOIS
PORCIEN
CÔTE CHAMPENOISE
CHAMPAGNE POUILLEUSE
CHAMPAGNE HUMIDE
PERTHOIS
Val de Seine
Montois
GÂTINAIS
PAYS D'OTHE
Forêt d'Othe
CHÂTILLONNAIS
CÔTE DES BARS
AUXERROIS
PUISAYE
Terre Plaine
Collines du Sancerrois
Val d'Orléans
AUXOIS
Forêt de Fontainebleau
19
26
30
7 8 9 10 11 12
A B C D E F

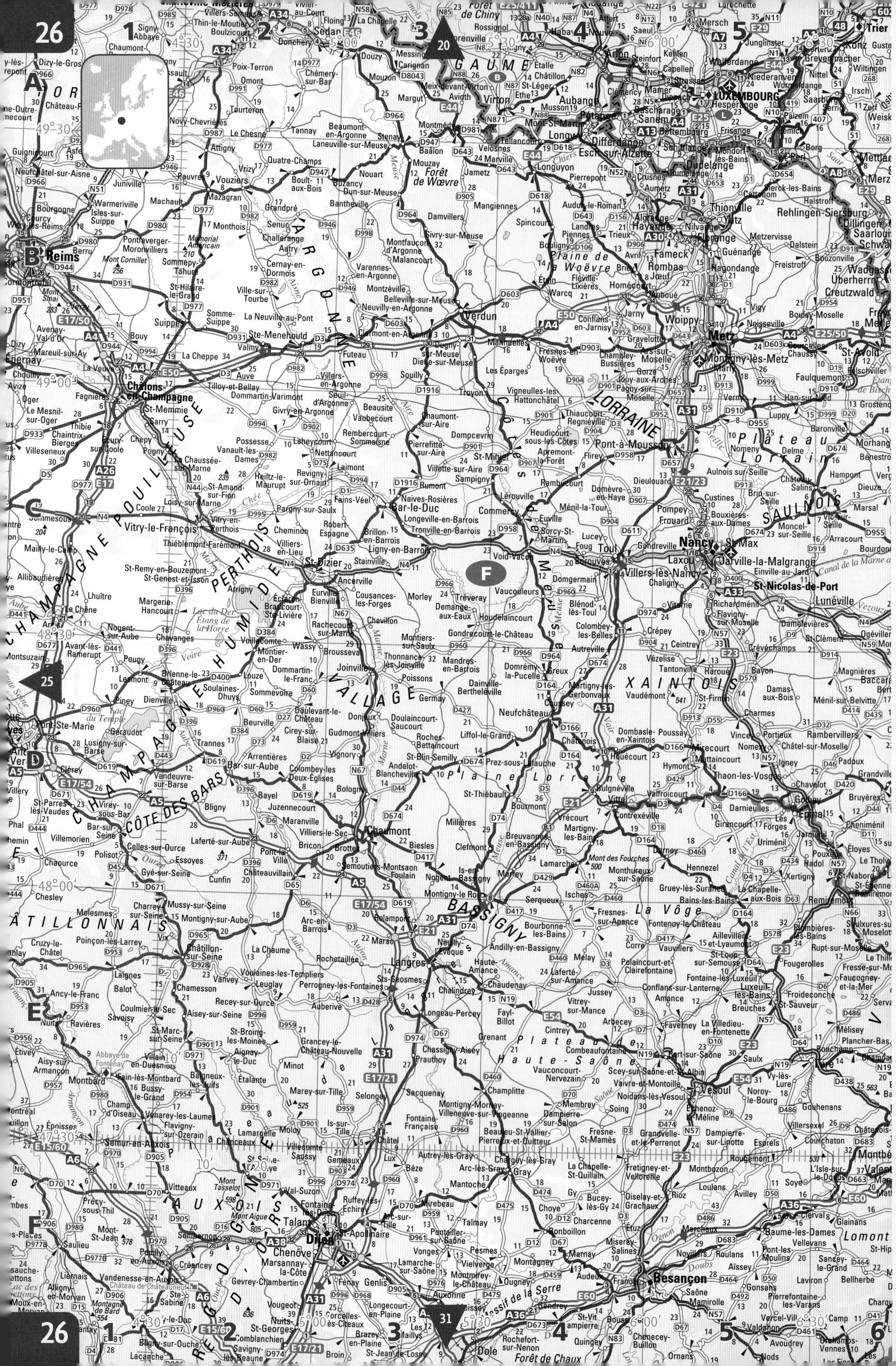

Reims
Châlons-en-Champagne
Verdun
Metz
Nancy
LUXEMBOURG
Arlon
Sedan
Trier
Thionville
Bar-le-Duc
St-Dizier
Toul
Épinal
Chaumont
Langres
Dijon
Besançon
Vesoul
Neufchâteau
Vitry-le-François
Troyes
Châtillon-sur-Seine
Montbard
Gray
Dole
Lunéville
St-Nicolas-de-Port
Pont-à-Mousson
Commercy
Joinville
Bar-sur-Aube
Vittel
Contrexéville
Remiremont
Luxeuil-les-Bains
Baume-les-Dames
Ste-Menehould
ARGONNE
LORRAINE
CHAMPAGNE POUILLEUSE
CHAMPAGNE HUMIDE
PERTHOIS
VALLAGE
BASSIGNY
XAINTOIS
SAULNOIS
GAUME
Plateau Lorrain
Plaine de la Woëvre
Plaine Lorraine
Plateau de Haute-Saône
La Vôge
AUXOIS
CÔTE DES BARS
CHÂTILLONNAIS
Massif de la Serre
Forêt de Chaux
Forêt de Wœvre

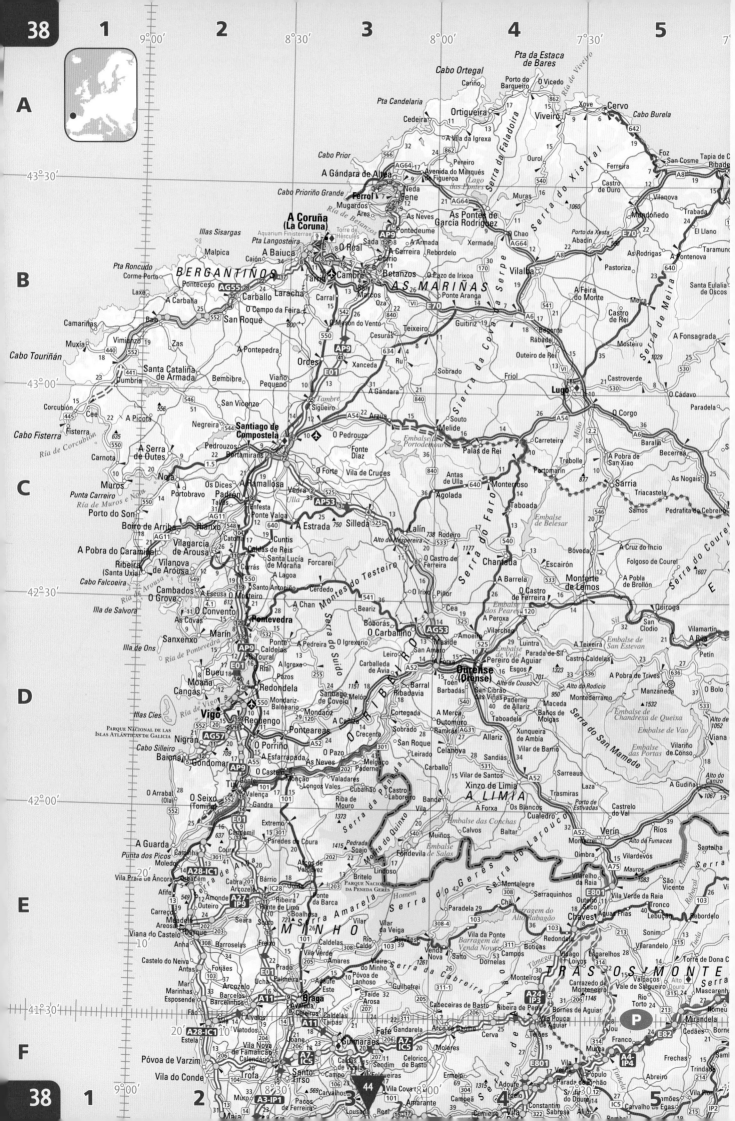

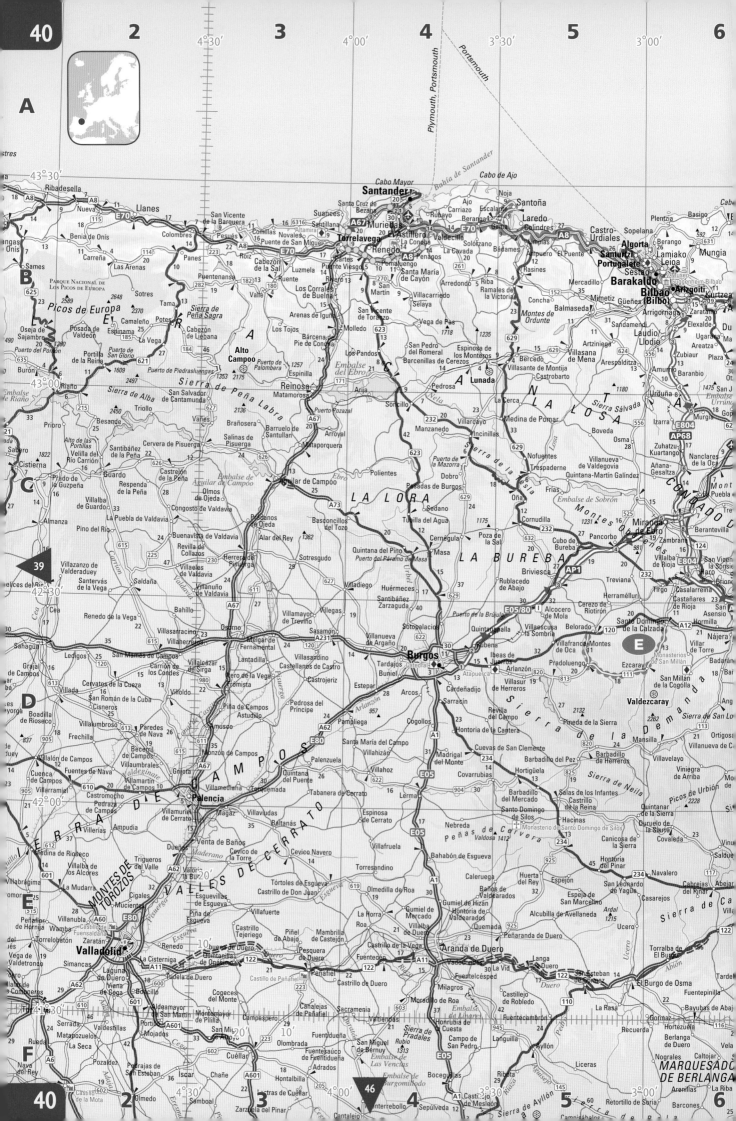

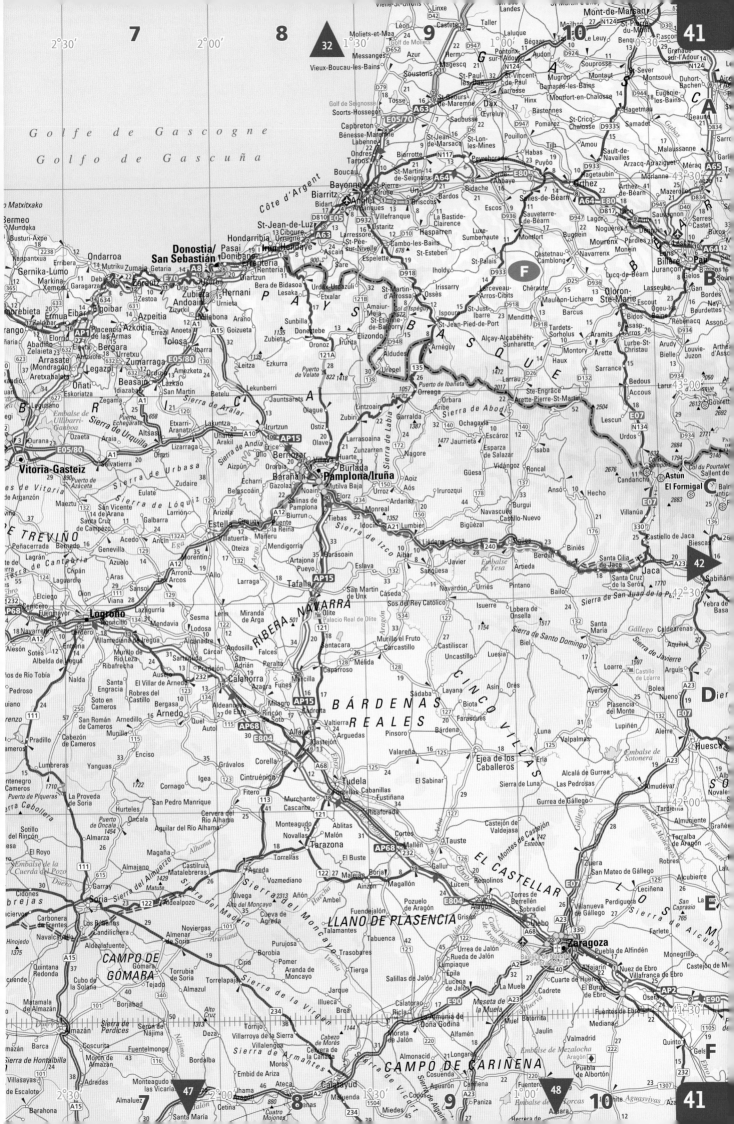

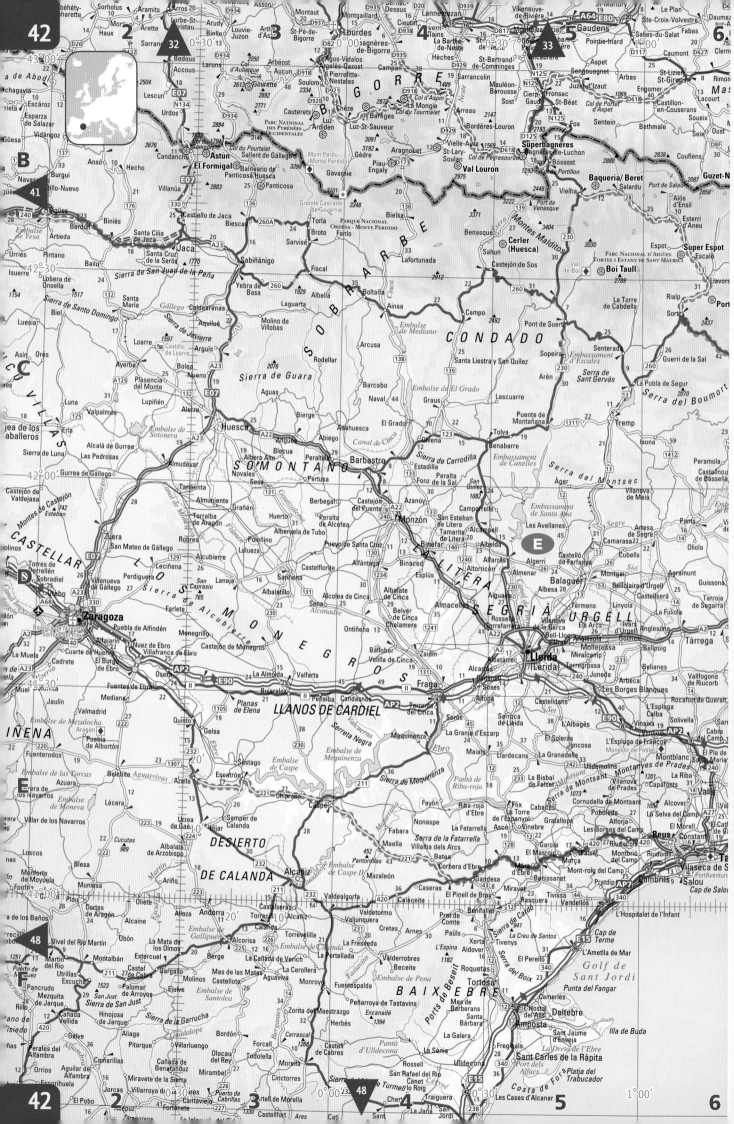

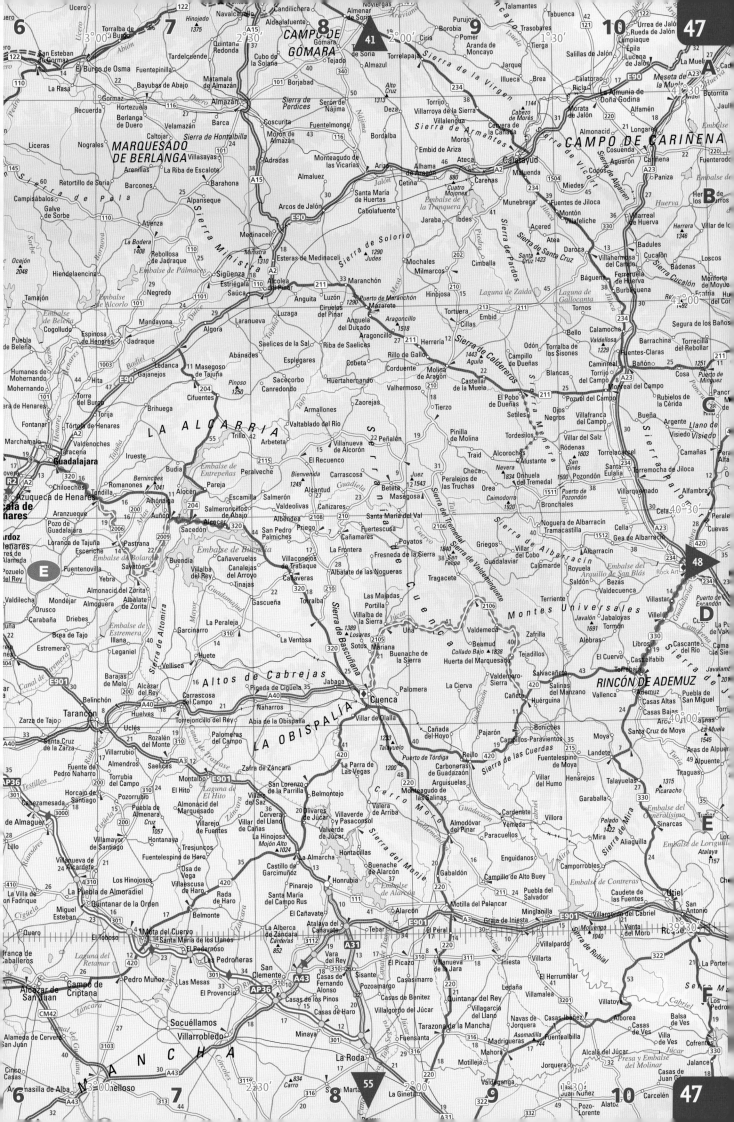

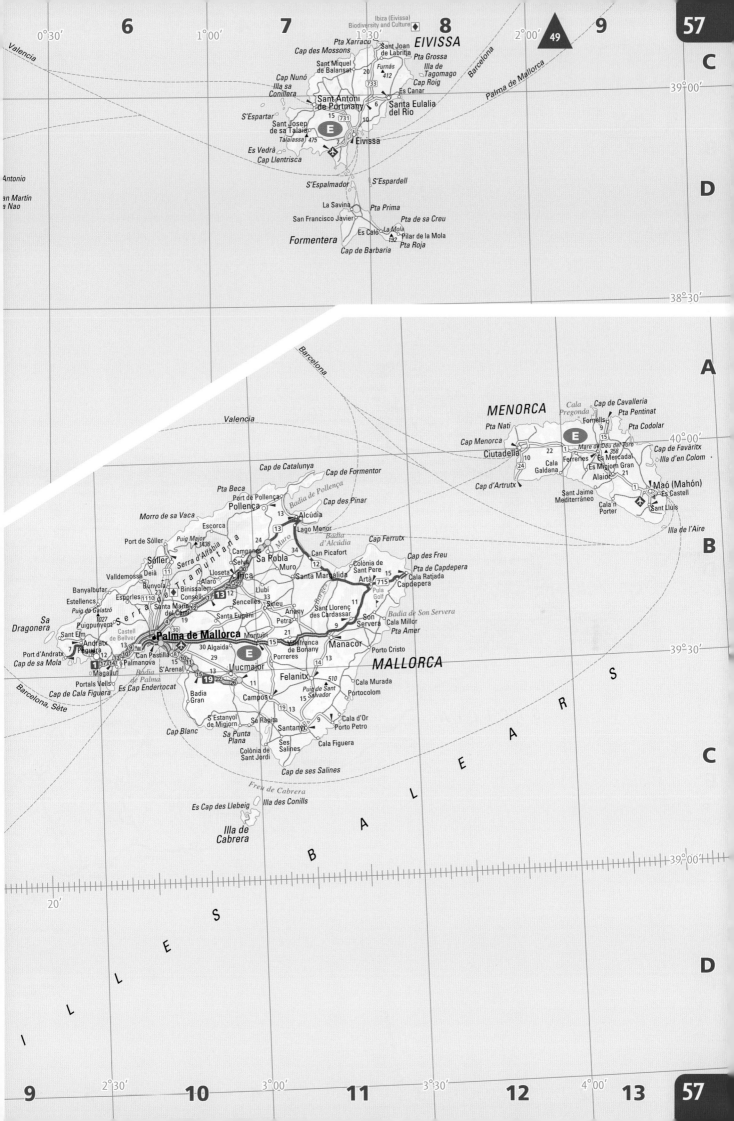

6   0°30'   1°00'   **7**   1°30'   **8**   2°00'   49   **9**

C

Ibiza (Eivissa)
Biodiversity and Culture

Pta Xarracó
Cap des Mossons
Sant Joan de Labritja
EIVISSA
Pta Grossa
Illa de Tagomago
Sant Miquel de Balansat
Furnás 412
Cap Nunó
Cap Roig
Illa sa Conillera
20
Es Canar
733
Sant Antoni de Portmany
39°00'
Santa Eulalia del Río
S'Espartar
6
731
Sant Josep de sa Talaia
E
10
Talaiassa 475
Eivissa
Es Vedrà
Cap Llentrisca

Valencia

an Antonio
an Martín
a Nao

D

S'Espalmador
S'Espardell

La Savina
Pta Prima
San Francisco Javier
Pta de sa Creu
Es Caló
La Mola
Pilar de la Mola
Formentera
192
Pta Roja
Cap de Barbaria

38°30'

Barcelona

A

Valencia

MENORCA
Cala Pregonda
Cap de Cavalleria
Pta Pentinat
Pta Nati
Fornells
Pta Codolar
9
Cap Menorca
E
40°00'
Ciutadella
22
Mare de Déu del Toro
Cap de Favàritx
10
Ferreries
358
Illa d'en Colom
Cala Galdana
24
Es Mercadal
Es Migjorn Gran
21
Alaior
1
Maó (Mahón)
Cap d'Artrutx
Sant Jaime Mediterráneo
Es Castell
Cala'n Porter
Sant Lluís
Illa de l'Aire

Cap de Catalunya
Cap de Formentor
Pta Beca
Port de Pollença
Badia de Pollença
Morro de sa Vaca
Pollença
Cap des Pinar
13
Alcúdia
Escorca
13
Lago Menor
Port de Sóller
Puig Major
24
Badia d'Alcúdia
Cap Ferrutx
Muro
Sóller
1436
Campanet
Can Picafort
Cap des Freu
Serra d'Alfàbia
Selva
Sa Pobla
34
Pta de Capdepera
Valldemossa
Deià
11
Lloseta
30
Muro
Artà
Cala Ratjada
Tramuntana
Alaró
Inca
12
Santa Margalida
715
Capdepera
Banyalbufar
Bunyola
23
Binissalem
25
Pula Golf
Estellencs
Esporles
1110
Consell
13
12
Sencelles
Llubí
33
Sineu
Puig de Galatzó
Santa Maria del Camí
Sant Llorenç des Cardassar
11
1027
Santa Eugeni
Petra
Badia de Son Servera
Puigpunyent
Arany
21
Son Servera
Sa Dragonera
Castell de Bellver
9
Cala Millor
Sant Elm
30
Palma de Mallorca
Pta Amer
Andratx
Montuïri
Porto Cristo
Peguera
13
Algaida
15
Porreres
Manacor
39°30'
Port d'Andratx
17 14
10
30
Can Pastilla
8
29
Villafranca de Bonany
Cap de sa Mola
1
Magaluf
11
Llucmajor
14
MALLORCA
Palmanova
S'Arenal
Felanitx
Portals Vells
19 22
13
510
Cala Murada
Cap de Cala Figuera
26
11
Puig de Sant Salvador
Portocolom
Barcelona, Sète
Es Cap Enderrocat
Badia de Palma
15
S Estanyol de Migjorn
Campos
Cala d'Or
Badia Gran
19 13
Porto Petro
Cap Blanc
Santanyí
9
Sa Punta Plana
Sa Rápita
Cala Figuera
Colònia de Sant Jordi
Ses Salines
Cap de ses Salines

B
A
L
E
A
R
S

C

Freu de Cabrera
Es Cap des Llebeig
Illa des Conills
Illa de Cabrera

39°00'

I
L
L
E
S

20'

B
A
L
E
A
R
S

I

D

9   2°30'   **10**   3°00'   **11**   3°30'   **12**   4°00'   **13**

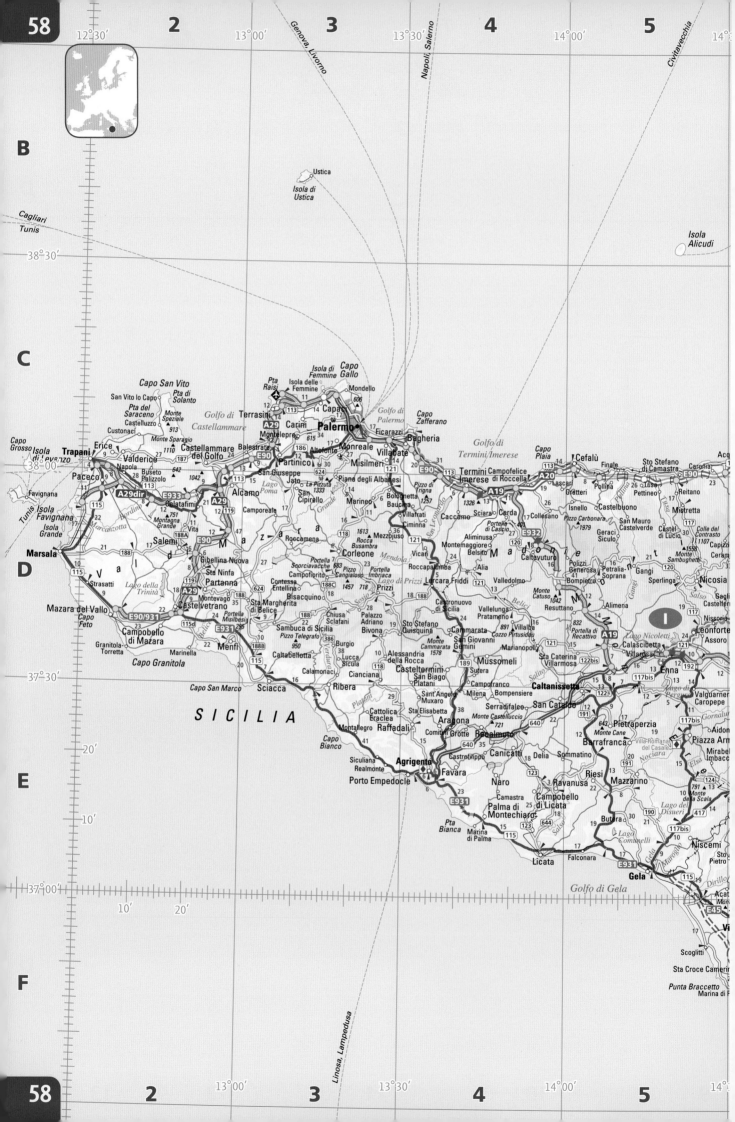

2　13°00'　3　13°30'　4　14°00'　5

B

Genova, Livorno

Napoli, Salerno

Civitavecchia

Cagliari
Tunis

Ustica
Isola di
Ustica

Isola
Alicudi

38°30'

C

Capo San Vito
San Vito lo Capo
Pta di
Solanto
Pta del
Saraceno
Monte
Speziale
913
Monte Sparagio
Castelluzzo
Custonaci
Golfo di
Castellammare
Terrasini
Isola di
Femmine
Capo
Gallo
Pta
Raisi
Isola delle
Femmine
12
14
11
Mondello
606
Capo
Zafferano
Golfo di
Palermo
Golfo di
Termini Imerese
Capo
Plaia
Cefalù
Finale
Sto Stefano
di Camastra
Acq
Caronia

Capo
Grosso
Isola
di Levanzo
Trapani
Erice
Valderice
Napola
Paceco
9
4
9
9
28
Buseto
Palizzolo
642
Castellammare
del Golfo
24
Balestrate
E90
Montelepre
586
Altofonte
Palermo
Monreale
17
Ficarazzi
Bagheria
31
Termini
Imerese
Campofelice
di Roccella
A20
Lascari
19
14
Grattei
Pollina
Isnello
Castelbuono
San Mauro
Castelverde
117
Reitano
Mistretta
23
E90

38°00'

Favignana
Isola
Favignana
Isola
Grande
Tunis
113
A29dir
E933
Calatafimi
21
Alcamo
113
15
Lago
Poma
San Giuseppe
Jato
La Pizzuta
615
34
30
Partinico
12
Piana degli Albanesi
Misilmeri
114
121
E90
A19
1326
13
Cerda
Sciara
Collesano
Pizzo Carbonara
1979
Pizzo
di Cascio
E932
120
Geraci
Siculo
Castel
di Lucio
Colle del
Contrasto
1107
Monte
Sambughetti
120
Capiz
Cerami

D

Marsala
115
Strasatti
9
188
115
22
Va
l
Marcanzotta
Montagna
Grande
751
Vita
Salemi
Gibellina Nuova
Sta Ninfa
Partanna
119
187
e
Lago
Grande
M
a
d
o
n
Roccamena
Camporeale
16
1613
Rocca
Busambra
1333
Corleone
36
Mezzojuso
118
Mendola
Vicari
121
Roccapalumba
Caccamo
Montemaggiore
Belsito
Alia
24
Valledolmo
Bompietro
Monte
Catuso
1042
Resuttano
Petralia
Soprana
Gangi
Sperlinga
Nicosia
Salso
Gagli
Castell

37°30'

Mazara del Vallo
Capo
Feto
E90/931
Granitola-
Torretta
Campobello
di Mazara
Marinella
115d
Castelvetrano
E931
Montevago
188
Pizzo Telegrafo
950
Sambuca di Sicilia
Sta Margherita
di Belice
386
188
Menfi
22
Caltabellotta
188B
115
Contessa
Entellina
Bisacquino
Palazzo
Adriano
Chiusa
Sclafani
19
Prizzi
718
1457
Sosio
18
188
Castronuovo
di Sicilia
Vallelunga
Pratameno
891
Villalba
832
Portella
di Recattivo
A19
Lago Nicoletti
Calascibetta
Villadoro
I
Leonforte
Assoro
121
10
192
Enna
117bis

E

Sciacca
16
Capo San Marco
Ribera
Calamonaci
Cianciana
118
10
Alessandria
della Rocca
Sta Elisabetta
Cattolica
Eraclea
Montallegro
Capo
Bianco
41
Raffadali
Siculiana
Realmonte
Porto Empedocle
Agrigento
Favara
6
6
Naro
123
Castrofilippo
Canicattì
Delia
Sommatino
Riesi
191
Butera
Castelluccio
721
Monte
Cane
643
Pietraperzia
Barrafranca
Villa Romana
del Casale
Nociara
Piazza Arm
Mirabel
Imbacc
124
Monte
della Scala
791
117bis
Niscemi
Sto
Pietro

S I C I L I A

37°20'

37°10'

Campobello
di Licata
25
Palma di
Montechiaro
Pta
Bianca
Marina
di Palma
123
644
15
115
Licata
Falconara
17
E931
Gela
115
Golfo di Gela
Dirillo

F

Linosa, Lampedusa

Scoglitti
Sta Croce Camerin
Punta Braccetto
Marina di

37°00'

2　13°00'　3　13°30'　4　14°00'　5

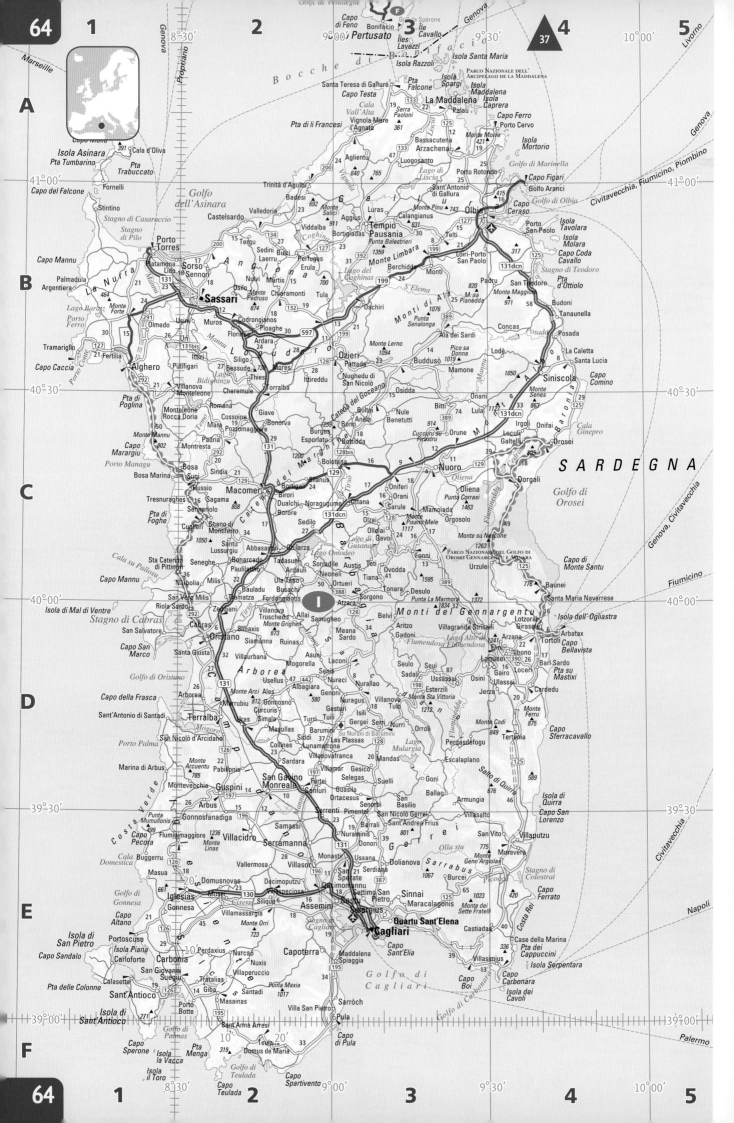

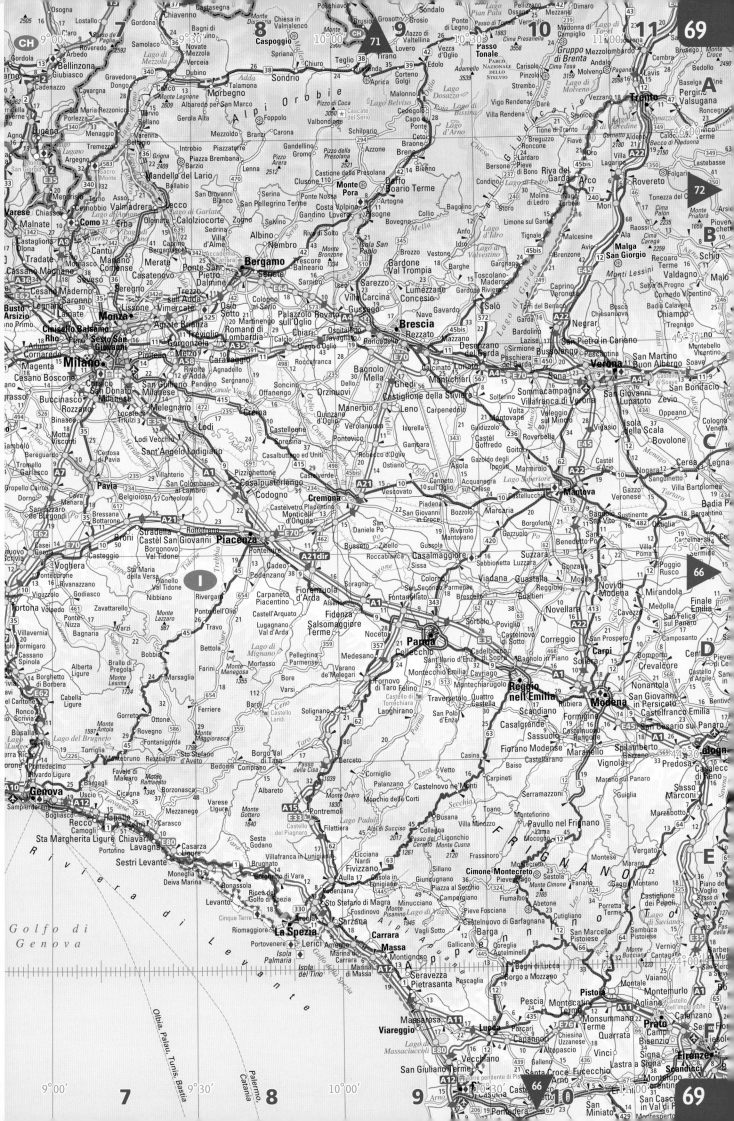

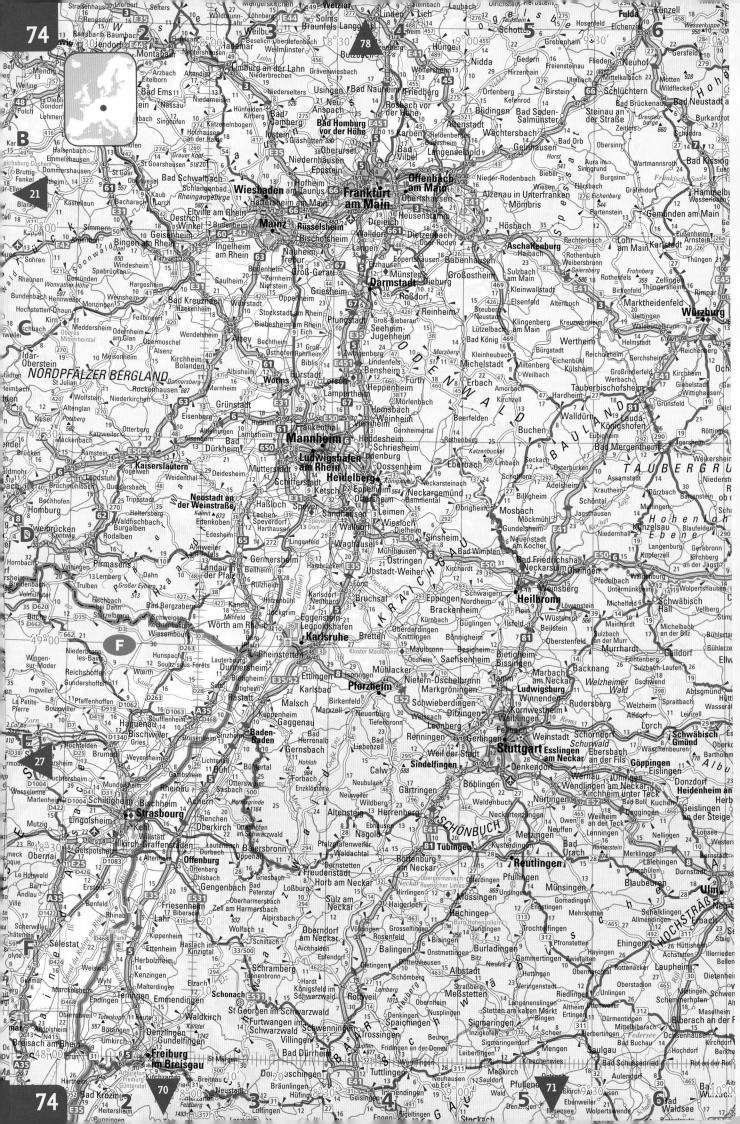

80
75
72
73
1
2
3
4
5
6
B
C
D
E
F
VOGTLAND
Fichtelgebirge
Oberpfälzer Wald
Český les
Böhmerwald
Bayerischer Wald
Šumava
Dunau Gau
Holledau
Mühlviertel
Innviertel
Hausruck
Doupovské Hory
Tepelská Vrchovina
Slavkovský les
Rakovnická Pahorkatina
Křivoklátská Vrchovina
Brdy
Plauen
Auerbach
Oelsnitz
Klingenthal
Selb
Aš
Cheb
Marktredwitz
Wunsiedel
Waldsassen
Mitterteich
Tirschenreuth
Weiden in der Oberpfalz
Neustadt an der Waldnaab
Amberg
Schwandorf
Burglengenfeld
Regensburg
Kelheim
Neustadt an der Donau
Abensberg
Mainburg
Landshut
Straubing
Deggendorf
Plattling
Cham
Roding
Furth im Wald
Bodenmais
Zwiesel
Regen
Grafenau
Sankt Englmar
Dingolfing
Landau an der Isar
Vilshofen
Passau
Pfarrkirchen
Eggenfelden
Vilsbiburg
Erding
Dorfen
Waldkraiburg
Mühldorf am Inn
Altötting
Burghausen
Braunau am Inn
Trostberg
Traunreut
Traunstein
Rosenheim
Wasserburg am Inn
Bad Füssing
Pocking
Schärding
Ried im Innkreis
Vöcklabruck
Gmunden
Wels
Linz
Traun
Leonding
Ansfelden
Marchtrenk
Kremsmünster
Grieskirchen
Eferding
Rohrbach in Oberösterreich
Český Krumlov
Vimperk
Prachatice
Strakonice
Písek
Sušice
Klatovy
Domažlice
Horažďovice
Blatná
Příbram
Dobříš
Beroun
Rokycany
Plzeň
Stříbro
Tachov
Mariánské Lázně
Karlovy Vary
Sokolov
Ostrov
Chodov
Kadaň
Chomutov
Most
Žatec
Louny
Slaný
Kladno
Rakovník
Kralupy nad Vltavou
Roudnice
Praha
Techmania
NATIONALPARK BAYER.WALD
Zoo Praha

PRAHA
Mladá Boleslav
Mělník
Brandýs nad Labem-Stará Boleslav
Poděbrady
Nymburk
Jičín
Hradec Králové
Pardubice
Náchod
Kłodzko
Kolín
Kutná Hora
Chrudim
Čáslav
Havlíčkův Brod
Jihlava
Benešov
Tábor
Pelhřimov
Jindřichův Hradec
České Budějovice
Třeboň
Svitavy
Litomyšl
Ústí nad Orlicí
Šumperk
Olomouc
Prostějov
Boskovice
Blansko
Brno
Vyškov
Třebíč
Velké Meziříčí
Žďár nad Sázavou
Znojmo
Mikulov
Břeclav
Hodonín
Zwettl
Krems an der Donau
St Pölten
Melk
Tulln
Stockerau
Mistelbach
Hollabrunn
WIEN
Schwechat
Mödling
Baden
BRATISLAVA
Malacky
Amstetten
Waidhofen an der Ybbs
Enns
ČESKOMORAVSKÁ VYSOČINA
WALDVIERTEL
WACHAU
Železné Hory
Orlické Hory
Žďárské Vrchy
Novohradské Hory
Weinsberger Wald
CZ
PL
SK
A
81
146
148
149

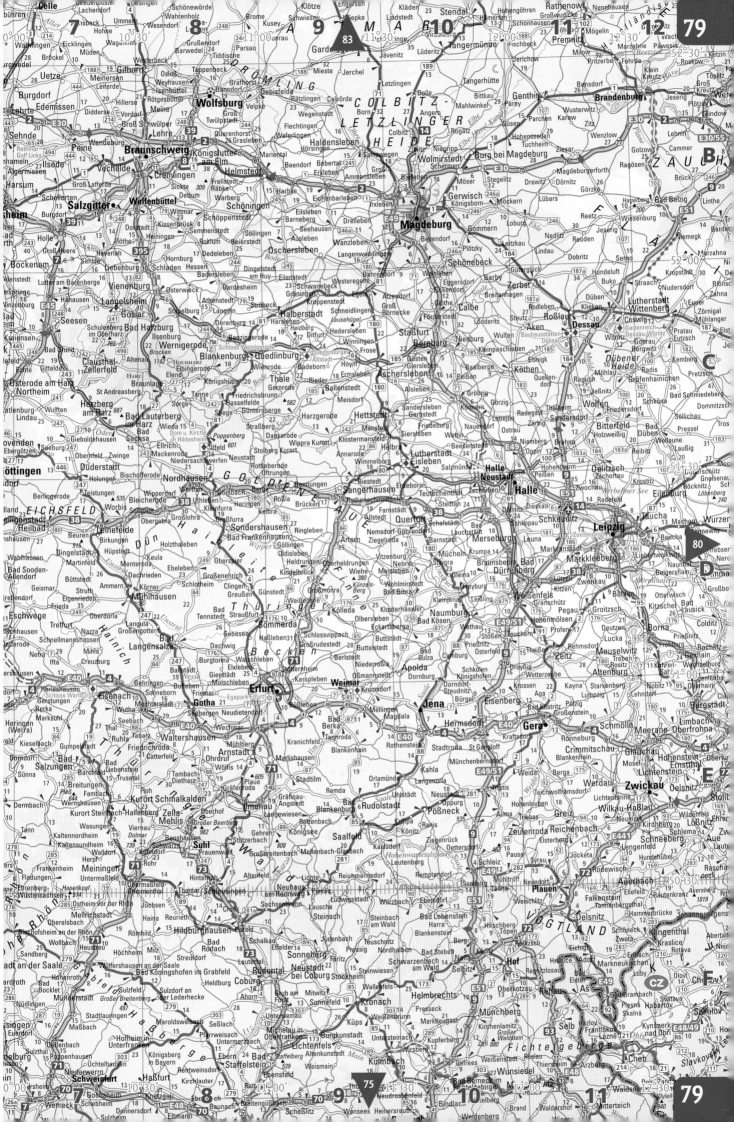

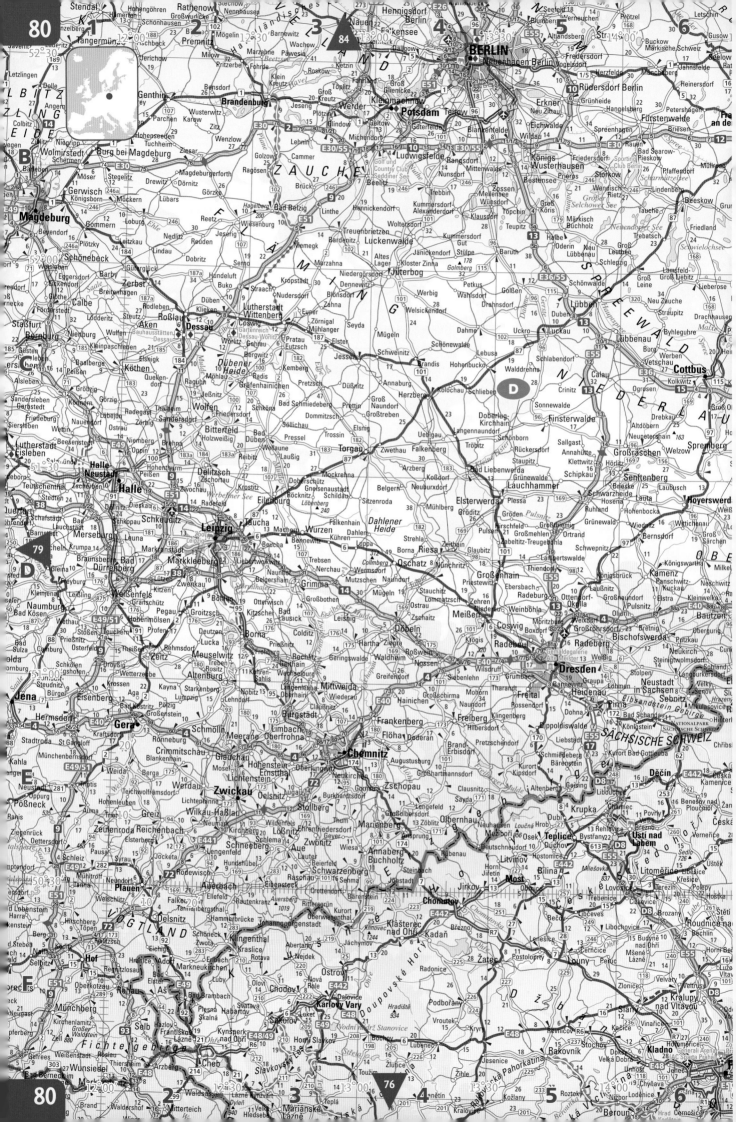

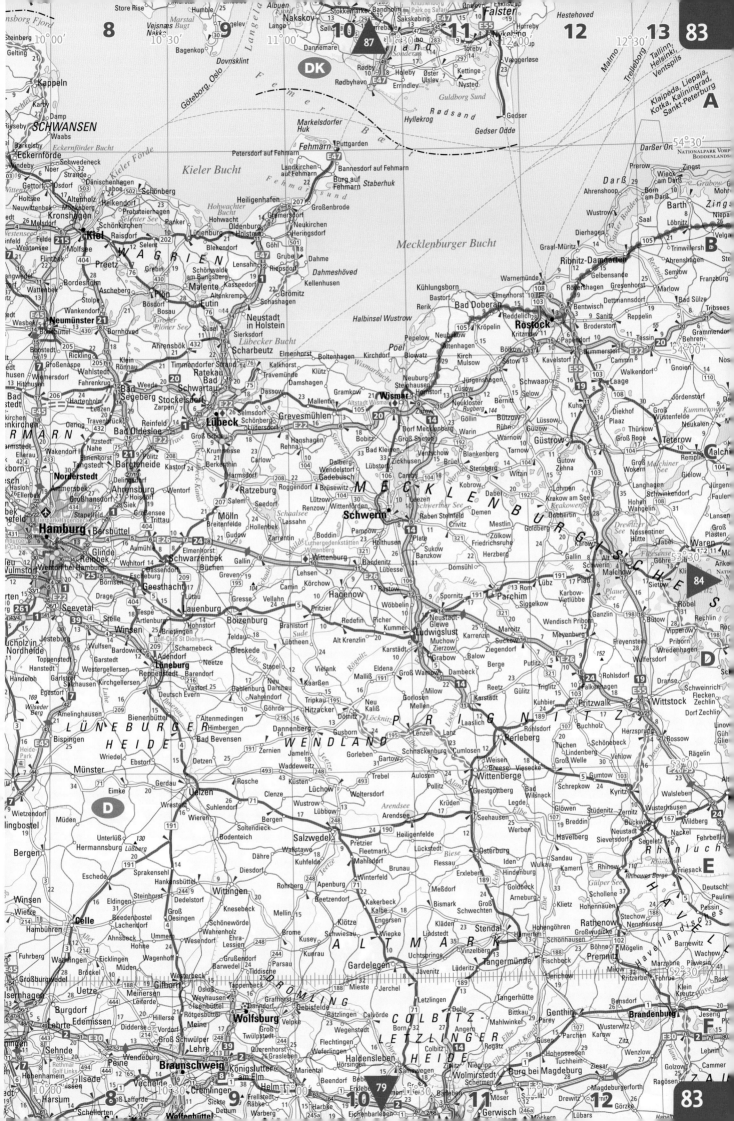

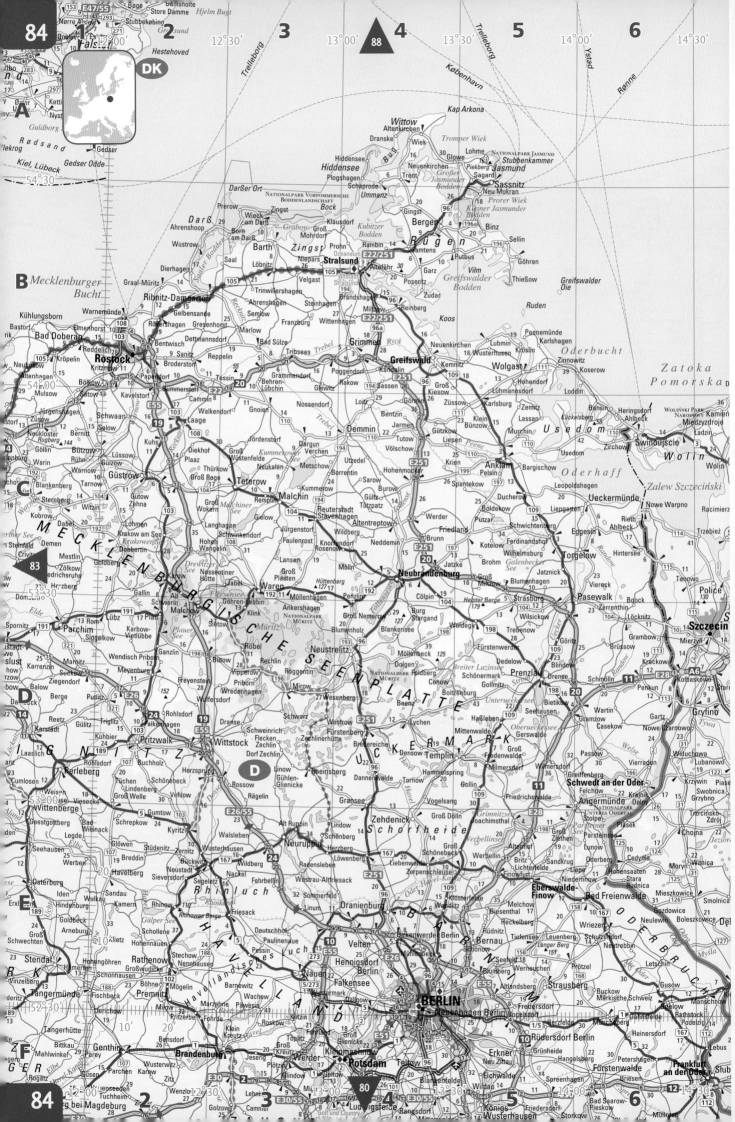

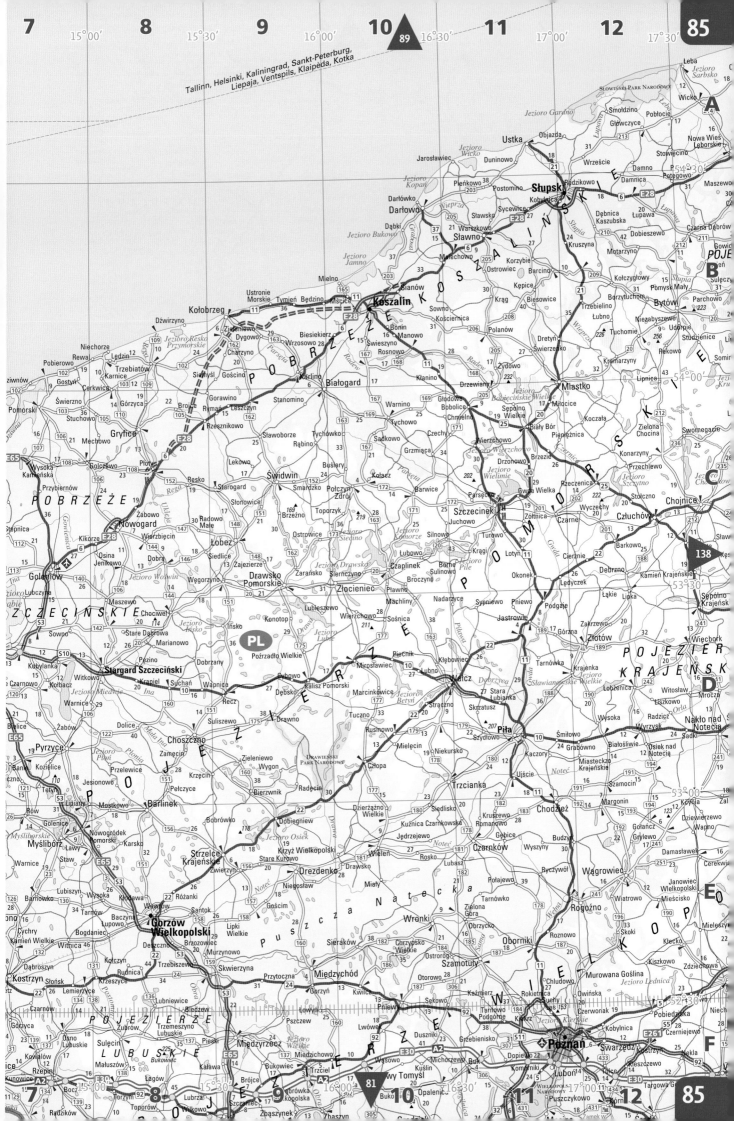

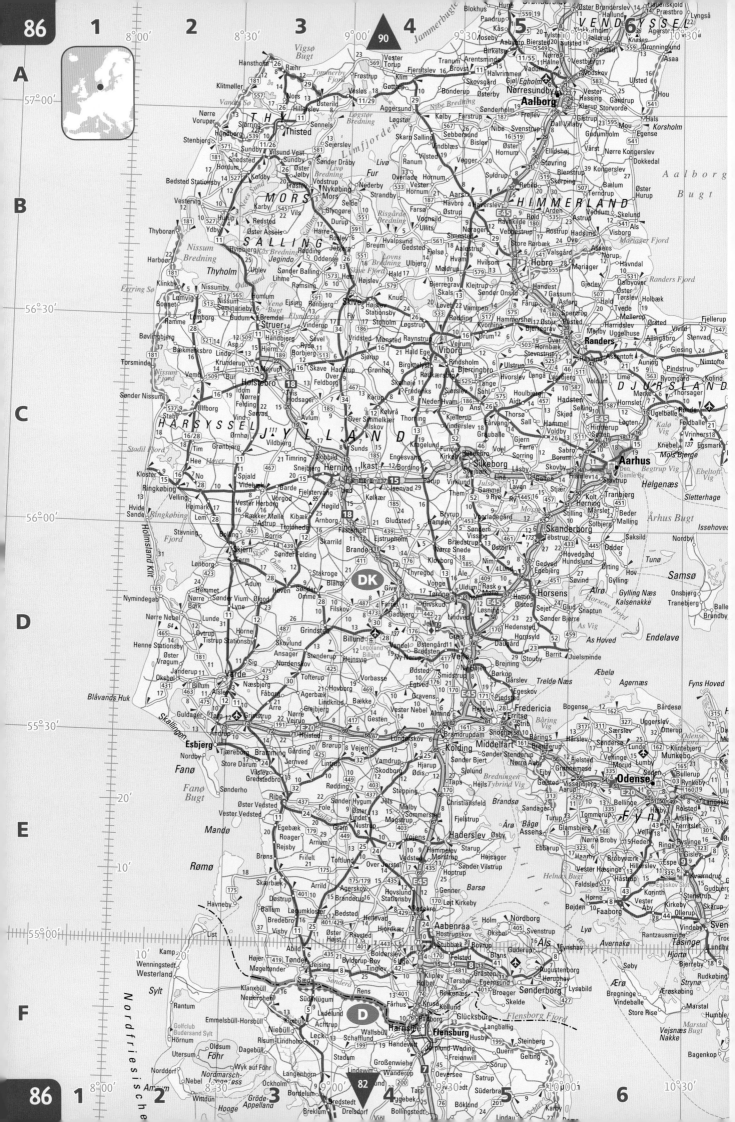

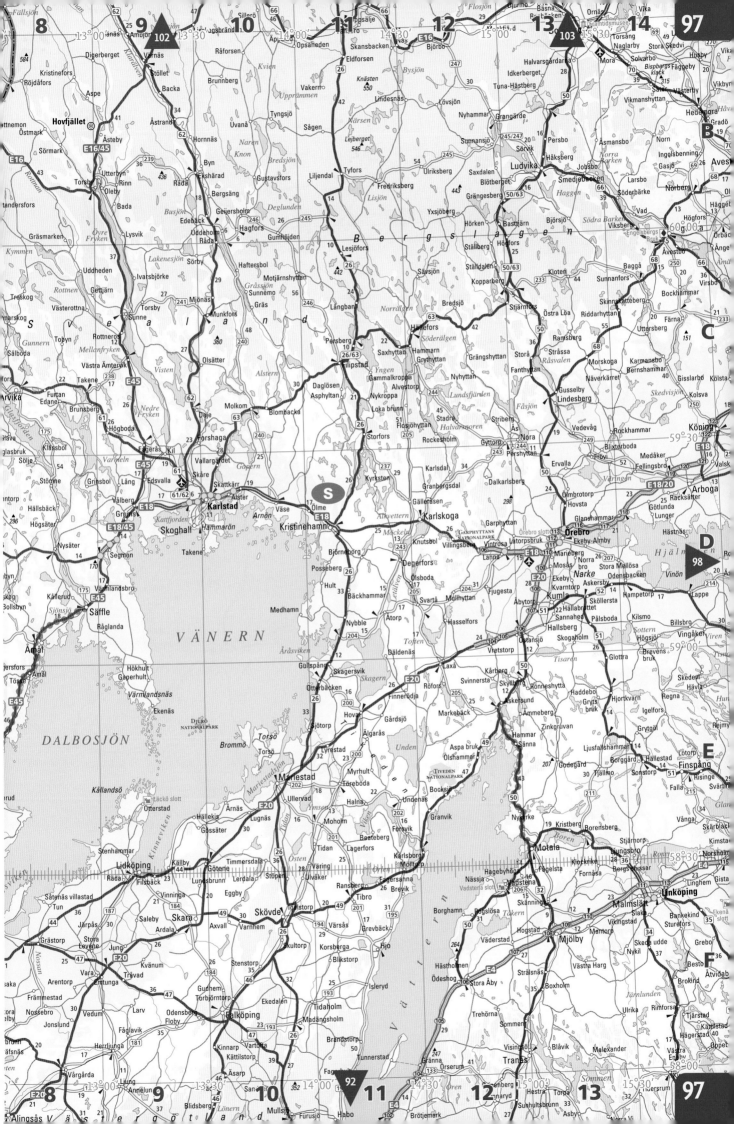

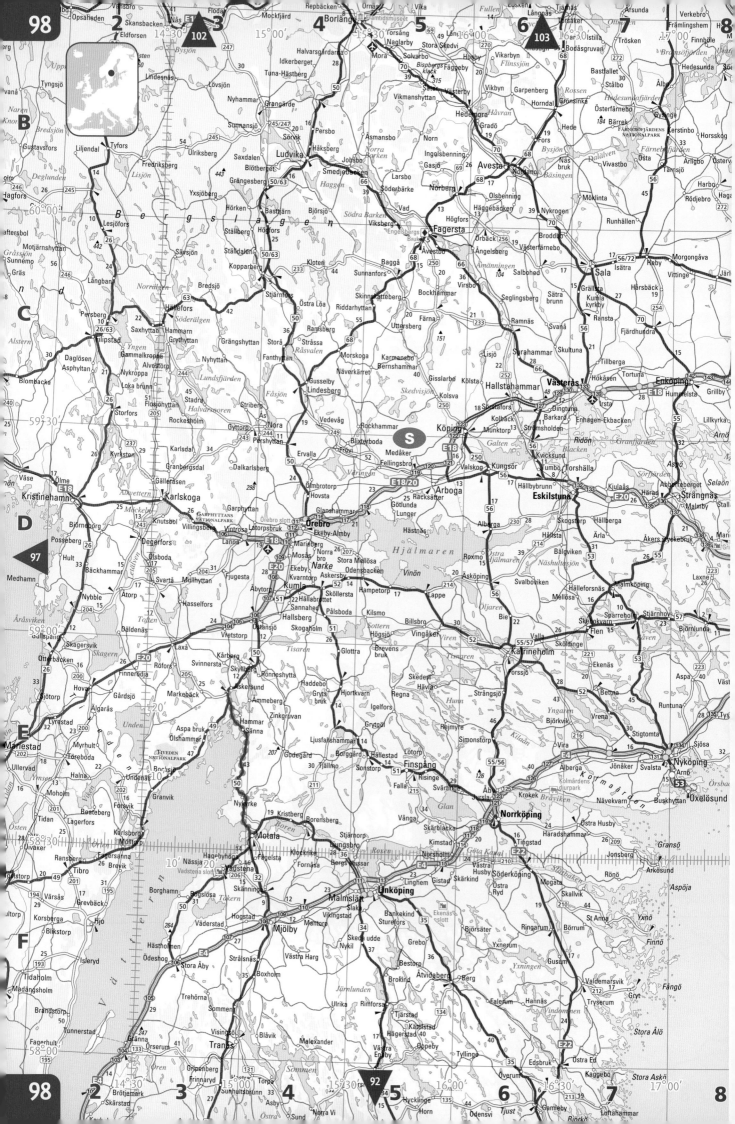

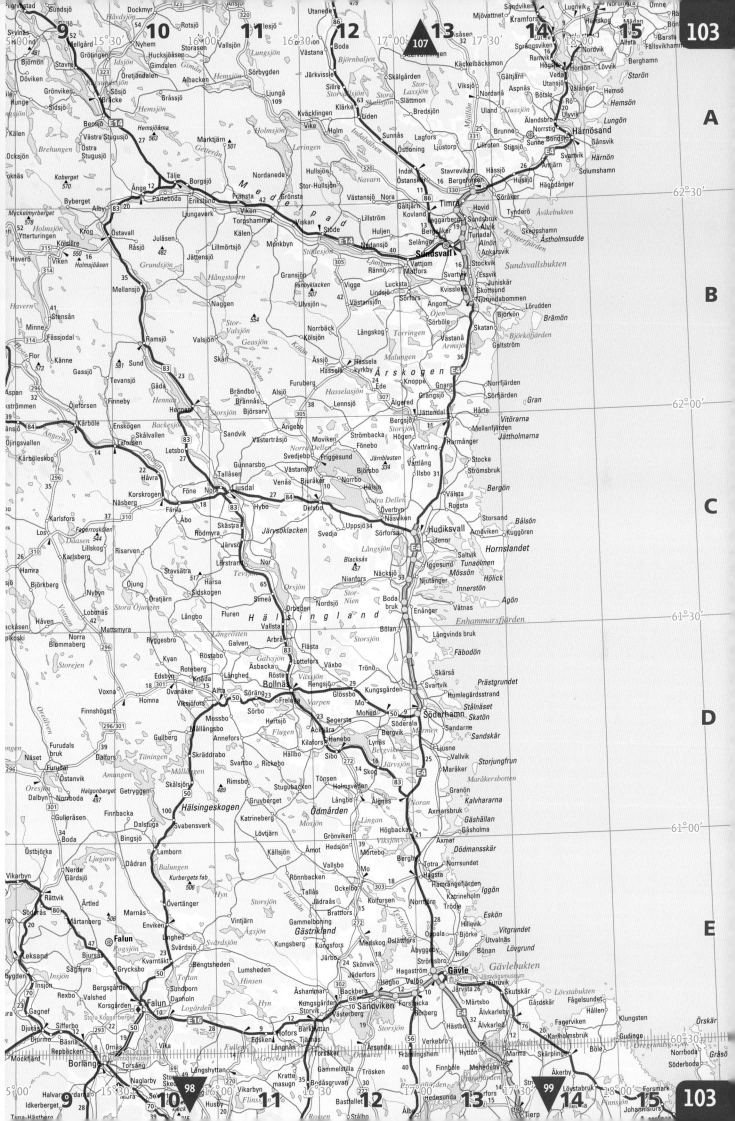

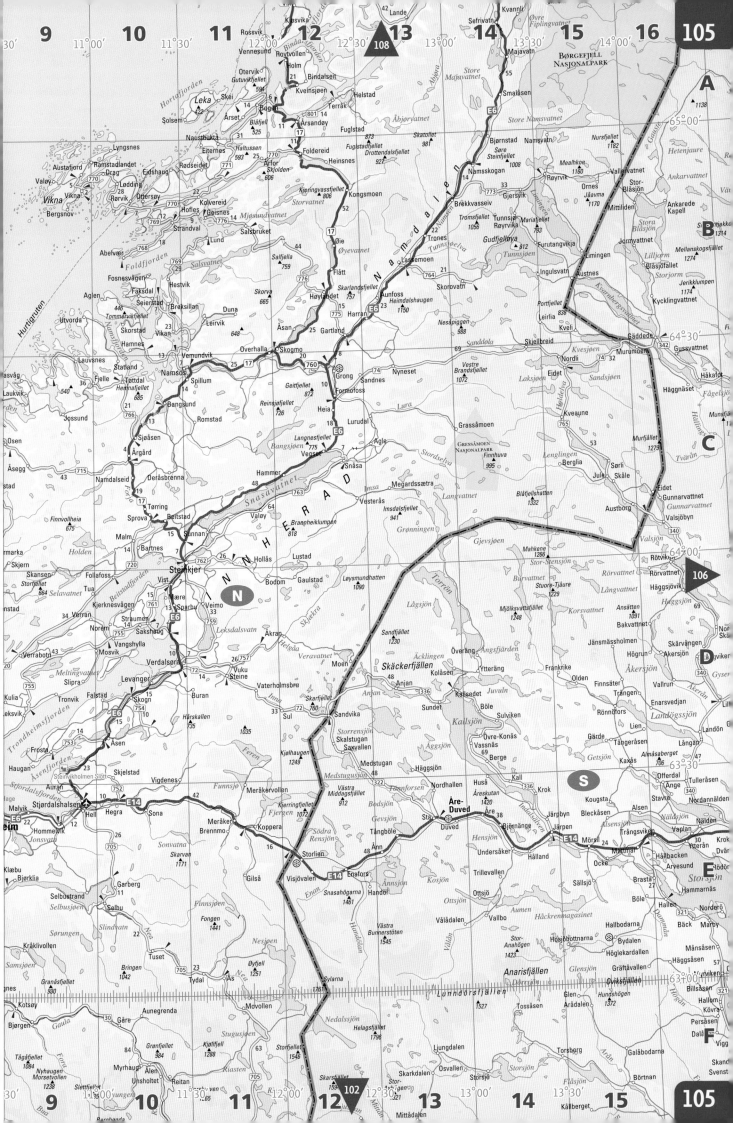

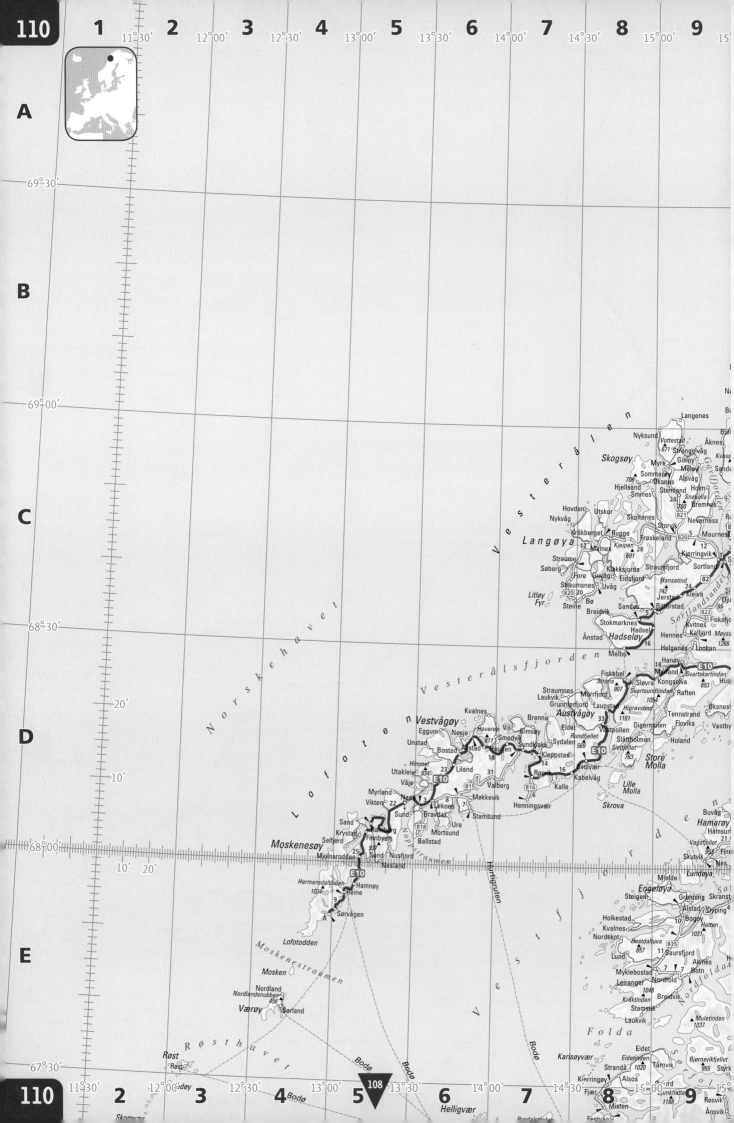

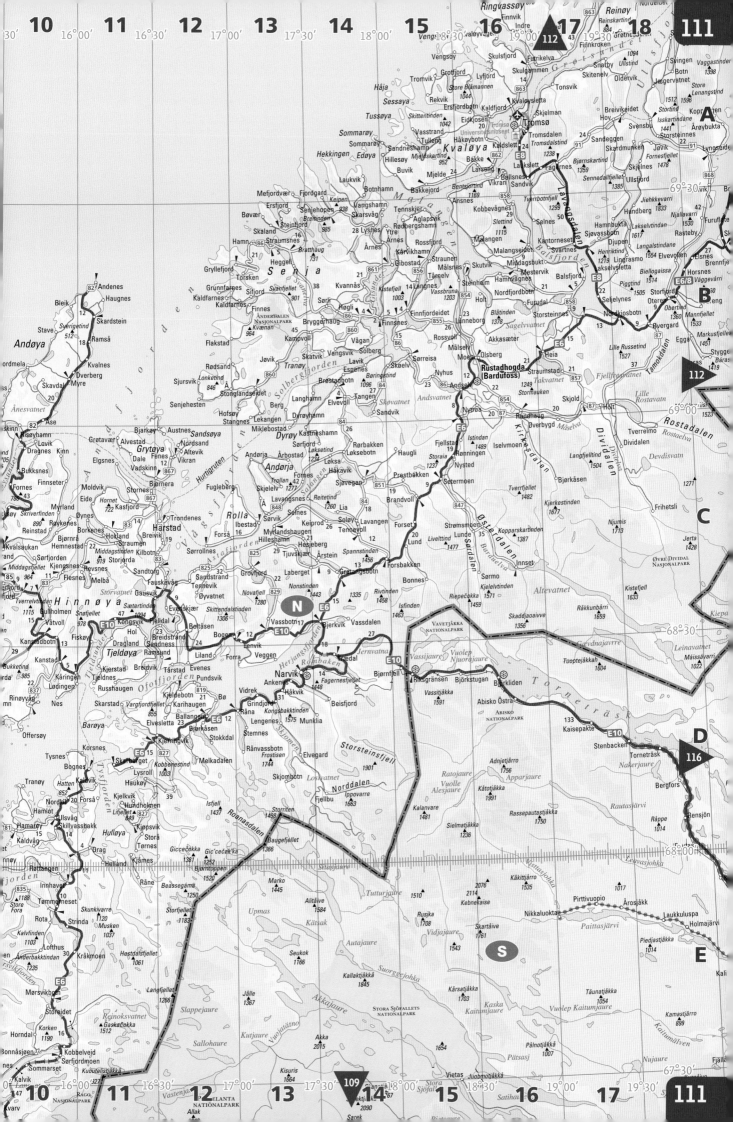

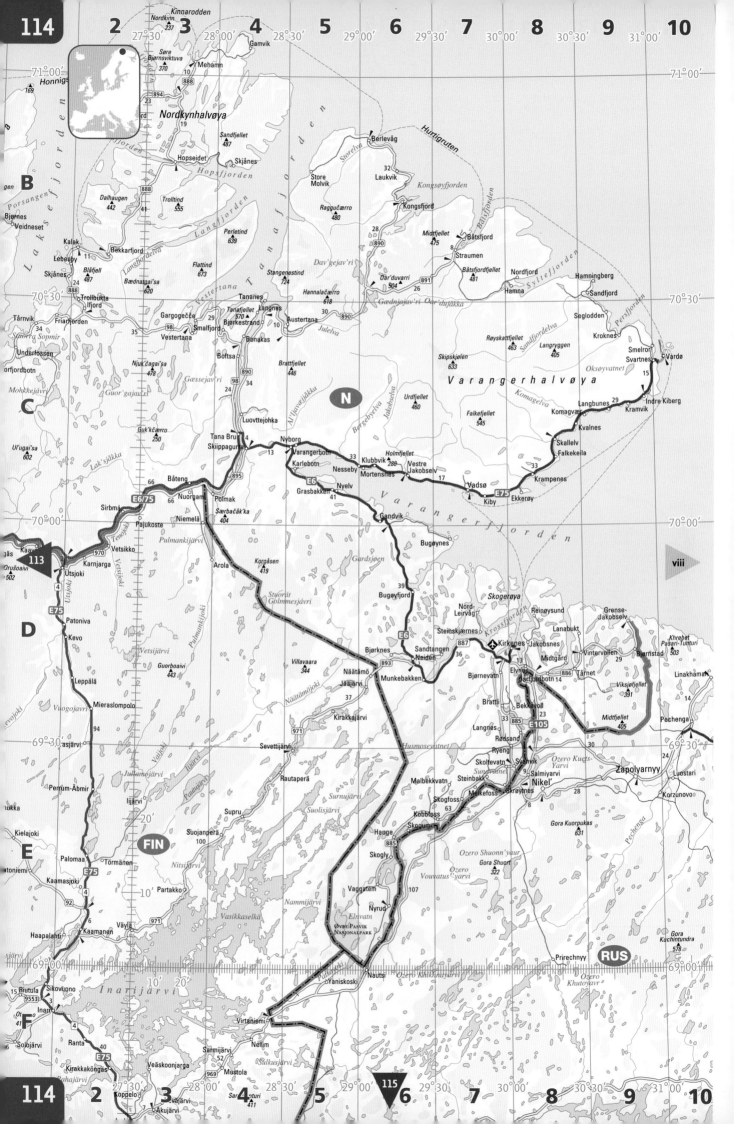

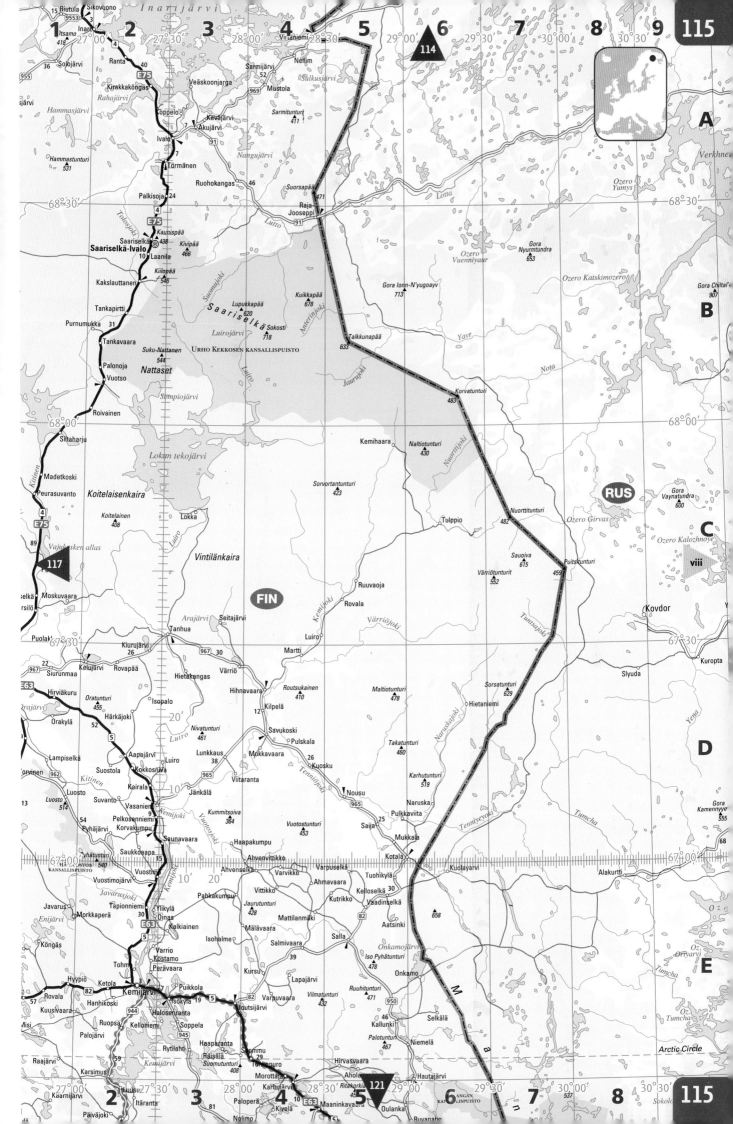

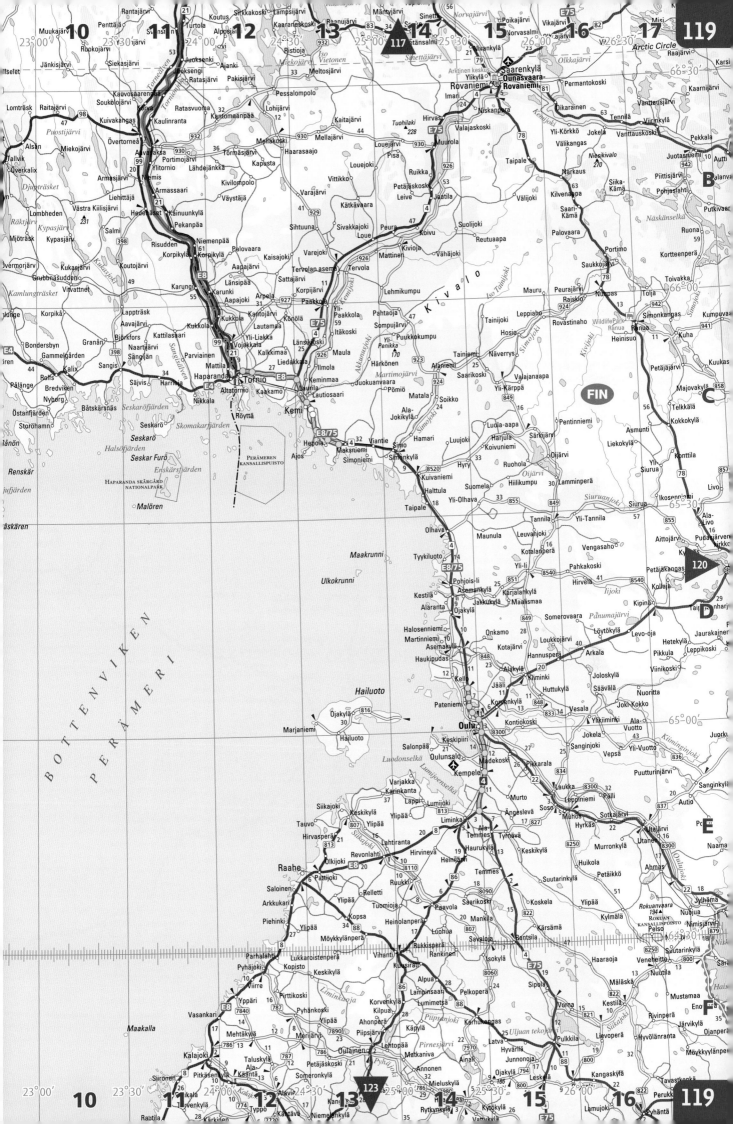

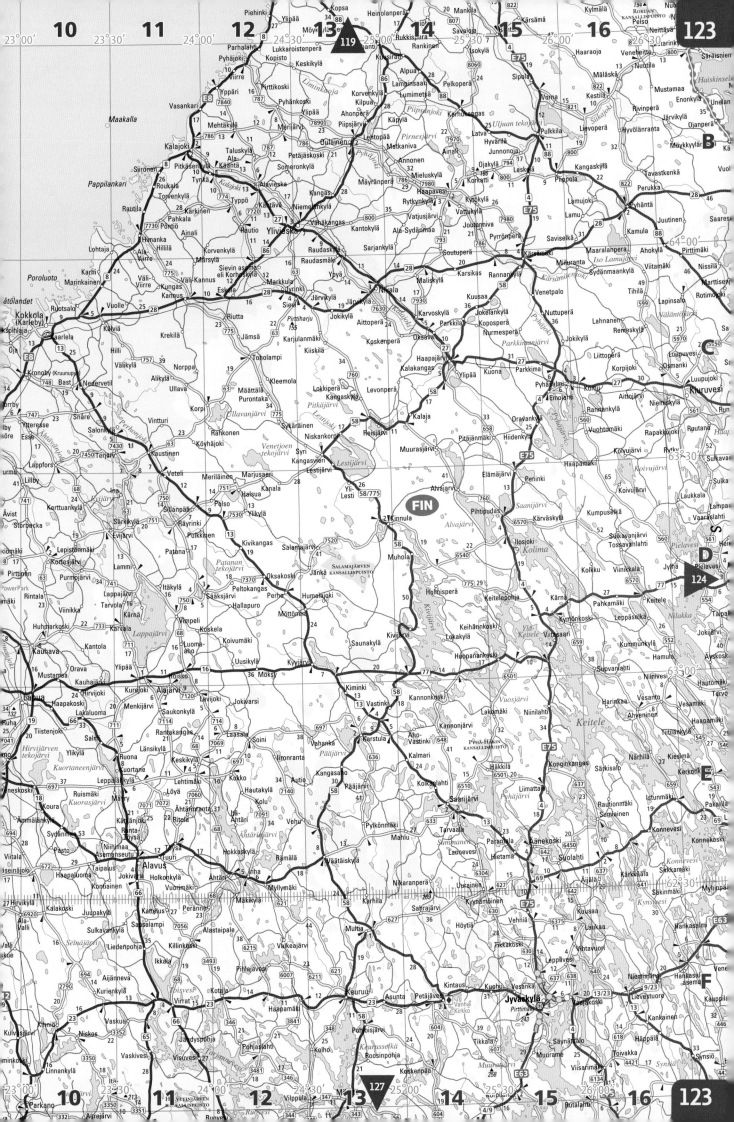

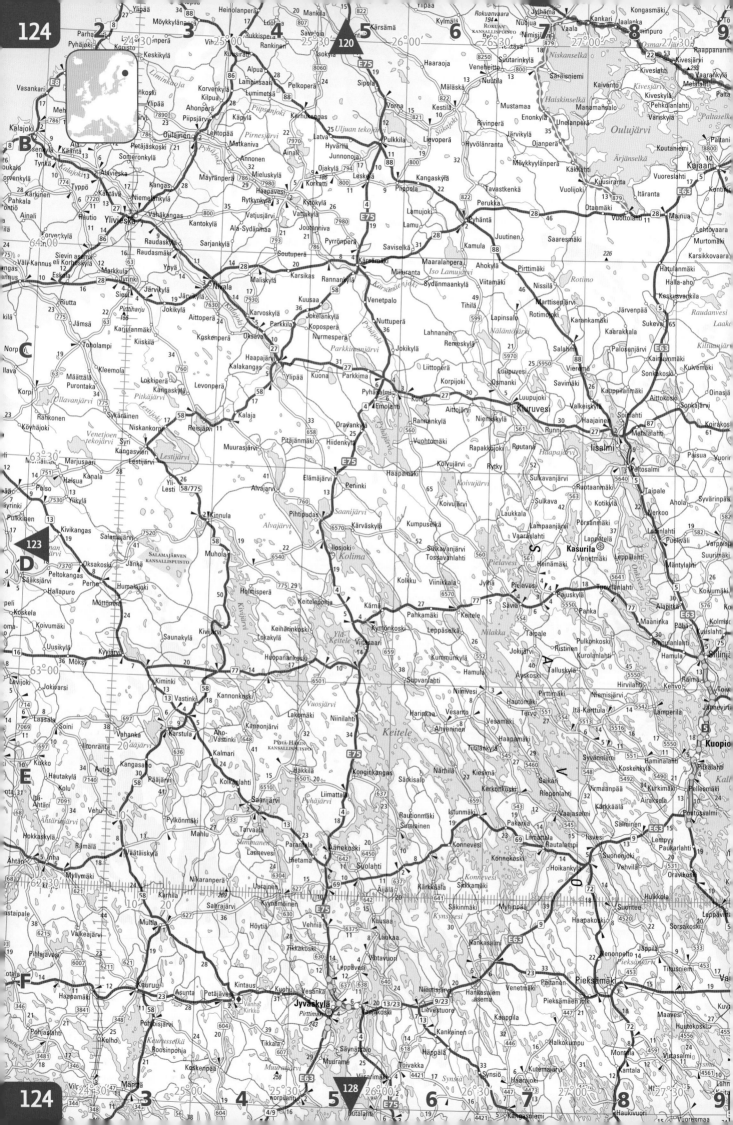

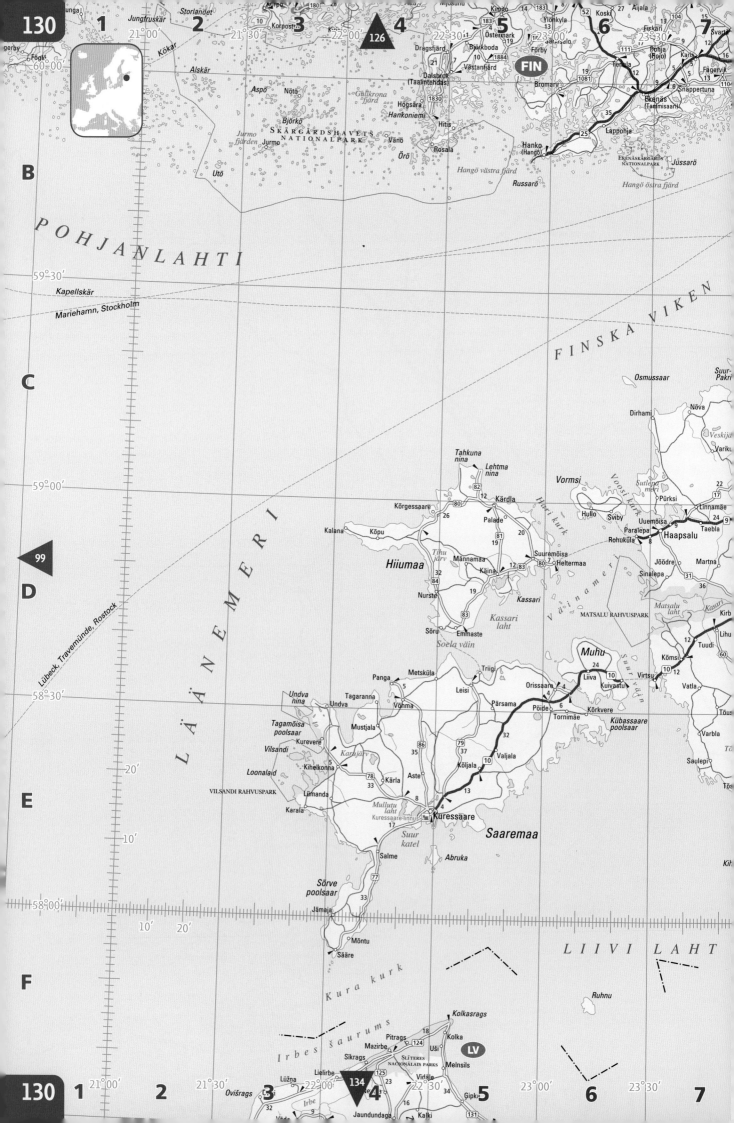

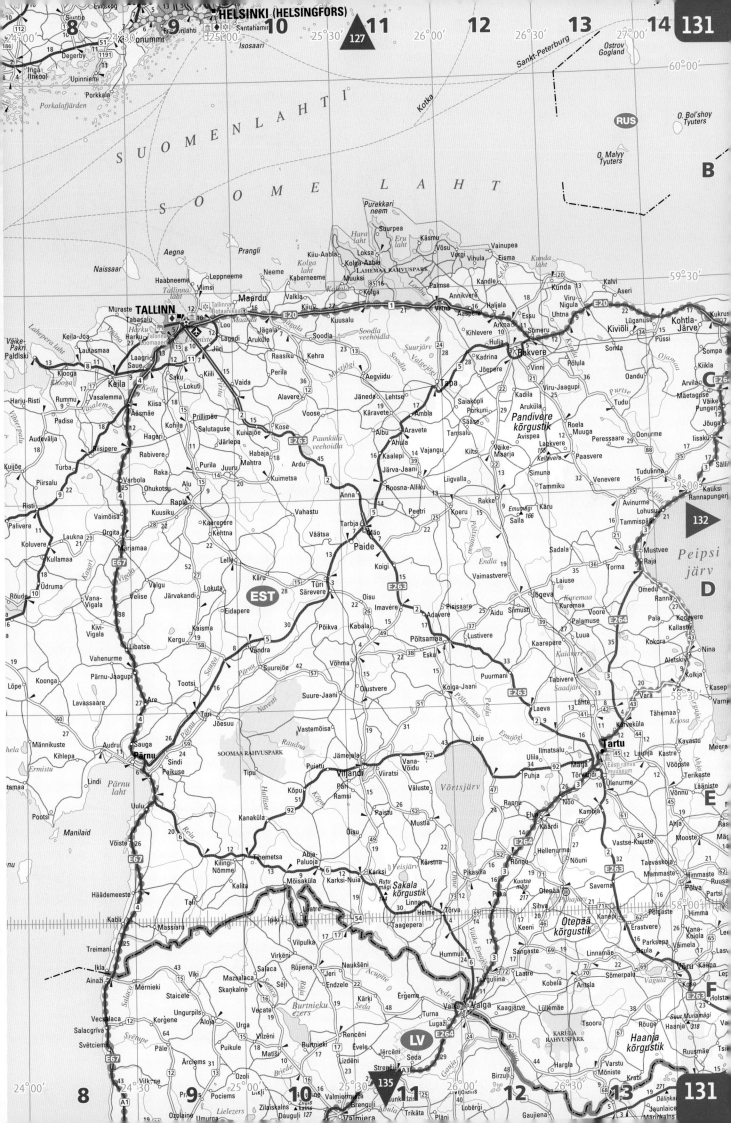

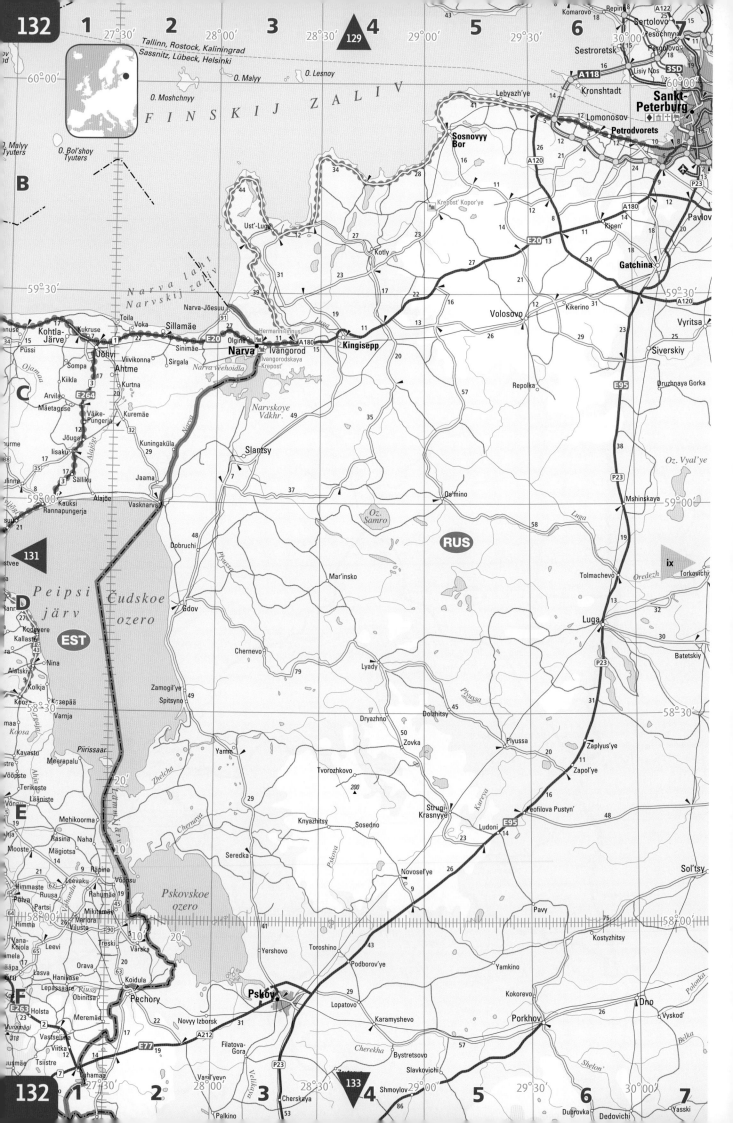

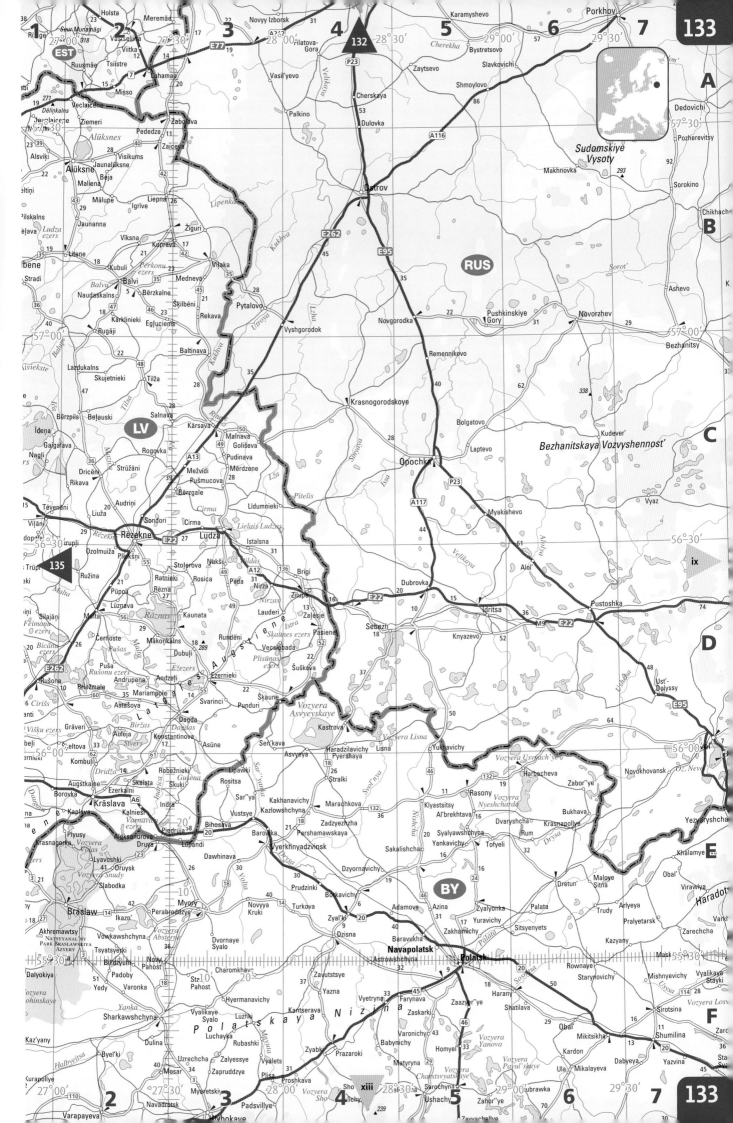

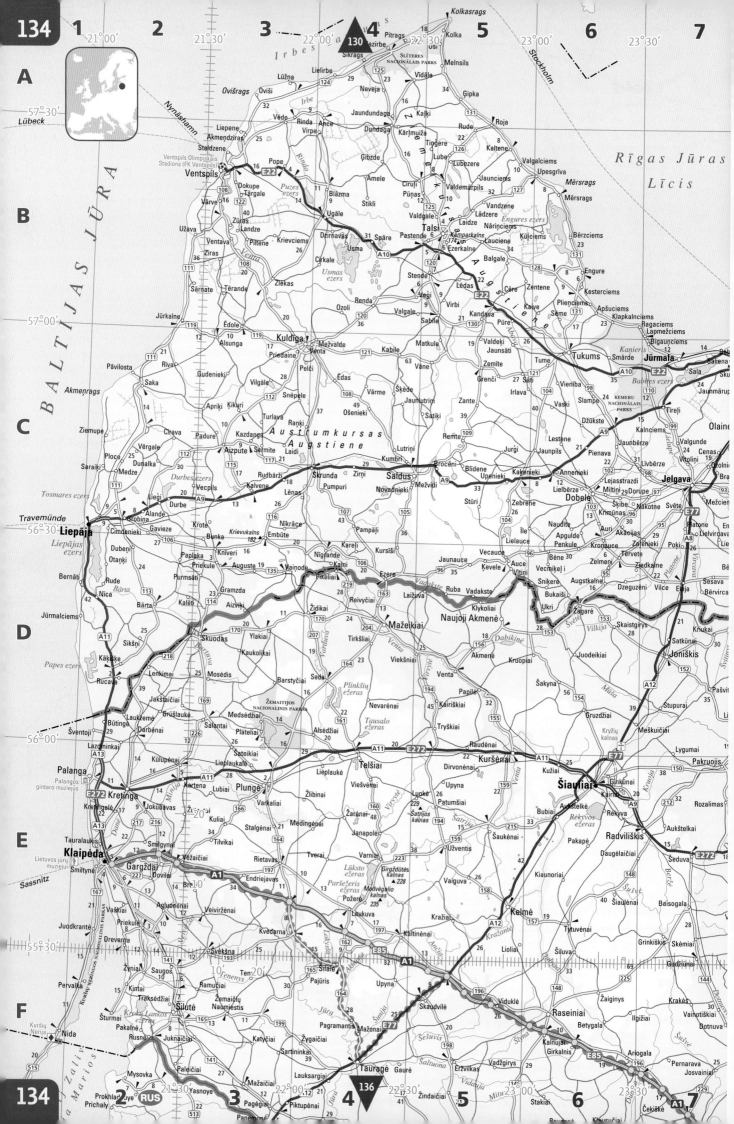

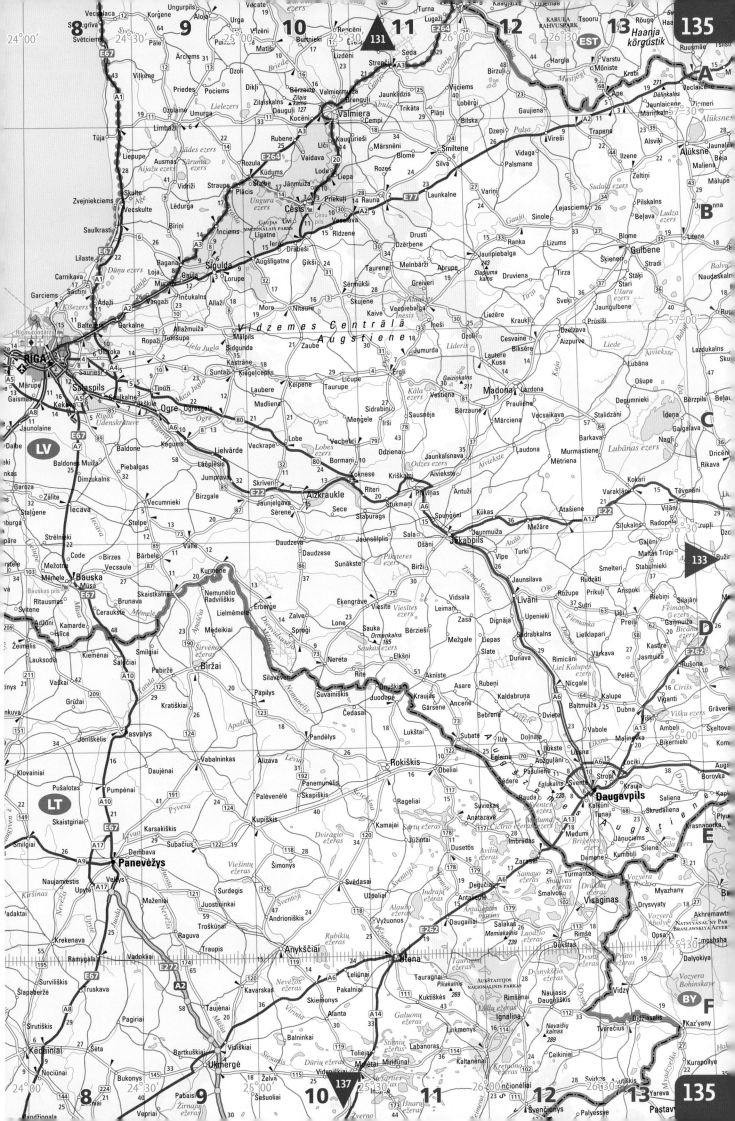

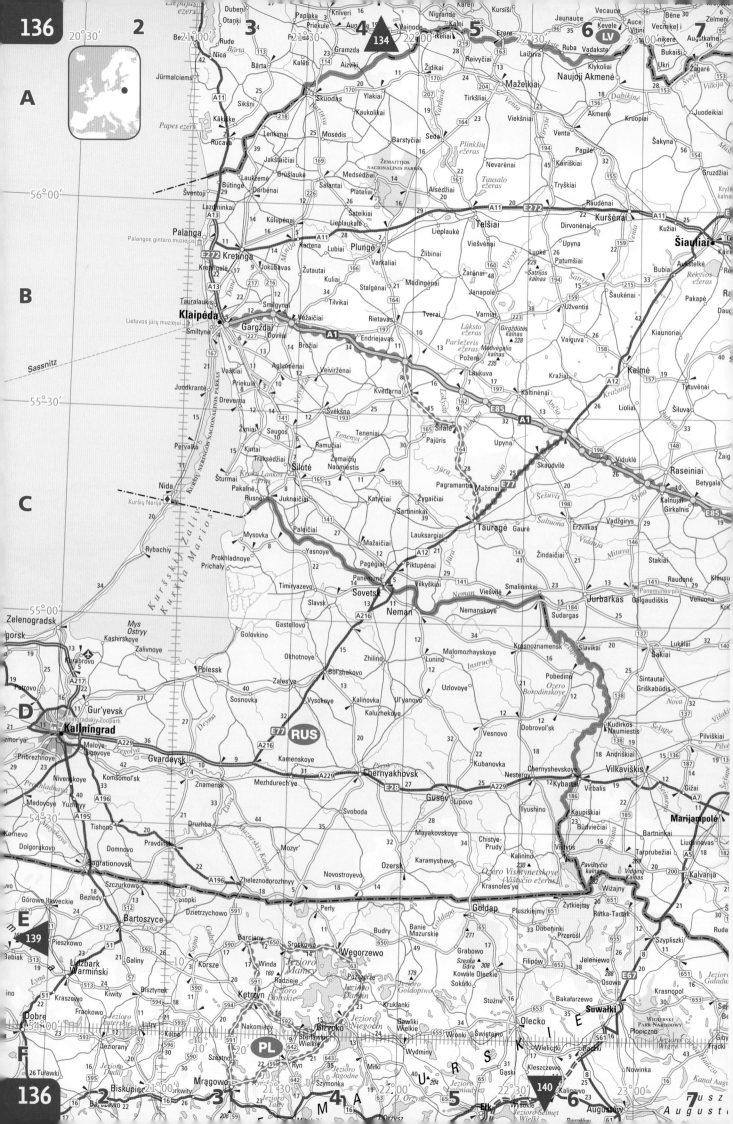

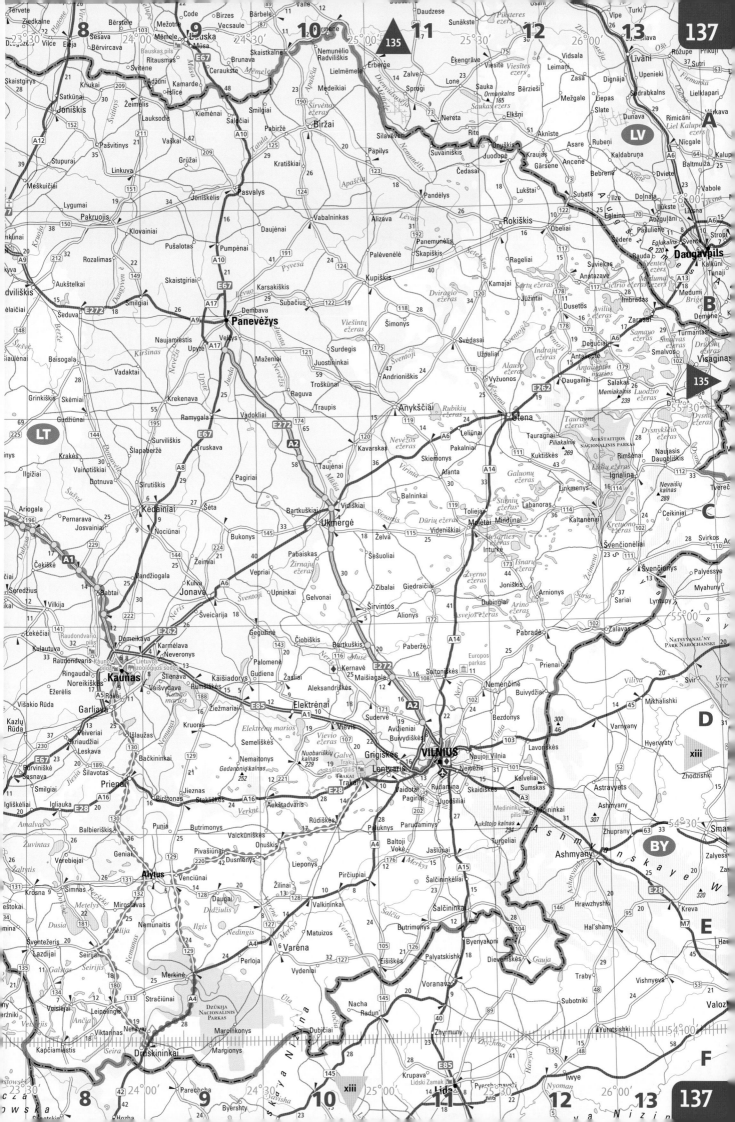

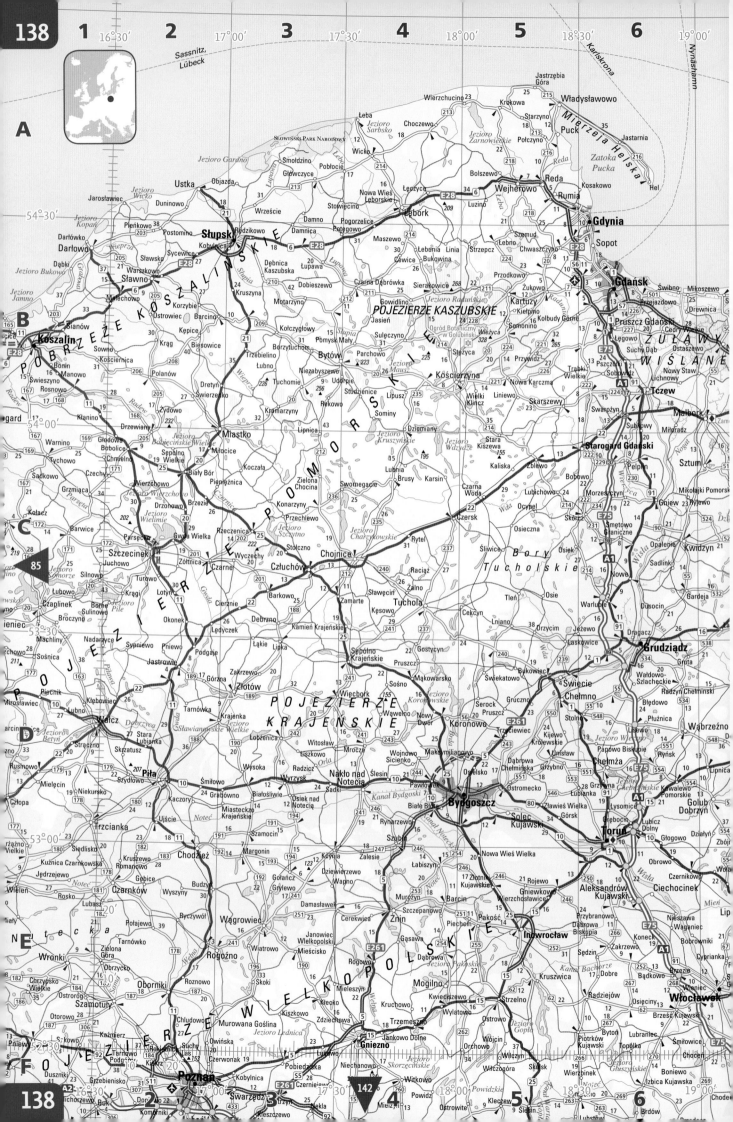

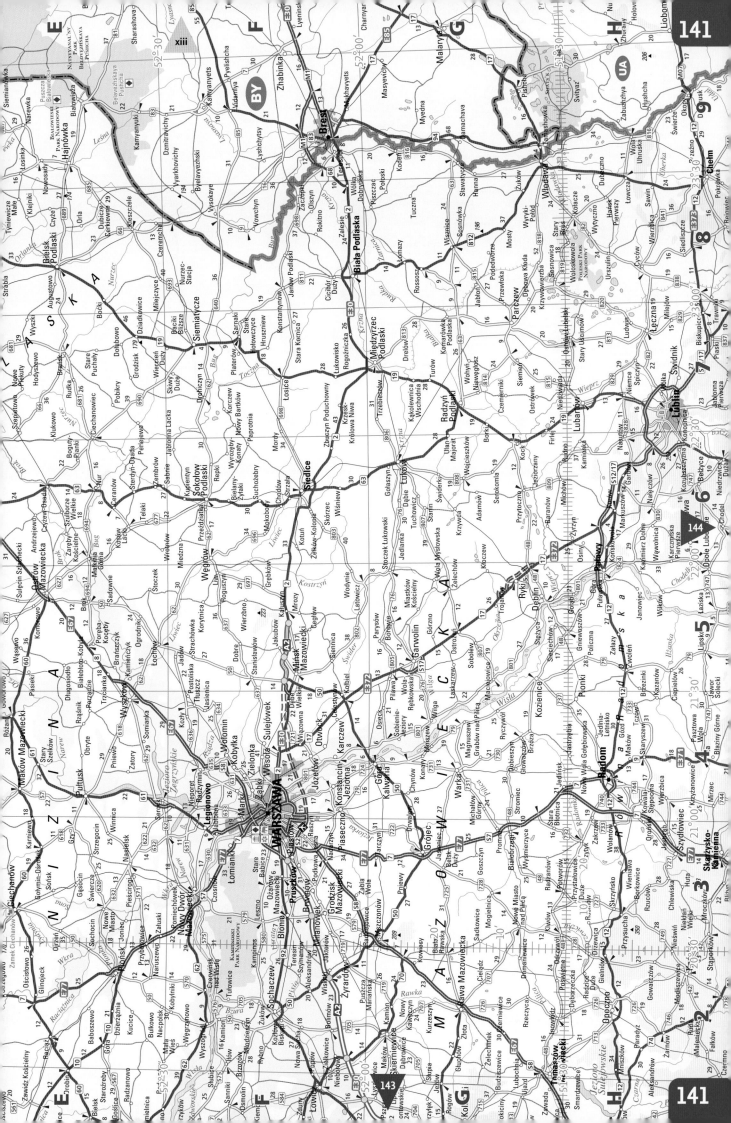

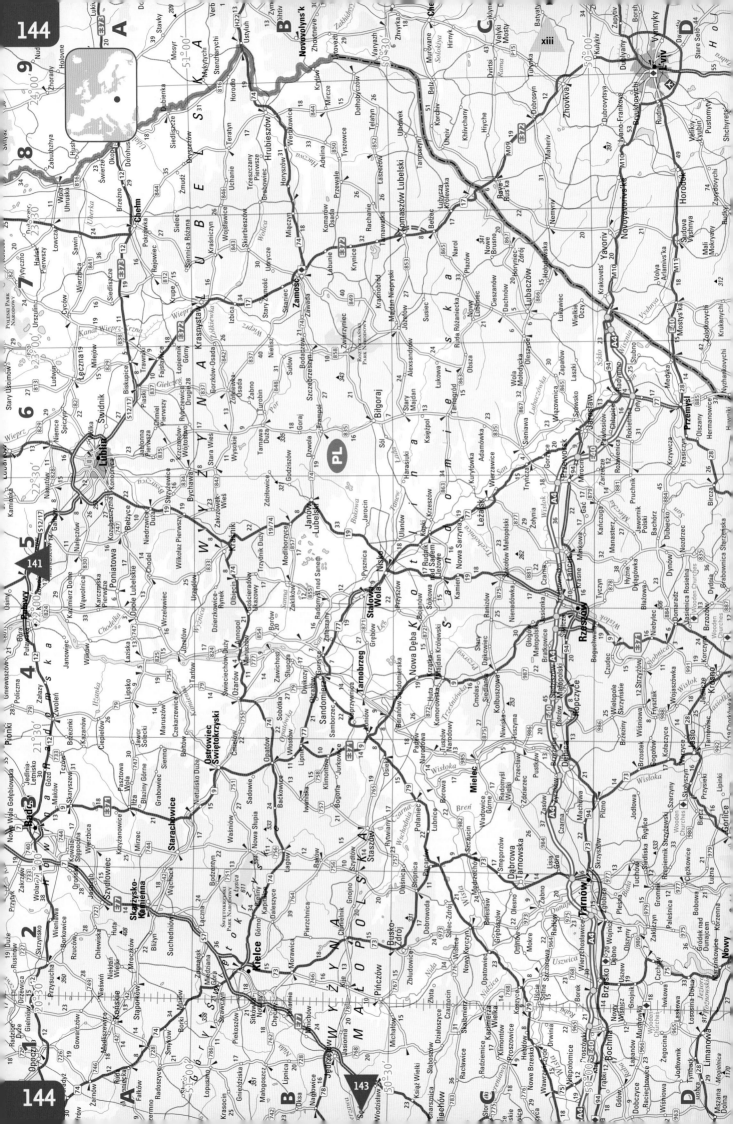

1
2
3
4
5
6
A
B
C
D
E
F
16°00'
16°30'
17°00'
17°30'
18°00'
50°00'
49°30'
49°00'
48°30'
48°00'
142
77
149
CZ
A
Hradec Králové
Pardubice
Chrudim
Náchod
Nové Město nad Metují
Kłodzko
Nysa
Krapkowice
Opolskie
Kędzierzyn-Koźle
Racibórz
Głuchołazy
Prudnik
Głubczyce
Jeseník
Šumperk
Krnov
Opava
Ostrava
Havířov
Frýdek-Místek
Bohumín
Hlučín
Bruntál
Ústí nad Orlicí
Vysoké Mýto
Litomyšl
Svitavy
Polička
Žďár nad Sázavou
Nové Město na Moravě
Velké Meziříčí
Třebíč
Zábřeh
Mohelnice
Moravská Třebová
Lanškroun
Šternberk
Uničov
Litovel
Olomouc
Prostějov
Přerov
Hranice
Nový Jičín
Kopřivnice
Valašské Meziříčí
Vsetín
Zlín
Kroměříž
Holešov
Otrokovice
Vyškov
Boskovice
Blansko
Brno
Tišnov
Bučovice
Kyjov
Hodonín
Břeclav
Mikulov
Znojmo
Uherské Hradiště
Uherský Brod
Veselí nad Moravou
Skalica
Senica
Myjava
Trnava
Hlohovec
Piešťany
Nové Mesto nad Váhom
Trenčín
Nitra
Topoľčany
Bánovce nad Bebravou
Púchov
Galanta
Šaľa
Sereď
Pezinok
Senec
Malacky
Bratislava
Šamorín
Dunajská Streda
Nové Zámky
Komárno
Kolárovo
Mosonmagyaróvár
Wien
Mödling
Baden
Bad Vöslau
Wiener Neustadt
Eisenstadt
Neusiedler See
Bruck an der Leitha
Hainburg an der Donau
Schwechat
Klosterneuburg
Stockerau
Korneuburg
Tulln
Hollabrunn
Mistelbach
Laa an der Thaya
Poysdorf
Deutsch-Wagram
Gänserndorf
Marchfeld
Orlické Hory
Góry Bystrzyckie
Hrubý Jeseník
Rychlebské Hory
Žďárské Vrchy
Oderské vrchy
Moravskoslezské Beskydy
Javorník
Chřiby
Ždánický Les
Biele Karpaty
Malé Karpaty
Považský Inovec
Tribeč
Pohronská pahorkatina
Moravia
Płaskowyż Głubczycki

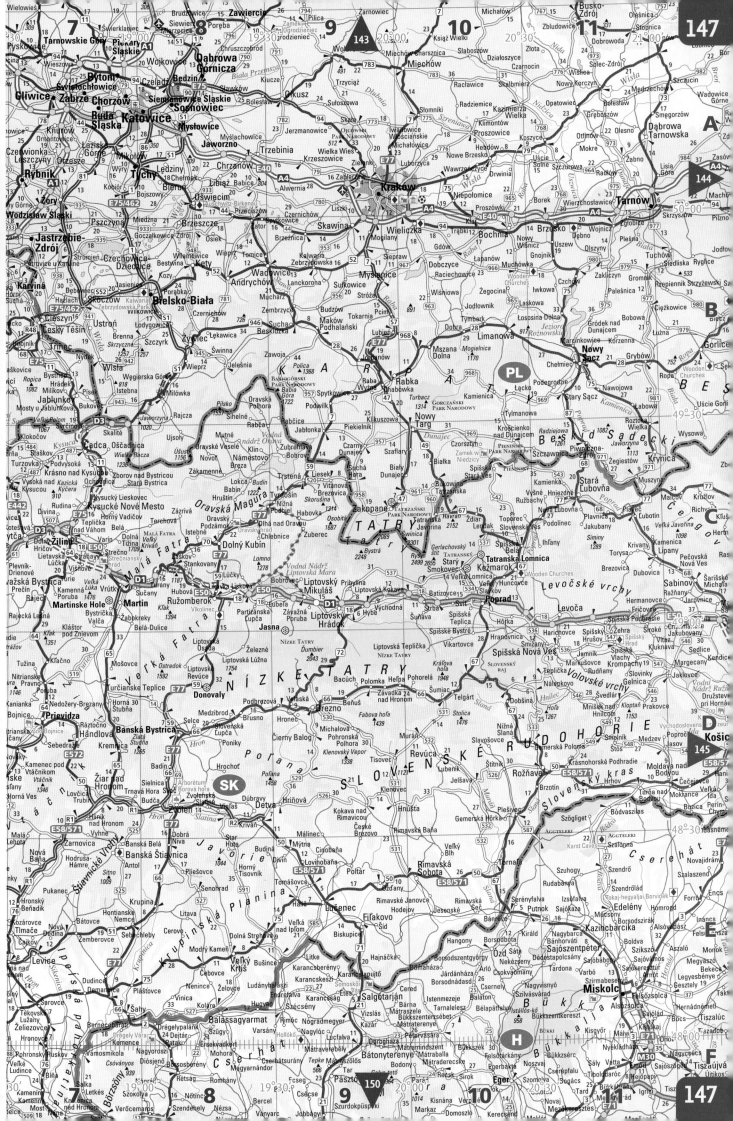

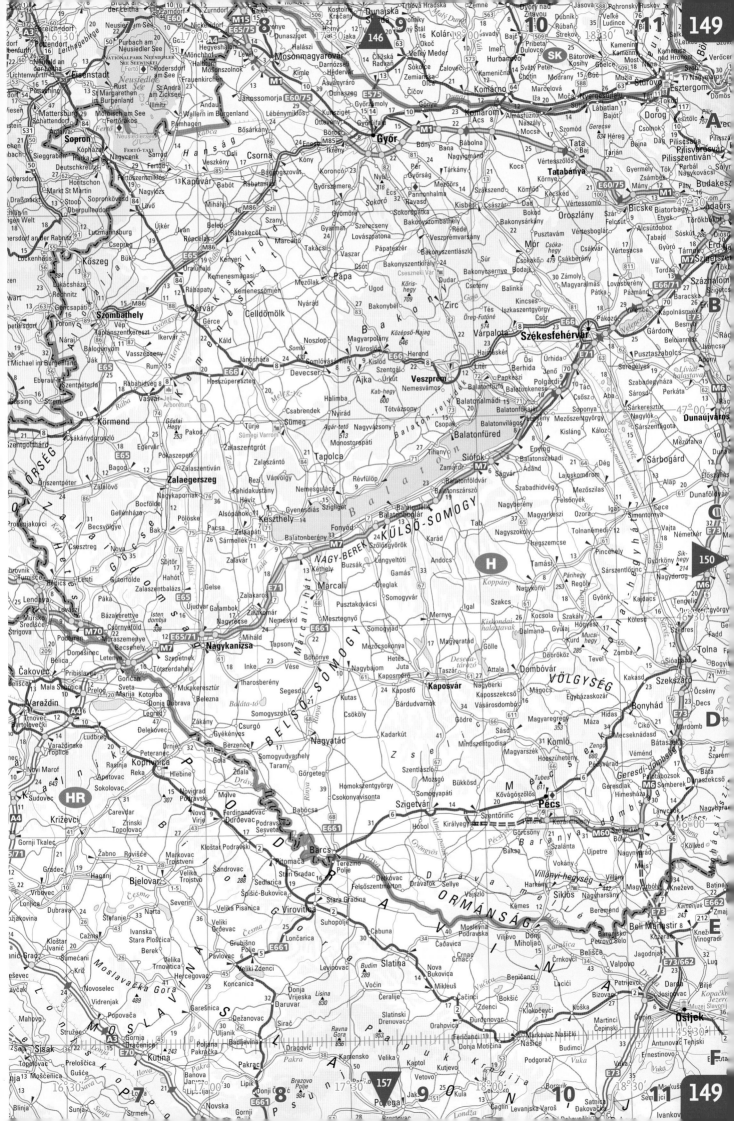

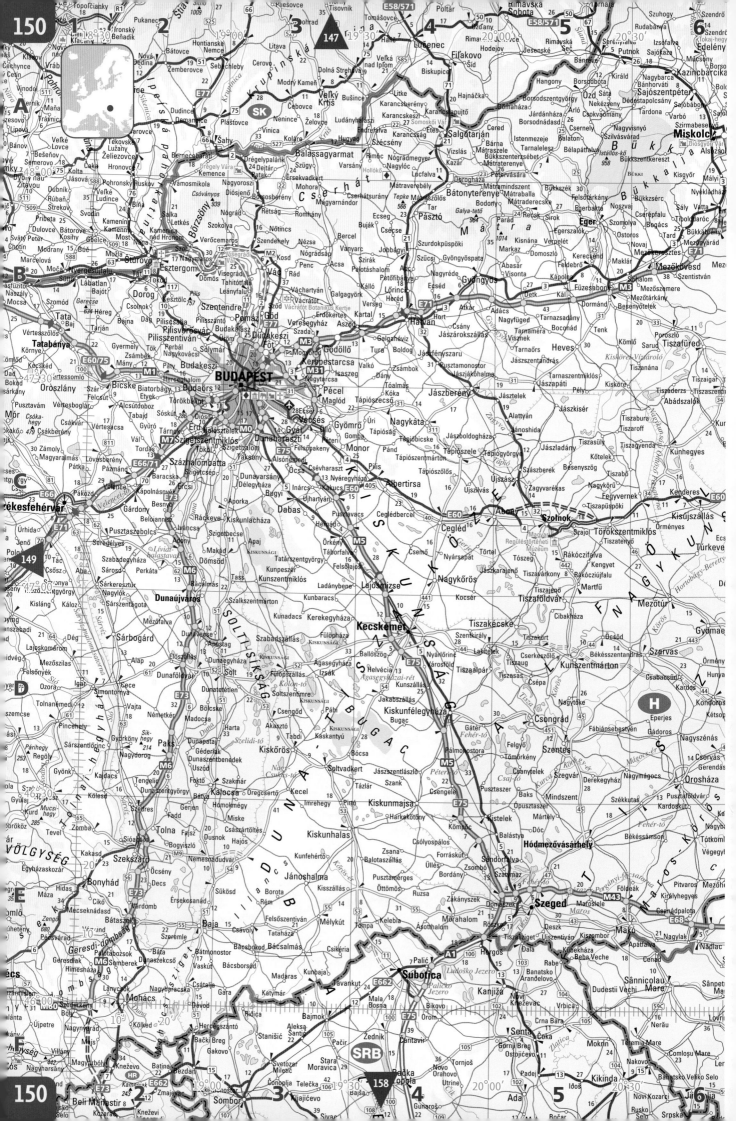

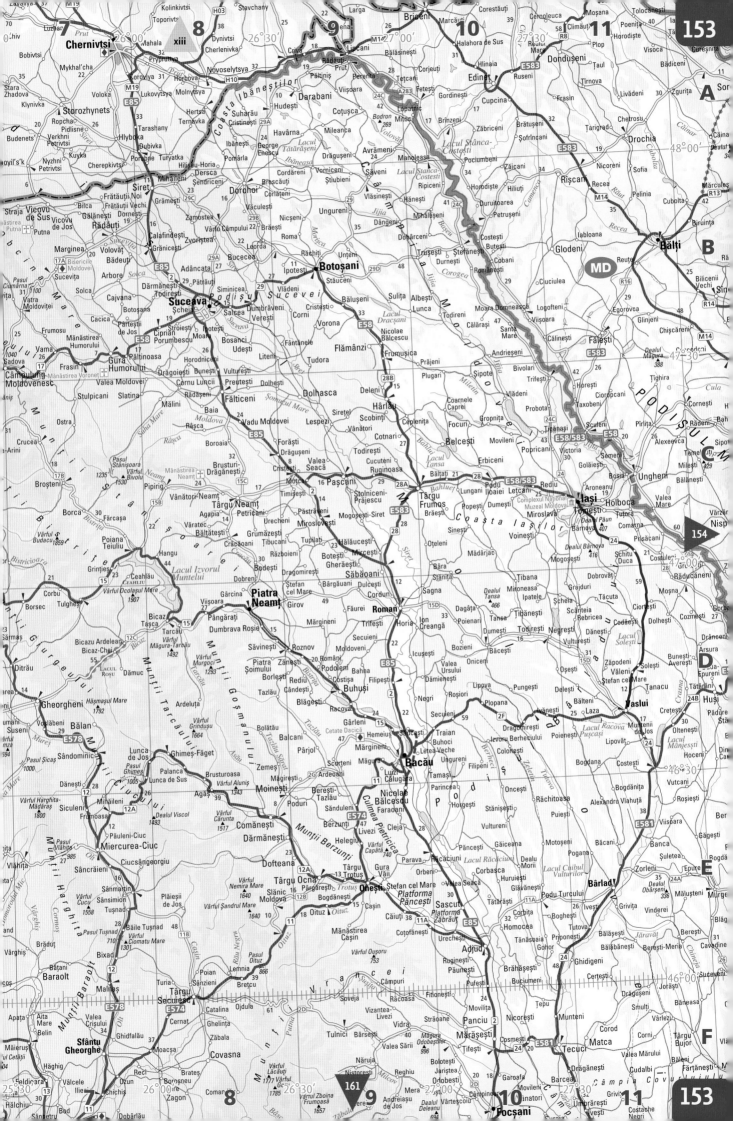

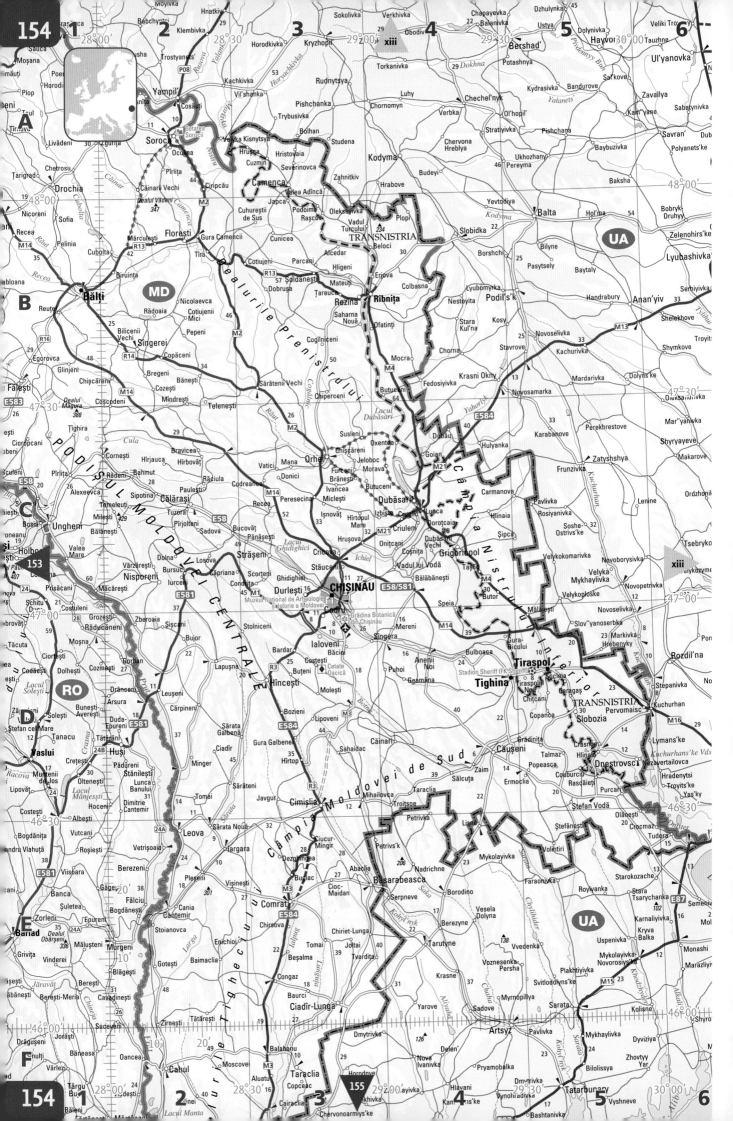

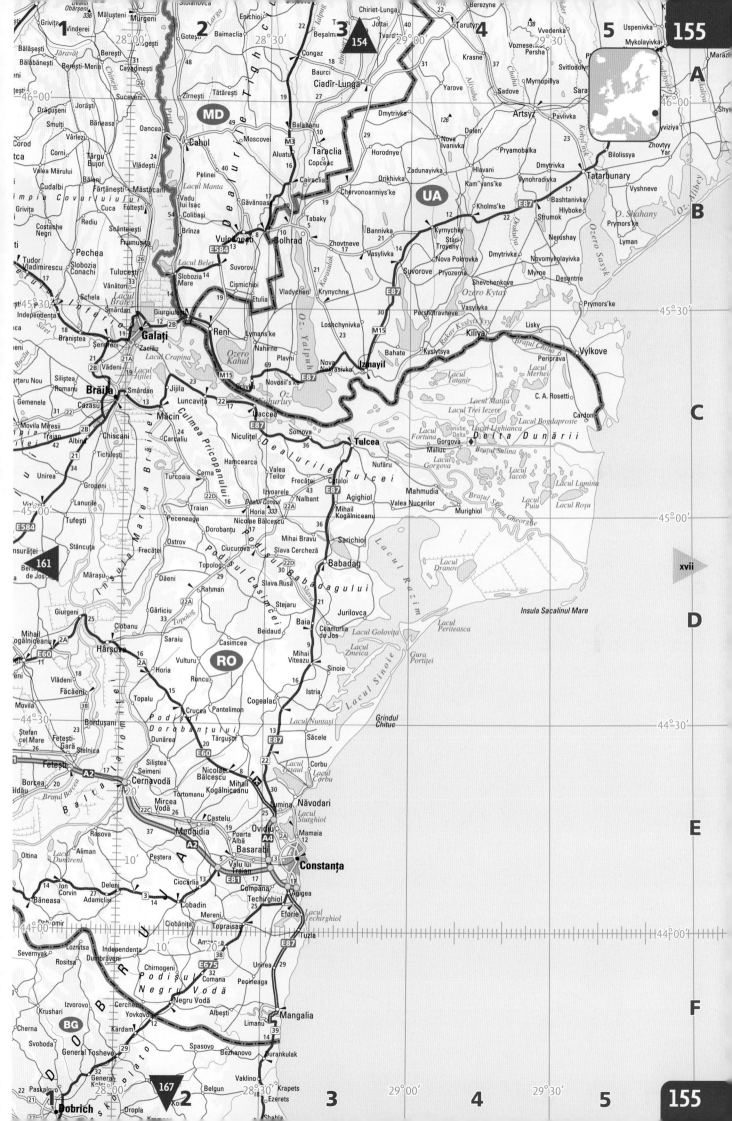

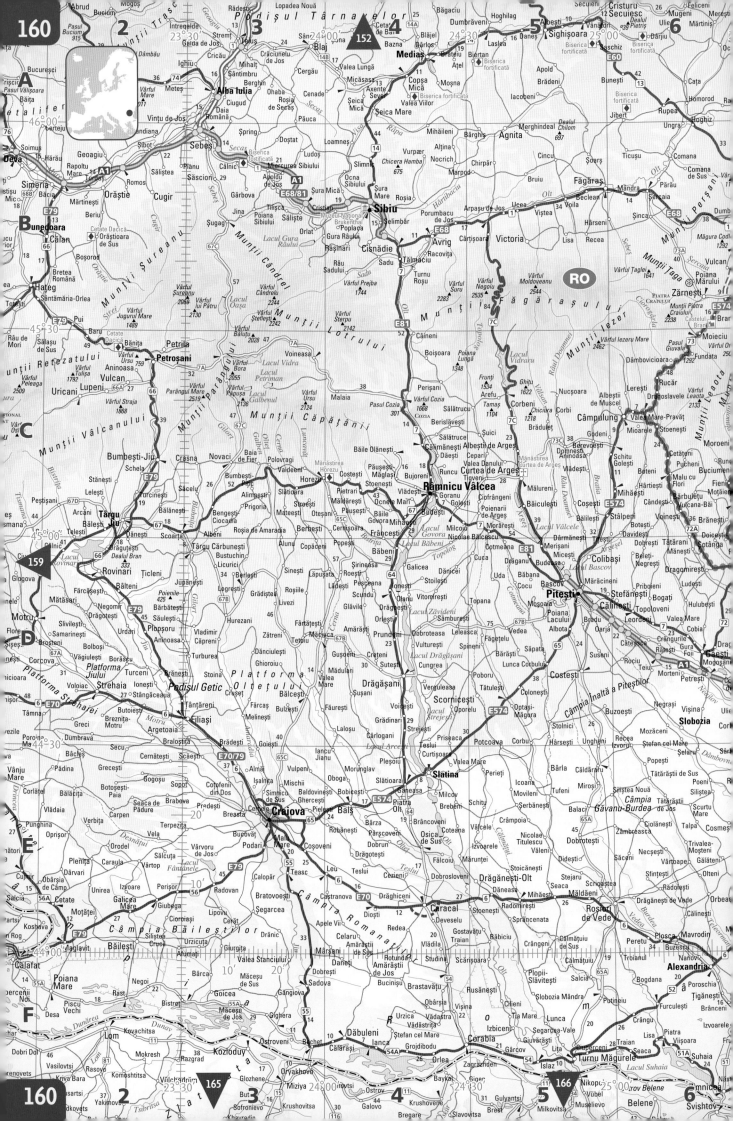

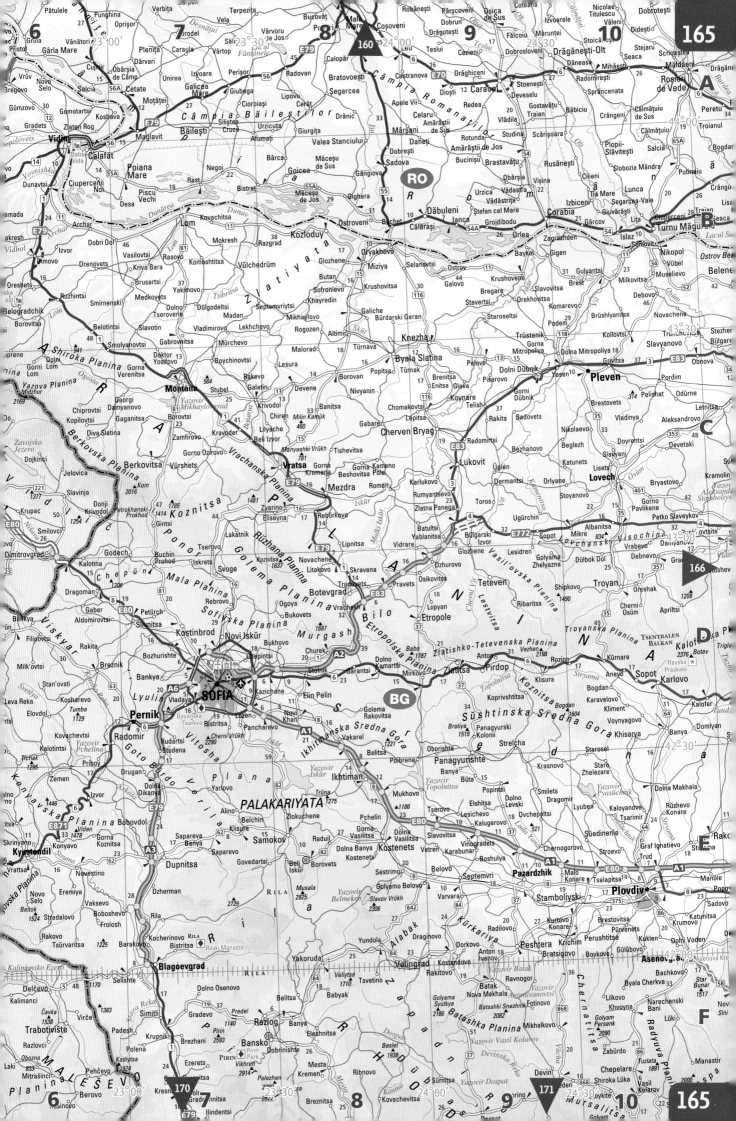

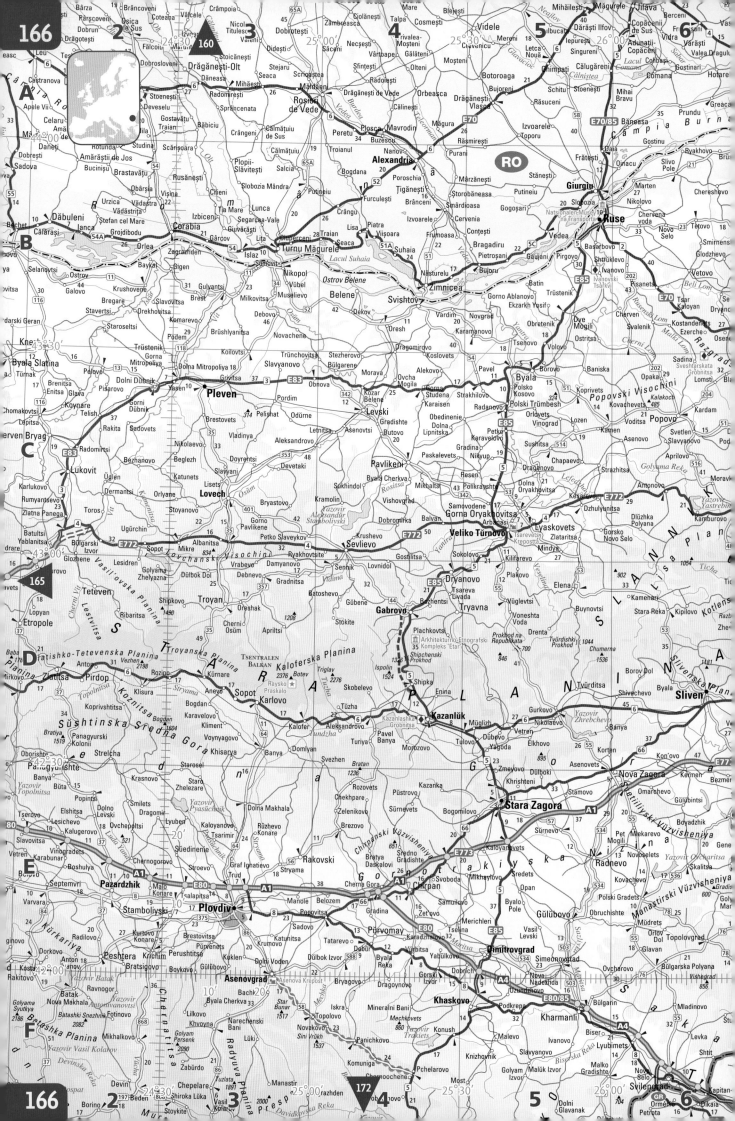

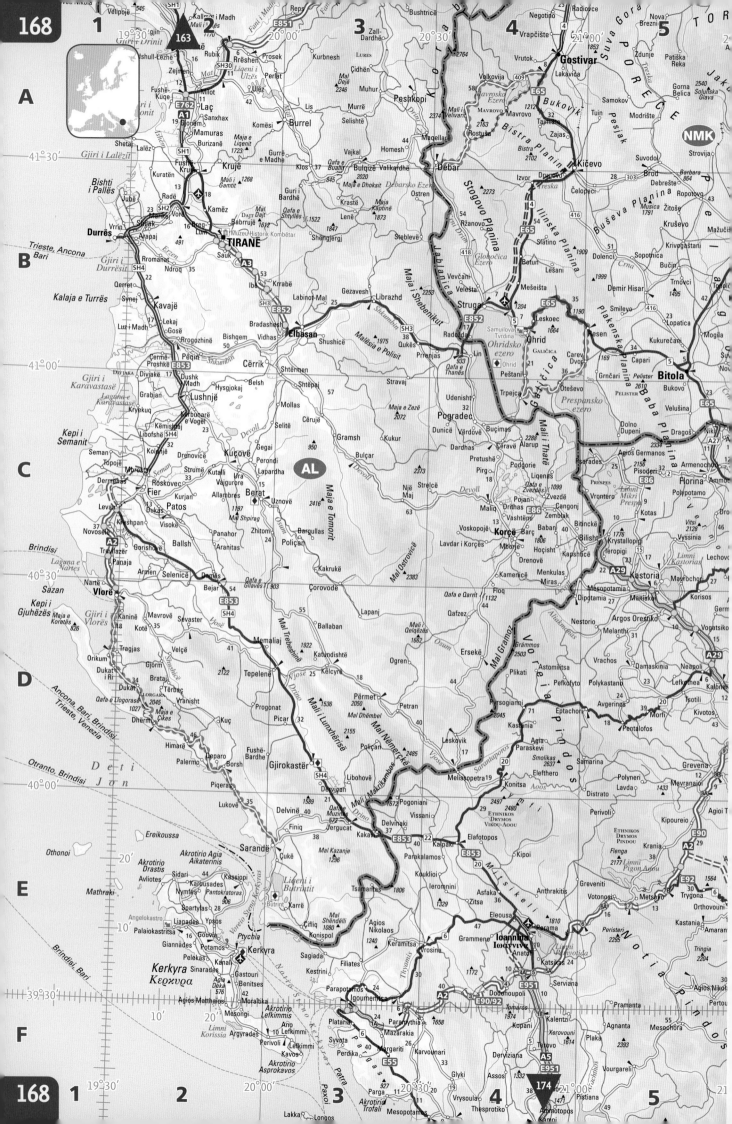

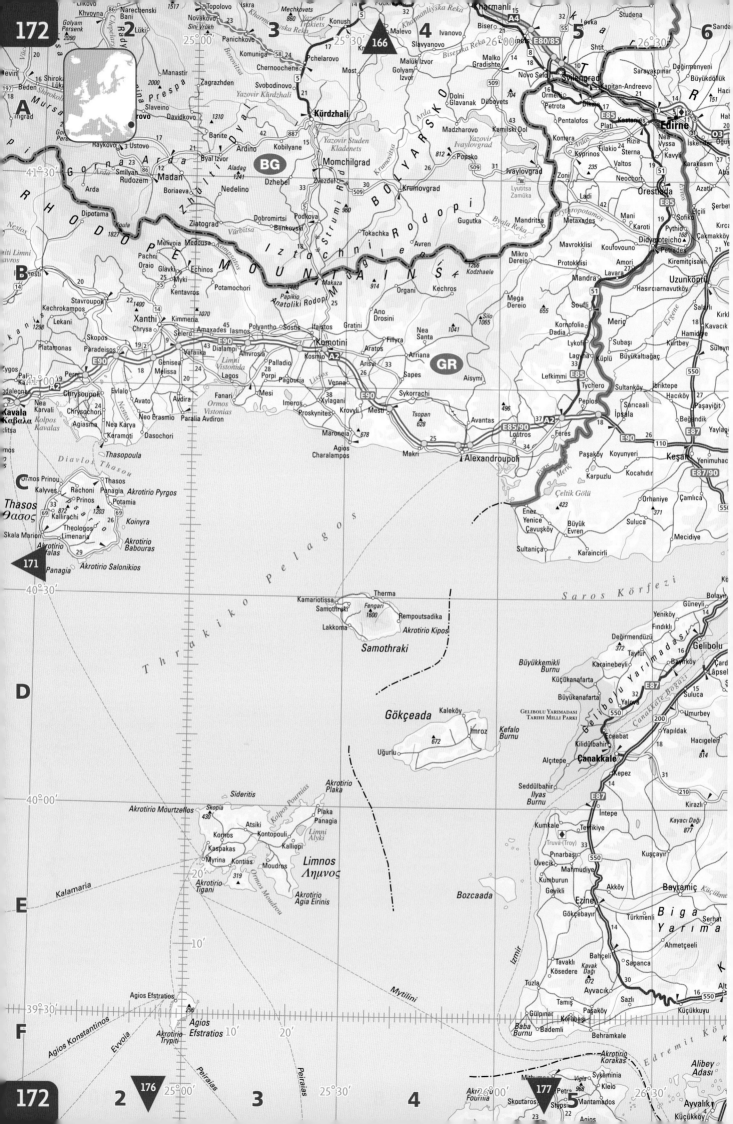

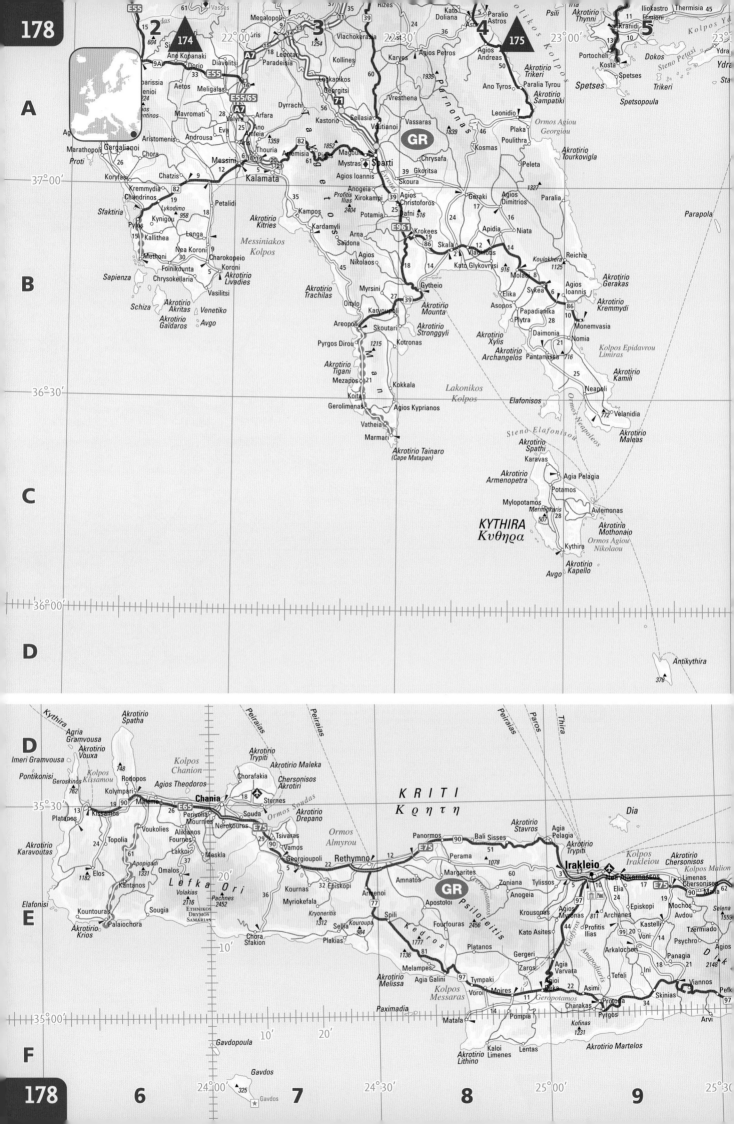

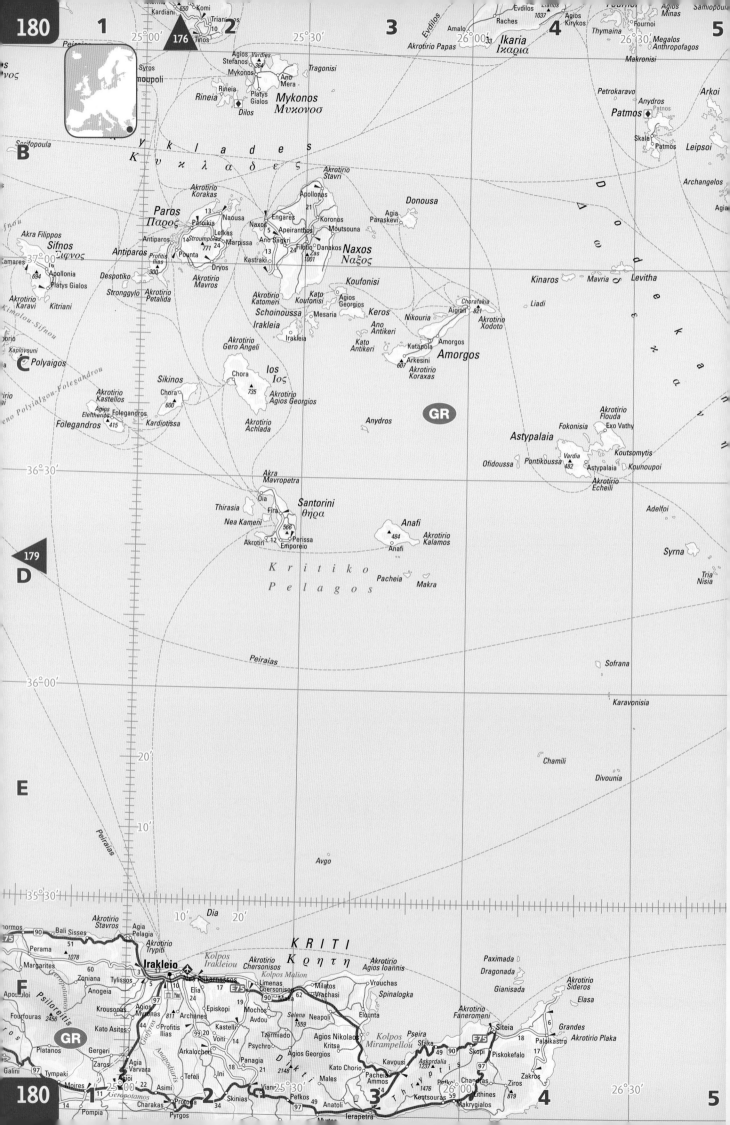

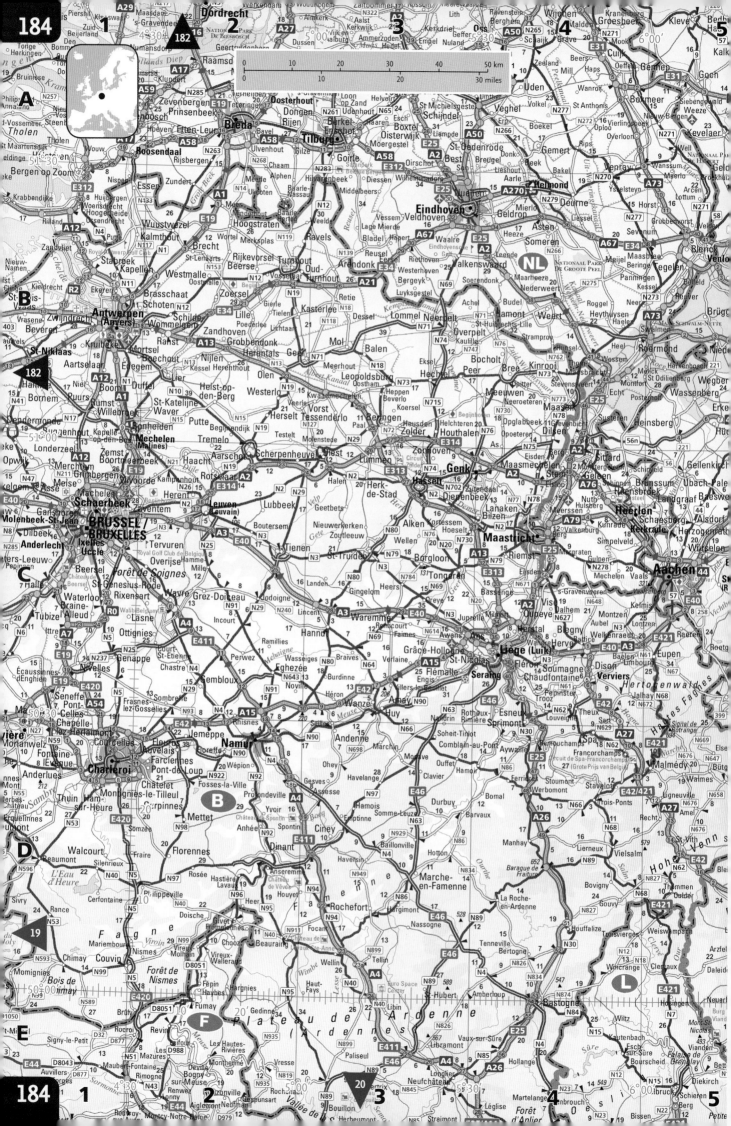

Nettetal D 183 C8
Neubrunn D 187 B8
Neubulach D 187 D6
Neuenbürg D 187 D6
Neuenkirchen-Seelscheid D 185 C7
Neuenrade D 185 B8
Neuenstadt am Kocher D 187 C7
Neuenstein D 187 C8
Neuerburg D 185 D5
Neufchâteau B 184 E3
Neuffen D 187 D7
Neufmanil F 184 E2
Neufra D 187 E7
Neuhausen D 187 D6
Neuhofen D 187 C5
Neu-Isenburg D 187 A6
Neuler D 187 D9
Neumagen D 185 E6
Neunkirchen D 185 C9
Neunkirchen D 186 C3
Neuss D 183 C9
Neustadt (Wied) D 185 C7
Neustadt an der Weinstraße D 186 C5
Neu-Ulm D 187 E9
Neuves-Maisons F 186 D1
Neuweiler D 187 D6
Neuwied D 185 D7
Nevele B 182 C3
Newel D 185 E6
Niederanven L 186 B1
Niederbrechen D 185 D9
Niederbreitbach D 185 C7
Niederbronn-les-Bains F 186 D4
Niederfischbach D 185 C8
Niederkassel D 183 D10
Niederkirchen D 186 B4
Niederkrüchten D 183 C8
Niederneisen D 185 D9
Niedernhall D 187 C8
Niedernhausen D 185 D9
Nieder-Olm D 185 E9
Nieder-Rodenbach D 187 A7
Niederselters D 185 D9
Niederstetten D 187 C8
Niederwerrn D 187 A9
Niederwörresbach D 186 B3
Niederzissen D 185 D7
Niefern-Öschelbronn D 187 D6
Niel B 182 C4
Nierstein D 185 E9
Nieuw-Bergen NL 183 B8
Nieuwegein NL 183 A6
Nieuwerkerk NL 182 B4
Nieuwerkerk aan de IJssel NL 182 B5
Nieuwerkerken B 183 D6
Nieuwe-Tonge NL 182 B4
Nieuw-Heeten NL 183 A8
Nieuwkoop NL 182 A5
Nieuw-Loosdrecht NL 183 A6
Nieuw-Milligen NL 183 A7
Nieuw-Namen NL 182 C4
Nieuwveen NL 182 A5
Nieuw-Vennep NL 182 A5
Nieuw-Vossemeer NL 182 B4
Nievern D 185 D8
Nijkerk NL 183 A6
Nijlen B 182 C5
Nijmegen NL 183 B7
Nijverdal NL 183 A8
Nilvange F 186 C1
Ninove B 182 D4
Nismes B 184 D2
Nispen NL 182 C4
Nistelrode NL 183 B7
Nittel D 186 B1
Nivelles B 182 D4
Nohfelden D 186 B3
Noisseville F 186 C1
Nomeny F 186 D1
Nomexy F 186 E1
Nonnenweier D 186 E4
Nonnweiler D 186 B2
Noordwijk aan Zee NL 182 A4
Noordwijk-Binnen NL 182 A4
Noordwijkerhout NL 182 A5
Nootdorp NL 182 A4
Nordheim D 187 C7
Nordkirchen D 185 A8
Nouzonville F 184 E2
Noville B 182 D5
Nüdlingen D 187 A9
Nuenen NL 183 C7
Nuland NL 183 B6
Numansdorp NL 182 B4
Nunkirchen D 186 C2
Nunspeet NL 183 A7
Nürtingen D 187 D7
Nuth NL 183 D7

O

Oberderdingen D 187 C6
Oberfell D 185 D7
Oberharmersbach D 186 E5
Oberhausen D 183 C9
Oberhausen-Rheinhausen D 187 C5
Oberhoffen-sur-Moder F 186 D4
Oberkirch D 186 D5
Oberkochen D 187 D9
Obermoschel D 186 B4
Obernai F 186 E3
Obernburg am Main D 187 B7
Oberndorf am Neckar D 187 E6
Obernheim-Kirchenarnbach D 186 C4
Ober-Olm D 185 E9
Ober-Roden D 187 B6
Oberrot D 187 C8
Obersinn D 187 A8
Obersontheim D 187 C8
Oberstenfeld D 187 C7
Oberthal D 186 B3
Oberthulba D 187 A8
Obertshausen D 187 A6
Oberursel (Taunus) D 187 A6
Oberwesel D 185 D8
Oberwolfach D 187 E5
Obrigheim D 187 C7
Obrigheim (Pfalz) D 187 B5
Ochsenfurt D 187 B9
Ochtrup D 183 A10
Odernheim am Glan D 186 B4
Oedelem B 182 C2
Oeffelt NL 183 B7
Oegstgeest NL 182 A5
Oene NL 183 A8
Oerlenbach D 187 A9
Oestrich-Winkel D 185 D8
Offenbach am Main D 187 A6
Offenbach an der Queich D 187 C5
Offenburg D 186 E4
Ofterdingen D 187 E7
Oftersheim D 187 C6
Ogéviller F 186 D2
Ohey B 183 E6
Ohlsbach D 186 E4
Öhringen D 187 C7
Oignies F 182 E1
Oijen NL 183 B6
Oirschot NL 183 B6
Oisterwijk NL 183 B6
Oldenzaal NL 183 A9
Olen B 182 C5
Olfen D 185 A7
Olpe D 185 B8
Olst NL 183 A8
Onstmettingen D 187 E6
Ooltgensplaat NL 182 B4
Oostakker B 182 C3
Oostburg NL 182 C2
Oostende B 182 C1
Oosterbeek NL 183 B7
Oosterhout NL 182 B5
Oosterland NL 182 B4
Oosterzele B 182 D3
Oostham B 183 C6
Oostkamp B 182 C2
Oostkapelle NL 182 B3
Oostmalle B 182 C5
Oost-Souburg NL 182 C3
Oostvoorne NL 182 B4
Ootmarsum NL 183 A9
Opglabbeek B 183 C7
Opheusden NL 183 B7
Opitter B 183 C7
Oploo NL 183 B7
Opoeteren B 183 C7
Oppenau D 187 E5
Oppenheim D 185 E9
Oppenweiler D 187 D7
Opwijk B 182 D4
Orchies F 182 E2
Orenhofen D 185 E6
Oreye B 183 D6
Ortenberg D 186 E4
Osburg D 186 B2
Oss NL 183 B7
Ossendrecht NL 182 C4
Ostend B 182 C1
Osterburken D 187 C7
Ostfildern D 187 D7
Osthofen D 187 B5
Ostricourt F 182 E2
Östringen D 187 C6
Ostwald F 186 D4
Ötigheim D 187 D5
Ötisheim D 187 D6
Ottenheim D 186 E4
Ottenhöfen im Schwarzwald D 187 D5
Otterbach D 186 C4
Otterberg D 186 B4
Otterlo NL 183 A7
Ottersweier D 186 D5
Ottignies B 182 D5
Ottweiler D 186 C3
Oud-Beijerland NL 182 B4
Ouddorp NL 182 B3
Oudenaarde B 182 D3
Oudenbosch NL 182 B5
Oudenburg B 182 C2
Oude-Tonge NL 182 B4
Oudewater NL 182 A5
Oud-Gastel NL 182 B4
Oud-Turnhout B 182 C5
Oud-Vossemeer NL 182 B4
Oudzele B 182 C2
Ouffet B 183 E6
Oulder B 184 D5
Oupeye B 183 D7
Overath D 185 C7
Overdinkel NL 183 A10
Overijse B 182 D5
Overloon NL 183 B7
Overpelt B 183 C6
Ovezande NL 182 C3
Owen D 187 D7

P

Paal B 183 C6
Padoux F 186 E2
Paliseul B 184 E3
Palzem D 186 B1
Pange F 186 C1
Panningen NL 183 C7
Papendrecht NL 182 B5
Partenstein D 187 A8
Pâturages B 182 E3
Pecq B 182 D2
Peer B 183 C6
Pelm D 185 D6
Pepingen B 182 D4
Pepinster B 183 D7
Perl D 186 C1
Péruwelz B 182 D3
Perwez B 182 D5
Petite-Rosselle F 186 C2
Petitmont F 186 D2
Pexonne F 186 E2
Pfaffenhofen an der Roth D 187 E9
Pfaffenhoffen F 186 D4
Pfalzfeld D 185 D8
Pfalzgrafenweiler D 187 D6
Pfedelbach D 187 C7
Pforzheim D 187 D6
Pfronstetten D 187 E7
Pfullingen D 187 E7
Pfungstadt D 187 B6
Phalsbourg F 186 D3
Philippeville B 184 D2
Philippine NL 182 C3
Philippsburg D 187 C5
Piershil NL 182 B4
Piesport D 185 E6
Pijnacker NL 182 A4
Pirmasens D 186 C4
Pittem B 182 D2
Plaidt D 185 D7
Plettenberg D 185 B8
Pliezhausen D 187 D7
Plobsheim F 186 E4
Plochingen D 187 D7
Ploegsteert B 182 D1
Plüderhausen D 187 D8
Poederlee B 182 C5
Polch D 185 D7
Polsbroek NL 182 B5
Pompey F 186 D1
Pont-à-Celles B 182 D4
Pont-à-Marcq F 182 D2
Pont-de-Loup B 182 E5
Poppenhausen D 187 A9
Portieux F 186 E1
Posterholt NL 183 C8
Poussay F 186 E1
Pracht D 185 C8
Prinsenbeek NL 182 B5
Profondeville B 184 D2
Pronsfeld D 185 D5
Provenchères-sur-Fave F 186 E3
Prüm D 185 D5
Puderbach D 185 C8
Pulheim D 183 C9
Putte B 182 C5
Putte NL 182 C4
Puttelange-aux-Lacs F 186 C2
Putten NL 183 A7
Püttlingen D 186 C2
Puurs B 182 C4

Q

Quaregnon B 182 E3
Queidersbach D 186 C4
Quendorf D 183 A10
Quesnoy-sur-Deûle F 182 D2
Quierschied D 186 C3
Quiévrain B 182 E3
Quiévrechain F 182 E3

R

Raalte NL 183 A8
Raamsdonksveer NL 182 B5
Radevormwald D 185 B7
Raeren B 183 D8
Raesfeld D 183 B9
Ralingen D 185 E6
Rambervillers F 186 E2
Rambrouch L 184 E4
Ramillies B 182 D5
Rammelsbach D 186 B3
Rammingen D 187 D9
Ramstein D 186 C4
Rance B 184 D1
Randersacker D 187 B8
Rangendingen D 187 E6
Ransbach-Baumbach D 185 D8
Ranst B 182 C5
Raon-l'Étape F 186 E2
Rastatt D 187 D5
Ratingen D 183 C9
Raubach D 185 C8
Ravels B 182 C5
Ravenstein NL 183 B7
Rebecq B 182 D4
Réchicourt-le-Château F 186 D2
Recht B 184 D5
Rechtenbach D 187 B8
Recklinghausen D 183 B10
Réding F 186 D3
Rees D 183 B8
Rehlingen-Siersburg D 186 C2
Reichelsheim (Odenwald) D 187 B6
Reichenbach D 187 B6
Reichenberg D 187 B8
Reicholzheim D 187 B8
Reichshoffen F 186 D4
Reichstett F 186 D4
Reil D 185 D7
Reilingen D 187 C6
Reinheim D 187 B6
Reinsfeld D 186 B2
Reken D 183 B10
Rekken NL 183 A9
Remagen D 185 C7
Remich L 186 B1
Remicourt B 183 D6
Remouchamps B 183 E7
Remscheid D 183 C10
Renchen D 186 D5
Renesse NL 182 B3
Rengsdorf D 185 C7
Renkum NL 183 B7
Rennerod D 185 C9
Renningen D 187 D6
Renswoude NL 183 A7
Renwez F 184 E2
Retie B 183 C6
Reusel NL 183 C6
Reutlingen D 187 E7
Reuver NL 183 C8
Revin F 184 E2
Rhaunen D 185 E7
Rhede D 183 B9
Rheden NL 183 A8
Rheinau D 186 D4
Rheinbach D 183 D9
Rheinberg D 183 B9
Rheinböllen D 185 E8
Rheinbreitbach D 185 C7
Rheinbrohl D 185 D7
Rheinstetten D 187 D5
Rheinzabern D 187 C5
Rhenen NL 183 B7
Rhens D 185 D8
Rhinau F 186 E4
Rhisnes B 182 D5
Rhoon NL 182 B4
Richardménil F 186 D1
Ridderkerk NL 182 B5
Riegelsberg D 186 C2
Riemst B 183 D7
Rieneck D 187 A8
Riethoven NL 183 C6
Rijen NL 182 B5
Rijkevorsel B 182 C5
Rijnsburg NL 182 A4
Rijsbergen NL 182 B5
Rijsel F 182 D2
Rijssen NL 183 A9
Rijswijk NL 182 A4
Rilland NL 182 C4
Rimbach D 187 B6
Rimogne F 184 E2
Rips NL 183 B7
Rittersdorf D 185 D5
Rixensart B 182 D5
Rochefort B 184 D3
Rochehaut B 184 E3
Rochin F 182 D2
Rockanje NL 182 B4
Rockenhausen D 186 B4
Rocroi F 184 E2
Rodalben D 186 C4
Roermond NL 183 C7
Roeselare B 182 D2
Roetgen D 183 D8
Roggel NL 183 C7
Röhlingen D 187 D9
Rohrbach-lès-Bitche F 186 C3
Rombas F 186 C1
Rommerskirchen D 183 C9
Ronse B 182 D3
Roosendaal NL 182 B4
Rosée B 184 D2
Rosenfeld D 187 E6
Rosheim F 186 D3
Rosmalen NL 183 B6
Rösrath D 185 C7
Roßdorf D 187 B6
Rossum NL 183 B6
Rot am See D 187 C9
Rothenberg D 187 B6
Rothenbuch D 187 B7
Rothenburg ob der Tauber D 187 C9
Rothenfels D 187 B8
Rotheux-Rimière B 183 D6
Rotselaar B 182 D5
Rottenacker D 187 E8
Rottenburg am Neckar D 187 E6
Rottendorf D 187 B9
Rotterdam NL 182 B5
Röttingen D 187 B8
Roubaix F 182 D2
Roulers B 182 D2
Rouvroy F 182 E1
Rouvroy-sur-Audry F 184 E2
Rozenburg NL 182 B4
Rozendaal NL 183 A7
Ruddervoorde B 182 C2
Rudersberg D 187 D8
Rüdesheim D 185 E8
Ruiselede B 182 C2
Rülzheim D 187 C5
Rumes B 182 D2
Rumigny F 184 E1
Rumst B 182 C4
Runkel D 185 D9
Rüsselsheim D 187 A5
Rutesheim D 187 D6
Rüthen D 185 B9
Rütten-Scheid D 183 C9
Ruurlo NL 183 A8

S

Saales F 186 E3
Saarbrücken D 186 C2
Saarburg D 186 B2
Saarlouis D 186 C2
Saarwellingen D 186 C2
Sachsenheim D 187 D7
St-Amand-les-Eaux F 182 E2
St-Avold F 186 C2
St-Blaise-la-Roche F 186 E3
St-Clément F 186 D2
St-Dié F 186 E2
Ste-Marguerite F 186 E2
Ste-Marie-aux-Mines F 186 E3
St-Firmin F 186 E1
St-Ghislain B 182 E3
St-Hubert B 184 D3
St-Louis-lès-Bitche F 186 D3
St-Max F 186 D1
St-Michel F 184 E1
St-Michel-sur-Meurthe F 186 E2
St-Nicolas B 183 D7
St-Nicolas-de-Port F 186 D1
St-Oedenrode NL 183 B6
St-Quirin F 186 D3
St-Vith B 184 D5
Salmtal D 185 E6
Sandhausen D 187 C6
Sankt Augustin D 185 C7
Sankt Goar D 185 D8
Sankt Goarshausen D 185 D8
Sankt Ingbert D 186 C3
Sankt Julian D 186 B4
Sankt Katharinen D 185 C7
Sankt Wendel D 186 C3
Santpoort NL 182 A5
Sarralbe F 186 D3
Sarrebourg F 186 D3
Sarreguemines F 186 C3
Sarre-Union F 186 D3
Sart B 183 D7
Sasbach D 186 D5
Sasbachwalden D 186 D5
Sassenheim NL 182 A5
Sas Van Gent NL 182 C3
Satteldorf D 187 C9
Saulheim D 185 E9
Saverne F 186 D3
Schaafheim D 187 B7
Schaarsbergen NL 183 A7
Schaerbeek B 182 D4
Schaesberg NL 183 D8
Schaijk NL 183 B7
Schalkhaar NL 183 A8
Schalksmühle D 185 B8
Scharendijke NL 182 B3
Schebheim D 187 B9
Schefflenz D 187 C7
Schelklingen D 187 E8
Schenkenzell D 187 E5
Schermbeck D 183 B9
Scherpenheuvel B 182 D5
Scherpenzeel NL 183 A6
Scherwiller F 186 E3
Schiedam NL 182 B4
Schieren L 184 E5
Schifferstadt D 187 C5
Schiffweiler D 186 C3
Schijndel NL 183 B6
Schilde B 182 C5
Schillingen D 186 B2
Schiltach D 187 E5
Schiltigheim F 186 D4
Schinnen NL 183 D7
Schinveld NL 183 D7
Schipluiden NL 182 B4
Schirmeck F 186 E3
Schlangenbad D 185 D9
Schleiden D 183 D8
Schmallenberg D 185 B9
Schmelz D 186 C2
Schnelldorf D 187 C9
Schnürpflingen D 187 E8
Schoenberg B 185 D5
Schöllkrippen D 187 A7
Schömberg D 187 D6
Schönaich D 187 D7
Schondra D 187 A8
Schönecken D 185 D5
Schönenberg-Kübelberg D 186 C3
Schöntal D 187 C8
Schoondijke NL 182 C3
Schoonhoven NL 182 B5
Schorndorf D 187 D8
Schoten B 182 C4
Schriesheim D 187 C6
Schrozberg D 187 C8
Schuttertal D 186 E4
Schutterwald D 186 E4
Schüttorf D 183 A10
Schwäbisch Gmünd D 187 D8
Schwäbisch Hall D 187 C8
Schwaigern D 187 C7
Schwalbach D 186 C2
Schwegenheim D 187 C5
Schweich D 185 E6
Schweigen-Rechtenbach D 186 C4
Schweighouse-sur-Moder F 186 D4
Schweinfurt D 187 A9
Schwelm D 185 B7
Schwerte D 185 B8
Schwieberdingen D 187 D7
Seckach D 187 C7
Seclin F 182 D2
Seebach D 187 D5
Seeheim-Jugenheim D 187 B6
Seilles B 183 E6
Seinsheim D 187 B9
Sélestat F 186 E3
Seligenstadt D 187 A6
Selm D 185 A7
Selters (Westerwald) D 185 C8
Seltz F 186 D5
Senden D 187 E9
Seneffe B 182 D4
Senones F 186 E2
Seraing B 183 D7
Serooskerke NL 182 B3
Serrig D 186 B2
Sevenum NL 183 C8
's-Gravendeel NL 182 B5
's-Gravenhage NL 182 A4
's-Gravenmoer NL 182 B5
's-Gravenpolder NL 182 C3
's-Gravenvoeren B 183 D7
's-Gravenzande NL 182 B4
's-Heerenberg NL 183 B8
's-Heerenhoek NL 182 C3
's-Hertogenbosch NL 183 B6
Siebengewald NL 183 B8
Siegburg D 185 C7
Siegen D 185 C9
Sierck-les-Bains F 186 C1
Siershahn D 185 D8
Signy-le-Petit F 184 E1
Sijsele B 182 C2
Silenrieux B 184 D1
Simmerath D 183 D8
Simmern (Hunsrück) D 185 E8
Simpelveld NL 183 D7
Sindelfingen D 187 D6
Singhofen D 185 D8
Sinn D 185 C9
Sinsheim D 187 C6
Sint Annaland NL 182 B4
Sint Anthonis NL 183 B7
Sint-Genesius-Rode B 182 D4
Sint-Gillis-Waas B 182 C4
Sint-Huibrechts-Lille B 183 C6
Sint Jansteen NL 182 C4
Sint-Katelijne-Waver B 182 C5
Sint-Laureins B 182 C3
Sint-Lenaarts B 182 C5
Sint Maartensdijk NL 182 B4
Sint-Margriete B 182 C3
Sint-Maria-Lierde B 182 D3
Sint-Martens-Latem B 182 C3
Sint Michielsgestel NL 183 B6
Sint-Niklaas B 182 C4
Sint Odilienberg NL 183 C8
Sint-Pauwels B 182 C4
Sint Philipsland NL 182 B4
Sint-Pieters-Leeuw B 182 D4
Sint-Truiden B 183 D6
Sinzheim D 187 D5
Sinzig D 185 C7
Sittard NL 183 D7
Sivry B 184 D1
Sleidinge B 182 C3
Sliedrecht NL 182 B5
Sluis NL 182 C2
Sluiskil NL 182 C3
Soerendonk NL 183 C7
Soest D 185 A9
Soest NL 183 A6
Soesterberg NL 183 A6
Soheit-Tinlot B 183 E6
Sohren D 185 E7
Soignies B 182 D4
Solingen D 183 C10
Sombreffe B 182 D5
Someren NL 183 C7
Somme-Leuze B 184 D3
Somzée B 184 D1
Son NL 183 B6
Soufflenheim F 186 D4
Soultz-sous-Forêts F 186 D4
Soumagne B 183 D7
Spa B 183 E7
Spabrücken D 185 E8
Spay D 185 D8
Speicher D 185 E6
Speyer D 187 C5
Spiere B 182 D2
Spiesen-Elversberg D 186 C3
Spijkenisse NL 182 B4
Spontin B 184 D3
Spraitbach D 187 D8
Sprendlingen D 185 E8
Sprimont B 183 D7
Sprockhövel D 185 B7
Stabroek B 182 C4
Staden B 182 D2
Stadtkyll D 185 D6
Stadtlohn D 183 B9
Staig D 187 E8
Standdaarbuiten NL 182 B5
Stavelot B 184 D4
Stavenisse NL 182 B4
Steenbergen NL 182 B4
Steenderen NL 183 A8
Stein NL 183 D7
Steinach D 186 E5
Steinfeld D 186 C5
Steinfeld D 187 B8
Steinheim am Albuch D 187 D9
Steinheim an der Murr D 187 D7
Steinsfeld D 187 C9
Steinwenden D 186 C4
Stekene B 182 C4
Stellendam NL 182 B4
Stevensweert NL 183 C7
Stimpfach D 187 C9
Stiring-Wendel F 186 C2
Stockstadt am Rhein D 187 B5
Stolberg (Rheinland) D 183 D8
Stoumont B 183 E7
Straelen D 183 C8
Straimont B 184 E3
Stramproy NL 183 C7
Strasbourg F 186 D4
Strassen L 186 B1
Straßenhaus D 185 C8
Strijen NL 182 B5
Stromberg D 185 E8
Sturzelbronn F 186 C4
Stuttgart D 187 D7
Suddendorf D 183 A10
Südlohn D 183 B9
Sulz am Neckar D 187 E6
Sulzbach am Main D 187 B7
Sulzbach an der Murr D 187 C7
Sulzbach-Laufen D 187 D8
Sulzbach/Saar D 186 C3
Sulzfeld D 187 C6
Sulzthal D 187 A9
Sundern (Sauerland) D 185 B9
Susteren NL 183 C7
Swalmen NL 183 C8

T

Taintrux F 186 E2
Talange F 186 C1
Tamm D 187 D7
Tantonville F 186 E1
Tauberbischofsheim D 187 B8
Tawern D 186 B2
Tegelen NL 183 C8
Tellin B 184 D3
Templeuve F 182 D2
Temse B 182 C4
Tenneville B 184 D4
Ter Aar NL 182 A5
Terborg-Silvolde NL 183 B8
Terheijden NL 182 B5
Terneuzen NL 182 C3
Tervuren B 182 D5
Tessenderlo B 183 C6
Testelt B 182 C5
Teteringen NL 182 B5
Thaleischweiler-Fröschen D 186 C4
Thalfang D 186 B2
Thaon-les-Vosges F 186 E1
't Harde NL 183 A7
Theux B 183 D7
Thionville F 186 C1
Tholen NL 182 B4
Tholey D 186 C3
Thommen B 184 D5
Thorn NL 183 C7
Thuin B 184 D1
Thüngen D 187 B8
Thüngersheim D 187 B8
Tiefenbronn D 187 D6
Tiel NL 183 B6
Tielen B 182 C5
Tielt B 182 D2
Tienen B 182 D5
Tilburg NL 183 B6
Tongeren B 183 D6
Tönisvorst D 183 C8
Torhout B 182 C2
Tourcoing F 182 D2
Tournai B 182 D2
Traar D 183 C9
Traben D 185 E7
Trarbach D 185 E7
Trebur D 187 B5
Treis D 185 D7
Tremelo B 182 D5
Trier D 186 B2
Trierweiler D 186 B2
Trippstadt D 186 C4
Trittenheim D 185 E6
Trochtelfingen D 187 E7
Troisdorf D 183 D10
Troisfontaines F 186 D3
Trois-Ponts B 184 D4
Troisvierges L 184 D5
Trooz B 183 D7
Truchtersheim F 186 D4
Trulben D 186 C4
Tubbergen NL 183 A9
Tübingen D 187 D7
Tubize B 182 D4
Turnhout B 182 C5
Twello NL 183 A8

U

Übach-Palenberg D 183 D8
Überherrn D 186 C2
Ubstadt-Weiher D 187 C6
Uccle B 182 D4
Üchtelhausen D 187 A9
Uckange F 186 C1
Uddel NL 183 A7
Uden NL 183 B7
Udenhout NL 183 B6
Üdersdorf D 185 D6
Uettingen D 187 B8
Uffenheim D 187 B9
Uhingen D 187 D8
Uithoorn NL 182 A5
Ulft NL 183 B8
Ulicoten NL 182 C5
Ulm D 187 E8
Ulmen D 185 D6
Ulvenhout NL 182 B5
Undingen D 187 E7
Unkel D 185 C7
Unna D 185 A8
Unnau D 185 C8
Untermünkheim D 187 C8
Unterpleichfeld D 187 B9
Urbach D 185 C8
Urbar D 185 D8
Urberach D 187 B6
Utrecht NL 183 A6
Üxheim D 185 D6

V

Vaals NL 183 D8
Vaassen NL 183 A7
Valkenburg NL 183 D7
Valkenswaard NL 183 C6
Vallendar D 185 D8
Vandœvre-lès-Nancy F 186 D1
Varik NL 183 B6
Varsseveld NL 183 B8
Vaux-sur-Sûre B 184 E4
Veenendaal NL 183 A7
Veere NL 182 B3
Veerle B 182 C5
Veghel NL 183 B7
Velbert D 183 C10
Veldegem B 182 C2
Velden NL 183 C8
Veldhoven NL 183 C6
Velen D 183 B9
Vellberg D 187 C8
Velp NL 183 B7
Vendenheim F 186 D4
Venlo NL 183 C8
Venray NL 183 B7
Vergaville F 186 D2
Verlaine B 183 D6
Verny F 186 C1
Verviers B 183 D7
Vessem NL 183 C6
Vettelschoss D 185 C7
Vianden L 184 E5
Vianen NL 183 B6
Vic-sur-Seille F 186 D2
Vielsalm B 184 D4
Vierlingsbeek NL 183 B7
Viernheim D 187 B6
Viersen D 183 C8
Vieux-Condé F 182 E3
Vigy F 186 C1
Villé F 186 E3
Villeneuve-d'Ascq F 182 D2
Villers-le-Bouillet B 183 D6
Villers-lès-Nancy F 186 D1
Villmar D 185 D9
Vilvoorde B 182 D4
Vincey F 186 E1
Vinkt B 182 C2
Vinningen D 186 C4
Vireux-Molhain F 184 D2
Vireux-Wallerand F 184 D2
Visé B 183 D7
Vlaardingen NL 182 B4
Vleuten NL 183 A6
Vlijmen NL 183 B6
Vlissingen NL 182 C3
Voerde (Niederrhein) D 183 B9
Vogelenzang NL 182 A5
Vogelweh D 186 C4
Vöhringen D 187 E6
Vöhringen D 187 E9
Volkach D 187 B9
Volkel NL 183 B7
Völklingen D 186 C2
Volmunster F 186 C3
Voorburg NL 182 A4
Voorhout NL 182 A4
Voorschoten NL 182 A4
Voorst NL 183 A8
Voorthuizen NL 183 A7
Vorden NL 183 A8
Vorst B 183 C6
Vosselaar B 182 C5
Vrasene B 182 C4
Vreden D 183 A9
Vreeland NL 183 A6
Vresse B 184 E2
Vriezenveen NL 183 A9
Vrouwenpolder NL 182 B3
Vught NL 183 B6

W

Waalre NL 183 C6
Waalwijk NL 183 B6
Waarschoot B 182 C3
Wachenheim an der Weinstraße D 187 C5
Wachtebeke B 182 C3
Wächtersbach D 187 A7
Waddinxveen NL 182 A5
Wadern D 186 B2
Wadersloh D 185 A9
Wadgassen D 186 C2
Wageningen NL 183 B7
Waghäusel D 187 C6
Waiblingen D 187 D7
Waibstadt D 187 C6
Waigolshausen D 187 B9
Waimes B 183 E8
Walcourt B 184 D1
Waldachtal D 187 E6
Waldböckelheim D 185 E8
Waldbreitbach D 185 C7
Waldbröl D 185 C8
Waldbrunn-Lahr D 185 C9
Waldbüttelbrunn D 187 B8
Waldenbuch D 187 D7
Waldenburg D 187 C8
Waldesch D 185 D8
Waldfischbach-Burgalben D 186 C4
Wald-Michelbach D 187 B6
Waldmohr D 186 C3
Waldrach D 186 B2
Waldsee D 187 C5
Waldstetten D 187 D8
Walferdange L 186 B1
Walldorf D 187 A6
Walldorf D 187 C6
Walldürn D 187 B7
Wallhausen D 185 E8
Wallhausen D 187 C9
Wamel NL 183 B6
Wandre B 183 D7
Wanne-Eikel D 183 B10
Wanroij NL 183 B7
Wanssum NL 183 B8
Wanze B 183 D6
Wapenveld NL 183 A8
Waregem B 182 D2
Waremme B 183 D6
Warmond NL 182 A5
Warnsveld NL 183 A8
Warstein D 185 B9
Wartmannsroth D 187 A8
Wäschenbeuren D 187 D8
Waspik NL 182 B5
Wasseiges B 183 D6
Wasselonne F 186 D3

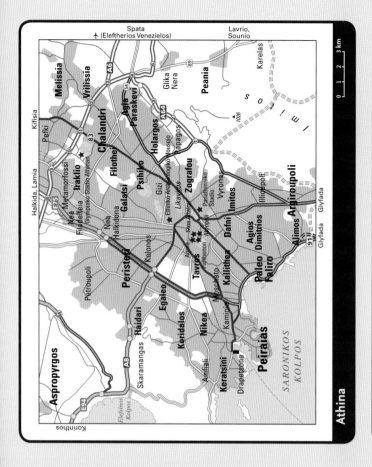

Athina

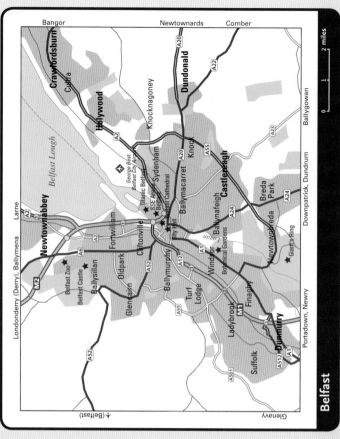

Belfast

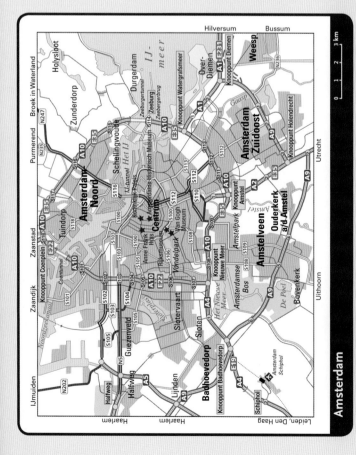

Amsterdam

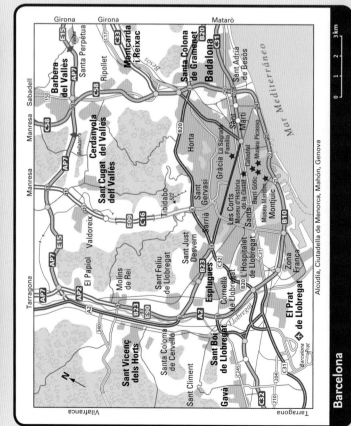

Barcelona

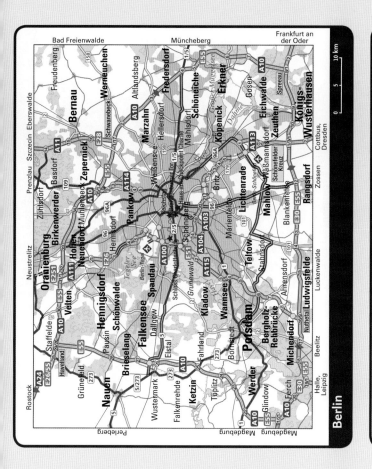

Berlin

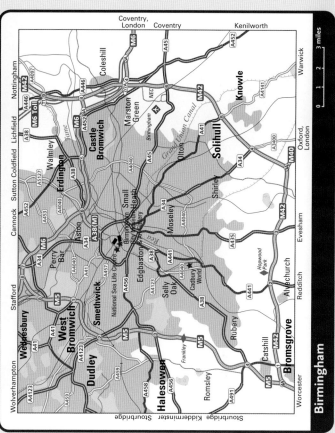

Birmingham

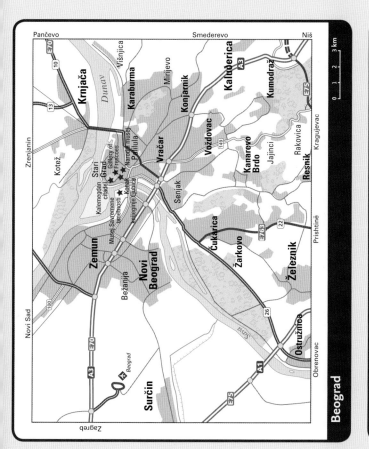

Beograd

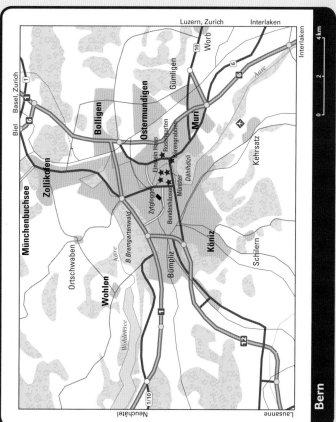

Bern

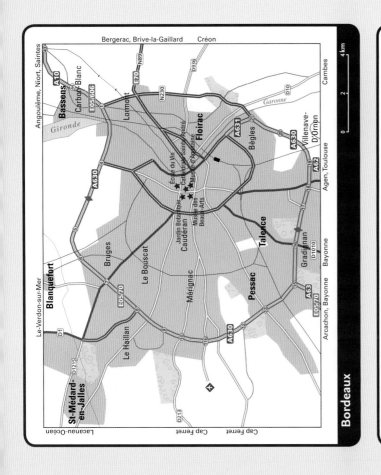

Bordeaux

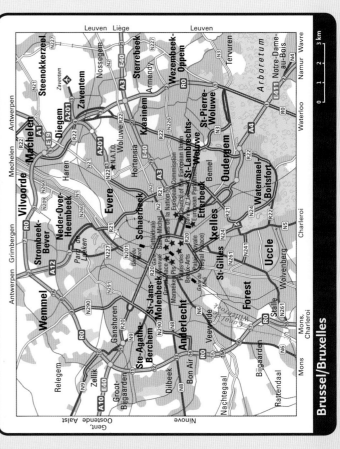

Brussel/Bruxelles

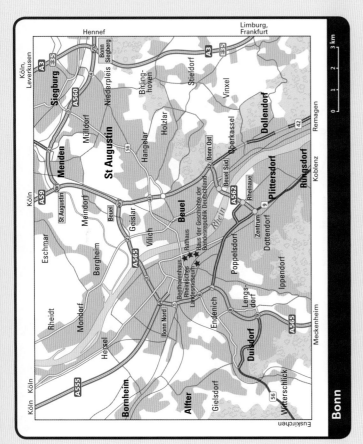

Bonn

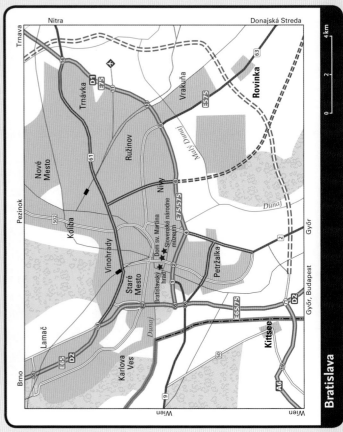

Bratislava

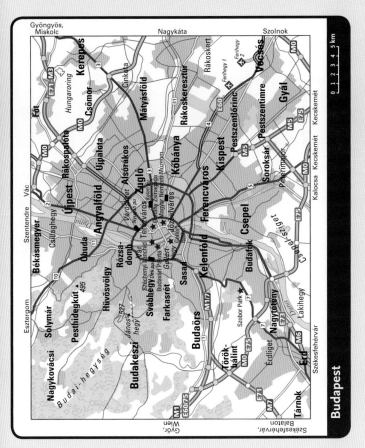

Budapest

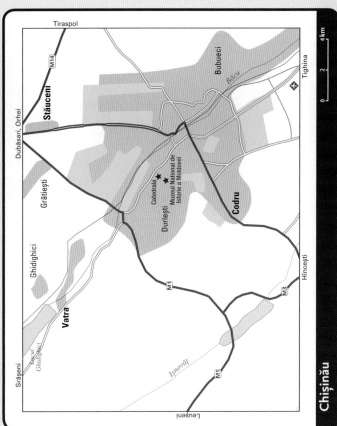

Chișinău

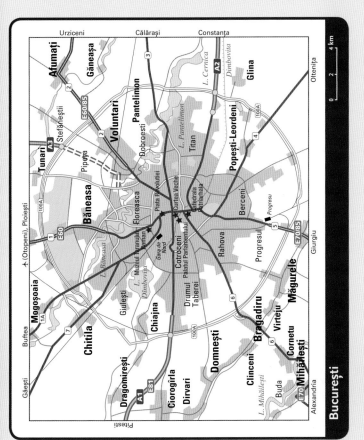

București

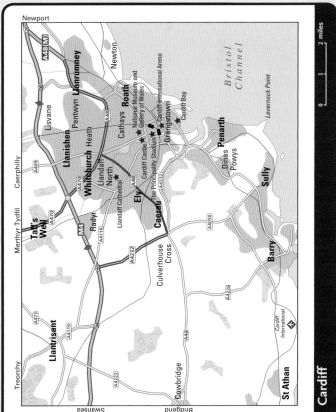

Cardiff

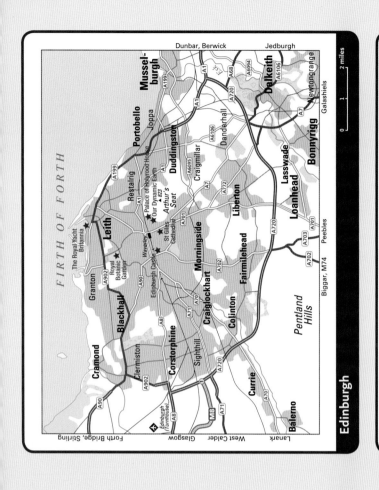

Edinburgh

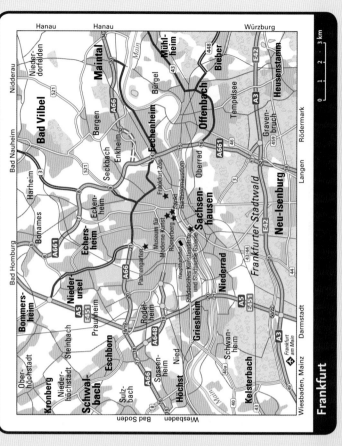

Frankfurt

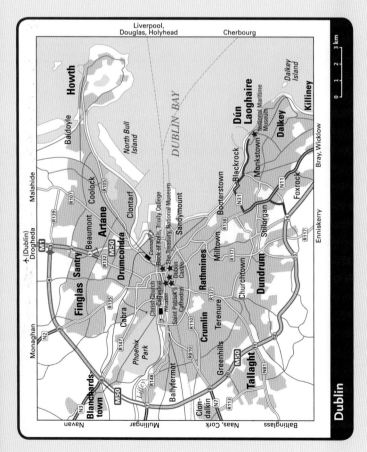

Dublin

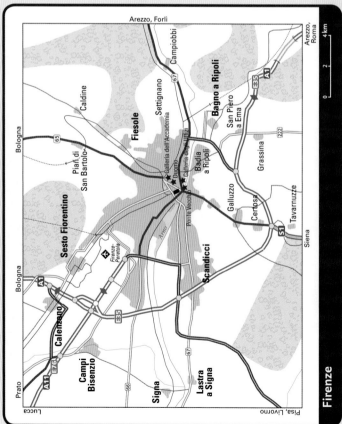

Firenze

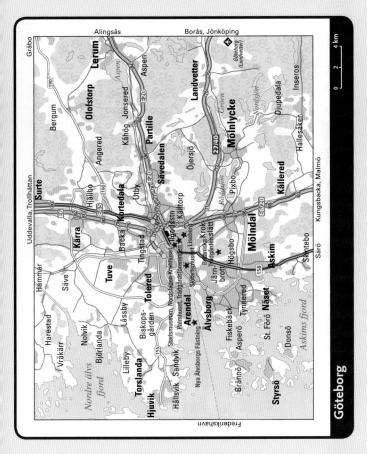

Göteborg

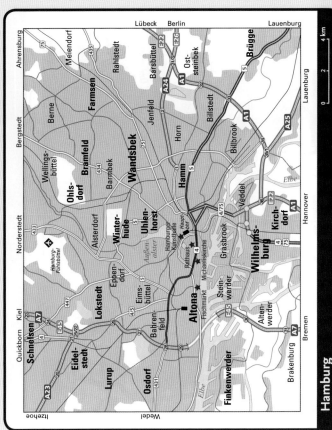

Hamburg

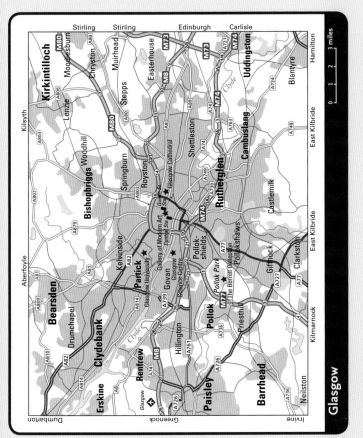

Glasgow

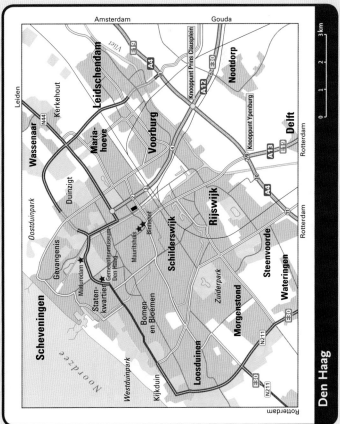

Den Haag

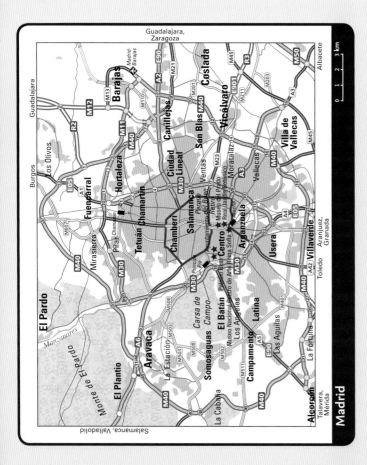

Madrid

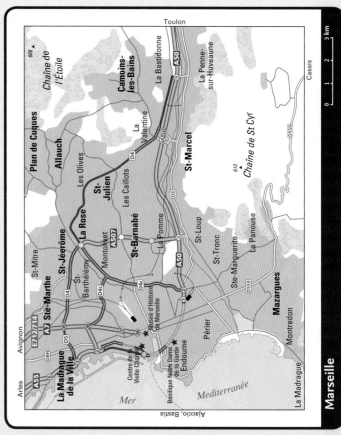

Marseille

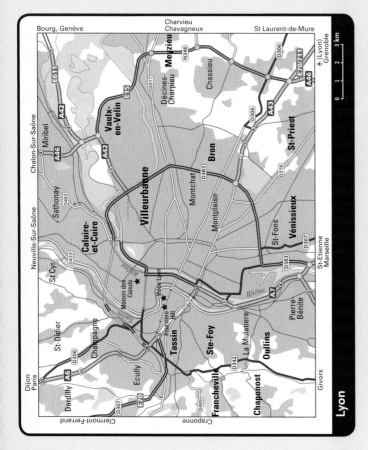

Lyon

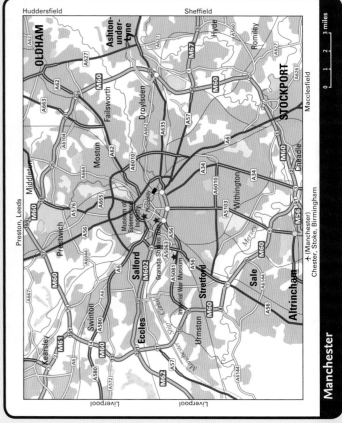

Manchester

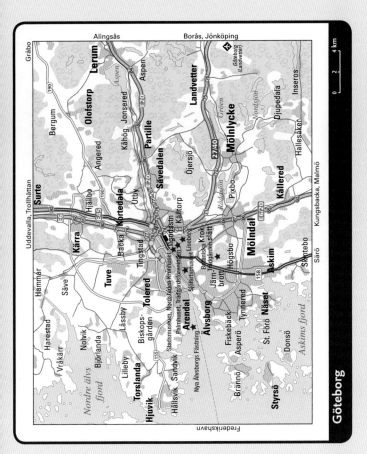

Göteborg

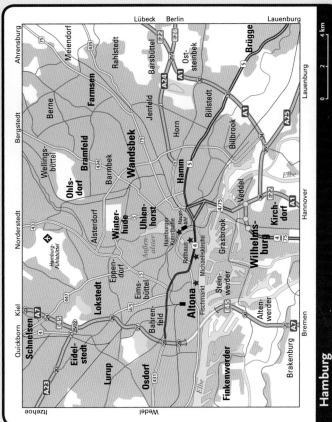

Hamburg

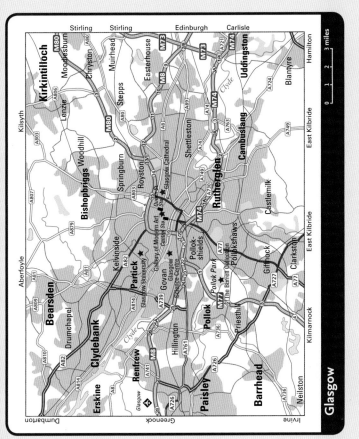

Glasgow

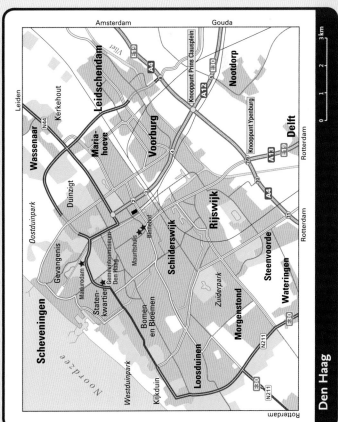

Den Haag

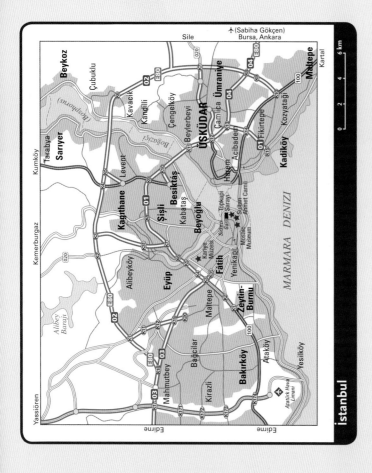

İstanbul

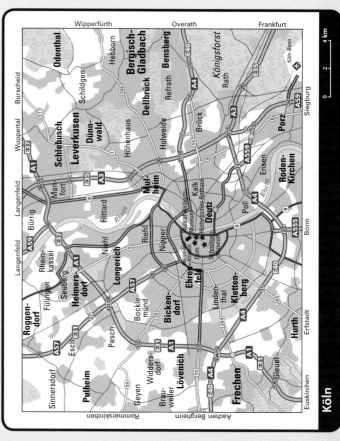

Köln

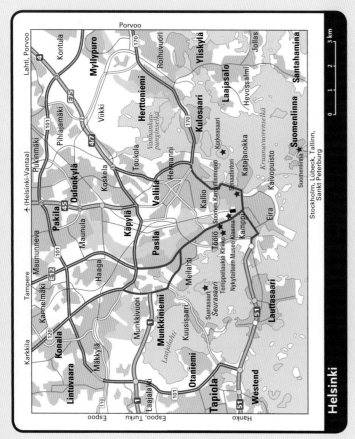

Helsinki

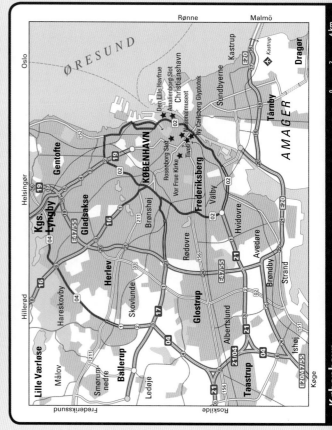

København

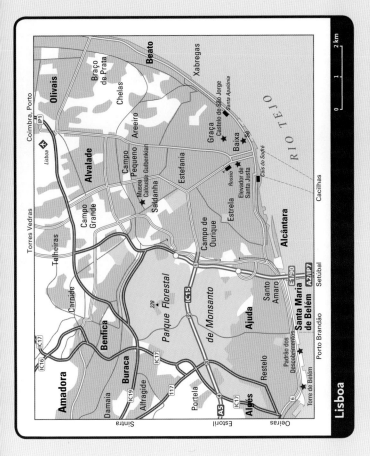

Lisboa

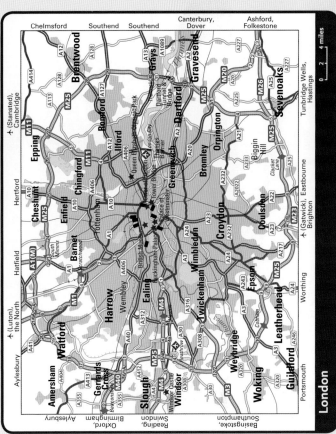

London

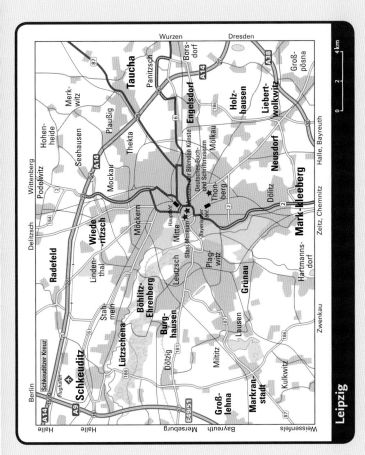

Leipzig

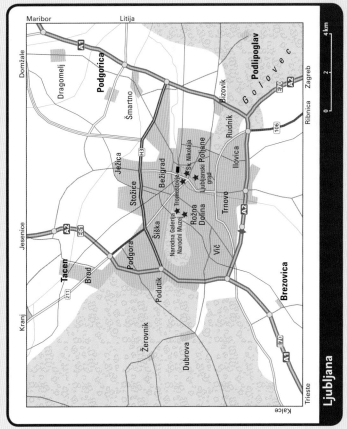

Ljubljana

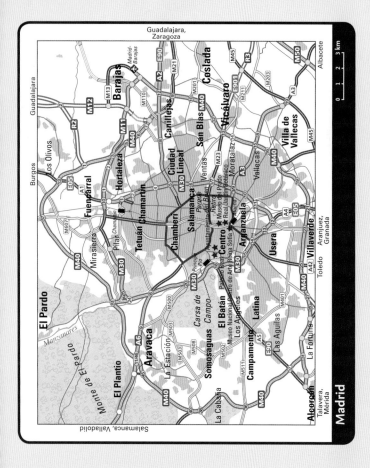

Madrid

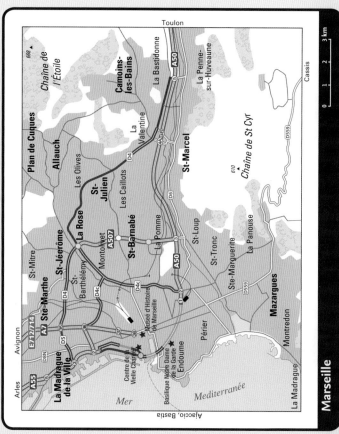

Marseille

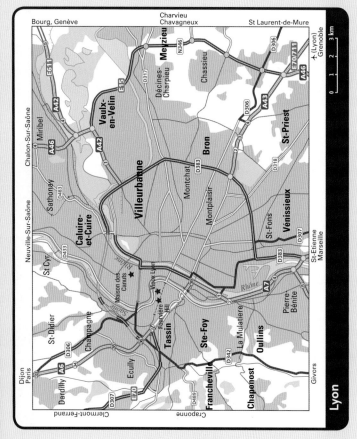

Lyon

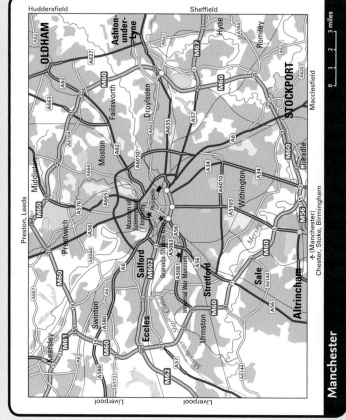

Manchester

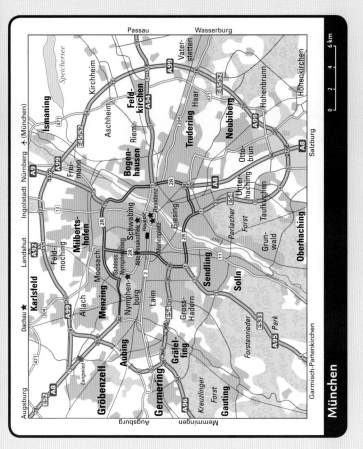

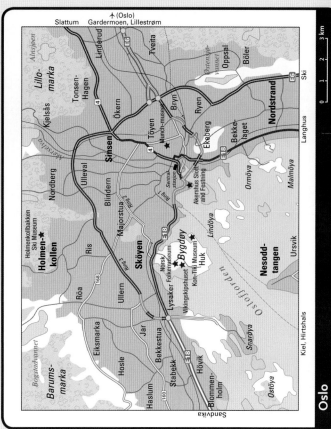

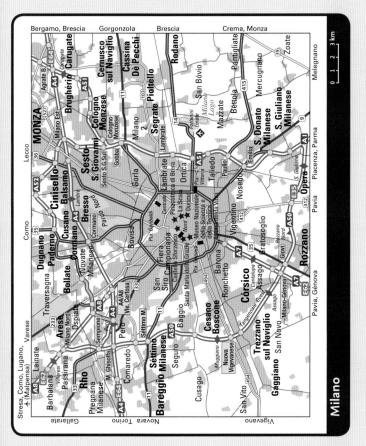

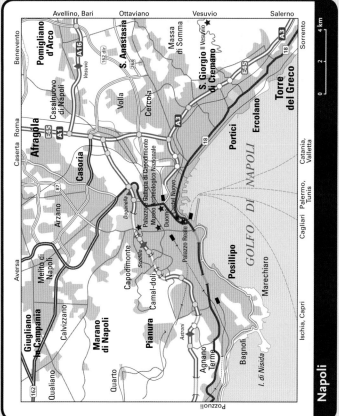

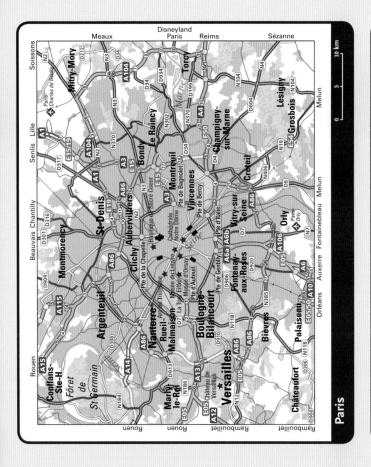

Paris

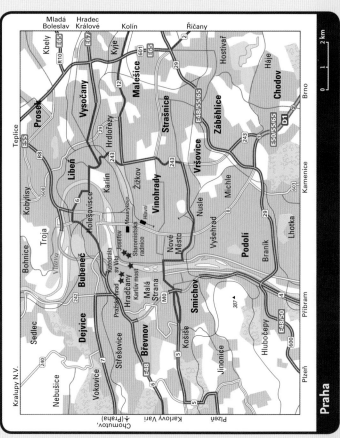

Praha

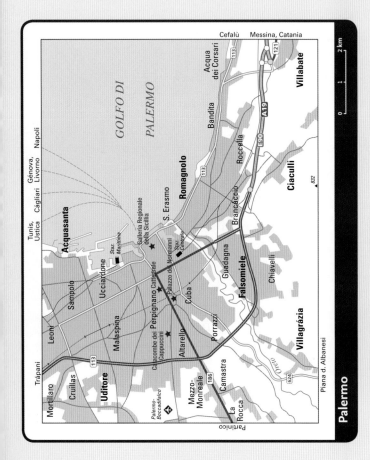

Palermo

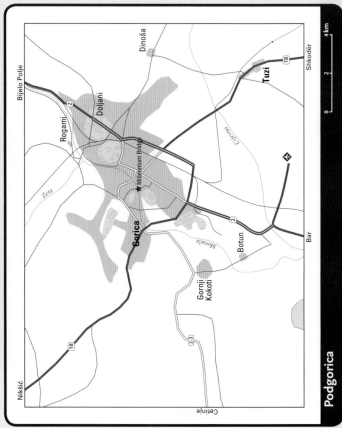

Podgorica

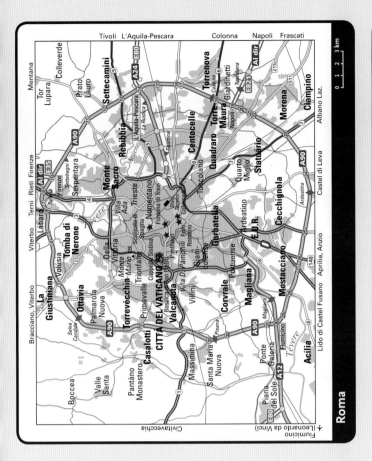

Roma

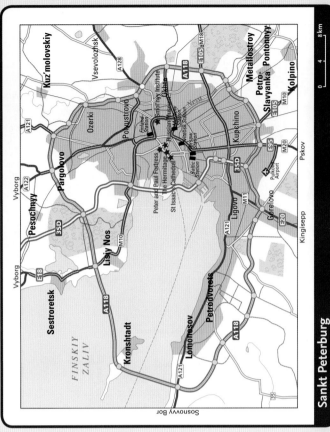

Sankt Peterburg

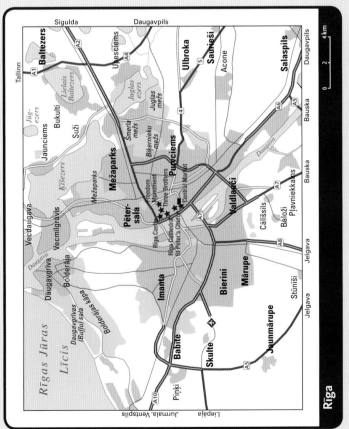

Rīga

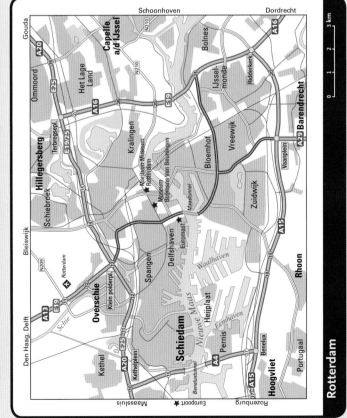

Rotterdam

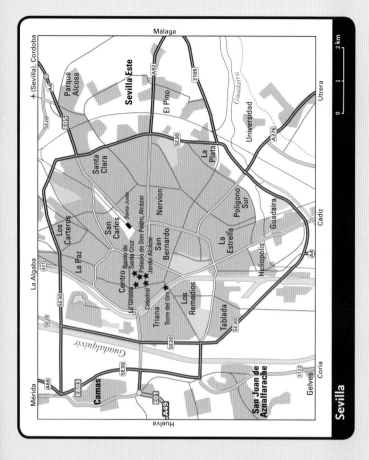

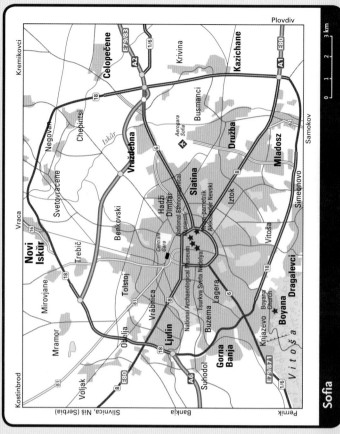

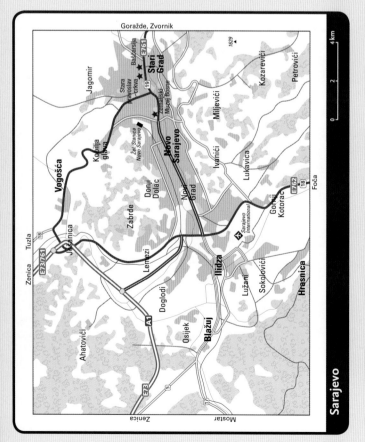

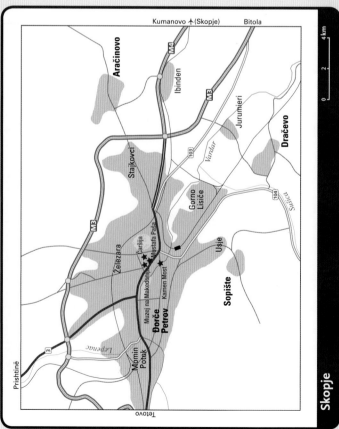

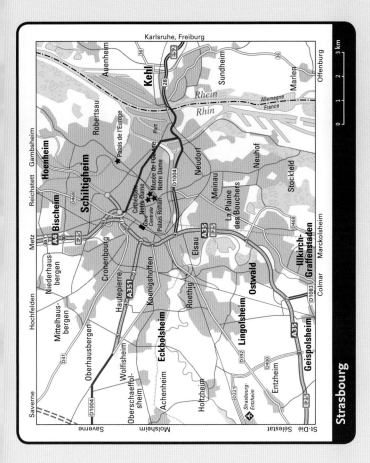

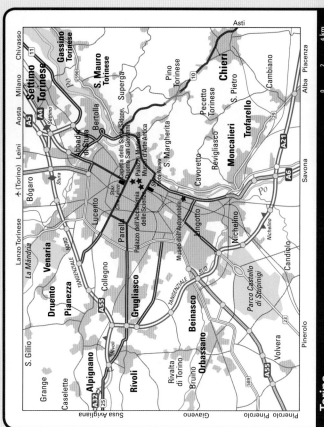

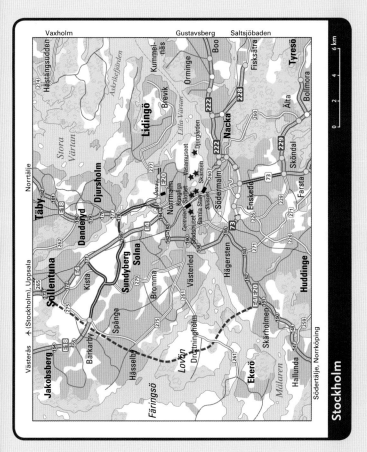

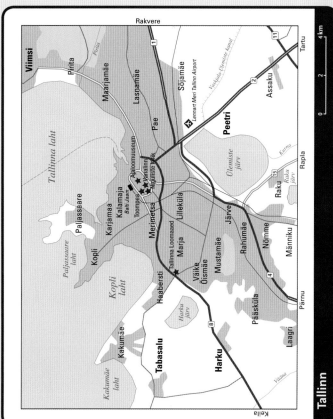

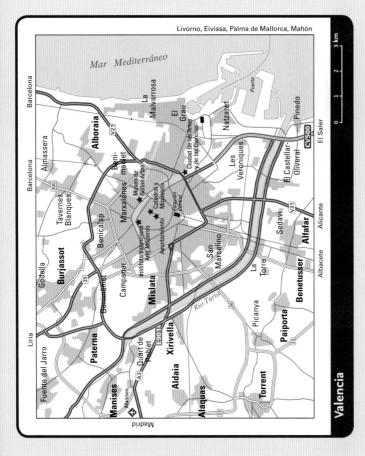

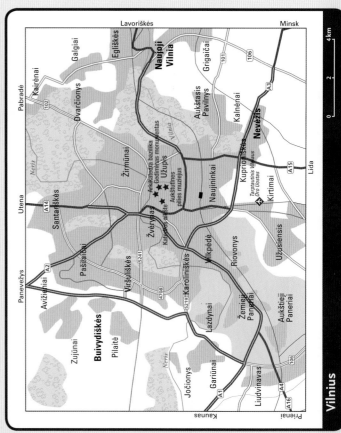

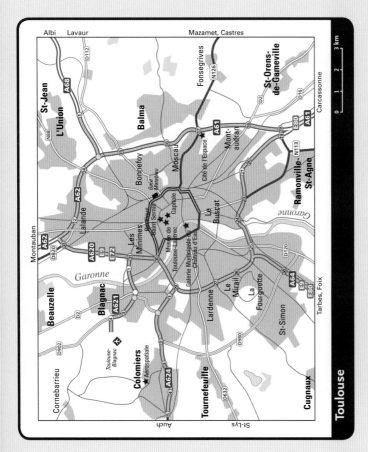

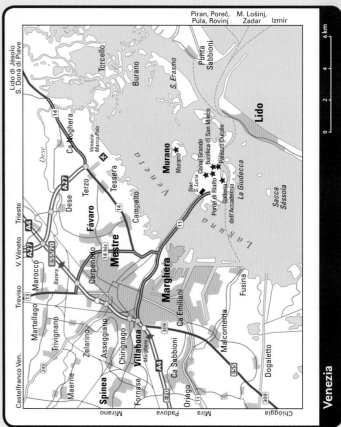

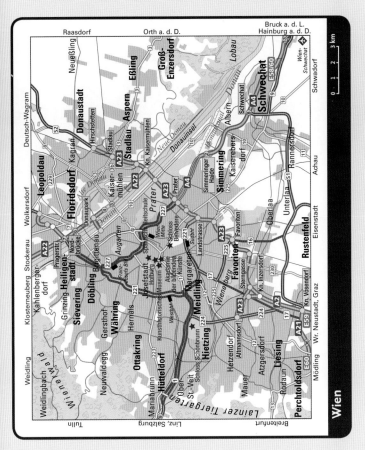

Wien

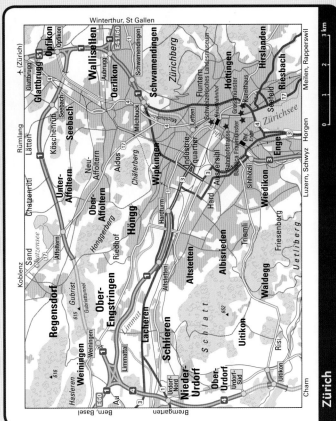

Zürich

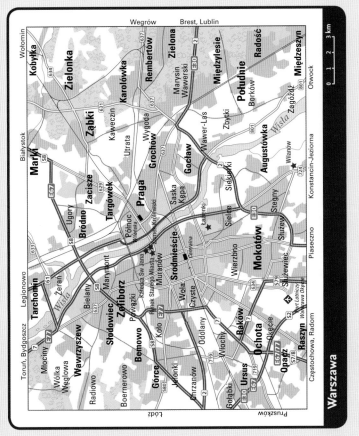

Warszawa

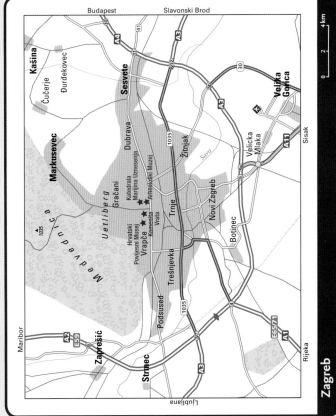

Zagreb

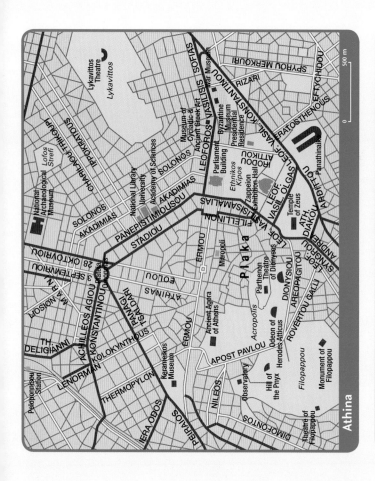

Athina

Bern

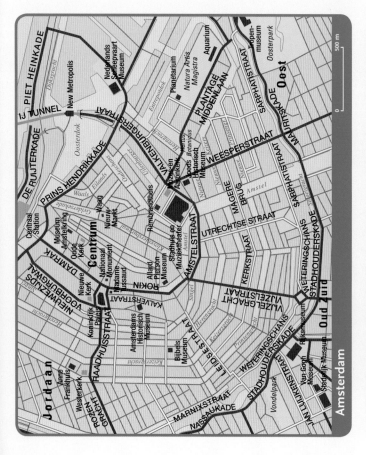

Amsterdam

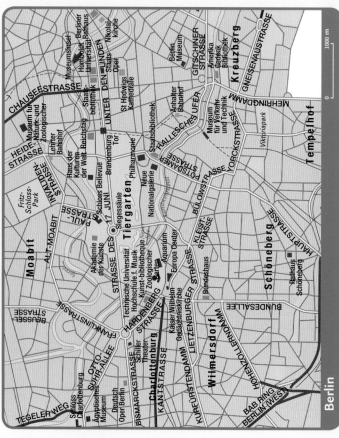

Berlin

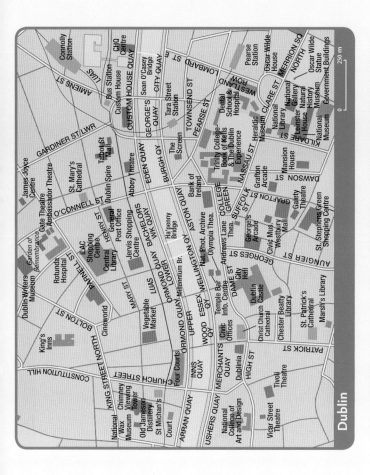

Dublin

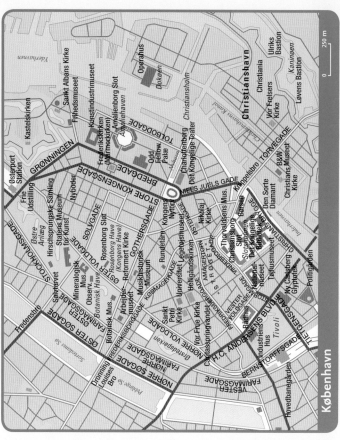

København

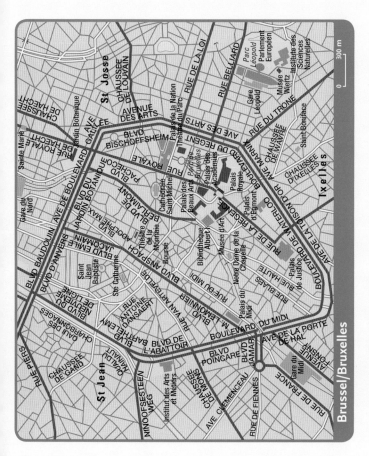

Brussel/Bruxelles

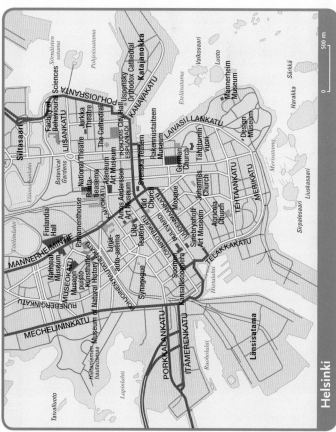

Helsinki

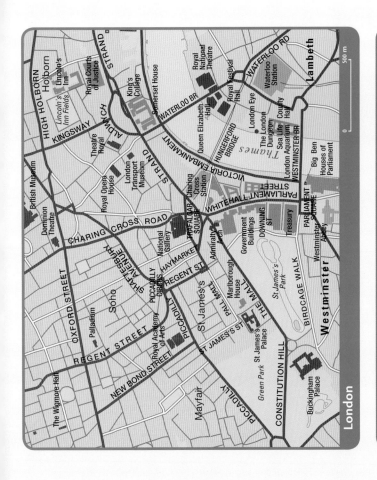

London

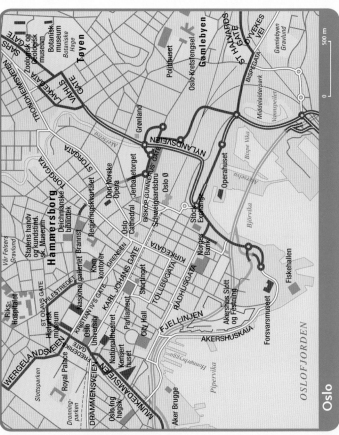

Oslo

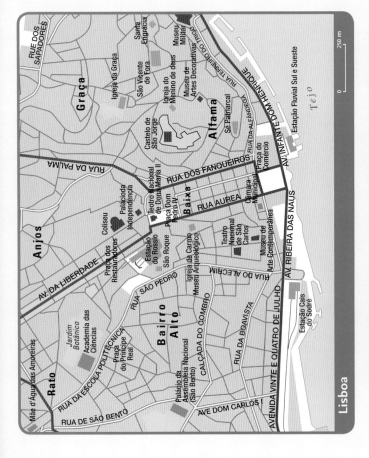

Lisboa

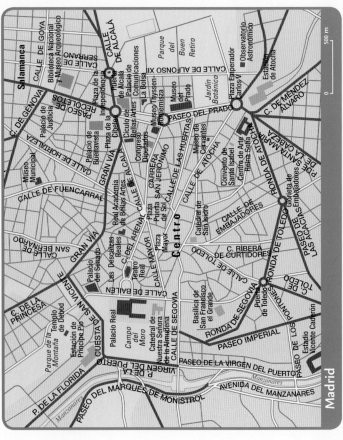

Madrid

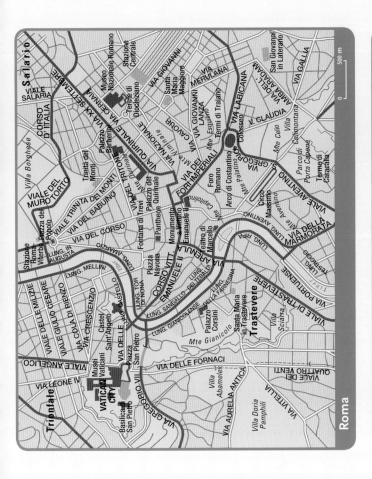

Roma

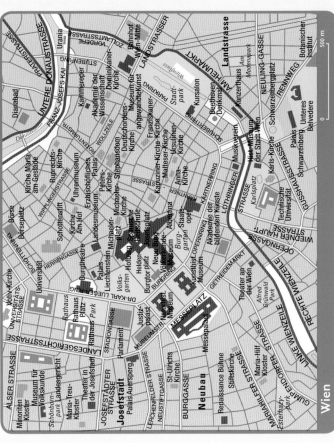

Wien

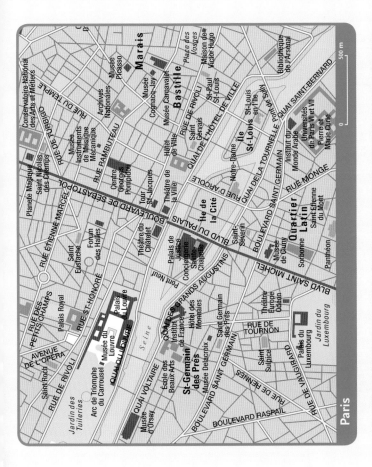

Paris

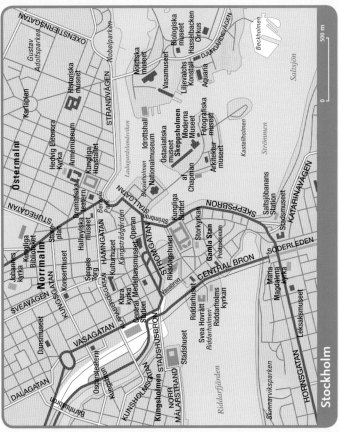

Stockholm

A

Å N 104 F7
Å N 110 E4
Å N 111 B12
Å N 111 C13
Aabenraa DK 86 E4
Aabybro DK 86 A5
Aachen D 20 C6
Aadorf CH 27 F10
Aakirkeby DK 89 E7
Aalborg DK 86 A5
Aalen D 75 E7
Aalestrup DK 86 B4
Aalsmeer NL 16 D3
Aalst B 19 C9
Aalst NL 183 B6
Aalten NL 17 E7
Aalter B 19 B7
Äänekoski FIN 123 E15
Aapajärvi FIN 115 D2
Aapajärvi FIN 119 B12
Aapajoki FIN 119 B12
Aapua S 117 E11
Aarau CH 27 F9
Aarberg CH 31 A11
Aardenburg NL 19 B7
Aareavaara S 117 D10
Aarhus DK 86 C6
Aarle NL 16 F5
A Armada E 38 B3
Aars DK 86 B5
Aarschot B 19 C10
Aartrijke B 182 C2
Aartselaar B 19 B9
Aarup DK 86 E6
Aarwangen CH 27 F8
Aasleagh IRL 6 E3
Ääsmäe EST 131 C9
Aaspere EST 131 C12
Aatsinki FIN 115 E5
Aavajärvi S 119 C11
Aavasaksa FIN 119 B11
Aba H 149 B11
Abaclia MD 154 E3
Abades E 46 C4
Abadín E 38 B5
Abadiño-Zelaieta E 41 B6
Abádszalók H 150 C6
A Baiuca E 38 B3
Abak TR 181 A7
Abalar TR 172 A6
Abánades E 47 C8
Abanilla E 56 E2
Abano Terme I 66 B4
Abarán E 55 C10
A Barrela E 38 C4
Abasár H 150 B5
Abaújszántó H 145 G3
Abbadia San Salvatore I 62 B1
Abbasanta I 64 C2
Abbekås S 87 E13
Abbeville F 18 D4
Abbey IRL 6 F6
Abbeydorney IRL 8 D3
Abbeyfeale IRL 8 D4
Abbeyleix IRL 9 C8
Abbey Town GB 5 F10
Abbiategrasso I 69 C6
Abborrberg S 109 F12
Abborreberget S 98 D8
Abborrträsk S 109 F17
Abbotsbury GB 13 D9
Abbots Langley GB 15 D8
Abcoude NL 16 D3
Abejar E 40 E6
Abejuela E 48 E3
Abela P 50 C2
Abelvær N 105 B10
Abenberg D 75 D8
Abenójar E 54 B4
Abensberg D 75 E10
Aberaeron GB 12 A6
Aberaman GB 13 B8
Aberchirder GB 3 K11
Aberdare GB 13 B8
Aberdaron GB 10 F2
Aberdeen GB 3 L12
Aberdovey GB 10 F3
Aberfeldy GB 5 B9
Aberffraw GB 10 E3
Aberford GB 11 D9
Aberfoyle GB 5 C8
Abergavenny GB 13 B8
Abergele GB 10 E4
Åberget S 109 E18
Abergwaun GB 12 B5
Abergynolwyn GB 10 F4
Aberlady GB 5 C11
Aberlour GB 3 L10
Abernethy GB 5 C10
Aberporth GB 12 A5
Abersoch GB 10 F2
Abertamy CZ 75 B12
Abertawe GB 13 B7
Abertillery GB 13 B8
Abertura E 45 F9
Aberuthven GB 5 C9
Aberystwyth GB 12 A6
Abetone I 66 D2
Abfaltersbach A 72 C6
Abhainnsuidhe GB 2 K2
Abia de la Obispalía E 47 D8
Abiego E 42 C3
Abild DK 86 F3
Abilly F 29 B7
Abingdon GB 13 B12
Abington GB 5 E9
Abisko Östra S 111 D16
Abja-Paluoja EST 131 E10
Abla E 55 E7
Ablis F 24 C6
Ablitas E 41 E8
Abmelaseter N 112 E6
Abo FIN 126 E7
Åbo S 103 C10
Åbodarna S 107 E14
Åbogen N 96 B7
Abondance F 31 C10
Abony H 150 C5
Åbosjö S 107 D13
Aboyne GB 5 A11
Abragão P 44 B4
Abram RO 151 C9
Abrămuț RO 151 C9
Abrantes P 44 F4
Abraur S 109 D16
Abreiro P 38 F5
Abreschviller F 27 C7
Abrest F 30 C3
Abriès F 31 F10
Abrigada P 44 F2
Abriola I 60 B5
Abrucena E 55 E7
Abrud RO 151 E11
Abrupe LV 135 B11
Absam A 72 B4
Absberg D 75 D8
Absdorf A 77 F9
Abtenau A 73 A7
Abtsgmünd D 74 E6
Abukhava BY 140 C10
Åby S 89 A7
Åby S 93 B8
Åbyen DK 90 D7
Åbyggeby S 103 E13
Åbyn S 118 D6
Åbytorp S 92 A6
Acaill IRL 6 E3
A Cañiza E 38 D3
A Carballa E 38 B2
Acarlar TR 177 D10
A Carreira E 38 B3
Acâș RO 151 B10
Acate I 58 E5
Accadia I 60 A4
Acceglio I 36 C5
Accettura I 60 C6
Acciano I 62 C5
Acciaroli I 60 C4
Accous F 32 E4
Accrington GB 11 D7
Accumoli I 62 B4
Acebo E 45 D7
Acedera E 45 F9
Acedo E 32 E1
Acehuche E 45 E7
Aceituna E 45 D8
Acered E 47 B9
Acerenza I 60 B5
Acerno I 60 B4
Acerra I 60 B2
Aceuchal E 51 B7
Ach A 76 F3
Achadh Mòr GB 2 J3
A Chan E 38 D3
Acharacle GB 4 B5
Acharnes GR 175 C8
Achavanich GB 3 J10
Achel B 183 C6
Achenkirch A 72 A4
Achern D 27 C9
Acheux-en-Amiénois F 18 D6
Achicourt F 18 D6
Achill IRL 6 E3
Achilleio GR 175 A6
Achim D 17 B12
Achintee GB 2 L6
Achladochori GR 169 B10
Achladokampos GR 175 D6
Achnacroish GB 4 B6
Achnasheen GB 2 K6
Achosnich GB 4 B4
Achstetten D 71 A9
Achtrup D 82 A6
Aci Castello I 59 D7
Aci Catena I 59 D7
Acireale I 59 D7
Aci Sant'Antonio I 59 D7
Aci Trezza I 59 D7
Acktjära S 103 D11
Acle GB 15 B12
A Coruña E 38 B3
Acquacalda I 59 B6
Acqualagna I 67 E6
Acquanegra sul Chiese I 66 B1
Acquapendente I 62 B1
Acquappesa I 60 E5
Acquaro I 59 B9
Acquarossa CH 71 E7
Acquasanta Terme I 62 B4
Acquasparta I 62 B3
Acquaviva Picena I 62 B5
Acquedolci I 59 C6
Acquigny F 24 B5
Acqui Terme I 37 B8
Acri I 61 E6
A Cruz do Incio E 38 C5
Ács H 149 A10
Acsa H 150 B3
Acuto I 62 D4
Ada SRB 150 F5
Adács H 150 B4
Adahuesca E 42 C3
Adak S 109 F16
Ådalsliden S 107 E11
Adamas GR 179 B7
Adamclisi RO 155 E1
Adamov CZ 77 D11
Adamova BY 133 E4
Adamów PL 141 G6
Adamówka PL 144 C6
Adamstown IRL 9 D9
Adămuș RO 152 E4
Adamuz E 53 A7
Adâncata RO 153 B8
Adâncata RO 161 D8
Ádánd H 149 C10
Adanero E 46 C3
Adão P 45 D6
Adare IRL 8 C5
Adatepe TR 173 D6
Adaúfe P 38 E3
Adavere EST 131 D11
Ādažl LV 135 B8
Adderbury GB 13 A12
Addlestone GB 15 E8
Adegem B 182 C2
Adelboden CH 31 C12
Adelebsen D 78 C6
Adelfia I 61 A7
Adelina PL 144 B8
Adelmannsfelden D 187 D8
Adelschlag D 75 E9
Adelsheim D 27 B11
Adelsried D 75 F8
Ademuz E 47 D10
Adenau D 21 D7
Adendorf D 83 D8
Adendro GR 169 C8
Adenstedt D 78 C6
Adjud RO 153 E10
Adlešiči SLO 148 E4
Adliswil CH 27 F10
Adlkofen D 75 E11
Admont A 73 A9
Adolfsström S 109 D12
Adony H 149 B11
Adorf D 75 B11
Adorf (Diemelsee) D 17 F11
Adoufe P 38 F4
Adra E 55 F6
Adradas E 41 F7
Adrados E 40 F3
Adrano I 59 D6
Adria I 66 B5
Adriani GR 171 B6
Adriers F 29 C7
Aduard NL 17 B6
Adulsbruk N 101 E14
Ådum DK 86 D3
Adunați RO 161 C7
Adunații-Copăceni RO 161 E8
Adutiškis LT 135 F13
Adzaneta de Albaida E 56 D4
Adžūni LV 135 D8
Aegviidu EST 131 C11
Aerino GR 169 F8
Ærøskøbing DK 86 F6
Aerzen D 17 D12
A Escusa E 38 C2
A Esfarrapada E 38 D2
A Estrada E 38 C3
Aetos GR 169 C6
Aetos GR 174 B3
Aetos GR 174 E4
Äetsä FIN 126 C8
Afantou GR 181 D8
Åfarnes N 100 A7
A Feira do Monte E 38 B4
Affing D 75 F8
Afife P 38 E2
Afissos GR 169 F9
Åfjord N 104 D8
Aflenz Kurort A 73 A11
A Fonsagrada E 38 B5
A Forxa E 38 D4
A Forxa E 38 D4
Åfoss N 90 A6
Afragola I 60 B2
Afritz A 73 C8
Afumați RO 160 E2
Afumați RO 161 D8
Afytos GR 169 D9
Aga D 79 E11
Ağaçli TR 173 B10
Ağaköy TR 173 D7
Agalas GR 174 D2
Agallas E 45 D8
A Gándara E 38 B3
A Gándara de Altea E 38 A3
Agapia RO 153 C8
Agăș RO 153 D8
Ágasegyháza H 150 D3
Agde F 34 D5
Agen F 33 B7
Àger E 42 C5
Agerbæk DK 86 D3
Agerskov DK 86 E4
Agersted DK 86 A6
Ågerup DK 87 D10
Ágfalva H 149 A7
Aggersund DK 86 A4
Aggius I 64 B3
Aggsbach Markt A 77 F8
Aghaboe IRL 9 C7
Aghagallon GB 7 C10
Aghalee GB 7 C10
Aghanloo GB 4 E3
Aghaville IRL 8 E4
Aghern IRL 8 D6
Aghione F 37 G10
Aghireșu RO 151 D11
Aghleam IRL 6 D2
Aghnagar Bridge IRL 8 E2
Agia GR 169 E8
Agia Anna GR 175 B7
Agia Anna GR 175 C6
Agia Effimia GR 174 C2
Agia Efthymia GR 174 C5
Agia Galini GR 178 E8
Agia Kyriaki GR 174 E4
Agia Marina GR 175 B6
Agia Marina GR 175 C9
Agia Marina GR 177 E8
Agia Paraskevi GR 168 D4
Agia Paraskevi GR 174 A3
Agia Paraskevi GR 177 E6
Agia Pelagia GR 178 C4
Agia Pelagia GR 178 E9
Agiasma GR 171 C7
Agiasos GR 177 A7
Agia Triada GR 174 D4
Agia Triada GR 175 D6
Agia Varvara GR 169 D7
Agia Varvara GR 178 E9
Agigea RO 155 E3
Agighiol RO 155 C3
Agino Selo BIH 157 C7
Agiofyllo GR 169 E6
Agioi Anargyroi GR 169 E7
Agioi Apostoloi GR 175 C8
Agioi Deka GR 178 E8
Agioi Theodoroi GR 169 E5
Agioi Theodoroi GR 175 A6
Agioi Theodoroi GR 175 D7
Agiokampos GR 169 E8
Agiokampos GR 175 B7
Agionori GR 175 D6
Agios Andreas GR 175 E6
Agios Athanasios GR 169 C8
Agios Athanasios GR 171 B6
Agios Charalampos GR 171 C9
Agios Christoforos GR 175 F5
Agios Dimitrios GR 169 D7
Agios Dimitrios GR 175 D8
Agios Dimitrios GR 175 F6
Agios Efstratios GR 171 E7
Agios Georgios GR 169 C7
Agios Georgios GR 174 B4
Agios Georgios GR 175 C6
Agios Georgios GR 177 F6
Agios Georgios GR 178 E9
Agios Germanos GR 168 C5
Agios Ioannis GR 174 E5
Agios Ioannis GR 175 C7
Agios Ioannis GR 178 B4
Agios Kirykos GR 177 D7
Agios Konstantinos GR 174 B3
Agios Konstantinos GR 174 D5
Agios Konstantinos GR 175 B6
Agios Konstantinos GR 175 D9
Agios Kyprianos GR 178 C3
Agios Leon GR 174 D2
Agios Loukas GR 169 C7
Agios Loukas GR 175 C9
Agios Mamas GR 169 D9
Agios Matthaios GR 168 F2
Agios Myronas GR 178 E9
Agios Nikolaos GR 168 E3
Agios Nikolaos GR 168 E5
Agios Nikolaos GR 169 D10
Agios Nikolaos GR 174 B2
Agios Nikolaos GR 174 B4
Agios Nikolaos GR 174 B4
Agios Nikolaos GR 178 B3
Agios Nikolaos GR 179 E10
Agios Panteleïmonas GR 169 C6
Agios Paraskevi GR 171 F10
Agios Petros GR 169 C8
Agios Petros GR 174 B2
Agios Petros GR 175 E6
Agios Spyridonas GR 169 D7
Agios Spyridonas GR 174 A2
Agios Stefanos GR 175 C8
Agios Stefanos GR 176 E5
Agios Thomas GR 175 C8
Agios Vasileios GR 169 C9
Agios Vasileios GR 175 D6
Agira I 59 D6
Agivey GB 4 E3
Agkathia GR 169 C7
Agkistro GR 169 B9
Aglapsvik N 111 B15
Aglasterhausen D 187 C6
Agle N 105 C13
Aglen N 105 B10
Agliana I 66 E3
Aglientu I 64 A3
Aglish IRL 9 D7
Agluonėnai LT 134 E2
Agnadello I 69 C8
Agnagar Bridge IRL 8 E2
Agnanta GR 168 F5
Agnantero GR 169 F6
Agneaux F 23 B9
Agnita RO 152 F5
Agno CH 69 A6
Agnone I 63 D6
Agolada E 38 C3
Agoncillo E 32 F1
Agon-Coutainville F 23 B8
Agordo I 72 D5
Agost E 56 E3
Agos-Vidalos F 32 D5
Ågotnes N 94 B2
Agra GR 177 A7
Agramón E 55 C9
Agramunt E 42 D6
Agrate Brianza I 69 B7
Agreda E 41 E8
Agrés E 56 D4
Agria GR 169 F9
Agridi GR 174 D4
Agrigento I 58 E4
Agrij RO 151 C11
Agrili GR 174 E4
Agrinio GR 174 B3
Agriovotano GR 175 A7
Agrochão P 39 E5
Agropoli I 60 C3
Ågskaret N 108 C5
Aguadulce E 53 B7
Aguadulce E 55 F7
A Guarda E 38 E2
Aguarón E 41 F9
Aguas E 42 C3
Águas Belas P 44 E4
Aguas de Busot E 56 D4
Águas de Moura P 50 B2
Águas Frias P 38 E5
Aguaviva E 42 F3
A Gudiña E 38 D5
Agudo E 54 B3
Águeda P 44 C4
Aguessac F 34 B5
Agugliano I 67 E7
Aguiar P 50 C4
Aguiar da Beira P 44 C5
Aguilafuente E 46 B4
Aguilar de Alfambra E 42 F2
Aguilar de Campóo E 40 C3
Aguilar de la Frontera E 53 A7
Aguilar del Río Alhama E 41 E8
Águilas E 55 E9
Agullana E 34 F4
Agullent E 56 D3
Aha S 109 F14
Ahafona IRL 8 C3
Aham D 75 E11
Ahascragh IRL 6 F6
Ahaus D 17 D8
Åheim N 100 B3
Ahelva FIN 121 E11
Ahigal E 45 D8
Ahigal de Villarino E 45 B8
Ahillones E 51 C8
Ahja EST 131 E14
Ahjola FIN 121 D12
Ahlainen FIN 126 B6
Ahlatli TR 167 E8
Ahlbeck D 84 C6
Ahlbeck D 84 C6
Ahlden (Aller) D 82 E7
Ahlen D 17 E9
Ahlerstedt D 17 B12
Ahlhorn D 17 C10
Ahmas FIN 119 E17
Ahmavaara FIN 115 E4
Ahmetbey TR 173 B8
Ahmetbeyli TR 177 C9
Ahmetçeeli TR 172 E6
Ahmetli TR 177 C9
Ahmovaara FIN 125 D13
Ahnsbeck D 79 A7
Ahoghill GB 4 F4
Ahoinen FIN 127 D11
Ahokylä FIN 123 C17
Ahola FIN 121 B11
Ahola FIN 121 C13
Ahola FIN 121 D13
Ahola FIN 124 D9
Aholanvaara FIN 115 E5
Ahonperä FIN 119 F13
Ahorn D 75 B8
Aho-Vastinki FIN 123 E14
Ahrbrück D 21 D7
Ahrensbök D 83 B9
Ahrensburg D 83 C8
Ahrenshagen D 83 B13
Ahrenshoop D 83 B12
Ähtäri FIN 123 E12
Ähtärinranta FIN 123 E12
Ahtme EST 132 C1
Ahula EST 131 C11
Ahun F 29 C10
Åhus S 88 D6
Ahveninen FIN 123 E16
Ahvenisto FIN 127 C16
Ahvensalmi FIN 125 F10
Ahvenselkä FIN 115 E4
Ahvenvittikko FIN 115 D4
Ahvionsaari FIN 129 B10
Aiani GR 169 D6
Aianteio GR 175 D7
Aibar E 32 E3
Aibl A 73 C11
Aichach D 75 F9
Aichhalden D 27 D9
Aichstetten D 71 B10
Ai'dejav'ri N 117 A10
Aidenbach D 76 E4
Aidipsos GR 175 B7
Aidone I 58 E5
Aidonochori GR 169 C10
Aidt DK 86 C5
Aidu EST 131 D12
Aiello Calabro I 59 A9
Aielo de Malferit E 56 D3
Aieta I 60 D5
Aiffres F 28 C5
Aigeira GR 174 C5
Aigen im Ennstal A 73 A9
Aigen im Mühlkreis A 76 E5
Aigiali GR 177 F6
Aigina GR 175 D7
Aiginio GR 169 D8
Aigio GR 174 C5
Aigle CH 31 C10
Aiglemont F 184 E2
Aignan F 33 C6
Aignay-le-Duc F 25 E12
Aigre F 28 D6
Aigrefeuille-d'Aunis F 28 C4
Aigrefeuille-sur-Maine F 28 A3
A Igrexa E 38 D3
Aiguafreda E 43 D8
Aiguebelle F 31 D9
Aigueblanche F 31 D10
Aigueperse F 30 C3
Aigues-Mortes F 35 C7
Aigues-Vives F 33 E9
Aigues-Vives F 34 D4
Aigues-Vives F 35 C7
Aiguilhe F 30 E4
Aiguilles F 31 F10
Aiguillon F 33 B6
Aigurande F 29 C9
Äijäjoki FIN 116 B10
Äijälä FIN 123 E16
Aijala FIN 127 E9
Aijänneva FIN 123 F11
Aillant-sur-Tholon F 25 E9
Aillas F 32 B5
Aillevillers-et-Lyaumont F 26 E5
Ailly-le-Haut-Clocher F 18 D4
Ailly-sur-Noye F 18 E5
Ailly-sur-Somme F 18 E5
Ailt an Chorráin IRL 6 C6
Aimargues F 35 C7
Aime F 31 D10
Ainali FIN 119 F14
Ainali FIN 123 B11
Ainay-le-Château F 29 B11
Ainaži LV 131 F8
Aindling D 75 E8
Ainet A 73 C6
Ainsa E 33 F6
Ainzón E 41 E9
Airaines F 18 E4
Airaksela FIN 124 E8
Airasca I 31 F11
Aird Asaig GB 2 K3
Airdrie GB 5 D9
Aire-sur-l'Adour F 32 C5
Aire-sur-la-Lys F 18 C5
Airidh a'Bhruaich GB 2 J3
Airola I 60 A3
Airole I 37 D7
Airolo CH 71 D7
Airvault F 28 B5
Aisey-sur-Seine F 25 E12
Aïssey F 26 F5
Aisymi GR 171 B9
Aisy-sur-Armançon F 25 E11
Aitamännikkö FIN 117 D12
Aita Mare RO 153 F7
Aiterhofen D 75 E12
Aith GB 3 E14
Aith GB 3 G11
Aitolahti FIN 127 B10
Aitoliko GR 174 C3
Aiton RO 152 D3
Aitona E 42 E4
Aitoo FIN 127 C11
Aitrach D 71 B10
Aitrang D 71 B11
Aittaniemi FIN 121 B10
Aittijoki FIN 113 D17
Aittojärvi FIN 119 D17
Aittojärvi FIN 123 C16
Aittokoski FIN 124 C8
Aittokylä FIN 121 E10
Aittoperä FIN 123 C13
Aittovaara FIN 121 D13
Aiud RO 152 E3
Aiviekste LV 135 C11
Aix-en-Othe F 25 D10
Aix-en-Provence F 35 C9
Aixe-sur-Vienne F 29 D8
Aix-les-Bains F 31 D8
Aizenay F 28 B2
Aizkraukle LV 135 C10
Aizpún E 32 E2
Aizpurve LV 135 C12
Aizpute LV 134 C3
Aizvīķi LV 134 D3
Ajaccio F 37 H9
Ajanki FIN 117 E12
Ajankijärvi FIN 117 E12
Ajat F 29 E8
Ajaureforsen S 109 E10
Ajdovščina SLO 73 E8
Ajka H 149 B9
Ajo E 40 B4
Ajofrín E 46 E5
Ajos FIN 119 C13
Akācijas LV 134 C6
Åkarp S 87 D12
Äkäsjokisuu FIN 117 D11
Äkäslompolo FIN 117 C12
Akasztó H 150 D3
Akçaova TR 181 B7
Akçasusurluk TR 173 D9
Akeld GB 5 D12
Aken D 79 C11
Åkerbränna S 107 D11
Åkerby S 99 B9
Åkerholmen S 118 C6
Åkersberga S 99 D10
Akersjön S 105 D16
Åkers styckebruk S 98 D8
Åkerstrømmen N 101 C14
Akheloy BG 167 D9
Akhremawtsy BY 133 E2
Akhtopol BG 167 E9
Akkan S 109 F12
Akkarfjord N 113 B12
Akkarvik N 112 C5
Akkasæter N 111 B16
Akkavare S 109 E17
Akkerhaugen N 95 D10
Akköy TR 171 E10
Akköy TR 177 E9
Akkrum NL 16 B5
Akmeņdziras LV 134 B3
Akmenė LT 134 D5
Åknes N 110 C9
Aknīste LV 135 D11
Akonkoski FIN 121 F13
Akonpohja FIN 125 D10
Akpinar TR 173 B10
Akraifnio GR 175 C7
Åkran N 105 D12
Akrata GR 174 C5
Åkrehamn N 94 D2
Akrini GR 169 D6
Akrolimni GR 169 C7
Akropotamos GR 170 C6
Akrotiri GR 179 C9
Aksakal TR 173 D9
Aksaz TR 173 D7
Aksdal N 94 D2
Aksnes N 104 F4
Akujärvi FIN 114 F3
Åkullsjön S 118 F5
Åkvisslan S 107 E13
Ål N 101 E9
Ala I 69 B11
Ala S 93 E13
Alacaat TR 173 E10
Alacant E 56 E4
Alacaoğlu TR 173 B7
Alaçati TR 177 C7
Alà dei Sardi I 64 B3
Ala di Stura I 31 E11
Alaejos E 39 F9
Alagna Valsesia I 68 B4
A Lagoa E 38 C2
Alagoa P 44 F5
Alagón E 41 E9
Alahärmä FIN 122 D9
Ala-Honkajoki FIN 126 B7
Alaigne F 33 D10
Alaior E 57 B13
Alájar E 51 D6
Alajärvi FIN 117 E15
Alajärvi FIN 121 E12
Alajärvi FIN 123 D11
Alajõe EST 132 C1
Ala-Jokikylä FIN 119 C14
Ala-Kääntä FIN 119 F12
Ala-Keyritty FIN 125 D10
Alakurtti RUS 115 E8
Alakylä FIN 117 D13
Alakylä FIN 119 D15
Alakylä FIN 126 B6
Ala-Livo FIN 119 D17
Alameda E 53 B7
Alameda de Cervera E 47 F6
Alameda de la Sagra E 46 D5
Alamedilla E 55 D6
Alamillo E 54 B3
Alan HR 67 B10
Ala-Nampa FIN 117 E16
Alanäs S 106 C9
Ālande LV 134 C2
Alandroal P 50 B5
Älandsbro S 103 A14
Alange E 51 B7
Alaniemi FIN 119 C14
Alanís E 51 C8
Alanta LT 135 F10
Alap H 149 C11
Alapitkä FIN 124 D9
Alaquàs E 48 F4
Alaranta FIN 119 D14
Alaraz E 45 C10
Alarcón E 47 E8
Alar del Rey E 40 C3
Alaró E 49 E10
Alarup AL 168 C4
Ålåsen S 106 D7
Alaskylä FIN 127 B8
Alassio I 37 C8
Alastaipale FIN 123 F11
Alastaro FIN 126 D8
Ala-Sydänmaa FIN 123 B14
Alata F 37 H9
Ala-Temmes FIN 119 E15
Alatoz E 47 F10
Alatri I 62 D4
Alatskivi EST 131 D14
Alattyán H 150 C5
Ala-Valli FIN 123 F9
Alavattnet S 106 C9
Alavere EST 131 C10
Ala-Vieksi FIN 121 F12
Alavieska FIN 119 F12
Ala-Viirre FIN 123 B11
Ala-Vuokki FIN 121 E13
Ala-Vuotto FIN 119 D16
Alavus FIN 123 E11
Alba I 37 B8
Alba Adriatica I 62 B5
Albac RO 151 E10
Albacete E 55 A9
Albacken S 103 A11
Alba de Tormes E 45 C9
Ålbæk DK 90 D7
Albagiara I 64 D2
Albaida E 56 D4
Alba Iulia RO 152 E3
Albaladejo E 55 B7
Alba-la-Romaine F 35 A8
Albalate de Arzobispo E 42 E3
Albalate de Cinca E 42 D4
Albalate de las Nogueras E 47 D8
Albalate de Zorita E 47 D7
Albalatillo E 42 D3
Alban F 33 C10
Albánchez E 55 E8
Albanella I 60 C4
Albanitsa BG 165 C10
Albano di Lucania I 60 B6
Albano Laziale I 62 D3
Albano Vercellese I 68 C5
Albanyà E 43 C9
Albaredo per San Marco I 69 A8
Albaret-le-Comtal F 30 F3
Albareto I 69 E8
Albaret-Ste-Marie F 30 F3
Albaron F 35 C7
Albarracín E 47 D10
Albatana E 55 B9
Albatàrrec E 42 D5
Albatera E 56 E3
Albbruck D 27 E9
Albelda E 42 D4
Albelda de Iregua E 41 D7
Albella E 32 F5
Albendea E 47 C8
Albendín E 53 A8
Albenga I 37 C8
Albeni RO 160 C3
Albens F 31 D8
Albentosa E 48 D3
Ålberga S 93 B9
Alberga S 98 D6
Albergaria-a-Velha P 44 C4
Albergaria dos Doze P 44 E3
Albergen NL 183 A9
Alberic E 48 F4
Alberndorf in der Riedmark A 77 F6
Albernoa P 50 D4
Albero Alto E 41 D11
Alberobello I 61 B8
Alberona I 60 A4
Alberoni I 66 B5
Alberschwende A 71 C9
Albersdorf D 82 B6
Albert F 18 E6
Albertacce F 37 G9
Alberta Ligure I 37 B10
Albertirsa H 150 C4
Albertshofen D 187 B9
Albertville F 31 D9
Alberuela de Tubo E 42 D3
Albesa E 42 D5
Albești RO 152 E5
Albești RO 153 B10
Albești RO 153 D11
Albești RO 155 F2
Albești RO 161 D10
Albeștii de Argeș RO 160 C5
Albeștii de Muscel RO 160 C6
Albești-Paleologu RO 161 D8
Albestroff F 27 C6
Albi F 33 C10
Albias F 33 B8
Albidona I 61 D6
Albignasego I 66 B4
Albina RO 155 C1
Albino I 69 B8
Albires E 39 D9
Albisheim (Pfrimm) D 21 E10
Albisola Marina I 37 C9
Albisola Superiore I 37 C9
Alblasserdam NL 16 E3
Ålbo S 98 B7
Albocàsser E 48 D5
Alboloduy E 55 E7
Albolote E 53 B9
Albon F 30 E6
Albondón E 55 F6
Alboraya E 48 E4
Alborea E 47 F10
Albota RO 160 D5
Albox E 55 E8
Albrechtice nad Orlicí CZ 77 B10
Al'brekhtava BY 133 E5
Albstadt D 27 D11
Albu EST 131 C11
Albudeite E 55 C10
Albufeira P 50 E3
Albujón E 56 F2
Albuñol E 55 F6
Albuñuelas E 53 C9
Alburquerque E 45 F7
Alby S 89 C11
Alby S 103 A9
Alby-sur-Chéran F 31 D9
Alcácer E 48 F4
Alcácer do Sal P 50 C2
Alcáçovas P 50 C3
Alcadozo E 55 B9
Alcafozes P 45 E6
Alcaine E 42 F2
Alcains P 44 E6
Alcalá de Guadaira E 51 E8
Alcalá de Gurrea E 41 D10
Alcalá de Henares E 46 D6
Alcalá del Júcar E 47 F10
Alcalá de los Gazules E 52 D5
Alcalá del Río E 51 D8
Alcalá del Valle E 51 F9
Alcalà de Xivert E 48 D5
Alcalá la Real E 53 B9
Alcalalí E 56 D4
Alcamo I 58 D2
Alcampell E 42 D4
Alcanadre E 32 F1
Alcanede P 44 F3
Alcanena P 44 F3
Alcanhões P 44 F3
Alcañices E 39 E7
Alcañiz E 42 E3
Alcántara E 45 E7
Alcantarilla E 56 F2
Alcantud E 47 C8
Alcaracejos E 54 C3
Alcara li Fusi I 59 C6
Alcaraz E 55 B8
Alcaria Ruiva P 50 D4
Alcarràs E 42 D5
Alcaucín E 53 C8
Alcaudete E 53 A8
Alcaudete de la Jara E 46 E3
Alçay-Alçabéhéty-Sunharette F 32 D4
Alcázar del Rey E 47 D7
Alcázar de San Juan E 47 F6
Alcedar MD 154 B3
Alcester GB 13 A11
Alçitepe TR 171 D10
Alcoba E 46 F4
Alcobaça P 44 E3
Alcobendas E 46 C5
Alcocer E 47 D7
Alcocero de Mola E 40 D5
Alcochete P 50 B2
Alcoentre P 44 F3
Alcoi E 56 D4
Alcolea E 53 A7
Alcolea E 55 F7
Alcolea de Calatrava E 54 B4
Alcolea de Cinca E 42 D4
Alcolea del Pinar E 47 B8
Alcolea del Río E 51 D8
Alcollarín E 45 F9
Alconchel E 51 B5
Alcóntar E 55 E7
Alcorcón E 46 D5
Alcorisa E 42 F3
Alcoroches E 47 C9
Alcossebre E 48 D5
Alcoutim P 50 E5
Alcover E 42 E6
Alcoy E 56 D4
Alcsútdoboz H 149 B11
Alcubierre E 41 E11
Alcubilla de Avellaneda E 40 E5
Alcubillas E 55 B6
Alcublas E 48 E3
Alcúdia E 57 B11
Alcudia de Guadix E 55 E6
Alcudia de Monteagud E 55 E8
Alcuéscar E 45 F8
Aldbrough GB 11 D11
Aldeacentenera E 45 E9

Aldeadávila de la Ribera E 45 B7
Aldea del Cano E 45 F8
Aldea del Fresno E 46 D4
Aldea del Obispo E 45 C7
Aldea del Rey E 54 B5
Aldea de Trujillo E 45 E9
Aldealafuente E 41 E7
Aldealpozo E 41 E7
Aldeamayor de San Martín E 39 E10
Aldeanueva de Barbarroya E 45 E10
Aldeanueva de Ebro E 41 D8
Aldeanueva de Figueroa E 45 B9
Aldeanueva de la Vera E 45 D9
Aldeanueva del Camino E 45 D9
Aldeanueva de San Bartolomé E 45 E10
Aldeaquemada E 55 C6
Aldea Real E 46 B4
Aldearrodrigo E 45 B9
Aldeaseca E 46 B3
Aldeatejada E 45 C9
Aldeavieja E 46 C4
Aldeburgh GB 15 C12
Aldehuela de la Bóveda E 45 C8
Aldehuela de Yeltes E 45 C8
Aldeia da Mata P 44 F5
Aldeia da Ponte P 45 D7
Aldeia de João Pires P 45 D6
Aldeia do Bispo P 45 D6
Aldeia dos Elvas P 50 D3
Aldeia dos Fernandes P 50 D3
Aldeia dos Palheiros P 50 D3
Aldeia Velha P 44 F4
Aldenhoven D 20 C6
Aldeno I 69 B11
Alderbury GB 13 C11
Alderholt GB 13 D11
Alderley Edge GB 11 E7
Aldersbach D 76 E4
Aldershot GB 15 E7
Aldinac SRB 164 B5
Aldinci NMK 164 F3
Aldingham GB 10 C5
Aldomirovtsi BG 165 D6
Aldover E 42 F5
Aldridge GB 11 F8
Aldudes F 32 D3
Åle DK 86 D5
Åled S 87 B11
Aledo E 55 D9
Alekovo BG 161 F10
Alekovo BG 166 C4
Aleksandriškės LT 137 D10
Aleksandrova LV 133 E2
Aleksandrovac SRB 159 E7
Aleksandrovac SRB 163 C11
Aleksandrovo BG 165 C10
Aleksandrovo BG 166 D4
Aleksandrovo BG 167 E7
Aleksandrów PL 141 F2
Aleksandrów PL 141 H1
Aleksandrów Kujawski PL 138 E6
Aleksandrów Łódzki PL 143 C7
Aleksa Šantić SRB 150 F3
Aleksinac SRB 164 B4
Ålem S 89 B10
Ålen N 101 A14
Alençon F 23 D12
Alenquer P 44 F3
Alénya F 34 E4
Alerheim D 75 E8
Aléria F 37 G11
Alerre E 41 D11
Alès F 35 B7
Ales I 64 D2
Aleșd RO 151 C9
Alesón E 41 D6
Alessandria I 37 B9
Alessandria del Carretto I 61 D6
Alessandria della Rocca I 58 D3
Alessano I 61 D10
Ålesund N 100 B4
Alet-les-Bains F 33 D10
Alexandreia GR 169 C7
Alexandria GB 4 D7
Alexandria RO 160 F6
Alexandroupoli GR 171 C9
Alexandru Vlahuță RO 153 E11
Alexeevca MD 153 C11
Alexeni RO 161 D9
Alexsandrów PL 144 C6
Alezio I 61 C10
Alf D 21 D8
Alfacar E 53 B9
Alfafar E 48 F4
Alfaiates P 45 D7
Alfajarín E 41 E10
Alfambra E 42 F1
Alfambras P 50 E2
Alfamén E 41 F9
Alfândega da Fé P 39 F6
Alfántega E 42 D4
Alfarim P 50 C1
Alfaro E 41 D8
Alfarràs E 42 D5
Alfatar BG 161 F10
Alfdorf D 74 E6
Alfedena I 62 D6
Alfeizerão P 44 E2
Alfeld (Leine) D 78 C6
Alfena P 44 B3
Alferce P 50 E3
Alfhausen D 17 C9
Alfonsine I 66 D5
Alford GB 3 L11
Alford GB 11 E12
Alforja E 42 E5
Alfredshem S 107 E15
Alfreton GB 11 E9
Alfta S 103 D11
Alfundão P 50 C3
Algaida E 57 B10
Algajola F 37 F9
Algámitas E 53 B6
Algar E 52 C5
Älgarås S 92 B4
Ålgård N 94 E3
Algarinejo E 53 B8
Algarrobo E 53 C8
Algatocín E 53 C6
Algeciras E 53 D6
Algemesí E 48 F4
Älgered S 103 B12
Algermissen D 79 B6
Algerri E 42 D5
Algestrup DK 87 E10
Algete E 46 C6
Alghero I 64 B1
Älghult S 89 A9
Alginet E 48 F4
Ålgnäs S 103 D12
Algodonales E 51 F9
Algodor P 50 D4
Algora E 47 C7
Algorta E 40 B6
Algoso P 39 F6
Algoz P 50 E3
Algrange F 20 F6
Alguaire E 42 D5
Alguazas E 56 E2
Algueirão-Mem Martins P 50 B1
Algueña E 56 E3
Algutsrum S 89 B11
Alhabia E 55 F7
Alhama de Almería E 55 F7
Alhama de Aragón E 41 F8
Alhama de Granada E 53 B9
Alhama de Murcia E 55 D10
Alhambra E 55 B6
Alhamn S 118 D7
Alhaurín de la Torre E 53 C7
Alhaurín el Grande E 53 C7
Alhendín E 53 B9
Alhojärvi FIN 127 B13
Alhóndiga E 47 C7
Ålhult S 92 D7
Alía E 45 F10
Alia I 58 D4
Aliaga E 42 F2
Aliağa TR 177 B8
Aliaguilla E 47 E10
Aliano I 60 C6
Aliartos GR 175 C7
Alibunar SRB 159 C6
Alicante E 56 E4
Alicún de Ortega E 55 D6
Alife I 60 A2
Alija del Infantado E 39 D8
Alijó P 38 F5
Alikianos GR 178 E6
Alikylä FIN 123 C11
Aliman RO 155 E1
Alimena I 58 D5
Aliminusa I 58 D4
Alimpești RO 160 C3
Alingsås S 91 D12
Alino BG 165 E7
Alionys 1 LT 137 C11
Aliseda E 45 F7
Alistrati GR 170 B5
Alì Terme I 59 C7
Aliveri GR 175 C9
Alizava LT 135 E10
Aljaraque E 51 E5
Aljezur P 50 E2
Aljinovići SRB 163 C8
Aljubarrota P 44 E3
Aljucén E 51 A7
Aljustrel P 50 D3
Alken B 19 C11
Alkkia FIN 122 F9
Alkmaar NL 16 C3
Allai I 64 D2
Allaire F 23 E7
Allambres AL 168 C2
Allan F 35 A8
Allanche F 30 E2
Allariz E 38 D4
Allarmont F 27 D7
Allassac F 29 E8
Allaži LV 135 B9
Allažmuiža LV 135 B9
Alle CH 27 F7
Alleghe I 72 D5
Allègre F 30 E4
Alleins F 35 C9
Allemond F 31 E9
Allen IRL 7 F9
Allendale Town GB 5 F12
Allendorf (Eder) D 21 B11
Allenheads GB 5 F12
Allensbach D 27 E11
Allentsteig A 77 E8
Allenwood IRL 7 F9
Allepuz E 42 G2
Allerona I 62 B1
Allersberg D 75 D9
Allershausen D 75 F10
Allerslev DK 87 E10
Allevard F 31 E9
Allex F 30 F6
Allibaudières F 25 C11
Alligny-en-Morvan F 25 F11
Allihies IRL 8 E2
Allingåbro DK 86 C6
Allinges F 31 C9
Allinge-Sandvig DK 89 E7
Alliste I 61 D10
Allmendingen D 74 F6
Allo E 32 E1
Alloa GB 5 C9
Allogny F 25 F7
Ålloluokta S 109 B17
Allonby GB 5 F10
Allonnes F 23 E12
Allonnes F 23 F12
Allons F 32 B5
Allos F 36 C5
Alloue F 29 C7
Alloza E 42 F2
Allschwil CH 27 E8
Allsta S 103 A15
Allstad N 110 D6
Allstedt D 79 D9
Allumiere I 62 C1
Alluy F 30 A4
Almacelles E 42 D4
Almáchar E 53 C8
Almada P 50 B1
Almadén E 54 B3
Almadén de la Plata E 51 D7
Almadenejos E 54 B3
Almagro E 54 B5
Almăj RO 160 E3
Almajano E 41 E7
Almalaguês P 44 D4
Almaluez E 41 F7
Almansa E 56 D2
Almansil P 50 E3
Almanza E 39 C9
Almaraz E 45 E9
Almargen E 53 B6
Almarza E 41 E7
Almaș RO 151 E9
Almásfüzitő H 149 A10
Almașu RO 151 D11
Almașu Mare RO 151 E11
Almazán E 41 F6
Almazora E 48 E4
Almazul E 41 E7
Almedina E 55 B7
Almedinilla E 53 B8
Almeida de Sayago E 39 F7
Almeirim P 44 F3
Almelo NL 17 D7
Almenar E 42 D5
Almenara E 48 E4
Almenar de Soria E 41 E7
Almendra E 45 B8
Almendra P 45 B6
Almendral E 51 B6
Almendralejo E 51 B7
Almendricos E 55 E9
Almendros E 47 E7
Almere NL 16 D4
Almería E 55 F8
Almerimar E 55 F7
Älmestad S 91 D13
Älmhult S 88 B6
Almind DK 86 D4
Almkerk NL 16 E3
Åmo N 104 E4
Almodôvar P 50 D3
Almodóvar del Campo E 54 B4
Almodóvar del Pinar E 47 E9
Almodóvar del Río E 53 A6
Almofala P 44 C5
Almogía E 53 C7
Almograve P 50 D2
Almoguera E 47 D7
Almoharín E 45 F8
Almonacid de la Sierra E 41 F9
Almonacid del Marquesado E 47 E7
Almonacid del Zorita E 47 D7
Almonacid de Toledo E 46 E5
Almonaster la Real E 51 D6
Almondsbury GB 13 B9
Almonte E 51 E6
Almoradí E 56 E3
Almorchón E 51 B9
Almorox E 46 D4
Álmosd H 151 C8
Almoster P 44 E4
Almsele S 107 C12
Almsjönäs S 107 E14
Älmsta S 99 C11
Almstedt D 79 B6
Almudema E 55 C9
Almudévar E 41 D10
Almuñécar E 53 C9
Almunge S 99 C10
Almuniente E 41 E11
Almünster A 73 A8
Álmuradiel E 55 B6
Almussafes E 48 F4
Almvik S 93 D9
Almyropotamos GR 175 C9
Almyros GR 175 A6
Alnes N 100 B4
Alness GB 3 K8
Alnwick GB 5 E13
Alobras E 47 D10
Alocén E 47 C7
Aloja LV 131 F9
Alol' RUS 133 D6
Alonia GR 169 D8
Álora E 53 C7
Alós d'Ensil E 33 E8
Alosno E 51 D5
Alost B 19 C9
Alost B 182 D4
Alovera E 47 C6
Alozaina E 53 C7
Alp E 33 F9
Alpalhão P 44 F5
Alpanseque E 41 F6
Alpbach A 72 B4
Alpedrinha P 44 D6
Alpedriz P 44 E3
Alpen D 17 E7
Alpenrod D 21 C9
Alpens E 43 C8
Alpera E 56 D2
Alphen NL 16 F3
Alphen aan den Rijn NL 16 D3
Alpiarça P 44 F3
Alpirsbach D 27 D9
Alpnach CH 70 D6
Alposjärvi FIN 117 E12
Alpua FIN 119 F14
Alpuente E 47 E11
Alpullu TR 173 B7
Alquería de la Condesa E 56 D4
Alquerías E 56 E2
Alqueva P 50 C4
Alquife E 55 E6
Alrance F 34 B4
Alrewas GB 11 F8
Als DK 86 B6
Alsager GB 11 E7
Alsån S 119 B9
Alsbach D 187 B6
Alsdorf D 20 C6
Alsėdžiai LT 134 D4
Alsen S 105 E15
Alsenborn D 21 F9
Alseno I 69 D8
Alsenz D 21 E9
Alsfeld D 21 C12
Alsheim D 185 E9
Alsike S 99 C9
Alsjö S 103 B11
Alsleben (Saale) D 79 C10
Alslev DK 86 D2
Alsmo N 100 D6
Alsónémedi H 150 C3
Alsópáhok H 149 C8
Alsos N 108 A8
Alsóvadász H 145 G2
Alsózsolca H 145 G2
Ålsrode DK 87 C7
Ålstad N 110 E9
Alstad S 87 E12
Alstahaug N 108 E3
Alstakan S 97 C8
Alster S 97 D10
Alsterbro S 89 B9
Alstermo S 89 B9
Alsting F 186 C2
Alston GB 5 F12
Alsunga LV 134 C3
Alsvåg N 110 C9
Alsvik N 108 B7
Alsviķi LV 133 B1
Alta N 113 D11
Älta S 99 D10
Altafulla E 43 E6
Altamura I 61 B7
Altare I 37 C8
Altatornio FIN 119 C12
Altaussee A 73 A8
Altavilla Irpina I 60 B3
Altavilla Silentina I 60 B4
Altdöbern D 80 C6
Altdorf CH 71 D7
Altdorf D 75 E11
Altdorf bei Nürnberg D 75 D9
Alt Duvenstedt D 82 B7
Alte P 50 E3
Altea E 56 D4
Altefähr D 84 B4
Alteglofsheim D 75 E11
Alteidet N 112 C9
Altena D 17 F9
Altenahr D 21 C7
Altenau D 79 C7
Altenberg D 80 E5
Altenberge D 17 D8
Altenbruch-Westerende D 17 A11
Altenbuch D 74 C5
Altenburg D 79 E11
Altendiez D 21 D9
Altenfeld D 75 A8
Altenfelden A 76 F5
Altenglan D 21 E8
Altenhagen D 83 B11
Altenheim D 27 D8
Altenhof D 84 E5
Altenholz D 83 B8
Altenkirchen D 84 A4
Altenkirchen (Westerwald) D 21 C9
Altenkrempe D 83 B9
Altenkunstadt D 75 B9
Altenmarkt an der Triesting A 77 F9
Altenmarkt bei Sankt Gallen A 73 A10
Altenmarkt im Pongau A 73 B7
Altenmedingen D 83 D9
Altenmünster D 75 F8
Altenstadt D 21 D11
Altenstadt D 71 A10
Altenstadt D 71 B11
Altensteig D 27 C10
Altentreptow D 84 C4
Alter do Chão P 44 F5
Altes Lager D 80 B4
Altevik N 111 C12
Altfraunhofen D 75 F11
Altheim A 76 F4
Altheim D 27 D11
Altheim (Alb) D 187 D9
Althengstett D 187 D6
Althofen A 73 C9
Altier F 35 B6
Altimir BG 165 B8
Alțina RO 152 F4
Altindag TR 177 C9
Altinoluk TR 172 E6
Altinova TR 177 A8
Altintaş TR 181 A8
Altkirch F 27 E7
Alt Krenzlin D 83 D10
Altlandsberg D 80 A5
Altleiningen D 21 E10
Altmannstein D 75 E10
Altnaharra GB 2 J8
Altofonte I 58 C3
Altomonte I 60 D6
Altomünster D 75 F9
Alton GB 11 F8
Alton GB 14 E7
Altopascio I 66 E2
Altorricón E 42 D4
Altötting D 75 F12
Altrich D 185 E6
Altrincham GB 11 E7
Alt Ruppin D 84 E3
Altsasu E 32 E1
Alt Schwerin D 83 C12
Altshausen D 71 B9
Altstätten CH 71 C9
Alttajärvi S 116 C5
Altura E 48 E4
Altusried D 71 B10
Alu EST 131 C9
Aluatu MD 154 F3
Alūksne LV 133 B2
Ålund S 118 D6
Alunda S 99 B10
Aluniș RO 152 C3
Aluniș RO 152 D5
Aluniș RO 161 C7
Alunu RO 160 C3
Alustante E 47 C9
Alva S 93 E12
Alvaiázere P 44 E4
Alvajarvi FIN 123 D14
Alvalade P 50 D3
Alvaneu CH 71 D9
Älvängen S 91 D11
Alvarenga P 44 C4
Álvares P 44 D4
Álvaro P 44 E5
Alvdal N 101 B13
Älvdalen S 102 D7
Alvega P 44 F4
Alveley GB 13 A10
Alvelos P 38 E2
Alverca P 50 B1
Alverca da Beira P 45 C6
Alvesta S 88 B7
Alvestad N 111 C11
Alvestorp S 97 C12
Alvettula FIN 127 C11
Alvhem S 91 C11
Älvho S 102 D8
Alviano I 62 B2
Alvie GB 3 L9
Alvignac F 29 F9
Ålvik N 94 B4
Alvik S 102 E8
Alvik S 103 B13
Alvik S 118 C7
Alvito I 62 D5
Alvito P 50 C4
Älvkarleby S 103 E13
Älvkarleö S 99 A8
Alvnes N 108 B9
Alvnes N 110 E9
Alvoco da Serra P 44 D5
Älvros S 102 B8
Älvsbyn S 118 C6
Älvsered S 87 A11
Ålvund N 101 A9
Ålvundeid N 101 A9
Alwernia PL 143 F8
Alyki GR 174 A3
Alyth GB 5 B10
Alytus LT 137 E9
Alzenau in Unterfranken D 21 D12
Alzey D 21 E10
Alzira E 48 F4
Alzon F 34 C5
Alzonne F 33 D10
Ämådalen S 102 D8
Amadora P 50 B1
Amaiur-Maia E 32 D3
Åmål S 91 A12
Åmål S 91 B12
Amalfi I 60 B3
Amaliada GR 174 D3
Amaliapoli GR 175 A6
Amalo GR 177 D6
Amance F 26 E5
Amancey F 31 A9
Amandola I 62 B4
Amantea I 60 E6
Amara RO 161 D10
Amarante P 38 F3
Amarantos GR 168 E5
Amărăști RO 160 D4
Amărăștii de Jos RO 160 F4
Amărăștii de Sus RO 160 F4
Amareleja P 51 C5
Amares P 38 E3
Amaroni I 59 B9
Amaru RO 161 D9
Amarynthos GR 175 C8
Amaseno I 62 E4
Amatrice I 62 B4
Amaxades GR 171 B8
Amay B 19 C11
Ambasaguas E 39 C9
Ambazac F 29 D8
Ambel E 41 E8
Ambeļi LV 135 D13
Amberg D 75 D10
Ambergate GB 11 E9
Ambérieu-en-Bugey F 31 D7
Amberloup B 19 D12
Ambert F 30 D4
Ambès F 28 E4
Ambierle F 30 C4
Ambillou F 24 F3
Ambjörby S 97 B9
Ambjörnarp S 91 E13
Ambla EST 131 C11
Amblainville F 24 B7
Amble GB 5 E13
Ambleside GB 10 C6
Ambleteuse F 15 F12
Amboise F 24 F4
Ambon F 22 E6
Ambrault F 29 B9
Ambrières-les-Vallées F 23 D10
Ambronay F 31 C7
Ambrosden GB 13 B12
Åmdals Verk N 95 D8
Ameglia I 69 E8
Ameide NL 182 B5
Ameixial P 50 E4
Amel B 20 D6
Amele LV 134 B4
Amelia I 62 B2
Amélie-les-Bains-Palalda F 34 F4
Amelinghausen D 83 D8
Amêndoa P 44 E4
Amendoeira P 50 D4
Amendolara I 61 D7
Amer E 43 C9
Amerang D 75 G11
A Merca E 38 D4
Amerongen NL 183 B6
Amersfoort NL 16 D4
Amersham GB 15 D7
Amesbury GB 13 C11
Amezketa E 32 D1
Amfikleia GR 175 B6
Amfilochia GR 174 B3
Amfipoli GR 169 C10
Amfissa GR 174 B5
Amieira P 50 C4
Amiens F 18 E5
Amilly F 25 E8
Åminne FIN 122 E7
Åminne S 87 A14
Åmland N 94 F5
Åmli N 90 A3
Åmli N 90 B3
Amlwch GB 10 E3
Ämmälänkylä FIN 123 E9
Ammanford GB 12 B7
Ämmänsaari FIN 121 E12
Ammarnäs S 109 E11
Åmmeberg S 92 B6
Ammenäs S 91 C10
Ammerbuch D 187 D6
Ammern D 79 D7
Ammersbek D 83 C8
Ammerzoden NL 183 B6
Ammochori GR 169 C5
Ammotopos GR 168 F4
Ammoudia GR 169 B9
Amnatos GR 178 E8
Amnéville F 186 C1
Amoeiro E 38 D4
Amonde P 38 E2
Amorbach D 21 E12
Amorebieta E 40 B6
Amorgos GR 177 F6
Amori GR 171 B10
Åmot N 94 C7
Åmot N 95 B11
Åmot N 95 C8
Åmot N 95 C11
Åmot S 103 E11
Åmotfors S 96 C7
Amou F 32 C4
Åmøyhamn N 108 C5
Ampelakia GR 169 E8
Ampeleia GR 169 F7
Ampelokipoi GR 169 C8
Ampelonas GR 169 E7
Ampezzo I 73 D6
Ampfing D 75 F11
Ampflwang im Hausruckwald A 76 F5
Amplepuis F 30 D5
Amposta E 42 F5
Ampthill GB 15 C8
Ampudia E 39 E10
Ampuero E 40 B5
Ampus F 36 D4
Amriswil CH 27 E11
Åmsele S 107 B16
Åmsosen N 94 D3
Amstelveen NL 16 D3
Amsterdam NL 16 D3
Amstetten A 77 F7
Amstetten D 187 D8
Amulree GB 5 B9
Amurrio E 40 B6
Amusco E 40 D3
Amvrosia GR 171 B8
Amygdaleonas GR 171 C6
Amygdalia GR 174 C5
Åmynnet S 107 E15
Amyntaio GR 169 C6
Amzacea RO 155 F2
Anacapri I 60 B2
Anadia P 44 D4
Anafi GR 180 D3
Anafonitria GR 174 D2
Anagaire IRL 6 B6
Anagni I 62 D4
An Aird Mhóir IRL 6 F3
Añana-Gesaltza E 40 C6
Anan'yiv UA 154 B5
Anarcs H 145 G5
Anargyroi GR 169 C6
Anarrachi GR 169 D6
Ånäset S 118 F6
Åna-Sira N 94 F4
Anatazavė LT 135 E11
Anatoli GR 168 E4
Anatoli GR 169 E8
Anatoli GR 179 E10
Anatoliki Fragkista GR 174 B4
Anatoliko GR 169 C6
Anatoliko GR 169 C8
Anavatos GR 177 C7
Anavra GR 174 A5
Anavra GR 175 A6
Anavyssos GR 175 D8
Anaya de Alba E 45 C10
An Baile Breac IRL 8 E2
An Baile Nua IRL 8 D5
An Bhlarna IRL 8 E5
An Bun Beag IRL 6 B6
An Cabhán IRL 7 E8
An Caiseal IRL 6 F3
An Caisleánn Riabhach IRL 6 E6
An Caisléan Nua IRL 7 F10
An Caisléan Nua IRL 8 D4
An Cathair IRL 9 D7
Ance LV 134 A4
Ancelle F 36 B4
Ancene LV 135 D11
Ancenis F 23 F9
Ancerville F 26 C3
An Charraig IRL 6 C5
An Cheathru Rua IRL 6 F3
An Chill IRL 7 F9
Ancín E 32 E1
An Cionn Garbh IRL 6 C6
An Clochán IRL 7 C7
An Clochán Liath IRL 6 C6
An Cóbh IRL 8 E6
An Coimín IRL 7 C7
An Coireán IRL 8 E2
Ancona I 67 E8
Ancroft GB 5 D13
Ancrum GB 5 D11
Ancy-le-Franc F 25 E11
Anda N 100 C4
Andalo I 69 A11
Åndalsnes N 100 A7
Andau A 149 A8
Andavías E 39 E8
Anddalsvågen N 108 E3
Andebu N 95 D12
Andechs D 75 G9
Andeer CH 71 D8
Andelfingen CH 27 E10
Andelot-Blancheville F 26 D3
Andelst NL 16 E5
Andenes N 111 B11
Andenne B 19 D11
Anderlecht B 19 C9
Anderlues B 19 D9
Andermatt CH 71 D7
Andernach D 185 D7
Andernos-les-Bains F 28 F3
Andersbo S 99 B9
Anderslöv S 87 E12
Anderstorp S 88 A5
Andervenne D 17 C9
Andfiskå N 108 D7
Andijk NL 16 C4
Andilly-en-Bassigny F 26 E4
Andlau F 27 D7
Andoain E 32 D1
Andocs H 149 C9
Andolsheim F 27 D7
Andorf A 76 F5
Andørja N 111 C13
Andorno Micca I 68 B5
Andorra E 42 F3
Andorra la Vella AND 33 E9
Andosilla E 32 F2
Andouillé F 23 D10
Andover GB 13 C12
Andrano I 61 D10
Andrășești RO 161 D10
Andratx E 49 E9
Andravida GR 174 D3
Andreas GBM 10 C3
Andreiașu de Jos RO 153 F9
Andrespol PL 143 C8
Andrest F 33 D6
Andretta I 60 B4
Andria I 60 A6
Andrid RO 151 B9
Andrieșeni RO 153 B10
Andrijaševci HR 157 B10
Andrijevica MNE 163 D8
Andrioniškis LT 135 E10
Andriškiai LT 136 D6
Andritsaina GR 174 E4
Andronianoi GR 175 B9
Andros GR 176 D4
Androusa GR 174 E4
Andrup DK 86 D3
Andrupene LV 133 D2
Andrychów PL 147 B8
Andrzejewo PL 141 E6
Andselv N 111 B15
Andsnes N 112 C7
An Dúchoraidh IRL 6 C6
Andújar E 53 A8
Anduze F 35 B6
Andzeļi LV 133 D3
An Eachléim IRL 6 D2
Åneby N 95 B13
Aneby S 92 D5
Anela I 64 C3
Anenii Noi MD 154 D4
Ånes N 104 E4
Anet F 24 C5
Anetjärvi FIN 121 C10
Anevo BG 165 D10
Aneza GR 174 A2
An Fál Carrach IRL 6 B6
An Féar Bán IRL 7 F7
An Fhairche IRL 6 E4
Anfo I 69 B9
Äng S 92 D5
Anga S 93 E13
Ånge S 103 A10
Änge S 105 E16
Ånge S 109 E14
An Geata Mór IRL 6 D2
Ängebo S 103 C11
Angeja P 44 C3
Ängelholm S 87 C11
Angeli FIN 113 F16
Angelniemi FIN 127 E8
Angelochori GR 169 C7
Angelokastro GR 174 B3
Angelokastro GR 175 D7
Ångelsberg S 97 C15
Angelstad S 87 B13
Angely F 25 E11
Anger D 73 A6
Angera I 68 B6
Angermünde D 84 D6
Angern D 79 B10
Angern an der March A 77 F11
Angers F 23 F10
Ångersjö S 102 C8
Ångersjö S 122 C3
Angersnes N 108 D4
Angervikko FIN 125 D10
Angerville F 24 D7
Ängesån S 116 E8
Ängeslevä FIN 119 E15
Ängesträsk S 118 B8
Anghiari I 66 E5
Anglade F 28 E4
Angle GB 9 E12
Anglès E 43 D9
Anglès F 34 C4
Anglesola E 42 D5
Anglesona E 42 D6
Angles-sur-l'Anglin F 29 B7
Anglet F 32 D2
Angliers F 29 B6
Anglure F 25 C10
Angnäs S 107 D16
Angoisse F 29 E8
Ängom S 103 B13
An Gort IRL 6 F5
Angoulême F 29 D6
Angoulins F 28 C3
Angri I 60 B3
Angrie F 23 E10
Angüés E 42 C3
Anguiano E 40 D6
Anguillara Sabazia I 62 C2
Anguillara Veneta I 66 B4
Anguita E 47 B8
Angvik N 100 A8
Anha P 38 E2
Anhée B 19 D10
Anholt DK 87 B9
Aniane F 35 C6
Aniche F 19 D7
Anif A 73 A7
Anina RO 159 C8
Aninoasa RO 160 C2
Aninoasa RO 160 C5
Aninoasa RO 160 D2
Aninoasa RO 161 D6
Anizy-le-Château F 19 E7
Anjalankoski FIN 128 D6
Anjan S 105 D13
Anjum NL 16 B6
Ankaran SLO 73 E8
Ankarede Kapell S 105 B16
Ankarsrum S 93 D8
Ankarsund S 109 F12
Ankarsvik S 103 B13
Ankenes N 111 D13
Ankerlia N 112 E6
Ankershagen D 84 D3
Anklam D 84 C5
Ankum D 17 C9
Anlaby GB 11 D11
An Leadhb Gharbh IRL 6 C5
Anlezy F 30 B4
An Longfort IRL 7 E7
An Mám IRL 6 E3
An Mhala Raithní IRL 6 E3
An Móta IRL 7 F7
An Muileann gCearr IRL 7 E8
Ånn S 105 E13
Anna E 56 C3
Anna EST 131 C11
Annaberg A 77 G8
Annaberg-Buchholtz D 80 E4
Annaburg D 80 C4
Annagassan IRL 7 E10
Annagry IRL 6 B6
Annahilt GB 7 D10
Annahütte D 80 C5
Annalong GB 7 D11
Annamoe IRL 7 F10
Annan GB 5 F10
Anna Paulowna NL 16 C3
Annarode D 79 C9
An Nás IRL 7 F9
Annayalla IRL 7 D9
Annbank GB 4 E7
Anneberg S 91 D11
Anneberg S 92 D5
Annecy F 31 D9
Annecy-le-Vieux F 31 D9
Annefors S 103 D11
Annelund S 91 D13
Annemasse F 31 C9
Annen NL 17 B7
Annenieki LV 134 C6
Annestown IRL 9 D8
Anneyron F 30 E6
Annikvere EST 131 C12
Annœullin F 182 D1
Annonay F 30 E6
Annonen FIN 119 F14
Annopol PL 144 B4
Annot F 36 D5
Annweiler am Trifels D 21 F9
Ano Agios Vlasios GR 174 B4
Ano Amfeia GR 174 E5
Ano Chora GR 174 B4
Ano Diakofto GR 174 C5
Ano Drosini GR 171 B9
Anoeta E 32 D1
Anogeia GR 174 F5
Anogeia GR 178 E8
Ano Kalliniki GR 168 C5
Ano Kardamyla GR 177 B7
Ano Kavallari GR 169 C9
Ano Komi GR 169 D6
Ano Kopanaki GR 174 E4
Ano Lechonia GR 169 F9
Ano Lefkimmi GR 168 F3
Ano Mera GR 176 E5
Añón E 41 E8
Ano Poroia GR 169 B9
Anor F 19 E9
Añora E 54 C3
Ano Sagkri GR 176 E5
Ano Steni GR 175 B8

Auby F 19 D7
Aucamville F 33 C8
Auce LV 134 D5
Auch F 33 C7
Auchallater GB 5 B10
Auchenbreck GB 4 D6
Auchencairn GB 5 F9
Auchencrow GB 5 D12
Auchnagatt GB 3 L12
Auchterarder GB 5 C9
Auchtermuchty GB 5 C10
Auchy-au-Bois F 18 C5
Aucun F 32 E5
Audenge F 32 A3
Auderville F 23 A8
Audeux F 26 F4
Audevälja EST 131 C8
Audierne F 22 D2
Audincourt F 27 F6
Audlem GB 10 F6
Audley GB 11 E7
Audnedal N 90 C1
Audon F 32 C4
Audresselles F 15 F12
Audriņi LV 133 C2
Audru EST 131 E8
Audruicq F 18 C5
Audun-le-Roman F 20 F5
Aue D 79 E12
Auerbach D 75 A11
Auerbach in der Oberpfalz D 75 C10
Auersthal A 77 F11
Auffay F 18 E3
Aufhausen D 75 E11
Augbrim IRL 6 F5
Auggen D 27 E8
Augher GB 7 D8
Aughnacloy GB 7 D9
Aughrim IRL 6 F5
Aughrim IRL 9 C10
Aughton GB 11 E9
Augignac F 29 D7
Augsburg D 75 F8
Augšlīgatne LV 135 B10
Augstkalne LV 133 E2
Augstkalne LV 134 D6
Augusta I 59 E7
Auguste LV 134 D3
Augustenborg DK 86 F5
Augustów PL 136 F6
Augustowo PL 141 E8
Augustusburg D 80 E4
Auho FIN 121 E10
Aukan N 104 E4
Aukra N 100 A5
Aukrug D 82 B7
Aukštadvaris LT 137 D10
Aukštelkai LT 134 E7
Aukštelkė LT 134 E6
Auktsjaur S 109 E17
Auleja LV 133 D2
Aulendorf D 71 B9
Auletta I 60 B4
Aulla I 69 E8
Aullène F 37 H10
Aulnat F 30 D3
Aulnay F 28 C5
Aulnay-sous-Bois F 25 C8
Aulnois sur-Seille F 26 C5
Aulnoye-Aymeries F 19 D8
Aulon F 33 D7
Aulosen D 83 E11
Ault F 18 D3
Aultbea GB 2 K5
Aultguish Inn GB 2 K7
Aulus-les-Bains F 33 E8
Auma D 79 E10
Aumale F 18 E4
Aumetz F 20 F5
Aumont F 31 B8
Aumont-Aubrac F 30 F3
Aumühle D 83 C8
Aunay-en-Bazois F 25 F10
Aunay-sur-Odon F 23 B10
Auneau F 24 D6
Aunegrenda N 105 F10
Aunfoss N 105 B13
Auning DK 86 C6
Auñón E 47 C7
Aups F 36 D4
Aura FIN 126 D8
Aurach D 75 D7
Aurach bei Kitzbühel A 72 B5
Aura im Sinngrund D 74 B6
Auran N 105 E9
Auray F 22 E6
Aurdal N 101 E10
Aure N 104 E5
Aurec-sur-Loire F 30 E5
Aureilhan F 33 D6
Aureille F 35 C8
Aurejärvi FIN 123 G10
Aurel F 35 A9
Aurel F 35 B9
Aurensan F 32 C5
Aureosen N 100 A6
Auri LV 134 C6
Aurich D 17 B8
Aurignac F 33 D7
Aurillac F 29 F10
Auriol F 35 D10
Aurisina I 73 E8
Auritz E 32 E3
Aurland N 100 E6
Aurolzmünster A 76 F4
Auron F 36 C5
Auronzo di Cadore I 72 C5
Auros F 32 A5
Auroux F 30 F4
Aurskog N 95 C14
Ausa-Corno I 73 E7
Ausejo E 32 F1
Auseu RO 151 C10
Ausleben D 79 B9
Ausmas LV 135 B9
Ausonia I 62 E5
Außervillgraten A 72 C5
Aussillon F 33 C10
Aussonne F 33 C8
Austafjord N 105 B9
Austbø N 95 C8
Austborg N 105 C15
Austertana N 114 C5
Austis I 64 C3
Austmannli N 94 C5
Austnes N 100 A4
Austnes N 105 B15
Austnes N 111 C12
Austråt N 104 D7
Austsmøla N 104 E4
Auterive F 33 D8
Authon F 24 E4
Authon F 36 C4
Authon-du-Perche F 24 D4
Autio FIN 119 E17
Autio FIN 123 E13
Autol E 41 D7
Autrans F 31 E8
Autreville F 26 D4
Autrey-lès-Gray F 26 F3
Autry F 19 F10
Autti FIN 119 B18
Auttoinen FIN 127 C13
Autun F 30 B5
Auve F 25 B12
Auvelais B 19 D10
Auvers-le-Hamon F 23 E11
Auvillar F 33 B7
Auvillers-les-Forges F 184 E1
Auxerre F 25 E10
Auxi-le-Château F 18 D5
Auxonne F 26 F3
Auxy F 30 B5
Auzances F 29 C10
Auzat F 33 E8
Auzat-la-Combelle F 30 E3
Aužguļāni LV 135 E12
Auzon F 30 E3
Äva FIN 126 E5
Ava S 107 D16
Avafors S 118 B8
Availles-Limouzine F 29 C7
Avaldsnes N 94 D2
Avallon F 25 E10
Avan S 118 C7
Avanäs S 107 C17
Avanca P 44 C3
Avançon F 36 B4
Avantas GR 171 C9
Avant-lès-Ramerupt F 25 D11
Avasjö S 107 C11
Avato GR 171 C7
Avaträsk S 107 C10
Avaviken S 109 E16
Avdira GR 171 C7
Avdou GR 178 E9
A Veiga E 39 D6
Aveiras de Cima P 44 F3
Aveiro P 44 C3
Avelar P 44 E4
Avelãs de Caminho P 44 D4
Aveleda P 38 E3
Aveleda P 39 E6
Avelgem B 19 C7
Avella I 60 B3
Avellino I 60 B3
Avenay-Val-d'Or F 25 B11
Avenches CH 31 B11
Avenhorn NL 16 C3
Avenida do Marqués de Figueroa E 38 A3
Avermes F 30 B3
Avers CH 71 E9
Aversa I 60 B2
Avesnes-le-Comte F 18 D6
Avesnes-sur-Helpe F 19 D8
Avesta S 98 B6
Åvestbo S 97 C14
Avetrano I 61 C9
Avezzano I 62 C4
Avgerinos GR 168 D5
Avià E 43 C7
Aviano I 73 D6
Aviemore GB 3 L9
Avigliana I 31 E11
Avigliano I 60 B5
Avigliano Umbro I 62 B2
Avignon F 35 C8
Ávila E 46 C3
A Vila da Igrexa E 38 A4
Avilés E 39 A8
Avilley F 26 F5
Avintes P 44 B3
Avinurme EST 131 D13
Avinyó E 43 D7
Avio I 69 B10
Avion F 18 D6
Avioth F 19 E11
Avis P 44 F5
Avispea EST 131 C12
Åvist FIN 122 D9
Avize F 25 C11
Avižieniai LT 137 D11
Avlakia GR 177 D8
Avlemonas GR 178 C5
Avliotes GR 168 E2
Avlonari GR 175 B9
Avlonas GR 175 C8
Avlum DK 86 C3
Avoca IRL 9 C10
Avoine F 23 F12
Avola I 59 F7
Avon F 25 D8
Avonmouth GB 13 B9
Avord F 29 A11
Avoriaz F 31 C10
Avoudrey F 26 F5
Avrămeni RO 153 A9
Avrămești RO 152 E6
Avram Iancu RO 151 D8
Avram Iancu RO 151 E10
Avranches F 23 C9
Avren BG 171 B9
Avricourt F 186 D2
Avrig RO 152 F4
Avril F 20 F5
Avrillé F 23 E10
Avrillé F 28 C3
Avtovac BIH 157 F10
Av'že N 112 E10
Awans B 183 D6
Axams A 72 B3
Axat F 33 E10
Axel NL 16 F1
Axente Sever RO 152 E4
Axintele RO 161 D9
Axioupoli GR 169 C8
Ax-les-Thermes F 33 E9
Axmar S 103 D13
Axmarsbruk S 103 D13
Axminster GB 13 D9
Axos GR 169 C7
Axvall S 91 C14
Ayamonte E 50 E5
Aycliffe GB 5 F13
Aydat F 30 D2
Aydemir BG 161 E10
Ayen F 29 E8
Ayerbe E 32 F4
Aying D 72 A4
Aylesbury GB 15 D7
Ayllón E 40 F5
Aylsham GB 15 B11
Aymavilles I 31 D11
Ayna E 55 B8
Aynac F 29 F9
Ayoo de Vidriales E 39 D7
Ayora E 47 F10
Ayr GB 4 E7
Ayrancilar TR 177 C9
Ayron F 28 B6
Ayşebaci TR 173 E8
Aysgarth GB 11 C8
Äyskoski FIN 123 D17
Äystö FIN 122 F7
Aytos BG 167 D8
Aytré F 28 C3
Ayvacik TR 171 E10
Ayvalik TR 172 F6
Aywaille B 19 D12
Azagra E 32 F2
Azaila E 41 F11
Azambuja P 44 F3
Azanja SRB 159 E6
Azanúy E 42 D4
Azaruja P 50 B4
Azatli TR 172 B6
Azay-le-Ferron F 29 B8
Azay-le-Rideau F 24 F3
Azé F 23 E10
Azerables F 29 C8
Azinhaga P 44 F3
Azinhal P 50 E5
Azinheira dos Barros P 50 C3
Azinhoso P 39 F6
Azkoitia E 32 D1
Aznalcázar E 51 E7
Aznalcóllar E 51 D7
Azóia P 50 C1
Azpeitia E 32 D1
Azuaga E 51 C8
Azuara E 41 F10
Azuel E 54 C4
Azuelo E 32 E1
Azuga RO 161 C7
Azuqueca de Henares E 47 C6
Azur F 32 C3
Azután E 45 E10
Azy-le-Vif F 30 B3
Azyory BY 140 C10
Azzano Decimo I 73 E6
Azzone I 69 B9

B

Baalberge D 79 C10
Baâlon F 19 F11
Baar CH 27 F10
Baarle-Hertog B 16 F3
Baarle-Nassau NL 16 F3
Baarn NL 16 D4
Baba Ana RO 161 D8
Babadag RO 155 D3
Babaeski TR 173 B7
Babaköy TR 173 E9
Baban AL 168 C4
Băbana RO 160 D5
Babberich NL 183 B8
Babchyntsi UA 154 A2
Babenhausen D 21 E11
Băbeni RO 151 C11
Băbeni RO 160 D4
Babiak PL 136 E1
Babiak PL 138 F6
Babice CZ 146 C4
Babice PL 143 F7
Babice nad Svitavou CZ 77 D11
Babići BIH 157 D7
Băbiciu RO 160 E5
Babilafuente E 45 C10
Babimost PL 81 B9
Babín SK 147 C8
Babina SRB 164 D5
Babina Greda HR 157 B10
Babino Polje HR 162 D4
Babīte LV 135 C7
Babno Polje SLO 73 E10
Babócsa H 149 D8
Bábolna H 149 A9
Baborów PL 142 F4
Baboszewo PL 139 E9
Babót H 149 A8
Babrujë AL 168 B2
Babtai LT 137 C8
Babuk BG 161 E10
Babušnica SRB 164 C5
Babyak BG 165 F8
Babynichy BY 133 F4
Bać MNE 163 D9
Bač SRB 158 C3
Băcani RO 153 E11
Bacares E 55 E8
Bacău RO 153 D9
Baccarat F 27 D6
Baceno I 68 A5
Băcești RO 153 D10
Bach A 71 C10
Bacharach D 21 D9
Bachkovo BG 165 F10
Bachórz PL 144 D5
Băcia RO 151 F11
Baciki Bliższe PL 141 F7
Băcioi MD 154 D3
Baciu RO 152 D3
Bäck S 105 E16
Backa S 91 E10
Backa S 97 A9
Backa S 97 B9
Backaland GB 3 G11
Bačka Palanka SRB 158 C3
Backaryd S 89 C8
Bačka Topola SRB 150 F4
Backberg S 103 E12
Backe S 107 D10
Bäckebo S 89 B10
Bäckefors S 91 B11
Bäckhammar S 91 A15
Bački Breg SRB 150 F2
Bački Brestovac SRB 158 B3
Bački Jarak SRB 158 C4
Bački Monoštor SRB 150 F2
Bačkininkai LT 137 D8
Bački Petrovac SRB 158 C4
Bäcklund S 109 E17
Bäckmark S 107 A11
Backnang D 27 C11
Bäcknäs S 109 F17
Bačko Dobro Polje SRB 158 B4
Bačko Gradište SRB 158 B5
Bačko Novo Selo SRB 157 B11
Bačko Petrovo Selo SRB 158 B5
Baćkowice PL 143 E11
Backträsk S 118 C6
Bäckvallen S 102 B8
Băcleș RO 159 E11
Bacoli I 60 B2
Bacqueville-en-Caux F 18 E2
Bácsalmás H 150 E3
Bácsbokod H 150 E3
Bácsborsód H 150 E3
Bacúch SK 147 D9
Baczyna PL 85 E8
Bada S 97 B9
Bad Abbach D 75 E11
Bad Aibling D 72 A5
Badajoz E 51 B6
Badalona E 43 E8
Badalucco I 37 D7
Bádames E 40 B5
Badarán E 40 D6
Bad Aussee A 73 A8
Bad Bayersoien D 71 B12
Bad Bederkesa D 17 A11
Bad Belzig D 79 B12
Bad Bentheim D 17 D8
Bad Bergzabern D 27 B8
Bad Berka D 79 E9
Bad Berleburg D 21 B10
Bad Berneck im Fichtelgebirge D 75 B10
Bad Bertrich D 21 D8
Bad Bevensen D 83 D9
Bad Bibra D 79 D10
Bad Birnbach D 76 F4
Bad Blankenburg D 79 E9
Bad Blumau A 148 B6
Bad Bocklet D 75 B7
Bad Boll D 74 E6
Bad Brambach D 75 B11
Bad Bramstedt D 83 C7
Bad Breisig D 185 D7
Bad Brückenau D 74 B6
Bad Buchau D 71 A9
Bad Camberg D 21 D10
Badcaul GB 2 K6
Badderen N 112 D9
Bad Doberan D 83 B11
Bad Driburg D 17 E12
Bad Düben D 79 C12
Bad Dürkheim D 21 F10
Bad Dürrenberg D 79 D11
Bad Dürrheim D 27 D10
Badeborn D 79 C9
Badefols-d'Ans F 29 E8
Bad Elster D 75 B11
Bademler TR 177 C8
Bademli TR 171 F10
Bademli TR 173 D10
Bademli TR 177 B8
Bad Ems D 21 D9
Baden A 77 F10
Baden CH 27 F9
Baden F 22 E6
Bádenas E 47 B10
Baden-Baden D 27 C9
Bad Endorf D 72 A5
Badenscoth GB 3 L12
Badenweiler D 27 E8
Baderna HR 67 B8
Badersleben D 79 C8
Badesi I 64 B2
Bad Essen D 17 D10
Bădeuți RO 153 B7
Bad Fallingbostel D 82 E7
Bad Feilnbach D 72 A5
Bad Frankenhausen (Kyffhäuser) D 79 D9
Bad Freienwalde D 84 E6
Bad Friedrichshall D 21 F12
Bad Füssing D 76 F4
Bad Gams A 73 C11
Bad Gandersheim D 79 C7
Badgastein A 73 B7
Bad Gleichenberg A 148 C5
Bad Goisern A 73 A8
Bad Griesbach im Rottal D 76 F4
Bad Grönenbach D 71 B10
Bad Großpertholz A 77 E7
Bad Grund (Harz) D 79 C7
Bad Hall A 76 F6
Bad Harzburg D 79 C8
Bad Herrenalb D 27 C9
Bad Hersfeld D 78 E6
Bad Hindelang D 71 B10
Badhoevedorp NL 182 A5
Bad Hofgastein A 73 B7
Bad Homburg vor der Höhe D 21 D11
Bad Honnef D 21 C8
Bad Hönningen D 185 C7
Badia I 72 C4
Badia Calavena I 69 B11
Badia Gran E 49 F10
Badia Polesine I 66 B3
Badia Tedalda I 66 E5
Bad Iburg D 17 D10
Bădiceni MD 153 A12
Badín SK 147 D8
Bad Ischl A 73 A8
Bad Karlshafen D 78 C5
Bad Kissingen D 75 B7
Bad Kleinen D 83 C10
Bad Kleinkirchheim A 73 C8
Bad König D 21 E12
Bad Königshofen im Grabfeld D 75 B7
Bad Kösen D 79 D10
Bad Köstritz D 79 E11
Bad Kötzting D 76 D3
Bądkowo PL 138 E6
Bad Kreuzen A 77 F7
Bad Kreuznach D 21 E9
Bad Krozingen D 27 E8
Bad Laasphe D 21 C10
Bad Laer D 17 D10
Bad Langensalza D 79 D8
Bad Lauchstädt D 79 D10
Bad Lausick D 79 D12
Bad Lauterberg im Harz D 79 C7
Bad Leonfelden A 76 E6
Bad Liebenstein D 79 E7
Bad Liebenwerda D 80 C4
Bad Liebenzell D 27 C10
Bad Lippspringe D 17 E11
Badljevina HR 149 E8
Bad Lobenstein D 75 B10
Bad Marienberg (Westerwald) D 21 C9
Bad Mergentheim D 74 D6
Bad Mitterndorf A 73 A8
Bad Münder am Deister D 78 B5
Bad Münstereifel D 21 C7
Bad Muskau D 81 C7
Bad Nauheim D 21 D11
Bad Nenndorf D 17 D12
Bad Neuenahr-Ahrweiler D 21 C8
Bad Neustadt an der Saale D 75 B7
Badolato I 59 B10
Badolatosa E 53 B7
Bad Oldesloe D 83 C8
Badonviller F 27 C6
Bad Orb D 21 D12
Badovinci SRB 158 D3
Bad Peterstal D 27 D9
Bad Pirawarth A 77 F11
Bad Pyrmont D 17 E12
Bad Radkersburg A 148 C5
Bad Ragaz CH 71 C9
Bad Rappenau D 187 C7
Bad Reichenhall D 73 A6
Bad Rodach D 75 B8
Bad Saarow-Pieskow D 80 B6
Bad Sachsa D 79 C8
Bad Säckingen D 27 E8
Bad Salzdetfurth D 79 B7
Bad Salzuflen D 17 D11
Bad Salzungen D 79 E7
Bad Sankt Leonhard im Lavanttal A 73 C10
Bad Sassendorf D 17 E10
Bad Schandau D 80 E6
Bad Schmiedeberg D 79 C12
Bad Schönborn D 187 C6
Bad Schussenried D 71 A9
Bad Schwalbach D 21 D10
Bad Schwartau D 83 C9
Bad Segeberg D 83 C8
Bad Sobernheim D 185 E8
Bad Soden-Salmünster D 74 B5
Bad Sooden-Allendorf D 79 D6
Bad Staffelstein D 75 B8
Bad Steben D 75 B10
Bad Sulza D 79 D10
Bad Sülze D 83 B13
Bad Tennstedt D 79 D8
Bad Tölz D 72 A4
Bad Überkingen D 187 D8
Badules E 47 B10
Bad Urach D 27 D11
Bad Vilbel D 21 D11
Bad Vöslau A 77 G10
Bad Waldsee D 71 B9
Bad Waltersdorf A 148 B6
Bad Wildbad im Schwarzwald D 187 D6
Bad Wildungen D 21 B12
Bad Wilsnack D 83 E11
Bad Wimpfen D 21 F12
Bad Windsheim D 75 C7
Bad Wörishofen D 71 B11
Bad Wurzach D 71 B9
Bad Zell A 77 F7
Bad Zurzach CH 27 E9
Bad Zwesten D 21 B12
Bad Zwischenahn D 17 B10
Bække DK 86 D4
Bækmarksbro DK 86 C2
Baelen B 183 D7
Bælum DK 86 B6
Baena E 53 A8
Bærums Verk N 95 C12
Baesweiler D 20 C6
Baeza E 53 A10
Baflo NL 17 B7
Bagà E 43 C7
Băgaciu RO 152 E4
Bagaladi I 59 C8
Bagamér H 151 C8
Bağarasi TR 177 B8
Bağarasi TR 177 D10
Bagard F 35 B7
Bağcilar TR 181 B8
Bâgé-le-Châtel F 30 C6
Bagenalstown IRL 9 C9
Bagenkop DK 83 A9
Bages F 34 E4
Baggå S 97 C14
Bagheria I 58 C4
Bagn N 101 E11
Bagnacavallo I 66 D4
Bagnac-sur-Célé F 33 A10
Bagnara Calabra I 59 C8
Bagnaria I 37 B10
Bagnaria Arsa I 73 E7
Bagnasco I 37 C8
Bagneaux-sur-Loing F 25 D8
Bagnères-de-Bigorre F 33 D6
Bagnères-de-Luchon F 33 E7
Bagni di Lucca I 66 D2
Bagni di Masino I 69 A8
Bagni di Rabbi I 71 E11
Bagno a Ripoli I 66 E3
Bagno di Romagna I 66 E4
Bagnoli del Trigno I 63 D6
Bagnoli di Sopra I 66 B4
Bagnoli Irpino I 60 B4
Bagnolo in Piano I 66 C2
Bagnolo Mella I 66 B1
Bagnolo Piemonte I 31 F11
Bagnolo San Vito I 66 B2
Bagnols-les-Bains F 35 A6
Bagnols-sur-Cèze F 35 B8
Bagnoregio I 62 B2
Bagod H 149 C7
Bagolino I 69 B9
Bagrationovsk RUS 136 E2
Bagrdan SRB 159 E7
Bagshot GB 15 E7
Báguena E 47 B10
Bágyogszovát H 149 A8
Bağyurdu TR 177 C10
Bağyüzü TR 173 F6
Bahabón de Esgueva E 40 E4
Bahate UA 155 C3
Bahçeburun TR 181 B7
Bahçeköy TR 173 B10
Bahçeli TR 171 E10
Bahillo E 39 D10
Bahmut MD 153 C12
Bahna RO 153 D9
Bahnea RO 152 E4
Báhoň SK 146 E4
Bahrenborstel D 17 C11
Bahrendorf D 79 C10
Baia RO 153 C8
Baia RO 155 D3
Baia de Aramă RO 159 D10
Baia de Arieș RO 151 E11
Baia de Criș RO 151 E10
Baia de Fier RO 160 C3
Baia della Zagare I 63 D10
Baia Mare RO 152 B3
Baiano I 60 B3
Baiardo I 37 D7
Baia Sprie RO 152 B3
Băicoi RO 161 C7
Băiculești RO 160 C5
Baiersbronn D 27 C9
Baiersdorf D 75 C9
Baignes-Ste-Radegonde F 28 E5
Baigneux-les-Juifs F 25 E12
Baile an Bhiataigh IRL 7 E10
Baile an Bhuinneánaigh IRL 8 C3
Baile an Chinnéidigh IRL 7 F10
Baile an Dúlaigh IRL 6 F4
Baile an Fheirtéaraigh IRL 8 D2
Baile an Mhóta IRL 6 D5
Baile an Mhuilinn IRL 8 D2
Baile an Róba IRL 6 E4
Baile an Sceilg IRL 8 E2
Baile Átha an Rí IRL 6 F5
Baile Átha Buí IRL 7 E9
Baile Átha Cliath IRL 7 F10
Baile Átha Fhirdhia IRL 7 E9
Baile Átha Í IRL 7 G9
Baile Átha Luain IRL 7 F7
Baile Átha Troim IRL 7 E9
Baile Brigín IRL 7 E10
Baile Coimín IRL 7 F9
Băile Govora RO 160 C4
Băile Herculane RO 159 D9
Baile Loch Riach IRL 6 F5
Baile Mhartainn GB 2 K2
Baile Mhic Andáin IRL 9 C8
Baile Mhic Íre IRL 8 E4
Baile Mhistéala IRL 8 D6
Bailén E 54 C5
Baile na Finne IRL 6 C6
Baile na Lorgan IRL 7 D9
Băile Olănești RO 160 C4
Baile Órthaí IRL 7 E9
Băilești RO 160 E2
Băile Tușnad RO 153 E7
Baile Uilcín IRL 7 E9
Bailieborough IRL 7 E9
Baillargues F 35 C7
Bailleau-le-Pin F 24 D5
Bailleul F 18 C6
Baillonville B 19 D11
Bailo E 32 E4
Baimaclia MD 154 E2
Bainbridge GB 11 C7
Bain-de-Bretagne F 23 E8
Baindt D 71 B9
Bains F 30 E4
Bains-les-Bains F 26 D5
Bainton GB 11 D10
Baio E 38 B2
Baiona E 38 D2
Bais F 23 D9
Bais F 23 D11
Baiso I 66 D2
Băișoara RO 151 D11
Baisogala LT 134 E7
Băița RO 151 E10
Băița de sub Codru RO 151 B11
Baix F 35 A8
Baixa da Banheira P 50 B1
Baixas F 34 E4
Baj H 149 A10
Baja H 150 E2
Bajč SK 146 F6
Bajgorë RKS 164 D3
Bajina Bašta SRB 158 F4
Bajmok SRB 150 F3
Bajna H 149 A11
Bajót H 149 A11
Bajovo Polje MNE 157 F10
Bajram Curri AL 163 E9
Bajša SRB 150 F4
Bak H 149 C7
Baka SK 146 F5
Bakacak TR 173 D7
Bakałarzewo PL 136 E6
Bakar HR 67 B10
Bakel NL 16 F5
Bakir TR 177 A10
Bakırköy TR 173 C10
Bakkasund N 94 B2
Bakke N 111 A16
Bakkeby N 112 D6
Bakkejord N 111 A15
Bakken N 101 E15
Bakko N 95 C9
Bakonszeg H 151 C7
Bakonybél H 149 B9
Bakonycsernye H 149 B10
Bakonysárkány H 149 B10
Bakonyszentkirály H 149 B9
Bakonyszentlászló H 149 B9
Bakonyszombathely H 149 B9
Bakov nad Jizerou CZ 77 B7
Baks H 150 D5
Baksa H 149 E10
Baksha UA 154 A5
Baktalórántháza H 145 H5
Baktsjaur S 109 F17
Bakum D 17 C10
Bakvattnet S 105 D16
Bål S 93 D13
Bala GB 10 F4
Bala RO 159 D10
Balabancik TR 173 C6
Bălăbănești MD 154 C4
Bălăbănești RO 153 E11
Balabanu MD 154 F3
Bălăceanu RO 161 C10
Balaci RO 160 E5
Bălăcița RO 159 E11
Balaciu RO 161 D9
Balaguer E 42 D5
Balallan GB 2 J3
Balan F 19 E10
Balan F 31 D7
Bălan RO 151 C11
Bălan RO 153 D7
Bălănești MD 153 C12
Bălănești RO 160 C2
Balanivka UA 154 A4
Balaruc-les-Bains F 35 D6
Bălășești RO 153 E11
Bălășinești MD 153 A9
Balassagyarmat H 147 E8
Balástya H 150 E5
Balat TR 177 D9
Balaton H 145 G1
Balatonalmádi H 149 B10
Balatonberény H 149 C8
Balatonboglár H 149 C9
Balatonfőkajár H 149 B10
Balatonföldvár H 149 C9
Balatonfüred H 149 C9
Balatonfűzfő H 149 B10
Balatonkenese H 149 B10
Balatonlelle H 149 C9
Balatonszabadi H 149 C10
Balatonszárszó H 149 C9
Balatonvilágos H 149 C10
Bălăușeri RO 152 E5
Balazote E 55 B8
Balbeggie GB 5 C10
Balbieriškis LT 137 D8
Balbigny F 30 D5
Balbriggan IRL 7 E10
Balcani RO 153 D9
Bălcești RO 160 D3
Balchik BG 167 C10
Balcilar TR 173 D6
Balçova TR 177 C9
Balderton GB 11 E10
Baldock GB 15 D8
Baldone LV 135 C8
Baldones Muiža LV 135 C8
Baldovinești RO 160 E4
Bale HR 67 B8
Baleizão P 50 C4
Balemartine GB 4 C3
Balen B 19 B11
Băleni RO 153 F11
Băleni RO 161 D7
Balephuil GB 4 C3
Balerma E 55 F7
Balești RO 159 C11
Balestrand N 100 D5
Balestrate I 58 C3
Balfour GB 3 G11
Balfron GB 5 C8
Balgale LV 134 B5
Balgown GB 2 K4
Bälgviken S 98 D6
Bali GR 178 E8
Baligród PL 145 E5
Balıkesir TR 173 E8
Balıklıçeşme TR 173 D7
Balikliova TR 177 C8
Bălilești RO 160 C5
Bälinge S 99 C9
Bälinge S 118 C7
Balingen D 27 D10
Balinka H 149 B10
Balinț RO 151 F8
Balintore GB 3 K9
Balje D 17 A12
Baljevac BIH 156 C4
Baljevac SRB 163 C10
Baljvine BIH 157 D7
Balk NL 16 C5
Balkány H 151 B8
Balkbrug NL 16 C6
Balla IRL 6 E4
Ballaban AL 168 D3
Ballabio I 69 B7
Ballachulish GB 4 B6
Ballaghaderreen IRL 6 E5
Ballaghkeen IRL 9 D10
Ballangen N 111 D12
Ballantrae GB 4 E6
Ballao I 64 D3
Ballasalla GBM 10 C2
Ballater GB 5 A10
Ballaugh GBM 10 C2
Balle DK 87 C7
Ballée F 23 E11
Ballee GB 7 D11
Ballen DK 86 D7
Ballenstedt D 79 C9
Balleroy F 23 B10
Ballerup DK 87 D10
Ballesteros de Calatrava E 54 B5
Balli TR 173 C7
Ballina IRL 6 D4
Ballina IRL 8 C6
Ballinaboy IRL 6 F2
Ballinafad IRL 6 D6
Ballinagar IRL 7 F8
Ballinagh IRL 7 E8
Ballinakill IRL 9 C8
Ballinalack IRL 7 E8
Ballinalee IRL 7 E7
Ballinamallard GB 7 D7
Ballinamore IRL 7 D7
Ballinamult IRL 9 D7
Ballinasloe IRL 6 F6
Ballincollig IRL 8 E5
Ballindine IRL 6 E5
Ballindooly IRL 6 F4
Ballineen IRL 8 E5
Ballingarry IRL 8 D5
Ballingarry IRL 9 C7
Ballingeary IRL 8 E4
Ballingry GB 5 C10
Ballingslöv S 87 C13
Ballingurteen IRL 8 E4
Ballinhassig IRL 8 E5
Ballinlough IRL 6 E5
Ballinluig GB 5 B9
Ballinrobe IRL 6 E4
Ballinskelligs IRL 8 E2
Ballinspittle IRL 8 E5
Ballintober IRL 6 E4
Ballintoy GB 4 E4
Ballintra IRL 6 C6
Ballintubber IRL 6 E4
Ballinure IRL 9 C7
Ballivor IRL 7 E9
Ballobar E 42 D4
Ballon F 23 D12
Ballon IRL 9 C9
Ballószög H 150 D4
Ballots F 23 E9
Ballsh AL 168 C2
Ballsnes N 111 A16
Ballstad N 110 D6
Ballstädt D 79 D8
Ballum DK 86 E3
Ballum NL 16 B5
Ballure IRL 6 C6
Ballybay IRL 7 D9
Ballybofey IRL 7 C7
Ballybrack IRL 7 F10
Ballybrack IRL 8 E2
Ballybrittas IRL 7 F8
Ballybunion IRL 8 C3
Ballybunnion IRL 8 C3
Ballycahill IRL 9 C7
Ballycanew IRL 9 C10
Ballycarry GB 4 F5
Ballycastle GB 4 E4
Ballycastle IRL 6 D4
Ballyclare GB 4 F5
Ballycolla IRL 9 C8
Ballyconneely IRL 6 F2
Ballyconnell IRL 7 D7
Ballycotton IRL 8 E6
Ballycroy IRL 6 D3
Ballydavid IRL 6 F6
Ballydehob IRL 8 E4
Ballydesmond IRL 8 D4
Ballydonegan IRL 8 E2
Ballyduff IRL 8 D3
Ballyduff IRL 8 D6
Ballyfarnan IRL 6 D6
Ballyfarnon IRL 6 D6
Ballyfeard IRL 8 E6

Ballyferriter IRL 8 D2
Ballyforan IRL 6 F6
Ballygar IRL 6 E6
Ballygarrett IRL 9 C10
Ballygawley GB 7 D8
Ballygeary IRL 9 D10
Ballyglass IRL 6 E5
Ballygorman IRL 4 E2
Ballygowan GB 7 C11
Ballyhaise IRL 7 D8
Ballyhalbert GB 7 D12
Ballyhale IRL 9 D8
Ballyhaunis IRL 6 E5
Ballyhean IRL 6 E4
Ballyheigue IRL 8 D3
Ballyjamesduff IRL 7 E8
Ballykeeran IRL 7 F7
Ballykelly GB 4 E2
Ballykilleen IRL 7 F8
Ballylanders IRL 8 D6
Ballylaneen IRL 9 D8
Ballylickey IRL 8 E4
Ballyliffen IRL 4 E2
Ballyliffin IRL 4 E2
Ballylynan IRL 9 C8
Ballymacarberry IRL 9 D7
Ballymacmague IRL 9 D7
Ballymadog IRL 9 E7
Ballymagorry GB 4 F2
Ballymahon IRL 7 E7
Ballymakeery IRL 8 E4
Ballymartin GB 7 D11
Ballymena GB 4 F4
Ballymoney GB 4 E3
Ballymore IRL 7 F7
Ballymote IRL 6 D5
Ballymurphy IRL 9 C9
Ballymurry IRL 6 E6
Ballynacally IRL 8 C4
Ballynafid IRL 7 E8
Ballynahinch GB 7 D11
Ballynahowen IRL 7 F7
Ballynakill IRL 7 F7
Ballynamona IRL 8 D5
Ballyneaner GB 4 F2
Ballynunty IRL 9 C7
Ballynure GB 4 F5
Ballyporeen IRL 8 D6
Ballyragget IRL 9 C8
Ballyroan IRL 9 C8
Ballyronan GB 4 F3
Ballyshannon IRL 6 C6
Ballyvaldon IRL 9 D10
Ballyvaughan IRL 6 F4
Ballyvoy GB 4 E4
Ballyvoyle IRL 9 D7
Ballywalter GB 7 C12
Ballyward GB 7 D10
Balma F 33 C9
Balmaha GB 4 C7
Balmaseda E 40 B5
Balmazújváros H 151 B7
Balme I 31 E11
Balmedie GB 3 L12
Balmuccia I 68 B5
Balnacra GB 2 L6
Balnapaling GB 3 K8
Balneario de Panticosa Huesca E 32 E5
Balninkai LT 135 F10
Balocco I 68 C5
Balogunyom H 149 B7
Balot F 25 E11
Balotaszállás H 150 E4
Balotești RO 161 D8
Balow D 83 D11
Balrath IRL 7 E10
Balș RO 160 E4
Balșa RO 151 E11
Balsa de Ves E 47 F10
Balsa Pintada E 56 F2
Balsareny E 43 D7
Balsfjord N 111 B17
Balsicas E 56 F3
Balsjö S 107 D16
Balsorano I 62 D5
Bålsta S 99 C9
Balsthal CH 27 F8
Balta RO 159 D10
Balta UA 154 B5
Balta Albă RO 161 C10
Balta Berilovac SRB 164 C5
Balta Doamnei RO 161 D8
Baltanás E 40 E3
Baltar E 38 E4
Baltasound GB 3 D15
Bălțătești RO 153 C8
Bălţaţi RO 153 C10
Bălteni RO 153 D11
Bălteni RO 159 D11
Baltezers LV 135 B8
Bălți MD 153 B11
Baltimore IRL 8 F4
Baltinava LV 133 C3
Baltinglass IRL 9 C9
Baltiysk RUS 139 A8
Baltmuiža LV 135 D13
Baltoji Vokė LT 137 E11
Baltora S 99 C11
Bałtów PL 143 D12
Baltray IRL 7 E10
Băluşeni RO 153 B9
Balvan BG 166 C4
Bălvănești RO 159 D10
Balvano I 60 B5
Balve D 17 F9
Balvi LV 133 B2
Balvicar GB 4 C5
Balya TR 173 E8
Balzers FL 71 C9
Bamberg D 75 C8
Bamburgh GB 5 D13
Bammental D 21 F11
Bampini GR 174 B3
Bampton GB 13 B11
Bampton GB 13 D8
Bana H 149 A9
Banafjäl S 107 E16
Banagher IRL 7 F7
Banarli TR 173 B7
Banassac F 34 B5
Banatski Brestovac SRB 159 D6
Banatski Dvor SRB 158 B6
Banatski Karlovac SRB 159 C7
Banatsko Aranđelovo SRB 150 E5
Banatsko Karađorđevo SRB 158 B6
Banatsko Novo Selo SRB 159 D6
Banatsko Veliko Selo SRB 150 F6
Banbridge GB 7 D10
Banbury GB 13 A12
Banca RO 153 E11
Banchory GB 5 A12
Band RO 152 D4
Bande E 38 D4
Bandenitz D 83 D10
Bandholm DK 83 A10
Bandirma TR 173 D8
Bandol F 35 D10
Bandon IRL 8 E5
Bandurove UA 154 A5
Băneasa RO 153 F11
Băneasa RO 155 E1
Băneasa RO 161 E8
Bănești MD 154 B2
Bănești RO 161 C7
Banevo BG 167 D8
Banff GB 3 K11
Bångnäs S 106 B9
Bangor GB 4 F5
Bangor GB 10 E3
Bangor IRL 6 D3
Bangor Erris IRL 6 D3
Bangsund N 105 C10
Banham GB 15 C11
Bánhorváti H 145 G2
Bănia RO 159 D9
Banie PL 85 D7
Banie Mazurskie PL 136 E5
Baniska BG 166 C5
Bănişor RO 151 C10
Băniţa RO 159 C11
Banite BG 171 A8
Banitsa BG 165 C8
Banja BIH 158 F3
Banja SRB 163 B8
Banja Lučica BIH 157 D10
Banja Luka BIH 157 C7
Banjani SRB 158 D4
Banja Vrućia BIH 157 C8
Bankekind S 92 C7
Bankeryd S 92 D4
Bankfoot GB 5 B9
Bankya BG 165 D6
Bankya BG 165 D7
Banloc RO 159 C7
Bannalec F 22 E4
Bannay F 25 F8
Bannesdorf auf Fehmarn D 83 B10
Bannewitz D 80 E5
Bannivka UA 155 B3
Bannockburn GB 5 C9
Bañobárez E 45 C7
Bañón E 47 C10
Banon F 35 B10
Baños de la Encina E 54 C5
Baños de Molgas E 38 D4
Baños de Montemayor E 45 D9
Baños de Río Tobía E 40 D6
Baños de Valdearados E 40 E4
Bánov CZ 146 D5
Bánov SK 146 E6
Banova Jaruga HR 149 F7
Bánovce nad Bebravou SK 146 D6
Banovići BIH 157 D10
Bánréve H 145 G1
Bansin D 84 C6
Banská Belá SK 147 E7
Banská Bystrica SK 147 D8
Banská Štiavnica SK 147 E7
Banské SK 145 F4
Bansko BG 165 F7
Bant NL 16 C5
Banteer IRL 8 D5
Banteln D 78 B6
Bantheville F 19 F11
Bantry IRL 8 E4
Banya BG 165 D10
Banya BG 165 E9
Banya BG 165 F8
Banya BG 166 D5
Banya BG 167 D9
Banyalbufar E 49 E10
Banyeres de Mariola E 56 D3
Banyliv UA 152 A6
Banyliv-Pidhirnyy UA 152 A7
Banyoles E 43 C9
Banyuls-sur-Mer F 34 F5
Banzi I 60 B6
Banzkow D 83 C11
Bapaume F 18 D6
Bar MNE 163 E7
Bara RO 151 F8
Bara RO 153 C10
Bara S 87 D12
Barabás H 145 G5
Baracska H 149 B11
Bărăganul RO 161 D11
Baragiano I 60 B5
Barahona E 41 F6
Barajas de Melo E 47 D7
Barajevo SRB 158 D5
Barakaldo E 40 B6
Barakovo BG 165 E7
Baralla E 38 C5
Barañain E 32 E2
Baranbio E 40 B6
Báránd H 151 C7
Baranello I 63 D7
Baranjsko Petrovo Selo HR 149 E10
Barano d'Ischia I 62 F5
Baranów PL 141 G6
Baranów PL 142 D5
Baranowo PL 139 D11
Baranów Sandomierska PL 143 F12
Barão de São João P 50 E2
Baraolt RO 153 E7
Baraqueville F 33 B10
Barásoain E 32 E2
Barassie GB 4 D7
Bărăşti RO 160 D5
Baravukha BY 133 E5
Barbacena P 51 B5
Barbadás E 38 D4
Barbadillo de Herreros E 40 D5
Barbadillo del Mercado E 40 D5
Barbadillo del Pez E 40 D5
Barban HR 67 B9
Barbarano Vicentino I 66 B4
Barbaraville GB 3 K8
Barbaros TR 173 C7
Barbaste F 33 B6
Barbastro E 42 C4
Barbat HR 67 C10
Barbate de Franco E 52 D5
Bărbătescu RO 161 D9
Bărbătești RO 160 D3
Barbatovac SRB 164 C3
Barbâtre F 28 B1
Bārbele LV 135 D9
Barbentane F 35 C8
Barberá del Vallès E 43 D8
Barberaz F 31 D8
Barberino di Mugello I 66 D3
Barbezieux-St-Hilaire F 28 E5
Barbonne-Fayel F 25 C10
Bărbuleţu RO 160 C6
Barbullush AL 163 F8
Barby (Elbe) D 79 C10
Barç AL 168 C4
Barca E 41 F6
Bârca RO 160 F3
Barcabo E 42 C4
Barcada BIH 157 B8
Barca de Alva P 45 B7
Bărcăneşti RO 161 D8
Bărcănești RO 161 D9
Barcani RO 161 B8
Barcarrota E 51 B6
Barcea RO 153 F10
Barcelinhos P 38 E2
Barcellona Pozzo di Gotto I 59 C7
Barcelona E 43 E8
Barcelonne-du-Gers F 32 C5
Barcelonnette F 36 C5
Barcelos P 38 E2
Bárcena del Monasterio E 39 B6
Bárcena de Pie de Concha E 40 B3
Barcenillas de Cerezos E 40 B4
Barchfeld D 79 E7
Barciany PL 136 E3
Barcillonnette F 35 B10
Barcin PL 138 E4
Barcino PL 85 B11
Barcis I 72 D6
Barcones E 40 F6
Barcos P 44 B5
Barcs H 149 E8
Barcus F 32 D4
Barczewo PL 136 F2
Bardal N 108 D5
Bardar MD 154 D3
Barde DK 86 C3
Bardejov SK 145 E3
Bârdena E 41 D9
Bardenitz D 80 B3
Bårdesø DK 86 D6
Bardi I 69 D8
Bardineto I 37 C8
Bardney GB 11 E11
Bardo PL 77 B11
Bardolino I 66 A2
Bardonecchia I 31 E10
Bardos F 32 D3
Bardowick D 83 D8
Bardsea GB 10 C5
Bárdudvarnok H 149 D9
Bare BIH 157 E10
Bare SRB 158 E6
Bare SRB 163 C8
Barefield IRL 8 C5
Barèges F 33 E6
Barenburg D 17 C11
Barendorf D 83 D9
Bärenklau D 81 C7
Bärenstein D 76 B4
Bärenstein D 80 E5
Barentin F 18 E2
Barenton F 23 C10
Barevo BIH 157 D7
Barfleur F 23 A9
Barga I 66 D1
Bargagli I 37 C10
Bargas E 46 E4
Bărgăuani RO 153 D9
Barge I 31 F11
Bargemon F 36 D5
Bargen CH 27 E10
Bargenstedt D 82 B6
Barghe I 69 B9
Bărghiș RO 152 F5
Bargischow D 84 C5
Bargłów Kościelny PL 140 C7
Bargoed GB 13 B8
Bargrennan GB 4 E7
Bargstedt D 17 B12
Bargteheide D 83 C8
Bargullas AL 168 C3
Barham GB 15 E11
Bar Hill GB 15 C9
Bari I 61 A7
Barić Draga HR 156 D3
Barile I 60 B5
Barilović HR 148 F5
Barinas E 56 E2
Båring DK 86 E5
Barì Sardo I 64 D4
Barisciano I 62 C5
Barjac F 35 B7
Bårjasnjar'ga N 113 D15
Barjols F 35 C11
Barkåkar N 95 D12
Barkåkra S 87 C11
Barkald N 101 C13
Barkarö S 98 C7
Barkava LV 135 C13
Barkelsby D 83 A7
Barkhyttan S 103 E11
Barkowo PL 85 C12
Barkston GB 11 F10
Bârla RO 160 E5
Barlad RO 153 E11
Barleben D 79 B10
Bar-le-Duc F 26 C3
Barles F 36 C4
Barletta I 60 A6
Barley GB 15 C9
Barlinek PL 85 E8
Barlingbo S 93 D12
Barmouth GB 10 F3
Barmstedt D 82 C7
Bârna H 147 E9
Barna IRL 6 F4
Bârna RO 159 B9
Barnaderg IRL 6 F5
Barnard Castle GB 11 B8
Bärnarp S 92 D4
Barnatra IRL 6 D3
Bârnau D 75 C11
Barnbach A 73 B11
Barneberg D 79 B9
Barneveld NL 16 D5
Barneville-Carteret F 23 B8
Barnewitz D 79 A12
Barneycarroll IRL 6 E5
Barnoldswick GB 11 D7
Bârnova RO 153 C11
Barnowko PL 85 E7
Barnsley GB 11 D9
Barnstädt D 79 D10
Barnstaple GB 12 C6
Barnstorf D 17 C11
Barntrup D 17 E12
Baronissi I 60 B3
Baronville F 26 C6
Baroševac SRB 158 E5
Barovo NMK 169 B7
Barowka BY 133 E3
Barqueros E 55 D10
Barr F 27 D7
Barr GB 4 E7
Barracas E 48 D3
Barrachina E 47 C10
Barraduff IRL 8 D4
Barrafranca I 58 E5
Barral E 38 D3
Barrali I 64 E3
Barranco do Velho P 50 E4
Barrancos P 51 C6
Barranda E 55 C9
Barrapoll GB 4 C3
Barrax E 55 A8
Barre-des-Cévennes F 35 B6
Barreiro P 50 B1
Barrek S 98 B7
Barrême F 36 D4
Barrhead GB 5 D8
Barrhill GB 4 E7
Barriada Nueva E 43 D8
Bàrrio P 38 E2
Barrio del Peral E 56 F3
Barrio Mar E 48 E4
Barrit DK 86 D5
Barr na Trá IRL 6 D3
Barroca P 44 D5
Barroselas P 38 E2
Barrowby GB 11 F10
Barrow-in-Furness GB 10 C5
Barruecopardo E 45 B7
Barruelo de Santullan E 40 C3
Barry GB 13 C8
Barry IRL 7 E7
Bârsa RO 151 E9
Barsac F 32 A5
Bârsana RO 145 H9
Bârsău RO 151 B11
Barsbüttel D 83 C8
Bårse DK 87 E9
Barsele S 107 A12
Bârsești RO 153 F9
Barsinghausen D 78 B5
Barßel D 17 B9
Barsta S 103 A15
Barstyčiai LT 134 D3
Bar-sur-Aube F 25 D12
Bar-sur-Seine F 25 D11
Bārta LV 134 D2
Bartenheim F 27 E7
Bartenstein D 74 D6
Barth D 83 B13
Bartholomä D 74 E6
Bartholomäberg A 71 C9
Bartkuškiai LT 135 F9
Bartkuškis LT 137 D10
Bartnes N 105 C10
Bartniki PL 139 D10
Bartninkai LT 136 E7
Barton GB 10 D6
Barton-upon-Humber GB 11 D11
Bartoszyce PL 136 E2
Baru RO 159 C11
Baruchowo PL 139 F7
Barulho P 45 F6
Barumini I 64 D3
Baruth D 80 B5
Barvas GB 2 J3
Barvaux B 19 D11
Barver D 17 C11
Barwedel D 79 A8
Barwice PL 85 C10
Barxeta E 56 C4
Bârza RO 160 E4
Bârzana E 39 B8
Bârzava RO 151 E9
Barzio I 69 B7
Bašaid SRB 158 B5
Basarabeasca MD 154 E3
Basarabi RO 155 E2
Basarbovo BG 161 F7
Bàscara E 43 C9
Baschi I 62 B2
Bascharage L 20 E5
Baschurch GB 10 F6
Basciano I 62 B5
Basconcillos del Tozo E 40 C4
Bascons F 32 C5
Bascous F 33 C6
Bascov RO 160 D5
Basdahl D 17 B12
Basècles B 19 C8
Basel CH 27 E8
Baselga di Pinè I 69 A11
Baselice I 60 A3
Bas-en-Basset F 30 E5
Băsești RO 151 C11
Bâsheim N 95 B10
Bashtanivka UA 154 F4
Basigo E 40 B6
Basildon GB 15 D9
Basiliano I 73 D7
Basingstoke GB 13 C12
Baška CZ 146 B6
Baška HR 67 C10
Baška Voda HR 157 F6
Baskemölla S 88 D6
Bäsksele S 107 B11
Bäsksjö S 107 B12
Basksjön S 107 A12
Baslow GB 11 E8
Bäsna S 97 A13
Bassacutena I 64 A3
Bassano del Grappa I 72 E4
Bassano Romano I 62 C2
Bassecourt CH 27 F7
Basse-Goulaine F 23 F9
Bassenge B 19 C12
Bassens F 28 F4
Bassiano I 62 D4
Bassoues F 33 C6
Bassum D 17 C11
Bassy F 31 D8
Bast FIN 123 C10
Båstad S 87 C11
Bastardo I 62 B3
Bastasi BIH 156 D5
Bastasi BIH 157 F10
Bastelica F 37 G10
Bastelicaccia F 37 H9
Bastennes F 32 C4
Bastfallet S 98 B7
Bastia F 37 F10
Bastia I 62 A3
Bastogne B 19 D12
Bastorf D 83 B11
Basttjärn S 97 B12
Bastumarks by S 118 E3
Bastuträsk S 107 C16
Bastuträsk S 118 E4
Báta H 149 D11
Bata RO 151 E9
Batajnica SRB 158 D5
Batak BG 165 F9
Batalha P 44 E3
Băţani RO 153 E7
Batăr RO 151 D8
Bătarci RO 145 G7
Båtas S 106 B8
Bátaszék H 149 D11
Batea E 42 E4
Batelov CZ 77 D8
Båteng N 113 C20
Baterno E 54 B3
Batetskiy RUS 132 D7
Bath GB 13 C10
Bathford GB 13 C10
Bathgate GB 5 D9
Bathmen NL 16 D6
Batin BG 161 F7
Batina HR 149 E11
Batizovce SK 145 E1
Batković BIH 158 D3
Batley GB 11 D8
Batllavë RKS 164 D3
Båtmonostor H 150 E2
Båtnfjordsøra N 100 A7
Batočina SRB 159 E7
Bátonyterenye H 147 F9
Batorove Kosihy SK 146 F6
Batoş RO 152 D5
Batoshevo BG 166 D4
Bátovce SK 147 E7
Batovo BG 167 C9
Batrina HR 157 B8
Båtsfjord N 114 B7
Batsi GR 176 D4
Båtsjaur S 109 D13
Båtskärsnäs S 119 C10
Battenberg (Eder) D 21 B11
Bätterkinden CH 27 F8
Battice B 183 D7
Battipaglia I 60 B3
Battle GB 15 F9
Battonya H 151 E7
Batultsi BG 165 C9
Bátya H 150 E2
Batyatychi UA 144 C9
Batz-sur-Mer F 22 F7
Baucina I 58 D4
Baud F 22 E5
Bauduen F 36 D4
Bauen CH 71 D7
Baugé F 23 E11
Baugy F 25 F8
Bauladu I 64 C2
Baulon F 23 E8
Baume-les-Dames F 26 F5
Baumholder D 186 B3
Baunach D 75 C8
Baunei I 64 C4
Baurci MD 154 E3
Bausendorf D 21 D7
Bauska LV 135 D8
Băuţar RO 159 B10
Bautzen D 80 D6
Bavanište SRB 159 D6
Bavay F 19 D8
Bavel NL 182 B5
Baveno I 68 B6
Bavilliers F 27 E6
Bavorov CZ 76 D6
Bawdeswell GB 15 B11
Bawdsey GB 15 C11
Bawinkel D 17 C8
Bawn Cross Roads IRL 8 D5
Bayárcal E 55 E7
Bayarque E 55 E8
Baybuzivka UA 154 A5
Baye F 25 C10
Bayel F 25 D12
Bayerbach D 76 F4
Bayerbach bei Ergoldsbach D 75 E11
Bayerisch Eisenstein D 76 D4
Bayeux F 23 B10
Bayindir TR 177 C10
Bayir TR 181 B8
Bayirköy TR 172 D6
Baykal BG 160 F4
Bayon F 26 D5
Bayonne F 32 D3
Bayramiç TR 172 E6
Bayramiç TR 173 C6
Bayramli TR 173 B6
Bayreuth D 75 C10
Bayrischzell D 72 A5
Bayston Hill GB 10 F6
Baytaly UA 154 B5
Bayubas de Abajo E 40 E6
Baza E 55 D7
Bázakerettye H 149 C7
Bazas F 32 B5
Bazet F 33 D6
Bazièɡe F 33 D9
Bazillac F 33 D6
Bazna RO 152 E4
Bazoches F 25 F10
Bazoches-au-Houlme F 23 C11
Bazoches-les-Gallerandes F 24 D7
Bazoches-sur-Hoëne F 24 C3
Bazougers F 23 D10
Bazouges F 23 E10
Bazzano I 66 D3
Beaconsfield GB 15 D7
Beadnell GB 5 D13
Beagh IRL 6 E5
Bealach A Doirín IRL 6 E5
Bealach Conglais IRL 9 C9
Bealach Feich IRL 7 C7
Bealaclugga IRL 6 F4
Béal an Átha IRL 6 D4
Béal an Mhuirthead IRL 6 D3
Béal Átha an Ghaorthaidh IRL 8 E4
Béal Átha Beithe IRL 7 D9
Béal Átha hAmhnais IRL 6 E5
Béal Átha Liag IRL 7 E7
Béal Átha na Muice IRL 6 E5
Béal Átha na Sluaighe IRL 6 F6
Béal Átha Seanaidh IRL 6 C6
Béal Deirg IRL 6 D3
Béal Easa IRL 6 E4
Bealnablath IRL 8 E5
Beaminster GB 13 D9
Beamud E 47 D9
Beannchar IRL 7 F7
Beantraí IRL 8 E4
Beariz E 38 D3
Bearna IRL 6 F4
Bearsden GB 5 D8
Beas E 51 E6
Beasain E 32 D1
Beas de Granada E 53 B10
Beas de Segura E 55 C7
Beateberg S 92 B4
Beattock GB 5 E10
Beaucaire F 35 C8
Beaucamps-le-Vieux F 18 E4
Beauchastel F 30 F6
Beaucouzé F 23 F10
Beaufay F 24 D3
Beaufort F 31 B7
Beaufort F 31 D10
Beaufort IRL 8 D3
Beaufort-en-Vallée F 23 F11
Beaugency F 24 E6
Beaujeu F 30 C6
Beaujeu F 36 C4
Beaujeu-St-Vallier-Pierrejux-et-Quitteur F 26 E4
Beaulieu F 35 C7
Beaulieu-lès-Loches F 24 F5
Beaulieu-sur-Dordogne F 29 F9
Beaulieu-sur-Loire F 25 E8
Beaulon F 30 B4
Beauly GB 2 L8
Beaumarchés F 33 C6
Beaumaris GB 10 E3
Beaumesnil F 24 B4
Beaumetz-lès-Loges F 18 D6
Beaumont B 19 D9
Beaumont F 23 A8
Beaumont F 29 B6
Beaumont F 29 F7
Beaumont-de-Lomagne F 33 C7
Beaumont-de-Pertuis F 35 C10
Beaumont-en-Argonne F 19 E11
Beaumont-en-Véron F 23 F12
Beaumont-le-Roger F 24 B4
Beaumont-lès-Valence F 30 F6
Beaumont-sur-Oise F 25 B7
Beaumont-sur-Sarthe F 23 D12
Beaune F 30 A6
Beaune-La Rolande F 25 D7
Beaupréau F 23 F10
Beauquesne F 18 D5
Beauraing B 19 D10
Beaurepaire F 31 E7
Beaurepaire-en-Bresse F 31 B7
Beaurières F 35 A10
Beausite F 26 C3
Beausoleil F 37 D6
Beautor F 19 E7
Beauvais F 18 F5
Beauval F 18 D5
Beauvezer F 36 C5
Beauville F 33 B7
Beauvoir-sur-Mer F 28 B1
Beauvoir-sur-Niort F 28 C5
Beauzac F 30 E5
Beauzelle F 33 C8
Beba Veche RO 150 E5
Bebertal D 79 B9
Bebington GB 10 E5
Bebra D 78 E6
Bebrene LV 135 D12
Bebrina HR 157 B8
Beccles GB 15 C12
Becedas E 45 D9
Beceite E 42 F4
Bečej SRB 158 B5
Beceni RO 161 C9
Becerreá E 38 C5
Becerril de Campos E 39 D10
Becherbach D 186 B4
Bécherel F 23 D8
Bechet RO 160 F3
Bechhofen D 21 F8
Bechhofen D 75 D8
Bechlín CZ 76 B6
Bechtheim D 21 E10
Bechyně CZ 77 D6
Becicherecu Mic RO 151 F7
Bečići MNE 163 E6
Becilla de Valderaduey E 39 D9
Beçin TR 181 B7
Beckdorf D 82 D7
Beckedorf D 17 D12
Beckeln D 17 C11
Beckingen D 21 F7
Beckingham GB 11 E10
Beckov SK 146 D5
Beckum D 17 E10
Beclean RO 152 C4
Beclean RO 152 F5
Bécon-les-Granits F 23 F10
Bečov CZ 76 B5
Becsehely H 149 D7
Becsvölgye H 149 C7
Bečváry CZ 77 C8
Bedale GB 11 C8
Bédar E 55 E9
Bédarieux F 34 C5
Bédarrides F 35 B8
Bedburg D 21 C7
Bedburg-Hau D 183 B8
Beddgelert GB 10 E3
Beddingestrand S 87 E12
Bédée F 23 D8
Bedekovčina HR 148 D5
Beden BG 165 F9
Beder DK 86 C6
Bedford GB 15 C8
Bedihošť CZ 77 D12
Bjdków PL 143 C8
Bedlington GB 5 E13
Bedlno PL 143 B8
Bedmar E 53 A10
Bednja HR 148 D5
Bédoin F 35 B9
Bedollo I 69 A11
Bedonia I 37 B11
Bedous F 32 D4
Bedsted DK 86 E4
Bedsted Stationsby DK 86 B2
Bédueг F 33 A9
Bedum NL 17 B7
Bedwas GB 13 B8
Bedworth GB 13 A12
Bjdzin PL 143 F7
Bjdzino PL 85 B9
Beedenbostel D 79 A7
Beeford GB 11 D11
Beek NL 16 E5
Beek NL 16 E5
Beek NL 183 D7
Beekbergen NL 183 A7
Beelitz D 80 B3
Beendorf D 79 B9
Beenz D 84 D4
Beerfelden D 21 E11
Beernem B 19 B7
Beers NL 16 E5
Beerse B 16 F3
Beersel B 19 C9
Beerst B 182 C1
Beerta NL 17 B8
Beesd NL 183 B6
Beesenstedt D 79 C10
Beeskow D 80 B6
Beesten D 17 D9
Beeston GB 11 F9
Beetsterzwaag NL 16 B6
Beetzendorf D 83 E10
Bégaar F 32 C4
Bégadan F 28 E4
Begaljica SRB 158 D6
Bégard F 22 C5
Begejci SRB 158 B6
Beğendik TR 172 C6
Begijar E 53 A9
Begijnendijk B 19 B10
Begležh BG 165 C10
Begnište NMK 169 B6
Begonte E 38 B4
Begur E 43 D10
Behramkale TR 171 F10
Behren-lès-Forbach F 27 B6
Behren-Lübchin D 83 B13
Behringen D 79 D8
Beica de Jos RO 152 D5
Beidaud RO 155 D3
Beierfeld D 79 E12
Beierstedt D 79 B8
Beilen NL 17 C7
Beilngries D 75 D9
Beilstein D 27 B11
Beimerstetten D 187 E8
Beinasco I 37 A7
Beinette I 37 C7
Beinwil CH 27 F9
Beirã P 44 F6
Beisfjord N 111 D14
Beisland N 90 C3
Beith GB 4 D7
Beitostølen N 101 D9
Beitstad N 105 C10
Beiuş RO 151 D9
Beja LV 133 B2
Beja P 50 C4
Bejar AL 168 D2
Béjar E 45 D9
Bejís E 48 E3
Bekecs H 145 G3
Békés H 151 D7
Békéscsaba H 151 D7
Békéssámson H 150 E6
Békésszentandrás H 150 D5
Bekkarfjord N 113 B19
Bekken N 101 C15
Bekkevoll N 114 D8
Belá SK 147 C7
Bélâbre F 29 B8
Bela Crkva SRB 159 D7
Beladice SK 146 E6
Belá-Dulice SK 147 C7
Belalcázar E 51 B9
Belá nad Cirochou SK 145 F5
Bělá nad Radbuzou CZ 75 C12
Belanovce NMK 164 E4
Belanovica SRB 158 E5
Bela Palanka SRB 164 C5
Bélapátfalva H 145 G1
Bělá pod Bezdězem CZ 77 A7
Bělá pod Pradědem CZ 77 B12
Belascoáin E 32 E2
Belauski LV 133 C2
Belava LV 135 B13
Belazaima do Chão P 44 C4
Belcaire F 33 E9
Belcastel F 33 B10
Belceşti RO 153 C10
Bełchatów PL 143 D7
Belchin BG 165 E7
Belchite E 41 F10
Bělčice CZ 76 C5
Belciugatele RO 161 E8
Belclare IRL 6 F5
Belcoo GB 7 D7
Belderg IRL 6 D3
Beldibi TR 181 C8
Beled H 149 B8
Belegiš SRB 158 C5
Belej HR 67 C9
Belene BG 160 F6
Belësta F 33 E9
Beleţi-Negreşti RO 160 D6
Belevi TR 177 C9
Belezna H 149 D7
Belfast GB 7 C11
Belfeld NL 16 F6
Belford GB 5 D13
Belfort F 27 E6
Belfort-du-Quercy F 33 B9
Belforte del Chienti I 67 F7
Belgern D 80 D4
Belgershain D 79 D12
Belgioioso I 69 C7
Belgodère F 37 F10
Belgooly IRL 8 E6
Belgun BG 155 F2
Belhomert-Guéhouville F 24 C5
Beli HR 67 B9
Belianes E 42 D6
Belica HR 149 D7
Beli Iskŭr BG 165 E8
Beli Izvor BG 165 C7
Beli Manastir HR 149 E11
Belin RO 153 F7
Belin-Béliet F 32 B4
Belinchón E 47 D6
Belinț RO 151 F8
Beli Potok SRB 164 B5
Beliș RO 151 D11
Belišće HR 149 E10
Belitsa BG 161 F9
Belitsa BG 165 D8
Belitsa BG 165 F8
Beliu RO 151 E9
Bělkovice-Lašťany CZ 146 B4
Bell D 21 D8
Bell (Hunsrück) D 185 D7
Bella I 60 B5
Bellac F 29 C8
Bellacorick IRL 6 D3
Bellaghy GB 4 F3
Bellaghy IRL 6 E5
Bellagio I 69 B7
Bellahy IRL 6 E5
Belanicë RKS 163 E10
Bellano I 69 A7

Bellante I 62 B5
Bellaria I 66 D5
Bellavary IRL 6 E4
Bellavista E 51 E8
Bellclaire d'Urgell E 42 D5
Belleek GB 7 D10
Bellegarde F 25 E7
Bellegarde F 35 C8
Bellegarde-en-Marche F 29 D10
Bellegarde-sur-Valserine F 31 C8
Belle-Isle-en-Terre F 22 C5
Bellême F 24 D4
Bellenaves F 30 C3
Bellenberg D 71 A10
Bellencombre F 18 E3
Bellerive-sur-Allier F 30 C3
Belles-Forêts F 27 C6
Belleu F 19 F7
Bellevaux F 31 C10
Belleville F 30 C6
Belleville-sur-Meuse F 26 B3
Belleville-sur-Vie F 28 B3
Bellevue-la-Montagne F 30 E4
Belley F 31 D8
Bellheim D 21 F10
Bellherbe F 26 F6
Bellignat F 31 C8
Bellinge DK 86 E6
Bellingham GB 5 E12
Bellingwolde NL 17 B8
Bellinzago Novarese I 68 B6
Bellinzona CH 69 A7
Bellizzi I 60 B3
Bell-Lloc d'Urgell E 42 D5
Bello E 47 C10
Bellobradë RKS 163 C10
Bellopojë RKS 163 D10
Bellou-en-Houlme F 23 C11
Bellpuig E 42 D6
Bellreguard E 56 D4
Bellshill GB 5 D8
Belluno I 72 D5
Bellver de Cerdanya E 33 F9
Bellvik S 107 C10
Belm D 17 D10
Bélmegyer H 151 D7
Bélmez E 51 C9
Bélmez de la Moraleda E 53 A10
Belmont GB 3 D15
Belmont-de-la-Loire F 30 C5
Belmonte E 39 B7
Belmonte E 47 E7
Belmonte P 45 D6
Belmonte Calabro I 60 E6
Belmonte del Sannio I 63 D6
Belmonte in Sabina I 62 C3
Belmontejo E 47 E8
Belmont-sur-Rance F 34 C4
Belmullet IRL 6 D3
Belo Brdo RKS 163 C10
Beloci MD 154 B4
Belœil B 19 C8
Belogradchik BG 159 F10
Beloiannisz H 149 B11
Belojin SRB 164 C3
Belorado E 40 D5
Beloslav BG 167 C9
Bělotín CZ 146 B5
Belotintsi BG 165 B6
Belovo BG 165 E9
Belozem BG 166 E4
Belp CH 31 B11
Belpasso I 59 D6
Belpech F 33 D9
Belper GB 11 E9
Belsay GB 5 E13
Belsh AL 168 C2
Belsk Duży PL 141 G3
Beltheim D 21 D8
Beltinci SLO 148 C6
Beltiug RO 151 B10
Beltra IRL 6 D5
Beltra IRL 6 E4
Beltrum NL 183 A9
Belturbet IRL 7 D8
Beluša SK 146 C6
Belušić SRB 159 F7
Belvédère-Campomoro F 37 H9
Belvedere Marittimo I 60 D5
Belvedere Ostrense I 67 E7
Belver de Cinca E 42 D4
Belver de los Montes E 39 E9
Belvès F 29 F8
Belvèze-du-Razès F 33 D10
Belvì I 64 D3
Belville IRL 6 D4
Belvís de la Jara E 46 E3
Belz F 22 E5
Belz UA 144 C9
Bełżec PL 144 C7
Bełżyce PL 141 H6
Bembibre E 38 B2
Bembibre E 39 C7
Bemmel NL 16 E5
Bemposta P 39 F7
Bemposta P 44 F4
Bempton GB 11 C11
Benabarre E 42 C4
Benacazón E 51 E7
Benahadux E 55 F8
Benahavís E 53 C6
Benalmádena E 53 C7
Benalúa de Guadix E 55 E6
Benalúa de las Villas E 53 B9
Benalup de Sidonia E 52 D5
Benamargosa E 53 C8
Benamaurel E 55 D7
Benamejí E 53 B7
Benamocarra E 53 C8
Benaocaz E 53 C6
Benaoján E 53 C6
Benasal E 48 D4
Benasau E 56 D4
Benasque E 33 E7
Benassay F 28 B6
Benatae E 55 C7
Benátky nad Jizerou CZ 77 B7
Benavente E 39 D8
Benavente P 50 B2
Benavides de Orbigo E 39 D8
Benavila P 44 F5
Benburb GB 7 D9
Bencatel P 50 B5
Bendorf D 21 D9
Bēne LV 134 D6
Benecko CZ 81 E9
Beneden-Leeuwen NL 16 E4
Benediktbeuren D 72 A3
Benedita P 44 F3
Benegiles E 39 E8
Bénéjacq F 32 D5
Benejama E 56 D3
Benejúzar E 56 E3
Benesat RO 151 C11
Benešov CZ 77 C7
Benešov nad Černou CZ 77 E7
Benešov nad Ploučnicí CZ 80 E6
Bénesse-Maremne F 32 C3
Benestare I 59 C9
Bénestroff F 27 C6
Benet F 28 C4
Benetutti I 64 C3
Bene Vagienna I 37 B7
Bénévent-l'Abbaye F 29 C9
Benevento I 60 A3
Benfeld F 27 D8
Benfica do Ribatejo P 44 F3
Bengești-Ciocadia RO 160 C3
Bengtsfors S 91 A11
Bengtsheden S 103 E10
Benia de Onís E 39 B10
Beniarbeig E 56 D5
Beniarrés E 56 D4
Beničanci HR 149 E10
Benicarló E 48 D5
Benicasim E 48 D5
Benidorm E 56 D4
Beniel E 56 E3
Benifaió E 48 F4
Benifallet E 42 F5
Benifallim E 56 D4
Benigánim E 56 D4
Benilloba E 56 D4
Benissa E 56 D5
Benissanet E 42 E5
Benitachell E 56 D5
Benitses GR 168 E2
Benizalón E 55 E8
Benizar y la Tercia E 55 C9
Benken CH 27 F11
Benkovac HR 156 D4
Benkovski BG 161 F10
Benkovski BG 171 B8
Benllech GB 10 E3
Benlloch E 48 D5
Bennebroek NL 182 A5
Bennekom NL 183 A7
Bennewitz D 79 D12
Bennungen D 79 D9
Bénodet F 22 E3
Benquerença P 45 D6
Benquerenças P 44 E5
Benquerencia de la Serena E 51 B9
Benquet F 32 C4
Bensafrim P 50 E2
Bensbyn S 118 C8
Bensdorf D 79 B11
Benshausen D 79 E8
Bensheim D 21 E11
Bensjö S 103 A9
Benson GB 13 B12
Bentelo NL 17 D7
Bentivoglio I 66 C3
Bentley GB 11 D9
Bentwisch D 83 B12
Bentzin D 84 C4
Beňuš SK 147 D9
Benzingerode D 79 C8
Beočin SRB 158 C4
Beograd SRB 158 D5
Bera de Bidasoa E 32 D2
Beragh GB 7 C8
Berane MNE 163 D8
Beranga E 40 B4
Berango E 40 B6
Berantevilla E 40 C6
Berat AL 168 C2
Bérat F 33 D8
Beratzhausen D 75 D10
Berbegal E 42 D3
Berbești RO 160 C3
Berca RO 161 C9
Bercedo E 40 B5
Bercel H 147 F8
Berceni RO 161 D8
Berceni RO 161 E8
Bercero E 39 E9
Berceto I 69 D8
Berchem B 19 C8
Berchidda I 64 B3
Berching D 75 D9
Berchtesgaden D 73 A7
Bérchules E 55 F6
Bercianos del Páramo E 39 D8
Berck F 15 G12
Bercu RO 145 H6
Berdal N 104 E6
Berdalen N 94 D6
Berducedo E 39 B6
Berdún E 32 E4
Bere Alston GB 12 E6
Beregdaróc H 145 G6
Beregsurgardo I 69 C7
Berehomet UA 152 A6
Berehove UA 145 G6
Berek HR 149 E7
Berekböszörmény H 151 C8
Berekfürdő H 150 C6
Beremend H 149 E10
Berești RO 153 E11
Berești-Meria RO 153 E11
Berești-Tazlău RO 153 E9
Berettyóújfalu H 151 C8
Berevoești RO 160 C5
Berezeni RO 154 E2
Berezyne UA 154 E4
Berg D 71 B9
Berg D 75 B10
Berg D 183 D9
Berg L 20 E6
Berg N 96 B7
Berg N 108 F3
Berg N 111 B13
Berg NL 19 C12
Berg NL 183 D7
Berg S 92 C8
Berg S 102 A7
Berg S 107 E10
Berg (Pfalz) D 27 C9
Berga D 79 D9
Berga D 79 E11
Berga E 43 C7
Berga S 89 A10
Bergagård S 87 B11
Bergaland N 94 D4
Bergama TR 177 A9
Bergamo I 69 B8
Bergantino I 66 B3
Bergara E 32 D1
Bergasa E 32 F1
Bergatreute D 71 B9
Berg bei Neumarkt in der Oberpfalz D 75 D9
Bergby S 103 E13
Berge D 17 C9
Berge D 83 D11
Berge E 42 F3
Berge S 102 A8
Berge S 105 D14
Bergeforsen S 103 A13
Bergeggi I 37 C8
Bergen D 73 A6
Bergen D 83 E7
Bergen D 84 B4
Bergen N 94 B2
Bergen NL 16 C3
Bergen (Dumme) D 83 E9
Bergen op Zoom NL 16 F2
Berger N 95 C12
Bergerac F 29 F6
Bergères-lès-Vertus F 25 C11
Bergesserin F 30 C6
Berget N 108 D6
Bergeyk NL 16 F4
Bergfors S 111 D18
Berghamn S 103 A15
Bergharen NL 183 B7
Berghaupten D 186 E4
Bergheim A 73 A7
Bergheim D 75 E9
Bergheim (Edertal) D 21 B12
Bergheim (Erft) D 21 C7
Berghem NL 16 E5
Berghem S 91 E12
Berghin RO 152 E3
Berghülen D 74 F6
Berg im Drautal A 73 C7
Bergisch Gladbach D 21 C8
Bergkamen D 17 E9
Bergkarlås S 102 D8
Bergkvara S 89 C10
Bergland S 107 A10
Berglia N 105 C15
Bergmo N 112 D7
Bergnäs S 109 E13
Bergnäset S 118 C8
Bergnäsudden S 109 E15
Bergnäsviken S 109 D15
Bergneustadt D 185 B8
Bergö FIN 99 B13
Bergö FIN 122 E6
Bergom S 107 E15
Bergsåker S 103 B13
Bergsäng S 97 B10
Bergsäter S 107 B12
Bergsbyn S 118 E6
Bergschenhoek NL 182 B5
Bergsgården S 103 E10
Bergshamra S 99 C11
Bergsjö S 103 C13
Bergsnov N 105 B9
Bergs slussar S 92 C7
Bergstod N 95 D9
Bergstrøm N 96 D6
Bergsviken S 118 D6
Bergtheim D 75 C7
Bergues F 18 C5
Bergün CH 71 D9
Bergvik S 103 D12
Bergviken S 109 D16
Bergwitz D 79 C12
Berhida H 149 B10
Beringe NL 183 C7
Beringel P 50 C4
Beringen B 19 B11
Berislăvești RO 160 C4
Beriu RO 151 F11
Berja E 55 F7
Berka D 79 E7
Berkåk N 101 A12
Berkel NL 16 E2
Berkel-Enschot NL 16 E4
Berkeley GB 13 B10
Berkenthin D 83 C9
Berkheim D 71 A10
Berkhout NL 16 C4
Berkoviči BIH 157 F9
Berkovitsa BG 165 C7
Berlanga E 51 C8
Berlanga de Duero E 40 F6
Berlești RO 160 D3
Berlevåg N 114 B6
Berlicum NL 183 B6
Berlin D 80 A4
Berlingerode D 79 D7
Berliște RO 159 D7
Berlstedt D 79 D9
Bermatingen D 27 E11
Bermeo E 40 B6
Bermillo de Sayago E 39 F7
Bern CH 31 B11
Bernac-Dessus F 33 D6
Bernalda I 61 C7
Bernardos E 46 B4
Bernartice CZ 76 D6
Bernartice CZ 81 E9
Bernāti LV 134 D1
Bernau D 27 E9
Bernau D 84 E5
Bernau am Chiemsee D 72 A5
Bernaville F 18 D5
Bernay F 24 B4
Bernbeuren D 71 B11
Bernburg (Saale) D 79 C10
Berndorf A 77 G10
Berne D 17 B10
Bernecebaráti H 147 E7
Bernedo E 41 C7
Bernhardsthal A 77 E11
Bernhardswald D 75 D11
Bernin F 31 E8
Bernis F 35 C7
Bernisdale GB 2 L4
Bernissart B 19 D8
Bernitt D 83 C11
Bernkastel-Kues D 21 E8
Bernolákovo SK 146 E4
Bernsdorf D 80 D6
Bernshammar S 97 C14
Bernstadt D 74 E7
Bernstadt D 81 D7
Bernstein A 148 B6
Beromünster CH 27 F9
Beronovo BG 167 D7
Beroun CZ 76 C6
Berovo NMK 165 F6
Berra I 66 C4
Berre-l'Étang F 35 D9
Berriedale GB 3 J9
Berrien F 22 D4
Berriozar E 32 E2
Berru F 19 F9
Berry-au-Bac F 19 F8
Bersenbrück D 17 C9
Bershad' UA 154 A5
Beršići SRB 158 E5
Bersone I 69 B10
Bērstele LV 135 D7
Bertamirans E 38 C2
Bertea RO 161 C7
Berteștii de Jos RO 155 D1
Bertinoro I 66 D5
Bertnes N 108 B8
Bertogne B 19 D12
Bertrange L 186 B1
Bertrichamps F 27 D6
Bertrix B 19 E11
Běrunice CZ 77 B8
Berveni RO 151 B9
Bērvircava LV 134 D7
Berwick-upon-Tweed GB 5 D12
Bērzaine LV 131 F10
Berzasca RO 159 D8
Bērzaune LV 135 C12
Bērzciems LV 134 B6
Berzence H 149 D8
Bērzgale LV 133 C3
Bērzieši LV 135 D11
Bērzkalne LV 133 B2
Berźniki PL 137 E7
Berzovia RO 159 C8
Bērzpils LV 133 C2
Berzunți RO 153 E9
Beșalma MD 154 E3
Besalú E 43 C9
Besançon F 26 F5
Besande E 39 C10
Bescanó E 43 D9
Beselich-Obertiefenbach D 21 D10
Beseňov SK 146 E6
Besenyőtelek H 150 B5
Besenyszög H 150 C5
Besigheim D 27 C11
Beşiktaş TR 173 B11
Beška SRB 158 C5
Besko PL 145 D4
Besni Fok SRB 158 D5
Besnyő H 149 B11
Besozzo I 68 B6
Bessacarr GB 11 D9
Bessaker N 104 C8
Bessan F 34 D5
Bessay-sur-Allier F 30 C3
Bessbrook GB 7 D10
Besse F 31 E9
Besse-et-St-Anastaise F 30 D2
Bessèges F 35 B7
Bessenbach D 187 B7
Bessé-sur-Braye F 24 E4
Besse-sur-Issole F 36 E4
Bessières F 33 C9
Bessines-sur-Gartempe F 29 C8
Bessude I 64 B2
Best NL 16 E4
Bestensee D 80 B5
Bestorp S 92 C7
Bestwig D 17 F10
Bestwina PL 147 B8
Beszterec H 145 G4
Betanzos E 38 B3
Betelu E 32 D2
Bétera E 48 E4
Beteta E 47 C8
Bethausen RO 151 F8
Betheln D 78 B6
Bethesda GB 10 E3
Bethmale F 33 E8
Bethon F 25 C10
Béthune F 18 C6
Betna N 104 E4
Beton-Bazoches F 25 C9
Betschdorf F 186 D4
Betsele S 107 B15
Bettelainville F 186 C1
Bettembourg L 20 E6
Bettendorf L 20 E6
Bettingen D 20 E6
Bettna S 93 B9
Bettola I 37 B11
Betton F 23 D8
Bettyhill GB 3 H8
Bettystown IRL 7 E10
Betws-y-coed GB 10 E4
Betxi E 48 E4
Betygala LT 134 F6
Betz F 25 B8
Betzdorf D 21 C9
Betzdorf L 186 B1
Betzenstein D 75 C9
Betzigau D 71 B10
Beucha D 79 D12
Beuil F 36 C5
Beuningen NL 16 E5
Beuren D 79 D7
Beuron D 27 D10
Beurville F 25 D12
Beuvrages F 182 E2
Beuvry F 18 C6
Beuzeville F 18 F1
Bevagna I 62 B3
Bevaix CH 31 B10
Beveren B 19 B9
Beverley GB 11 D11
Beverlo B 183 C6
Bevern D 78 C5
Beverstedt D 17 B11
Beverungen D 21 A12
Beverwijk NL 16 D3
Béville-le-Comte F 24 D6
Bewdley GB 13 A10
Bex CH 31 C11
Bexbach D 21 F8
Bexhill GB 15 F9
Beyağaç TR 181 B9
Beyazköy TR 173 B8
Beyçayiri TR 173 D6
Beyel TR 173 E10
Beyendorf D 79 B10
Beykoz TR 173 B11
Beynac-et-Cazenac F 29 F8
Beynat F 29 E9
Beynost F 31 D7
Beyoba TR 177 B10
Beyobasi TR 181 C9
Bezas E 47 D10
Bezau A 71 C9
Bezdan SRB 150 F2
Bezdead RO 161 C6
Bezdonys LT 137 D12
Bèze F 26 F3
Bezenye H 146 F4
Bezhanitsy RUS 133 C7
Bezhanovo BG 155 F2
Bezhanovo BG 165 C9
Béziers F 34 D5
Bezledy PL 136 E2
Bezmer BG 161 F10
Bezmer BG 166 E6
Bezouce F 35 C8
Bežovce SK 145 F5
Biadki PL 142 C4
Biała PL 142 F4
Biała-Parcela Pierwsza PL 142 D5
Biała Piska PL 139 C13
Biała Podlaska PL 141 F8
Biała Rawska PL 141 G2
Białe Błota PL 138 D4
Białebłoto-Kobyla PL 139 E12
Białka PL 145 E1
Białobrzegi PL 141 G3
Białogard PL 85 C9
Białośliwie PL 85 D12
Białowieża PL 141 E9
Biały Bór PL 85 C11
Biały Dunajec PL 147 C10
Białystok PL 140 D8
Biancavilla I 59 D6
Bianco I 59 C9
Biandrate I 68 C5
Bians-les-Usiers F 31 B9
Bianzè I 68 C5
Biar E 56 D3
Biarritz F 32 D2
Biarrotte F 32 C3
Biars-sur-Cère F 29 F9
Bias F 32 B3
Bias F 33 B7
Biasca CH 71 E7
Biatorbágy H 149 B11
Bibbiena I 66 E4
Bibbona I 66 F2
Biberach D 27 D9
Biberach an der Riß D 71 A9
Biberbach D 75 E8
Biberist CH 27 F8
Bibinje HR 156 D3
Bibione I 73 E7
Biblis D 21 E10
Bibury GB 13 B11
Bicaz RO 151 C11
Bicaz RO 153 D8
Bicaz-Chei RO 153 D7
Bicazu Ardelean RO 153 D7
Biccari I 60 A4
Bicester GB 13 B12
Bichiș RO 152 E4
Bichl D 72 A3
Bichlbach A 71 C11
Bickleigh GB 13 D7
Bicorp E 48 F3
Bicos P 50 D3
Bicske H 149 A11
Bicton GB 10 F6
Bidache F 32 D3
Bidart F 32 D2
Biddenden GB 15 E10
Biddinghuizen NL 16 D5
Biddulph GB 11 E7
Bideford GB 12 C6
Bidjovagge N 112 E10
Bidos F 32 D4
Bidovce SK 145 F3
Bie S 93 A8
Bieber D 21 D12
Biebesheim am Rhein D 21 E10
Biecz PL 144 D3
Biedenkopf D 21 C11
Biel CH 27 F7
Biel E 32 F4
Bielany-Żyłaki PL 141 F6
Bielawa PL 81 E11
Bielawy PL 143 B8
Bielefeld D 17 D11
Bielice PL 85 D7
Bieliny Kapitulne PL 143 E10
Biella I 68 B5
Bielle F 32 D5
Bielsa E 33 E6
Bielsk PL 139 E8
Bielsko-Biała PL 147 B8
Bielsk Podlaski PL 141 E8
Bienenbüttel D 83 D8
Bieniów PL 81 C8
Bienno I 69 B9
Bienservida E 55 B7
Bienvenida E 51 C7
Bierawa PL 142 F5
Bierdzany PL 142 E5
Bière CH 31 B9
Bierge E 42 C3
Bierné F 23 E10
Biersted DK 86 A5
Biert F 33 E8
Biertan RO 152 E5
Bieruń PL 143 F7
Bierutów PL 142 D4
Bierzwienna-Długa PL 142 B6
Bierzwnik PL 85 D9
Biesaidgohppi N 113 C16
Biescas E 32 E5
Biesenthal D 84 E5
Biesiekierz PL 85 B10
Biesles F 26 D3
Biesowice PL 85 B11
Biessenhofen D 71 B11
Bietigheim D 27 C9
Bietigheim-Bissingen D 27 C11
Bietikow D 84 D5
Bièvre B 19 E11
Bieżuń PL 139 E8
Biga TR 173 D7
Bigadiç TR 173 F9
Biganos F 32 A4
Bigastro E 56 E3
Bigauņciems LV 134 C7
Bigbury-on-Sea GB 13 E7
Biggar GB 5 D9
Biggleswade GB 15 C8
Bignan F 22 E6
Bignasco CH 71 E7
Bigor MNE 163 E7
Bigüézal E 32 E3
Biguglia F 37 F10
Bihać BIH 156 C4
Biharia RO 151 C8
Biharkeresztes H 151 C8
Biharnagybajom H 151 C7
Bihartorda H 151 C7
Biharugra H 151 D8
Bihosava BY 133 E3
Bijela MNE 163 E6
Bijele Poljane MNE 163 D6
Bijeljani BIH 157 F9
Bijeljina BIH 158 D3
Bijelo Brdo HR 149 E11
Bijelo Bučje BIH 157 D8
Bijelo Polje MNE 163 C8
Biķernieki LV 135 E13
Bikovo SRB 150 F4
Biksēre LV 135 C12
Bílá Lhota CZ 77 C11
Bilalovac BIH 157 D9
Bilbao E 40 B6
Bilbo E 40 B6
Bilbor RO 153 C7
Bilca RO 153 B7
Bilciurești RO 161 D7
Bil'dzyuhi BY 133 F2
Bileća BIH 162 D5
Biled RO 151 F6
Biłgoraj PL 144 B6
Bilicenii Vechi MD 153 B12
Bílina CZ 80 E5
Bilisht AL 168 C4
Biljača SRB 164 E4
Bilje HR 149 E11
Bilky UA 145 G7
Billdal S 91 D10
Billerbeck D 17 E8
Billère F 32 D5
Billericay GB 15 D9
Billesholm S 87 C11
Billiat F 31 C8
Billigheim D 21 F12
Billingham GB 11 B9
Billinghay GB 11 E11
Billingsfors S 91 B11
Billingshurst GB 15 E8
Billom F 30 D3
Billsåsen S 105 F16
Billsbro S 92 A7
Billsta S 107 E15
Billum DK 86 D2
Billund DK 86 D4
Billy F 30 C3
Bilolissya UA 154 F5
Bílovec CZ 146 B6
Bílovice CZ 146 C5
Bilska LV 135 B11
Bilston GB 5 D10
Bilthoven NL 16 D4
Bilto N 112 E7
Bilton GB 11 D11
Bilyayivka UA 154 E6
Bilychi UA 145 E6
Bilyn UA 152 A4
Bilyne UA 154 B5
Bilzen B 19 C12
Bimbister GB 3 G10
Bíňa SK 147 F7
Binaced E 42 D4
Binas F 24 E5
Binasco I 69 C7
Binbrook GB 11 E11
Binche B 19 D9
Bindalseit N 105 A12
Bindlach D 75 C10
Bindslev DK 90 D7
Binefar E 42 D4
Bingen D 27 D11
Bingen am Rhein D 21 E9
Bingerden NL 183 B8
Bingham GB 11 F10
Binghamstown IRL 6 D2
Bingley GB 11 D8
Bingsjö S 103 D10
Binic F 22 C6
Biniés E 32 E4
Binissalem E 49 E10
Binnen D 17 C12
Binz D 84 B5
Binzen D 27 E8
Biograd na Moru HR 156 E3
Biokovina BIH 157 D7
Biol F 31 E7
Bionaz I 31 D11
Biorra IRL 7 F7
Biosca E 43 D6
Biot F 36 D6
Biota E 41 D9
Birchington GB 15 E11
Birchiș RO 151 F9
Bircza PL 144 D5
Birdhill IRL 8 C6
Birgittelyst DK 86 C4
Biri H 151 B8
Biri N 101 E13
Bīriņi LV 135 B9
Biristrand N 101 D12
Birkeland N 90 C3
Birkelse DK 86 A5
Birkenau D 187 B6
Birkenfeld D 21 E8
Birkenfeld D 27 C10
Birkenfeld D 74 C6
Birkenhead GB 10 E5
Birken-Honigsessen D 185 C8
Birkenwerder Berlin D 84 E4
Birkerød DK 87 D10
Birket DK 87 F8
Birketveit N 90 C2
Birkfeld A 148 B5
Birkungen D 79 D7
Birmingham GB 13 A11
Birnbaum A 73 C6
Biron F 33 A7
Birori I 64 C2
Birr IRL 7 F7
Birresborn D 21 D7
Birsay GB 3 G10
Birstall GB 11 F9
Birstein D 21 D12
Birštonas LT 137 D9
Birtavarre N 112 E6
Birtley GB 5 F13
Biruința MD 153 B12
Biržai LT 135 D9
Birzes LV 135 D8
Birži LV 135 D11
Birzuļi LV 131 F12
Biš SLO 148 C5
Bisaccia I 60 A4
Bisacquino I 58 D3
Biscarrosse F 32 B3
Biscarrosse-Plage F 32 B3
Bisceglie I 61 A7
Bischberg D 75 C8
Bischbrunn D 187 B7
Bischhausen (Waldkappel) D 78 D6
Bischheim F 27 C8
Bischoffen D 21 C10
Bischofferode D 79 D7
Bischoffsheim F 186 E3
Bischofsheim D 21 E10
Bischofsheim an der Rhön D 74 B7
Bischofshofen A 73 B7
Bischofsmais D 76 E4
Bischofswerda D 80 D6
Bischofswiesen D 73 A6
Bischofszell CH 27 E11
Bischwiller F 27 C8
Bisenti I 62 B5
Biser BG 166 F5
Bisertsi BG 161 F9
Bishop Auckland GB 5 F13
Bishop's Castle GB 10 G6
Bishop's Cleeve GB 13 B10
Bishop's Lydeard GB 13 C8
Bishop's Stortford GB 15 D9
Bishop's Waltham GB 13 D12
Bishqem AL 168 B2
Bishtazhin RKS 163 E10
Bisignano I 60 D6
Bisingen D 27 D10
Biskupice PL 141 H7
Biskupice PL 142 D5
Biskupice SK 147 E9
Biskupiec PL 136 F2
Biskupiec PL 139 C7
Bislev DK 86 B5
Bismark (Altmark) D 83 E11
Bismervik N 113 B11
Bismo N 101 C8
Bisoca RO 161 B9
Bispgården S 107 E11
Bispingen D 83 D8
Bissen L 20 E6
Bissendorf D 17 D10
Bissendorf (Wedemark) D 78 A6
Bissingen D 75 E8
Bistagno I 37 B8
Bistarac BIH 157 C10
Bistra RO 151 E11
Bistra RO 152 B4
Bistreț RO 160 F3
Bistrets BG 167 E8
Bistrica BIH 157 B7
Bistrica BIH 157 C7
Bistrica BIH 157 E8
Bistrica BIH 157 E10
Bistrica SLO 73 D9
Bistrica SLO 148 D5
Bistričak BIH 157 D8
Bistrița RO 152 C5
Bistrița Bârgăului RO 152 C5
Bistritsa BG 165 D7
Bistritsa BG 165 E7
Bisztynek PL 136 E2
Bitburg D 21 E7
Bitche F 27 B7
Bitetto I 61 A7
Bitinckë AL 168 C4
Bitola NMK 168 B5
Bitonto I 61 A7
Bitritto I 61 A7
Bitschwiller-lès-Thann F 27 E7
Bitterfeld D 79 C11
Bitterstad N 110 C9
Bitti I 64 C3
Bittkau D 79 B10
Bitton GB 13 C10
Bitz D 27 D11
Biurrun E 32 E2
Bivio CH 71 E9
Bivolari RO 153 B10
Bivona I 58 D4
Bixad RO 145 H7
Bixad RO 153 E7
Bixter GB 3 E14
Biyikali TR 173 B7
Biyikli TR 177 D10
Bizanet F 34 D4
Bizanos F 32 D5
Bizovac HR 149 E10
Bjåen N 94 C6
Bjærangen N 108 C6
Bjæverskov DK 87 E10
Bjännberg S 122 C3
Bjarkøy N 111 C12
Bjärnum S 87 C13
Bjärred S 87 D12
Bjärsjölagård S 87 D13
Bjärtrå S 107 F13
Bjästa S 107 E15
Bjela BIH 157 F10
Bjelajci BIH 157 B6
Bjelopolje HR 156 C4
Bjelovar HR 149 E7
Bjergby DK 90 D7
Bjerge DK 87 D8
Bjerka N 108 D6
Bjerkvik N 111 C14
Bjerreby DK 86 F7
Bjerregrav DK 86 B5
Bjerringbro DK 86 C5
Bjøllånes N 108 C8
Bjoneroa N 95 A12
Bjønnes N 108 D7
Björbo S 97 B12
Björboholm S 91 D11
Bjordal N 94 E4
Bjørgen N 105 F9
Bjørgo N 101 E10
Björkå S 107 E13
Bjørkåsen N 111 C17
Bjørkåsen N 111 D12
Björkberg S 103 C9
Björkberg S 107 B13
Björkberg S 118 C5
Björkboda FIN 126 E8
Björke S 93 D12
Björke S 103 E13
Bjørkeflåta N 95 B9
Bjørkelangen N 95 C15
Bjørkeset N 95 C10
Bjørkestrand N 114 C4
Bjørketorp S 91 E12
Björkfors S 119 C10
Björkheden S 109 E12
Björkhöjden S 107 E10
Björkholmen S 109 C17
Björkland S 109 F16
Bjørklia N 105 E9
Björkliden S 111 D16
Björklinge S 99 B9
Björknäset S 107 F12
Bjørknes N 96 B6
Bjørknes N 114 D6
Björköby FIN 122 D6
Björköby S 92 D5
Björkön S 103 B14
Björksele S 107 B15
Björksele S 107 D12
Björksjön S 107 E13
Björkstugan S 111 D15
Björkvik S 93 B9
Bjorli N 100 B8
Bjørn N 108 D4
Björna S 107 D15
Björnänge S 105 E14
Björndalen S 91 C11
Björneborg S 97 D11
Bjørnengen N 113 D11

Boveda E 40 C5
Bovegno I 69 B9
Bovenden D 78 C6
Bøverfjord N 104 E5
Boves F 18 E5
Boves I 37 C7
Bovigny B 20 D5
Boviken S 118 E6
Boville Ernica I 62 D4
Bovino I 60 A4
Bøvlingbjerg DK 86 C2
Bovolone I 66 B3
Bovrup DK 86 F5
Bow GB 3 H10
Bowes GB 11 B7
Bowmore GB 4 D4
Box FIN 127 E13
Boxberg D 81 D7
Boxberg D 187 C8
Boxdorf D 80 D5
Boxholm S 92 C6
Boxmeer NL 16 E5
Boxtel NL 16 E4
Boyadzhik BG 166 E6
Boyanovo BG 167 E7
Boychinovtsi BG 165 C7
Boykovo BG 165 E10
Boyle IRL 6 E6
Bøylefoss N 90 B4
Boynes F 25 D7
Boynitsa BG 159 F10
Bøyum N 100 D5
Božava HR 67 D10
Bozburun TR 181 C8
Bozeat GB 15 C7
Bozel F 31 E10
Boževac SRB 159 D7
Bożewo PL 139 E8
Bozhentsi BG 166 D4
Bozhurishte BG 165 D7
Božica SRB 164 D5
Božice CZ 77 E10
Bozieni MD 154 D3
Bozieni RO 153 D10
Bozioru RO 161 C8
Božjakovina HR 148 E6
Bozlar TR 173 D7
Bozouls F 34 B4
Bozovici RO 159 D9
Bozveliysko BG 167 C8
Bozzolo I 66 B1
Bra I 37 B7
Braås S 89 A8
Bråbo S 89 A10
Brabova RO 160 E2
Bracadale GB 2 L4
Bracciano I 62 C2
Brach F 28 E4
Brachbach D 185 C8
Bracieux F 24 E6
Bräcke S 103 A9
Brackenheim D 27 B11
Brackley GB 13 A12
Bracknagh IRL 7 F8
Bracknell GB 15 E7
Braco GB 5 C9
Brad RO 151 E10
Bradashesh AL 168 B3
Brădeanu RO 161 D9
Brădeni RO 152 E5
Brădești RO 152 E6
Brădești RO 160 E3
Bradford GB 11 D8
Bradford-on-Avon GB 13 C10
Bradpole GB 13 D9
Bradu RO 160 D5
Brădulet RO 160 C5
Brăduț RO 153 E7
Bradwell GB 15 B12
Bradwell Waterside GB 15 D10
Brae GB 3 E14
Brædstrup DK 86 D5
Braehead of Lunan GB 5 B11
Braemar GB 5 A10
Brăești RO 153 B8
Brăești RO 153 C10
Brăești RO 161 C9
Brăfim E 43 E6
Braga P 38 E3
Bragadiru RO 161 E7
Bragadiru RO 161 F7
Bragança P 39 E6
Bragar GB 2 J3
Brăhășești RO 153 E10
Brahlstorf D 83 D9
Brăila RO 155 C1
Brailsford GB 11 F8
Braine F 19 F8
Braine-l'Alleud B 19 C9
Braine-le-Comte B 19 C9
Braintree GB 15 D10
Braives B 19 C11
Brajkovići BIH 157 D8
Brake (Unterweser) D 17 B10
Brakel B 19 C8
Brakel D 17 E12
Bräkne-Hoby S 89 C8
Brålanda S 91 B11
Bralin PL 142 D4
Brallo di Pregola I 37 B10
Bralos GR 174 B5
Braloștița RO 160 D3
Bram F 33 D10
Bramans F 31 E10
Bramberg am Wildkogel A 72 B5
Bramdrupdam DK 86 D4
Bramming DK 86 E3
Brampton GB 5 F11
Brampton GB 15 C12
Bramsche D 17 D8
Bramsche D 17 D10
Bramstedt D 17 B11
Bran RO 160 B6
Brånaberg S 109 E11
Branäs S 102 E4
Brancaleone I 59 D9
Brancaster GB 15 B10
Brânceni RO 160 F6
Brâncovenești RO 152 D5
Brâncoveni RO 160 E4
Brand A 71 C9
Brand D 75 C10
Brandal N 100 B4
Brändåsen S 102 B4
Brändbo S 103 B11
Brandbu N 95 B13
Brande DK 86 D4
Brande-Hörnerkirchen D 82 C7
Brandenberg A 72 B4
Brandenburg D 79 B12
Brand-Erbisdorf D 80 E4
Branderup DK 86 E4
Brandesburton GB 11 D11
Brandis D 80 C4
Brand-Nagelberg A 77 E8
Brando F 37 F10
Brändö FIN 126 E5
Brandon GB 15 C10
Brändön S 118 C8
Brändövik FIN 122 D6
Brandshagen D 84 B4
Brandstorp S 92 C4
Brandsvoll N 90 C2
Brandval N 96 B7
Brandvoll N 111 C15
Brandýs nad Labem-Stará Boleslav CZ 77 B7
Brandýs nad Orlicí CZ 77 B10
Branes N 96 A6
Brănești MD 154 C3
Brănești RO 160 C6
Brănești RO 160 D2
Brănești RO 161 E8
Branice PL 142 F4
Braniewo PL 139 B8
Branik SLO 73 E8
Brănișca RO 151 F10
Braniștea RO 152 C4
Braniștea RO 155 C1
Braniștea RO 161 D7
Brankas LV 134 C7
Bränna S 91 B11
Brännåker S 107 B9
Brännäs S 103 B11
Brännberg S 118 C6
Branne F 28 F5
Brännland S 107 D16
Brännland S 122 C4
Brañosera E 40 C3
Brańsk PL 141 E7
Branston GB 11 E11
Brańszczyk PL 139 E12
Brantevik S 88 D6
Brantice CZ 142 F4
Brantôme F 29 E7
Branzi I 69 A8
Braojos E 46 B5
Braone I 69 B9
Braskereidfoss N 101 E15
Braslaw BY 133 E2
Brașov RO 161 B7
Brassac F 33 C10
Brasschaat B 16 F2
Brassy F 25 F10
Brasta S 105 E16
Brastad S 91 C10
Brastavățu RO 160 F4
Břasy CZ 76 C5
Brataj AL 168 D2
Bratca RO 151 D10
Bråte N 95 C14
Brateiu RO 152 E4
Brateljevići BIH 157 D10
Brateș RO 153 F8
Bratislava SK 77 F12
Bratkowice PL 144 C4
Bratovoești RO 160 E3
Bratsigovo BG 165 E9
Brattåker S 107 A11
Brattbäcken S 107 C9
Bratten S 107 B14
Brattfors S 103 E12
Brattfors S 107 D17
Brattli N 114 D7
Brattmon S 102 E4
Bratton GB 13 C10
Brattsbacka S 107 D16
Brattsele S 107 D12
Brattset N 104 E5
Brattvåg N 100 A4
Bratunac BIH 158 E3
Brătușeni MD 153 A10
Bratya Daskalovi BG 166 E4
Braubach D 21 D9
Braud-et-St-Louis F 28 E4
Braunau am Inn A 76 F4
Brauneberg D 185 E6
Braunfels D 21 C10
Braunlage D 79 C8
Bräunlingen D 27 E9
Braunsbach D 187 C8
Braunsbedra D 79 D10
Braunschweig D 79 B8
Braunton GB 12 C6
Bravicea MD 154 C2
Bravnica BIH 157 D7
Bray IRL 7 F10
Bray-sur-Seine F 25 D9
Bray-sur-Somme F 18 E6
Brazatortas E 54 B4
Brazey-en-Plaine F 26 F3
Brazi RO 161 D8
Brazii RO 151 E9
Brazii RO 161 D8
Brbinj HR 67 D11
Brčigovo BIH 157 E11
Brčko BIH 157 C10
Brdów PL 138 F6
Bré IRL 7 F10
Brea E 41 E8
Brea de Tajo E 47 D6
Breaghva IRL 8 C3
Breascleit GB 2 J3
Breasta RO 160 E3
Breaza RO 152 B6
Breaza RO 152 D5
Breaza RO 161 C7
Breaza RO 161 C9
Brebeni RO 160 E4
Brebu RO 159 C8
Brebu RO 161 C7
Brebu Nou RO 159 C9
Brécey F 23 C9
Brech F 22 E6
Brechfa GB 12 B6
Brechin GB 5 B11
Brecht B 16 F3
Breckerfeld D 185 B7
Břeclav CZ 77 E11
Brecon GB 13 B8
Breda E 43 D9
Breda NL 16 E3
Bredared S 91 D12
Bredaryd S 87 A13
Bredbyn S 107 E14
Breddenberg D 17 C9
Breddin D 83 E12
Bredebro DK 86 E3
Bredene B 18 B6
Bredereiche D 84 D4
Bredevoort NL 17 E7
Bredkälen S 106 D8
Bredsätra S 89 B11
Bredsel S 118 C4
Bredsjö S 97 C12
Bredsjön S 103 A13
Bredstedt D 82 A5
Bredsten DK 86 D4
Bredträsk S 107 D15
Bredvik S 107 D17
Bredviken S 108 D8
Bredviken S 119 C10
Bree B 19 B12
Breese D 83 D11
Bregana HR 148 E5
Breganze I 72 E4
Bregare BG 165 B9
Bregeni MD 153 B12
Bregenz A 71 B9
Breg-Lum AL 163 E9
Breg-Lum AL 168 B2
Bregninge DK 86 F6
Bregovo BG 159 E10
Breguzzo I 69 B10
Bréhal F 23 C8
Bréhan F 22 D6
Brehna D 79 C11
Breidenbach D 21 C10
Breidenbach F 27 B7
Breidstrand N 111 C12
Breidvik N 108 B9
Breidvik N 110 C8
Breidvik N 110 E9
Breidvik N 111 D11
Breiholz D 82 B7
Breil CH 71 D8
Breil-sur-Roya F 37 D7
Breisach am Rhein D 27 D8
Breistein N 94 B2
Breitenbach CH 27 F8
Breitenbach D 21 F8
Breitenbach (Schauenburg) D 17 F12
Breitenbach am Herzberg D 78 E6
Breitenbach am Inn A 72 B4
Breitenberg D 76 E5
Breitenbrunn D 75 D10
Breitenburg D 82 C7
Breitenfelde D 83 C9
Breitengüßbach D 75 C8
Breitenhagen D 79 C10
Breitnau D 27 E9
Breitscheid D 183 C9
Breitscheid D 185 C7
Breitscheid D 185 C9
Breitungen D 79 E7
Breivik N 111 C12
Breivik N 112 B9
Breivikbotn N 112 B9
Breivikeidet N 111 A18
Brejning DK 86 D5
Brekka N 108 B9
Brekken N 101 A15
Brekken N 108 E5
Brekkestø N 90 C3
Brekkhus N 100 E4
Brekkvasseiv N 105 B14
Breklum D 82 A5
Brekovo SRB 158 F5
Breksillan N 105 B10
Brekstad N 104 D7
Brélès F 22 D2
Brelingen (Wedemark) D 78 A6
Bremdal DK 86 B3
Bremen D 17 B11
Bremerhaven D 17 A11
Bremervörde D 17 B12
Bremgarten CH 27 F9
Bremm D 21 D8
Bremnes N 94 C2
Bremnes N 110 C9
Brem-sur-Mer F 28 B2
Brenderup DK 86 E5
Brenes E 51 D8
Brenguli LV 131 F11
Brenitsa BG 165 C9
Brenna N 108 F5
Brenna N 110 D7
Brenna PL 147 B7
Brennero I 72 C4
Brennes N 112 D5
Brennfjell N 112 E5
Brenngam N 113 B19
Brennhaug N 101 C10
Brennmo N 105 E11
Brennsvik N 113 B13
Breno I 69 B9
Brénod F 31 C8
Brens F 33 C9
Brensbach D 187 B6
Brent Knoll GB 13 C9
Brentwood GB 15 D9
Brenzone I 69 B10
Bresalc RKS 164 E3
Brescello I 66 C2
Brescia I 66 A1
Breskens NL 16 F1
Bresnica SRB 158 F6
Bressana Bottarone I 69 C7
Bressanone I 72 C4
Bressols F 33 C8
Bressuire F 28 B5
Brest BG 160 F5
Brest BY 141 F9
Brest F 22 D3
Brestak BG 167 C9
Brestanica SLO 148 E4
Bresternica SLO 148 C5
Brestova HR 67 B9
Brestovac SRB 159 E9
Brestovac SRB 164 C4
Brestovac Požeški HR 149 F9
Brestovăț RO 151 F8
Brestovene BG 161 F9
Brestovets BG 165 C10
Brestovitsa BG 165 E10
Bretagne-d'Armagnac F 33 C6
Brețcu RO 153 E8
Bretea Română RO 159 B11
Breteil F 23 D8
Bretenoux F 29 F9
Breteuil F 18 E5
Breteuil F 24 C4
Brétignolles-sur-Mer F 28 B2
Bretnig D 80 D6
Bretocino E 39 E8
Bretoncelles F 24 D4
Bretten D 27 B10
Bretton GB 10 E6
Brettville-sur-Laize F 23 B11
Bretzenheim D 185 E8
Bretzfeld D 187 C7
Breuberg-Neustadt D 21 E12
Breuches F 26 E5
Breugel NL 183 B7
Breuil-Cervinia I 68 B4
Breuil-Magné F 28 D4
Breuilpont F 24 C5
Breukelen NL 16 D4
Breum DK 86 B4
Breuna D 17 F12
Breuvannes-en-Bassigny F 26 D4
Brevens bruk S 92 A7
Brevik N 90 A6
Brevik S 92 C4
Brevik S 93 A12
Brevik S 99 D10
Breviken S 96 D7
Brevörde D 78 C5
Breza BIH 157 D9
Breza SK 147 C8
Brežde SRB 158 E5
Breze SLO 148 D4
Brezhani BG 165 F7
Březí CZ 77 E11
Brezičani BIH 157 B6
Brežice SLO 148 E5
Brezna SRB 163 B10
Breznica HR 148 D6
Breznica SK 145 E4
Březnice CZ 76 C5
Breznik BG 165 D6
Breznița-Motru RO 159 D11
Breznița-Ocol RO 159 D10
Breznitsa BG 165 F8
Březno CZ 76 B4
Brezno SK 147 D9
Brezoaele RO 161 D7
Brézolles F 24 C5
Březolupy CZ 146 C5
Březová CZ 146 D5
Březová nad Svitavou CZ 77 C11
Brezová pod Bradlom SK 146 D5
Brezovica SK 145 E2
Brezovica SK 147 C9
Brezovica SLO 73 D9
Brezovo BG 166 E4
Brezovo Polje BIH 157 C10
Brezovo Polje HR 156 B5
Briançon F 31 F10
Briare F 25 E8
Briatexte F 33 C9
Briceni MD 153 A10
Bricherasio I 31 F11
Bricon F 26 D2
Bricquebec F 23 B8
Brides-les-Bains F 31 E10
Brideswell IRL 6 F6
Bridgeland IRL 9 C9
Bridgend GB 4 C6
Bridgend GB 4 D4
Bridgend GB 13 B7
Bridge of Cally GB 5 B10
Bridge of Don GB 3 L12
Bridge of Dye GB 5 B11
Bridge of Earn GB 5 C10
Bridge of Orchy GB 4 B7
Bridge of Weir GB 4 D7
Bridgetown IRL 9 D9
Bridgnorth GB 11 F7
Bridgwater GB 13 C8
Břidličná CZ 146 B4
Bridlington GB 11 C11
Bridport GB 13 D9
Brie F 29 D6
Briec F 22 D4
Brie-Comte-Robert F 25 C8
Briedel D 185 D7
Brielle NL 16 E2
Brienne-le-Château F 25 D12
Briennon F 30 C5
Brienon-sur-Armançon F 25 D10
Brienz CH 70 D6
Brienza I 60 C5
Briesen D 80 B6
Brieske D 80 D5
Brieskow-Finkenheerd D 81 B7
Briesnig D 81 C7
Brietlingen D 83 D8
Briey F 20 F5
Brig CH 68 A4
Brigg GB 11 D11
Brighstone GB 13 D12
Brightlingsea GB 15 D11
Brighton GB 15 F8
Brigi LV 133 D4
Brignais F 30 D6
Brignogan-Plage F 22 C3
Brignoles F 36 E4
Brigstock GB 15 C7
Brihuega E 47 C7
Brijesta HR 162 D4
Brillon-en-Barrois F 26 C3
Brilon D 17 F11
Brimington GB 11 E9
Brimnes N 94 B5
Brinches P 50 C4
Brincones E 45 B8
Brindisi I 61 B9
Brindisi Montagna I 60 B5
Bringsinghaug N 100 B2
Bringsli N 108 B9
Brinian GB 3 G11
Brinje HR 67 B11
Brinkum D 17 B9
Brinkum D 17 B11
Brinlack IRL 6 B6
Brinon-sur-Beuvron F 25 F9
Brinon-sur-Sauldre F 25 E7
Brin-sur-Seille F 26 C5
Brînza MD 155 B2
Brînzeni MD 153 A10
Brion F 30 F3
Briones E 40 C6
Brionne F 24 B4
Brioude F 30 E3
Brioux-sur-Boutonne F 28 C5
Briouze F 23 C11
Briscous F 32 D3
Brisighella I 66 D4
Brissac-Quincé F 23 F11
Bristol GB 13 C9
Briston GB 15 B11
Britelo P 38 E3
Britof SLO 73 D9
Briton Ferry GB 13 B7
Brittas IRL 7 F10
Brittas Bay IRL 9 C10
Britvica BIH 157 F8
Britz D 84 E5
Brive-la-Gaillarde F 29 E9
Briviesca E 40 C5
Brix F 23 A8
Brixen im Thale A 72 B5
Brixham GB 13 E7
Brixworth GB 15 C7
Brka BIH 157 C10
Brložnik BIH 157 D11
Brna HR 162 D2
Brnaze HR 157 E6
Brněnec CZ 77 C11
Brniště CZ 81 E7
Brnjica SRB 159 D8
Brnjica SRB 163 C9
Brno CZ 77 D11
Bro S 93 D12
Bro S 99 C9
Broadford GB 2 L5
Broadford IRL 8 C5
Broadford IRL 8 D5
Broad Haven GB 9 E12
Broadheath GB 13 A10
Broadstairs GB 15 E11
Broadway GB 13 A11
Broadwey GB 13 D10
Broadwindsor GB 13 D9
Broager DK 86 F5
Broaryd S 87 A12
Broby S 88 C6
Broby S 99 C11
Brobyværk DK 86 E6
Broc CH 31 B11
Broćanac BIH 157 F7
Brocas F 32 B4
Broceni LV 134 C5
Bröckel D 79 A7
Brockum D 17 D10
Brockworth GB 13 B10
Broczyno PL 85 C10
Brod BIH 157 F10
Brod NMK 168 A5
Brod NMK 169 C6
Brod RKS 163 F10
Brod RKS 164 E3
Brodalen S 91 C10
Brodarevo SRB 163 C8
Broddbo S 98 C6
Brodek u Prostějova CZ 77 D12
Broderstorf D 83 B12
Brodica SRB 159 E8
Brodick GB 4 D6
Brodilovo BG 167 E9
Brodina RO 152 B6
Brodnica PL 81 B11
Brodnica PL 139 D7
Brodosanë RKS 163 E10
Brodské SK 77 E12
Brodski Stubnik HR 157 B8
Brody PL 81 B8
Brody PL 81 C7
Broekhuizenvorst NL 183 C8
Broglie F 24 B4
Brohl D 185 D7
Brohm D 84 C5
Broin F 26 F3
Brójce PL 81 B9
Brojce PL 85 C8
Brójce PL 143 C8
Brok PL 139 E12
Brokdorf D 17 A12
Brokind S 92 C7
Brokka N 90 C2
Brokstedt D 83 C7
Brolo I 59 C6
Bromarv FIN 127 F9
Brome D 79 A8
Bromma N 95 B10
Bromnes N 112 C2
Bromölla S 88 C6
Brömsebro S 89 C10
Bromsgrove GB 13 A10
Bromyard GB 13 A9
Bron F 30 D6
Bronchales E 47 C9
Brønderslev DK 86 A5
Broni I 69 C7
Bronice PL 81 C7
Brønnøysund N 108 F3
Bronnytsya UA 154 A1
Brøns DK 86 E3
Bronte I 59 D6
Bronzani Majdan BIH 157 C6
Brooke GB 15 B11
Brookeborough GB 7 D8
Broons F 23 D7
Broquiès F 34 B4
Brora GB 3 J9
Brørup DK 86 E4
Brösarp S 88 D6
Broscăuți RO 153 B8
Broseley GB 10 F7
Broshniv Osada UA 145 F9
Brossac F 28 E5
Brøstadbotn N 111 B14
Broșteni RO 153 C7
Broșteni RO 153 F10
Broșteni RO 159 D10
Brotas P 50 B3
Brötjemark S 92 D4
Broto E 32 E5
Brottby S 99 C10
Brottes F 26 D3
Brotton GB 11 B10
Brøttum N 101 D13
Brou F 24 D5
Brough GB 3 H10
Brough GB 11 B7
Broughshane GB 4 F4
Broughton GB 5 D10
Broughton GB 10 E6
Broughton in Furness GB 10 C5
Broughtown GB 3 G11
Broughty Ferry GB 5 C11
Broumov CZ 81 E10
Brousseval F 26 D2
Broutzaiika GR 175 D6
Brouvelieures F 26 D6
Brouwershaven NL 16 E1
Brovst DK 86 A5
Brownhills GB 11 F8
Broxburn GB 5 D10
Brozany CZ 76 B6
Brozas E 45 E7
Brožiai LT 134 E3
Brozzo I 69 B9
Brštanovo HR 156 E5
Brtnice CZ 77 D9
Bruay-la-Bussière F 18 D6
Bruchhausen-Vilsen D 17 C12
Bruchköbel D 187 A6
Bruchmühlbach D 21 F8
Bruchsal D 27 B10
Bruchweiler-Bärenbach D 186 C4
Brück D 79 B12
Bruck an der Großglocknerstraße A 73 B6
Bruck an der Leitha A 77 F11
Bruck an der Mur A 73 B11
Brücken D 21 E8
Brücken (Helme) D 79 D9
Brücken (Pfalz) D 21 F8
Brückl A 73 C10
Bruckmühl D 72 A4
Brudzeń Duży PL 139 E8
Brudzew PL 142 B6
Brudzowice PL 143 E7
Brue-Auriac F 35 C10
Brüel D 83 C11
Bruère-Allichamps F 29 B10
Bruff IRL 8 D5
Brugelette B 182 D3
Bruges B 19 B7
Bruges B 182 C2
Brugg CH 27 F9
Brugge B 19 B7
Brüggen D 16 F6
Brüggen D 78 B6
Brugnato I 69 E8
Brugnera I 72 E6
Bruguières F 33 C8
Bruhagen N 104 E3
Brühl D 21 C7
Brühl D 187 C6
Bruinisse NL 16 E2
Bruiu RO 152 F5
Bruksvallarna S 102 A3
Brûlon F 23 E11
Brûly B 19 E10
Brumath F 27 C8
Brummen NL 183 A8
Brumov-Bylnice CZ 146 C6
Brumunddal N 101 E13
Brumundsag N 101 E13
Brunau D 83 E10
Brunava LV 135 D8
Brundby DK 86 D7
Brundish GB 15 C11
Brunehamel F 19 E9
Brunete E 46 D5
Brunflo S 106 E7
Brunico I 72 C4
Bruniquel F 33 B9
Brunkeberg N 95 D8
Brunn D 84 C4
Brunna S 99 C8
Brunna S 99 C9
Brunn am Gebirge A 77 F10
Brunnberg S 97 B10
Brunne S 103 A14
Brunnen CH 71 C7
Brunnsberg S 102 D6
Brunsberg S 97 C8
Brunsbüttel D 17 A12
Brunssum NL 20 C5
Bruntál CZ 142 G3
Bruravik N 94 B5
Bruree IRL 8 D5
Brus SRB 163 C11
Brusago I 69 A11
Brusand N 94 E3
Brušane HR 156 C3
Brusartsi BG 159 F11
Brüsewitz D 83 C10
Brüshlen BG 161 F8
Brüshlyanitsa BG 165 B10
Brusio CH 69 A9
Brusnik SRB 159 E9
Brusnika Velika BIH 157 B9
Brusno SK 147 D8
Brusque F 34 C4
Brussel B 19 C9
Brusson I 68 B4
Brüssow D 84 D6
Brusturi RO 151 C9
Brusturi-Drăgănești RO 153 C8
Brusturiv UA 152 A5
Brusturoasa RO 153 D8
Brusy PL 138 C4
Bruton GB 13 C10
Bruttig-Fankel D 21 D8
Bruvno HR 156 D4
Bruxelles B 19 C9
Bruyères F 26 D6
Bruz F 23 D8
Bruzaholm S 92 D6
Brvnište SK 146 C6
Brwinów PL 141 F3
Bryagovo BG 166 F4
Bryastovo BG 165 C10
Bryggerhaug N 111 B14
Brymbo GB 10 E5
Brynamman GB 13 B7
Bryne N 94 E3
Brynford GB 10 E5
Brynge S 107 E14
Bryngelhögen S 102 B7
Brynje S 102 A8
Brynje S 103 E7
Brynmawr GB 13 B8
Bryrup DK 86 C5
Bryukhovychi UA 144 D8
Brzan SRB 159 E7
Brza Palanka SRB 159 E9
Brzeće SRB 163 C10
Brzeg PL 142 E3
Brzeg Dolny PL 81 D11
Brześć Kujawski PL 138 E6
Brzesko PL 143 G10
Brzeszcze PL 143 G7
Brzezie PL 85 C11
Brzezie PL 138 E6
Brzezinki PL 141 H5
Brzeziny PL 142 C5
Brzeziny PL 143 C8
Brzeziny PL 144 D4
Brzeźnica PL 81 C8
Brzeźnica PL 143 F11
Brzeźnica PL 147 B9
Brzeźno PL 85 C9
Brzeźno PL 141 H9
Brzeźno PL 142 B5
Brzostek PL 144 D3
Brzotín SK 145 F1
Brzóza PL 141 G4
Brzozów PL 141 F2
Brzozów PL 144 D5
Brzozowiec PL 81 A8
Brzuze PL 139 D7
Bû F 24 C6
Bua S 87 A10
Buais F 23 C10
Buarcos P 44 D3
Buavågen N 94 C2
Bubbio I 37 B8
Bubiai LT 134 E6
Bubry F 22 E5
Bubwith GB 11 D10
Búč SK 149 A10
Buca TR 177 C9
Bučany SK 146 E5
Buccheri I 59 E6
Bucchianico I 63 C6
Buccinasco I 69 C7
Buccino I 60 B4
Bucecea RO 153 B8
Bucelas P 50 B1
Buceș RO 151 E10
Bucey-lès-Gy F 26 F4
Buch D 71 A10
Buch am Erlbach D 75 F11
Buchbach D 75 F11
Buchboden A 71 C9
Büchel D 21 D8
Büchen D 83 D9
Buchen (Odenwald) D 27 A11
Büchenbeuren D 185 E7
Buchholz D 83 D12
Buchholz (Aller) D 82 E7
Buchholz (Westerwald) D 21 C8
Buchin RO 159 C9
Buchin Prohod BG 165 D7
Buch in Tirol A 72 B4
Buchkirchen A 76 F6
Büchlberg D 76 E5
Buchloe D 71 A11
Buchlovice CZ 146 C4
Bucholz in der Nordheide D 83 D7
Buchs CH 71 C8
Buchy F 18 E3
Bučim NMK 164 F5
Buçimas AL 168 C4
Bučin NMK 168 B5
Bucine I 66 F4
Bucinișu RO 160 F4
Bučište NMK 164 F5
Bucium RO 151 E11
Buciumeni RO 153 F10
Buciumeni RO 161 C6
Buciumi RO 151 C11
Bučje SRB 159 F9
Bučje SRB 163 C7
Buckden GB 11 C7
Bückeburg D 17 D12
Bücken D 17 C12
Buckfastleigh GB 13 E7
Buckhaven GB 5 C10
Buckie GB 3 K11
Buckingham GB 14 D7
Buckley GB 10 E5
Buckode IRL 6 D6
Buckow Märkische Schweiz D 80 A6
Bückwitz D 83 E12
Bucoșnița RO 159 C9
Bucov RO 161 D8
Bucovăț MD 154 C2
Bucovăț RO 160 E3
Bucovica BIH 157 E7
Bučovice CZ 77 D12
Bucsa H 151 C7
Bucșani RO 161 D7
Bucșani RO 161 E7
Bucu RO 161 D11
București RO 151 E10
București RO 161 E8
Bucy-lès-Pierrepont F 19 E8
Bucz PL 81 B10
Buczek PL 143 D7
Bud N 100 A5
Buda RO 161 B9
Budacu de Jos RO 152 C5
Budakalász H 150 B3
Budakeszi H 149 A11
Budakovo NMK 168 B5
Budaörs H 149 B11
Budapest H 150 C3
Budča SK 147 D8
Buddusò I 64 B3
Bude GB 12 D5
Budeasa RO 160 D5
Budel NL 16 F5
Büdelsdorf D 82 B7
Budenets' UA 153 A7
Budenheim D 21 D10
Budens P 50 E2
Büdesheim D 21 D11
Budești RO 152 C5
Budești RO 152 D4
Budești RO 160 C4
Budești RO 161 E8
Budeyi UA 154 A4
Budia E 47 C7
Budila RO 161 B7
Budimci HR 149 F10
Budimlič Japra BIH 156 C5
Budiná SK 147 E8
Büdingen D 21 D12
Budinščina HR 148 D6
Budišov CZ 77 D9
Budišov nad Budišovkou CZ 146 B5
Budkovce SK 145 F4
Budleigh Salterton GB 13 D8
Budmerice SK 146 E4
Budoia I 72 D6
Budoni I 64 B4
Budrio I 66 C4
Budry PL 136 E4
Budureasa RO 151 D10
Buduslău RO 151 C9
Budva MNE 163 E6
Būdviečiai LT 136 D6
Budyně nad Ohří CZ 76 B6
Budziszewice PL 141 G1
Budzów PL 147 B9
Budzyń PL 85 E11
Bue N 94 E3
Bueña E 47 C10
Buenache de Alarcón E 47 E8
Buenache de la Sierra E 47 D8
Buenaventura E 46 D3
Buenavista de Valdavia E 39 C10
Buendía E 47 D7
Buer D 183 B10
Buer N 96 D6
Bueu E 38 D2
Bufleben D 79 D8
Buftea RO 161 D7
Bugac H 150 D4
Bugarra E 48 E3
Buğdayli TR 173 D8
Bugeat F 29 D9
Buggenhout B 182 C4
Buggerru I 64 E1
Buggingen D 27 E8
Bugiac MD 154 E3
Bugnara I 62 C5
Bugnein F 32 D4
Bugojno BIH 157 D7
Bugøyfjord N 114 D6
Bugøynes N 114 D7
Bugyi H 150 C3
Bühl D 27 C9
Bühlertal D 27 C9
Bühlertann D 74 D6
Bühlerzell D 74 D6

Caorle I 73 E6
Capaccio I 60 C4
Capaci I 58 C3
Capafonts E 42 E6
Capalbio I 65 C4
Căpâlna RO 151 D9
Căpâlniţa RO 153 E6
Capannoli I 66 E2
Capannori I 66 E2
Caparde BIH 157 D10
Capari NMK 168 B5
Caparica P 50 B1
Caparrosa P 44 C4
Caparroso E 32 F2
Cap-Blanc E 48 F4
Capbreton F 32 C3
Cap d'Agde F 34 D6
Capdenac F 33 A10
Capdenac-Gare F 33 A10
Capdepera E 57 B11
Capel Curig GB 10 E4
Capelins P 51 B5
Capelle aan de IJssel NL 16 E3
Capellen L 20 E6
Capel St Mary GB 15 C11
Capendu F 34 D4
Capestang F 34 D5
Capestrano I 62 C5
Cap Ferret F 32 A3
Capileira E 55 F6
Capilla E 54 B2
Capinha P 44 D6
Capistrello I 62 D4
Capizzi I 58 D5
Căpleni RO 151 B10
Čaplje BIH 157 C6
Čapljina BIH 157 F8
Capodimonte I 62 B1
Capo di Ponte I 69 A9
Capo d'Orlando I 59 C6
Capoliveri I 65 B2
Capolona I 66 E4
Caposele I 60 B4
Capoterra I 64 E2
Cappadocia I 62 C4
Cappagh White IRL 8 C6
Cappamore IRL 8 C6
Cappawhite IRL 8 C6
Cappeen IRL 8 E5
Cappelle sul Tavo I 62 C6
Cappeln (Oldenburg) D 17 C10
Cappercleuch GB 5 E10
Cappoquin IRL 9 D7
Capracotta I 63 D6
Capraia Isola I 65 A1
Capranica I 62 C2
Caprarola I 62 C2
Căpreni RO 160 D3
Capri I 60 B2
Căpriana MD 154 C2
Capriati a Volturno I 63 E6
Capri Leone I 59 C6
Caprino Bergamasco I 69 B7
Caprino Veronese I 69 B10
Captieux F 32 B5
Capua I 60 A2
Capurso I 61 A7
Căpuşu Mare RO 151 D11
Capvern-les-Bains F 33 D6
Carabaña E 47 D6
Caracal RO 160 E4
Caracuel de Calatrava E 54 B4
Caragaş MD 154 D5
Caragele RO 161 D10
Caraglio I 37 C6
Caraman F 33 C9
Caramanico Terme I 62 C6
Caramulo P 44 C4
Cărand RO 151 E9
Caranga E 39 B7
Caranguejeira P 44 E3
Caransebeş RO 159 C9
Carantec F 22 C4
Carapelle I 60 A5
Carapinheira P 44 D3
Carasco I 37 C10
Caraşova RO 159 C8
Caraula RO 159 E11
Caravaca de la Cruz E 55 C9
Caravaggio I 69 C8
Carbajales de Alba E 39 E8
Carballeda de Avia E 38 D3
Carballo E 38 B2
Carballo E 38 D4
Carbellino E 45 B8
Carbonera de Frentes E 41 E6
Carboneras E 55 F9
Carboneras de Guadazaón E 47 E9
Carbonero El Mayor E 46 B4
Carboneros E 54 C5
Carbonia I 64 E2
Carbonin I 72 C5
Carbonne F 33 D8
Carbost GB 2 L4
Carbost GB 2 L4
Cărbunari RO 159 D8
Cărbuneşti RO 161 C8
Carbury IRL 7 F9
Carcaboso E 45 D8
Carcabuey E 53 B8
Carcaixent E 48 F4
Carcaliu RO 155 C2
Carcans F 28 E3
Carcans-Plage F 28 E3
Carção P 39 E6
Cárcar E 32 F2
Carcare I 37 C8
Carcassonne F 33 D10
Carcastillo E 32 F3
Carcelén E 47 F10
Carcès F 36 E4
Carchelejo E 53 A9
Carcoforo I 68 B5
Cardaillac F 29 F9
Çardak TR 172 D6
Cardedeu E 43 D8
Cardedu I 64 D4
Cardeña E 54 C4
Cardeñadijo E 40 D4
Cardenden GB 5 C10
Cardenete E 47 E9
Cardeñosa E 46 C3
Cardeto I 59 C8
Cardiff GB 13 C8
Cardigan GB 12 A5
Cardigos P 44 E4
Cardinale I 59 B9
Cardito I 62 D5
Cardon RO 155 C5
Cardona E 43 D7
Cardosas P 50 E2
Carei RO 151 B9
Carenas E 41 F8
Carentan F 23 B9
Carentoir F 23 E7
Carevdar HR 149 D7
Carev Dvor NMK 168 B5
Cargenbridge GB 5 E9
Cargèse F 37 G9
Carhaix-Plouguer F 22 D4
Caria P 44 D6
Cariati I 61 E7
Caridade P 50 C4
Carife I 60 A4
Carignan F 19 E11
Carignano I 37 B7
Cariñena E 41 F9
Carini I 58 C3
Carinish GB 2 K2
Cariño E 38 A4
Carinola I 60 A1
Carisio I 68 C5
Carisolo I 69 A10
Cârjiţi RO 151 F10
Carland GB 7 C9
Carlanstown IRL 7 E9
Carlantino I 63 D7
Carlat F 29 F11
Carlentini I 59 E7
Carlet E 48 F3
Cârlibaba RO 152 B6
Cârligele RO 153 F10
Carling F 186 C2
Carlingford IRL 7 D10
Carlisle GB 5 F11
Carloforte I 64 E1
Cârlogani RO 160 D4
Cârlomăneşti RO 161 C9
Carlopoli I 59 A9
Carlops GB 5 D10
Carlow D 83 C9
Carlow IRL 9 C9
Carloway GB 2 J3
Carlsberg D 186 C5
Carlton GB 11 F9
Carlton Colville GB 15 C12
Carluke GB 5 D9
Carlux F 29 F8
Carmagnola I 37 B7
Carmanova MD 154 C5
Carmarthen GB 12 B6
Carmaux F 33 B10
Cármena E 46 E4
Cármenes E 39 C8
Carmiano I 61 C10
Carmona E 51 E8
Carmonita E 45 F8
Carmyllie GB 5 B11
Carnac F 22 E5
Carnagh GB 7 D9
Carndonagh IRL 4 E2
Carnew IRL 9 C10
Carnforth GB 10 C6
Carnières F 19 D7
Carnikava LV 135 B8
Carnlough GB 4 F5
Carno GB 10 F4
Carnota E 38 C1
Carnoules F 36 E4
Carnoustie GB 5 B11
Carnoux-en-Provence F 35 D10
Carnteel GB 7 D9
Carnwath GB 5 D9
Carolei I 60 E6
Carolles F 23 C8
Carona I 69 A8
Caronia I 58 C5
C. A. Rosetti RO 155 C5
C. A. Rosetti RO 161 C10
Carosino I 61 C8
Carovigno I 61 B9
Carovilli I 63 D6
Carpaneto Piacentino I 69 D8
Carpegna I 66 E5
Carpen RO 159 E11
Carpenedolo I 66 B1
Carpentras F 35 B9
Carpi I 66 C2
Carpignano Salentino I 61 C10
Carpignano Sesia I 68 B5
Cărpineni MD 154 D2
Cărpinet RO 151 E10
Carpineti I 66 D1
Carpineto Romano I 62 D4
Cărpiniş RO 151 F6
Carpino I 63 D9
Carpinone I 63 D6
Carpio E 40 F1
Carpiquet F 23 B11
Carquefou F 23 F9
Carqueiranne F 36 E4
Carracastle IRL 6 E5
Carracedelo E 39 C6
Carradale East GB 4 D6
Carragh IRL 7 F9
Carraig Airt IRL 7 B7
Carraig na Siuire IRL 9 D8
Carraig Thuathail IRL 8 E6
Carral E 38 B3
Carralevë RKS 163 E10
Carranque E 46 D5
Carrapateira P 50 E2
Carrapichana P 44 C6
Carrara I 69 E9
Carraroe IRL 6 F3
Carrascal del Obispo E 45 C9
Carrascosa E 47 C8
Carrascosa del Campo E 47 D7
Carratraca E 53 C7
Carrazeda de Ansiães P 45 B6
Carrazeda de Montenegro P 38 E5
Carrbridge GB 3 L9
Carreço P 38 E2
Carregado P 50 A2
Carregal do Sal P 44 D5
Carregueiros P 44 E4
Carreira P 44 E3
Carreña E 39 B10
Carreteira E 38 C4
Carriazo E 40 B4
Carrick IRL 6 C5
Carrick IRL 9 D9
Carrickart IRL 7 B7
Carrickfergus GB 4 F5
Carrickmacross IRL 7 E9
Carrickmore GB 4 F2
Carrick-on-Shannon IRL 6 E6
Carrick-on-Suir IRL 9 D8
Carriço P 44 E3
Carrigaholt IRL 8 C3
Carrigallen IRL 7 E7
Carriganima IRL 8 E4
Carriganimmy IRL 8 E4
Carrigart IRL 7 B7
Carrigkerry IRL 8 D4
Carrig Mhachaire IRL 7 E9
Carrigtohill IRL 8 E6
Carrigtwohill IRL 8 E6
Carrio E 38 B3
Carrión de Calatrava E 54 A5
Carrión de los Céspedes E 51 E7
Carrión de los Condes E 39 D10
Carrizo de la Ribera E 39 C8
Carrizosa E 55 B7
Carronbridge GB 5 E9
Carros F 37 D6
Carrouges F 23 C11
Carrowkeel IRL 4 E2
Carrowkeel IRL 7 B7
Carrowkennedy IRL 6 E3
Carrù I 37 C7
Carryduff GB 7 D11
Carry-le-Rouet F 35 D9
Cars F 28 E4
Carsac-Aillac F 29 F8
Carsluith GB 5 F8
Carsoli I 62 C4
Carspach F 27 E7
Carsphairn GB 5 E8
Carstairs GB 5 D9
Cartagena E 56 F3
Cártama E 53 C7
Cartaxo P 44 F3
Cartaya E 51 E5
Cartelègue F 28 E4
Carteret F 23 B8
Carterton GB 13 B11
Cartes E 40 B3
Cârţişoara RO 152 F5
Cartoceto I 67 E6
Carucedo E 39 D6
Caruncho I 63 D7
Carvalhal P 44 E4
Carvalhal P 50 C2
Carvalho de Egas P 38 F5
Carvalhosa P 38 F3
Carviçais P 45 B7
Carvin F 18 D6
Carvoeira P 44 F2
Carvoeiro P 50 E3
Čáry SK 77 E12
Casabermeja E 53 C8
Casabona I 61 E7
Casa Branca P 50 B3
Casa Branca P 50 B4
Casacalenda I 63 D7
Casagiove I 60 A2
Casaglione F 37 G9
Casa l'Abate I 61 C10
Casalanguida I 63 C6
Casalarreina E 40 C6
Casalbordino I 63 C7
Casalbore I 60 A4
Casalborgone I 68 C4
Casalbuono I 60 C5
Casalbuttano ed Uniti I 69 C8
Casàl Cermelli I 37 B9
Casàl di Principe I 60 A2
Casalecchio di Reno I 66 D3
Casale Monferrato I 68 C5
Casaletto Spartano I 60 C5
Casalfiumanese I 66 D4
Casalgrande I 66 C2
Casalgrasso I 37 B7
Casalmaggiore I 66 C1
Casalnuovo Monterotaro I 63 D8
Casalpusterlengo I 69 C8
Casalvecchio di Puglia I 63 D8
Casàl Velino I 60 C4
Casamassima I 61 B7
Casamozza F 37 F10
Casarabonela E 53 C7
Casarano I 61 C10
Casar de Cáceres E 45 E8
Casar de Palomero E 45 D8
Casarejos E 40 E5
Casares E 39 B7
Casares E 53 D6
Casares de las Hurdes E 45 D8
Casariche E 53 B7
Casarrubios del Monte E 46 D4
Casarsa della Delizia I 73 E6
Casarza Ligure I 37 C10
Casas Altas E 47 D10
Casas Bajas E 47 D10
Casas de Benítez E 47 F8
Casas de Don Pedro E 45 F10
Casas de Fernando Alonso E 47 F8
Casas de Haro E 47 F8
Casas de Juan Gil E 47 F10
Casas de Juan Núñez E 47 F9
Casas de Lázaro E 55 B8
Casas del Monte E 45 D9
Casas de los Pinos E 47 F8
Casas del Puerto E 56 E2
Casas de Millán E 45 E8
Casas de Reina E 51 C8
Casas de Ves E 47 F10
Casas-Ibáñez E 47 F10
Casasimarro E 47 F8
Casas Novas de Mares P 50 B5
Casasola de Arión E 39 E9
Casatejada E 45 E9
Casatenovo I 69 B7
Casavieja E 46 D3
Cascais P 50 B1
Cascante E 41 D8
Cascante del Río E 47 D10
Cascia I 62 B4
Casciana Terme I 66 E2
Cascina I 66 E2
Căscioarele RO 161 E8
Casebres P 50 B2
Cáseda E 32 E3
Case della Marina I 64 E4
Casei Gerola I 37 A9
Căşeiu RO 152 C3
Casekow D 84 D6
Casella I 37 B9
Caselle in Pittari I 60 C5
Caselle Torinese I 68 C4
Case Perrone I 61 B7
Caseras E 42 E4
Caserta I 60 A2
Casével P 50 D3
Cashel IRL 6 E5
Cashel IRL 6 F3
Cashel IRL 7 B7
Cashel IRL 7 G8
Cashel IRL 9 C7
Cashla IRL 6 F5
Casillas E 46 D3
Casillas de Flores E 45 D7
Casimcea RO 155 D2
Caşin RO 153 E9
Casina I 66 C1
Casinos E 48 E3
Casla IRL 6 F3
Čáslav CZ 77 C8
Casnewydd GB 13 B9
Casola in Lunigiana I 66 D1
Casola Valsenio I 66 D4
Casole d'Elsa I 66 F3
Casoli I 63 C6
Casoria I 60 B2
Caspe E 42 E3
Casperia I 62 C3
Cassà de la Selva E 43 D9
Cassagnes-Bégonhès F 33 B11
Cassaniouze F 29 F10
Cassano allo Ionio I 61 D6
Cassano delle Murge I 61 B7
Cassano Magnano I 69 B6
Cassano Spinola I 37 B9
Cassaro I 59 E6
Cassel F 18 C5
Casseneuil F 33 B7
Casserres E 43 C7
Cassibile I 59 F7
Cassine I 37 B9
Cassino I 62 E5
Cassis F 35 D10
Cassola I 72 E4
Cassuéjouls F 30 F2
Častá SK 146 E4
Castagliona Olona I 69 B6
Castagnaro I 66 B3
Castagneto Carducci I 66 F2
Castagnole delle Lanze I 37 B8
Castagnole Monferrato I 37 B8
Castalla E 56 D3
Castañar de Ibor E 45 E10
Castañares de Rioja E 40 C6
Castanet-Tolosan F 33 C9
Castanheira P 44 C6
Castanheira de Pêra P 44 D4
Castano Primo I 68 B6
Castasegna CH 69 A8
Casteggio I 37 A10
Castejón E 41 D8
Castejón del Puente E 42 D4
Castejón de Monegros E 42 D3
Castejón de Sos E 33 E6
Castejón de Valdejasa E 41 E10
Castèlbellino I 67 F7
Castèl Bolognese I 66 D4
Castelbuono I 58 D5
Castelcivita I 60 C4
Castèl d'Ario I 66 B2
Castel de Cabra E 42 F2
Casteldelfino I 36 B6
Castèl del Monte I 62 C5
Castèl del Piano I 65 B5
Castèl del Rio I 66 D4
Castèl di Iudica I 59 E6
Castèl di Lama I 62 B5
Castèl di Lucio I 58 D5
Castèl di Sangro I 62 D6
Casteleiro P 45 D6
Castelfidardo I 67 F8
Castelfiorentino I 66 E2
Castelflorite E 42 D3
Castelfocognano I 66 E4
Castelforte I 62 E5
Castelfranci I 60 B4
Castelfranco di Sopra I 66 E4
Castelfranco di Sotto I 66 E2
Castelfranco Emilia I 66 C3
Castelfranco in Miscano I 60 A4
Castelfranco Veneto I 72 E4
Castèl Frentano I 63 C6
Castèl Gandolfo I 62 D3
Castelginest F 33 C8
Castèl Giorgio I 62 B1
Castèl Goffredo I 66 B1
Castelgrande I 60 B4
Casteljaloux F 33 B6
Castellabate I 60 C3
Castell'Alfero I 37 B8
Castellalto I 62 B5
Castellammare del Golfo I 58 C2
Castellammare di Stabia I 60 B2
Castellamonte I 68 C4
Castellana Grotte I 61 B8
Castellane F 36 D5
Castellaneta I 61 B7
Castellanos de Castro E 40 D3
Castellarano I 66 C2
Castellar de la Frontera E 53 D6
Castellar de la Muela E 47 C9
Castellar de la Ribera E 43 C6
Castellar de Santiago E 55 B6
Castellar de Santisteban E 55 C6
Castell'Arquato I 69 D8
Castell'Azzara I 62 B1
Castellazzo Bormida I 37 B9
Castelldans E 42 E5
Castell de Cabres E 42 F4
Castell de Castells E 56 D4
Castelldefels E 43 E7
Castell de Ferro E 55 F6
Castelleone I 69 C8
Castelletto sopra Ticino I 68 B6
Castellfort E 42 F3
Castellina in Chianti I 66 F3
Castellina Marittima I 66 F2
Castelliri I 62 D5
Castellnou de Bassella E 43 C6
Castellnovo E 48 E4
Castelló d'Argile I 66 C3
Castelló de Farfanya E 42 D5
Castelló de la Plana E 48 E4
Castelló d'Empúries E 43 C10
Castelló de Rugat E 56 D4
Castello di Annone I 37 B8
Castellón de la Plana E 48 E4
Castellote E 42 F3
Castello Tesino I 72 D4
Castellserà E 42 D5
Castellterçol E 43 D8
Castellucchio I 66 B2
Castelluccio dei Sauri I 60 A4
Castelluccio Inferiore I 60 C5
Castellucio Valmaggiore I 60 A4
Castell'Umberto I 59 C6
Castelluzzo I 58 C2
Castell-y-Nedd GB 13 B7
Castèl Madama I 62 D3
Càstel Magno I 66 C3
Castelmagno I 37 C6
Castelmassa I 66 B3
Castelmauro I 63 D7
Castelmoron-sur-Lot F 33 B6
Castelnau-Barbarens F 33 C7
Castelnaudary F 33 D9
Castelnau-d'Auzan F 33 C6
Castelnau-de-Médoc F 28 E4
Castelnau-de-Montmiral F 33 C9
Castelnau d'Estréfonds F 33 C8
Castelnau-le-Lez F 35 C6
Castelnau-Magnoac F 33 D7
Castelnau-Montratier F 33 B8
Castelnau-Rivière-Basse F 32 C5
Castelnovo di Sotto I 66 C2
Castelnovo ne'Monti I 66 D1
Castelnuovo Berardenga I 66 F4
Castelnuovo della Daunia I 63 D8
Castelnuovo di Garfagnana I 66 D1
Castelnuovo di Porto I 62 C3
Castelnuovo di Val di Cecina I 66 F2
Castelnuovo Don Bosco I 68 C4
Castelnuovo Rangone I 66 C2
Castelnuovo Scrivia I 37 B9
Castelo Bom P 45 C7
Castelo Branco P 39 F6
Castelo Branco P 44 E6
Castelo de Paiva P 44 B4
Castelo de Vide P 44 F6
Castelo do Neiva P 38 E2
Castelões P 44 B4
Castelplanio I 67 F7
Castelraimondo I 67 F7
Castèl Ritaldi I 62 B3
Castelrotto I 72 C4
Castelsagrat F 33 B7
Castèl San Giovanni I 69 C7
Castèl San Lorenzo I 60 C4
Castèl San Niccolò I 66 E4
Castèl San Pietro Terme I 66 D4
Castèl Sant'Angelo I 62 C4
Castelsantangelo sul Nera I 62 B4
Castelsaraceno I 60 C5
Castelsardo I 64 B2
Castelsarrasin F 33 B8
Castelseras E 42 F3
Casteltermini I 58 D4
Castelu RO 155 E2
Castelverde I 69 C8
Castelvetere in Val Fortore I 60 A3
Castelvetrano I 58 D2
Castelvetro Placentino I 69 C8
Castèl Viscardo I 62 B2
Castèl Volturno I 60 A1
Castenaso I 66 C3
Castéra-Verduzan F 33 C6
Castetnau-Camblong F 32 D4
Castets F 32 C3
Castiadas I 64 E4
Castielfabib E 47 D10
Castiello de Jaca E 32 E4
Castiglioncello I 66 F1
Castiglione dei Pepoli I 66 D3
Castiglione del Lago I 66 F5
Castiglione della Pescaia I 65 B3
Castiglione delle Stiviere I 66 B1
Castiglione di Sicilia I 59 D7
Castiglione d'Orcia I 65 A5
Castiglione in Teverina I 62 B2
Castiglione Messer Marino I 63 D6
Castiglion Fiorentino I 66 F4
Castignano I 62 B5
Castilblanco E 45 F10
Castilblanco de los Arroyos E 51 D8
Castiliscar E 32 F3
Castilleja de la Cuesta E 51 E7
Castillejar E 55 D7
Castillejo de Martin Viejo E 45 C7
Castillejo de Mesleón E 40 F4
Castillejo de Robledo E 40 E5
Castillo de Bayuela E 46 D3
Castillo de Garcimuñoz E 47 E8
Castillo de Locubín E 53 A9
Castillon-en-Couserans F 33 E8
Castillon-la-Bataille F 28 F5
Castillonnès F 33 A7
Castillo-Nuevo E 32 E3
Castilruiz E 41 E7
Castione della Presolana I 69 B9
Castiòns di Strada I 73 E7
Castlebar IRL 6 E4
Castlebay GB 4 B2
Castlebellingham IRL 7 E10
Castleblakeney IRL 6 F6
Castleblayney IRL 7 D9
Castlebridge IRL 9 D10
Castle Carrock GB 5 F11
Castle Cary GB 13 C9
Castlecomer IRL 9 C8
Castleconnell IRL 8 C5
Castlecor IRL 8 D5
Castledawson GB 4 F3
Castlederg GB 4 F1
Castledermot IRL 9 C9
Castle Douglas GB 5 F9
Castleellis IRL 9 D10
Castlefinn IRL 4 F1
Castleford GB 11 D9
Castlegal IRL 6 D6
Castlegregory IRL 8 D2
Castlehill IRL 6 D4
Castleisland IRL 8 D4
Castle Kennedy GB 4 F7
Castlellis IRL 9 D10
Castlemaine IRL 8 D3
Castlemartin GB 12 B4
Castlemartyr IRL 8 E6
Castleplunket IRL 6 E6
Castlepollard IRL 7 E8
Castlerea IRL 6 E6
Castlereagh GB 7 C11
Castlerock GB 4 E3
Castletown GB 3 H10
Castletown GB 11 F7
Castletown GBM 10 C2
Castletown IRL 7 G8
Castletown Bere IRL 8 E3
Castletownshend IRL 8 E4
Castlewellan GB 7 D11
Castranova RO 160 E4
Castrejón de la Peña E 39 C10
Castrelo do Val E 38 E5
Castres F 33 C10
Castricum NL 16 C3
Castries F 35 C6
Castrignano del Capo I 61 D10
Castril E 55 D7
Castrillo de Don Juan E 40 E3
Castrillo de Duero E 40 E3
Castrillo de la Reina E 40 E5
Castrillo de la Vega E 40 E4
Castrillo Tejeriego E 40 E3
Castro I 61 C10
Castrobarto E 40 B5
Castrocalbón E 39 D8
Castro Caldelas E 38 D5
Castrocaro Terme I 66 D4
Castrocontrigo E 39 D7
Castro Daire P 44 C5
Castro dei Volsci I 62 D5
Castro del Río E 53 A8
Castro de Ouro E 38 A5
Castro de Rei E 38 B5
Castrofilippo I 58 E4
Castrogonzalo E 39 E8
Castrojeriz E 40 D3
Castro Laboreiro P 38 D3
Castro Marim P 50 E5
Castromocho E 39 D10
Castromonte E 39 E9
Castronuevo E 39 E8
Castronuño E 39 F9
Castronuovo di Sant'Andrea I 60 C6
Castronuovo di Sicilia I 58 D4
Castropignano I 63 D7
Castropodame E 39 C7
Castropol E 39 A5
Castrop-Rauxel D 17 E8
Castroreale I 59 C7
Castro-Urdiales E 40 B5
Castroverde E 38 B5
Castro Verde P 50 D3
Castroverde de Campos E 39 E9
Castrovillari I 60 D6
Cața RO 152 E6
Catadau E 48 F3
Çatalca TR 173 B9
Catalina RO 153 F8
Cataloi RO 155 C3
Catania I 59 E7
Catanzaro I 59 B10
Catanzaro Marina I 59 B10
Catarroja E 48 F4
Cățcău RO 152 C3
Căteasca RO 160 D6
Catenanuova I 59 D6
Caterham GB 15 E8
Cateri F 37 F9
Cathair Dónall IRL 8 E2
Cathair na Mart IRL 6 E3
Cathair Saidhbhín IRL 8 E2
Catherdaniel IRL 8 E2
Catí E 42 G4
Čatići BIH 157 D9
Catignano I 62 C5
Cătina RO 152 D4
Cătina RO 161 C8
Cativelos P 44 C5
Catoira E 38 C2
Caton GB 10 C6
Catral E 56 E3
Cattenom F 20 F6
Catterfeld D 79 E8
Catterick GB 11 C8
Catterline GB 5 B12
Cattolica I 67 E6
Cattolica Eraclea I 58 E3
Cătunele RO 159 D10
Catus F 33 A8
Căuaş RO 151 B10
Caudan F 22 E5
Caudebec-lès-Elbeuf F 18 F3
Caudecoste F 33 B7
Caudete E 56 D3
Caudete de las Fuentes E 47 E10
Caudiel E 48 E3
Caudiès-de-Fenouillèdes F 33 E10
Caudry F 19 D7
Caujac F 33 D8
Caulnes F 23 D7
Caulonia I 59 C9
Caumont F 33 B8
Caumont F 33 D8
Caumont-l'Éventé F 23 B10
Caumont-sur-Durance F 35 C8
Caunes-Minervois F 34 D4
Cauro F 37 H9
Căuşeni MD 154 D4
Causeway IRL 8 D3
Causeway Head GB 4 E3
Caussade F 33 B9
Cautano I 60 A3
Cauterets F 32 E5
Cava de'Tirreni I 60 B3
Cavadineşti RO 153 E12
Cavaglià I 68 C5
Cavaillon F 35 C9
Cavalaire-sur-Mer F 36 E5
Cavaleiro P 50 D2
Cavalese I 72 D3
Cavallermaggiore I 37 B7
Cavallino I 66 B6
Cava Manara I 69 C7
Cavan IRL 7 E8
Cavanagarven IRL 7 D9
Cavargna I 69 A7
Cavarzere I 66 B5
Cavazzo Carnico I 73 D7
Cave I 62 D3
Cave del Predil I 73 D8
Caveirac F 35 C7
Cavezzo I 66 C3
Cavignac F 28 E5
Čavle HR 67 B9
Cavnic RO 152 B3
Cavour I 68 D3
Cavriago I 66 C2
Cavriglia I 66 E3
Cavtat HR 162 D5
Çavuşköy TR 171 C10
Cawdor GB 3 K9
Cawood GB 11 D9
Cawston GB 15 B11
Caxarias P 44 E3
Çaybaşi TR 177 C9
Çayboyu TR 181 B8
Cayeux-sur-Mer F 18 D4
Çayirdere TR 173 B9
Caylus F 33 B9
Cazalegas E 46 D3
Cazalilla E 53 A9
Cazalla de la Sierra E 51 D8
Cazals F 33 A8
Cazals F 33 B9
Căzăneşti RO 159 D10
Căzăneşti RO 161 D10
Cazasu RO 155 C1
Cazaubon F 32 C5
Cazères F 33 D8
Cazes-Mondenard F 33 B8
Cazilhac F 33 D10
Cazin BIH 156 C4
Cazis CH 71 D8
Čažma HR 149 E7
Cazorla E 55 D7
Cazoulès F 29 F8
Cea E 38 D4
Cea E 39 D10
Ceahlău RO 153 C7
Ceamurlia de Jos RO 155 D3
Ceanannus Mór IRL 7 E9
Ceann Toirc IRL 8 D5
Ceann Trá IRL 8 D2
Ceanu Mare RO 152 D3
Cearsiadar GB 2 J3
Ceatharlach IRL 9 C9
Ceaucé F 23 D10
Ceauşu de Câmpie RO 152 D5
Céaux-d'Allègre F 30 E4
Cébazat F 30 D3
Čebín CZ 77 D10
Cebolla E 46 E3
Čebovce SK 147 E8
Cebreros E 46 D4
Ceccano I 62 D4
Cece H 149 C11
Čečejovce SK 145 F3
Čechtice CZ 77 C8
Čechynce SK 146 E6
Cecina I 66 F2
Ceclavín E 45 E7
Cecuni MNE 163 D8
Cedães P 38 F5
Čedasai LT 135 D10
Cedegolo I 69 A9
Cedeira E 38 A3
Cedillo E 44 E6
Cedillo del Condado E 46 D5
Cedrillas E 48 D3
Cedry Wielkie PL 138 B6
Cedynia PL 84 E6
Cee E 38 C1
Cefa RO 151 D8
Cefalù I 58 C5
Cefn-mawr GB 10 F5
Ceggia I 73 E6
Cegléd H 150 C4
Ceglédbercel H 150 C4
Ceglie Messapica I 61 B9
Cegłów PL 141 F5
Čegrane NMK 163 F10
Cehal RO 151 C10
Cehegín E 55 C9
Cehu Silvaniei RO 151 C11
Ceica RO 151 D9
Ceikiniai LT 135 F12
Ceilhes-et-Rocozels F 34 C5
Ceinos de Campos E 39 D9
Ceintrey F 26 C5
Ceira P 44 D4
Čejč CZ 77 E11
Cejkov SK 145 G4
Cekcyn PL 138 C5
Çekirdekli TR 173 F9
Čekiškė LT 134 F7
Ceków-Kolonia PL 142 C5
Celadas E 47 D10
Čeladná CZ 146 B6
Čelákovice CZ 77 B7
Celaliye TR 173 A7
Celano I 62 C5
Celanova E 38 D4
Čelarevo SRB 158 C4
Celaru RO 160 E4
Celbridge IRL 7 F9
Čelebić BIH 157 E6
Čelebići BIH 157 F10
Celeiros P 38 E3
Celenza Valfortore I 63 D7
Celestynów PL 141 F4
Čelič BIH 157 C10
Celico I 61 E6
Čelinac Donji BIH 157 C7
Celje SLO 148 D4
Cella E 47 D10
Celldömölk H 149 B8
Celle D 79 A7
Celle Ligure I 37 C9
Cellere I 62 C1
Celles B 19 C7
Celles-sur-Belle F 28 C5
Celles-sur-Ource F 25 D11
Cellettes F 24 E5
Cellino Attanasio I 62 B5
Cellole I 62 E5
Čelopeci NMK 168 B5
Čelopek NMK 164 F3
Celorico da Beira P 44 C6
Celorico de Basto P 38 F4
Celrà E 43 C9
Çeltikçi TR 173 D9
Cembra I 69 A11
Čemerno BIH 157 F10
Cempi LV 135 A11
Cénac-et-St-Julien F 29 F8
Cenad RO 150 E6
Cenade RO 152 E4
Cenas LV 134 C7
Cencenighe Agordino I 72 D4
Cendras F 35 B7
Cendrieux F 29 F7
Cenei RO 159 B6
Ceneselli I 66 B3
Cengio I 37 C8
Cenicero E 41 D6
Ceniclentos E 46 D4
Čenta SRB 158 C5
Centallo I 37 B7
Centelles E 43 D8
Cento I 66 C3
Centola I 60 C4
Centuri F 37 F10
Centuripe I 59 D6
Cepagatti I 62 C6
Cepari RO 160 C5
Čepin HR 149 E11
Ceplenița RO 153 C9
Čepovan SLO 73 D8
Ceppaloni I 60 A3
Ceppo Morelli I 68 B5
Ceprano I 62 D5
Ceptura RO 161 C8
Ćeralije HR 149 E9
Cerami I 59 D6
Cerani BIH 157 C8
Cerano I 68 C6
Ceranów PL 141 E6
Cérans-Foulletourte F 23 E12
Cerasi I 59 C8
Ceraso I 60 C4
Cerașu RO 161 C8
Cerăt RO 160 E3
Ceraukste LV 135 D8
Çërravë AL 168 C4
Cerbăl RO 151 F10

Civitella Roveto I 62 D4
Civray F 29 B10
Civray F 29 C6
Cizer RO 151 C10
Čížkovice CZ 76 B6
Čkyně CZ 76 D5
Clabhach GB 4 B3
Clachan GB 2 L4
Clachan GB 4 C7
Clachan of Glendaruel GB 4 C6
Clachtoll GB 2 J6
Clackmannan GB 5 C9
Clacton-on-Sea GB 15 D11
Cladich GB 4 C6
Clady GB 4 F1
Clady GB 4 F3
Claggan GB 4 B5
Clairac F 33 B6
Clairoix F 18 F6
Clairvaux-les-Lacs F 31 B8
Claix F 31 E8
Clamecy F 25 F10
Clane IRL 7 F9
Clans F 36 C6
Claonadh IRL 7 F9
Claonaig GB 4 D6
Clapham GB 11 C7
Clapham GB 15 C8
Clara IRL 7 F7
Clár Chlainne Mhuiris IRL 6 E5
Clarecastle IRL 8 C5
Claremorris IRL 6 E5
Claret F 35 B10
Claro CH 69 A7
Clary F 19 D7
Clashmore IRL 9 D7
Clashnessie GB 2 J6
Claudy GB 4 F2
Clausnitz D 80 E4
Claußnitz D 80 E3
Clausthal-Zellerfeld D 79 C7
Claut I 72 D6
Clauzetto I 73 D6
Clavering GB 15 D9
Clavier B 19 D11
Clay Cross GB 11 E9
Claydon GB 15 C11
Clayton GB 15 F8
Cleady IRL 8 E3
Cleat GB 3 H11
Cleator Moor GB 10 B4
Clécy F 23 C11
Cléder F 22 C3
Cleethorpes GB 11 D11
Clefmont F 26 D4
Cléguérec F 22 D5
Cleja RO 153 E9
Clelles F 31 F8
Clémency L 20 E5
Clenze D 83 E9
Cleobury Mortimer GB 13 A10
Cléon F 18 F3
Cléon-d'Andran F 35 A8
Cléré-les-Pins F 24 F3
Clères F 18 E3
Clérey F 25 D11
Clermain F 30 C6
Clermont F 18 F5
Clermont F 33 D8
Clermont-en-Argonne F 26 B3
Clermont-Ferrand F 30 D3
Clermont-l'Hérault F 34 C5
Clerval F 26 F6
Clervaux L 20 D6
Cléry-St-André F 24 E6
Cles I 72 D3
Clevedon GB 13 C9
Cleveleys GB 10 D5
Clifden IRL 6 F2
Cliffe GB 15 E9
Cliffoney IRL 6 D6
Climăuți MD 153 A11
Clinge NL 16 F2
Clingen D 79 D8
Clion F 29 B8
Clisson F 28 A3
Clitheroe GB 11 D7
Cloch na Rón IRL 6 F3
Clogh GB 4 F4
Clogh IRL 9 C7
Clogh IRL 9 C8
Clogh IRL 9 C10
Cloghan IRL 7 C7
Cloghan IRL 7 F7
Clogheen IRL 8 D7
Clogher GB 7 D8
Clogherhead IRL 7 E10
Cloghy GB 7 D12
Clohars-Carnoët F 22 E4
Clohernagh IRL 9 D8
Cloich na Coillte IRL 8 E5
Clonakilty IRL 8 E5
Clonaslee IRL 7 F7
Clonbern IRL 6 E5
Clonbulloge IRL 7 F8
Clonbur IRL 6 E4
Clondrohid IRL 8 E4
Clondulane IRL 8 D6
Clonea IRL 9 D8
Clonee IRL 7 F10
Cloneen IRL 9 D7
Clones IRL 7 D8
Clonmel IRL 9 D7
Clonmellon IRL 7 E8
Clonoulty IRL 9 C7
Clonroche IRL 9 D9
Clontibret IRL 7 D9
Clonygowan IRL 7 F8
Cloonbannin IRL 8 D4
Cloonboo IRL 6 F4
Cloonfad IRL 6 E5
Cloonfad IRL 6 F6
Cloonkeen IRL 6 E4
Cloppenburg D 17 C10
Closeburn GB 5 E9
Clough GB 7 D11
Cloughjordan IRL 8 C6
Cloughmills GB 4 E4
Cloughton GB 11 C11
Clova GB 5 B10
Clovelly GB 12 D6
Clovullin GB 4 B6
Cloyes-sur-le-Loir F 24 E5
Cloyne IRL 8 E6
Cluain Bú IRL 6 F4
Cluain Eois IRL 7 D8
Cluainín IRL 6 D6
Cluain Meala IRL 9 D7
Cluis F 29 B9
Cluj-Napoca RO 152 D3
Clumanc F 36 C4
Clun GB 13 A8
Cluny F 30 C6
Cluses F 31 C10
Clusone I 69 B8
Clydach GB 13 B7
Clydebank GB 5 D8
Clynderwen GB 12 B5
Clyro GB 13 A8
Ćmielów PL 143 E12
Cmolas PL 143 F12
Coachford IRL 8 E5
Coagh GB 4 F3
Coalburn GB 5 D9
Coalisland GB 7 C9
Coalville GB 11 F9
Coaña E 39 A6
Coarnele Caprei RO 153 C10
Coarraze F 32 D5
Coast GB 2 K5
Coatbridge GB 5 D8
Cobadin RO 155 E2
Cobani MD 153 B10
Cobeja E 46 D5
Cobeta E 47 C8
Cobh IRL 8 E6
Cobia RO 160 D6
Coburg D 75 B8
Coca E 46 B3
Cocentaina E 56 D4
Cochem D 21 D8
Cochirleanca RO 161 C10
Cociuba Mare RO 151 D9
Cockburnspath GB 5 D12
Cockenzie and Port Seton GB 5 D11
Cockerham GB 10 D6
Cockermouth GB 5 F10
Cockett GB 12 B7
Cocora RO 161 D10
Cocu RO 160 D5
Cocumont F 32 B6
Codăești RO 153 D11
Coddington GB 11 E10
Code LV 135 D8
Codevigo I 66 B5
Codigoro I 66 C5
Codlea RO 161 B6
Codogno I 69 C8
Codos E 41 F9
Codreanca MD 154 C3
Codroipo I 73 E6
Codrongianos I 64 B2
Codru MD 154 D3
Coesfeld D 17 E8
Coevorden NL 17 C7
Coëx F 28 B2
Cofrentes E 47 F10
Cogealac RO 155 D3
Cogeces del Monte E 40 E3
Coggeshall GB 15 D10
Coggia F 37 G9
Coggiola I 68 B5
Cogîlniceni MD 154 B3
Çöğmen TR 181 C10
Cognac F 28 D5
Cognac-la-Forêt F 29 D8
Cogne I 31 D11
Cognin F 31 D8
Cogoleto I 37 C9
Cogolin F 36 E5
Cogollos E 40 D4
Cogollos Vega E 53 B9
Cogolludo E 47 C6
Cogula P 45 C6
Coillan Chollaigh IRL 7 E9
Coimbra P 44 D4
Coimbrão P 44 E3
Coín E 53 C7
Coincy F 25 B9
Coja P 44 D5
Cojasca RO 161 D7
Cojocna RO 152 D3
Čoka SRB 150 F5
Colares P 50 B1
Colayrac-St-Cirq F 33 B7
Colbasna MD 154 B4
Cölbe D 21 C11
Colbitz D 79 B10
Colbordola I 67 E6
Colceag RO 161 D8
Colchester GB 15 D10
Coldingham GB 5 D12
Colditz D 79 D12
Coldstream GB 5 D12
Coleford GB 13 B9
Coleraine GB 4 E3
Colibași MD 155 B2
Colibași RO 160 D5
Colibași RO 161 E8
Colibița RO 152 C5
Colico I 69 A7
Coligny F 31 C7
Colijnsplaat NL 182 B3
Colindres E 40 B5
Colintraive GB 4 D6
Collado Hermoso E 46 B5
Collado Villalba E 46 C5
Collagna I 66 D1
Collanzo E 39 B8
Collarmele I 62 C5
Collazzone I 62 B2
Collecchio I 66 C1
Collecorvino I 62 C5
Colledara I 62 B5
Colle di Val d'Elsa I 66 F3
Colleferro I 62 D4
Collegno I 68 C4
Colle Isarco I 72 C3
Collelongo I 62 D5
Collepardo I 62 D4
Collepasso I 61 C10
Collesalvetti I 66 E1
Colle Sannita I 60 A3
Collesano I 58 D4
Colletorto I 63 D7
Colliano I 60 B4
Colli a Volturno I 62 D6
Collieston GB 3 L13
Collinas I 64 D2
Collinée F 22 D6
Collinghorst (Rhauderfehn) D 17 B9
Collio I 69 B9
Collioure F 34 E5
Collobrières F 36 E4
Collombey CH 31 C10
Collon IRL 7 E10
Collonges F 31 C8
Collonges-la-Rouge F 29 E9
Collooney IRL 6 D6
Colmar F 27 D7
Colmars F 36 C5
Colmberg D 75 D7
Colmeal P 44 D5
Colmenar E 53 C8
Colmenar del Arroyo E 46 D4
Colmenar de Montemayor E 45 D9
Colmenar de Oreja E 46 D6
Colmenar Viejo E 46 C5
Colméry F 25 F9
Colmonell GB 4 E7
Colne GB 11 D7
Colobraro I 61 C6
Cologna Veneta I 66 B3
Cologne F 33 C7
Cologno al Serio I 69 B8
Colombelles F 23 B11
Colombey-les-Belles F 26 C4
Colombey-les Deux-Églises F 25 D12
Colombier CH 31 B10
Colombiès F 33 B10
Colombres E 39 B10
Colomers E 43 C9
Colomiers F 33 C8
Colonești RO 153 D10
Colonești RO 160 D5
Colònia de Sant Jordi E 57 C11
Colònia de Sant Pere E 57 B11
Colonnella I 62 B5
Colorno I 66 C1
Colos P 50 D3
Cölpin D 84 C4
Colquhar GB 5 D10
Colroy-la-Grande F 27 D7
Colsterworth GB 11 F10
Colți RO 161 C8
Coltishall GB 15 B11
Colunga E 39 B9
Colwyn Bay GB 10 E4
Coly F 29 E8
Colyford GB 13 D8
Comacchio I 66 C5
Comana RO 152 F6
Comana RO 155 F2
Comana RO 161 E8
Comana de Sus RO 152 F6
Comandău RO 153 F8
Comănești RO 153 E8
Comares E 53 C8
Comarna RO 153 C11
Comarnic RO 161 C7
Combeaufontaine F 26 E4
Combe Martin GB 12 C6
Comber GB 7 C11
Comberton GB 15 C9
Comblain-au-Pont B 19 D12
Comblanchien F 26 F2
Combles F 18 D6
Combloux F 31 D10
Combourg F 23 D8
Combronde F 30 D3
Comeglians I 73 C6
Comèlico Superiore I 72 C6
Comillas E 40 B3
Comines B 18 C6
Comișani RO 161 D7
Comiso I 59 F6
Comitini I 58 E4
Comloșu Mare RO 150 F6
Commeen IRL 7 C7
Commenailles F 31 B7
Commensacq F 32 B4
Commentry F 30 C2
Commequiers F 28 B2
Commer F 23 D10
Commercy F 26 C4
Como I 69 B7
Cómpeta E 53 C9
Compiano I 37 B11
Compiègne F 18 F6
Compolibat F 33 B10
Comporta P 50 C2
Compreignac F 29 D8
Comps-sur-Artuby F 36 D5
Comrat MD 154 E3
Comrie GB 5 C9
Comunanza I 62 B4
Cona I 66 B5
Conca F 37 H10
Concarneau F 22 E4
Concas I 64 B4
Conceição P 50 E4
Concesio I 69 B9
Concha E 40 B5
Conches-en-Ouche F 24 C4
Concordia Sagittaria I 73 E6
Concorès F 33 A8
Concots F 33 B9
Condat F 30 E2
Condé-en-Brie F 25 B10
Condeixa-a-Nova P 44 D4
Condé-sur-Huisne F 24 D4
Condé-sur-l'Escaut F 182 E3
Condé-sur-Noireau F 23 C10
Condé-sur-Vire F 23 B9
Condino I 69 B10
Condofuri I 59 C8
Condom F 33 C6
Condove I 31 E11
Condrieu F 30 E6
Condrița MD 154 C3
Conegliano I 72 E5
Conflans-en-Jarnisy F 26 B4
Conflans-sur-Lanterne F 26 E5
Conflenti I 59 A9
Confolens F 29 C7
Cong IRL 6 E4
Congaz MD 154 E3
Congdon's Shop GB 12 D6
Congleton GB 11 E7
Congosto E 39 C7
Congosto de Valdavia E 39 C10
Congrier F 23 E9
Conil de la Frontera E 52 D4
Coningsby GB 11 E11
Coniston GB 10 C5
Conlie F 23 D11
Conliège F 31 B8
Conlig GB 4 F5
Connah's Quay GB 10 E5
Connantre F 25 C10
Connaux F 35 B8
Connel GB 4 C6
Connerré F 24 D3
Connolly IRL 8 C4
Connor GB 4 F4
Conon Bridge GB 2 K8
Conop RO 151 E8
Čonoplja SRB 150 F3
Conow D 84 D4
Conques F 33 A10
Conques-sur-Orbiel F 33 D10
Conquista E 54 C3
Consandolo I 66 C4
Consdorf L 186 B1
Conselice I 66 C4
Consell E 49 E10
Conselve I 66 B4
Consett GB 5 F13
Constância P 44 F4
Constanța RO 155 E3
Constantí E 42 E6
Constantim P 38 F4
Constantim P 39 E7
Constantina E 51 D8
Constantin Daicoviciu RO 159 B9
Constanzana E 46 C3
Consuegra E 46 F5
Contarina I 66 B5
Contes F 37 D6
Contessa Entellina I 58 D3
Contești RO 161 D7
Contești RO 161 F6
Conthey CH 31 C11
Contigliano I 62 C3
Contis-Plage F 32 B3
Contres F 24 F5
Contrexéville F 26 D4
Controne I 60 B4
Contursi Terme I 60 B4
Contwig D 21 F8
Conty F 18 E5
Conversano I 61 B8
Convoy IRL 7 C7
Conwy GB 10 E4
Conza della Campania I 60 B4
Cookstown GB 4 F3
Coola IRL 6 D6
Coolbaun IRL 6 G6
Coole F 25 C11
Coole IRL 7 E8
Coolmore IRL 6 C6
Coombe Bissett GB 13 C11
Cootehill IRL 7 D8
Copăcel RO 151 D9
Copăcele RO 159 C9
Copăceni MD 154 B2
Copăceni RO 160 D3
Copăcenii de Sus RO 161 E8
Copalnic-Mănăștur RO 152 B3
Copanca MD 154 D5
Copanello I 59 B10
Copceac MD 154 F3
Copertino I 61 C10
Çöpköy TR 173 B6
Copley GB 5 F13
Copons E 43 D7
Copparo I 66 C4
Coppeen IRL 8 E5
Copplestone GB 13 D7
Coppull GB 10 D6
Copșa Mică RO 152 E4
Copythorne GB 13 D11
Corabia RO 160 F4
Cora Chaitlín IRL 8 E5
Cora Droma Rúisc IRL 6 E6
Čoralići BIH 156 C4
Corato I 61 A6
Coray F 22 D4
Corbalán E 47 D11
Corbally IRL 6 D4
Corbasca RO 153 E10
Corbeanca RO 161 D8
Corbeil-Essonnes F 25 C7
Corbeilles F 25 D8
Corbeni RO 160 C5
Corbeny F 19 F8
Corbera E 48 F4
Corbera d'Ebre E 42 E4
Corbi RO 160 C5
Corbie F 18 E6
Corbières CH 31 B11
Corbières F 35 C10
Corbigny F 25 F10
Corbii Mari RO 161 D6
Corbița RO 153 E10
Corbridge GB 5 F12
Corbu RO 153 D7
Corbu RO 155 E3
Corbu RO 160 D5
Corby GB 11 G10
Corçà E 43 D10
Corcaigh IRL 8 E6
Corcelles-lès-Cîteaux F 26 F3
Corchiano I 62 C2
Corciano I 66 F5
Corcieux F 27 D6
Corcova RO 159 D11
Corcubión E 38 C1
Cordăreni RO 153 B9
Cordemais F 23 F8
Cordenòns I 73 E6
Cordes-sur-Ciel F 33 B9
Córdoba E 53 A7
Cordobilla de Lácara E 45 F8
Corduente E 47 C9
Cordun RO 153 D9
Coreglia Antelminelli I 66 D2
Corella E 41 D8
Coreses E 39 E8
Corestăuți MD 153 A10
Corfe Castle GB 13 D10
Corfinio I 62 C5
Cori I 62 D3
Coria E 45 E7
Coria del Río E 51 E7
Coriano I 66 E6
Corigliano Calabro I 61 D7
Corinaldo I 67 E7
Coripe E 51 F9
Corjeuți MD 153 A10
Cork IRL 8 E6
Corlătel RO 159 E10
Corlăteni RO 153 B9
Corlay F 22 D5
Corlea IRL 7 E7
Corleone I 58 D3
Corleto Perticara I 60 C6
Çorlu TR 173 B8
Cormatin F 30 B6
Cormeilles F 18 F1
Corme Porto E 38 B2
Cormicy F 19 F8
Cormons I 73 E7
Cormontreuil F 20 F2
Cornafulla IRL 6 F7
Cornago E 41 D7
Cornamona IRL 6 E4
Cornaredo I 69 B7
Cornas F 30 F6
Cornățelu RO 161 D7
Cornau D 17 C10
Cornea RO 159 C9
Cornedo all'Isarco I 72 D3
Cornedo Vicentino I 69 B11
Corneilla-del-Vercol F 34 E4
Cornellà de Llobregat E 43 E8
Cornellà de Terri E 43 C9
Cornellana E 39 B7
Cornereva RO 159 C9
Cornești MD 153 C12
Cornești RO 152 C3
Cornești RO 161 D7
Cornetu RO 161 E7
Corni RO 153 B9
Corni RO 153 F11
Corniglio I 69 E9
Cornimont F 27 E6
Cornu RO 161 C7
Cornuda I 72 E5
Cornudella de Montsant E 42 E5
Cornudilla E 40 C5
Cornu Luncii RO 153 C8
Cornus F 34 C5
Corod RO 153 F11
Corofin IRL 8 C4
Coroieni RO 152 C3
Coroisânmărtin RO 152 E5
Coron F 23 F10
Çorovodë AL 168 C3
Corps F 31 F8
Corps-Nuds F 23 E8
Corral de Almaguer E 47 E6
Corral de Calatrava E 54 B4
Corrales E 39 F8
Corral-Rubio E 55 B10
Corre F 26 E5
Correggio I 66 C2
Corrèze F 29 E9
Corridonia I 67 F8
Corrie GB 4 D6
Corris GB 10 F4
Corr na Móna IRL 6 E4
Corrobert F 25 C10
Corry IRL 6 D6
Corsano I 61 D10
Corseul F 23 D7
Corsham GB 13 C10
Corsico I 69 C7
Corsock GB 5 E9
Cortale I 59 B9
Corte F 37 G10
Corteconcepción E 51 D7
Corte de Peleas E 51 B6
Cortegada E 38 D3
Cortegana E 51 D6
Cortemilia I 37 B8
Corteno Golgi I 69 A9
Corteolona I 69 C7
Cortes E 41 E9
Cortes de Aragón E 42 F2
Cortes de Arenoso E 48 D3
Cortes de Baza E 55 D7
Cortes de la Frontera E 53 C6
Cortes de Pallás E 48 F3
Cortiçadas do Lavre P 50 B3
Cortijo de Arriba E 46 F4
Cortijos Nuevos E 55 C7
Cortina d'Ampezzo I 72 C5
Corton GB 15 B12
Cortona I 66 F4
Coruche P 50 B2
Corullón E 39 C6
Corund RO 152 E6
Corvara in Badia I 72 C4
Corvera E 56 F2
Corwen GB 10 F5
Coryton GB 15 D10
Cosa E 47 C10
Cosâmbești RO 161 D10
Cosăuți MD 154 A2
Coșbuc RO 152 C4
Cosby GB 11 F9
Coșcodeni MD 153 B12
Coscurita E 41 F7
Coșeiu RO 151 C11
Cosenza I 60 E6
Coșereni RO 161 D9
Cosești RO 160 C5
Coshieville GB 5 B9
Čosići BIH 157 D8
Cosio di Arroscia I 37 C7
Coslada E 46 D5
Cosmești RO 153 F10
Cosmești RO 160 E6
Cosminele RO 161 C7
Cosne-Cours-sur-Loire F 25 F8
Cosne-d'Allier F 30 C2
Coșnița MD 154 C4
Cosoleto I 59 C8
Coșoveni RO 160 E3
Cossato I 68 B5
Cossé-le-Vivien F 23 E10
Cossoine I 64 C2
Cossonay CH 31 B10
Costacciaro I 67 F6
Costache Negri RO 153 F11
Costa da Caparica P 50 B1
Costa di Rovigo I 66 B4
Costa Volpino I 69 B9
Coșteiu RO 151 F8
Costelloe IRL 6 F3
Costești MD 153 B10
Costești MD 154 D3
Costești RO 153 D11
Costești RO 160 C4
Costești RO 160 D5
Costești RO 161 C9
Costeștii din Vale RO 161 D6
Costigliole Saluzzo I 37 B6
Costișa RO 153 D9
Costuleni RO 153 C11
Cosuenda E 41 F9
Coswig D 79 C11
Coswig D 80 D5
Coteana RO 160 E4
Cotești RO 161 B10
Cothen NL 16 D4
Coti-Chiavari F 37 H9
Cotignac F 36 D4
Cotignola I 66 D4
Cotiujeni MD 154 B3
Cotiujenii Mici MD 154 B2
Cotmeana RO 160 D5
Cotnari RO 153 C9
Coțofănești RO 153 E9
Coțofenii din Dos RO 160 E3
Cotronei I 61 E7
Cottanello I 62 C3
Cottbus D 80 C6
Cottenham GB 15 C9
Cottesmore GB 11 F10
Cottingham GB 11 F10
Cotușca RO 153 A9
Coubon F 30 E4
Couburciu MD 154 D5
Couches F 30 B6
Couço P 50 B3
Coucy-le-Château-Auffrique F 19 E7
Coudekerque-Branche F 18 B5
Couëron F 23 F8
Couflens F 33 E8
Coufouleux F 33 C9
Couhé F 29 C6
Couiza F 33 E10
Coulaines F 23 D12
Coulanges-la-Vineuse F 25 E10
Coulanges-sur-Yonne F 25 E10
Coulaures F 29 E7
Couleuvre F 30 B2
Coullons F 25 E7
Coulmier-le-Sec F 25 E11
Coulmiers F 24 E6
Coulogne F 15 F12
Coulombiers F 29 C6
Coulombs F 24 C6
Coulommiers F 25 C9
Coulonges-sur-l'Autize F 28 C4
Coulounieix-Chamiers F 29 E7
Coulport GB 4 C7
Coupar Angus GB 5 B10
Couptrain F 23 D11
Coura P 38 E2
Courcelles B 182 E4
Courcelles-Chaussy F 26 B5
Courcelles-sur-Nied F 186 C1
Courchaton F 26 E6
Courchevel F 31 E10
Cour-Cheverny F 24 E5
Courcité F 23 D11
Courçon F 28 C4
Courcy F 19 F9
Courgains F 23 D12
Courgenay CH 27 F7
Courgenay F 25 D10
Courlay F 28 B4
Courmayeur I 31 D10
Courmelles F 19 F7
Cournon-d'Auvergne F 30 D3
Courpière F 30 D4
Courrendlin CH 27 F7
Courrensan F 33 C6
Courrières F 182 E1
Coursac F 29 E7
Coursan F 34 D5
Coursegoules F 36 D6
Courseulles-sur-Mer F 23 B11
Cours-la-Ville F 30 C5
Courson-les-Carrières F 25 E9
Court CH 27 F7
Courtalain F 24 D5
Courtelary CH 27 F7
Courtenay F 25 D9
Courthézon F 35 B8
Courtmacsherry IRL 8 E5
Courtomer F 24 C3
Courtown IRL 9 C10
Courtrai B 19 C7
Courtrai B 182 D2
Court-St-Etienne B 19 C10
Courville-sur-Eure F 24 D5
Cousance F 31 B7
Cousances-les-Forges F 26 C3
Coussac-Bonneval F 29 D8
Coussay-les-Bois F 29 B7
Coussegrey F 25 E11
Coussey F 26 D4
Coustouges F 34 F4
Coutances F 23 B9
Couterne F 23 C11
Couto de Cima P 44 C5
Coutras F 28 E5
Couvet CH 31 B10
Couvin B 19 D10
Couze-et-St-Front F 29 F7
Couzeix F 29 D8
Covaleda E 40 E6
Covarrubias E 40 D5
Covăsinț RO 151 E8
Covasna RO 153 F8
Cove GB 2 K5
Cove Bay GB 3 L12
Coventry GB 13 A11
Covilhã P 44 D6
Cowbit GB 11 F11
Cowbridge GB 13 C8
Cowdenbeath GB 5 C10
Cowes GB 13 D12
Cox E 56 E3
Cox F 33 C8
Coxheath GB 15 E9
Coxhoe GB 5 F13
Coylumbridge GB 3 L9
Cózar E 55 B6
Cozes F 28 D4
Cozești MD 154 B2
Cozieni RO 161 C9
Cozmești RO 153 D11
Cozzano F 37 H10
Craanford IRL 9 C10
Crăcăoani RO 153 C8
Crach F 22 E5
Crăciunelu de Jos RO 152 E3
Crăciunești RO 152 E5
Craco I 61 C6
Craidorolț RO 151 B10
Craig GB 2 L6
Craigavad GB 4 F5
Craigavon GB 7 D10
Craigellachie GB 3 L10
Craignure GB 4 C5
Crail GB 5 C11
Crailsheim D 75 D7
Craiova RO 160 E3
Craiva RO 151 D8
Cramlington GB 5 E13
Crâmpoia RO 160 E5
Cranage GB 11 E7
Cranagh GB 4 F2
Cranford IRL 7 B7
Crângeni RO 160 E5
Cran-Gevrier F 31 D9
Crângu RO 160 F6
Crângurile RO 160 D6
Cranleigh GB 15 E8
Crans-sur-Sierre CH 31 C11
Craon F 23 E10
Craonne F 19 F8
Craponne-sur-Arzon F 30 E4
Crask Inn GB 2 J7
Crasna RO 151 C10
Crasna RO 160 C3
Crasnoe MD 154 D5
Crathie GB 5 A10
Crato P 44 F5
Cravagliana I 68 B5
Cravant F 25 E10
Craven Arms GB 13 A9
Crawfordjohn GB 5 E9
Crawfordsburn GB 4 F5
Crawley GB 15 E8
Creaca RO 151 C11
Creagh IRL 8 E4
Creagorry GB 2 L2
Creamhghort IRL 7 B7
Créances F 23 B8
Créancey F 25 F12
Crecente E 38 D3
Crêches-sur-Saône F 30 C6
Crécy-en-Ponthieu F 18 D4
Crécy-la-Chapelle F 25 C8
Crécy-sur-Serre F 19 E8
Credenhill GB 13 A9
Crediton GB 13 D7
Creeslough IRL 7 B7
Creevagh IRL 6 D4
Creggan GB 4 F2
Creggan GB 7 D9
Cregganbaun IRL 6 E3
Creggs IRL 6 E6
Creglingen D 75 D7
Cregneash GBM 10 C2
Créhange F 186 C2
Creil F 18 F5
Creil NL 16 C5
Creissels F 34 B5
Crema I 69 C8
Cremeaux F 30 D4
Crémenes E 39 C9
Crémieu F 31 D7
Cremlingen D 79 B8
Cremona I 69 C9
Črenšovci SLO 148 C6
Créon F 28 F5
Crepaja SRB 158 C6
Crépey F 26 C4
Crépy F 19 E8
Crépy-en-Valois F 18 F6
Cres HR 67 C9
Crescentino I 68 C5
Crespina I 66 E2
Crespino I 66 C4
Crespos E 46 C3
Cressensac F 29 E9
Crest F 31 F7
Creswell GB 11 E9
Cretas E 42 F4
Créteil F 25 C7
Crețeni RO 160 D4
Crețești RO 153 D11
Creußen D 75 C10
Creutzwald F 21 F7
Creuzburg D 79 D7
Crevalcore I 66 C3
Crevant F 29 C9
Crévéchamps F 26 C5
Crèvecœur-le-Grand F 18 E5
Crevedia RO 161 D7
Crevedia Mare RO 161 E7
Crevenicu RO 161 E7
Crevillente E 56 E3
Crevoladossola I 68 A5
Crewe GB 10 E7
Crewkerne GB 13 D9
Crianlarich GB 4 C7
Cricău RO 152 E3
Criccieth GB 10 F3
Criciova RO 159 B9
Crickhowell GB 13 B8
Cricklade GB 13 B11
Cricova MD 154 C3
Crieff GB 5 C9
Criel-sur-Mer F 18 D3
Crikvenica HR 67 B10
Crimmitschau D 79 E11
Crimond GB 3 K13
Crinan GB 4 C5
Cringleford GB 15 B11
Crinitz D 80 C5
Cripán E 41 C7
Cripp's Corner GB 15 F10
Criquetot-l'Esneval F 18 E1
Crișcior RO 151 E10
Crișeni RO 151 C11
Crispiano I 61 B8
Crissolo I 31 F11
Cristești RO 152 D4
Cristești RO 153 B9
Cristești RO 153 C9
Cristian RO 152 F4
Cristian RO 161 B6
Cristinești RO 153 A8
Criștioru de Jos RO 151 E10
Cristóbal E 45 D9
Cristolț RO 151 C11
Cristuru Secuiesc RO 152 E6
Criuleni MD 154 C4
Criva MD 153 A9
Crivitz D 83 C11
Crkvice BIH 157 D8
Crkvice HR 162 D3
Crkvice MNE 163 D6
Crkvina BIH 157 B9
Crkvine SRB 163 C9
Crljivica BIH 156 D5
Črmošnjice SLO 73 E11
Črna SLO 73 D10
Crna Bara SRB 150 F5
Crna Bara SRB 158 D3
Crnac HR 149 E9
Crnajka SRB 159 E9
Crna Trava SRB 164 D5
Crnča SRB 158 E3
Crni Lug BIH 156 D6
Crni Lug HR 67 B10
Crnjelovo BIH 157 C11
Crnkovci HR 149 E10
Crnoklište SRB 164 C5
Črnomelj SLO 148 E4
Crock D 75 B8
Crocketford GB 5 E9
Crockets Town IRL 6 D4
Crockmore IRL 7 C7
Crocmaz MD 154 E5
Crocq F 29 D10
Crodo I 68 A5
Crofty GB 12 B6
Croghan IRL 6 E6
Crognaleto I 62 B4
Croisilles F 18 D6
Croithlí IRL 6 B6
Crolles F 31 E8
Crolly IRL 6 B6
Cromadh IRL 8 C5
Cromarty GB 3 K8
Cromer GB 15 B11
Cromhall GB 13 B10
Cronat F 30 B4
Crook GB 5 F13
Crookham GB 5 D12
Crookhaven IRL 8 F3
Crookstown IRL 8 E5
Croom IRL 8 C5
Cropalati I 61 D7
Cropani I 59 B10
Crosbost GB 2 J4

Column 7

Digny F 24 C5
Digoin F 30 C4
Dihtiv UA 144 B9
Dijon F 26 F3
Dikaia GR 166 F6
Dikanäs S 107 A10
Dikancë RKS 163 E10
Dikili TR 177 A8
Dikkebus B 18 C6
Dikļi LV 131 F10
Diksmuide B 18 B6
Dilar E 53 B9
Dilbeek B 182 D4
Dilesi GR 175 C8
Dilinata GR 174 C2
Dillenburg D 21 C10
Dilling N 95 D13
Dillingen (Saar) D 21 F7
Dillingen an der Donau D 75 E7
Dilove UA 145 H9
Dilsen B 19 B12
Dimaro I 71 E11
Diminio GR 169 F8
Dimitrie Cantemir RO 153 D12
Dimitritsi GR 169 C9
Dimitrovgrad BG 166 E5
Dimitrovgrad SRB 165 C6
Dimitsana GR 174 D5
Dimovo BG 159 F10
Dimzukalns LV 135 C8
Dinami I 59 B9
Dinan F 23 D7
Dinant B 19 D10
Dinard F 23 C7
Dingé F 23 D8
Dingelstädt D 79 D7
Dingelstedt am Huy D 79 C8
Dingle IRL 8 D2
Dingle S 91 B10
Dingolfing D 75 E12
Dingtuna S 98 C6
Dingwall GB 2 K8
Dinjiška HR 67 D11
Dinkelsbühl D 75 D7
Dinkelscherben D 75 F8
Dinklage D 17 C10
Dinnet GB 5 A11
Dinslaken D 17 E7
Dinteloord NL 16 E2
Dinther NL 183 B6
Dinxperlo NL 17 E6
Diö S 88 B6
Dion GR 169 D7
Diósd H 149 B11
Diosig RO 151 C9
Diósjenő H 147 F8
Dioşti RO 160 E4
Diou F 30 B4
Dipignano I 60 E6
Dipotama GR 171 B7
Dipotamia GR 168 D4
Dippach L 20 E6
Dippoldiswalde D 80 E5
Dirdal N 94 E4
Dirhami EST 130 C7
Dirivaara S 116 E8
Dirkshorn NL 16 C3
Dirksland NL 16 E2
Dirlewang D 71 A11
Dirmstein D 187 B5
Dirvonėnai LT 134 E5
Dischingen D 75 E7
Disentis Muster CH 71 D7
Diseröd S 91 D11
Dison B 19 C12
Diss GB 15 C11
Dissay F 29 B6
Dissay-sous-Courcillon F 24 E3
Dissen am Teutoburger Wald D 17 D10
Distington GB 10 B4
Distomo GR 175 C6
Distrato GR 168 D5
Ditfurt D 79 C9
Ditrău RO 153 D7
Ditton GB 15 E9
Ditzingen D 27 C11
Divača SLO 73 E8
Divarata GR 174 C2
Diva Slatina BG 165 C6
Divci SRB 158 E5
Divčibare SRB 158 E5
Dives-sur-Mer F 23 B11
Dividalen N 111 C18
Divieto I 59 C7
Divín SK 147 E9
Divina SK 147 C7
Divion F 18 D6
Divišov CZ 77 C7
Divjakë AL 168 C2
Divonne-les-Bains F 31 C9
Divuša HR 156 B5
Dixmont F 25 D9
Dizy F 25 B10
Dizy-le-Gros F 19 E9
Djäkneboda S 122 B5
Djäkneböle S 122 C4
Djupen N 111 B18
Djupfjord N 110 C9
Djupfors S 109 E11
Djupsjö S 107 E14
Djuptjärn S 107 D15
Djupvik N 109 B10
Djupvik N 112 D5
Djupvik S 89 A11
Djura S 103 E8
Djurås S 97 A13
Djurmo S 97 A13
Djurö S 99 D11
Dlhá nad Oravou SK 147 C8
Dlouhá Loučka CZ 77 C12
Dlouhá Třebová CZ 77 C10
Długołęka PL 81 D12
Długołęka PL 140 D7
Długosiodło PL 139 E12
Dłutów PL 143 C7
Dlŭzhka Polyana BG 166 C6
Dmytrivka UA 154 F3
Dmytrivka UA 154 F4
Dmytrivka UA 155 B4
Dnestrovsc MD 154 D5
Dno RUS 132 F6
Doagh GB 4 F4
Doba RO 151 B10
Dobanovci SRB 158 D5
Dobârceni RO 153 B10
Dobârlău RO 153 F7
Dobbertin D 83 C12
Dobbiaco I 72 C5
Dobczyce PL 144 D1
Dobele LV 134 C6
Döbeln D 80 D4
Doběřçan RKS 164 E4
Doberlug-Kirchhain D 80 C5
Döbern D 81 C7
Dobersberg A 77 E8
Doberschütz D 79 D12
Dobiegniew PL 85 E9
Dobieszewo PL 85 B12
Dobieszyn PL 141 G4
Doboj BIH 157 C9
Dobova SLO 148 E5
Doboz H 151 D7
Dobrá CZ 146 B6
Dobra PL 85 C8
Dobra PL 142 C6
Dobra PL 144 D1
Dobra RO 151 F10
Dobra RO 161 D7
Dobra SRB 159 D8
Dobrá Niva SK 147 E8
Dobřany CZ 76 C4
Dobre PL 138 E6
Dobre PL 139 F12
Dobre Miasto PL 136 F1
Dobreni RO 153 D8
Dobrešinci NMK 169 A8
Dobreşti RO 151 D9
Dobreşti RO 160 D6
Dobreşti RO 160 F3
Dobrevo NMK 164 E5
Dobrica SRB 159 C6
Dobričevo SRB 159 D7
Dobrich BG 155 F1
Dobrich BG 166 E5
Dobri Do SRB 164 D3
Dobri Dol BG 159 F11
Dobrin RO 151 C11
Dobrinishte BG 165 F8
Dobříš CZ 76 C6
Dobritz D 79 B11
Dobřív CZ 76 C5
Dobrljin BIH 156 B5
Dobrna SLO 73 D11
Dobrnič SLO 73 E10
Dobrnja BIH 157 C7
Dobrnja BIH 157 C10
Dobrnje SRB 159 E7
Dobro E 40 C4
Dobrodzień PL 142 E5
Döbrököz H 149 D10
Dobromierz PL 81 E10
Dobromir RO 155 E1
Dobromirka BG 166 C4
Dobromirtsi BG 171 B8
Dobromyl' UA 145 D6
Dobroń PL 143 C7
Dobron' UA 145 G5
Dobronín CZ 77 D9
Dobro Polje BIH 157 E10
Dobro Polje SRB 159 F9
Dobrošane NMK 164 E4
Dobrosloveni RO 160 E4
Dobrosyn UA 144 C8
Dobroszyce PL 81 D12
Dobroteasa RO 160 D4
Dobroteşti RO 160 E5
Dobrotić SRB 164 C4
Dobrotich BG 167 C8
Dobrotino NMK 169 B6
Dobrotitsa BG 161 F9
Dobrovăţ RO 153 D11
Dobrovci BIH 157 C9
Dobrovice CZ 77 B7
Dobrovnik SLO 149 C6
Dobrovol'sk RUS 136 D5
Dobrowoda PL 143 F10
Dobruchi RUS 132 D2
Dobrun BIH 158 F3
Dobrun RO 160 E4
Dobruşa MD 154 B3
Dobruševo NMK 169 B5
Dobruška CZ 77 B10
Dobrzankowo PL 139 E10
Dobrzany PL 85 D8
Dobrzeń Wielki PL 142 E4
Dobrzyca PL 142 C4
Dobrzyków PL 139 F8
Dobrzyń nad Wisłą PL 139 E7
Dobšiná SK 145 F1
Dóc H 150 E5
Docking GB 15 B10
Dockmyr S 103 A10
Docksta S 107 E14
Dockweiler D 21 D7
Doclin RO 159 C8
Doddington GB 5 D12
Dodewaard NL 183 B7
Dodonoupoli GR 168 E4
Dödre S 102 A8
Doesburg NL 16 D6
Doetinchem NL 16 E6
Dofteana RO 153 E9
Doğanbey TR 177 C8
Doğanbey TR 177 D9
Doğanci TR 173 D10
Doğanköy TR 173 D10
Döge H 145 G5
Dogliani I 37 B7
Dognecea RO 159 C8
Doğüşbelen TR 181 C9
Dohna D 80 E5
Dohňany SK 146 C6
Dohren D 17 C9
Doiceşti RO 160 D6
Doïrani GR 169 B8
Doire lorrais IRL 6 F3
Doische B 19 D10
Dojč SK 146 D4
Dojkinci SRB 165 C6
Dokka N 101 E12
Dokkas S 116 D6
Dokkedal DK 86 B6
Dokkum NL 16 B5
Doksy CZ 76 B6
Doksy CZ 81 E7
Doktor Yosifovo BG 165 C7
Dokupe LV 134 B3
Dolanog GB 10 F5
Dolbenmaen GB 10 F3
Dolceacqua I 37 D7
Dol-de-Bretagne F 23 C8
Dole BIH 157 D10
Dole F 26 F3
Dølemo N 90 B3
Dolenci NMK 168 B5
Dolenja Vas SLO 73 E10
Dolenjske Toplice SLO 73 E11
Dolgarrog GB 10 E4
Dolgellau GB 10 F4
Dolgen D 84 D4
Dolgorukovo RUS 136 E2
Dolhan TR 167 F8
Dolhasca RO 153 C9
Dolheşti RO 153 C9
Dolheşti RO 153 D11
Dołhobyczów PL 144 B9
Dolianova I 64 E3
Dolice PL 85 D8
Dolichi GR 169 D7
Doljani BIH 157 E8
Doljani HR 156 D5
Doljevac SRB 164 C4
Dolla IRL 8 C6
Dolle D 79 B10
Dollern D 82 C7
Döllnitz D 79 D11
Dollnstein D 75 E9
Dollon F 24 D4
Dolna MD 154 C2
Dolna Banya BG 165 E8
Dolna Dikanya BG 165 E7
Dolna Gradeshnitsa BG 165 F7
Dolnaja LV 135 D12
Dolná Krupá SK 146 E5
Dolna Lipnitska BG 166 C4
Dolna Makhala BG 165 E10
Dolna Melna BG 164 D6
Dolna Mitropoliya BG 165 C10
Dolna Oryakhovitsa BG 166 C5
Dolná Strehová SK 147 E8
Dolná Súča SK 146 D6
Dolná Tižina SK 147 C7
Dolna Vasilitsa BG 165 E8
Dolné Orešany SK 146 E4
Dolné Vestenice SK 146 D6
Dolní Bousov CZ 77 B8
Dolní Bukovsko CZ 77 D7
Dolní Čermná CZ 77 C11
Dolni Chiflik BG 167 D9
Dolní Dobrouč CZ 77 C11
Dolni Dŭbnik BG 165 C9
Dolní Dvořiště CZ 77 E6
Dolni Glavanak BG 166 F5
Dolní Kounice CZ 77 D10
Dolni Lom BG 165 C6
Dolní Loučky CZ 77 D10
Dolní Němčí CZ 146 D5
Dolní Podluží CZ 81 E7
Dolní Újezd CZ 77 C10
Dolní Újezd CZ 146 B5
Dolni Voden BG 165 E10
Dolní Šandov CZ 75 B12
Dolno Dupeni NMK 168 C5
Dolno Ezerovo BG 167 D8
Dolno Kamartsi BG 165 D8
Dolno Konjare NMK 164 F4
Dolno Levski BG 165 E9
Dolno Osenovo BG 165 F7
Dolno Selo BG 164 E5
Dolno Tserovene BG 159 F11
Dolno Uyno BG 164 E6
Dolný Hričov SK 147 C7
Dolný Kubín SK 147 C8
Dolný Pial SK 146 E6
Dolný Štál SK 146 F5
Dolo I 66 B5
Dolomieu F 31 D8
Dolores E 56 E3
Dolovo SRB 159 D6
Dölsach A 73 C6
Dolsk PL 81 C12
Dołubowo PL 141 E7
Dolus-d'Oléron F 28 D3
Dolyna UA 145 F8
Dolynivka UA 154 A5
Dolyns'ke UA 154 B5
Dolzhitsy RUS 132 D5
Domaháza H 147 E10
Domaniewice PL 141 G2
Domaniewice PL 143 B8
Domanín CZ 146 C4
Domaradz PL 144 D4
Domart-en-Ponthieu F 18 D5
Domaševo BIH 162 D5
Domašinec HR 149 D7
Domaşnea RO 159 C9
Domaszek H 150 E5
Domaszków PL 77 B11
Domaszowice PL 142 D4
Domat Ems CH 71 D8
Domats F 25 D9
Domažlice CZ 76 D3
Dombås N 101 B10
Dombasle-en-Xaintois F 26 D4
Dombasle-sur-Meurthe F 186 D1
Dombegyház H 151 E7
Dombóvár H 149 D10
Dombrád H 145 G4
Dombresson CH 31 A10
Domburg NL 16 E1
Domegge di Cadore I 72 D5
Domeikava LT 137 D8
Domène F 31 E8
Domeniko GR 169 E7
Domérat F 29 C11
Domèvre-en-Haye F 26 C4
Domèvre-sur-Vezouze F 27 C6
Domfront F 23 C10
Domgermain F 26 C4
Dominće HR 162 D3
Domingo Pérez E 46 E4
Dömitz D 83 D10
Domlyan BG 165 D10
Dommartin-le-Franc F 26 D2
Dommartin-Varimont F 25 C12
Domme F 29 F8
Dommershausen D 21 D8
Dommitzsch D 80 C3
Domneşti RO 160 C5
Domneşti RO 161 E7
Domnitsa GR 174 B4
Domnovo RUS 136 E2
Domodossola I 68 A5
Domokos GR 174 A5
Domont F 25 B7
Domoroc RKS 164 D4
Dömös H 149 A11
Domoszló H 147 F10
Dompcevrin F 26 C3
Dompierre-les-Ormes F 30 C5
Dompierre-sur-Besbre F 30 B4
Dompierre-sur-Mer F 28 C3
Dompierre-sur-Yon F 28 B3
Domrémy-la-Pucelle F 26 D4
Dömsöd H 150 C3
Domsühl D 83 D11
Domus de Maria I 64 F2
Domusnovas I 64 E2
Domvaina GR 175 C6
Domžale SLO 73 D10
Donagh GB 7 D8
Donaghadee GB 4 F5
Donaghmore GB 7 C9
Donaghmore IRL 7 F10
Don Álvaro E 51 B7
Doña Mencía E 53 A8
Donard IRL 7 F9
Donaueschingen D 27 E9
Donauwörth D 75 E8
Don Benito E 51 B8
Doncaster GB 11 D9
Donchery F 19 E10
Donduşeni MD 153 A11
Donegal IRL 6 C6
Doneraile IRL 8 D5
Doneztebe E 32 D2
Dønfoss N 100 C8
Dongen NL 16 E3
Donges F 23 F7
Dongo I 69 A7
Donici MD 154 C3
Doñinos de Salamanca E 45 C9
Donja Banya BG 165 E8
Donja Bela Reka SRB 159 E9
Donja Brela HR 157 F6
Donja Bukovica MNE 163 C7
Donja Dubrava HR 149 D7
Donja Kupčina HR 148 E5
Donja Lepenica BIH 157 B8
Donja Mahala BIH 157 B10
Donja Motičina HR 149 F10
Donja Šatornja SRB 158 E6
Donja Stubica HR 148 E5
Donja Višnjica HR 148 D6
Donja Vrijeska HR 149 E8
Donja Zelina HR 148 E6
Donje Pazarište HR 67 C11
Donjeux F 26 D3
Donji Andrijevci HR 157 B9
Donji Čaglić HR 149 F8
Donji Dubovnik BIH 156 C5
Donji Dušnik SRB 164 C5
Donji Kosinj HR 156 C3
Donji Krčin SRB 159 F7
Donji Krivodol SRB 165 C6
Donji Lapac HR 156 C4
Donji Miholjac HR 149 E10
Donji Milanovac SRB 159 E9
Donji Proložac HR 157 F7
Donji Rujani BIH 157 E6
Donji Seget HR 156 E5
Donji Srb HR 156 D5
Donji Striževac SRB 164 C5
Donji Svilaj BIH 157 B9
Donji Vakuf BIH 157 D7
Donji Vijačani BIH 157 C8
Donji Zemunik HR 156 D3
Donji Širovac HR 156 B5
Donk NL 183 B7
Donkerbroek NL 16 B6
Donnalucata I 59 F6
Donnas I 68 B4
Donnemarie-Dontilly F 25 D9
Donnersbach A 73 B9
Donnersdorf D 75 C7
Donohill IRL 8 C6
Donori I 64 E3
Donostia E 32 D2
Donskoye RUS 139 A8
Donville-les-Bains F 23 C8
Donzdorf D 74 E6
Donzenac F 29 E9
Donzère F 35 B8
Donzy F 25 F9
Dooagh IRL 6 E2
Doochary IRL 6 C6
Dooish GB 4 F2
Doolin IRL 6 F4
Doon IRL 8 C6
Doonbeg IRL 8 C3
Doorn NL 16 D4
Doornspijk NL 183 A7
Dopiewo PL 81 B11
Đorče Petrov NMK 164 E3
Dorchester GB 13 D10
Dørdal N 90 B5
Dordives F 25 D8
Dordrecht NL 16 E3
Dore-l'Église F 30 E4
Dörentrup D 17 D12
Dores GB 3 L8
Dorfen D 75 F11
Dorfgastein A 73 B7
Dorfmark D 82 E7
Dorf Mecklenburg D 83 C10
Dorf Zechlin D 83 D13
Dorgali I 64 C4
Dorgoş RO 151 E8
Dorio GR 174 E4
Dorking GB 15 E8
Dorkovo BG 165 E9
Dorlisheim F 186 D3
Dormagen D 21 B7
Dormánd H 150 B5
Dormans F 25 B10
Dor Mărunt RO 161 E9
Dorna-Arini RO 152 C6
Dorna Candrenilor RO 152 C6
Dornava SLO 148 D5
Dörnberg (Habichtswald) D 17 F12
Dornbirn A 71 C9
Dornburg (Saale) D 79 D10
Dornburg-Frickhofen D 185 C9
Dornbusch D 17 A12
Dorndorf D 79 E7
Dorndorf-Steudnitz D 79 D10
Dornelas P 38 E4
Dornes F 30 B3
Dorneşti RO 153 B8
Dornhan D 187 E6
Dornie GB 2 L5
Dornişoara RO 152 C6
Dörnitz D 79 B11
Dorno I 69 C6
Dornoch GB 3 K8
Dornstadt D 74 F6
Dornstetten D 27 D9
Dornum D 17 A8
Dornumersiel D 17 A8
Dorobanţu RO 155 D2
Dorobanţu RO 161 E9
Dorog H 149 A11
Dorogháza H 147 F9
Dorohoi RO 153 B8
Dorohusk PL 141 H9
Dorolţ RO 151 B10
Dorotcaia MD 154 C4
Dorotea S 107 C10
Dörpen D 17 C8
Dorras N 112 D8
Dorris S 107 B9
Dorstadt D 79 B8
Dorsten D 17 E7
Dorstfeld D 185 A7
Dortan F 31 C8
Dortmund D 17 E8
Dörtepe TR 177 E10
Doruchów PL 142 D5
Dorum D 17 A11
Dorupe LV 134 C7
Dörverden D 17 C12
Dörzbach D 74 D6
Dos Aguas E 48 F3
Dosbarrios E 46 E6
Dos Hermanas E 51 E8
Dospat BG 165 F9
Dossenheim D 21 F11
Doştat RO 152 F3
Dos Torres E 54 C3
Døstrup DK 86 E3
Dotnuva LT 134 F7
Dotternhausen D 27 D10
Döttingen CH 27 E9
Douai F 19 D7
Douarnenez F 22 D3
Doubrava CZ 147 B7
Doubravice nad Svitavou CZ 77 D11
Doubs F 31 B9
Douchy F 25 E9
Douchy-les-Mines F 19 D7
Doucier F 31 B8
Doudeville F 18 E2
Doudleby nad Orlicí CZ 77 B10
Doué-la-Fontaine F 23 F11
Douglas GB 5 D9
Douglas GBM 10 C3
Douglas IRL 8 E6
Douglas Bridge GB 4 F2
Doulaincourt-Saucourt F 26 D3
Doulevant-le-Château F 25 D12
Doullens F 18 D5
Dounaiika GR 174 D3
Doune GB 5 C8
Dounreay GB 3 H9
Dour B 19 D8
Dourdan F 24 C7
Dourgne F 33 D10
Douriez F 18 D4
Doussard F 31 D9
Douvaine F 31 C9
Douvres-la-Délivrande F 23 B11
Douzy F 19 E11
Dovadola I 66 D4
Dover GB 15 E11
Dovhe UA 145 G7
Döviken S 103 A9
Dovilai LT 134 E2
Dovre N 101 C10
Dowally GB 5 B9
Downham Market GB 11 F12
Downpatrick GB 7 D11
Downton GB 13 D11
Dowra IRL 6 D6
Dowsby GB 11 F11
Doxato GR 171 B6
Doyet F 30 C2
Doyrentsi BG 165 C10
Dozulé F 23 B11
Drabeši LV 135 B10
Drâby DK 86 C7
Dračevo BIH 162 D5
Dračevo NMK 164 F4
Drachhausen D 80 C6
Drachselsried D 76 D4
Drachten NL 16 B6
Drag N 105 B10
Drag N 111 D11
Dragacz PL 138 C6
Dragalijevac BIH 157 C11
Dragalina RO 161 E10
Dragalovci BIH 157 C8
Drăgăneşti RO 151 D9
Drăgăneşti RO 153 F10
Drăgăneşti RO 161 D8
Drăgăneşti de Vede RO 160 E6
Drăgăneşti-Olt RO 160 E5
Drăgăneşti-Vlaşca RO 161 E7
Draganići HR 148 E5
Draganovo BG 166 C5
Drăganu RO 160 D5
Drăgăşani RO 160 D4
Dragash RKS 163 E10
Dragatuš SLO 67 A11
Drage D 83 D8
Drage HR 156 E4
Drăgeşti RO 151 D9
Drăghiceni RO 160 E4
Draginac SRB 158 D3
Draginje SRB 158 D4
Draginovo BG 165 E8
Dragland N 111 C11
Dragnes N 111 C10
Dragnić BIH 157 D7
Dragobi AL 163 E8
Dragočaj BIH 157 C7
Dragocvet SRB 159 F7
Dragodana RO 160 D6
Drăgoeşti RO 160 D4
Drăgoeşti RO 161 D9
Dragoevo BG 167 C7
Dragoevo NMK 164 F5
Drăgoieşti RO 153 B8
Dragoman BG 165 D6
Dragomance NMK 164 E4
Dragomir BG 165 E9
Dragomireşti RO 152 B4
Dragomireşti RO 153 C9
Dragomireşti RO 153 D10
Dragomireşti RO 160 D6
Dragomirovo BG 166 B4
Dragoni I 60 A2
Dragør DK 87 D11
Dragoš NMK 168 C5
Dragoslavele RO 160 C6
Dragoş Vodă RO 161 E10
Drăgoteşti RO 159 D11
Drăgoteşti RO 160 E4
Dragotina HR 156 B5
Dragović HR 149 F8
Dragovishtitsa BG 165 E6
Dragoychintsi BG 164 D5
Dragoynovo BG 166 F4
Dragsfjärd FIN 126 E7
Draguignan F 36 D4
Drăguşeni RO 153 A9
Drăguşeni RO 153 C8
Drăguşeni RO 153 F11
Drăguţeşti RO 159 D11
Drahnsdorf D 80 C5
Drahovce SK 146 D5
Drahove UA 145 G8
Drahovica Donja BIH 157 C9
Drajna RO 161 C8
Draka BG 167 E8
Drakenburg D 17 C12
Draksenič BIH 157 B6
Dralfa BG 167 C6
Drama GR 170 B6
Drammen N 95 C12
Drănceni RO 153 D12
Drange N 94 F5
Drangedal N 90 A5
Drangstedt D 17 A11
Drănic RO 160 E3
Dranse D 83 D13
Dransfeld D 78 D6
Dranske D 84 A4
Draperstown GB 4 F3
Drasenhofen A 77 E11
Draßmarkt A 149 A6
Drávafok H 149 E9
Dravagen S 102 B6
Draviskos GR 170 C5
Dravograd SLO 73 C11
Drawno PL 85 D9
Drawsko PL 85 E10
Drawsko Pomorskie PL 85 C9
Drayton GB 15 B11
Drążdżewo PL 139 D11
Dražen Vrh SLO 148 C5
Draževac SRB 158 D5
Dražgoše SLO 73 D9
Drebber D 17 C10
Drebkau D 80 C6
Drégelypalánk H 147 E8
Dreieich D 21 D11
Dreileben D 79 B9
Dreis D 21 E7
Drelów PL 141 G7
Drelsdorf D 82 A6
Drem GB 5 C11
Drenchia I 73 D8
Drenovac SRB 159 F7
Drenovci HR 157 C10
Drenovë AL 168 C4
Drenovets BG 159 F10
Drenovicë AL 168 C2
Drenovo NMK 164 F4
Drenovo NMK 169 B6
Drense D 84 D5
Drensteinfurt D 17 E9
Drenta BG 166 D5
Drentwede D 17 C11
Drepano GR 169 D6
Drepano GR 175 D6
Dresden D 80 D5
Dretun' BY 133 E6
Dretyń PL 85 B11
Dreumel NL 183 B6
Dreux F 24 C5
Dreverna LT 134 E2
Drevja N 108 E5
Drevjesætra N 102 D4
Dřevohostice CZ 146 C5
Drevsjø N 102 C3
Drevvatn N 108 D5
Drewitz D 79 B11
Drewnica PL 138 B6
Drezdenko PL 85 E9
Drežnica BIH 157 E8
Drežnik SRB 158 F4
Dricēni LV 133 C2
Dridu RO 161 D8
Driebergen NL 16 D4
Driebes E 47 D6
Driedorf D 185 C9
Drienov SK 145 E3
Drietoma SK 146 D5
Driffield GB 11 C11
Drimmo IRL 7 F7
Drimnin GB 4 B5
Drimoleague IRL 8 E4
Drinić BIH 156 C5
Drinjača BIH 157 D11
Drinovci BIH 157 F7
Dripsey IRL 8 E5
Drisht AL 163 E8
Dříteň CZ 76 D6
Drithas AL 168 C4
Driva N 101 A11
Drivstua N 101 B11
Drmno SRB 159 D7
Drnholec CZ 77 E11
Drniš HR 156 E5
Drnje HR 149 D7
Drnovice CZ 77 D11
Drnovice CZ 77 D11
Dro I 69 B10
Drøbak N 95 C13
Drobeta-Turnu Severin RO 159 D10
Drobin PL 139 E8
Drochia MD 153 A11
Drochtersen D 17 A12
Drogheda IRL 7 E10
Drohiczyn PL 141 F7
Drohobych UA 145 E8
Droichead Abhann IRL 8 C5
Droichead Átha IRL 7 E10
Droichead na Bandan IRL 8 E5
Droichead Nua IRL 7 F9
Droitwich Spa GB 13 A10
Drolshagen D 185 B8
Drolsum N 95 B12
Dromara GB 7 D10
Dromina IRL 8 D5
Drommahane IRL 8 D5
Drömme S 107 E14
Dromod IRL 7 E7
Dromore GB 7 C8
Dromore GB 7 D10
Dromore West IRL 6 D5
Dronero I 37 C6
Dronfield GB 11 E9
Drongan GB 5 E8
Drongen B 182 C3
Dronninglund DK 86 A6
Dronrijp NL 16 B5
Dronten NL 16 C5
Dropla BG 155 F2
Drosato GR 169 B8
Drosbacken S 102 C3
Drosendorf A 77 E9
Drosia GR 175 C8
Drösing A 77 E11
Drosopigi GR 168 C5
Droué F 24 D5
Droyßig D 79 D11
Drugan BG 165 E7
Drugovo NMK 168 B4
Druid GB 10 F5
Druimdrishaig GB 4 D5
Drulingen F 27 C7
Drumandoora IRL 6 G5
Drumanespick IRL 7 E8
Drumatober IRL 6 F6
Drumbeg GB 2 J6
Drumbilla IRL 7 D10
Drumcard GB 7 D7
Drumcollogher IRL 8 D5
Drumcondra IRL 7 E9
Drumconrath IRL 7 E9
Drumcree IRL 7 E8
Drumettaz-Clarafond F 31 D8
Drumevo BG 167 C8
Drumfree IRL 4 E2
Drumkeeran IRL 6 D6
Drumlea IRL 7 D7
Drumlish IRL 7 E7
Drumlithie GB 5 B12
Drummin IRL 9 D9
Drummore GB 4 F7
Drumnadrochit GB 2 L8
Drumquin GB 4 F2
Drumshanbo IRL 6 D6
Drung IRL 7 D8
Drusenheim F 27 C8
Druskininkai LT 137 F9
Drusti LV 135 B11
Druten NL 183 B7
Druviena LV 135 B12
Druya BY 133 E2
Druyes-les-Belles-Fontaines F 25 E9
Druysk BY 133 E2
Družbice PL 143 D7
Druzhba RUS 136 E3
Druzhnaya Gorka RUS 132 C7
Družstevná pri Hornáde SK 145 F3
Drvenik HR 157 F7
Drwalew PL 141 G4
Drwinia PL 143 F9
Dryanovets BG 161 F8
Dryanovo BG 166 D4
Dryazhno RUS 132 E4
Drygały PL 139 C13
Drymaia GR 175 B6
Drymen GB 5 C8
Drymos GR 169 C8
Dryna N 100 A5
Dryopida GR 175 E9
Dryos GR 176 E5
Drysvyaty BY 135 E13
Dryszczów PL 144 A8
Drzewce PL 142 B6
Drzewiany PL 85 C11
Drzewica PL 141 H2
Drzonowo PL 85 C11
Drzycim PL 138 C5
Duagh IRL 8 D4
Dualchi I 64 C2
Dually IRL 9 C7
Duas Igrejas P 39 F7
Dub SRB 158 F4
Dubá CZ 77 A7
Dubăsari MD 154 C4
Dubăsarii Vechi MD 154 C4
Duba Stonska HR 162 D4
Dubău MD 154 C4
Dubeczno PL 141 H8
Düben D 79 C11
Duben D 80 C5
Dübendorf CH 27 F10
Dubeņi LV 134 D2
Dubeninki PL 136 E6
Dubí CZ 80 E5
Dubičiai LT 137 E10
Dubicko CZ 77 C11
Dubicze Cerkiewne PL 141 E8
Dubidze PL 143 D7
Dubiecko PL 144 D5
Dubienka PL 144 A8
Dubingiai LT 137 C11
Dubino I 69 A7
Dubivka UA 153 A8
Dublin IRL 7 F10
Dublje SRB 158 D4
Dublovice CZ 76 C6
Dublyany UA 144 D9
Dublyany UA 145 E7
Dubna LV 135 D13
Dub nad Moravou CZ 146 C4
Dubňany CZ 77 E12
Dubnica nad Váhom SK 146 D6
Dubník SK 146 F6
Dubošbica BIH 157 D9
Dubova RO 159 D9
Dubovac SRB 159 D7
Dubove UA 145 G8
Dŭbovets BG 166 F5
Dubovica SK 145 E2
Dŭbovo BG 166 D5
Dubovo SRB 164 C4
Dubovsko BIH 156 C5
Dubrava BIH 157 C8
Dubrava HR 149 E7
Dubrave BIH 157 C10
Dubrave BIH 157 D6
Dubrave BIH 157 D10
Dubravica BIH 157 D8
Dubravica HR 148 E5
Dubravica SRB 159 D7
Dúbravy SK 147 D8
Dubrawka BY 133 F6
Dubrovka RUS 129 F14
Dubrovka RUS 132 F6
Dubrovka RUS 133 D5
Dubrovnik HR 162 D5
Dubrovytsya UA 144 D8
Dubuļi LV 133 D3
Dubynove UA 154 A6
Ducey F 23 C9
Ducherow D 84 C5
Duchov CZ 80 E5
Duck End GB 15 D9
Duclair F 18 F2
Duda-Epureni RO 153 D12
Dudar H 149 B9
Duddo GB 5 D12
Dudelange L 20 F6
Dudeldorf D 21 E7
Duderstadt D 79 C7
Dudeşti RO 161 D10
Dudestii Vechi RO 150 E5
Dudince SK 147 E7
Düdingen CH 31 B11
Dudley GB 11 F7
Dudovica SRB 158 E5
Dueñas E 40 E2
Duesund N 100 E2
Dueville I 72 E4
Duffel B 19 B10
Dufftown GB 3 L10
Duga Poljana SRB 163 C9
Duga Resa HR 148 F5
Dugi Rat HR 156 F6
Dugny-sur-Meuse F 26 B3
Dugopolje HR 156 E6
Dugo Selo HR 148 E6
Düğüncübaşi TR 173 B7
Duhort-Bachen F 32 C5
Duino I 73 E8
Duirinish GB 2 L5
Duisburg D 17 F7
Dukas AL 168 C2
Dukat AL 168 D2
Dukat i Ri AL 168 D1

Dukla PL 145 D4
Dūkštas LT 135 E12
Dŭlbok Dol BG 165 D10
Dŭlboki BG 166 E5
Dŭlbok Izvor BG 166 E4
Dulceşti RO 153 D9
Duleek IRL 7 E10
Dŭlgodeltsi BG 160 F2
Dŭlgopol BG 167 C8
Dulina BY 133 F2
Duljci BIH 157 D7
Dullingham GB 15 C9
Dülmen D 17 E8
Dulnain Bridge GB 3 L9
Dulovce SK 146 F6
Dulovka RUS 133 A4
Dulovo BG 161 F10
Dulverton GB 13 C7
Dumbarton GB 4 D7
Dumbrava RO 151 F9
Dumbrava RO 159 D11
Dumbrava RO 161 D8
Dumbrava Roşie RO 153 D8
Dumbrăveni RO 152 E5
Dumbrăveni RO 153 B8
Dumbrăveni RO 155 F1
Dumbrăveni RO 161 B10
Dumbrăveşti RO 161 C7
Dumbrăviţa RO 151 F7
Dumbrăviţa RO 152 B3
Dumbrăviţa RO 153 F6
Dumbría E 38 B1
Dumeşti RO 153 C10
Dumeşti RO 153 D10
Dumfries GB 5 E9
Dumitra RO 152 C4
Dumitreşti RO 161 B9
Dummerstorf D 83 C12
Dumnicë e Poshtme RKS 164 D3
Dümpelfeld D 21 D7
Dun F 33 D9
Duna N 105 B11
Dunaegyháza H 149 C11
Dunaföldvár H 149 C11
Dunaharaszti H 150 C3
Dunajská Lužná SK 146 E4
Dunajská Streda SK 146 F5
Dunakeszi H 150 B3
Dunalka LV 134 C2
Dún an Rí IRL 7 E9
Dunapataj H 150 D3
Dunărea RO 155 E2
Dunaszeg H 149 A9
Dunaszekcső H 149 D11
Dunaszentbenedek H 149 C11
Dunaszentgyörgy H 149 C11
Dunasziget H 146 F4
Dunatetétlen H 150 D3
Dunaújváros H 149 C11
Dunava LV 135 D12
Dunavarsány H 150 C3
Dunavecse H 150 D2
Dunavtsi BG 159 F10
Dunbar GB 5 C11
Dunbeath GB 3 J10
Dunblane GB 5 C9
Dunboyne IRL 7 F10
Dún Búinne IRL 7 F10
Duncannon IRL 9 D9
Dún Chaoin IRL 8 D2
Dunchurch GB 13 A12
Duncormick IRL 9 D9
Dundaga LV 134 A4
Dundalk IRL 7 D10
Dún Dealgan IRL 7 D10
Dun Dealgan IRL 7 D10
Dundee GB 5 C11
Dunderland N 108 D8
Dundonald GB 7 C11
Dundreggan GB 2 L7
Dundrennan GB 5 F9
Dundrum GB 7 D11
Dundrum IRL 8 C6
Dunecht GB 3 L12
Dunes F 33 B7
Dunfanaghy IRL 7 B7
Dunfermline GB 5 C10
Dungannon GB 7 C9
Dún Garbhán IRL 9 D7
Dungarvan IRL 9 C8
Dungarvan IRL 9 D7
Düngenheim D 185 D7
Dungiven GB 4 F3
Dungloe IRL 6 C6
Dungourney IRL 8 E6
Dunholme GB 11 E11
Dunicë AL 168 C4
Dunières F 30 E5
Duninowo PL 85 A11
Dunje NMK 169 B6
Dunkeld GB 5 B9
Dunkerque F 18 B5
Dunkerrin IRL 9 C7
Dunkitt IRL 9 D8
Dún Laoghaire IRL 7 F10
Dunlavin IRL 7 F9
Dunleer IRL 7 E10
Dún Léire IRL 7 E10
Dun-le-Palestel F 29 C9
Dun-les-Places F 25 F11
Dunlop GB 4 D7
Dunloy GB 4 E4
Dún Mánmhaí IRL 8 E4
Dunmanway IRL 8 E4
Dún Mór IRL 9 D9
Dunmore IRL 6 E5
Dunmore East IRL 9 D9
Dunmurry GB 7 C11
Dunnamanagh GB 4 F2
Dún na nGall IRL 6 C6
Dunning GB 5 C9
Dunoon GB 4 D7
Dunquin IRL 8 D2
Duns GB 5 D12
Dunscore GB 5 E9
Dünsen D 17 C11
Dunshaughlin IRL 7 E9
Dunstable GB 15 D7
Dunster GB 13 C8
Dun-sur-Auron F 29 B11
Dun-sur-Meuse F 19 F11
Dunure GB 4 E7
Dunvant GB 12 B6
Dunvegan GB 2 L3
Duplica SLO 73 D10
Dupnitsa BG 165 E7
Durach D 71 B10
Durak TR 173 E9
Durana E 41 C6
Durance F 33 B6
Durango E 41 B6
Durankulak BG 155 F3
Duras F 33 A6
Durbach D 27 C9
Durban-Corbières F 34 E4
Durbe LV 134 C2
Durbuy B 184 D3
Dúrcal E 53 C9
Durdat-Larequille F 29 C11
Đurđenovac HR 149 E10
Đurđevac HR 149 D8
Đurđevića Tara MNE 163 C7
Đurđevik BIH 157 D10
Đurđevo SRB 158 C5
Đurđevo SRB 159 E6
Düren D 20 C6
Durfort F 35 C6
Durham GB 5 F13
Ďurkov SK 145 F3
Durlas IRL 9 C7
Durleşti MD 154 C3
Durmanec HR 148 D5
Dürmentingen D 71 A9
Durmersheim D 27 C9
Durness GB 2 H7
Durneşti RO 153 B10
Dürnkrut A 77 F11
Durrës AL 168 B1
Durrington GB 13 C11
Dürrlauingen D 75 F7
Durrow IRL 9 C8
Durrus IRL 8 E3
Dürrwangen D 75 D7
Dursley GB 13 B10
Dursunbey TR 173 E10
Durtal F 23 E11
Duruelo de la Sierra E 40 E6
Duruitoarea MD 153 B10
Durup DK 86 B3
Durusu TR 173 B10
Dusetos LT 135 E11
Dushk i Madh AL 168 C2
Dusina BIH 157 E8
Dŭskotna BG 167 D8
Duškovci SRB 158 F5
Dusmenys LT 137 E9
Dusnok H 150 E2
Dusocin PL 138 C6
Düsseldorf D 21 B7
Dussen NL 16 E3
Dußlingen D 187 E7
Düßnitz D 79 C12
Duszniki PL 81 B10
Dutluca TR 173 E11
Dutovlje SLO 73 E8
Duvberg S 102 B7
Duved S 105 E13
Düvertepe TR 173 F9
Duži BIH 162 D5
Dvärsätt S 106 E6
Dvaryshcha BY 133 E6
Dve Mogili BG 161 F7
Dverberg N 111 B10
Dviete LV 135 D12
Dvirtsi UA 144 C9
Dvor HR 156 B5
Dvorce CZ 146 B5
Dvornaye Syalo BY 133 E3
Dvorníky SK 146 E5
Dvory nad Šitavou SK 146 F6
Dvůr Králové CZ 77 B9
Dwikozy PL 144 B4
Dwingeloo NL 16 C6
Dyan GB 7 D9
Dyankovo BG 161 F9
Dybvad DK 90 E7
Dyce GB 3 L12
Dychów PL 81 C8
Dydnia PL 144 D5
Dyfjord N 113 B19
Dygowo PL 85 B9
Dyke GB 3 K9
Dykehead GB 5 B11
Dykhtynets' UA 152 A6
Dylągówka PL 144 D5
Dylaki PL 142 E5
Dylewo PL 139 D11
Dymchurch GB 15 E10
Dymock GB 13 B10
Dynäs S 107 F13
Dynivtsi UA 153 A8
Dynów PL 144 D5
Dyo F 30 C5
Dyping N 110 E9
Dyrnes N 104 E3
Dyrøyhamn N 111 B13
Dyrrachi GR 174 E5
Dyulevo BG 167 E8
Dyulino BG 167 D9
Dyviziya UA 154 F5
Dywity PL 136 F1
Dzeguzēni LV 134 D6
Dzelzava LV 135 C12
Dzeņi LV 135 B12
Dzērbene LV 135 B11
Dzhebel BG 171 A8
Dzherman BG 165 E7
Dzhulynka UA 154 A5
Dzhulyunitsa BG 166 C5
Dzhuriv UA 152 A6
Dzhurovo BG 165 D9
Dziadkowice PL 141 E7
Dziadowa Kłoda PL 142 D4
Działdowo PL 139 D9
Działoszyce PL 143 F9
Działoszyn PL 142 D6
Działyń PL 138 D7
Dziemiany PL 138 B4
Dziergowice PL 142 F5
Dzierzążnia PL 139 E9
Dzierżążno Wielkie PL 85 E10
Dzierzgoń PL 139 C7
Dzierzgowo PL 139 D10
Dzierzkowice-Rynek PL 144 B5
Dzierżoniów PL 81 E11
Dzietrzniki PL 142 D6
Dzietrzychowo PL 136 E3
Dziewierzewo PL 85 E13
Džigolj SRB 164 C4
Dzirnavas LV 134 B4
Dzisna BY 133 E4
Dziwnów PL 85 B7
Dzmitravichy BY 141 F9
Džūkste LV 134 C6
Džumajlija NMK 164 F4
Dźwierzuty PL 139 C10
Dźwirzyno PL 85 B8
Dzwola PL 144 B6
Dzwonowice PL 143 E8
Dzyornavichy BY 133 E4

E

Éadan Doire IRL 7 F8
Eaglesfield GB 5 E10
Eardisley GB 13 A8
Earith GB 15 C9
Earl Shilton GB 11 F9
Earlston GB 5 D11
Earl Stonham GB 15 C11
Earsairidh GB 4 B2
Easdale GB 4 C5
Easington GB 5 F14
Easington GB 11 D12
Easingwold GB 11 C9
Easky IRL 6 D5
Eastbourne GB 15 F9
Eastburn GB 11 D11
Eastfield GB 11 C11
Eastgate GB 5 F12
East Grinstead GB 15 E8
East Harling GB 15 C10
East Kilbride GB 5 D8
Eastleigh GB 13 D12
East Linton GB 5 D11
East Looe GB 12 E6
Eastoft GB 11 D10
Easton GB 13 D10
East Retford GB 11 E10
Eastriggs GB 5 F10
Eastry GB 15 E11
East Wemyss GB 5 C10
East Wittering GB 15 F7
Eastwood GB 11 E9
Eaton Socon GB 15 C8
Eaunes F 33 D8
Eauze F 33 C6
Ebberup DK 86 E5
Ebbs A 72 A5
Ebbw Vale GB 13 B8
Ebecik TR 181 A9
Ebeleben D 79 D8
Ebelsbach D 75 C8
Ebeltoft DK 86 C7
Ebene Reichenau A 73 C8
Ebenfurth A 77 G10
Eben im Pongau A 73 B7
Ebensee A 73 A8
Ebensfeld D 75 B8
Ebenthal A 73 C9
Ebenweiler D 71 B9
Eberau A 149 B6
Eberbach D 21 F11
Ebergötzen D 79 C7
Ebermannsdorf D 75 D10
Ebermannstadt D 75 C9
Ebern D 75 B8
Eberndorf A 73 C10
Ebersbach D 80 D5
Ebersbach D 81 D7
Ebersbach an der Fils D 74 E6
Ebersberg D 75 F10
Eberschwang A 76 F5
Ebersdorf A 148 B5
Ebersdorf D 17 A12
Ebersdorf D 75 B10
Ebersmunster F 186 E4
Eberstein A 73 C10
Eberswalde-Finow D 84 E5
Ebes H 151 C8
Ebhausen D 27 C10
Ebikon CH 27 F9
Ebnat-Kappel CH 27 F11
Eboli I 60 B4
Ebrach D 75 C7
Ebreichsdorf A 77 G10
Ébreuil F 30 C3
Ebsdorfergrund-Dreihausen
D 21 C11
Ebstorf D 83 D8
Écaussinnes-d'Enghien B
182 D4
Ecclefechan GB 5 E10
Eccles GB 5 D12
Eccleshall GB 11 F7
Eceabat TR 171 D10
Echallens CH 31 B10
Echarri E 32 E2
Échauffour F 24 C3
Échenoz-la-Méline F 26 E5
Eching D 75 E11
Eching D 75 F10
Echinos GR 171 B7
Échiré F 28 C5
Échirolles F 31 E8
Échourgnac F 29 E6
Echsenbach A 77 E8
Echt GB 3 L12
Echt NL 19 B12
Echte D 79 C7
Echternach L 20 E6
Écija E 53 A6
Ečka SRB 158 C5
Eckartsberga D 79 D10
Eckbolsheim F 186 D4
Eckental D 75 C9
Eckernförde D 83 B7
Eckerö FIN 99 B13
Eckington GB 11 E9
Eckington GB 13 A10
Éclaron-Braucourt-Ste-Livière
F 25 C12
Écommoy F 23 E12
Écos F 24 B6
Écouché F 23 C11
Écouflant F 23 E10
Écouis F 18 F3
Écrouves F 26 C4
Écs H 149 A9
Ecséd H 150 B4
Ecseg H 147 F9
Ecsegfalva H 151 C6
Ecser H 150 C3
Écueillé F 29 A8
Écuisses F 30 B6
Écury-sur-Coole F 25 C11
Ed S 91 B10
Ed S 107 E12
Eda glasbruk S 96 C7
Edam NL 16 C4
Edane S 97 C8
Ēdas LV 134 C4
Eddelak D 82 C6
Edderton GB 3 K8
Eddleston GB 5 D10
Ede NL 16 D5
Ede S 103 B12
Edebäck S 97 B10
Edefors S 118 B5
Edegem B 19 B9
Edelény H 145 G2
Edelschrott A 73 B11
Edemissen D 79 B7
Eden GB 4 F5
Eden S 107 D12
Edenderry IRL 7 F8
Edenkoben D 21 F10
Edermünde D 78 D5
Ederny GB 7 C7
Edesheim D 21 F10
Edessa GR 169 C7
Edewecht D 17 B9
Edewechterdamm D 17 B9
Edgeworthstown IRL 7 E7
Edgmond GB 11 F7
Ediger-Eller D 21 D8
Edinburgh GB 5 D10
Edincik TR 173 D8
Edineţ MD 153 A10
Edirne TR 171 A11
Edland N 94 C7
Edling D 75 F11
Edlingham GB 5 E13
Edlitz A 148 A6
Edmondstown IRL 6 E5
Edmundbyers GB 5 F13
Ēdole LV 134 B3
Edolo I 69 A9
Edremit TR 173 E7
Edrosa P 39 E6
Edroso P 39 E6
Edsbro S 99 C10
Edsbruk S 93 C8
Edsbyn S 103 D10
Edsele S 107 F11
Edsken S 98 A6
Edsvalla S 97 D9
Edzell GB 5 B11
Eefde NL 183 A8
Eeklo B 19 B8
Eelde-Paterswolde NL 17 B7
Eerbeek NL 16 D6
Eernegem B 182 C2
Eersel NL 16 F4
Eferding A 76 F6
Effelder D 75 B9
Effeltrich D 75 C9
Effretikon CH 27 F10
Efkarpia GR 169 B8
Efkarpia GR 169 C10
Eforie RO 155 E3
Efpalio GR 174 C4
Efringen-Kirchen D 27 E8
Eftimie Murgu RO 159 D9
Efxeinoupoli GR 175 A6
Egby S 89 B11
Egebæk DK 86 E3
Egebjerg DK 86 D5
Egebjerg DK 87 D9
Egeln D 79 C9
Egense DK 86 B6
Eger H 145 H1
Egerbakta H 145 H1
Egernsund DK 86 F5
Egersund N 94 F4
Egerszalók H 145 H1
Egervár H 149 C7
Egeskov DK 86 D5
Egestorf D 83 D8
Egga N 111 B19
Eggby S 91 C14
Eggebek D 82 A6
Eggenburg A 77 E9
Eggenfelden D 75 F12
Eggenstein-Leopoldshafen
D 27 B9
Eggersdorf D 79 C10
Eggersdorf bei Graz A 148 B5
Eggesbønes N 100 B3
Eggesin D 84 C6
Eggingen D 27 E9
Eggiwil CH 70 D5
Egglham D 76 E4
Eggolsheim D 75 C9
Eggstätt D 72 A5
Eggum N 110 D6
Eghezée B 19 C10
Eging am See D 76 E4
Eglaine LV 135 E12
Égletons F 29 E10
Egling D 72 A4
Eglingham GB 5 E13
Eglinton GB 4 E2
Eglisau CH 27 E10
Eglish GB 7 D9
Egluciems LV 133 B2
Eglwys Fach GB 10 F4
Eglwyswrw GB 12 A5
Egmond aan Zee NL 16 C3
Egna I 69 A11
Egorovca MD 153 B11
Egremont GB 10 C4
Egsmark DK 86 C7
Egtved DK 86 D4
Éguilles F 35 C9
Eguisheim F 27 D7
Éguzon-Chantôme F 29 C9
Egyek H 151 B6
Egyházaskozár H 149 D10
Ehekirchen D 75 E9
Ehingen D 75 D8
Ehingen (Donau) D 71 A9
Ehlen (Habichtswald) D 17 F12
Ehningen D 187 D6
Ehra-Lessien D 79 A8
Ehrenberg-Wüstensachsen
D 74 B7
Ehrenburg D 17 C11
Ehrenfriedersdorf D 80 E3
Ehrenhausen A 148 C5
Ehringshausen D 21 C10
Eibar E 41 B7
Eibelstadt D 74 C7
Eibenstock D 75 B12
Eibergen NL 17 D7
Eibiswald A 148 C4
Eich D 21 E10
Eichenbarleben D 79 B9
Eichenbühl D 27 A11
Eichendorf D 76 E3
Eichenzell D 74 B6
Eichgraben A 77 F9
Eichigt D 75 B11
Eichstätt D 75 E9
Eichwalde D 80 B5
Eickendorf D 79 C10
Eicklingen D 79 A7
Eidapere EST 131 D9
Eide N 100 A6
Eide N 104 D8
Eide N 111 C11
Eidem N 108 E2
Eidet N 105 C15
Eidet N 105 C16
Eidet N 108 A9
Eidet N 110 D8
Eidfjord N 94 B6
EiŠi FO 2 A2
Eidkjosen N 111 A16
Eidsbugarden N 101 D8
Eidsdal N 100 B6
Eidsfjord N 110 C8
Eidsfoss N 95 C12
Eidshaug N 105 B10
Eidsnes N 112 C10
Eidsøra N 100 A8
Eidstranda N 111 A19
Eidsund N 94 D3
Eidsvåg N 100 A8
Eidsvoll N 95 B14
Eidsvoll Verk N 95 B14
Eidvågeid N 113 B12
Eigeltingen D 27 E10
Eigenrieden D 79 D7
Eijsden NL 183 D7
Eik N 94 D3
Eikelandsosen N 94 B3
Eiken N 94 F6
Eikesdal N 100 B8
Eikjaberg N 100 D6
Eikjeskog N 94 E4
Eikjil N 90 B1
Eiksund N 100 B3
Eilenburg D 79 D12
Eilenstedt D 79 C9
Eilsleben D 79 B9
Eime D 78 B6
Eimen D 78 C6
Eimke D 83 E8
Eina N 101 E13
Einacleit GB 2 J3
Einbeck D 78 C6
Eindhoven NL 16 F4
Einsiedeln CH 27 F10
Einville-au-Jard F 26 C5
Einvollen N 108 F3
Eisden B 183 D7
Eiselfing D 75 F11
Eisenach D 79 E7
Eisenberg D 79 E10
Eisenberg (Pfalz) D 21 E10
Eisenerz A 73 A10
Eisenhüttenstadt D 81 B7
Eisenkappel A 73 D10
Eisenstadt A 77 G11
Eisfeld D 75 B8
Eišiškės LT 137 E10
Eislandet N 100 E3
Eisleben, Lutherstadt D 79 C10
Eislingen (Fils) D 74 E6
Eisma EST 131 B12
Eitelborn D 21 D9
Eiterfeld D 78 E6
Eiternes N 105 B11
Eiterstraum N 108 E5
Eitorf D 21 C8
Eivinvik N 100 E2
Eivissa E 57 D7
Eja P 44 B4
Ejby DK 86 E5
Ejby DK 87 D9
Ejby DK 87 E10
Ejea de los Caballeros E 41 D9
Ejsing DK 86 B3
Ejstrupholm DK 86 D4
Ejulve E 42 F2
Ekeby S 87 C11
Ekeby S 92 A6
Ekeby S 99 D9
Ekeby-Almby S 97 D13
Ekedalen S 91 C14
Ekenäs FIN 127 F9
Ekenäs S 91 B13
Ekenäs S 93 B9
Ekenässjön S 92 E6
Ēkengrāve LV 135 D11
Ekeren B 182 C4
Ekerö S 99 D9
Eket S 87 C12
Ekkerøy N 114 C8
Ekmekçi TR 173 D9
Ekola FIN 122 D9
Ekorrträsk S 107 B16
Eksaarde B 182 C3
Eksel B 183 C6
Ekshärad S 97 B9
Eksjö S 92 D5
Eksta S 93 E12
Ekträsk S 118 F3
Ekzarkh-Antimovo BG 167 D7
Ekzarkh Yosif BG 161 F7
Elafos GR 169 D7
Elafotopos GR 168 E4
Elaiochori GR 171 C6
Elaionas GR 169 B10
Elaionas GR 174 B5
Elaionas GR 175 C7
El Álamo E 46 D5
El Algar E 56 F3
El Almendro E 51 D5
El Alquián E 55 F8
Elämäjärvi FIN 123 D15
El Arahal E 51 E8
El Arenal E 45 D10
Elassona GR 169 E7
El Astillero E 40 B4
Elateia GR 175 B6
Elati GR 169 E6
Elati GR 169 E6
Elatochori GR 169 D7
Elatou GR 174 B4
El Ballestero E 55 B8
El Barco de Ávila E 45 D9
El Barraco E 46 D3
Elbasan AL 168 B3
Elbergen D 17 D8
Elbeuf F 18 F3
Elbigenalp A 71 C10
Elbingerode (Harz) D 79 C8
Elbląg PL 139 B7
El Bodón E 45 D7
El Bonillo E 55 B7
El Bosque E 53 C6
El Bullaque E 46 F4
El Burgo E 53 C7
El Burgo de Ebro E 41 E10
El Burgo de Osma E 40 E5
El Burgo Ranero E 39 D9
El Buste E 41 E8
El Cabaco E 45 C8
El Cabildo y la Campana E 55 E9
El Cabo de Gata E 55 F8
El Campillo E 51 D6
El Campillo de la Jara E 45 E10
El Campo de Peñaranda
E 45 C10
El Cañavate E 47 E8
El Carpio E 53 A8
El Carpio de Tajo E 46 E4
El Casar E 46 C6
El Casar de Escalona E 46 D3
El Castellar E 48 D3
El Castillo de las Guardas
E 51 D7
El Catllar de Gaià E 43 E6
El Centenillo E 54 C5
El Cerro de Andévalo E 51 D6
Elche E 56 E3
Elche de la Sierra E 55 C8
Elchingen D 187 E9
Elciego E 41 C6
Elçili TR 172 B6
El Coronil E 51 E8
El Cubo de Don Sancho E 45 C8
El Cubo de Tierra del Vino E 39 F8
El Cuervo E 47 D10
El Cuervo E 51 F7
Elda E 56 E3
Eldalsosen N 100 D4
Eldena D 83 D10
Eldforsen S 97 B11
Eldingen D 83 E8
Eldsberga S 87 B12
Elduvík FO 2 A3
Elefsina GR 175 C8
Eleftheres GR 171 C6
Elefthero GR 168 D4
Eleftheroupoli GR 171 C6
Eleja LV 134 D7
El Ejido E 55 F7
Elek H 151 D7
Elektrėnai LT 137 D10
Elemir SRB 158 C5
Elena BG 166 D5
Elend D 79 C8
Eleousa GR 168 E4
El Escorial E 46 C4
Eleshnitsa BG 165 F8
El Espinar E 46 C4
El Estrecho E 56 F3
Elexalde E 40 B6
El Fendek MA 53 E5
Elfershausen D 187 A8
El Fresno E 46 C3
Elgå N 101 B15
El Garrobo E 51 D7
Elgershausen (Schauenburg)
D 21 B12
Elgeta E 41 B7
Elgin GB 3 K10
Elgoibar E 32 D1
Elgol GB 2 L4
El Grado E 42 C4
El Granado E 50 D5
El Grau de Borriana E 48 E4
Elgsnes N 111 C11
El Herrumblar E 47 F9
El Hito E 47 E7
El Hoyo de Pinares E 46 C4
Elia GR 178 E9
Elice I 62 B5
Elie GB 5 C11
Elika GR 178 B4
Elimäki FIN 127 D15
Eling GB 13 D12
Elini I 64 D4
Elin Pelin BG 165 D8
Elisenvaara RUS 129 C12
Eliseyna BG 165 C8
Elizondo E 32 D2
Eljas E 45 D7
Ełk PL 136 F5
Elkenroth D 185 C8
Elkhovo BG 166 D5
Elkhovo BG 167 E7
Elkšņi LV 135 D11
Ellan S 99 B11
Elland GB 11 D8
Ellefeld D 75 B11
Ellenberg D 187 C9
Ellerau D 83 C7
Ellerbek D 83 C7
Ellesmere GB 10 F6
Ellesmere Port GB 10 E6
Ellezelles B 19 C8
Ellidshøj DK 86 B5
Elling DK 90 E7
Ellingen D 75 D8
Ellington GB 5 E13
El Llano E 38 B5
Ellmau A 72 A5
Ellon GB 3 L12
Ellös S 91 C9
El Losar del Barco E 45 D9
Elloughton GB 11 D10
Ellrich D 79 C8
Ellwangen (Jagst) D 75 E7
Ellwürden D 17 B10
Elm CH 71 D8
Elm D 17 A12
Elmacik TR 167 F8
El Masroig E 42 E5
Elmen A 71 C11
Elmenhorst D 83 B12
Elmenhorst D 83 C8
Elmenhorst D 83 C9
Elmenhorst D 83 C10
El Molar E 46 C5
El Molinillo E 46 F4
El Moral E 55 D8
El Morell E 42 E6
Elmshorn D 82 C7
Elne F 34 E4
Elnesvågen N 100 A6
Elorrio E 41 B6
Elorz E 32 E2
Elos GR 178 E6
El Oso E 46 C3
Előszállás H 149 C11
Elounta GR 179 E10
Elovdol BG 165 D6
Éloyes F 26 D6
El Palmar E 56 F2
El Palo E 53 C8
El Payo E 45 D7
El Pedernoso E 47 F7
El Pedroso E 51 D8
El Pedroso de la Armuña
E 45 B10
El Peral E 47 E9
El Perdigón E 39 F8
El Perelló E 42 F5
El Perelló E 48 F4
Elpersbüttel D 82 B6
Elphin GB 2 J6
Elphin IRL 6 E6
El Picazo E 47 F8
El Pinell de Bray E 42 E5
El Piñero E 39 F8
El Pla de Santa María E 43 E6
El Pobo E 42 F2
El Pobo de Dueñas E 47 C9
El Pont d'Armentera E 43 E6
El Port E 48 E4
El Port de la Selva E 34 F5
El Prat de Llobregat E 43 E8
El Provencio E 47 F7
El Puente E 40 B5
El Puente de Arzobispo E 45 E10
El Puerto de Santa María
E 52 C4
El Real de la Jara E 51 D7
El Real de San Vicente E 46 D3
El Recuenco E 47 C8
El Robledo E 46 F4
El Rocío E 51 E7
El Romeral E 46 E6
El Rompido E 51 E5
El Ronquillo E 51 D7
El Royo E 41 E6
El Rubio E 53 B7
El Sabinar E 41 D9
El Sabinar E 55 C8
El Saler E 48 F4
El Salobral E 55 B9
Els Arcs E 42 D5
El Saucejo E 53 B6
El Saugo E 45 D7
Elsdon GB 5 E12
Elsdorf D 21 C7
Elsenborn B 20 D6
Elsendorf D 75 E10
Elsenfeld D 21 E12
El Serrat AND 33 E9
Elsfjord N 108 D6
Elsfleth D 17 B10
Elshitsa BG 165 E9
Elsloo NL 183 D7
Elsnes N 111 B19
Elsnig D 80 C3
Elsnigk D 79 C11
El Soleràs E 42 E5
Elspeet NL 16 D5
Els Prats de Rei E 43 D7
Elst NL 16 E5
Elst NL 183 B6
Elster D 79 C12
Elsterberg D 79 E11
Elsterwerda D 80 D5
Elstra D 80 D6
El Tiemblo E 46 D4
Eltmann D 75 C8
El Toboso E 47 E7
Elton GB 11 F11
Elton IRL 8 D6
El Torno E 45 D9
El Trincheto E 46 F4
El Tumbalejo E 51 E6
Eltville am Rhein D 21 D10
Elva EST 131 E12
Elvål N 101 C14
Elvanfoot GB 5 E9
Elvas P 51 B5
Elvebakken N 113 D11
Elvegard N 111 D13
Elvekrok N 113 B17
Elvelund N 112 E6
Elvemund N 113 E16
Elven F 22 E6
El Vendrell E 43 E7
El Verger E 56 D5
Elverum N 101 E15
Elvesletta N 111 D12
Elvevoll N 111 B14
Elvevollen N 111 B18
El Villar de Arnedo E 32 F1
Elvington GB 11 D10
El Viso E 54 C3
El Viso del Alcor E 51 E8
Elvnes N 114 D8
Elx E 56 E3
Elxleben D 79 D8
Ely GB 13 C8
Ely GB 15 C9
Elz D 185 D9
Elzach D 27 D9
Elze D 78 B6
Elze (Wedemark) D 78 A6
Embid E 47 C9
Embid de Ariza E 41 F8
Embleton GB 5 E13
Embrun F 36 B4
Emburga LV 135 C7
Embūte LV 134 C3
Emden D 17 B8
Emecik TR 181 C7
Emiralem TR 177 B9
Emirali TR 173 B8
Emlichheim D 17 C7
Emly IRL 8 D6
Emmaboda S 89 B9
Emmaljunga S 87 C13
Emmanouil Pappas GR 169 B10
Emmaste EST 130 D5
Emmeloord NL 16 C5
Emmelsbüll-Horsbüll D 82 A5
Emmelshausen D 21 D9
Emmen CH 27 F9
Emmen NL 17 C7
Emmendingen D 27 D8
Emmer-Compascuum
NL 17 C8
Emmerich D 16 E6
Emmoo IRL 6 E6
Emőd H 145 H2
Emolahti FIN 123 C15
Empel NL 16 E4
Empesos GR 174 A3
Empfingen D 187 E6
Empoli I 66 E2
Emponas GR 181 D7
Emporeio GR 179 C9
Emporeios GR 177 C7
Emptinne B 19 D11
Emsbüren D 17 D8
Emsdetten D 17 D9
Emsfors S 89 A10
Emskirchen D 75 C8
Emst NL 16 D5
Emstek D 17 C10
Emsworth GB 15 F7
Emtinghausen D 17 C11
Emtunga S 91 C12
Emyvale IRL 7 D9
Enafors S 105 E12
Enäjärvi FIN 128 D7
Enånger S 103 C13
Enarsvedjan S 105 D16
Encamp AND 33 E9
Encinas de Abajo E 45 C10
Encinasola E 51 C6
Encinas Reales E 53 B8
Encinedo E 39 D6
Enciso E 41 D7
Encs H 145 G3
Encsencs H 151 B9
Endingen D 27 D8
Endre S 93 D12
Endrefalva H 147 E9
Endriejavas LT 134 E3
Endrinal E 45 C9

Gittelde D 79 C7
Gittun S 109 D16
Giubega RO 160 E2
Giubiasco CH 69 A7
Giugliano in Campania I 60 B2
Giulești RO 152 B3
Giuliano di Roma I 62 D4
Giulianova I 62 B5
Giulvăz RO 159 B6
Giuncugnano I 66 D1
Giurgeni RO 155 D1
Giurgița RO 160 E3
Giurgiu RO 161 F7
Giurgiulești MD 155 C2
Giuvărăști RO 160 F5
Give DK 86 D4
Givet F 19 D10
Givors F 30 D6
Givry B 19 D9
Givry F 30 B6
Givry-en-Argonne F 25 C12
Givskud DK 86 D4
Gižai LT 136 D7
Gizałki PL 142 B4
Gizeux F 23 F12
Giżycko PL 136 E4
Gizzeria I 59 B9
Gjakovë RKS 163 E9
Gjærnes N 90 B5
Gjegjan AL 163 E9
Gjegjan AL 163 F9
Gjengstø N 104 E6
Gjerde N 100 C6
Gjerdebakken N 113 C11
Gjerdrum N 95 B14
Gjerlev DK 86 B6
Gjermungshamn N 94 B3
Gjern DK 86 C5
Gjerrild DK 87 C7
Gjerstad N 90 B5
Gjersvik N 105 B14
Gjesing DK 86 C6
Gjesvær N 113 A15
Gjevaldshaugen N 101 D15
Gjilan RKS 164 E3
Gjirokastër AL 168 D3
Gjógv FO 2 A3
Gjøl DK 86 A5
Gjøljelia N 104 D7
Gjølme N 104 E7
Gjonaj RKS 163 E10
Gjonëm AL 168 A2
Gjøra N 101 A10
Gjorm AL 168 D2
Gjøvåg N 94 B2
Gjøvik N 101 E13
Gjurakoc RKS 163 D9
Gjuvberget N 102 E3
Gkoritsa GR 175 E6
Gladbeck D 17 E7
Gladenbach D 21 C11
Gladsaxe DK 87 D10
Gladstad N 108 E2
Glainans F 26 F6
Glamis GB 5 B11
Glamoč BIH 157 D6
Glåmos N 101 A14
Glamsbjerg DK 86 E6
Glandage F 35 A10
Glandon F 29 E8
Glandore IRL 8 E4
Glandorf D 17 D10
Glanegg A 73 C9
Glanerbrug NL 17 D7
Glanshammar S 97 D13
Glanworth IRL 8 D6
Glarryford GB 4 F4
Glarus CH 71 C8
Glasbury GB 13 A8
Glasgow GB 5 D8
Gläshütten D 21 D10
Glashütten D 75 C9
Glaslough IRL 7 D9
Glassan IRL 7 F7
Glastonbury GB 13 C9
Glaubitz D 80 D4
Glauchau D 79 E12
Glava BG 165 C9
Glava S 97 C8
Glava glasbruk S 96 C7
Glavan BG 166 E6
Glăvănești RO 153 E10
Glavanovtsi BG 164 D6
Glavatićevo BIH 157 F9
Glavice HR 157 E6
Glavičice BIH 157 C11
Glăvile RO 160 D4
Glavinitsa BG 161 F9
Glavki GR 171 B7
Gleann Cholm Cille IRL 6 C5
Gleann Doimhin IRL 7 C7
Gleann na Muaidhe IRL 6 D3
Gleđica SRB 163 C9
Glein N 108 D4
Gleina D 79 D10
Gleisdorf A 148 B5
Gleizé F 30 D6
Glejbjerg DK 86 D3
Glemsford GB 15 C10
Glen S 102 A6
Glenade IRL 6 D6
Glenamaddy IRL 6 E5
Glenamoy IRL 6 D3
Glenariff GB 4 E4
Glenarm GB 4 F5
Glenavy GB 7 C10
Glenbarr GB 4 D5
Glenbeg GB 4 B5
Glenbeigh IRL 8 D3
Glencaple GB 5 E9
Glencar IRL 6 D6
Glencoe GB 4 B6
Glencolumbkille IRL 6 C5
Glendowan IRL 7 C7
Gleneagles GB 5 C9
Glenealy IRL 7 G10
Gleneely IRL 4 E2
Glenegedale GB 4 D4
Glenelg GB 2 L5
Glenfield GB 11 F9
Glenfinnan GB 4 B6
Glengarriff IRL 8 E3
Glengavlen IRL 7 D7
Glenhead GB 4 E2
Glenluce GB 4 F7
Glenmore IRL 9 D8
Glenoe GB 4 F5
Glenrothes GB 5 C10
Glenties IRL 6 C6
Glère F 27 F6
Glesborg DK 87 C7
Gletsch CH 71 D6
Glewitz D 84 B3
Glibaći MNE 163 C7
Glimåkra S 88 C6
Glimboca RO 159 C9
Glin IRL 8 C4
Glina HR 148 F6
Glina RO 161 E8
Glinde D 83 C8
Glindow D 79 B12
Glinjeni MD 153 B11
Glinojeck PL 139 E9
Glinsce IRL 6 F3
Glinsk IRL 6 F3
Glinton GB 11 F11
Glissjöberg S 102 B7
Gliwice PL 142 F6
Gllamnik RKS 164 D3
Globoçicë RKS 164 E3
Glogoc RKS 163 D10
Glodeanu-Sărat RO 161 D9
Glodeanu-Siliștea RO 161 D9
Glodeni MD 153 B11
Glodeni MD 152 D5
Glodeni RO 161 C6
Glödnitz A 73 C9
Głodowa PL 85 C11
Glodzhevo BG 161 F8
Gloggnitz A 148 A5
Glogova RO 159 D10
Glogovac SRB 159 E7
Głogów PL 81 C10
Głogówek PL 142 F4
Głogów Małopolski PL 144 C4
Glogowo PL 138 D6
Glomfjord N 108 C6
Glommen S 87 B10
Glommersträsk S 107 A17
Glonn D 75 G10
Glória P 50 B4
Glória do Ribatejo P 44 F3
Glos-la-Ferrière F 24 C4
Glossa GR 175 A8
Glössbo S 103 D12
Glossop GB 11 E8
Glöte S 102 B5
Glöthe D 79 C10
Glottra S 92 B6
Gloucester GB 13 B10
Glounthaune IRL 8 E6
Głowaczów PL 141 G4
Główczyce PL 85 A12
Glowe D 84 A4
Glöwen D 83 E12
Głowno PL 143 C8
Gložan SRB 158 C4
Glozhene BG 160 F3
Glozhene BG 165 C9
Głubczyce PL 142 F4
Głuchołazy PL 142 F3
Głuchów PL 141 G2
Glücksburg (Ostsee) D 82 A7
Glückstadt D 17 A12
Glud DK 86 D5
Gludsted DK 86 C4
Gluggvasshaugen N 108 E5
Glumslöv S 87 D11
Glumsø DK 87 E9
Glusburn GB 11 D8
Glušci SRB 158 D4
Głuszyca PL 81 E10
Glyfa GR 175 B6
Glyfada GR 175 D8
Glyki GR 168 F4
Glyn Ceiriog GB 10 F5
Glyngøre DK 86 B3
Glynn GB 4 F5
Glynn IRL 9 D9
Glynneath GB 13 B7
Gmünd A 73 C8
Gmünd A 77 E7
Gmund am Tegernsee D 72 A4
Gmunden A 73 A8
Gnarp S 103 B13
Gnarrenburg D 17 B12
Gneisenaustadt Schildau D 80 D3
Gnesta S 93 A10
Gniebing A 148 C5
Gniew PL 138 C6
Gniewkowo PL 138 E5
Gniewoszów PL 141 H5
Gnieździska PL 143 E9
Gniezno PL 85 E13
Gnisvärd S 93 D12
Gnocchetta I 66 C5
Gnoien D 83 C13
Gnojna PL 81 E12
Gnojnice BIH 157 F8
Gnojnik PL 144 D2
Gnojno PL 143 E10
Gnosall GB 11 F7
Gnosjö S 91 E14
Gnotzheim D 75 D8
Gnutz D 83 B7
Göbel TR 173 D9
Gobowen GB 10 F5
Göçbeyli TR 177 A9
Göcek TR 181 C9
Göçerler TR 173 B8
Goch D 16 E6
Gochsheim D 75 B7
Goczałkowice-Zdrój PL 147 B7
Göd H 150 B3
Godačica SRB 159 F6
Godal N 95 D11
Godalming GB 15 E7
Godby FIN 99 B13
Goddelau D 187 B6
Goddelsheim (Lichtenfels) D 21 B11
Godeanu RO 159 D10
Godech BG 165 C7
Godega di Sant'Urbano I 72 E5
Godegård S 92 B6
Godelleta E 48 F3
Godeni RO 160 C5
Goderville F 18 E1
Godiasco I 37 B10
Godimilje BIH 157 E11
Godinești RO 159 C10
Godinje MNE 163 E7
Godkowo PL 139 B8
Godmanchester GB 15 C8
Gödöllő H 150 B3
Godovič SLO 73 E9
Gödre H 149 D9
Godstone GB 15 E8
Goduš BIH 157 C10
Godziesze Wielkie PL 142 C5
Godziszów PL 144 B5
Goedereede NL 16 E1
Goes NL 16 E1
Göfritz an der Wild A 77 E8
Göggingen D 187 D8
Gogolin PL 142 F5
Gogołów PL 144 D4
Gogoșari RO 161 F7
Gogoșu RO 159 E10
Gogoșu RO 160 E2
Göhl D 83 B9
Gohor RO 153 E10
Gohrau D 79 C11
Göhrde D 83 D9
Göhren D 84 B5
Göhren-Lebbin D 83 D13
Goian MD 154 C4
Goicea RO 160 F3
Goiești RO 160 E3
Goirle NL 16 E4
Góis P 44 D4
Goito I 66 B2
Goizueta E 32 D2
Gojść PL 143 D7
Gökçealan TR 177 D9
Gökçebayir TR 171 E10
Gökçedağ TR 173 E10
Gökçeören TR 181 B9
Gökçeyazi TR 173 E8
Gokels D 82 B6
Gökova TR 181 B8
Göktepe TR 181 B9
Göktürk TR 173 B10
Gol N 101 E9
Gola HR 149 D8
Gołąb PL 141 H5
Golac SLO 67 A9
Golăiești RO 153 C11
Golaj AL 163 E9
Gołańcz PL 85 E12
Gołaszyn PL 141 G6
Golbey F 26 D5
Gölby FIN 99 B13
Gölcük TR 173 F8
Golčův Jeníkov CZ 77 C8
Golczewo PL 85 C7
Goldach CH 71 C8
Gołdap PL 136 E5
Goldbeck D 83 E11
Goldberg D 83 C12
Goldegg A 73 B7
Goldelund D 82 A6
Golden IRL 9 D7
Golden Pot GB 14 E7
Goldenstedt D 17 C10
Goleen IRL 8 F3
Golegã P 44 F4
Golemanovo BG 159 F9
Golema Rakovitsa BG 165 D8
Golema Rečica NMK 163 F10
Golenice PL 85 E7
Goleniów PL 85 C7
Golesh BG 161 F11
Golești RO 153 F10
Golești RO 160 C4
Golfo Aranci I 64 B4
Golina PL 142 B5
Golinhac F 33 A11
Goliševa LV 133 C3
Gölköy TR 177 E9
Gölle H 149 D10
Göllersdorf A 77 F10
Göllheim D 186 B5
Göllin D 83 C11
Gollin D 84 D5
Golling an der Salzach A 73 A7
Göllingen D 79 D9
Gollmitz D 84 D5
Golmes E 42 D5
Golnik SLO 73 D9
Gøløse DK 87 D10
Golovkino RUS 136 D3
Golpejas E 45 B9
Gols A 77 G11
Golspie GB 3 K9
Golßen D 80 C5
Golubac SRB 159 D8
Golub-Dobrzyń PL 138 D7
Golubić HR 156 D5
Golubinje SRB 159 D9
Golyama Zhelyazna BG 165 D9
Golyam Izvor BG 166 F5
Golyam Manastir BG 166 E6
Golyamo Belovo BG 165 E8
Gölyazi TR 173 D10
Gołymin-Ośrodek PL 139 E10
Golzow D 79 B12
Gomadingen D 27 D11
Gómara E 41 E7
Gomaringen D 187 E7
Gomati GR 169 D10
Gomba H 150 C4
Gömeç TR 173 F7
Gomecello E 45 B9
Gomes Aires P 50 D3
Gomirje HR 67 B11
Gommern D 79 B10
Gomotartsi BG 159 E10
Gomunice PL 143 D7
Gönc H 145 G3
Gonçalo P 44 D6
Goncelin F 31 E8
Gondelsheim D 187 C6
Gondershausen D 185 D7
Gondomar E 38 D2
Gondomar P 44 B3
Gondorf D 21 D8
Gondrecourt-le-Château F 26 C4
Gondreville F 26 C4
Gondrin F 33 C6
Gönen TR 173 D8
Gonfaron F 36 E4
Gonfreville-l'Orcher F 18 E1
Goni I 64 D3
Goniądz PL 140 D7
Gonnesa I 64 E1
Gonnoi GR 169 E7
Gonnosfanadiga I 64 E2
Gonnosnò I 64 D2
Gonsans F 26 F5
Gönyű H 149 A9
Gonzaga I 66 C2
Goodwick GB 12 A5
Goole GB 11 D10
Goonhavern GB 12 E4
Goor NL 17 D7
Gopegi E 40 C6
Göppingen D 74 E6
Gor E 55 E7
Góra PL 81 C11
Góra PL 139 E9
Gorafe E 55 E6
Goraj PL 144 B6
Góra Kalwaria PL 141 G4
Goranu RO 160 C4
Góra Puławska PL 141 H5
Gorawino PL 85 C8
Goražde BIH 157 E10
Gorban RO 153 D12
Görbeháza H 151 B7
Görcsöny H 149 E10
Gördalen S 102 C3
Gordaliza del Pino E 39 D9
Gordes F 35 C9
Gordinești MD 153 A10
Gørding DK 86 E3
Gordola CH 69 A6
Gordon GB 5 D11
Gordona I 69 A7
Gorebridge GB 5 D10
Görece TR 177 C9
Gorenja Straža SLO 73 E11
Gorenja vas SLO 73 D9
Gorey IRL 9 C10
Görgeteg H 149 D8
Gorgoglione I 60 C6
Gorgonzola I 69 B7
Gorgota RO 161 D8
Gorgova RO 155 C4
Gorica BIH 157 D7
Gorica BIH 157 F7
Gorica BIH 162 D5
Gorica MNE 163 E7
Goričan HR 149 D7
Gorinchem NL 16 E3
Gorino I 66 C5
Gorishovë AL 168 C2
Görisried D 71 B11
Goritsa BG 167 D9
Goritsa BG 167 D9
Göritz D 84 D5
Gorizia I 73 E8
Gorleben D 83 D10
Gørlev DK 87 D8
Gorlice PL 144 D3
Görlitz D 81 D7
Gorlosen D 83 D10
Gormanston IRL 7 E10
Gormanstown IRL 7 E10
Gormaz E 40 E6
Görmin D 84 C4
Gorna Belica NMK 164 F3
Gorna Beshovitsa BG 165 C8
Gorna Breznitsa BG 165 F7
Gorna Koznitsa BG 165 E6
Gorna Kremena BG 165 C8
Gorna Mitropoliya BG 165 C9
Gorna Oryakhovitsa BG 166 C5
Gorna Studena BG 166 C4
Gornau D 80 E4
Gorna Vasilitsa BG 165 E8
Gorna Verenitsa BG 165 C7
Gornești RO 152 D5
Gornet RO 161 C8
Gornet-Cricov RO 161 C8
Gorni Dŭbnik BG 165 C9
Gorni Lom BG 165 C6
Gornja Golubinja BIH 157 D8
Gornja Grabovica BIH 157 E8
Gornja Gračenica HR 149 E7
Gornja Ljubata SRB 164 D5
Gornja Ljuta BIH 157 E9
Gornjane SRB 159 E9
Gornja Ploča HR 156 D4
Gornja Radgona SLO 148 C5
Gornja Sanica BIH 157 C6
Gornja Slatina BIH 157 C9
Gornja Toponica SRB 164 C4
Gornja Trnava SRB 159 E6
Gornja Tuzla BIH 157 C10
Gornje Jelenje HR 67 B10
Gornje Peulje BIH 156 D6
Gornje Ratkovo BIH 157 C6
Gornje Vratno HR 148 D6
Gornji Agići BIH 156 C5
Gornji Babin Potok HR 156 C4
Gornji Breg SRB 150 F5
Gornji Dolac HR 157 E6
Gornji Grad SLO 73 D10
Gornji Humac HR 157 F6
Gornji Kosinj HR 156 C3
Gornji Lapac HR 156 C5
Gornji Lukavac BIH 157 F9
Gornji Majkovi HR 162 D4
Gornji Malovan BIH 157 E7
Gornji Matejevac SRB 164 C4
Gornji Milanovac SRB 158 E5
Gornji Očcauš BIH 157 C8
Gornji Podgradći BIH 157 B7
Gornji Rajić HR 157 B7
Gornji Ribnik BIH 157 D6
Gornji Tkalec HR 149 E6
Gornji Vakuf BIH 157 E8
Górno PL 143 E10
Gorno Ablanovo BG 161 F7
Gorno Aleksandrovo BG 167 D7
Gorno Orizari NMK 164 F4
Gorno Ozirovo BG 165 C7
Gorno Pavlikene BG 165 C10
Goro I 66 C5
Gorobinci NMK 164 F4
Górowo Iławeckie PL 136 E2
Gorredijk NL 16 B6
Gorreto I 37 B10
Gorron F 23 D10
Görsbach D 79 D8
Gorseinon GB 12 B6
Górsk PL 138 D5
Gorska Polyana BG 167 E7
Gorski Izvor BG 166 E4
Gorsko Novo Selo BG 166 C5
Gorssel NL 16 D6
Gort IRL 6 F5
Gortahork IRL 6 B6
Gort an Choirce IRL 6 B6
Gortavoy Bridge GB 7 C9
Gorteen IRL 6 E5
Gorteen IRL 6 E6
Gorteeny IRL 6 F6
Gortin GB 4 F2
Goruia RO 159 C8
Görükle TR 173 D10
Gorun BG 167 B10
Görvik S 106 D9
Görwihl D 27 E9
Gorxheimertal D 21 E11
Gorzanów PL 77 B11
Gorze F 26 B5
Görzig D 79 C10
Görzke D 79 B11
Gorzkowice PL 143 D8
Gorzków-Osada PL 144 B7
Górzna PL 85 D11
Górzno PL 139 D8
Górzno PL 141 G5
Gorzów Śląski PL 142 D5
Gorzów Wielkopolski PL 85 E8
Górzyca PL 81 B7
Górzyca PL 85 C8
Gorzyce PL 144 B4
Gorzyce PL 144 C6
Gorzyce PL 146 B6
Gorzyń PL 81 A9
Górzyn PL 81 C7
Gosaldo I 72 D4
Gosau A 73 A8
Gosberton GB 11 F11
Gościeradów Ukazowy PL 144 B4
Gościm PL 85 E9
Gościno PL 85 B9
Gósciszów PL 81 D8
Gosdorf A 148 C5
Gosë AL 168 B2
Gosfield GB 15 D10
Gosforth GB 5 E13
Gosforth GB 10 C5
Goslar D 79 C7
Goślice PL 139 E8
Gosné F 23 D9
Gospić HR 156 C3
Gospođinci SRB 158 C4
Gosport GB 13 D12
Gössäter S 91 B13
Gossau CH 27 F11
Gössendorf A 148 C5
Gößl A 73 A8
Gostavățu RO 160 E5
Gostil AL 163 E9
Gostilitsa BG 166 C4
Gostinari RO 161 E8
Gostinu RO 161 E8
Gostivar NMK 163 F10
Göstling an der Ybbs A 73 A10
Gostoviči BIH 157 D9
Gostycyn PL 138 D4
Gostyń PL 81 C12
Gostyń PL 85 B7
Gostynin PL 139 F7
Goszcz PL 142 D3
Goszczanów PL 142 C6
Goszczyn PL 141 G3
Göta S 91 C11
Göteborg S 91 D10
Götene S 91 B13
Gotești MD 154 E2
Gotha D 79 E8
Gothem S 93 D13
Götlunda S 97 D14
Gotse Delchev BG 169 A10
Gottböle FIN 122 F6
Gotteszell D 76 E3
Gottfrieding D 75 E12
Göttingen D 78 C6
Gottmadingen D 27 E10
Gottne S 107 E14
Gøttrup DK 86 A4
Götzis A 71 C9
Gouarec F 22 D5
Gouda NL 16 D3
Goudswaard NL 182 B4
Gouesnou F 22 D3
Gouhenans F 26 E5
Goult F 35 C9
Goumenissa GR 169 C7
Goumois F 27 F6
Gourdan-Polignan F 33 D7
Gourdon F 29 F8
Gourdon GB 5 B12
Gourette F 32 E5
Gourgançon F 25 C11
Gouria GR 174 C3
Gourin F 22 D4
Gournay-en-Bray F 18 F4
Goussainville F 25 B7
Gout-Rossignol F 29 E6
Gouveia P 44 D5
Gouvia GR 168 E2
Gouvieux F 25 B7
Gouvy B 20 D5
Gouzon F 29 C10
Gove P 44 B4
Goveđari HR 162 D3
Govedartsi BG 165 E7
Goven F 23 D8
Gowarczów PL 141 H2
Gowidlino PL 138 B4
Goworowo PL 139 E12
Gowran IRL 9 C8
Goxhill GB 11 D11
Göynükbelen TR 173 E11
Gózd PL 141 H4
Gozdnica PL 81 D8
Gozdowice PL 84 E6
Gözsüz TR 173 C6
Gozzano I 68 B5
Graal-Müritz D 83 B12
Grab BIH 157 F10
Grab BIH 162 D5
Graben-Neudorf D 187 C5
Grabica PL 143 D8
Grabjan AL 168 C2
Gråbo S 91 D11
Grabovac HR 157 F7
Grabovci SRB 158 D4
Grabovica SRB 159 E10
Grabow D 83 D11
Grabów PL 143 B7
Grabowiec PL 143 D11
Grabowiec PL 144 B8
Grabówka PL 140 D8
Grabów nad Pilicą PL 141 G4
Grabów nad Prosną PL 142 C5
Grabownica Starzeńska PL 144 D5
Grabówno PL 85 D12
Grabowno Wielkie PL 142 D3
Grabowo PL 136 E5
Grabowo PL 139 D13
Grabs CH 71 C8
Gračac HR 156 D4
Gračanica BIH 157 C9
Gračanica BIH 157 D10
Gračanica BIH 157 E8
Graçay F 24 F6
Grâce-Hollogne B 19 C11
Grâces F 22 C5
Gračianica BIH 157 E8
Gracze PL 142 E4
Grad SLO 148 C6
Gradac BIH 162 D5
Gradac HR 157 F7
Gradac SLO 148 E4
Gradačac BIH 157 C9
Gradara I 67 E6
Grăddö S 99 C12
Gradec HR 149 E6
Gradec NMK 169 B7
Gradefes E 39 C9
Gradets BG 159 E10
Gradets BG 167 D7
Gradevo BG 165 F7
Gradina BG 166 C5
Gradina BG 166 E4
Gradina BIH 157 F9
Gradina SRB 163 C9
Grădinari RO 159 C8
Grădinari RO 160 D4
Grădinița MD 154 D5
Gradishte BG 166 C4
Gradište HR 157 B10
Gradište SRB 164 B5
Gradište SRB 164 C5
Grădiștea RO 160 D3
Grădiștea RO 161 C10
Grădiștea RO 161 D8
Grădiștea RO 161 E10
Gradište Bekteško HR 149 F9
Gradnitsa BG 165 D10
Grado E 39 B7
Grado I 73 E7
Gradö S 97 B15
Gradojević SRB 158 D4
Gradoli I 62 B1
Gradsko NMK 169 A6
Gradskovo SRB 159 E9
Graena E 55 E6
Græsted DK 87 C10
Gräfelfing D 75 F9
Grafenau D 76 E4
Gräfenberg D 75 C9
Grafendorf D 74 B6
Grafendorf bei Hartberg A 148 B5
Gräfenhainichen D 79 C11
Grafenhausen D 27 E9
Grafenrheinfeld D 187 B9
Gräfenroda D 79 E8
Grafenstein A 73 C9
Grafenwöhr D 75 C10
Grafenworth A 77 F9
Graffignano I 62 B2
Grafhorst D 79 B8
Graf Ignatievo BG 165 E10
Gräfinau-Angstedt D 79 E9
Grafing bei München D 75 F10
Grafrath D 75 F9
Gräfsnäs S 91 C11
Gräftåvallen S 105 E15
Gragnano I 60 B3
Grahovac MNE 163 D6
Grahovo MNE 163 D6
Grahovo SLO 73 D8
Gráig na Manach IRL 9 C9
Graigue IRL 9 C9
Graiguenamanagh IRL 9 C9
Grain GB 15 E10
Grainau D 71 C12
Grainet D 76 E5
Graissac F 30 F2
Graissessac F 34 C5
Graja de Iniesta E 47 E9
Grajal de Campos E 39 D9
Grajduri RO 153 D11
Grajewo PL 140 C6
Grällsta S 98 C7
Grålum N 95 D14
Gram DK 86 E4
Gramada BG 159 F10
Gramastettan A 76 F6
Gramat F 29 F9
Gramatikovo BG 167 E9
Grambow D 84 D6
Grămești RO 153 B8
Gramkow D 83 C10
Grammatiko GR 169 F7
Grammendorf D 83 B13
Grammenitsa GR 174 A2
Grammeno GR 168 E4
Grammichele I 59 E6
Gramsbergen NL 17 C7
Gramsh AL 168 C3
Gramzda LV 134 D3
Gramzow D 84 D6
Gran N 95 B13
Granabeg IRL 7 F10
Granada E 53 B9
Granån S 119 C10
Granard IRL 7 E8
Granarolo dell'Emilia I 66 C3
Granåsen S 107 C11
Granátula de Calatrava E 54 B5
Granberg S 118 D3
Granberget N 102 D3
Granbergsdal S 97 D12
Granbergsträsk S 107 A17
Grančarevo BIH 162 D5
Grancey-le-Château-Nouvelle F 26 E3
Grandas E 39 B6
Grandcamp-Maisy F 23 B9
Grand-Champ F 22 E6
Grand-Couronne F 18 F3
Grande-Synthe F 18 B5
Grande-Vabre F 33 A10
Grand-Fort-Philippe F 18 B5
Grand-Fougeray F 23 E8
Grândola P 50 C2
Grandpré F 19 F10
Grandpuits-Bailly-Carrois F 25 C8
Grandrieu F 30 F4
Grandris F 30 C5
Grandson CH 31 B10
Grandtully GB 5 B9
Grandvelle-et-le-Perrenot F 26 E5
Grandvillars F 27 E6
Grandvillers F 26 D6
Grandvilliers F 18 E4
Grañén E 41 E11
Grangärde S 97 B12
Grange IRL 7 E10
Grange IRL 9 E7
Grangemouth GB 5 C9
Grange-over-Sands GB 10 C6
Grängesberg S 97 B13
Granges-sur-Vologne F 27 D6
Grängshyttan S 97 C12
Grängsjö S 103 B13
Granhult S 116 D7
Granica BIH 162 D5
Grăniceri RO 151 D7
Grănicești RO 153 B8
Granitola-Torretta I 58 D2
Granitsa GR 174 A4
Granja P 51 C5
Granja de Moreruela E 39 E8
Granja de Torrehermosa E 51 C8
Granja do Ulmeiro P 44 D3
Gränna S 92 C4
Grannäs S 107 A10
Grannäs S 109 E13
Granneset N 108 E6
Granö S 107 C16
Granollers E 43 D8
Granön S 103 D13
Granowiec PL 142 D4
Granowo PL 81 B11
Granschütz D 79 D11
Gransee D 84 D4
Granselet S 109 E14
Gränsgård S 109 F15
Gransjö S 107 A15
Gransjön S 103 B11
Gränssjö S 108 F8
Grantham GB 11 F10
Grantown-on-Spey GB 3 L9
Granträsk S 107 C14
Granträskmark S 118 D6
Grantshouse GB 5 D12
Granum S 88 C7
Granvik S 92 B5
Granville F 23 C8
Granvin N 94 A5
Grapska BIH 157 C9
Gräs S 97 C10
Grasbakken N 114 C5
Gräsgård S 89 C11
Grasleben D 79 B9
Gräsmarken S 97 B8
Grasmere GB 10 C5
Gräsmyr S 107 D17
Grassåmoen N 105 C14
Grassano I 60 B6
Grassau D 72 A5
Grasse F 36 D5
Grassington GB 11 C8
Gråssjö S 103 A10
Gråsten DK 86 F5
Grästorp S 91 C12
Gratallops E 42 E5
Gratangsbotn N 111 C14
Gratens F 33 D8
Gratia RO 161 E6
Gratini GR 171 B9
Gratkorn A 148 B4
Grätnäs S 107 E14
Gråträsk S 118 D3
Gratteri I 58 D4
Gratwein A 148 B4
Grauballe DK 86 C5
Graulhet F 33 C9
Graupa D 80 D5
Graus E 42 C4
Grávalos E 41 D8
Gravberget N 102 E3
Gravbränna S 106 D7
Gravdal N 110 D6
Grave NL 16 E5
Gravedona I 69 A7
Gravelines F 18 C5
Gravellona Toce I 68 B5
Gravelotte F 26 B5
Gravens DK 86 D4
Grävenwiesbach D 21 D10
Grāveri LV 133 D2
Gravesend GB 15 E9
Gravia GR 174 B5
Gravigny F 24 B5
Gråvika N 100 E1
Gravina di Catania I 59 D7
Gravina in Puglia I 61 B6
Gravmark S 118 F4
Gray F 26 F4
Grayan-et-l'Hôpital F 28 E3
Grays GB 15 E9
Graz A 148 B4
Grazalema E 53 C6
Grążawy PL 139 D8
Grazzanise I 60 A2
Grčak SRB 163 C10
Grdelica SRB 164 D5
Greaca RO 161 E8
Greåker N 95 D14
Gréalou F 33 A9
Great Baddow GB 15 D10
Great Bircham GB 15 B10
Great Clifton GB 5 F10
Great Cornard GB 15 C10
Great Dunmow GB 15 D9
Great Glen GB 11 F9
Great Gonerby GB 11 F10
Greatham GB 11 B9
Great Harwood GB 11 D7
Great Haywood GB 11 F8
Great Linford GB 15 C7
Great Malvern GB 13 A10
Great Ponton GB 11 F10
Great Salkeld GB 5 F11
Great Shelford GB 15 C9
Great Torrington GB 12 D6
Great Wakering GB 15 D10
Great Yarmouth GB 15 B12
Grebănu RO 161 C9
Grebaštica HR 156 E4
Grebbestad S 91 B9
Grebci BIH 162 D5
Grebenac SRB 159 D7
Grebendorf (Meinhard) D 79 D7
Grebenhain D 21 D12
Grebenișu de Câmpie RO 152 D4
Grebenstein D 21 B12
Grebin D 83 B8
Grjbków PL 141 F6
Grebo S 92 C7
Grjbocin PL 138 D6
Grjboszów PL 143 F10
Grjbów PL 144 B4
Greccio I 62 C3
Grecești RO 160 E2
Greci I 60 A4
Greci RO 159 D11
Gredelj BIH 157 F10
Greding D 75 D9
Gredstedbro DK 86 E3
Greencastle GB 4 F2
Greencastle GB 7 D10
Greencastle IRL 4 E3
Greene D 78 C6
Greengairs GB 5 D9
Greenhead GB 5 F11
Greenigo GB 3 H10
Greenisland GB 4 F5
Greenlaw GB 5 D12
Greenloaning GB 5 C9
Greenock GB 4 D7
Greenodd GB 10 C5
Greenore IRL 7 D10
Greenway GB 12 B5
Greggio I 68 C5
Greifenburg A 73 C7
Greifendorf D 80 D4
Greifenstein D 21 C10
Greiffenberg D 84 D5
Greifswald D 84 B4
Grein A 77 F7

Greiveri LV 135 B11
Greiz D 79 E11
Grejs DK 86 D5
Gremersdorf D 83 B9
Grenaa DK 87 C7
Grenade F 33 C8
Grenade-sur-l'Adour F 32 C5
Grenant F 26 E4
Grenås S 106 D8
Grenchen CH 27 F7
Grenči LV 134 C5
Grenoble F 31 E8
Grense-Jakobselv N 114 D9
Gréoux-les-Bains F 35 C10
Gresenhorst D 83 B12
Gress GB 2 J4
Gressan I 31 D11
Gresse D 83 D9
Gressoney-la-Trinite I 68 B4
Gressvik N 91 A8
Gresten A 77 G8
Grésy-sur-Aix F 31 D8
Grésy-sur-Isère F 31 D9
Gretna GB 5 F10
Greußen D 79 D8
Greux F 26 D4
Grevbäck S 92 C4
Greve in Chianti I 66 E3
Greven D 17 D9
Greven D 83 D9
Grevena GR 168 D5
Grevenbicht NL 183 C7
Grevenbroich D 21 B7
Greveniti GR 168 E5
Grevenmacher L 20 E6
Grevesmühlen D 83 C10
Greve Strand DK 87 D10
Grevie S 87 C11
Grevinge DK 87 D9
Greyabbey GB 7 C11
Greystoke GB 5 F11
Greystones IRL 7 F10
Grez-Doiceau B 19 C10
Grez-en-Bouère F 23 E10
Grgar SLO 73 D8
Grgurevci SRB 158 C4
Griegos E 47 D9
Grijota E 40 D2
Grijpskerk NL 16 B6
Grillby S 98 C8
Grillon F 35 B8
Grimaldi I 60 E6
Grimaud F 36 E5
Grimbergen B 19 C9
Grimma D 79 D12
Grimmen D 84 B4
Grimoldby GB 11 E12
Grimsås S 91 E14
Grimsbu N 101 B12
Grimsby GB 11 D11
Grimslöv S 88 B7
Grimstad N 90 C4
Grimston GB 11 F13
Grimstorp S 92 D5
Grimstrup DK 86 D3
Grindafjord N 94 D2
Grindaheim N 101 D9
Grindal N 101 A11
Grindelwald CH 70 D6
Grinder N 96 B7
Grindjord N 111 D13
Grindsted DK 86 A6
Grindsted DK 86 D3
Grindu RO 161 D9
Grinkiškis LT 134 E7
Griñón E 46 D5
Grins A 71 C11
Grinsbol S 97 C8
Grinties RO 153 C7
Gripenberg S 92 D5
Grisén E 41 E9
Griškabūdis LT 136 D7
Grisolia I 60 D5
Grisolles F 33 C8
Grisslehamn S 99 B11
Gritley GB 3 H11
Grivița RO 153 E11
Grivița RO 153 F11
Grivița RO 161 D10
Grivitsa BG 165 C10
Grkinja SRB 164 C4
Grljan SRB 159 F9
Grnčari NMK 168 B5
Grobbendonk B 19 B10
Gröbenzell D 75 F9
Grobina LV 134 C2
Gröbming A 73 B8
Gröbzig D 79 C10
Grocka SRB 158 D6
Gródby S 93 A11
Gródek PL 140 D9
Gródek nad Dunajcem PL 144 D2
Gröden D 80 D5
Grödig A 73 A7
Gröditz D 80 D4
Gródki PL 139 D9
Grodków PL 142 E3
Grodziec PL 142 B5
Grodzisk PL 141 E7
Grodzisk Mazowiecki PL 141 F3
Grodzisk Wielkopolski PL 81 B10
Groenlo NL 17 D7
Groesbeek NL 183 B7
Grohnde (Emmerthal) D 78 B5
Groitzsch D 79 D11
Groix F 22 E5
Grojdibodu RO 160 F4
Grójec PL 141 G3
Grom PL 139 C10
Gromadka PL 81 D9
Grömitz D 83 B9
Gromnik PL 144 D2
Gromo I 69 B8
Gronau (Westfalen) D 17 D8
Grønbjerg DK 86 C3
Grönbo S 118 C5
Gröndal S 108 E8

Grong N 105 C12
Grönhögen S 89 C10
Grønhøj DK 86 C4
Gröningen D 79 C9
Groningen NL 17 B7
Grønnemose DK 86 E6
Grønning N 110 E9
Grønningen N 104 D7
Gronowo PL 138 B6
Grönsinka S 98 B7
Grönskåra S 89 A9
Grönsta S 103 A11
Grønvik N 94 D4
Grönviken S 103 A9
Grönviken S 103 D12
Groomsport GB 4 F5
Grootegast NL 16 B6
Gropello Cairoli I 69 C6
Gropeni RO 155 C1
Gropnița RO 153 C10
Grorud N 95 C11
Groscavallo I 31 E11
Groși RO 152 B3
Grosio I 69 A9
Grošnica SRB 159 F6
Grosotto I 69 A9
Großaitingen D 71 A11
Groß Ammensleben D 79 B10
Großarl A 73 B7
Groß-Bieberau D 21 E11
Groß Börnecke D 79 C9
Großbothen D 79 D12
Großbottwar D 27 C11
Großbreitenbach D 79 E9
Großburgwedel (Burgwedel) D 78 B6
Groß Dölln D 84 E5
Grosselfingen D 27 D10
Großenaspe D 83 C7
Großenbrode D 83 B10
Großenehrich D 79 D8
Groß Engersdorf A 77 F11
Großengottern D 79 D8
Großenhain D 80 D5
Großenkneten D 17 C10
Großenlüder D 78 E6
Großensee D 83 C8
Großenstein D 79 E11
Großenwiehe D 82 A6
Groß-Enzersdorf A 77 F11
Grosseto I 65 B4
Grosseto-Prugna I 37 H9
Groß Fredenwalde D 84 D5
Großfurra D 79 D8
Groß-Gerau D 21 E10
Groß-Gerungs A 77 E7
Groß Glienicke D 80 B4
Großgmain D 73 A6
Groß Grönau D 83 C9
Großhabersdorf D 75 D8
Großhansdorf D 83 C8
Großharras A 77 E11
Groß Hartmannsdorf D 80 E4
Groß Heere (Heere) D 79 B7
Großhennersdorf D 81 E7
Groß-Hesepe D 17 C8
Großheubach D 187 B7
Grössjö S 107 F14
Großkarolinenfeld D 72 A5
Groß Kiesow D 84 B4
Großklein A 148 C4
Groß Köris D 80 B5
Groß Kreutz D 79 B12
Großkrut A 77 E11
Groß Lafferde (Lahstedt) D 79 B7
Großlangheim D 187 B9
Groß Leine D 80 B6
Groß Leuthen D 80 B6
Großlittgen D 21 D7
Großlohra D 79 D8
Großmaischeid D 185 C8
Großmehlen D 80 D5
Groß Miltzow D 84 D4
Groß Mohrdorf D 84 B3
Großmonra D 79 D9
Groß Naundorf D 80 C3
Großnaundorf D 80 D5
Groß Nemerow D 84 D4
Groß Oesingen D 79 A7
Großolbersdorf D 80 E4
Großörner D 79 C9
Großostheim D 21 E12
Großpetersdorf A 149 B6
Groß Plasten D 83 C13
Großraming A 73 A10
Großräschen D 80 C6
Großrinderfeld D 74 C6
Groß Roge D 83 C13
Groß-Rohrheim D 21 E10
Großröhrsdorf D 80 D6
Großrosseln D 186 C2
Großrudestedt D 79 D9
Großrußbach A 77 F10
Groß Sankt Florian A 148 C4
Groß Särchen D 80 D6
Großschirma D 80 E4
Großschönau A 77 E7
Groß Schöneebeck D 84 E5
Groß Schwechten D 83 E11
Groß Schwülper (Schwülper) D 79 B7
Groß Stieten D 83 C11
Großthiemig D 80 D5
Großtreben D 80 C3
Groß Twülpstedt D 79 B8
Groß-Umstadt D 187 B6
Großwallstadt D 187 B7
Groß Warnow D 83 D11
Großweikersdorf A 77 F9
Groß Welle D 83 D12
Groß Wittensee D 83 B7
Groß Wokern D 83 C12
Großwudicke D 79 A11
Groß Wüstenfelde D 83 C13
Groß Ziethen D 84 D5
Groß-Zimmern D 187 B6
Grostenquin F 27 C7
Grosuplje SLO 73 E10
Grøtavær N 111 C12
Grotfjord N 111 A16
Grötholen S 102 D7
Grötingen S 103 A9
Grotli N 100 B7
Grötlingbo S 93 E12
Grotnesdalen N 111 A18
Grottaferrata I 62 D3
Grottaglie I 61 B8
Grottaminarda I 60 A4
Grottammare I 62 B5
Grottazzolina I 62 A5

Grotte I 58 E4
Grotte di Castro I 62 B1
Grotteria I 59 C9
Grottole I 61 B7
Grou NL 16 B5
Grova N 90 A4
Grove GB 13 B12
Grövelsjön S 102 B3
Grovfjord N 111 C13
Grozd'ovo BG 167 C9
Grozești RO 153 D12
Grub am Forst D 75 B9
Grubbenvorst NL 183 C8
Grubbnäsudden S 119 B10
Grube D 83 B10
Grubišno Polje HR 149 E8
Gruczno PL 138 D5
Gruda HR 162 D5
Grudusk PL 139 D10
Grudziądz PL 138 D6
Gruey-lès-Surance F 26 D5
Grugliasco I 68 C4
Gruia RO 159 E10
Gruissan F 34 D5
Gruiu RO 161 D8
Grullos E 39 B7
Grumăzești RO 153 C8
Grumbach D 80 D5
Grumo Appula I 61 A7
Grums S 97 C9
Grünau A 73 A8
Grünau A 77 F9
Grünberg D 21 C11
Grünburg A 76 G6
Grundagssätern S 102 B4
Grundfors S 106 A8
Grundfors S 107 B11
Grundforsen S 102 C3
Grundsanden S 118 B5
Grundsel S 107 C11
Grundsjö S 107 C11
Grundsuna S 107 E16
Grundsund S 91 C9
Grundtjärn S 107 D12
Grundträsk S 109 F11
Grundträsk S 109 F17
Grundträsk S 118 B7
Grundvattnet S 118 C4
Grünendeich D 82 C7
Grünewald D 80 D5
Grünheide D 80 C5
Grünkraut D 71 B9
Grunnfarnes N 111 B12
Grunnfjord N 112 C4
Grunnførfjord N 110 D8
Grunow D 80 B6
Grünsfeld D 74 C6
Grünstadt D 21 E10
Grünwald D 75 F10
Grupčin NMK 164 F3
Grury F 30 B4
Grūšlaukė LT 134 D2
Grußendorf (Sassenburg) D 79 A8
Gruta PL 138 D5
Gruvberget S 103 D11
Gruyères CH 31 B11
Gruža SRB 159 F6
Grūžai LT 135 D8
Gruždžiai LT 134 D6
Grybów PL 145 D2
Grycksbo S 103 E9
Gryfice PL 85 C8
Gryfino PL 84 D6
Gryfów Śląski PL 81 D8
Grygov CZ 146 B4
Grylewo PL 85 E12
Gryllefjord N 111 B13
Grynberget S 107 C11
Gryt S 93 C9
Grytan S 106 E7
Grytgöl S 92 B7
Grythyttan S 97 C12
Gryts bruk S 92 B6
Grytsjö S 106 A9
Gryttjom S 99 B8
Gryżliny PL 139 C9
Grzebienisko PL 81 B11
Grzmiąca PL 85 C10
Grzybno PL 84 D7
Grzybno PL 138 D5
Grzymiszew PL 142 B5
Grzywna PL 138 D5
Gschnitz A 72 B3
Gschwandt A 73 A8
Gschwend D 74 D6
Gstaad CH 31 C11
Gsteig CH 31 C11
Guadahortuna E 53 A10
Guadajoz E 53 D8
Guadalajara E 47 C6
Guadalaviar E 47 D9
Guadalcanal E 51 C8
Guadalcázar E 53 A7
Guadalest E 56 D4
Guadalmez E 54 B3
Guadarrama E 46 C4
Guadassuar E 48 F4
Guadix E 55 E6
Guaire IRL 9 C10
Guájar-Faraguit E 53 C9
Gualäv S 88 C5
Gualdo Cattaneo I 62 B3
Gualdo Tadino I 67 F6
Gualtieri I 66 C2
Guarcino I 62 D4
Guarda P 45 C6
Guardamar del Segura E 56 E4
Guardavalle I 59 B9
Guardea I 62 B2
Guardiagrele I 63 C6
Guardia Lombardi I 60 B4
Guardia Perticara I 60 C6
Guardia Piemontese I 60 E6
Guardia Sanframondi I 60 A3
Guardias Viejas E 55 F7
Guardiola de Berguedà E 43 C7
Guardo E 39 C10
Guardramiro E 45 B8
Guareña E 51 B7
Guaro E 53 C7
Guarromán E 54 C5
Guasila I 64 E3
Guastalla I 66 C2
Gubaveeny IRL 7 D7
Gubbhögen S 106 C9
Gubbio I 66 F6
Gubbträsk S 107 A13
Guben D 81 C7
Gübene BG 166 D4

Gubin PL 81 C7
Guča SRB 158 F5
Guča Gora BIH 157 D8
Gudar E 48 D3
Gudavac BIH 156 C5
Gudbjerg DK 86 E7
Gudenieki LV 134 C3
Guderup DK 86 F5
Gudhem S 91 C14
Gudhjem DK 89 A9
Gudiena LT 137 D9
Gudinge S 99 A9
Gudme DK 87 E7
Gudmont-Villiers F 26 D3
Gudow D 83 C9
Gudum DK 86 B2
Gudumholm DK 86 B6
Gudvangen N 100 E5
Gudžiūnai LT 134 E7
Guebwiller F 27 E7
Guégon F 22 E6
Güéjar-Sierra E 53 B10
Guémar F 27 D7
Guémené-Penfao F 23 E8
Guémené-sur-Scorff F 22 D5
Guénange F 20 F6
Güenes E 40 B5
Guenrouet F 23 E8
Guer F 23 E7
Guérande F 22 F7
Guéret F 29 C9
Guérigny F 25 F9
Guerri de la Sal E 33 F8
Güesa E 32 E3
Gueugnon F 30 B5
Gugești RO 161 B10
Güglingen D 27 B10
Guglionesi I 63 D7
Gugutka BG 171 B9
Gühlen-Glienicke D 83 D13
Guia P 44 E3
Guia P 50 E3
Guichen F 23 E8
Guidel F 22 E5
Guide Post GB 5 E13
Guidizzolo I 66 B2
Guidonia-Montecelio I 62 D3
Guiglia I 66 D2
Guignen F 23 E8
Guignes F 25 C8
Guijo de Coria E 45 D8
Guijo de Galisteo E 45 D8
Guijo de Granadilla E 45 D8
Guijuelo E 45 C9
Guildford GB 15 E7
Guilers F 22 D2
Guilherand F 30 F6
Guilhofrei P 38 E3
Guilhovai P 44 C3
Guillaumes F 36 C5
Guillena E 51 D7
Guillestre F 36 B5
Guilliers F 22 D7
Guillon F 25 E11
Guillos F 32 A4
Guilvinec F 22 E3
Guimarães P 38 F3
Guînes F 15 F12
Guingamp F 22 C5
Guipavas F 22 D3
Guipry F 23 E8
Guisando E 45 D10
Guisborough GB 11 B9
Guiscard F 19 E7
Guise F 19 E8
Guissény F 22 C3
Guissona E 42 D6
Guist GB 15 B10
Guitiriz E 38 B4
Guîtres F 28 E5
Gujan-Mestras F 32 A3
Gulács I 145 G5
Gülbahçe TR 177 C8
Gulbene LV 135 B13
Guldager DK 86 D2
Guldborg DK 84 A1
Gulgamme N 113 B16
Gulianca RO 161 C11
Gülitz D 83 D11
Gullabo S 89 C9
Gullane GB 5 C11
Gullberg S 103 C10
Gullbrå N 100 E4
Gullbrandstorp S 87 B11
Gullbranna S 87 B11
Gulleråsen S 103 D9
Gullholmen N 111 C10
Gullön S 109 F11
Gullringen S 92 D7
Gullspång S 91 B15
Gullträsk S 118 B6
Güllük TR 177 E10
Güllük TR 177 E10
Gullverket N 95 B14
Gulpen NL 183 D7
Gülpinar TR 171 E10
Gulsele S 107 D12
Gulsvik N 95 B11
Gültz D 84 C4
Gülübintsi BG 166 E6
Gülübovo BG 165 E10
Gülübovo BG 166 E5
Gulyantsi BG 160 F5
Gülzow D 83 C12
Gumhöjden S 97 B10
Gumiel de Hizán E 40 E4
Gumiel de Mercado E 40 E4
Gummark S 118 E5
Gummersbach D 21 B9
Gumpelstadt D 79 E7
Gumtow D 83 E12
Gümüşçay TR 173 D7
Gümüşsuyu TR 177 C9
Gümüşyaka TR 173 B9
Gümzovo BG 159 E10
Gunaroš SRB 150 F4
Gundelfingen D 27 D11
Gundelfingen an der Donau D 75 E7
Gundelsheim D 21 F12
Gundershoffen F 27 C8
Gundinci HR 157 B9
Gündoğan TR 173 D8
Gündoğdu TR 173 D7
Güneyli TR 172 D6
Gunja HR 157 C10
Gunnarn S 107 A13
Gunnarnes N 113 A13
Gunnarsbo S 103 C11

Gunnarsbyn S 118 B7
Gunnarskog S 97 C8
Gunnarvattnet S 105 C16
Gunnebo S 93 D9
Günstedt D 79 D9
Güntersberge D 79 C8
Guntersdorf A 77 E10
Güntersleben D 187 B8
Guntramsdorf A 77 F10
Günzburg D 75 F7
Gunzenhausen D 75 D8
Gura-Biculului MD 154 D4
Gura Caliței RO 161 B9
Gura Camencii MD 154 B2
Gura Foii RO 160 D6
Gura Galbenei MD 154 D3
Gurahonț RO 151 E9
Gura Humorului RO 153 B7
Gurasada RO 151 F10
Gura Ocniței RO 160 D6
Gura Râului RO 152 F3
Gura Teghii RO 161 B9
Gura Vadului RO 161 C8
Gura Văii RO 153 E9
Gura Vitioarei RO 161 C8
Gurbănești RO 161 E9
Gurghiu RO 152 D5
Guri i Bardhë AL 168 B3
Guri i Zi AL 163 E8
Gurk A 73 C9
Gurkovo BG 166 D5
Gurkovo BG 167 C10
Gürlyano BG 164 C6
Gurrea de Gállego E 41 D10
Gurrë e Madhe AL 168 A3
Gurteen IRL 6 E6
Gur'yevsk RUS 136 D3
Gusborn D 83 D10
Gušće HR 149 F7
Gusev RUS 136 D5
Gusinje MNE 163 E9
Gușoeni RO 160 D4
Gusow D 84 A5
Guspini I 64 E2
Gussago I 69 B9
Gusselby S 97 C13
Güssing A 149 B6
Gussola I 66 B1
Gussvattnet S 105 C16
Güsswerk A 148 A4
Güsten D 79 C10
Gustavsberg S 99 D10
Gustavsfors S 97 B10
Gusten D 79 C10
Güstrow D 83 C12
Gusum S 93 C8
Gutach (Schwarzwaldbahn) D 187 E5
Gutau A 77 F7
Gutcher GB 3 D14
Güterfelde D 80 B4
Güterglück D 79 C10
Gütersloh D 17 E10
Gutow D 83 C12
Guttannen CH 70 D6
Guttaring A 73 C10
Gützkow D 84 C4
Guvåg N 110 C8
Güvemalanı TR 173 D7
Güvercinlik TR 177 E10
Guxhagen D 78 D5
Güzelbahçe TR 177 C8
Güzelçamlı TR 177 D10
Gvardeysk RUS 136 D3
Gvarv N 95 D10
Gvozd HR 148 F5
Gvozd MNE 163 D7
Gvozdansko HR 156 B5
Gwda Wielka PL 85 C11
Gweedore IRL 6 B6
Gwithian GB 12 E4
Gy F 26 F5
Gyál H 150 C3
Gyarmat H 149 B8
Gyékényes H 149 D8
Gyenesdiás H 149 C8
Gyermely H 149 A11
Gyé-sur-Seine F 25 D11
Gyhum D 17 B12
Gyljen S 118 B8
Gylling DK 86 D6
Gymno GR 175 C8
Gyomaendrőd H 150 D6
Gyömöre H 149 A9
Gyömrő H 150 C3
Gyöngyös H 150 B4
Gyöngyöspata H 150 B4
Gyönk H 149 C10
Győr H 149 A9
Györköny H 149 C11
Györság H 149 A9
Győrszemere H 149 A9
Györtelek H 145 H5
Győrújbarát H 149 A9
Győrújfalu H 149 A9
Györzámoly H 149 A9
Gyrstinge DK 87 E9
Gysinge S 98 B7
Gytheio GR 178 B4
Gyttorp S 97 C12
Gyueshevo BG 164 E5
Gyula H 151 D7
Gyulaháza H 145 G5
Gyulaj H 149 C10
Gyúró H 149 B11
Gzy PL 139 E10

H

Haabneeme EST 131 B9
Haacht B 19 C10
Häädemeeste EST 131 B9
Haaften NL 183 B6
Haag A 77 F7
Haag am Hausruck A 76 F5
Haag in Oberbayern D 75 F11
Haajainen FIN 123 E17
Haaksbergen NL 17 D7
Haaltert B 19 C9
Haanja EST 131 F14
Haapajärvi FIN 123 C15
Haapa-Kimola FIN 127 D15
Haapakoski FIN 123 E17
Haapakoski FIN 124 F8
Haapakumpu FIN 115 D3
Haapalahti FIN 113 E19
Haapaluoma FIN 123 E10
Haapamäki FIN 123 C16

Haapamäki FIN 123 E17
Haapamäki FIN 123 F12
Haapamäki FIN 125 E10
Haaparanta FIN 115 C3
Haapavesi FIN 119 F14
Haapsalu EST 130 D7
Haar D 75 F10
Haarajoki FIN 123 F17
Haarajoki FIN 127 E13
Haaraoja FIN 119 F16
Haarasaajo FIN 119 B13
Haarbach D 76 E4
Haarby DK 86 E6
Haaren NL 183 B6
Haarlem NL 16 D3
Haastrecht NL 16 E3
Haavisto FIN 127 D11
Habaja EST 131 C10
Habartov CZ 75 B12
Habas F 32 C4
Habay-la-Neuve B 19 E12
Häbbersliden S 118 E4
Habiller TR 167 F7
Hablingbo S 93 E12
Habo S 91 C14
Håbol S 91 B11
Habovka SK 147 C9
Habry CZ 77 D8
Habsheim F 27 E7
Hachenburg D 21 C9
Haciaslanlar TR 167 F7
Hacidanişment TR 171 E10
Hacigelen TR 172 D6
Hacıköy TR 172 C6
Hacinas E 40 E5
Haciırahmanli TR 177 B10
Haciumur TR 167 F7
Hacivelioba TR 173 D8
Hackås S 102 A8
Hackenheim D 21 E9
Hacketstown IRL 9 C9
Hackleton GB 15 C7
Hacksjö S 107 B13
Hadamar D 21 D10
Hadanberg S 107 D14
Haddebo S 92 B6
Haddington GB 5 D11
Haddiscoe GB 15 B12
Haderslev DK 86 E4
Haderup DK 86 C3
Hadim TR 173 B10
Hadımköy TR 173 B10
Hadleigh GB 15 C10
Hadleigh GB 15 D10
Hadley GB 10 F7
Hadol F 26 D5
Hadsel N 110 C8
Hadsten DK 86 C6
Hadsund DK 86 B6
Hadžići BIH 157 E9
Haelen NL 183 C7
Hafnerbach A 77 F8
Haftersbol S 97 C10
Haga S 99 D10
Haganj HR 149 E7
Hagaström S 103 E13
Hagby S 89 B10
Hagebyhöga S 92 C5
Hagen D 17 F8
Hagenbach D 187 C5
Hagenburg D 17 D12
Hagenow D 83 D10
Hagenwerder D 81 D7
Hageri EST 131 C9
Hägerstad S 92 C7
Hagetaubin F 32 C4
Hagetmau F 32 C4
Hagfors S 97 B10
Häggås S 107 C11
Häggdånger S 103 A14
Häggebäcken S 98 B6
Häggenås S 106 E7
Häggnäset S 105 C16
Häggsåsen S 105 E16
Häggsjön S 105 D13
Häggsjövik S 105 D16
Haghig RO 152 F7
Hagley GB 13 A9
Hagondange F 20 F6
Hagsta S 103 E13
Haguenau F 27 C8
Hahausen D 79 C7
Hahnbach D 75 C10
Hahnstätten D 185 D9
Hahót H 149 C7
Haibach D 21 E12
Haibach D 75 D12
Haidmühle D 76 E5
Haiger D 21 C10
Haigerloch D 27 D10
Häijää FIN 127 B9
Hailsham GB 15 F9
Hailuoto FIN 119 D13
Haiming D 76 F3
Haimoo FIN 127 E11
Haina D 75 B8
Haina (Kloster) D 21 B11
Hainburg an der Donau A 77 F11
Hainfeld A 77 F9
Hainichen D 80 E4
Haiterbach D 187 D6
Haitzendorf A 77 F9
Hajala FIN 127 E8
Hajdúbagos H 151 C8
Hajdúdorog H 151 B8
Hajdúhadház H 151 B8
Hajdúnánás H 145 H3
Hajdúsámson H 151 B8
Hajdúszoboszló H 151 C7
Hajdúszovát H 151 C7
Hajmáskér H 149 B10
Hajnáčka SK 147 E10
Hajnøc RKS 164 E3
Hajnówka PL 141 E9
Hajós H 150 E3
Hakadal N 95 B13
Håkafot S 105 C16
Håkansvallen S 102 B7
Hakkavik N 111 C14
Hakkas S 116 E7
Hakkenpää FIN 126 D6
Häkkilä FIN 123 E12
Hakokylä FIN 121 E12
Håkøybotn N 111 A16
Hakstabben N 112 C11
Håkvik N 111 D13
Halahora de Sus MD 153 A10
Håland N 94 E3
Halapić BIH 157 D6
Halászi H 146 F4
Halásztelek H 150 C2

Hălăucești RO 153 C9
Halbe D 80 B5
Halbenrain A 148 C5
Hälberg S 109 F18
Halberstadt D 79 C9
Halblech D 71 B11
Halbturn A 77 G11
Hălchiu RO 153 F7
Hald DK 86 B4
Hald DK 86 B6
Haldarsvik FO 2 A2
Hald Ege DK 86 C4
Halden N 91 A9
Haldensleben D 79 B9
Hale GB 11 E7
Halen B 183 D6
Halenkov CZ 146 C6
Halenkovice CZ 146 C4
Halesowen GB 13 A10
Halesworth GB 15 C12
Halfing D 72 A5
Halfway IRL 8 E5
Halfweg NL 16 D3
Halhjem N 94 B2
Halič SK 147 E9
Halifax GB 11 D8
Halikko FIN 127 E9
Halimba H 149 B9
Halitpaşa TR 177 B10
Haljala EST 131 C12
Häljarp S 87 C12
Hälkia FIN 127 C13
Halkirk GB 3 H10
Halkivaha FIN 127 C9
Halkokumpu FIN 124 F7
Hall S 93 D13
Hälla S 107 D12
Halla-aho FIN 124 C9
Hallabro S 89 C8
Hällabrottet S 92 A6
Halla Heberg S 91 E10
Halland GB 15 F9
Hålland S 105 E14
Hallapuro FIN 123 D12
Hällaryd S 89 C7
Hällbacken S 109 E16
Hällbacken S 109 D12
Hällberga S 98 D7
Hällbo S 103 D11
Hallbodarna S 105 E15
Hällbybrunn S 98 D6
Halle B 19 C9
Halle D 78 C6
Halle NL 183 B8
Halle (Saale) D 79 D10
Halle (Westfalen) D 17 D11
Hällefors S 97 C12
Hälleforsnäs S 93 A9
Hallein A 73 A7
Hällekis S 91 B13
Hällen S 103 E14
Hallen S 105 E16
Hallenberg D 21 B11
Hallencourt F 18 E4
Halle-Neustadt D 79 D10
Hallerndorf D 75 C9
Hällesjö S 103 A11
Hällestad S 92 B7
Hällevadsholm S 91 B10
Hällevik S 88 D7
Hälleviksstrand S 91 C9
Hall-Häxåsen S 106 D8
Hallingby N 95 B13
Hallingeberg S 93 D8
Hällinmäki FIN 124 F9
Hall in Tirol A 72 B4
Hällnäs S 107 C17
Hällnäs S 109 D15
Hällnäs S 109 D13
Hallom S 102 A7
Hallow GB 13 A10
Hällsbäck S 97 D8
Hallsberg S 92 A6
Hällsjö S 107 E13
Hallsta S 98 D6
Hallstahammar S 98 C6
Hallstatt A 73 A8
Hallstavik S 99 B11
Halltorp S 89 C10
Halluin B 19 C7
Hallund DK 86 A6
Hällvik S 109 D14
Hallviken S 106 D8
Hallworthy GB 12 D5
Hälmägel RO 151 E9
Hälmagiu RO 151 E10
Halmeu RO 145 H7
Halmstad S 87 B11
Halna S 92 B4
Halosenniemi FIN 119 D13
Halosenranta FIN 115 E2
Halovo SRB 159 E9
Hals DK 86 B6
Halsa N 104 E4
Halsenbach D 21 D9
Hal'shany BY 137 E13
Hälsingby FIN 122 D7
Hälsjo S 103 C12
Halsøy N 108 B5
Halsskov DK 87 E8
Halstead GB 15 D10
Halstenbek D 83 C7
Halsteren NL 16 E2
Halstroff F 20 F6
Halsua FIN 123 D12
Haltern D 17 E8
Halttula FIN 119 C14
Haltwhistle GB 5 F12
Haluna FIN 125 D10
Hälvä FIN 129 B11
Halvarsgårdarna S 97 B13
Halver D 185 B7
Halvrimmen DK 86 A5
Halwell GB 13 E7
Halže CZ 75 C12
Ham F 19 E7
Ham GB 3 E12
Hamar N 101 E14
Hamari FIN 119 C14
Hamarøy N 108 C5
Hamarøy N 111 D10
Hambach F 27 B7
Hambergen D 17 B11
Hambledon GB 13 D12
Hambrücken D 21 F11
Hamburg D 83 C7
Hamburgsund S 91 B9
Hambye F 23 C9
Hamcearca RO 155 C2
Hamdibey TR 173 E7
Hämeenkoski FIN 127 C13

Himmaste *EST* 131 E14
Himmelberg *A* 73 C9
Himmelpforten *D* 17 A12
Hînceşti *MD* 154 D3
Hinckley *GB* 11 F9
Hindås *S* 91 D11
Hindenburg *D* 83 E11
Hinderwell *GB* 11 B10
Hindhead *GB* 15 E7
Hindley *GB* 10 D6
Hindon *GB* 13 C10
Hindrem *N* 104 D8
Hinganmaa *FIN* 117 D15
Hingham *GB* 15 B10
Hinnerjöki *FIN* 126 C6
Hinnerup *DK* 86 C6
Hinneryd *S* 87 B13
Hinojal *E* 45 E8
Hinojales *E* 51 C6
Hinojares *E* 55 D7
Hinojasas de Calatrava *E* 54 B4
Hinojos *E* 51 E7
Hinojosa *E* 47 B9
Hinojosa de Duero *E* 45 C7
Hinojosa de Jarque *E* 42 F2
Hinojosa del Duque *E* 51 B9
Hinojosa del Valle *E* 51 C7
Hinojosa de San Vicente *E* 46 D3
Hinova *RO* 159 D10
Hinte *D* 17 B8
Hinterhermsdorf *D* 80 E6
Hinternah *D* 75 A8
Hinterrhein *CH* 71 D8
Hintersee *A* 73 A7
Hintersee *D* 84 C6
Hinterweidenthal *D* 186 C4
Hinterzarten *D* 27 E9
Hinthaara *FIN* 127 E13
Hinwil *CH* 27 F10
Hinx *F* 32 C4
Hippolytushoef *NL* 16 C3
Hîrbovăţ *MD* 154 C2
Hîrjauca *MD* 154 C2
Hirka *TR* 181 B9
Hirnyk *UA* 144 C9
Hirrlingen *D* 27 D10
Hirschaid *D* 75 C9
Hirschau *D* 75 C10
Hirschberg *D* 75 B10
Hirschfeld *D* 80 D5
Hirschhorn (Neckar) *D* 187 C6
Hirsilä *FIN* 127 B11
Hirsingue *F* 27 E7
Hirson *F* 19 E9
Hîrtop *MD* 154 D3
Hîrtopul Mare *MD* 154 C3
Hirtshals *DK* 90 D6
Hirvas *FIN* 119 B14
Hirvaskoski *FIN* 120 D9
Hirvasperä *FIN* 119 E13
Hirvasvaara *FIN* 115 E5
Hirvelä *FIN* 119 D16
Hirvelä *FIN* 121 F14
Hirvensalmi *FIN* 128 B6
Hirviäkuru *FIN* 115 D1
Hirvihaara *FIN* 127 D13
Hirvijoki *FIN* 123 E10
Hirvikylä *FIN* 123 F9
Hirvilahti *FIN* 124 D8
Hirvineva *FIN* 119 E14
Hirvivaara *FIN* 121 E13
Hirvlax *FIN* 122 D8
Hirwaun *GB* 13 B7
Hirzenhain *D* 21 D12
Hisarönü *TR* 181 C8
Hishult *S* 87 C12
Hissjön *S* 122 C4
Histon *GB* 15 C9
Hita *E* 47 C6
Hitchin *GB* 15 D8
Hitis *FIN* 126 F8
Hittarp *S* 87 C11
Hittisau *A* 71 C9
Hitzacker *D* 83 D10
Hitzendorf *A* 148 B4
Hitzhusen *D* 83 C7
Hiukkajoki *FIN* 129 B12
Hiyche *UA* 144 C8
Hjäggsjö *S* 122 C3
Hjallerup *DK* 86 A6
Hjältevad *S* 92 D6
Hjärnarp *S* 87 C11
Hjärsås *S* 88 C6
Hjärtum *S* 91 C11
Hjarup *DK* 86 E4
Hjelle *N* 100 C6
Hjellestad *N* 94 B2
Hjellsand *N* 110 C8
Hjelmeland *N* 94 D4
Hjelset *N* 100 A7
Hjerkinn *N* 101 B11
Hjerm *DK* 86 C3
Hjo *S* 92 C4
Hjordkær *DK* 86 E4
Hjørring *DK* 90 E7
Hjorted *S* 93 D8
Hjortkvarn *S* 92 B6
Hjortsberga *S* 88 B6
Hjørungavåg *N* 100 B4
Hjuvik *S* 91 D10
Hlavani *UA* 154 F4
Hlebine *HR* 149 D7
Hligeni *MD* 154 B3
Hlinaia *MD* 153 A10
Hlinaia *MD* 154 C4
Hlinaia *MD* 154 D5
Hliník nad Hronom *SK* 147 D7
Hlinné *SK* 145 F4
Hlinsko *CZ* 77 C9
Hlohovec *SK* 146 E5
Hlubočky *CZ* 146 B4
Hluboká nad Vltavou *CZ* 77 D6
Hlučín *CZ* 146 B6
Hlyboka *UA* 153 A7
Hlybokaye *BY* 133 F3
Hlyboke *UA* 155 B5
Hnatkiv *UA* 154 A2
Hněvotín *CZ* 77 C12
Hniezdné *SK* 145 E2
Hnizdychiv *UA* 145 E9
Hnojník *CZ* 147 B7
Hnúšťa *SK* 147 D9
Hobol *H* 149 D9
Hobøl *N* 95 C13
Hobro *DK* 86 B5
Hoburg *S* 93 F12
Hoçë e Qytetit *RKS* 163 E10
Hoceni *RO* 153 D12
Hochdonn *D* 82 B6
Hochdorf *CH* 27 F9
Hochdorf *D* 71 A9
Hochfelden *F* 27 C8
Höchheim *D* 75 B7
Hochspeyer *D* 186 C4
Hochstadt (Pfalz) *D* 187 C5
Höchstadt an der Aisch *D* 75 C8
Höchstädt an der Donau *D* 75 E8
Hochstetten-Dhaun *D* 21 E8
Höchst im Odenwald *D* 187 B6
Hoçisht *AL* 168 C4
Hockenheim *D* 187 C6
Hoczew *PL* 145 E5
Hodac *RO* 152 D5
Hodalen *N* 101 B14
Hoddesdon *GB* 15 D8
Hodejov *SK* 147 E10
Hodenhagen *D* 82 E7
Hodkovice nad Mohelkou *CZ* 81 E8
Hódmezővásárhely *H* 150 E5
Hodnet *GB* 10 F6
Hodod *RO* 151 C11
Hodonice *CZ* 77 E10
Hodonín *CZ* 77 E12
Hodoşa *RO* 152 D5
Hodruša-Hámre *SK* 147 E7
Hodsager *DK* 86 C3
Hodyszewo *PL* 141 E7
Hoek *NL* 16 F1
Hoek van Holland *NL* 16 E2
Hoem *N* 104 F4
Hoenderloo *NL* 183 A7
Hœnheim *F* 186 D4
Hoensbroek *NL* 19 C12
Hœrdt *F* 186 D4
Hoeselt *B* 19 C11
Hoevelaken *NL* 16 D4
Hoeven *NL* 16 E3
Hof *D* 21 C10
Hof *D* 75 B10
Hof *N* 95 C12
Hofbieber *D* 78 E6
Hoffstad *N* 104 C8
Hofgeismar *D* 21 B12
Hofheim am Taunus *D* 21 D10
Hofheim in Unterfranken *D* 75 B8
Hofles *N* 105 B11
Hofors *S* 98 A6
Hofsøy *N* 111 B13
Hofterup *S* 87 D11
Höganäs *S* 87 C11
Högås *S* 108 E9
Högbacka *S* 103 D12
Högbo *S* 103 E12
Högboda *S* 97 C9
Högbränna *S* 109 F15
Högen *S* 103 C13
Högfors *S* 97 B15
Högfors *S* 97 C13
Höghilag *RO* 152 E5
Höghiz *RO* 152 F6
Høgild *DK* 86 C3
Högland *S* 107 B9
Høglekardallen *S* 105 E15
Høgli *N* 111 B14
Höglunda *S* 107 E9
Hogosht *RKS* 164 D4
Högrun *S* 105 D16
Högsåra *FIN* 126 F7
Högsäter *S* 91 B11
Högsäter *S* 96 C6
Högsäter *S* 97 D8
Högsby *S* 89 A10
Høgset *N* 104 F3
Högsjö *S* 92 A7
Högsjö *S* 103 A14
Hogstad *S* 92 C6
Högstorp *S* 91 C10
Högträsk *S* 116 E5
Högvålen *S* 102 B4
Hőgyész *H* 149 C10
Hohberg *D* 186 E4
Hohen-Altheim *D* 75 E8
Hohenaspe *D* 82 C7
Hohenau *D* 76 E5
Hohenau an der March *A* 77 E11
Hohenberg *A* 77 G9
Hohenbocka *D* 80 D6
Hohenbucko *D* 80 C4
Hohenburg *D* 75 D10
Hohendorf *D* 84 B5
Hoheneich *A* 77 E8
Hohenems *A* 71 C9
Hohenfels *D* 75 D10
Hohenfurch *D* 71 B11
Hohengöhren *D* 79 A11
Hohenhameln *D* 79 B7
Hohenkammer *D* 75 F10
Hohenkirchen *D* 17 A9
Höhenkirchen-Siegertsbrunn *D* 75 F10
Hohenleuben *D* 79 E11
Hohenlockstedt *D* 82 C7
Hohenmocker *D* 84 C4
Hohenmölsen *D* 79 D11
Hohennauen *D* 83 E12
Hohenpeißenberg *D* 71 B12
Hohenroth *D* 75 B7
Hohensaaten *D* 84 E6
Hohenseeden *D* 79 B11
Hohenstein-Ernstthal *D* 79 E12
Hohenthann *D* 75 E11
Hohenthurm *D* 79 C11
Hohen Wangelin *D* 83 C12
Hohenwart *D* 75 E9
Hohenwarth *D* 76 D3
Hohenwestedt *D* 82 B7
Höhn *D* 21 C9
Höhn *D* 82 B7
Hohne *D* 79 A7
Hohnhorst *D* 17 D12
Hohnstorf (Elbe) *D* 83 D9
Höhr-Grenzhausen *D* 21 D9
Hohwacht (Ostsee) *D* 83 B9
Hoikankylä *FIN* 124 E7
Hoikka *FIN* 121 E12
Hoisdorf *D* 83 C8
Hoisko *FIN* 123 D11
Højby *DK* 86 E6
Højby *DK* 87 D9
Højer *DK* 86 F3
Højmark *DK* 86 C2
Højslev *DK* 86 B4
Højslev Stationsby *DK* 86 B4
Hok *S* 92 D4
Hökåsen *S* 98 C7
Hökerum *S* 91 D13
Hökhult *S* 91 A13
Hökhuvud *S* 99 B10
Hokka *FIN* 128 B6
Hökkaskylä *FIN* 123 E12
Hokksund *N* 95 C11
Hokland *N* 111 C11
Hökmark *S* 118 F6
Hökön *S* 88 C6
Hol *N* 101 E8
Hol *N* 111 C11
Holand *N* 110 D9
Holandsvika *N* 108 E5
Holasovice *CZ* 142 G4
Holbæk *DK* 86 B6
Holbæk *DK* 87 D9
Holbeach *GB* 11 F12
Holboca *RO* 153 C11
Holbøl *DK* 86 F4
Holbrook *GB* 15 D11
Holdorf *D* 17 C10
Holeby *DK* 83 A10
Hølen *N* 95 C13
Holešov *CZ* 146 C5
Holevik *N* 100 D1
Holguera *E* 45 E8
Holíč *SK* 77 E12
Holice *CZ* 77 B9
Höljes *S* 102 E4
Holkestad *N* 110 E8
Holkonkylä *FIN* 123 E11
Hollabrunn *A* 77 E10
Hollandscheveld *NL* 17 C7
Hollange *B* 19 E12
Hollås *N* 105 C11
Holle *D* 79 B7
Høllen *N* 90 C2
Hollenbach *D* 75 F9
Hollenbek *D* 83 C9
Hollenegg *A* 73 C11
Hollenstedt *D* 82 D7
Hollenstein an der Ybbs *A* 73 A10
Hollern-Twielenfleth *D* 82 C7
Hollfeld *D* 75 C9
Hollingstedt *D* 82 B6
Hollington *GB* 15 F10
Hollingworth *GB* 11 E8
Hollóháza *H* 145 F3
Hollola *FIN* 127 D14
Hollum *NL* 16 B5
Hollybush *GB* 4 E7
Hollyford *IRL* 8 C6
Hollywood *IRL* 7 F9
Holm *D* 82 C7
Holm *DK* 86 E5
Holm *N* 105 A12
Holm *N* 110 C9
Holm *S* 103 A12
Holm *S* 107 E13
Hol'ma *UA* 154 B5
Holmajärvi *S* 111 E18
Holme-Olstrup *DK* 87 E9
Holme-on-Spalding-Moor *GB* 11 D10
Holmestrand *N* 95 D12
Holmfirth *GB* 11 D8
Holmfors *S* 118 D4
Holmisperä *FIN* 123 D14
Holmsjö *S* 89 C9
Holmsjö *S* 107 A14
Holmsjö *S* 107 D12
Holmsund *S* 122 C4
Holmsvattensel *S* 118 B6
Holmsveden *S* 103 D12
Holmträsk *S* 107 B16
Hölö *S* 93 A11
Holod *RO* 151 D9
Hołodowska *PL* 144 C7
Holoşniţa *MD* 153 A12
Holoubkov *CZ* 76 C5
Holovets'ko *UA* 145 E6
Holovne *UA* 141 H10
Holsbybrunn *S* 92 E6
Holsljunga *S* 91 E12
Holsta *EST* 131 F14
Holstebro *DK* 86 C3
Holsted *DK* 86 D3
Hölstein *CH* 27 F8
Holsworthy *GB* 12 D6
Holt *GB* 10 E6
Holt *GB* 15 B11
Holt *N* 111 B16
Holt *N* 111 B17
Holte *DK* 87 D10
Holten *NL* 17 D6
Holtet *N* 102 E3
Holtgast *D* 17 A9
Holthusen *D* 83 C10
Holtsee *D* 83 B7
Holungen *D* 79 D7
Holwerd *NL* 16 B5
Holycross *IRL* 9 C7
Holyhead *GB* 10 E2
Holywell *GB* 7 D7
Holywell *GB* 10 E5
Holywood *GB* 4 F5
Holzappel *D* 185 D8
Holzen *D* 78 C6
Holzgerlingen *D* 187 D7
Holzhausen an der Haide *D* 21 D9
Holzheim *D* 21 D11
Holzheim *D* 75 E8
Holzheim *D* 75 E8
Holzheim *D* 75 F7
Holzkirchen *D* 72 A4
Holzminden *D* 21 A12
Holzthaleben *D* 79 D8
Holzweißig *D* 79 C11
Holzwickede *D* 17 E9
Hom *DK* 87 E9
Homberg (Efze) *D* 21 B12
Homberg (Ohm) *D* 21 C11
Hombourg-Budange *F* 186 C1
Hombourg-Haut *F* 186 C2
Homburg *D* 21 F8
Homécourt *F* 20 F5
Homersfield *GB* 15 C11
Homesh *AL* 168 A3
Hommelstø *N* 108 F4
Hommelvik *N* 105 E9
Hommersåk *N* 94 E3
Homna *S* 103 D10
Homocea *RO* 153 E10
Homokmégy *H* 150 E3
Homokszentgyörgy *H* 149 D9
Homoroade *RO* 151 B11
Homorod *RO* 152 E6
Homrogd *H* 145 G2
Homyel' *BY* 133 F5
Hondarribia *E* 32 D2
Hondón de las Nieves *E* 56 E3
Hondón de los Frailes *E* 56 E3
Hondschoote *F* 18 C6
Hône *I* 68 B4
Hønefoss *N* 95 B12
Honfleur *F* 23 B12
Høng *DK* 87 D8
Honiton *GB* 13 D8
Honkajoki *FIN* 122 G8
Honkakoski *FIN* 126 B7
Honkakylä *FIN* 122 E9
Honkilahti *FIN* 126 D7
Honley *GB* 11 D8
Honningsvåg *N* 100 B2
Honningsvåg *N* 113 B16
Hönö *S* 91 D10
Honoratka *PL* 142 B5
Honrubia *E* 47 E8
Honrubia de la Cuesta *E* 40 F4
Hønseby *N* 113 B11
Hontacillas *E* 47 E8
Hontalbilla *E* 40 F3
Hontanaya *E* 47 E7
Hontianske Nemce *SK* 147 E7
Hontoria de la Cantera *E* 40 D4
Hontoria del Pinar *E* 40 E5
Hontoria de Valdearados *E* 40 E4
Hoofddorp *NL* 16 D3
Hoogerheide *NL* 16 F2
Hoogersmilde *NL* 16 C6
Hoogeveen *NL* 17 C6
Hoogezand-Sappemeer *NL* 17 B7
Hoogkarspel *NL* 16 C4
Hoog-Keppel *NL* 183 B8
Hoogkerk *NL* 17 B6
Hoogland *NL* 183 A6
Hoogstede *D* 17 C7
Hoogstraten *B* 16 F3
Hoogvliet *NL* 16 E2
Hook *GB* 11 D10
Hook *GB* 14 E7
Hooksiel *D* 17 A10
Höör *S* 87 D13
Hoorn *NL* 16 C4
Hoornaar *NL* 182 B5
Hopârta *RO* 152 E3
Hope *GB* 10 E5
Hope *N* 100 E3
Hopeman *GB* 3 K10
Hopen *N* 111 E10
Hopfgarten im Brixental *A* 72 B5
Hopfgarten in Defereggen *A* 72 C6
Hopland *N* 100 C4
Hoppstädten *D* 21 E8
Hoppula *FIN* 115 F2
Hopseidet *N* 113 B20
Hopsten *D* 17 D9
Hopton *GB* 15 B12
Hoptonheath *GB* 13 A9
Hoptrup *DK* 86 E4
Horam *GB* 15 F9
Horažďovice *CZ* 76 D5
Horb am Neckar *D* 27 D10
Horbova *UA* 153 A8
Hörbranz *A* 71 B9
Hørby *DK* 90 E7
Hörby *S* 87 D13
Horcajo de las Torres *E* 45 B10
Horcajo de los Montes *E* 46 F3
Horcajo de Santiago *E* 47 E7
Horcajo Medianero *E* 45 C10
Horda *N* 94 C5
Horda *S* 88 A6
Hörde *D* 185 B7
Horden *GB* 11 B9
Hordum *DK* 86 B3
Horea *RO* 151 E10
Horeb *GB* 12 A6
Horeşti *MD* 153 C11
Horezu *RO* 160 C3
Horgen *CH* 27 F10
Horgenzell *D* 71 B9
Horgeşti *RO* 153 E10
Horgoš *SRB* 150 E4
Horia *RO* 153 D9
Horia *RO* 155 C2
Horia *RO* 155 D2
Hořice *CZ* 77 B9
Horinchove *UA* 145 G7
Horitschon *A* 149 A7
Horjul *SLO* 73 D9
Horka *D* 81 D7
Hôrka *SK* 145 E1
Hörken *S* 97 B12
Horley *GB* 15 E8
Hörlitz *D* 80 C5
Hormakumpu *FIN* 117 C14
Hormilla *E* 40 D6
Horn *A* 77 E9
Horn *N* 95 A12
Horn *N* 108 E3
Horn *S* 92 D7
Hornachos *E* 51 B7
Hornachuelos *E* 51 D9
Horná Kraľová *SK* 146 E5
Horná Potôň *SK* 146 E4
Horná Streda *SK* 146 D5
Horná Štubňa *SK* 147 D7
Horná Súča *SK* 146 D5
Horná Ves *SK* 146 D6
Hornbach *D* 21 F8
Horn-Bad Meinberg *D* 17 E11
Hornbæk *DK* 87 C10
Hornburg *D* 79 B8
Hornby *GB* 10 C6
Horncastle *GB* 11 E11
Horndal *N* 109 A10
Horndal *S* 98 B6
Horndean *GB* 14 F6
Horne *DK* 86 D3
Horne *DK* 86 E6
Horne *DK* 90 D6
Horneburg *D* 82 C7
Hörnefors *S* 122 C3
Horné Obdokovce *SK* 146 E6
Horné Orešany *SK* 146 E4
Horné Saliby *SK* 146 E5
Horné Srnie *SK* 146 C6
Horní Bečva *CZ* 146 C6
Horní Benešov *CZ* 146 B5
Horní Beřkovice *CZ* 76 B6
Horní Cerekev *CZ* 77 D8
Horní Jelení *CZ* 77 B10
Horní Jiřetín *CZ* 80 E5
Horní Lideč *CZ* 146 C6
Horní Maršov *CZ* 81 E9
Horní Moštěnice *CZ* 146 C4
Hornindal *N* 100 C5
Hørning *DK* 86 C6
Horní Planá *CZ* 76 E6
Horní Slavkov *CZ* 75 B12
Horní Štěpánov *CZ* 77 C11
Horní Stropnice *CZ* 77 E7
Horní Suchá *CZ* 146 B6
Hornmyr *S* 107 C14
Hornnäs *S* 97 B9
Hornnes *N* 90 B2
Hornön *S* 103 A14
Hornos *E* 55 C7
Hornow *D* 81 C7
Hornoy-le-Bourg *F* 18 E4
Hornsea *GB* 11 D11
Hörnsjö *S* 107 D17
Hornslet *DK* 86 C6
Hornstorf *D* 83 C11
Hornsyld *DK* 86 D5
Hörnum *D* 82 A4
Hornum *DK* 86 B4
Horný Bar *SK* 146 F4
Horný Tisovník *SK* 147 E8
Horný Vadičov *SK* 147 C7
Horoatu Crasnei *RO* 151 C10
Horodişte *MD* 153 A11
Horodişte *MD* 153 B10
Horodkivka *UA* 154 A3
Horodło *PL* 144 B9
Horodniceni *RO* 153 B8
Horodnye *UA* 154 F3
Horodok *UA* 144 D8
Horoměřice *CZ* 76 B6
Horonda *UA* 145 G6
Horonkylä *FIN* 122 E7
Hořovice *CZ* 76 C5
Horrabridge *GB* 12 D6
Horreby *DK* 83 A11
Horred *S* 91 E11
Hörsching *A* 76 F6
Horsdal *N* 108 B7
Horseleap *IRL* 6 F5
Horsens *DK* 86 D5
Horsforth *GB* 11 D8
Horsham *GB* 15 E8
Hørsholm *DK* 87 D10
Hörsingen *D* 79 B9
Horslunde *DK* 87 F8
Horsmanaho *FIN* 125 E12
Horsnes *N* 111 B18
Horšovský Týn *CZ* 76 C3
Horsskog *S* 98 B8
Horst *NL* 16 F6
Horst (Holstein) *D* 82 C7
Horstedt *D* 17 B12
Hörstel *D* 17 D9
Horstmar *D* 17 D8
Hort *H* 150 B4
Horten *N* 95 D12
Hortezuela *E* 40 F6
Hortigüela *E* 40 D5
Hortlax *S* 118 D6
Hortobágy *H* 151 B7
Horton in Ribblesdale *GB* 11 C7
Høruphav *DK* 86 F5
Hørve *DK* 87 D8
Hörvik *S* 89 C7
Horw *CH* 70 C6
Horwich *GB* 10 D6
Horyniec-Zdrój *PL* 144 C7
Horyszów *PL* 144 B8
Hösbach *D* 21 D12
Hosena *D* 80 D6
Hosenfeld *D* 74 A5
Hoset *N* 108 B8
Hosingen *L* 20 D6
Hosio *FIN* 119 C15
Hosjö *S* 106 E8
Hosjöbottnarna *S* 105 E15
Hoşköy *TR* 173 C7
Hospital *IRL* 8 D6
Hossa *FIN* 121 D14
Hössjö *S* 122 C3
Hossjön *S* 107 D9
Hoßkirch *D* 27 E11
Hosszúhetény *H* 149 D10
Hosszúpályi *H* 151 C8
Hosszúpereszteg *H* 149 B8
Hošťálková *CZ* 146 C5
Hostalric *E* 43 D9
Hostens *F* 32 B4
Hostěradice *CZ* 77 E10
Hostie *SK* 146 E6
Hostinné *CZ* 81 E9
Hoštka *CZ* 76 B6
Hostomice *CZ* 76 C6
Hostomice *CZ* 80 E5
Hoston *N* 104 E7
Höstoppen *S* 106 C8
Hostouň *CZ* 75 C12
Hostrupskov *DK* 86 E4
Höstsätern *S* 102 C4
Hot *AL* 163 E7
Hotarele *RO* 161 E8
Hoting *S* 107 C10
Hotinja vas *SLO* 148 D5
Hotonj *BIH* 162 D4
Hotton *B* 19 D11
Hou *DK* 86 A6
Houbie *GB* 3 D15
Houdain *F* 18 D6
Houdan *F* 24 C6
Houdelaincourt *F* 26 C3
Houécourt *F* 26 D4
Houeillès *F* 32 B6
Houeydets *F* 33 D6
Houffalize *B* 19 D12
Houghton le Spring *GB* 5 F14
Houghton Regis *GB* 15 D7
Houlbjerg *DK* 86 C5
Houlgate *F* 23 B11
Hourtin *F* 28 E3
Hourtin-Plage *F* 28 E3
Houten *NL* 16 D4
Houthalen *B* 19 B11
Houthulst *B* 18 C6
Houton *GB* 3 H10
Houtsala *FIN* 126 E6
Houtskär *FIN* 126 E5
Houyet *B* 184 D3
Hov *DK* 86 D6
Hov *N* 101 E12
Hov *N* 108 D4
Hov *N* 111 A18
Hova *S* 92 B4
Hovborg *DK* 86 D3
Hovda *N* 94 D4
Hovde *N* 90 B4
Hovden *N* 110 C8
Hovdevik *N* 100 B2
Hove *GB* 15 F8
Hovedgård *DK* 86 D5
Hövelhof *D* 17 E11
Hoven *DK* 86 D3
Hoveton *GB* 15 B11
Hovězí *CZ* 146 C6
Hovid *S* 103 B13
Hovin *N* 104 E8
Hovingham *GB* 11 C10
Hovmantorp *S* 89 B8
Høvringen *N* 101 C10
Hovslund Stationsby *DK* 86 E4
Hovsta *S* 97 D13
Howden *GB* 11 D10
Howth *IRL* 7 F10
Höxter *D* 17 E12
Hoya *D* 17 C12
Hoya Gonzalo *E* 55 B9
Høyanger *N* 100 D4
Høydal *N* 90 A5
Hoyerswerda *D* 80 D6
Hoylake *GB* 10 E5
Høylandet *N* 105 B12
Hoym *D* 79 C9
Hoyocasero *E* 46 D3
Hoyo de Manzanares *E* 46 C5
Hoyos *E* 45 D7
Hoyos del Espino *E* 45 D10
Höytiä *FIN* 123 F14
Hoyvík *FO* 2 A3
Hozha *BY* 137 F8
Hrabove *UA* 154 A4
Hrabyně *CZ* 146 B6
Hradec Králové *CZ* 77 B9
Hradec nad Moravicí *CZ* 146 B5
Hradec nad Svitavou *CZ* 77 C10
Hrádek *CZ* 147 B7
Hrádek nad Nisou *CZ* 81 E7
Hradenytsi *UA* 154 D6
Hradešice *CZ* 76 D5
Hradište *SK* 146 D6
Hradište pod Vrátnom *SK* 146 D5
Hradištko *CZ* 76 C6
Hraň *SK* 145 F4
Hranice *CZ* 75 B11
Hranice *CZ* 146 B5
Hranovnica *SK* 145 F1
Hrasnica *BIH* 157 E9
Hrastnik *SLO* 73 D11
Hrawzhyshki *BY* 137 E12
Hrebenyky *UA* 154 D5
Hreljin *HR* 67 B10
Hrhov *SK* 145 F2
Hrimne *UA* 145 D8
Hriňová *SK* 147 D9
Hristovaia *MD* 154 A3
Hrnjadi *BIH* 156 D5
Hrob *CZ* 80 E5
Hrochot *SK* 147 D8
Hrochův Týnec *CZ* 77 C9
Hrodna *BY* 140 C9
Hromnice *CZ* 76 C4
Hronec *SK* 147 D9
Hronov *CZ* 77 B10
Hronovce *SK* 147 E7
Hronský Beñ Beňx *SK* 147 E7
Hrotovice *CZ* 77 D10
Hroznová Lhota *CZ* 146 D4
Hrtkovci *SRB* 158 D4
Hrubieszów *PL* 144 B8
Hruşca *MD* 154 A3
Hrušky *CZ* 77 E11
Hruşova *MD* 154 C3
Hrušovany *SK* 146 E6
Hrušovany nad Jevišovkou *CZ* 77 E10
Hruštín *SK* 147 C8
Hruszniew *PL* 141 F7
Hrvaćani *BIH* 157 C7
Hrvace *HR* 156 E6
Hrvatska Dubica *HR* 157 B6
Hrvatska Kostajnica *HR* 156 B6
Hrynyava *UA* 152 B5
Huaröd *S* 88 D5
Huarte *E* 32 E2
Hubová *SK* 147 C8
Hückelhoven *D* 20 B6
Hückeswagen *D* 21 B8
Hucknall *GB* 11 E9
Hucksjöåsen *S* 103 A10
Hucqueliers *F* 15 F12
Huddersfield *GB* 11 D8
Hüde *D* 17 C10
Hude (Oldenburg) *D* 17 B10
Hudeşti *RO* 153 A9
Hudiksvall *S* 103 C13
Huécija *E* 55 F7
Huedin *RO* 151 D11
Huélago *E* 55 E6
Huelgoat *F* 22 D4
Huelma *E* 53 A10
Huelva *E* 51 E6
Huelves *E* 47 D7
Huércal de Almería *E* 55 F8
Huércal-Overa *E* 55 E9
Huérguina *E* 47 D9
Huérmeces *E* 40 C4
Huerta del Marquesada *E* 47 D9
Huerta del Rey *E* 40 E5
Huerta de Valdecarábanos *E* 46 E5
Huertahernando *E* 47 C8
Huerto *E* 42 D3
Huesa *E* 55 D6
Huesa del Común *E* 42 E2
Huesca *E* 41 D11
Huéscar *E* 55 D7
Huete *E* 47 D7
Huétor-Tájar *E* 53 B8
Huétor-Vega *E* 53 B9
Huévar *E* 51 E7
Hüfingen *D* 27 E9
Hufthamar *N* 94 B2
Hugh Town *GB* 12 F2
Hugulia *N* 101 D11
Hugyag *H* 147 E8
Huhdasjärvi *FIN* 127 C16
Huhmarkoski *FIN* 123 D10
Huhtamo *FIN* 127 C8
Huhti *FIN* 127 C10
Huhtilampi *FIN* 125 F14
Huhus *FIN* 125 E15
Huijbergen *NL* 182 C4
Huikola *FIN* 119 E16
Huisheim *D* 75 E8
Huisinis *GB* 2 K2
Huissen *NL* 16 E5
Huissinkylä *FIN* 122 E8
Huittinen *FIN* 126 C8
Huizen *NL* 16 D4
Hujakkala *FIN* 128 D8
Hukijärvi *FIN* 121 D10
Hukkajärvi *FIN* 125 B14
Hulín *CZ* 146 C4
Hulja *EST* 131 C12
Huljen *S* 103 B12
Hulkkola *FIN* 124 E8
Hull *GB* 11 D11
Hüllhorst *D* 17 D11
Hullo *EST* 130 D6
Hullsjön *S* 103 A12
Hüls *D* 183 C8
Hulsberg *NL* 183 D7
Hulst *NL* 16 F2
Hult *S* 91 A15
Hult *S* 92 D6
Hulterstad *S* 89 C11
Hultsfred *S* 92 D7
Hulu *S* 91 D13
Hulubeşti *RO* 160 D6
Hulyanka *UA* 154 C4
Hum *BIH* 157 F10
Hum *BIH* 162 D5
Humalajoki *FIN* 123 D13
Humanes de Madrid *E* 46 D5
Humanes de Mohernando *E* 47 C6
Humberston *GB* 11 D11
Humbie *GB* 5 D11
Humble *DK* 83 A9
Humenné *SK* 145 F4
Humilladero *E* 53 B7
Humlebæk *DK* 87 D11
Humlegärdsstrand *S* 103 D13
Humlum *DK* 86 B3
Hummelholm *S* 107 D17
Hummelo *NL* 183 A8
Hummelsta *S* 98 C7
Hummuli *EST* 131 F12
Hum na Sutli *HR* 148 D5
Humpolec *CZ* 77 C8
Humppila *FIN* 127 D9
Humshaugh *GB* 5 E12
Huncovce *SK* 145 E1
Hundåla *N* 108 E4
Hundberg *N* 111 B18
Hundberg *S* 109 F16
Hundborg *DK* 86 B3
Hundeluft *D* 79 C11
Hunderdorf *D* 75 E12
Hundested *DK* 87 D9
Hundholmen *N* 111 D11
Hundorp *N* 101 C11
Hundsangen *D* 21 D9
Hundshübel *D* 79 E12
Hundsjön *S* 118 C7
Hundslund *DK* 86 D6
Hundvin *N* 100 E2
Hune *DK* 86 A5
Hunedoara *RO* 151 F10
Hünfeld *D* 78 E6
Hünfelden-Kirberg *D* 21 D10
Hunge *S* 103 A9
Hungen *D* 21 D11
Hungerford *GB* 13 C11
Hunnebostrand *S* 91 C9
Hunsel *NL* 19 B12
Hunspach *F* 27 C8
Hunstanton *GB* 11 F12
Huntingdon *GB* 15 C8
Huntlosen *D* 17 C10
Huntly *GB* 3 L11
Hünxe *D* 183 B9
Hunya *H* 151 D6
Huopanankoski *FIN* 123 D15
Hüpstedt *D* 79 D7
Hurbanovo *SK* 146 F6
Hurdal *N* 95 B14
Hurdalsverk *N* 95 B14
Hurezani *RO* 160 D3
Huriel *F* 29 C10
Hurissalo *FIN* 128 C8
Hurler's Cross *IRL* 8 C5
Hursley *GB* 13 C12
Hurst Green *GB* 15 E9
Hurstpierpoint *GB* 15 F8
Hurteles *E* 41 D7
Hürth *D* 21 C7
Huruieşti *RO* 153 E10
Huruksela *FIN* 128 D6
Hurup *DK* 86 B2
Hurva *S* 87 D12
Huså *S* 105 E14
Husås *S* 106 E7
Husasău de Tinca *RO* 151 D8
Husbands Bosworth *GB* 13 A12
Husberget *S* 102 B6
Husbondliden *S* 107 B15
Husby *D* 82 A7
Husby *S* 97 B15
Husby *S* 99 B9
Hushcha *UA* 141 H9
Huşi *RO* 153 D12
Husinec *CZ* 76 D5
Husjorda *N* 111 D9
Huskvarna *S* 92 D4
Husnes *N* 94 C3
Husnicioara *RO* 159 D10
Husøy *N* 108 D3
Hussjö *S* 103 A14
Hustopeče *CZ* 77 E11
Hustopeče nad Bečvou *CZ* 146 B5
Husum *D* 17 C12
Husum *D* 82 B6
Husum *S* 107 E16
Husvik *N* 108 E4
Huta *PL* 141 H3
Huta Komorowska *PL* 143 F12
Hutisko-Solanec *CZ* 146 C6
Hutovo *BIH* 162 D4
Hütschenhausen *D* 186 C3
Hüttau *A* 73 B7
Hüttenberg *A* 73 C10
Hüttisheim *D* 74 F6
Hüttlingen *D* 75 E7
Huttoft *GB* 11 E12
Hüttschlag *A* 73 B7
Huttukylä *FIN* 119 D15
Huttwil *CH* 27 F8
Huuhilonkylä *FIN* 121 F13
Huuki *S* 117 D11
Huutijärvi *FIN* 127 C11
Huutokoski *FIN* 124 F9
Huutokoski *FIN* 125 E12
Huutoniemi *FIN* 113 E18
Huvåsen *S* 118 D4
Hüven *D* 17 C9
Huwniki *PL* 145 D6
Huy *B* 19 C11
Hvalpsund *DK* 86 B4
Hvalsø *DK* 87 D9
Hvalvik *FO* 2 A2
Hvam *DK* 86 B5
Hvannasund *FO* 2 A3
Hvar *HR* 156 F5
Hvidbjerg *DK* 86 B3
Hvide Sande *DK* 86 C2
Hvidovre *DK* 87 D10
Hvilsom *DK* 86 B5
Hvittingfoss *N* 95 D11
Hvorslev *DK* 86 C5
Hwlffordd *GB* 12 B5
Hybe *SK* 147 C9
Hybo *S* 103 C11
Hycklinge *S* 92 D7
Hyères *F* 36 E4
Hyermanavichy *BY* 133 F3

Hyervyaty BY 137 D13
Hylen N 94 C5
Hylleråsen N 102 C3
Hyllestad N 100 D2
Hyllinge DK 87 E9
Hyllinge S 87 C11
Hyltebruk S 87 A12
Hymont F 26 D5
Hyönölä FIN 127 E10
Hyrkäs FIN 119 E16
Hyry FIN 119 C14
Hyrynsalmi FIN 121 E11
Hysgjokaj AL 168 C2
Hyssna S 91 D12
Hythe GB 13 D12
Hythe GB 15 E11
Hytti FIN 129 D9
Hyttön S 99 B8
Hyväneula FIN 127 D13
Hyväniemi FIN 121 B11
Hyvärilä FIN 119 F15
Hyvikkälä FIN 127 D12
Hyvinkää FIN 127 D12
Hyvölänranta FIN 119 F16
Hyvönmäki FIN 129 B12
Hyypiö FIN 115 E1
Hyyppä FIN 122 F8
Hyżne PL 144 D5

I

Iablanița RO 159 D9
Iabloana MD 153 B11
Iacobeni RO 152 C6
Iacobeni RO 152 E5
Ialoveni MD 154 D3
Iam RO 159 C7
Ianca RO 160 F4
Ianca RO 161 C10
Iancu Jianu RO 160 E4
Iara RO 152 D3
Iargara MD 154 E2
Iarova MD 153 A12
Iași RO 153 C11
Iasmos GR 171 B8
Ibahernando E 45 F9
Iballë AL 163 E9
Ibănești RO 152 D5
Ibănești RO 153 A8
Ibarra E 32 D1
Ibbenbüren D 17 D9
Ibdes E 47 B9
Ibë AL 168 B2
Ibeas de Juarros E 40 D4
Ibestad N 111 C13
Ibi E 56 D3
Ibos F 32 D5
Ibrány H 145 G4
İbriktepe TR 171 B10
Ibros E 53 A10
Ibstock GB 11 F9
Ichenhausen D 75 F7
Ichenheim D 186 E4
Ichtegem B 18 B7
Icking D 72 A3
Icklesham GB 15 F10
Icklingham GB 15 C10
Iclănzel RO 152 D4
Iclod RO 152 D3
Icoana RO 160 E5
Icușești RO 153 D9
Idanha-a-Nova P 45 E6
Idanha-a-Velha P 45 E6
Idar-Oberstein D 21 E8
Ideciu de Jos RO 152 D5
Iden D 83 E11
Īdeņa LV 133 C1
Idenor S 103 C13
Idestrup DK 83 A11
Idiazabal E 32 D1
Idivuoma S 116 B8
Idkerberget S 97 B13
Idmiston GB 13 C11
Idocin E 32 E3
Idom DK 86 C2
Iđoš SRB 150 F5
Idre S 102 C4
Idrigil GB 2 K4
Idrija SLO 73 D9
Idritsa RUS 133 D5
Idro I 69 B9
Idstedt D 82 A7
Idstein D 21 D10
Idvattnet S 107 C12
Iecava LV 135 C8
Iedera RO 161 C7
Ieper B 18 C6
Iepurești RO 161 E7
Ierapetra GR 179 E10
Ieriķi LV 135 B10
Ierissos GR 170 D5
Iernut RO 152 E4
Ieromnini GR 168 E4
Ieropigi GR 168 C5
Ieșelnița RO 159 D9
Ifaistos GR 171 B8
Iffendic F 23 D7
Iffezheim D 187 D5
Ifjord N 113 C19
Ifs F 23 B11
Ifta D 79 D7
Ig SLO 73 E10
Igal H 149 C9
Igalo MNE 162 E6
Igar H 149 C11
Igé F 24 D4
Igea E 41 D7
Igel D 186 B2
Igelfors S 92 B7
Igelstorp S 91 C14
Igensdorf D 75 C9
Igerøy N 108 E3
Igersheim D 74 D6
Iggelheim D 187 C5
Iggensbach D 76 E4
Iggesund S 103 C13
Ighiu RO 152 E3
Igis CH 71 D9
Iglesias I 64 E2
Igliauka LT 137 D8
Igling D 71 A11
Igliškėliai LT 137 D8
Ignalina LT 135 F12
Ignatievo BG 167 C9
İğneada TR 167 F9
Ignești RO 151 E9
Igney F 26 D5
Igornay F 30 A5
Igoumenitsa GR 168 E3
Igralishte BG 169 A9
Igrejinha P 50 B4
Igrici H 145 H2
Igrīve LV 133 B2
Igualada E 43 D7
Igualeja E 53 C6
Igueña E 39 C7
Iguerande F 30 C5
Iharosberény H 149 D8
Ihľany SK 145 E2
Ihlienworth D 17 A11
Ihlowerhörn (Ihlow) D 17 B9
Ihode FIN 126 D6
Iholdy F 32 D3
Ihrhove D 17 B8
Ihrlerstein D 75 E10
İhsaniye TR 173 B10
Ii FIN 119 D14
Iijärvi FIN 113 E20
Iinattijärvi FIN 121 D9
Iironranta FIN 123 E12
Iisalmi FIN 124 C8
Iisvesi FIN 124 E8
Iitti FIN 127 D15
Iitto FIN 116 A6
Iivantiira FIN 121 F13
IJlst NL 16 B5
IJmuiden NL 16 D3
IJsselmuiden NL 16 C5
IJsselstein NL 16 D4
IJzendijke NL 16 F1
Ikaalinen FIN 127 B9
Ikast DK 86 C4
Ikazn' BY 133 E2
Ikervár H 149 B7
Ikhtiman BG 165 E8
İkizdere TR 177 D10
Ikkala FIN 123 F11
Ikkala FIN 127 E11
Ikkeläjärvi FIN 122 F9
Ikla EST 131 F8
Ikornes N 100 B5
Ikosenniemi FIN 119 C17
Ikrény H 149 A9
Ikšķile LV 135 C8
Ilandža SRB 159 C6
Ilanz CH 71 D8
Ilava SK 146 D6
Iława PL 139 C8
Ilbono I 64 D4
Ilchester GB 13 C9
Ildir TR 177 C7
Īle LV 134 C6
Ileana RO 161 D9
Ileanda RO 152 C3
Ilfeld D 79 C8
Ilford GB 15 D9
Ilfracombe GB 12 C6
Ilgižiai LT 134 F6
Ílhavo P 44 C3
Ilia RO 151 F10
Ilica TR 173 E8
Ilidza BIH 157 E9
Ilieni RO 153 F7
Ilijaš BIH 157 E9
Ilindentsi BG 165 F7
Iliokastro GR 175 E7
Ilirska Bistrica SLO 73 E9
Ilk H 145 G5
Ilkeston GB 11 F9
Ilkley GB 11 D8
Illana E 47 D7
Illar E 55 F7
Illats F 32 A5
Illerrieden D 71 A10
Illertissen D 71 A10
Illescas E 46 D5
Ille-sur-Têt F 34 E4
Illiers-Combray F 24 D5
Illingen D 21 F8
Illingen D 187 D6
Illkirch-Graffenstaden F 27 C8
Illmensee D 27 E11
Illmitz A 149 A7
Íllora E 53 B9
Illschwang D 75 D10
Illueca E 41 E8
Illzach F 27 E7
Ilmajoki FIN 122 E9
Ilmatsalu EST 131 E13
Ilmenau D 79 E8
Ilminster GB 13 D9
Ilmmünster D 75 F10
Ilmola FIN 119 C13
Il'nytsya UA 145 G7
Ilok HR 158 C3
Ilola FIN 127 E14
Ilomantsi FIN 125 E15
Ilosjoki FIN 123 D15
Ilovăț RO 159 D10
Ilovica NMK 169 B8
Ilovice BIH 157 E9
Ilovița RO 159 D9
Iłów PL 139 F9
Iłowa PL 81 C8
Iłowo Osada PL 139 D9
Ilsbo S 103 C13
Ilsede D 79 B7
Ilsenburg (Harz) D 79 C8
Ilseng N 101 E14
Ilsfeld D 27 B11
Ilskov DK 86 C4
Ilūkste LV 135 E12
Ilva Mare RO 152 C5
Ilva Mică RO 152 C5
Ilvesjoki FIN 122 F9
İlyaslar TR 173 F9
Ilyushino RUS 136 D6
Ilz A 148 B5
Iłża PL 141 H4
Ilze LV 135 D12
Ilzene LV 135 B13
Imari FIN 119 B15
Imatra FIN 129 C10
Imavere EST 131 D11
Imbradas LT 135 E12
Imeľ SK 146 F6
Imèr I 72 D4
Imeros GR 171 C8
Imielnica PL 139 E8
Immeln S 88 C6
Immendingen D 27 E10
Immenhausen D 78 D5
Immenreuth D 75 C10
Immenstaad am Bodensee D 27 E11
Immenstadt im Allgäu D 71 B10
Immingham GB 11 D11
Imnäs S 107 D11
Imola I 66 D4
Imotski HR 157 F7
Imperia I 37 D8
Imphy F 30 B3
Impilakhti RUS 129 B15
Impiö FIN 120 C9
Impruneta I 66 E3
Imrehegy H 150 E3
İmroz TR 171 D9
Imst A 71 C11
Ina FIN 123 D11
Inagh IRL 8 C4
Ináncs H 145 G3
Inárcs H 150 C3
Inari FIN 113 F19
Inari FIN 125 D15
Inca E 57 B10
Inch IRL 8 D3
Inch IRL 9 C10
Inchbare GB 5 B11
Incheville F 18 D3
Inchigeelagh IRL 8 E4
Inchnadamph GB 2 J7
Inciems LV 135 B9
Incinillas E 40 C4
İncirliova TR 177 D10
Incisa in Val d'Arno I 66 E3
Incourt B 19 C10
Inčukalns LV 135 B9
Indal S 103 A13
Indalstø N 100 E2
Independența RO 155 C1
Independența RO 155 F2
Inđija SRB 158 C5
Indra LV 133 E3
Indreabhán IRL 6 F4
Indre Arna N 94 B2
Indre Billefjord N 113 C15
Indre Brenna N 113 B16
Indre Kårvik N 111 A16
Indre Kiberg N 114 C9
Indre Kjæs N 113 B16
Indre Sortvik N 113 B15
Indura BY 140 D9
Indzhe Voyvoda BG 167 E8
İnece TR 167 F8
İnecik TR 173 C7
Ineši LV 135 B11
Ineu RO 151 C9
Ineu RO 151 E8
Infiesto E 39 B9
Ingå FIN 127 E11
Ingared S 91 D11
Ingatestone GB 15 D9
Ingatorp S 92 D6
Ingelfingen D 187 C8
Ingelheim am Rhein D 21 E10
Ingelmunster B 19 C7
Ingelstad S 89 B7
Ingenes N 94 B3
Ingersheim F 27 D7
Ingleton GB 5 F13
Ingleton GB 10 C7
Ingoldmells GB 11 E12
Ingolsbenning S 97 B14
Ingolstadt D 75 E9
Ingrandes F 23 F10
Ingrandes F 29 B7
Ingstrup DK 90 E6
Inguiniel F 22 E5
Ingulsvatn N 105 B14
Ingwiller F 27 C7
Inha FIN 123 E12
Ini GR 178 E9
Iniesta E 47 F9
Inis IRL 8 C5
Inis Córthaidh IRL 9 C9
Inis Diomáin IRL 8 C4
Inistioge IRL 9 D8
Injevo NMK 169 A7
Inkberrow GB 13 A11
Inke H 149 D8
Inkee FIN 121 C12
Inkere FIN 127 E9
Inkoo FIN 127 E11
Inndyr N 108 B7
Innerbraz A 71 C9
Innerleithen GB 5 D10
Innernzell D 76 E4
Innertällmo S 107 D13
Innertavle S 122 C4
Innertkirchen CH 70 D6
Innervik S 109 E14
Innervillgraten A 72 C5
Innhavet N 111 E10
Inniscrone IRL 6 D4
Innishannon IRL 8 E5
Innsbruck A 72 B3
Innset N 111 C16
Inntorget N 108 F3
Inowłódz PL 141 G2
Inowrocław PL 138 E5
Ins CH 31 A11
Insch GB 3 L11
Insjön S 103 E9
Ińsko PL 85 D9
Insming F 27 C6
Instefjord N 100 E2
Instinción E 55 F7
Însurăței RO 161 D11
İntepe TR 171 D10
Interlaken CH 70 D5
Întorsura Buzăului RO 161 B8
Întregalde RO 151 E11
Introbio I 69 B7
Inturkė LT 135 F11
Inver IRL 6 C6
Inverallochy GB 3 K13
Inveran IRL 6 F4
Inveraray GB 4 C6
Inverarity GB 5 B11
Inverarnan GB 4 C7
Inverbervie GB 5 B12
Invercassley GB 2 K7
Invercharnan GB 4 B6
Invergarry GB 4 A7
Invergordon GB 3 K8
Inverkeilor GB 5 B11
Inverkeithing GB 5 C10
Invermoriston GB 2 L7
Inverness GB 3 L8
Inverurie GB 3 L12
Inviken S 106 B8
Inzell D 73 A6
Inzigkofen D 27 D11
Inzing A 72 B3
Inzinzac-Lochrist F 22 E5
Ioannina GR 168 E4
Ion Corvin RO 155 E1
Ion Creangă RO 153 D9
Ionești RO 160 D2
Ionești RO 160 D4
Ion Luca Caragiale RO 161 D7
Ion Roată RO 161 D9
Iordăcheanu RO 161 C8
Ioulis GR 175 D9
Ip RO 151 C10
Ipatele RO 153 D10
Iphofen D 187 B9
Ipiķi LV 131 E10
Ipotești RO 153 B8
Ipotești RO 153 B9
Ippesheim D 75 C7
Ipplepen GB 13 E7
İpsala TR 171 C10
Ipsheim D 75 C7
Ipstones GB 11 E8
Ipswich GB 15 C11
Irakleia GR 169 B9
Irakleia GR 174 B5
Irakleia GR 176 F5
Irakleio GR 178 E9
Irancy F 25 E10
Iratoșu RO 151 E7
Irdning A 73 A9
Irechekovo BG 167 E7
Iregszemcse H 149 C10
Irgoli I 64 C4
Iria GR 175 E7
Irig SRB 158 C4
Irishtown IRL 6 E5
Irissarry F 32 D3
Irjanne FIN 126 C6
Irlava LV 134 C5
Irlbach D 75 E12
Irninniemi FIN 121 C13
Irodouër F 23 D8
Ironbridge GB 10 F7
Irrel D 20 E6
Irsch D 21 E7
Irsee D 71 B11
Irshava UA 145 G7
Irši LV 135 C11
Irsina I 60 B6
Irsta S 98 C7
Irueste E 47 C7
Irun E 32 D2
Iruña E 32 E2
Irurita E 32 D2
Irurozqui E 32 E3
Irurtzun E 32 E2
Irvine GB 4 D7
Irvinestown GB 7 D7
Irxleben D 79 B9
Isaba E 32 E4
Isaccea RO 155 C2
Isačić BIH 156 C4
Ișalnița RO 160 E3
Isane N 100 C3
Isaris GR 174 E5
Isaszeg H 150 B3
Isätra S 98 C7
Isbergues F 18 C5
Isbister GB 3 D14
Íscar E 40 F2
Isches F 26 D4
Ischgl A 71 C10
Ischia I 60 B1
Ischia di Castro I 62 B1
Ischitella I 63 D9
Isdes F 25 E7
Iselvmoen N 111 C16
Isen D 75 F11
Is-en-Bassigny F 26 D3
Isenbüttel D 79 B8
Isenvad DK 86 C4
Iseo I 69 B9
Iserlohn D 17 F9
Isernhagen D 78 B6
Isernia I 63 D6
Isfjorden N 100 A7
İshakçelebi TR 177 B10
Ishull-Lezhë AL 163 F8
Isigny-sur-Mer F 23 B9
Isili I 64 D3
İskele TR 173 F9
İskender TR 172 A6
Iškoras N 113 E16
Iskra BG 166 F4
Iskrets BG 165 D7
Isla Cristina E 51 E5
İslambeyli TR 167 F9
Isla Plana E 56 F2
Išlaužas LT 137 D8
Islaz RO 160 F5
Isle F 29 D8
Isle of Whithorn GB 5 F8
Isleryd S 92 C4
Isles-sur-Suippe F 19 F9
Īslīce LV 135 D8
İsmailli TR 177 B9
Ismaning D 75 F10
Ismundsundet S 106 E8
Isna P 44 E5
Isnäs FIN 127 E15
Isnello I 58 D5
Ișnovăț MD 154 C3
Isny im Allgäu D 71 B10
Iso-Äiniö FIN 127 C13
Iso-Evo FIN 127 C13
Isohalme FIN 115 E3
Isojoki FIN 122 F7
Isokumpu FIN 121 C11
Isokylä FIN 115 E3
Isokylä FIN 119 F14
Isokyrö FIN 122 E8
Isola F 36 C6
Isola 2000 F 37 C6
Isola d'Asti I 37 B8
Isola del Gran Sasso d'Italia I 62 B5
Isola della Scala I 66 B3
Isola delle Femmine I 58 C3
Isola del Liri I 62 D5
Isola di Capo Rizzuto I 61 F8
Isole del Cantone I 37 B9
Isona E 42 C6
Isopalo FIN 115 D2
Isorella I 66 B1
Iso-Vimma FIN 126 C7
Ispagnac F 35 B6
Isperikh BG 161 F9
Ispica I 59 F6
Ispoure F 32 D3
Ispra I 68 B6
Ispringen D 27 C10
Issakka FIN 125 C10
Isselburg D 17 E6
Issigeac F 29 F7
Issime I 68 B4
Isso E 55 C9
Issogne I 68 B4
Issoire F 30 D3
Issoudun F 29 B9
Issum D 17 E6
Is-sur-Tille F 26 E3
Issy-l'Évêque F 30 B4
Istalsna LV 133 D3
Istán E 53 C7
İstanbul TR 173 B10
Istead Rise GB 15 E9
Istebna PL 147 B7
Istebné SK 147 C8
Istenmezeje H 147 E10
Isternia GR 176 D5
Isthmia GR 175 D7
Istiaia GR 175 B7
Istibanja NMK 164 F5
Istog RKS 163 D9
Istres F 35 C8
Istria RO 155 D3
Istrio GR 181 D7
Istunmäki FIN 123 E16
Isuerre E 32 F3
Iszkaszentgyörgy H 149 B10
Itä-Ähtäri FIN 123 E12
Itä-Aure FIN 123 F10
Itä-Karttula FIN 124 E8
Itäkoski FIN 119 C13
Itäkoski FIN 125 C9
Itäkylä FIN 123 D11
Itäranta FIN 115 F2
Itäranta FIN 120 F9
Itea GR 169 C6
Itea GR 169 D6
Itea GR 169 F7
Itea GR 174 C5
Itero de la Vega E 40 D3
Iteuil F 29 C6
Ithaki GR 174 C2
Itrabo E 53 C9
Itri I 62 E5
Itterbeck D 17 C7
Ittireddu I 64 B2
Ittiri I 64 B2
Ittre B 19 C9
Ituero de Azaba E 45 D7
Itzehoe D 82 C7
Itzstedt D 83 C8
Iurceni MD 154 C2
Ivalo FIN 115 A3
Ivalon Matti FIN 117 B15
Iván H 149 B7
Ivana Franka UA 145 E7
Ivancea MD 154 C3
Ivančice CZ 77 D10
Ivančići BIH 157 D9
Iváncsa H 149 B11
Ivanec HR 148 D6
Ivănești RO 153 D10
Ivangorod RUS 132 C3
Ivanić=-Grad HR 149 E6
Ivanivka UA 145 G6
Ivanjica SRB 163 B9
Ivanjska BIH 157 C7
Ivankovo HR 149 F11
Ivano-Frankove UA 144 D8
Ivanovice na Hané CZ 77 D12
Ivanovo BG 161 F7
Ivanovo BG 166 F5
Ivanovo BG 167 C7
Ivanovo SRB 158 D6
Ivanska HR 149 E7
Ivanski BG 167 C8
Ivarrud N 108 F6
Ivarsbjörke S 97 C9
Ivars d'Urgell E 42 D5
Ivaylovgrad BG 171 A10
Iveland N 90 C2
Iver GB 15 D7
Ivești RO 153 E11
Ivești RO 153 F11
Ivrea I 68 C4
İvrindi TR 173 E7
Ivry-la-Bataille F 24 C5
Ivry-sur-Seine F 25 C7
Ivybridge GB 13 E7
Iwaniska PL 143 E11
Iwanowice Włościańskie PL 143 F8
Iwkowa PL 144 D2
Iwye BY 137 F12
Ixelles B 19 C9
Ixworth GB 15 C10
İyaslar TR 177 A10
Iža SK 149 A10
Iza UA 145 G7
Izarra E 40 C6
Izbica PL 144 B7
Izbica Kujawska PL 138 F6
Izbiceni RO 160 F5
Izbicko PL 142 E5
Izbiște MD 154 C4
Izbište SRB 159 C7
Izbižno BIH 157 E10
Izeaux F 31 E7
Izeda P 39 E6
Izegem B 19 C7
Izernore F 31 C8
Izeron F 31 E7
Izgrev BG 161 F9
Izgrev BG 167 E9
Iž Mali HR 67 D11
Izmayil UA 155 C3
İzmir TR 177 C9
Iznájar E 53 B8
Iznalloz E 53 B9
Izola SLO 67 A8
Izsák H 150 D3
Izsófalva H 145 G2
Izvoare RO 160 E2
Izvoarele RO 155 C3
Izvoarele RO 160 E5
Izvoarele RO 160 F6
Izvoarele RO 161 C8
Izvoarele RO 161 E7
Izvoarele Sucevei RO 152 B6
Izvor BG 159 F10
Izvor BG 165 E6
Izvor NMK 168 B4
Izvor NMK 169 A6
Izvor SRB 159 F8
Izvorovo BG 155 F1
Izvoru RO 160 E6
Izvoru Bârzii RO 159 D10
Izvoru Berheciului RO 153 D10
Izvoru Crișului RO 151 D11

J

Jääjärvi FIN 114 D6
Jaakonvaara FIN 125 D14
Jaala FIN 127 C15
Jaalanka FIN 120 D9
Jaalanka FIN 120 E9
Jääli FIN 119 D15
Jaama EST 132 C2
Jääskänjoki FIN 122 E9
Jääskö FIN 117 D14
Jaatila FIN 119 B14
Jabaga E 47 D8
Jabalanac HR 67 C10
Jabaloyas E 47 D10
Jabalquinto E 53 A9
Jabbeke B 19 B7
Jabel D 83 C13
Jablan Do BIH 162 D5
Jablanica BIH 157 E8
Jabłoń PL 141 G8
Jablonec nad Jizerou CZ 81 E8
Jablonec nad Nisou CZ 81 E8
Jablonica SK 146 D4
Jabłonka PL 147 C9
Jabłonka Kościelna PL 140 E6
Jabłonna PL 139 F10
Jabłonna Lacka PL 141 F6
Jabłonna Pierwsza PL 141 H7
Jablonné nad Orlicí CZ 77 B11
Jablonné v Podještědí CZ 81 E7
Jablonové SK 77 F12
Jabłonowo Pomorskie PL 139 D7
Jablůnka CZ 146 C5
Jablunkov CZ 147 B7
Jabugo E 51 D6
Jabuka BIH 157 E10
Jabuka SRB 158 D6
Jabuka SRB 163 C7
Jabukovac HR 149 F6
Jabukovac SRB 159 E9
Jabukovik SRB 164 D5
Jaca E 32 E4
Jachenau D 72 A3
Jáchymov CZ 76 B3
Jacovce SK 146 D6
Jäderfors S 103 E12
Jadów PL 139 F12
Jädraås S 103 E11
Jadranska Lešnica SRB 158 D3
Jadraque E 47 C7
Jægerspris DK 87 D9
Jægervatnet N 111 A18
Jaén E 53 A9
Jägala EST 131 C10
Jagare BIH 157 C7
Jagerberg A 148 C5
Jagodina SRB 159 F7
Jagodnjak HR 149 E11
Jagodzin PL 81 D8
Jagsthausen D 27 B11
Jagstzell D 75 D7
Jähdyspohja FIN 123 F11
Jahnsfelde D 80 A6
Jahodná SK 146 E5
Jah-Salih AL 163 E9
Jajce BIH 157 D7
Ják H 149 B7
Jakabszállás H 150 D4
Jäkälävaara FIN 121 C10
Jakkukylä FIN 119 D15
Jakkula FIN 122 E8
Jäkkvik S 109 D12
Jaklovce SK 145 F3
Jakobsbakken N 109 B10
Jakobsnes N 114 D8
Jakobstad FIN 122 C9
Jakokoski FIN 125 E13
Jakovlje HR 148 E5
Jakšić HR 149 F9
Jakštaičiai LT 134 D2
Jaktorów PL 141 F3
Jakubany SK 145 E2
Jakubov SK 77 F11
Jakubów PL 141 F5
Jalance E 47 F10
Jalasjärvi FIN 122 F9
Jalhay B 20 C5
Jaligny-sur-Besbre F 30 C4
Jallais F 23 F10
Jalovik SRB 158 D4
Jałówka PL 140 D9
Jalubí CZ 146 C4
Jämaja EST 130 E4
Jämäs FIN 125 B12
Jämejala EST 131 E11
Jameln D 83 D10
Jamena SRB 157 C11
Jamestown IRL 7 F8
Jametz F 19 F11
Jamielnik PL 139 C7
Jämijärvi FIN 126 B8
Jamilena E 53 A9
Jäminkipohja FIN 127 B11
Jämjö S 89 C9
Jammerdal N 96 B7
Jamník SK 145 F2
Jämsä FIN 123 C12
Jämsä FIN 127 B13
Jämsänkoski FIN 127 B13
Jämshög S 88 C7
Jämtön S 118 C8
Jamu Mare RO 159 C7
Janakkala FIN 127 D12
Janapolė LT 134 E4
Jánd H 145 G5
Jandelsbrunn D 76 E5
Janderup DK 86 D2
Jäneda EST 131 C11
Jänickendorf D 80 B4
Janja BIH 158 D3
Janjevë RKS 164 D3
Janjići BIH 158 F3
Janjina HR 162 D3
Jänkä FIN 123 D13
Jänkälä FIN 115 D3
Jänkisjärvi S 116 E10
Jánkmajtis H 145 H6
Janków PL 143 B7
Jankowo Dolne PL 138 E4
Jāņmuiža LV 135 B10
Jännevirta FIN 125 E9
Jánoshalma H 150 E3
Jánosháza H 149 B8
Jánoshida H 150 C5
Jánossomorja H 149 A8
Janovice nad Úhlavou CZ 76 D4
Janów PL 140 D8
Janów PL 143 E7
Janowice Wielkie PL 81 E9
Janowiec PL 141 H5
Janowiec Wlelkopolski PL 85 E12
Janów Lubelski PL 144 B5
Janowo PL 139 D10
Janów Podlaski PL 141 F8
Jansjö S 107 D10
Jänsmässholmen S 105 D15
Jāņuciems LV 135 E13
Janville F 24 D6
Janzé F 23 E9
Japca MD 154 B3
Jäppilä FIN 124 F8
Jaraba E 47 B9
Jaraczewo PL 81 C12
Jarafuel E 47 F10
Jaraicejo E 45 E9
Jaraiz de la Vera E 45 D9
Järämä S 116 B6
Jarandilla de la Vera E 45 D9
Järbo S 103 E12
Járdánháza H 145 G1
Jard-sur-Mer F 28 C2
Jaren N 95 B13
Jarfjordbotn N 114 D8
Jårgastat N 113 E16
Jargeau F 24 E7
Jarhoinen FIN 117 E11
Jarhois S 117 E11
Jariștea RO 153 F10
Jarkovac SRB 159 C6
Järkvissle S 103 A12
Järlåsa S 98 C8
Järlepa EST 131 C9
Jarmen D 84 C4
Jarménil F 26 D6
Jarmina HR 149 F11
Järna S 93 A11
Järna S 97 A11
Jarnac F 28 D5
Jarnages F 29 C10
Järnäs S 107 E17
Järnäsklubb S 107 E17
Järnforsen S 92 E7
Jarny F 26 B4
Jarocin PL 142 C4
Jarocin PL 144 B5
Jarok SK 146 E5
Jaroměř CZ 77 B9
Jaroměřice CZ 77 C11
Jaroměřice nad Rokytnou CZ 77 D9
Jaroslavice CZ 77 E10
Jarosław PL 144 C6
Jarosławiec PL 85 A11
Jarošov nad Nežárkou CZ 77 D8
Jarovnice SK 145 E3
Järpås S 91 C12
Järpbyn S 105 E14
Järpen S 105 E14
Järpliden S 102 E3
Jarplund-Weding D 82 A6
Jarque E 41 E8
Jarrow GB 5 F14
Järva-Jaani EST 131 C11
Järvakandi EST 131 D9
Järvberget S 107 D13
Järvennpää FIN 117 C12
Järvenpää FIN 122 E7
Järvenpää FIN 124 C8
Järvenpää FIN 125 D10
Järvenpää FIN 127 E13
Järvikylä FIN 119 F17
Järvikylä FIN 123 C13
Järvikylä FIN 123 C13
Jarville-la-Malgrange F 26 C5
Järvirova FIN 117 D12
Järvsand S 107 C9
Järvsjö S 107 B12
Järvsö S 103 C11
Järvsta S 103 E13
Järvtjärn S 118 E5
Järvträsk S 107 A16
Jarzé F 23 E11
Jaša Tomić SRB 159 C6
Jasen BIH 162 D5
Jasenak HR 67 B11
Jasenica BIH 156 C5
Jasenovac HR 157 B6
Jasenovo SRB 159 D7
Jasenovo SRB 163 B8
Jasień PL 81 C8
Jasień PL 85 B13
Jasienica PL 139 F11
Jasienica PL 147 B7
Jasienica Rosielna PL 144 D4
Jasieniec PL 141 G3
Jasika SRB 159 F7
Jasionka PL 144 C5
Jasionna PL 143 E9
Jasionówka PL 140 D8
Jaśliska PL 145 E4
Jasło PL 144 D3
Jašlūnai LT 137 E11
Jasmuiža LV 135 D13
Jasov SK 145 F2
Jásová SK 146 F6
Jassans-Riottier F 30 D6
Jasseron F 31 C7
Jastarnia PL 138 A6
Jastrebarsko HR 148 E5
Jastrowie PL 85 D11
Jastrząb PL 141 H3
Jastrzjbia PL 141 H4
Jastrzjbia Góra PL 138 A5
Jastrzjbie-Zdrój PL 147 B7
Jászapáti H 150 B5
Jászárokszállás H 150 B4
Jászberény H 150 C4
Jászboldogháza H 150 C4
Jászfényszaru H 150 B4
Jászjákóhalma H 150 B5
Jászkarajenő H 150 C5
Jászkisér H 150 C5
Jászladány H 150 C5
Jászszentandrás H 150 B5
Jászszentlászló H 150 D4
Jásztelek H 150 C5
Jatar E 53 C9
Jättendal S 103 C13
Jättensjö S 103 B10
Jatuni FIN 116 B9
Jatzke D 84 C5
Jatznick D 84 C5
Jaulín E 41 F10
Jaun CH 31 B11
Jaunalūksne LV 133 B2
Jaunanna LV 133 B2
Jaunauce LV 134 D5
Jaunay-Clan F 29 B6
Jaunbērze LV 134 C6
Jaunciems LV 134 B5
Jaundundaga LV 130 F4
Jaungulbene LV 135 B13
Jaunjelgava LV 135 C10
Jaunkalsnava LV 135 C11
Jaunklidzis LV 131 F11
Jaunlaicene LV 131 F13
Jaunlutriņi LV 134 C4
Jaunmārupe LV 135 C7
Jaunmuiža LV 135 C11
Jaunolaine LV 135 C7
Jaunpiebalga LV 135 B12
Jaunpils LV 134 C6
Jaunsāti LV 134 C5
Jaunsēlplis LV 135 C11
Jaunsilava LV 135 D12
Jauntsarats E 32 E2
Jaurakainen FIN 119 D17
Jaurakkajärvi FIN 121 D10
Jaurrieta E 32 E3
Jausiers F 36 C5
Javalí Viejo E 56 F2
Javarus FIN 115 E1
Jávea-Xábia E 56 D5

K

Korpela FIN 117 B14
Kőrperich D 20 E6
Korpi FIN 123 C12
Korpijärvi FIN 119 B13
Korpijoki FIN 123 C16
Korpikå S 119 C10
Korpikylä FIN 119 B11
Korpikylä FIN 121 E12
Korpikylä S 119 B11
Korpilahti FIN 123 F15
Korpilombolo S 116 E10
Korpilompolo FIN 117 E13
Korpinen FIN 121 D10
Korpinen FIN 125 D10
Korpisel'kya RUS 125 F16
Korpivaara FIN 125 E12
Korpo FIN 126 E6
Korpoström FIN 126 E6
Korsåmon S 103 A12
Korsbäck FIN 122 E6
Korsberga S 89 A8
Korsberga S 91 C15
Korsgården S 103 E10
Korsholm FIN 122 D7
Korskrogen S 103 C10
Korsmyrbränna S 106 E8
Korsnäs FIN 122 E6
Korsnes N 111 D11
Korso FIN 127 E13
Korsør DK 87 E8
Korssjön S 118 F5
Korssund N 100 D1
Korsträsk S 118 C5
Korsveggen N 104 E8
Korsvoll N 104 E4
Korsze PL 136 E3
Kortemark B 19 B7
Korten BG 166 D5
Kortenhoef NL 16 D4
Kortesalmi FIN 121 C14
Kortesjärvi FIN 123 D10
Kortessem B 19 C11
Kortevaara FIN 125 B13
Kortgene NL 16 E1
Korthi GR 176 D4
Kortrijk B 19 C7
Kortteenperä FIN 119 B17
Kortteinen FIN 125 D11
Korubaşi TR 171 E10
Korucu TR 173 F7
Koruköy TR 173 C6
Koruköy TR 177 E10
Korva S 119 B11
Korvakumpu FIN 115 D2
Korvala FIN 117 E16
Korvaluoma FIN 126 B8
Kõrveküla EST 131 E13
Korvenkylä FIN 119 D15
Korvenkylä FIN 119 F14
Korvenkylä FIN 123 B12
Korvua FIN 121 D12
Koryčany CZ 77 D12
Korycin PL 140 D8
Koryfasi GR 174 E4
Koryfi GR 169 C8
Korytnica PL 139 F12
Korzenna PL 144 D2
Korzeńsko PL 81 C11
Korzunovo RUS 114 E9
Korzybie PL 85 B11
Kos GR 177 F9
Kosakowo PL 138 A6
Kosanica MNE 163 C7
Košarovce SK 145 E4
Kösching D 75 E10
Kościan PL 81 B11
Kościelec PL 142 B6
Kościelna Wieś PL 142 C5
Kościernica PL 85 B10
Kościerzyna PL 138 B4
Kosd H 150 B3
Kose EST 131 C10
Kose EST 131 F14
Košeca SK 146 C6
Košecké Podhradie SK 146 D6
Kösedere TR 171 E10
Kösedere TR 177 B8
Köseilyas TR 173 B8
Kosel D 82 A7
Koselji BIH 157 E9
Koserow D 84 B6
Košetice CZ 77 C8
Kosharevo BG 165 D6
Koshava BG 159 E11
Košice SK 145 F3
Kosiv UA 152 A6
Kosivs'ka Polyana UA 145 G9
Kosjerić SRB 158 F4
Koška HR 149 E10
Koskama FIN 117 C14
Koskeby FIN 122 D8
Koskela FIN 119 E15
Koskela FIN 123 D11
Koskenkorva FIN 122 E8
Koskenkylä FIN 117 C16
Koskenkylä FIN 121 C14
Koskenkylä FIN 121 F11
Koskenkylä FIN 124 E8
Koskenkylä FIN 126 D7
Koskenmäki FIN 121 F13
Koskenniska FIN 113 F17
Koskenpää FIN 123 F14
Koskenperä FIN 123 C14
Koski FIN 127 D9
Koski FIN 127 E9
Koskimäki FIN 122 E7
Koskinou GR 181 D8
Koskioinen FIN 127 C9
Koškovce SK 145 E4
Koskue FIN 122 F9
Koskullskulle S 116 D5
Koslovets BG 166 C4
Kosmach UA 152 A5
Kosman BIH 157 F10
Kosmas GR 175 E6
Kosmio GR 171 B8
Kosmonosy CZ 77 B7
Kosola FIN 122 D9
Kosova Hora CZ 77 C6
Kosovo HR 156 E5
Kosovska Kamenicë RKS 164 D4
Kosów Lacki PL 141 E6
Koßdorf D 80 D4
Kössen A 72 A5
Kosta GR 175 E7
Kosta S 89 B8
Kostakioi GR 174 A2
Koštálov CZ 81 E8
Kostamo FIN 115 E2
Kostandenets BG 166 B6
Kostandovo BG 165 E9
Kostanjevac HR 148 E4
Kostanjevica SLO 148 E4
Kostel SLO 67 A10
Kostelec nad Černými Lesy CZ 77 C7
Kostelec nad Orlicí CZ 77 B10
Kostelec na Hané CZ 77 C12
Kostenets BG 165 E8
Kostenets BG 165 E8
Kostice CZ 77 E11
Kostinbrod BG 165 D7
Kostolac SRB 159 D7
Kostolné Kračany SK 146 F5
Kostomłoty PL 81 D11
Kostomuksha RUS 121 E16
Kostrzyn PL 81 A7
Kostrzyn PL 81 B12
Kostyzhitsy RUS 132 F6
Kosula FIN 125 E11
Košute HR 157 E6
Kosy UA 154 B5
Kosyny UA 145 G5
Koszalin PL 85 B10
Koszcjcin PL 142 E6
Kőszeg H 149 B7
Koszyce PL 143 F10
Kotajärvi FIN 119 D15
Kotala FIN 115 D5
Kotala FIN 123 F12
Kotalanperä FIN 119 D15
Kotas GR 168 C5
Kotë AL 168 D2
Kötegyán H 151 D7
Kotel BG 167 D6
Kötelek H 150 C5
Kotelow D 84 C5
Kotešová SK 147 C7
Köthen (Anhalt) D 79 C10
Kotikylä FIN 124 D8
Kotila FIN 121 E10
Kotiranta FIN 121 E13
Kotka FIN 128 E6
Kotlin PL 142 C4
Kotly RUS 132 B4
Kotor MNE 163 E6
Kotoriba HR 149 D7
Kotorsko BIH 157 C9
Kotor Varoš BIH 157 C7
Kotraža SRB 158 F5
Kotronas GR 178 B3
Kötschach A 73 C7
Kotsøy N 105 F9
Kottenheim D 185 D7
Kottes A 77 F8
Köttmannsdorf A 73 C9
Köttsjön S 107 E10
Kotuń PL 141 F6
Koudekerke NL 16 F1
Koudum NL 16 C4
Koufalia GR 169 C8
Koufovouno GR 171 B10
Kougsta S 105 E15
Kouklioi GR 168 E4
Koumanis GR 174 D4
Koura FIN 123 E10
Kouřim CZ 77 C7
Kourkouloi GR 175 B7
Kournas GR 178 E7
Koutaniemi FIN 121 F10
Koutojärvi S 119 B10
Koutsochero GR 169 E7
Koutsopodi GR 175 D6
Koutsouras GR 179 E10
Koutus FIN 117 E12
Kouva FIN 121 C10
Kouvola FIN 128 D6
Kovachevets BG 166 C6
Kovachevitsa BG 165 F8
Kovachevo BG 166 E6
Kovachevtsi BG 165 D6
Kovachitsa BG 160 F2
Kovači BIH 157 E7
Kovačica SRB 158 C6
Kővágószőlős H 149 D10
Kovallberget S 107 B13
Kovanj BIH 157 E10
Kovarce SK 146 E6
Kovářov CZ 76 C6
Kovdor RUS 115 C8
Kovelahti FIN 126 B8
Kovero FIN 125 E15
Kovilj SRB 158 C5
Kovin SRB 159 D6
Kovjoki FIN 122 C9
Kovland S 103 B13
Kövra S 102 A7
Kovren MNE 163 C8
Kowal PL 139 E7
Kowala-Stępocina PL 141 H4
Kowale PL 142 D5
Kowale Oleckie PL 136 E5
Kowale-Pańskie PL 142 C6
Kowalewo Pomorskie PL 138 D6
Kowalów PL 81 B7
Kowary PL 81 E9
Kowiesy PL 141 G2
Köyceğiz TR 181 C9
Köyhäjoki FIN 123 C11
Köyliö FIN 126 C7
Koynare BG 165 C9
Koyundere TR 177 B9
Koyunyeri TR 171 C10
Kozani GR 169 D6
Kozarac BIH 157 C6
Kozarac HR 149 E11
Kozar Belene BG 166 C4
Kozármisleny H 149 D10
Kozárovce SK 147 E7
Kozçeşme TR 173 D6
Kozica HR 157 F7
Koziegłowy PL 143 E7
Kozielice PL 85 D7
Kozienice PL 141 G5
Kozina SLO 73 E8
Kožlany CZ 76 C5
Kozloduy BG 160 F3
Kozłów Biskupi PL 141 F2
Kozłowo PL 139 D9
Kozluk BIH 157 C11
Koźły PL 139 F11
Koźminek PL 142 C5
Koźmin Wielkopolski PL 142 C3
Koz'ove UA 145 F7
Kozubszczyzna PL 141 H6
Kożuchów PL 81 C9
Kožuhe BIH 157 C9
Kozy PL 147 B8
Kozyörük TR 173 B6
Krabbendijke NL 16 F2
Krabi EST 131 F13
Kräckelbäcken S 102 C7
Krackow D 84 D6
Kraddsele S 109 E12
Kraftsdorf D 79 E10
Krąg PL 85 B11
Kragelund DK 86 C4
Kragerø N 90 B5
Kragi PL 85 C11
Kragujevac SRB 159 E6
Kraj HR 156 E6
Kraj HR 157 F7
Krajenka PL 85 D12
Krajišnik SRB 159 C6
Krajnik Dolny PL 84 D6
Krakača BIH 156 B4
Kråkberget N 110 C8
Kråken S 122 C3
Kråkenes N 100 B2
Kråkerøy N 91 A8
Krakės LT 134 F7
Krakhella N 100 D2
Kråklingbo S 93 E13
Kråklivollen N 105 E9
Kråkmoen N 111 E10
Krakovets' UA 144 D7
Kraków PL 143 F8
Krakow am See D 83 C12
Kråksmåla S 89 A9
Kråkstad N 95 C13
Kralevo BG 167 C7
Králíky CZ 77 B11
Kraljeva BIH 157 D9
Kraljevica HR 67 B10
Kraljevo SRB 158 F6
Kralovice CZ 76 C4
Kráľovský Chlmec SK 145 G4
Kralupy nad Vltavou CZ 76 B6
Králův Dvůr CZ 76 C6
Kramarzyny PL 85 B12
Kramfors S 103 A14
Kramolin BG 166 C4
Krampenes N 114 C8
Kramsach A 72 B4
Kramsk PL 142 B5
Kramvik N 114 C9
Kranenburg D 16 E6
Kranevo BG 167 C10
Krångfors S 118 E4
Krania GR 168 E5
Krania Elassonas GR 169 E6
Kranichfeld D 79 E9
Kranidi GR 175 E7
Kranj SLO 73 D9
Kranjska Gora SLO 73 D8
Krapanj HR 156 E4
Krapets BG 155 F3
Krąpiel PL 85 D8
Krapina HR 148 D5
Krapinske Toplice HR 148 D5
Krapkowice PL 142 F4
Krašić HR 148 E5
Krasiczyn PL 144 D6
Krasiv UA 145 D8
Krāslava LV 133 E2
Kraslice CZ 75 B12
Krasnagorka BY 133 E2
Krásná Hora nad Vltavou CZ 76 C6
Krasnapollye BY 133 E6
Krasne PL 139 E10
Krasne PL 144 C5
Krasne UA 154 E4
Kraśniczyn PL 144 B7
Kraśnik PL 144 B5
Krasni Okny UA 154 B4
Krasnobród PL 144 B7
Krasnogorodskoye RUS 133 C4
Krásnohorské Podhradie SK 145 F2
Krasnoles'ye RUS 136 E5
Krásno nad Kysucou SK 147 C7
Krasnopol PL 136 E7
Krasno Polje HR 67 C11
Krasnosel'skoye RUS 129 D11
Krasnosielc PL 139 D11
Krasnovo BG 165 E9
Krasnoyil's'k UA 153 A7
Krasnoznamensk RUS 136 D5
Krasnystaw PL 144 B7
Krasocin PL 143 E9
Krastë AL 168 B3
Kraszewice PL 142 C5
Kraszewo PL 136 E2
Kratigos GR 177 A8
Kratiškiai LT 135 D9
Kratovo NMK 164 E5
Kratte masugn S 98 B6
Krauchenwies D 27 D11
Krauja LV 135 E13
Kraujas LV 135 D11
Kraukļi LV 135 B12
Krauschwitz D 81 C7
Krautheim D 74 D6
Kravaře CZ 146 B6
Kravoder BG 165 C7
Kraymorie BG 167 E8
Kražiai LT 134 E5
Krčina BIH 157 C11
Krefeld D 17 F7
Kreiensen D 78 C6
Krekenava LT 135 E8
Krekhovychi UA 145 E9
Krekilä FIN 123 C11
Kremasti GR 181 D8
Kremen BG 165 F8
Kremena BG 155 F2
Kremintsi UA 152 A5
Kremmydia GR 174 F4
Kremna SRB 158 F4
Kremnica SK 147 D7
Krempe D 82 C7
Kremperheide D 17 A12
Krempna PL 145 D4
Krems an der Donau A 77 F9
Kremsbrücke A 73 C8
Kremsmünster A 76 F6
Křepice CZ 77 E11
Krepoljin SRB 159 E8
Kreševo BIH 157 E9
Kreshpan AL 168 C2
Křešice CZ 76 A6
Kresna BG 165 F7
Kresnice SLO 73 D10
Kressbronn am Bodensee D 71 B9
Krestena GR 174 D4
Kretinga LT 134 E2
Kretingalė LT 134 E2
Kreuth D 72 A4
Kreuzau D 20 C6
Kreuzlingen CH 27 E11
Kreuztal D 21 C9
Kreuzwertheim D 74 C6
Kreva BY 137 E13
Krezluk BIH 157 D7
Krichim BG 165 E9
Krieglach A 148 A5
Kriegstetten CH 27 F8
Krien D 84 C4
Kriens CH 70 C6
Krievciems LV 134 B3
Krieza GR 175 C9
Krikello GR 174 B4
Krikellos GR 174 B3
Krimpen aan de IJssel NL 16 E3
Krimūnas LV 134 C6
Křinec CZ 77 B8
Krinida GR 170 C5
Krinides GR 171 B6
Kriškalni LV 135 C11
Kriškovci BIH 157 C7
Kristberg S 92 B6
Kristdala S 93 E8
Kristiansand N 90 C2
Kristianstad S 88 C6
Kristiansund N 104 E3
Kristiinankaupunki FIN 122 F6
Kristineberg S 107 A15
Kristinefors S 97 B8
Kristinehamn S 97 D11
Kristinestad FIN 122 F6
Kristoni GR 169 C8
Kristvallabrunn S 89 D10
Kritinia GR 181 D7
Kritsa GR 179 E10
Kritzmow D 83 B12
Kriukai LT 134 D7
Kriūkai LT 137 C7
Kriva Bara BG 159 F11
Krivača BIH 157 G9
Kriva Feja SRB 164 D5
Krivaja BIH 157 D9
Kriváň SK 147 D8
Krivany SK 145 E2
Kriva Palanka NMK 164 E5
Krivelj SRB 159 E9
Krivi Put HR 67 B10
Krivi Vir SRB 159 F8
Krivodol BG 165 C7
Krivogaštani NMK 168 B5
Krivolak NMK 169 A7
Križ HR 149 E7
Křižanov CZ 77 D10
Križevci HR 149 D7
Křížová CZ 77 C9
Križpolje HR 67 B11
Krk HR 67 B10
Krka SLO 73 E10
Krmčina HR 156 D3
Krnča SK 146 D6
Krnica HR 67 C9
Krnjača SRB 158 D6
Krnja Jela MNE 163 D7
Krnjak HR 148 F5
Krnjeuša BIH 156 C5
Krnjevo SRB 159 E7
Krnov CZ 142 F4
Krobia PL 81 C11
Kroczyce PL 143 E8
Krøderen N 95 B11
Krofdorf Gleiberg D 21 C11
Krog S 103 B9
Krögis D 80 D4
Krok S 105 E14
Krokees GR 175 F6
Krokeide N 94 B2
Krokek S 93 B8
Kroken N 100 D6
Kroken N 108 F7
Krokfors S 108 E9
Krokfors S 118 B5
Krokio GR 175 A6
Kroknäs S 102 A8
Kroknes N 114 C9
Krokom S 106 E6
Krokos GR 169 D6
Krokowa PL 138 A5
Kroksjö S 107 B13
Kroksjö S 107 D15
Kroksjö S 118 F4
Krokstadelva N 95 C12
Krokstadøra N 104 E7
Krokstranda N 108 D9
Krokströmmen S 102 B8
Kroktjärn S 118 B4
Krokträsk S 118 C6
Królowy Most PL 140 D8
Krölpa D 79 E10
Kroměříž CZ 146 C4
Krommenie NL 16 C3
Krompachy SK 145 F2
Kromsdorf D 79 E9
Kronach D 75 B9
Kronau D 187 C6
Kronauce LV 134 C6
Kronberg im Taunus D 187 A5
Kronlund S 109 E14
Kronoby FIN 123 C10
Kronprinzenkoog D 82 C5
Kronshagen D 83 B8
Kronshtadt RUS 129 F12
Kronstorf A 77 F6
Kropa SLO 73 D9
Kröpelin D 83 B11
Kropp D 82 B7
Kroppenstedt D 79 C9
Kropstädt D 79 C12
Krościenko nad Dunajcem PL 145 E1
Kröslin D 84 B5
Krosna LT 137 E8
Krośnice PL 81 D12
Krośniewice PL 143 B7
Krosno PL 144 D4
Krosno Odrzańskie PL 81 B8
Krossen D 79 E10
Krossen N 90 C2
Krossen N 95 C8
Krossmoen N 94 E4
Krostitz D 79 D11
Krote LV 134 C3
Krotoszyce PL 81 D10
Krotoszyn PL 142 C3
Krottendorf A 148 B5
Krouna CZ 77 C10
Krousonas GR 178 E8
Kröv D 21 E8
Krovik S 111 E19
Krovyli GR 171 C9
Krrabë AL 168 B2
Krš HR 156 C3
Kršan HR 67 B9
Krško SLO 148 E4
Krstac MNE 157 F10
Krstinja HR 156 B4
Krtova BIH 157 C9
Kruchowo PL 138 E4
Krüden D 83 E11
Kruft D 185 D7
Kruibeke B 19 B9
Kruiningen NL 16 F2
Kruishoutem B 19 C8
Krujë AL 168 A2
Krukenychi UA 144 D7
Kruklanki PL 136 E4
Krukowo PL 139 D11
Krumbach A 71 C9
Krumbach A 148 A6
Krumbach (Schwaben) D 71 A10
Krumë AL 163 E9
Krummesse D 83 C9
Krumovgrad BG 171 B9
Krumovo BG 165 E10
Krumovo BG 166 E6
Krumpa (Geiseltal) D 79 D10
Krumvíř CZ 77 E11
Krün D 72 A3
Krunderup DK 86 C3
Kruonis LT 137 D9
Kruopiai LT 134 D6
Krupac BIH 157 E9
Krupac SRB 165 C6
Krupa na Vrbasu BIH 157 C7
Krupanj SRB 158 E3
Krupava BY 137 F11
Krupe PL 144 A7
Krupina SK 147 E8
Krupište NMK 164 F5
Krupka CZ 80 E5
Krupnik BG 165 F7
Kruså DK 82 A6
Kruševac SRB 164 B3
Kruševica SRB 158 E5
Kruševo NMK 168 B5
Kruševo Grdo BIH 157 D8
Krushari BG 155 F1
Krushë e Madhe RKS 164 E2
Krushel'nytsya UA 145 E8
Krushevets BG 167 E8
Krushevo BG 166 C4
Krushovene BG 160 F4
Krushovitsa BG 160 F3
Krušovce SK 146 D6
Kruszewo PL 85 E11
Kruszwica PL 138 E5
Kruszyna PL 85 B12
Kruszyna PL 143 E7
Krutådal N 108 E7
Krute MNE 163 E7
Kruunupyy FIN 123 C10
Kružlov SK 145 E3
Krya Vrysi GR 169 C7
Kryekuq AL 168 C2
Kryezi AL 163 E9
Kryłów PL 144 B9
Krynica PL 145 E2
Krynica Morska PL 139 B7
Krynice PL 144 B7
Krynki PL 140 D9
Krynychne UA 155 B3
Kryoneri GR 175 D6
Kryoneritis GR 175 B7
Kryopigi GR 169 D9
Krypno Kościelne PL 140 D7
Kryry CZ 76 B4
Krystad N 110 D5
Krystallopigi GR 168 C5
Kryva Balka UA 154 E5
Kryve Ozero UA 154 B6
Kryvorivnya UA 152 A5
Kryzhopil' UA 154 A3
Kržanja MNE 163 D7
Krzanowice PL 142 F5
Krzątka PL 144 C4
Krzczonów-Wójtostwo PL 144 A6
Krzcjcin PL 85 D9
Krzelów PL 81 D11
Krzemieniewo PL 81 C11
Krzepice PL 142 E6
Krzepielów PL 81 C10
Krzesk-Królowa Niwa PL 141 F7
Krzeszów PL 81 E10
Krzeszów PL 144 C5
Krzeszowice PL 143 F8
Krzeszyce PL 81 A8
Krzjtów PL 143 E8
Krzykosy PL 81 B12
Krzynowłoga Mała PL 139 D10
Krzystkowice PL 81 C8
Krzywcza PL 144 D6
Krzywda PL 141 G6
Krzywiń PL 81 C11
Krzywin PL 84 D6
Krzywowierzba PL 141 G8
Krzyżanów PL 143 B7
Krzyżanowice PL 141 H4
Krzyżanowice PL 146 B6
KrzyżKrzyż PL 85 E10
Ksar Sghir MA 53 E5
Książ Wielki PL 143 F9
Książ Wielkopolski PL 81 B12
Ksijżpol PL 144 C6
Kubanovka RUS 136 D5
Kubbe S 107 D14
Kübekháza H 150 E5
Kublichy BY 133 F4
Küblis CH 71 D9
Kubrat BG 161 F8
Kubuli LV 133 B2
Kuç AL 168 D2
Kučevo SRB 159 E8
Kuchen D 74 E6
Kuchl A 73 A7
Kuchurhan UA 154 D5
Kuchyňa SK 77 F12
Kucice PL 139 E9
Kuciny PL 143 C7
Kučište HR 162 D3
Kuçovë AL 168 C2
Küçükanafarta TR 171 D10
Küçükbahçe TR 177 B7
Küçükçekmece TR 173 B10
Küçükkariştiran TR 173 B7
Küçükkemerdere TR 177 C10
Küçükköy TR 172 F6
Küçükkumla TR 173 D11
Küçükkuyu TR 172 E6
Küçükyoncali TR 173 B8
Kucura SRB 158 B4
Kuczbork-Osada PL 139 D9
Kudever' RUS 133 C6
Kudirkos Naumiestis LT 136 D6
Kudowa-Zdrój PL 77 B10
Kūdums LV 135 B10
Kufstein A 72 A5
Kuggerud N 96 B6
Kuggören S 103 C14
Kuha FIN 119 C17
Kuhakoski FIN 129 B9
Kühbach D 75 F9
Kuhbier D 83 D12
Kuhfelde D 83 E10
Kühlungsborn D 83 B11
Kuhmalahti FIN 127 B12
Kuhmo FIN 121 F14
Kuhmoinen FIN 127 B13
Kühndorf D 79 E7
Kühren D 79 D12
Kuhs D 83 C12
Kuhstedt D 17 B11
Kuijõe EST 131 C7
Kuimetsa EST 131 C10
Kuinre NL 16 C5
Kuivajärvi FIN 121 E15
Kuivajõe EST 131 C10
Kuivakangas S 119 B11
Kuivalahti FIN 126 C6
Kuivaniemi FIN 119 C14
Kuivanto FIN 127 D15
Kuivasjärvi FIN 123 F9
Kuivastu EST 130 D6
Kujakowice Dolne PL 142 D5
Kūkas LV 135 C12
Kukasjärvi FIN 117 D15
Kukasjärvi S 119 B10
Kukës AL 163 E9
Kukko FIN 123 E12
Kukkola FIN 119 C12
Kukkola S 119 C12
Kuklen BG 165 E10
Kuklin PL 139 D9
Kuklinów PL 81 C12
Kukliš NMK 169 B8
Kukljić HR 156 D4
Kukljica HR 156 D3
Kukljin SRB 164 B3
Kukmirn A 148 B6
Kukruse EST 131 C14
Kuktiškės LT 135 F11
Kukulje BIH 157 C7
Kukur AL 168 C3
Kukurečani NMK 168 B5
Kula BG 159 F9
Kula HR 149 F9
Kula SRB 158 B4
Kulaši BIH 157 C8
Kulata BG 169 B9
Kulautuva LT 137 D8
Kūlciems LV 134 B6
Kuldīga LV 134 C3
Küllefli TR 173 D8
Kuleli TR 173 B6
Kulennoinen FIN 129 B11
Kulen Vakuf BIH 156 C5
Kulesze PL 140 D7
Kulho FIN 125 E13
Kulia N 105 D9
Kuliai LT 134 E3
Kulju FIN 127 C10
Kullaa FIN 126 C7
Kullamaa EST 131 D8
Kulleseid N 94 C2
Kulltorp S 88 A5
Kulmain D 75 C10
Kulmbach D 75 B9
Kulloharju FIN 121 C11
Külsheim D 27 A12
Kultima FIN 116 B9
Kuluntalahti FIN 121 F10
Kūlupėnai LT 134 E2
Kulva LT 137 C9
Kulvemäki FIN 124 C9
Kulykiv UA 144 D9
Kumachevo RUS 139 A9
Kumane SRB 158 B5
Kumanica SRB 163 C9
Kumanovo NMK 164 E4
Kumbağ TR 173 C7
Kumberg A 148 B5
Kumbri LV 134 C4
Kumbuļi LV 135 E13
Kumburun TR 171 E10
Kumhausen D 75 E11
Kumkadi TR 173 D9
Kumkale TR 171 E10
Kumköy TR 173 B11
Kumla S 92 A6
Kumla kyrkby S 98 C7
Kumlinge FIN 99 B15
Kummer D 83 D10
Kummerow D 83 C13
Kummersdorf-Alexanderdorf D 80 B4
Kummersdorf Gut D 80 B4
Kummunkylä FIN 123 D16
Kumpuranta FIN 125 G12
Kumpuselkä FIN 123 D16
Kumpuvaara FIN 119 C18
Kumrovec HR 148 D5
Kunadacs H 150 D3
Kunágota H 151 E7
Kunbaja H 150 E3
Kunbaracs H 150 D3
Kunčina CZ 77 C11
Kunda EST 131 B13
Kunes N 113 C18
Kunfehértó H 150 E3
Kungälv S 91 D10
Kungas FIN 123 C11
Kungsängen S 99 D9
Kungsäter S 88 A3
Kungsbacka S 91 E11
Kungsberg S 103 E11
Kungsfors S 103 E12
Kungsgården S 103 D12
Kungsgården S 103 E12
Kungshamn S 91 C9
Kungshult S 87 D12
Kungsör S 98 D6
Kunhegyes H 150 C6
Kunice PL 81 D10
Kunín CZ 146 B5
Kuningaküla EST 132 C2
Kuniów PL 142 E5
Kunmadaras H 150 C6
Kunovice CZ 146 C4
Kunowice PL 81 B7
Kunowo PL 81 C12
Kunpeszér H 150 C3
Kunrade NL 183 D7
Kunrau D 79 A9
Kunštát CZ 77 C11
Kunszállás H 150 D4
Kunszentmárton H 150 D5
Kunszentmiklós H 150 C3
Kunsziget H 149 A9
Kunvald CZ 77 B11
Kunžak CZ 77 D8
Künzell D 74 A6
Künzelsau D 74 D6
Künzing D 76 E4
Kuohatti FIN 125 C12
Kuohu FIN 123 F14
Kuoksajärvi FIN 117 E15
Kuoksu S 116 C7
Kuolayarvi RUS 115 E6
Kuolio FIN 121 C12
Kuomiokoski FIN 128 C7
Kuona FIN 123 C15
Kuopio FIN 124 E9
Kuoppala FIN 122 D9
Kuorevesi FIN 127 B12
Kuortane FIN 123 E11
Kuortti FIN 127 C15
Kuosku FIN 115 D4
Kuossakåbba S 116 D4
Kuouka S 116 E5
Kup PL 142 E4
Kupari HR 162 D5
Küpeler TR 173 E8
Kupferberg D 75 B10
Kupferzell D 74 D6
Kupientyn PL 141 F6
Kupinec HR 148 E5
Kupinovo SRB 158 D5
Kupiškis LT 135 E9
Kupjak HR 67 B10
Küplü TR 171 B10
Kuppenheim D 27 C9
Kuprava LV 133 B3
Kupres BIH 157 D7
Kuprešani BIH 157 D7
Küps D 75 B9
Kurapollye BY 135 F13
Kuratën AL 168 B2
Kurbnesh AL 163 F9
Kurd H 149 D10
Kŭrdzhali BG 171 A8
Kurejoki FIN 123 D11
Kuremaa EST 131 D13
Kuremäe EST 132 C2
Kuressaare EST 130 E4
Kurevere EST 130 E3
Kurienkylä FIN 123 F10
Kurikka FIN 122 E8
Kuřim CZ 77 D11
Kurima SK 145 E3
Kurjala FIN 125 E10
Kurjan AL 168 C2
Kurki FIN 121 D10
Kurkiharju FIN 125 E9
Kurkikylä FIN 121 D11
Kurkimäki FIN 124 E9
Kurmene LV 135 D9
Kürnach D 187 B9
Kürnare BG 165 D10
Kürnbach D 27 B10
Kurolanlahti FIN 124 D8
Kuropta RUS 115 D9
Kurort Bad Gottleuba D 80 E5
Kurort Kipsdorf D 80 E5
Kurort Oberwiesenthal D 76 B3
Kurort Schmalkalden D 79 E7
Kurort Steinbach-Hallenberg D 79 E8
Kurów PL 141 H6
Kurowice PL 143 C8
Kurravaara S 116 C4
Kurrokvejk S 109 E14
Kuršėnai LT 134 D5
Kursīši LV 134 D4
Kursu FIN 115 E4
Kuršumlija SRB 164 C3
Kuršumlijska Banja SRB 164 C3
Kurtakko FIN 117 D12
Kurtbey TR 172 B6
Kurtna EST 132 C2
Kurtovo Konare BG 165 E9
Kurtti FIN 121 D11
Kurtto FIN 121 E11
Kurtzea E 40 B6
Kuru FIN 127 B10
Kurvinen FIN 121 C14
Kuryłówka PL 144 C5
Kurzelów PL 143 E8
Kurzeszyn PL 141 G2
Kurzjtnik PL 139 D8
Kusa LV 135 C12
Kusadak SRB 159 E6
Kuşadasi TR 177 D9
Kuşçayir TR 172 E6
Kusel D 21 E8
Kusey D 79 A9
Kusfors S 118 E4
Kushnytsya UA 145 G7
Kušići SRB 163 C9
Kuside MNE 163 D6
Kuślin PL 81 B10
Kusmark S 118 E5
Küsnacht CH 27 F10
Küssnacht CH 27 F9
Kustavi FIN 126 D5
Küsten D 83 E10
Kusterdingen D 27 C11
Kuštilj SRB 159 C7
Kuta BIH 157 E10
Kutalli AL 168 C2
Kutas H 149 D8
Kutemajärvi FIN 124 F7
Kutenholz D 17 B12
Kuti MNE 163 D8
Kutina HR 149 F7
Kutjevo HR 149 F9
Kutlovo SRB 159 E6
Kutná Hora CZ 77 C8
Kutno PL 143 B7
Kutrikko FIN 115 E5
Kuttainen S 116 B9
Kuttanen FIN 116 B9
Kuttura FIN 117 B16
Kúty SK 77 E12
Kuty UA 152 A6
Kuukasjärvi FIN 119 C17
Kuumu FIN 121 E14
Kuurne B 19 C7
Kuurtola FIN 121 D12
Kuusaa FIN 123 C15
Kuusaa FIN 123 F15
Kuusajärvi FIN 117 C14
Kuusajoki FIN 117 C14
Kuusalu EST 131 C10
Kuusamo FIN 121 C13
Kuusamonkylä FIN 121 F13
Kuusankoski FIN 128 D6
Kuusijärvi FIN 121 D11
Kuusijoki FIN 126 B8
Kuusiku EST 131 D9
Kuusiranta FIN 120 F9
Kuusirati FIN 119 F14
Kuusivaara FIN 115 E2
Kuusjärvi FIN 125 E11
Kuusjoki FIN 127 D9
Kuuslahti FIN 124 D9
Kuvansi FIN 125 F9
Kuvaskangas FIN 126 B6
Kuyka UA 153 A7
Kuyvozi RUS 129 E13
Kužiai LT 134 E6
Kuzmice SK 145 F4

Llanllwchaiarn *GB* **10** F5
Llanllyfni *GB* **10** E3
Llannerch-y-medd *GB* **10** E3
Llan-non *GB* **12** A6
Llannon *GB* **12** B6
Llanrhaeadr-ym-Mochnant *GB* **10** F5
Llanrhidian *GB* **12** B6
Llanrhystud *GB* **12** A6
Llanrug *GB* **10** E3
Llanrumney *GB* **13** B8
Llanrwst *GB* **10** E4
Llansanffraid Glan Conwy *GB* **10** E4
Llansannan *GB* **10** E4
Llansawel *GB* **12** A6
Llantilio Pertholey *GB* **13** B8
Llantrisant *GB* **13** B8
Llantwit Major *GB* **13** C8
Llanuwchllyn *GB* **10** F4
Llanwddyn *GB* **10** F5
Llanwenog *GB* **12** A6
Llanwnda *GB* **10** E3
Llanwnog *GB* **10** F5
Llanwrtyd Wells *GB* **13** A7
Llanybydder *GB* **12** A6
Llapushnik *RKS* **163** D10
Llardecans *E* **42** E5
Llaurí *E* **48** F4
Llavorsí *E* **33** E8
Llay *GB* **10** E5
Lledrod *GB* **12** A7
Lleida *E* **42** D5
Llera *E* **51** C7
Llerena *E* **51** C7
Lliria *E* **48** E3
Llívia *E* **33** F9
Llodio *E* **40** B6
Llombai *E* **48** F3
Lloret de Mar *E* **43** D9
Lloseta *E* **49** E10
Llubí *E* **57** B11
Llucmajor *E* **57** C10
Lniano *PL* **138** C5
Lo *B* **18** C6
Loamneş *RO* **152** F4
Loano *I* **37** C8
Loarre *E* **32** F4
Löbau *D* **81** D7
Lobbæk *DK* **89** E7
Lobe *LV* **135** C10
Löbejün *D* **79** C10
Lobera de Onsella *E* **32** F3
Lobērģi *LV* **131** F12
Łobez *PL* **85** C9
Lobith *NL* **183** B8
Löbnitz *D* **83** B13
Łobodno *PL* **143** E6
Lobón *E* **51** B6
Lobonäs *S* **103** C9
Loburg *D* **79** B11
Łobżenica *PL* **85** D12
Locana *I* **31** E11
Locarno *CH* **68** A6
Locate di Triulzi *I* **69** C7
Loccum (Rehburg-Loccum) *D* **17** D12
Loceri *I* **64** D4
Lochaline *GB* **4** B5
Lochau *A* **71** B9
Lochawe *GB* **4** C6
Lochboisdale *GB* **2** L2
Lochcarron *GB* **2** L5
Lochdon *GB* **4** C5
Lochearnhead *GB* **5** C8
Lochem *NL* **16** D6
Lochen *A* **76** F4
Lochend *GB* **3** L8
Loches *F* **24** F4
Loch Garman *IRL* **9** D10
Lochgelly *GB* **5** C10
Lochgilphead *GB* **4** C6
Lochgoilhead *GB* **4** C7
Lochinver *GB* **2** J6
Lochmaben *GB* **5** E10
Lochmaddy *GB* **2** K2
Lochovice *CZ* **76** C5
Łochów *PL* **139** E12
Lochranza *GB* **4** D6
Lochristi *B* **19** B8
Loch Sgioport *GB* **2** L2
Lociki *LV* **135** E13
Lockenhaus *A* **149** B6
Lockerbie *GB* **5** E10
Lockne *S* **106** E7
Löcknitz *D* **84** D6
Locks Heath *GB* **13** D12
Lockton *GB* **11** C10
Locmaria-Plouzané *F* **22** D2
Locmariaquer *F* **22** E6
Locminé *F* **22** E6
Locorotondo *I* **61** B8
Locquirec *F* **22** C4
Locri *I* **59** C9
Locronan *F* **22** D3
Loctudy *F* **22** E3
Loculi *I* **64** C4
Löddeköpinge *S* **87** D12
Lödderitz *D* **79** C10
Loddin *D* **84** B6
Lødding *N* **105** B10
Loddiswell *GB* **13** E7
Loddon *GB* **15** B11
Lodè *I* **64** B4
Lode *LV* **135** B10
Loděnice *CZ* **76** B6
Löderup *S* **88** E6
Lodève *F* **34** C5
Lodi *I* **69** C8
Løding *N* **108** B8
Lødingen *N* **111** D10
Lodi Vecchio *I* **69** C7
Lodosa *E* **32** F1
Lödöse *S* **91** C11
Łodygowice *PL* **147** B8
Łódź *PL* **143** C7
Loeches *E* **46** D6
Loenen *NL* **183** A8
Löf *D* **21** D8
Løfallstrand *N* **94** B4
Lofer *A* **73** A6
Löffingen *D* **27** E9
Lofos *GR* **169** D7
Lofsdalen *S* **102** B5
Loftahammar *S* **93** D9
Lofthus *N* **94** B5
Lofthus *N* **111** E10
Loftus *GB* **11** B10
Log *SLO* **73** D8
Loga *N* **94** F5
Logan *GB* **5** E8
Logatec *SLO* **73** E9
Lögda *S* **107** C14
Lögdeå *S* **107** D16
Loggerheads *GB* **11** F7
Loghill *IRL* **8** C4
Logkanikos *GR* **174** E5
Logofteni *MD* **153** B11
Logreşti *RO* **160** D3
Logron *F* **24** D5
Logroño *E* **41** D7
Logrosán *E* **45** F10
Løgstør *DK* **86** B4
Løgstrup *DK* **86** B4
Løgten *DK* **86** C6
Løgumkloster *DK* **86** E3
Lohals *DK* **87** E7
Lohberg *D* **76** D4
Lohéac *F* **23** E8
Lohe-Rickelshof *D* **82** B6
Lohfelden *D* **78** D6
Lohijärvi *FIN* **119** B12
Lohilahti *FIN* **129** B10
Lohiluoma *FIN* **122** E8
Lohiniva *FIN* **117** D13
Lohiranta *FIN* **121** B12
Lohja *FIN* **127** E11
Lohjan kunta *FIN* **127** E11
Lohmar *D* **21** C8
Lohme *D* **84** A5
Lohmen *D* **80** E6
Lohmen *D* **83** C12
Löhnberg *D* **21** C10
Löhne *D* **17** D11
Lohne (Oldenburg) *D* **17** C10
Lohra *D* **21** C11
Lohr am Main *D* **74** C6
Lohsa *D* **80** D6
Lohtaja *FIN* **123** B11
Lohusuu *EST* **131** D14
Loiano *I* **66** D3
Loigny-la-Bataille *F* **24** D6
Loimaa *FIN* **127** D9
Loimaan kunta *FIN* **127** D8
Loiré *F* **23** E10
Loiri-Porto San Paolo *I* **64** B3
Loiron *F* **23** D10
Loisy-sur-Marne *F* **25** C12
Loitz *D* **84** C4
Loivos *P* **38** E5
Loivos do Monte *P* **44** B5
Loja *E* **53** B8
Loja *LV* **135** B9
Løjt Kirkeby *DK* **86** E4
Loka brunn *S* **97** C11
Lokakylä *FIN* **123** D14
Lokalahti *FIN* **126** D5
Lokavec *SLO* **73** E8
Lokca *SK* **147** C8
Loke *S* **106** F7
Løken *N* **95** C14
Lokeren *B* **19** B9
Loket *CZ* **75** B12
Lokev *SLO* **73** E8
Lokka *FIN* **115** C3
Løkken *DK* **90** E6
Løkken *N* **104** E7
Lokkiperä *FIN* **123** C13
Lőkösháza *H* **151** E7
Lokrume *S* **93** D13
Loksa *EST* **131** B11
Løksa *N* **111** C14
Løksebotn *N* **111** C14
Lokuta *EST* **131** D9
Lokuti *EST* **131** C9
Lokve *HR* **67** B10
Lokve *SLO* **73** D8
Lokve *SRB* **159** C7
Løkvoll *N* **112** D6
Lolishniy Shepit *UA* **152** A6
Lollar *D* **21** C11
L'Ollería *E* **56** D3
Lom *BG* **159** F11
Lom *N* **101** C9
Łomazy *PL* **141** G8
Lombez *F* **33** D7
Lombheden *S* **119** B9
Lomborg *DK* **86** B2
Lomello *I* **68** C6
Lomen *N* **101** D9
Łomianki *PL* **139** F10
Lomma *S* **87** D12
Lommatzsch *D* **80** D4
Lomme *F* **18** C6
Lommel *B* **19** B11
Łomnica *PL* **81** B9
Lomnice *CZ* **77** D10
Lomnice nad Lužnicí *CZ* **77** D7
Lomnice nad Popelkou *CZ* **77** A8
Lomonosov *RUS* **129** F12
Lompolo *FIN* **117** B13
Lomsdalen *N* **101** E12
Lomsjö *S* **107** C11
Lomsti *BG* **166** C6
Lomträsk *S* **109** E18
Lomträsk *S* **119** B9
Łomża *PL* **139** D13
Lonato *I* **66** B1
Lønborg *DK* **86** D2
Lončari *BIH* **157** C10
Lončarica *HR* **149** E8
Londa *I* **66** E4
Londerzeel *B* **19** C9
Londinières *F* **18** E3
London *GB* **15** D8
Londonderry *GB* **4** F2
Lone *LV* **135** D10
Long *F* **18** D4
Longa *GR* **174** F4
Longages *F* **33** D8
Longare *I* **66** B4
Longares *E* **41** F9
Longarone *I* **72** D5
Long Ashton *GB* **13** C9
Long Bennington *GB* **11** F10
Longbridge Deverill *GB* **13** C10
Longchaumois *F* **31** C8
Long Compton *GB* **13** B11
Long Crendon *GB* **14** D6
Long Eaton *GB* **11** F9
Longeau-Percey *F* **26** E3
Longecourt-en-Plaine *F* **26** F3
Longerak *N* **90** B2
Longeville-en-Barrois *F* **26** C3
Longeville-lès-St-Avold *F* **186** C2
Longeville-sur-Mer *F* **28** C3
Longford *IRL* **7** E7
Longframlington *GB* **5** E13
Longhope *GB* **3** H10
Longhope *GB* **13** B10
Longhorsley *GB* **5** E13
Longhoughton *GB* **5** E13
Long Itchington *GB* **13** A12
Longlier *B* **19** E11
Long Melford *GB* **15** C10
Longmorn *GB* **3** K10
Longny-au-Perche *F* **24** C4
Longobardi *I* **60** E6
Longobucco *I* **61** E7
Longomel *P* **44** F5
Longos *GR* **168** F3
Longos Vales *P* **38** D3
Long Preston *GB* **11** C7
Longré *F* **28** C5
Longridge *GB* **10** D6
Longroiva *P* **45** C6
Long Stratton *GB* **15** C11
Long Sutton *GB* **11** F12
Longton *GB* **10** D6
Longtown *GB* **5** E11
Longueau *F* **18** E5
Longué-Jumelles *F* **23** F11
Longuenesse *F* **18** C5
Longueville *F* **25** C9
Longueville-sur-Scie *F* **18** E3
Longuyon *F* **19** F12
Longwood *IRL* **7** F9
Longwy *F* **19** E12
Lonigo *I* **66** B3
Lonin *N* **95** C10
Löningen *D* **17** C9
Łoniów *PL* **143** E12
Lonja *HR* **149** F7
Lonjica *HR* **149** E6
Lonkan *N* **110** C9
Lonkka *FIN* **121** D13
Lonlay-l'Abbaye *F* **23** C10
Lönneberga *S* **92** D7
Lonneker *NL* **183** A9
Lonny *F* **184** E2
Lons *F* **32** D5
Lönsboda *S* **88** C6
Lonsee *D* **74** E6
Lons-le-Saunier *F* **31** B8
Lønstrup *DK* **90** E6
Lontzen *B* **183** D8
Lónya *H* **145** G5
Loo *EST* **131** C9
Loon op Zand *NL* **16** E4
Loos *F* **182** D2
Loosdorf *A* **77** F8
Loose *GB* **15** E10
Lopadea Nouă *RO* **152** E3
Lopar *HR* **67** C10
Lopare *BIH* **157** C10
Lopătari *RO* **161** C9
Lopate *NMK* **164** E4
Lopatica *NMK* **168** B5
Łopatki *PL* **143** C7
Lopatnic *MD* **153** A10
Lopatovo *RUS* **132** F4
Lopcombe Corner *GB* **13** C11
Lõpe *EST* **131** D7
Lopera *E* **53** A8
Łopiennik Górny *PL* **144** A7
Lopigna *F* **37** G9
Lopik *NL* **182** B5
Loppa *N* **112** C7
Loppersum *NL* **17** B7
Loppi *FIN* **127** D11
Lopra *FO* **2** C3
Lopushna *UA* **152** A6
Łopuszno *PL* **143** E9
Lopyan *BG* **165** D9
Lora *N* **101** B9
Lora del Río *E* **51** D8
Loranca de Tajuña *E* **47** D6
Lorås *S* **106** E8
Lörby *S* **88** C7
Lorca *E* **55** D9
Lorch *D* **21** D9
Lorch *D* **74** E6
Lorcha *E* **56** D4
Lordelo *P* **38** F4
Lordosa *P* **44** C5
Lørenskog *N* **95** C13
Loreo *I* **66** B5
Loreto *I* **67** F8
Loreto Aprutino *I* **62** C5
Lorgues *F* **36** D4
Lorient *F* **22** E5
Lorignac *F* **28** E4
Loriguilla *E* **48** E3
Lőrinci *H* **150** B4
Loriol-sur-Drôme *F* **30** F6
Lormes *F* **25** F10
Loro Ciuffenna *I* **66** E4
Loro Piceno *I* **67** F7
Lorquin *F* **186** D2
Lörrach *D* **27** E8
Lorrez-le-Bocage-Préaux *F* **25** D8
Lorris *F* **25** E8
Lorsch *D* **21** E11
Lørslev *DK* **90** E7
Lörstrand *S* **103** C11
Lörudden *S* **103** B14
Lorup *D* **17** C9
Lorupe *LV* **135** B9
Los *S* **103** C9
Losacino *E* **39** E7
Losa del Obispo *E* **48** E3
Los Alcázares *E* **56** F3
Los Algezares *E* **56** F2
Los Arcos *E* **32** E1
Losar de la Vera *E* **45** D9
Los Arenales del Sol *E* **56** E4
Los Barrios *E* **53** D6
Los Barrios de Luna *E* **39** C8
Los Belones *E* **56** F3
Los Cantareros *E* **55** D10
Los Corrales *E* **53** B7
Los Corrales de Buelna *E* **40** B3
Loscos *E* **42** E1
Los Dolores *E* **56** F2
Løset *N* **101** D14
Los Gallardos *E* **55** E9
Loshchynivka *UA* **155** C3
Losheim *D* **21** E7
Los Hinojosos *E* **47** E7
Łosice *PL* **141** F7
Łosinka *PL* **141** E9
Łosiów *PL* **142** E4
Los Maldonados *E* **56** F2
Los Molinos *E* **46** C4
Losna *N* **101** D12
Los Navalmorales *E* **46** E3
Los Navalucillos *E* **46** E3
Løsning *DK* **86** D5
Losomäki *FIN* **125** D11
Losone *CH* **68** A6
Łososina Dolna *PL* **144** D2
Losova *MD* **154** C2
Losovaara *FIN* **121** E11
Los Palacios y Villafranca *E* **51** E8
Los Pandos *E* **40** B4
Los Pedrones *E* **47** F10
Los Pozuelos de Calatrava *E* **54** B5
Los Rábanos *E* **41** E7
Los Royos *E* **55** D8
Los Santos *E* **45** C9
Los Santos de Maimona *E* **51** C7
Loßburg *D* **27** D9
Losse *F* **32** B5
Losser *NL* **17** D7
Lossiemouth *GB* **3** K10
Lößnitz *D* **79** E12
Lostallo *CH* **69** A7
Loštice *CZ* **77** C11
Los Tojos *E* **40** B3
Lostwithiel *GB* **12** E5
Los Villares *E* **53** A9
Los Yébenes *E* **46** E5
Löt *S* **89** B11
Lote *N* **100** C4
Loten *N* **94** D2
Løten *N* **101** E14
Lotenhulle *B* **182** C2
Loth *GB* **3** G11
Lothmore *GB* **3** J9
Lötorp *S* **92** B7
Lotte *D* **17** D9
Lottefors *S* **103** D11
Löttorp *S* **89** A11
Lottstetten *D* **27** E10
Lottum *NL* **183** C8
Lotyń *PL* **85** C11
Lotzorai *I* **64** D4
Louannec *F* **22** C5
Loučeň *CZ* **77** B8
Loučná nad Desnou *CZ* **77** B12
Loučovice *CZ* **76** E6
Loudéac *F* **22** D6
Loudes *F* **30** E4
Loudun *F* **28** A6
Loué *F* **23** E11
Loue *FIN* **119** B13
Louejärvi *FIN* **119** B14
Louejoki *FIN* **119** B14
Loughborough *GB* **11** F9
Loughbrickland *GB* **7** D10
Lougher *IRL* **8** D3
Loughgall *GB* **7** D9
Loughglinn *IRL* **6** E5
Loughrea *IRL* **6** F5
Loughton *GB* **15** D9
Lougratte *F* **33** A7
Louhans *F* **31** B7
Louka *CZ* **146** D4
Loukas *GR* **174** D5
Loukisia *GR* **175** C7
Loukkojärvi *FIN* **119** D15
Loukusa *FIN* **121** C10
Loulans *F* **26** F5
Loulay *F* **28** C4
Loulé *P* **50** E3
Louny *CZ* **76** B5
Loupiac *F* **32** A5
Lourdes *F* **32** D5
Lourdoueix-St-Pierre *F* **29** C9
Louriçal *P* **44** D3
Lourinhã *P* **44** F2
Lourmarin *F* **35** C9
Louros *GR* **174** A2
Loury *F* **24** E7
Lousã *P* **44** D4
Lousa *P* **50** B1
Lousada *P* **38** F3
Louth *GB* **11** E11
Louth *IRL* **7** E9
Loutra *GR* **175** E9
Loutra *GR* **177** A8
Loutra Aidipsou *GR* **175** B7
Loutra Eleftheron *GR* **170** C6
Loutraki *GR* **169** C6
Loutraki *GR* **174** B3
Loutraki *GR* **175** D6
Loutra Kyllinis *GR* **174** D3
Loutra Smokovou *GR* **174** A5
Loutra Ypatis *GR* **174** B5
Loutro *GR* **169** C7
Loutro *GR* **169** E6
Loutro *GR* **174** B3
Loutros *GR* **171** C10
Louvain *B* **19** C10
Louvain *B* **182** D5
Louveigné *B* **183** D7
Louverné *F* **23** D10
Louvie-Juzon *F* **32** D5
Louviers *F* **18** F3
Louvigné-du-Désert *F* **23** D9
Louvroil *F* **19** D8
Louze *F* **25** D12
Lov *DK* **87** E9
Lövånger *S* **118** F6
Lovas *HR* **157** B11
Lovasberény *H* **149** B11
Lovászi *H* **149** C7
Lovászpatona *H* **149** B9
Lovberg *S* **106** A7
Lövberga *S* **107** D9
Lovćenac *SRB* **158** B4
Lovčica-Trubín *SK* **147** D7
Løve *DK* **87** E8
Lovech *BG* **165** C10
Løvel *DK* **86** B4
Lovendegem *B* **19** B8
Lovere *I* **69** B9
Lovero *I* **69** A9
Lövestad *S* **88** D5
Loviisa *FIN* **127** E15
Lovik *N* **111** C10
Lovikka *S* **116** D9
Lovinac *HR* **156** D4
Lovinobaňa *SK* **147** E9
Lovisa *FIN* **127** E15
Lovište *HR* **157** F7
Lovliden *S* **107** B11
Løvlund *N* **101** D11
Lövnäs *S* **102** D5
Lövnäs *S* **107** B9
Lövnäs *S* **109** D14
Lövnäsvallen *S* **102** C6
Lovnidol *BG* **166** D4
Lövő *H* **149** A7
Lovosice *CZ* **76** A6
Lovraeid *N* **94** D4
Lovran *HR* **67** B9
Lovreč *HR* **67** B8
Lovreć *HR* **157** F7
Lovrenc *SLO* **148** C4
Lovrin *RO* **150** F6
Lövsele *S* **118** F6
Lövsjö *S* **106** B8
Lövsjön *S* **97** B12
Lövstabruk *S* **99** B9
Lövstalöt *S* **99** C9
Lövstrand *S* **107** C10
Lövtjärn *S* **103** D11
Lovund *N* **108** D3
Lövvik *S* **103** A15
Lövvik *S* **107** C9
Łowcza *PL* **141** H8
Löwenberg *D* **84** E4
Löwenstein *D* **27** B11
Lower Ballinderry *GB* **7** C10
Lower Cam *GB* **13** B10
Lower Kilchattan *GB* **4** C4
Lowestoft *GB* **15** C12
Lowick *GB* **5** D13
Łowicz *PL* **141** F1
Low Street *GB* **15** B11
Łowyń *PL* **81** B9
Loxstedt *D* **17** B11
Löyä *FIN* **123** E11
Loyettes *F* **31** D7
Loymola *RUS* **129** B16
Löytö *FIN* **128** B7
Löytökylä *FIN* **119** D16
Löytövaara *FIN* **121** C11
Lozarevo *BG* **167** D7
Lozen *BG* **165** D7
Lozen *BG* **166** C5
Lozenets *BG* **167** E9
Lozna *RO* **151** C11
Lozna *SRB* **159** F6
Loznica *SRB* **158** D3
Loznitsa *BG* **155** F1
Loznitsa *BG* **167** C7
Lozorno *SK* **77** F12
Lozovac *HR* **156** E4
Lozovik *SRB* **159** E7
Lozoya *E* **46** C5
Lozoyuela *E* **46** C5
Lozuvata *UA* **154** A6
Lozzo di Cadore *I* **72** D5
Lú *IRL* **7** E9
Luanco *E* **39** A8
Luarca *E* **39** A6
Lubaczów *PL* **144** C7
Lubań *PL* **81** D8
Lubāna *LV* **135** C13
Lubanowo *PL* **84** D7
Lübars *D* **79** B11
Lubartów *PL* **141** H7
Lubasz *PL* **85** E11
Lubawa *PL* **139** C8
Lubawka *PL* **81** E10
Lübbecke *D* **17** D11
Lübbeek *B* **19** C10
Lübben *D* **80** C5
Lübbenau *D* **80** C5
Lübbow *D* **83** E10
Lubczyna *PL* **85** C7
Lube *LV* **134** B5
Lübeck *D* **83** C9
Ľubeľa *SK* **147** C8
Lubenec *CZ* **76** B4
Lubeník *SK* **145** F1
Lubersac *F* **29** E8
Lübesse *D* **83** D10
Lubezere *LV* **134** B5
Lubiai *LT* **134** E3
Lubián *E* **39** D6
Łubianka *PL* **138** D6
Lubichowo *PL* **138** C5
Lubicz Dolny *PL* **138** D6
Lubijcin *PL* **81** C9
Lubień *PL* **147** B9
Lubień Kujawski *PL* **139** F7
Lubieszewo *PL* **85** D9
Lubiń *PL* **81** C11
Lubin *PL* **81** D10
Lubina *SK* **146** D5
Lubiszyn *PL* **85** E7
Lublin *PL* **141** H7
Lubliniec *PL* **142** E6
Lubmin *D* **84** B5
Lubnia *PL* **138** C4
Łubniany *PL* **142** E5
Lubnica *NMK* **169** A7
Lubnica *SRB* **159** F9
Łubnice *PL* **143** F11
Lubniewice *PL* **81** A8
Łubno *PL* **85** B12
Lubno *PL* **85** D10
Łubno *PL* **143** B7
Lubochnia *PL* **141** G2
Lubomierz *PL* **81** D9
Lubomino *PL* **139** B9
Luboń *PL* **81** B11
Luborzyca *PL* **143** F9
Ľubotice *SK* **145** E3
Ľubotín *SK* **145** E2
Lubowidz *PL* **139** D8
Łubowo *PL* **85** C10
Łubowo *PL* **85** E12
Lubraniec *PL* **138** E6
Lubrín *E* **55** E8
Lubrza *PL* **81** B8
Lubrza *PL* **142** F4
Lubsko *PL* **81** C7
Lübstorf *D* **83** C10
Lubstów *PL* **138** F5
Lubsza *PL* **142** E4
Lübtheen *D* **83** D10
Luby *CZ* **75** B11
Lubycza Królewska *PL* **144** C8
Lübz *D* **83** D12
Luc *F* **33** B11
Luc *F* **35** A6
Lucainena de las Torres *E* **55** E8
Lucan *IRL* **7** F10
Lučani *SRB* **158** F5
Lúcar *E* **55** E8
Luçay-le-Mâle *F* **24** F5
Lucca *I* **66** E2
Lucca Sicula *I* **58** D3
Lucé *F* **24** D5
Luče *SLO* **73** D10
Lucena *E* **53** B8
Lucena de Jalón *E* **41** E9
Lucena del Cid *E* **48** D4
Lucena del Puerto *E* **51** E6
Lucenay-lès-Aix *F* **30** B3
Lucenay-l'Évêque *F* **25** F11
Luc-en-Diois *F* **35** A9
Lučenec *SK* **147** E9
Luceni *E* **41** E9
Lucera *I* **63** D8
Lucéram *F* **37** D6
Lucey *F* **26** C4
Lucfalva *H* **147** E9
Luchayka *BY* **133** F3
Luché-Pringé *F* **23** E12
Lucheux *F* **18** D5
Lüchow *D* **83** E10
Luchy *F* **18** E5
Luciana *E* **54** B4
Lucień *PL* **139** F7
Lucieni *RO* **161** D6
Lucignano *I* **66** F4
Lucija *SLO* **67** A8
Lucillo de Somoza *E* **39** D7
Lučine *SLO* **73** D9
Lucito *I* **63** D7
Luciu *RO* **161** D10
Lucka *D* **79** D11
Luckau *D* **80** C5
Luckenwalde *D* **80** B4
Lucksta *S* **103** B13
Lückstedt *D* **83** E11
Lúčky *SK* **147** C8
Luco dei Marsi *I* **62** D4
Luçon *F* **28** C3
Lucq-de-Béarn *F* **32** D4
Luc-sur-Mer *F* **23** B11
Lucy-le-Bois *F* **25** E10
Ludag *GB* **2** L2
Ludanice *SK* **146** E6
Ludányhalászi *H* **147** E9
Ludbreg *HR* **149** D7
Lüdenscheid *D* **21** B9
Lüderitz *D* **79** A10
Lüdersdorf *D* **83** C9
Ludeşti *RO* **160** D6
Ludgershall *GB* **13** C11
Lüdinghausen *D* **17** E8
Ludlow *GB* **13** A9
Ludogortsi *BG* **161** F9
Ludoni *RUS* **132** E5
Ludoş *RO* **152** F3
Ludres *F* **186** D1
Luduş *RO* **152** E4
Ludvigsborg *S* **87** D13
Ludvika *S* **97** B13
Ludwigsau-Friedlos *D* **78** E6
Ludwigsburg *D* **27** C11
Ludwigsfelde *D* **80** B4
Ludwigshafen *D* **27** E11
Ludwigshafen am Rhein *D* **21** F10
Ludwigslust *D* **83** D10
Ludwigsstadt *D* **75** B9
Ludwin *PL* **141** H7
Ludza *LV* **133** C3
Lüe *F* **32** B4
Luelmo *E* **39** F7
Lüerdissen *D* **78** C6
Luesia *E* **32** F3
Lueta *RO* **153** E6
Lug *BIH* **162** D5
Lug *HR* **149** E11
Luga *RUS* **132** D6
Lugagnano Val d'Arda *I* **69** D8
Lugano *CH* **69** A6
Lüganuse *EST* **131** C14
Lugau *D* **79** E12
Lugaži *LV* **131** F11
Lügde *D* **17** E12
Luglon *F* **32** B4
Lugnano in Teverina *I* **62** B2
Lugnäs *S* **91** B14
Lugnvik *S* **103** A14
Lugnvik *S* **106** E7
Lugny-lès-Charolles *F* **30** C5
Lugo *E* **38** B4
Lugo *I* **66** D4
Lugo-di-Nazza *F* **37** G10
Lugoj *RO* **159** B8
Lugones *E* **39** B8
Lugos *F* **32** B4
Lugrin *F* **31** C10
Lugros *E* **55** E6
Luhačovice *CZ* **146** C5
Luhalahti *FIN* **127** B9
Luhamaa *EST* **132** F1
Luhanka *FIN* **127** B14
Luhden *D* **17** D12
Luhe-Wildenau *D* **75** C11
Lühmannsdorf *D* **84** B5
Luhtapohja *FIN* **125** E15
Luhtikylä *FIN* **127** D13
Luhy *UA* **152** A4
Luhy *UA* **154** A4
Luica *RO* **161** E9
Luica *RO* **161** E9
Luik *B* **19** C12
Luik *B* **183** D7
Luikonlahti *FIN* **125** E11
Luimneach *IRL* **8** C5
Luino *I* **68** B6
Luintra *E* **38** D4
Luiro *FIN* **115** C4
Luiro *FIN* **115** D3
Luisant *F* **24** D5
Luizi Călugăra *RO* **153** D9
Luka *BIH* **157** F9
Luka *SRB* **159** E9
Lukácsháza *H* **149** B7
Luka nad Jihlavou *CZ* **77** D9
Lukavac *BIH* **157** C10
Lukavec *CZ* **77** C7
Lukavica *BIH* **157** C9
Łukawiec *PL* **144** C7
Luke *NMK* **164** E5
Lukeswell *IRL* **9** D8
Lūki *BG* **165** F10
Lukivtsi *UA* **152** A6
Lukkaroistenperä *FIN* **119** F13
Lukov *CZ* **146** C5
Lukovë *AL* **168** E2
Lukovit *BG* **165** C9
Lukovo *HR* **67** C10
Lukovo *SRB* **159** F8
Lukovo *SRB* **163** C11
Lukovo Šugare *HR* **67** D11
Lukovytsya *UA* **153** A8
Łuków *PL* **141** G6
Łukowa *PL* **144** C6
Łukowisko *PL* **141** F7
Lukšiai *LT* **136** D7
Lukštai *LT* **135** D11
Luky *UA* **145** D7
Lula *I* **64** C3
Luleå *S* **118** C8
Lüleburgaz *TR* **173** B7
Lüllemäe *EST* **131** F12
Lullymore *IRL* **7** F9
Lümanda *EST* **130** E4
Lumbarda *HR* **162** D3
Lumbier *E* **32** E3
Lumbrales *E* **45** C7
Lumbreras *E* **41** D6
Lumbres *F* **18** C5
Lumby *DK* **86** E6
Lumezzane *I* **69** B9
Lumijoki *FIN* **119** E14
Lumimetsä *FIN* **119** F14
Lumina *RO* **155** E3
Lumio *F* **37** F9
Lummelunda *S* **93** D12
Lummen *B* **19** C11
Lumparland *FIN* **99** B14
Lumphanan *GB* **3** L11
Lumpiaque *E* **41** E9
Lumpzig *D* **79** E11
Lumsheden *S* **103** E11
Luna *E* **41** D10
Luna *RO* **152** D3
Lunamatrona *I* **64** D2
Lunano *I* **66** E5
Lunas *F* **34** C5
Lunca *MD* **154** C4
Lunca *RO* **151** D9
Lunca *RO* **152** D5
Lunca *RO* **153** B9
Lunca *RO* **160** F5
Lunca Banului *RO* **154** D2
Lunca Bradului *RO* **152** D6
Lunca Cernii de Jos *RO* **159** B10
Lunca Corbului *RO* **160** D5
Lunca de Jos *RO* **153** D7
Lunca de Sus *RO* **153** D7
Lunca Ilvei *RO* **152** C5
Lunca Mureşului *RO* **152** E3
Luncaviţa *RO* **155** C2
Luncaviţa *RO* **159** C9
Luncoiu de Jos *RO* **151** E10
Lund *DK* **86** D5
Lund *N* **105** B11
Lund *N* **110** E8
Lund *N* **111** C15
Lund *S* **87** D12
Lundamo *N* **104** E8
Lundbjörken *S* **102** E8
Lundby *DK* **86** F7
Lundby *DK* **87** E9
Lunde *DK* **86** D2
Lunde *DK* **86** E6
Lunde *N* **95** D10
Lunde *N* **111** C16
Lunde *S* **103** A14
Lundeborg *DK* **87** E7
Lundebyvollen *N* **102** E3
Lundegård *N* **94** F6
Lunden *D* **82** B6
Lunderskov *DK* **86** E4
Lundin Links *GB* **5** C11
Lundsbrunn *S* **91** C13
Lundsjön *S* **106** D7
Lünebach *D* **20** D6
Lüneburg *D* **83** D8
Lunel *F* **35** C7
Lünen *D* **17** E9
Lunery *F* **29** B10
Lunéville *F* **26** C5
Lungani *RO* **153** C10
Lunger *S* **97** D14
Lungern *CH* **70** D6
Lungro *I* **60** D6
Lungsjön *S* **107** E10
Lunguleţu *RO* **161** D7
Lunino *RUS* **136** D5
L'Union *F* **33** C8
Lunkkaus *FIN* **115** D3
Lunna *BY* **140** D10
Lunnäset *S* **102** A5
Lünne *D* **17** D8
Lunneborg *N* **111** B16
Lunow *D* **84** E6
Lunteren *NL* **183** A7
Luogosanto *I* **64** A3
Luohua *FIN* **119** E14
Luokė *LT* **134** E5
Luokkala *FIN* **121** D11
Luola-aapa *FIN* **119** C15
Luoma-aho *FIN* **123** D11
Luopa *FIN* **122** E9
Luopajärvi *FIN* **122** E9
Luopioinen *FIN* **127** C12
Luostari *RUS* **114** E10
Luosto *FIN* **115** D1
Luosu *FIN* **117** C12
Luotolahti *FIN* **128** C8
Luovankylä *FIN* **122** F7
Luovttejohka *N* **113** C21
Lupac *RO* **159** C8
Lupandi *LV* **133** E3
Łupawa *PL* **85** B12
Lupeni *RO* **152** E5
Lupeni *RO* **159** C11
Lupiac *F* **33** C6
Lupiñén *E* **41** D10
Lupión *E* **53** A9
Łupków *PL* **145** E5
Lupoglav *HR* **67** B9
Łupowo *PL* **85** E8
Luppa *D* **80** D3
Luppoperä *FIN* **121** D9
Luppy *F* **26** C5
Lupşa *RO* **151** E11
Lupşanu *RO* **161** E9
Luque *E* **53** A8
Luras *I* **64** B3
Lurbe-St-Christau *F* **32** D4
Lurcy-Lévis *F* **30** B2
Lure *F* **26** E5
Lurgan *GB* **7** D10
Lurgan *IRL* **6** E6
Luri *F* **37** F10
Lurøy *N* **108** D4
Lurs *F* **35** C10
Lurudal *N* **105** C13
Lury-sur-Arnon *F* **24** F7
Lusca *IRL* **7** E10
Lusciano *I* **60** B2
Luserna San Giovanni *I* **31** F11
Lushnjë *AL* **168** C2
Lusi *FIN* **127** C15
Lusignan *F* **29** C6
Lusigny-sur-Barse *F* **25** D11
Lusk *IRL* **7** E10
Lus-la-Croix-Haute *F* **35** A10
Lusminki *FIN* **121** C14
Lusnić *BIH* **157** E6
Luso *P* **44** D4
Luspa *FIN* **116** B8
Luspebryggan *S* **109** B18
Lussac *F* **28** F5
Lussac-les-Châteaux *F* **29** C7
Lussac-les-Églises *F* **29** C8
Lussan *F* **35** B7
Lüssow *D* **83** C12
Lusta *GB* **2** K3
Lustad *N* **105** C12
Lustadt *D* **187** C5
Lustenau *A* **71** C9
Luster *N* **100** D6
Lustivere *EST* **131** D12
Łuszkowo *PL* **81** B11
Luszyn *PL* **143** B8
Lutago *I* **72** C4
Lütau *D* **83** D9
Lütetsburg *D* **17** A8
Lutherstadt Wittenberg *D* **79** C12

Lütjenburg D 83 B9
Lutnes N 102 D4
Lutocin PL 139 E8
Lutomiersk PL 143 C7
Luton GB 15 D8
Lutowiska PL 145 E6
Lutriņi LV 134 C4
Lutry PL 136 E2
Luttenberg NL 183 A8
Lutter am Barenberge D 79 C7
Lutterbach F 27 E7
Lutterworth GB 13 A12
Lututów PL 142 D5
Lützelbach D 21 E12
Lützen D 79 D11
Lutzerath D 21 D8
Lutzingen D 75 E8
Lutzmannsburg A 149 B7
Lützow D 83 C10
Luua EST 131 D13
Luujoki FIN 119 C14
Luukkola FIN 129 C9
Luukkonen FIN 129 B9
Luumäen kk FIN 128 D8
Luumäki FIN 128 D8
Luunja EST 131 E13
Luupujoki FIN 123 C17
Luupuvesi FIN 123 C17
Luusniemi FIN 124 G7
Luusua FIN 115 F2
Luvia FIN 126 C6
Luvos S 109 C16
Lux F 26 F3
Luxembourg L 20 E6
Luxe-Sumberraute F 32 D3
Luxeuil-les-Bains F 26 E5
Luxey F 32 B4
Luyego de Somoza E 39 D7
Luyksgestel NL 183 C6
Luz P 50 E2
Luz P 50 E4
Luz P 51 C5
Luzaga E 47 C8
Lužani HR 157 B8
Luzarches F 25 B7
Luz-Ardiden F 32 E5
Luže CZ 77 C10
Luzech F 33 B8
Lužec nad Vltavou CZ 76 B6
Luzenac F 33 E9
Luzern CH 70 C6
Luzhany UA 153 A7
Luzhki BY 133 F3
Luzianes P 50 D3
Luz i Madh AL 168 B2
Luzino PL 138 A5
Luzmela E 40 B3
Łużna PL 144 D3
Lūžņa LV 130 F3
Lūznava LV 133 D2
Luzón E 47 B8
Luz-St-Sauveur F 32 E6
Luzy F 30 B4
Luzzara I 66 C2
Luzzi I 60 E6
L'viv UA 144 D9
Lwówek PL 81 B10
Lwówek Śląski PL 81 D9
Lyady RUS 132 D4
Lyaskelya RUS 129 B15
Lyaskovets BG 166 C5
Lyavoshki BY 133 E2
Lybokhora UA 145 F6
Lybster GB 3 J10
Lychen D 84 D4
Lycksaberg S 107 A14
Lycksele S 107 B15
Lydd GB 15 F10
Lyderslev DK 87 E10
Lydford GB 12 D6
Lydney GB 13 B9
Lyeninski BY 141 F10
Lyfjord N 111 A16
Lygna N 95 B13
Lygumiai LT 134 D7
Lykofi GR 171 B10
Lykoporia GR 175 C6
Lyly FIN 127 B11
Lylykylä FIN 121 E11
Lyman UA 155 B5
Lymans'ke UA 154 D5
Lymans'ke UA 155 C2
Lyme Regis GB 13 D9
Lymington GB 13 D11
Lymm GB 10 E7
Lynäs S 103 D12
Lyndhurst GB 13 D11
Lyne DK 86 D3
Lyneham GB 13 B11
Lynemore GB 3 L9
Lyness GB 3 H10
Lyngby DK 87 C7
Lyngdal N 94 F6
Lyngmoen N 112 D5
Lyngså DK 86 A7
Lyngseidet N 111 A19
Lyngsnes N 105 B10
Lynmouth GB 13 C7
Lynton GB 13 C7
Lyntupy BY 137 C13
Lyökki FIN 126 D5
Lyon F 30 D6
Lyons-la-Forêt F 18 F3
Lyrestad S 91 B15
Lyrkeia GR 175 D6
Lysabild DK 86 F6
Lysá pod Makytou SK 146 C6
Łyse PL 139 D12
Lysebotn N 94 D5
Lysekil S 91 C9
Lyshchytsy BY 141 F9
Lysice CZ 77 D11
Lysnes N 111 B14
Łysomice PL 138 D6
Lysøysund N 104 D7
Lysroll N 111 D11
Lyss CH 31 A11
Lysvik S 97 B9
Łyszkowice PL 141 G1
Lytchett Minster GB 13 D10
Lytham St Anne's GB 10 D5
Lytovezh UA 144 B9
Lyubashivka UA 154 B6
Lyuben BG 165 E10
Lyubimets BG 166 F6
Lyublino RUS 136 D1
Lyubomyrka UA 154 B4
Lyubyntsi UA 145 E8
Lyulyakovo BG 167 D8

M

Maakeski FIN 127 C13
Maalahti FIN 122 E7
Maalismaa FIN 119 D15
Maam IRL 6 E3
Maaninka FIN 124 D8
Maaninkavaara FIN 115 F4
Maanselkä FIN 125 C10
Maaralanpera FIN 123 C16
Maardu EST 131 B10
Maarheeze NL 183 C7
Maaria FIN 126 D7
Maarianvaara FIN 125 E11
Maarn NL 183 A6
Maarssen NL 16 D4
Maarssenbroek NL 183 A6
Maas IRL 6 C6
Maasbracht NL 19 B12
Maasbree NL 16 F6
Maasdam NL 182 B5
Maaseik B 19 B12
Maaselkä FIN 121 F14
Maasen D 17 C11
Maasland NL 16 E2
Maasmechelen B 19 C12
Maassluis NL 16 E2
Maastricht NL 19 C12
Määttälä FIN 123 C12
Määttälänvaara FIN 121 B14
Maavesi FIN 124 F9
Mablethorpe GB 11 E12
Macael E 55 E8
Maçanet de Cabrenys E 34 F4
Maçanet de la Selva E 43 D9
Mação P 44 E5
Măcărești MD 153 C11
Macastre E 48 F3
Maccagno I 68 A6
Macchiagodena I 63 D6
Macclesfield GB 11 E7
Macduff GB 3 K12
Macea RO 151 E7
Maceda E 38 D4
Maceda P 44 C3
Macedo de Cavaleiros P 39 E6
Maceira P 44 C6
Maceira P 44 E3
Macelj HR 148 D5
Macerata I 67 F7
Macerata Feltria I 66 E5
Măcești de Jos RO 160 F3
Măcești de Sus RO 160 F3
Machados P 50 C5
Machairas GR 174 B3
Machault F 19 F10
Machecoul F 28 B2
Machelen B 182 D4
Machen GB 13 B8
Machern D 79 D12
Machliny PL 85 D10
Machov CZ 77 A10
Machowa PL 143 F11
Machrihanish GB 4 E5
Machynlleth GB 10 F4
Maciejowice PL 141 G5
Măcin RO 155 C2
Macinaggio F 37 F10
Măciuca RO 160 D4
Mačkatica SRB 164 D5
Mackenbach D 21 F9
Mackenrode D 79 C8
Mačkovci SLO 148 C6
Macomer I 64 C2
Mâcon F 30 C6
Macosquin GB 4 E3
Macotera E 45 C10
Macroom IRL 8 E5
Macugnaga I 68 B4
Mačvanska Mitrovica SRB 158 D4
Mačvanski Pričinović SRB 158 D4
Mád H 145 G3
Madan BG 165 B7
Madan BG 171 A7
Mădan S 103 A15
Madängsholm S 91 C14
Madara BG 167 C8
Madaras H 150 E3
Mădăraș RO 151 D8
Mădârjac RO 153 C10
Maddalena Spiaggia I 64 E3
Maddaloni I 60 A2
Made NL 16 E3
Madekoski FIN 119 E15
Madeley GB 10 F7
Mäder A 71 C9
Madetkoski FIN 115 C1
Madiran F 32 C5
Madley GB 13 A9
Madliena LV 135 C10
Madocsa H 150 D2
Madona LV 135 C12
Madonna di Campiglio I 69 A10
Madrid E 46 D5
Madridejos E 46 F5
Madrigal de las Altas Torres E 45 B11
Madrigal de la Vera E 45 D10
Madrigal del Monte E 40 D4
Madrigalejo E 45 F9
Madrigueras E 47 F9
Madroñera E 45 F9
Mădulari RO 160 D4
Madzharovo BG 171 A9
Mæl N 95 C9
Maël-Carhaix F 22 D5
Maella E 42 E4
Maello E 46 C3
Maenclochog GB 12 B5
Maenza I 62 D4
Mære N 105 D10
Măeriște RO 151 C10
Mäetaguse EST 131 C14
Maeztu E 41 C7
Mafra P 50 B1
Magacela E 51 B8
Magallón E 41 E9
Magalluf E 49 E10
Magaña E 41 E7
Magašici BIH 158 E3
Magaz E 40 E3
Magdala D 79 E9
Magdeburg D 79 B10
Magdeburgerforth D 79 B11
Magenta I 69 C6
Magescq F 32 C3
Măgești RO 151 C9
Maggia CH 68 A6
Maghera GB 4 F3
Magherafelt GB 4 F3
Magheralin GB 7 D10
Măgherani RO 152 D5
Maghery GB 7 C9
Maghull GB 10 D6
Magione I 66 F5
Măgiotsa EST 132 E1
Măgirești RO 153 D9
Magisano I 59 A10
Maglaj BIH 157 C9
Magland F 31 C10
Maglavit RO 159 E11
Magliano de'Marsi I 62 C4
Magliano in Toscana I 65 B4
Magliano Sabina I 62 C2
Maglič SRB 158 F6
Maglie I 61 C10
Maglód H 150 C3
Magnac-Laval F 29 C8
Magné F 28 C4
Magnières F 26 D6
Magnor N 96 C7
Magnuszew PL 141 G4
Magny-Cours F 30 B3
Magny-en-Vexin F 24 B6
Mágocs H 149 D10
Magoula GR 174 E5
Magstrup DK 86 E4
Magueija P 44 B5
Maguilla E 51 C8
Maguiresbridge GB 7 D8
Măgura RO 153 D9
Măgura RO 160 E6
Măgura Ilvei RO 152 C5
Măgurele RKS 164 D3
Măgurele RO 161 C8
Măgurele RO 161 E8
Măgureni RO 161 C7
Măguri-Răcătău RO 151 D11
Magy H 145 H4
Magyaralmás H 149 B10
Magyaratád H 149 D9
Magyarbánhegyes H 151 E6
Magyarbóly H 149 E10
Magyaregregy H 149 D10
Magyarhomorog H 151 C8
Magyarkeszi H 149 C10
Magyarnándor H 147 F8
Magyarpolány H 149 B9
Magyarszék H 149 D10
Mahala UA 153 A8
Maheriv UA 144 C8
Mahíde E 39 E7
Mahlberg D 186 E4
Mahlsdorf D 83 E10
Mahlu FIN 123 E14
Mahlwinkel D 79 B10
Mahmudia RO 155 C4
Mahmudiye TR 171 E10
Mahmutköy TR 173 C6
Mahón E 57 B13
Mahora E 47 F9
Mahovo HR 149 E6
Mähring D 75 C12
Mahtra EST 131 C10
Maia P 44 B3
Maials E 42 E5
Măicănești RO 161 C10
Maîche F 27 F6
Maida I 59 B9
Maiden Bradley GB 13 C10
Maidenhead GB 15 D7
Maiden Newton GB 13 D9
Maidens GB 4 E7
Maidstone GB 15 E10
Maienfeld CH 71 C9
Maierato I 59 B9
Maierhöfen D 71 B10
Maieru RO 152 C5
Măieruș RO 153 F7
Maigh Chromtha IRL 8 E5
Maigh Cuilinn IRL 6 F4
Maiglean Rátha IRL 7 F8
Maignelay-Montigny F 18 E6
Maijanen FIN 117 D14
Maikammer D 186 C5
Maillas F 32 B5
Maillebois F 24 C5
Maillezais F 28 C4
Mailly-le-Camp F 25 C11
Mailly-le-Château F 25 E10
Mailly-Maillet F 18 D6
Mailovac SRB 159 D7
Mainaschaff D 187 B7
Mainbernheim D 75 C7
Mainburg D 75 E10
Mainham IRL 7 F9
Mainhardt D 74 D6
Mainiemi FIN 127 B16
Mainistir Eimhín IRL 7 F8
Mainistir Fhear Maí IRL 8 D6
Mainistir Laoise IRL 9 C8
Mainistir na Búille IRL 6 E6
Mainistir na Corann IRL 8 E6
Mainistir na Feile IRL 8 D4
Männikkö S 116 D8
Mainsat F 29 C10
Maintenon F 24 C6
Mainua FIN 121 F9
Mainvilliers F 24 D5
Mainz D 21 D10
Maiolati Spontini I 67 F7
Maiorca P 44 D3
Maiorga P 44 E3
Mairena del Alcor E 51 E8
Maisach D 75 F9
Maishofen A 73 B6
Maišiagala LT 137 D11
Maissau A 77 E9
Maisse F 25 D7
Maissin B 184 E3
Maivala FIN 121 B14
Maizières-lès-Metz F 186 C1
Majadahonda E 46 D5
Majadas de Tiétar E 45 E9
Majava FIN 121 C12
Majavatn N 105 A14
Majdan BIH 157 D7
Majdan Królewski PL 144 C4
Majdan Niepryski PL 144 C7
Majdanpek SRB 159 E8
Majovakylä FIN 119 C17
Majs H 149 E11
Majšperk SLO 148 D5
Majtum S 109 D18
Makád H 149 B11
Makarove UA 145 G6
Makarove UA 154 C6
Makarska HR 157 F7
Mäkelänranta FIN 121 E13
Makhnovka RUS 133 B6
Mäkikylä FIN 123 E12
Makkola FIN 125 G11
Makkoshotyka H 145 G4
Makkum NL 16 B4
Maklár H 147 F10
Makljenovac BIH 157 C9
Makó H 150 E5
Makoc RKS 164 D3
Mākoņkalns LV 133 D2
Mąkoszyce PL 142 E4
Makov SK 147 C7
Maków PL 141 G2
Maków PL 141 H4
Mąkowarsko PL 138 D4
Maków Mazowiecki PL 139 E11
Maków Podhalański PL 147 B9
Makrakomi GR 174 B5
Makresh BG 159 F10
Makri GR 171 C9
Makrisia GR 174 D4
Makrochori GR 169 C7
Makrychori GR 169 E7
Makrygialos GR 169 D8
Makrygialos GR 179 E10
Makrynitsa GR 169 F8
Makryrrachi GR 174 A5
Maksamaa FIN 122 D8
Maksniemi FIN 119 C13
Maksymilianowo PL 138 D5
Malá E 53 B9
Mala IRL 8 D5
Mala S 87 C13
Malå S 107 A15
Mala Bosna SRB 150 E4
Mala Čista HR 156 E4
Malacky SK 77 F12
Málaga E 53 C8
Malagón E 46 F5
Malahide IRL 7 F10
Malahvianvaara FIN 121 E14
Malaia RO 160 C4
Mălăiești MD 154 D5
Málainn Bhig IRL 6 C5
Málainn Mhóir IRL 6 C5
Mala Kladuša BIH 156 B4
Malalbergo I 66 C4
Malá Lehota SK 147 D7
Malamocco I 66 B5
Malancourt F 19 F11
Malandrino GR 174 C5
Malangen N 111 B16
Malangseidet N 111 B16
Malanów PL 142 C5
Malansac F 23 E7
Malaryta BY 141 G10
Mäläskä FIN 119 F16
Mala Subotica HR 149 D7
Malaucène F 35 B9
Malaunay F 18 E3
Malaussanne F 32 C5
Mälävaara FIN 115 E4
Malåvännäs S 107 A14
Mała Wieś PL 139 F9
Malax FIN 122 E7
Malaya Byerastavitsa BY 140 D9
Malbekkvatn N 114 E7
Malbork PL 138 B7
Malborn D 21 E7
Malbouzon F 30 F3
Malbuisson F 31 B9
Malcesine I 69 B10
Malchin D 83 C13
Malchow D 83 D12
Malcocinado E 51 C8
Malcov SK 145 E3
Malczyce PL 81 D10
Măldăeni RO 160 E5
Măldărești RO 160 C4
Maldegem B 19 B7
Malden NL 16 E5
Maldon GB 15 D10
Małdyty PL 139 C8
Malè I 71 E11
Malechowo PL 85 B11
Malején E 41 E8
Maleme GR 178 D6
Malemort-du-Comtat F 35 B9
Malemort-sur-Corrèze F 29 E9
Malente D 83 B9
Målerås S 89 B9
Males GR 179 E10
Malesco I 68 A6
Malesherbes F 25 D7
Malesina GR 175 B7
Malestroit F 23 E7
Maletto I 59 D6
Malevo BG 166 F5
Malexander S 92 C6
Malfa I 59 B6
Malgersdorf D 75 E12
Malgovik S 107 B10
Malgrat de Mar E 43 D9
Malhadas P 39 E7
Malia GR 178 E9
Malicorne-sur-Sarthe F 23 E11
Maliena LV 133 B2
Mali Iđoš SRB 158 B4
Malijai F 36 C4
Målilla S 92 E7
Mali Lošinj HR 67 C9
Mali Mokryany UA 144 D7
Malin IRL 4 E2
Malin Beg IRL 6 C5
Mälinec SK 147 D9
Malines B 19 B9
Malines B 182 C4
Mălini RO 153 C8
Malin More IRL 6 C5
Malinovka LV 135 E13
Malinska HR 67 B10
Maliq AL 168 C4
Malishevë RKS 163 E10
Maliskylä FIN 123 C14
Malissard F 30 F6
Maliuc RO 155 C4
Mali Zvornik SRB 157 D11
Maljasalmi FIN 125 E11
Malkara TR 173 C6
Małkinia Górna PL 139 E13
Malko Gradishte BG 166 F5
Malko Tŭrnovo BG 167 F9
Mallaig GB 4 A5
Mållångsbo S 103 D10
Mallén E 41 E9
Mallentin D 83 C10
Mallersdorf D 75 E11
Malles Venosta I 71 D11
Mallica TR 173 F7
Malling DK 86 C6
Mallíß D 83 D10
Mallnitz A 73 C7
Mallow IRL 8 D5
Mallusjoki FIN 127 D14
Mallwyd GB 10 F4
Malm N 105 C10
Malmån S 107 E12
Malmbäck S 92 D4
Malmberget S 116 D5
Malmby S 98 D8
Malmédy B 20 D6
Malmein N 94 E4
Malmesbury GB 13 B10
Malmköping S 93 A9
Malmö S 87 D12
Malmslätt S 92 C7
Malnaș RO 153 E7
Malnate I 69 B6
Malnava LV 133 C3
Malnes N 110 C8
Malo I 69 B11
Malo Crniće SRB 159 D7
Małogoszcz PL 143 E9
Malo Konare BG 165 E9
Małomice PL 81 C8
Malomir BG 167 E7
Malomozhayskoye RUS 136 D5
Malón E 41 E8
Malona GR 181 D8
Malonno I 69 A9
Malonty CZ 77 E7
Malorad BG 165 C8
Malošište SRB 164 C4
Malo Titavo BIH 156 D5
Malovăț RO 159 D10
Måløy N 100 C2
Maloye-Lugovoye RUS 136 D2
Maloye Sitna BY 133 E6
Malpartida P 45 C7
Malpartida de Cáceres E 45 F8
Malpartida de la Serena E 51 B8
Malpartida de Plasencia E 45 E8
Malpas GB 10 E6
Malpica E 38 B2
Malpica de Tajo E 46 E3
Malpica do Tejo P 44 E6
Mālpils LV 135 B9
Malsch D 27 C9
Målselv N 111 B16
Malsfeld D 78 D6
Malšice CZ 77 D7
Målsnes N 111 B16
Målsryd S 91 D13
Målsta S 106 E7
Malta A 73 C8
Malta LV 133 D2
Malta P 45 C6
Maltas Trūpi LV 135 D13
Maltby GB 11 E9
Maltby le Marsh GB 11 E12
Maltepe TR 173 D7
Malterdingen D 27 D8
Malters CH 70 C6
Malton GB 11 C10
Malu cu Flori RO 160 C6
Maluenda E 41 F8
Malŭk Izvor BG 166 F5
Malu Mare RO 160 E3
Malung S 102 E6
Malungsfors S 102 E6
Mālupe LV 133 B2
Mălureni RO 160 C5
Mălușteni RO 153 E11
Małuszów PL 81 B8
Maluszyn PL 143 E8
Malva E 39 E9
Malvaglia CH 71 E7
Malveira P 50 B1
Malvik N 105 E9
Malý Horeš SK 145 G4
Mályi H 145 G2
Mały Płock PL 139 D13
Malý Šariš SK 145 E3
Malyy Bereznyy UA 145 F5
Mamaia RO 155 E3
Mamarchevo BG 167 E7
Mamarrosa P 44 D3
Mambrilla de Castejón E 40 E4
Mamer L 20 E6
Mamers F 24 D3
Mamići BIH 157 F8
Mamirolle F 26 F5
Mammaste EST 131 E14
Mammendorf D 75 F9
Mammola I 59 C9
Mamoiada I 64 C3
Mamone I 64 B3
Mamonovo RUS 139 B8
Mamuras AL 168 A2
Mamushë RKS 163 E10
Mana MD 154 C3
Maňa SK 146 E6
Manacor E 57 B11
Manage B 19 D9
Manamansalo FIN 120 F9
Mañaria E 41 B6
Månäs S 97 A9
Manasia RO 161 D9
Manasterz PL 144 D5
Manastir BG 165 F10
Mănăstirea RO 161 E9
Mănăstirea Cașin RO 153 E9
Mănăstirea Humorului RO 153 B7
Manastirica SRB 159 D7
Manastirsko BG 167 C7
Mănăștiur RO 151 F9
Mancera de Abajo E 45 C10
Mancha Real E 53 A9
Manchester GB 11 E7
Manching D 75 E9
Manchita E 51 B7
Manciano I 65 B5
Manciet F 33 C6
Mandal N 90 C1
Måndalen N 100 A6
Mandalo GR 169 C7
Mandas I 64 D3
Mandatoriccio I 61 E7
Mandayona E 47 C7
Mandelbachtal-Ormesheim D 186 C3
Mandelieu-la-Napoule F 36 D5
Mandello del Lario I 69 B7
Manderscheid D 21 D7
Mandeure F 27 F6
Mandino Selo BIH 157 E7
Mándok H 145 G5
Mandra GR 175 C7
Măndra RO 152 F6
Mandraki GR 181 C6
Mandres-en-Barrois F 26 D3
Mandriko GR 181 D7
Mandritsa BG 171 B10
Manduria I 61 C9
Mane F 33 D7
Mane F 35 C10
Manea GB 11 G12
Mănăeciu RO 161 C7
Manerbio I 66 B1
Mañeru E 32 E2
Mănești RO 160 D6
Mănești RO 161 D7
Manětín CZ 76 C4
Manfredonia I 63 D9
Mangalia RO 155 F3
Manganeses de la Lampreana E 39 E8
Manganeses de la Polvorosa E 39 D8
Mångberg S 102 E8
Mångbyn S 118 F6
Manger N 100 E2
Mangiennes F 19 F12
Mangotsfield GB 13 C9
Mångsbodarna S 102 D6
Mangualde P 44 C5
Manhay B 19 D12
Manhuelles F 26 B4
Mani GR 171 B10
Maniace I 59 D6
Maniago I 73 D6
Maniakoi GR 168 D5
Manieczki PL 81 B11
Manilva E 53 D6
Manisa TR 177 B9
Manises E 48 E4
Manjärvträsk S 118 C4
Manjaur S 107 B16
Mank A 77 F8
Månkarbo S 99 B8
Mankila FIN 119 E15
Manlay F 25 F11
Manlleu E 43 D8
Manna GR 175 D6
Männamaa EST 130 D5
Mannersdorf an der Rabnitz A 149 B7
Mannheim D 21 F10
Männikuste EST 131 E8
Manningtree GB 15 D11
Manolada GR 174 C3
Manole BG 165 E10
Manoleasa RO 153 B10
Manoppello I 62 C6
Manorbier GB 12 B5
Manorhamilton IRL 6 D6
Manosque F 35 C10
Manowo PL 85 B10
Manresa E 43 D7
Månsåsen S 105 E16
Manschnow D 81 A7
Mansfeld D 79 C9
Mansfield GB 11 E9
Mansfield Woodhouse GB 11 E9
Mansilla E 40 D6
Mansilla de las Mulas E 39 D9
Mansle F 29 D6
Manso F 37 G9
Mansonville F 33 B7
Mansores P 44 C4
Manston GB 13 D10
Månsträsk S 109 E16
Mantamados GR 171 F10
Mantasia GR 174 A5
Manteigas P 44 D5
Mantel D 75 C11
Manternach L 186 B1
Mantes-la-Jolie F 24 C6
Mantes-la-Ville F 24 C6
Manthelan F 24 F4
Mantila FIN 122 F9
Mantoche F 26 F4
Mantorp S 92 C6
Mantoudi GR 175 B7
Mantova I 66 B2
Mäntsälä FIN 127 D13
Mänttä FIN 123 F13
Mäntyharju FIN 128 C6
Mäntyjärvi FIN 117 E14
Mäntyjärvi FIN 121 B10
Mäntylahti FIN 124 D8
Mäntyluoto FIN 126 B5
Mäntyvaara S 116 E7
Manuel E 56 C4
Manulla IRL 6 E4
Mány H 149 A11
Manyas TR 173 D8
Manzac-sur-Vern F 29 E7
Mănzălești RO 161 C9
Manzanal de Arriba E 39 E7
Manzanal del Puerto E 39 C7
Manzanares E 55 A6
Manzanares el Real E 46 C5
Manzaneda E 38 D5
Manzanedo E 40 C4
Manzaneque E 46 E5
Manzanera E 48 D3
Manzanilla E 51 E7
Manzano I 73 E7
Manzat F 30 D2
Manziana I 62 C2
Manziat F 30 C6
Maó E 57 B13
Māo EST 131 D11
Maoča BIH 157 C10
Maqellarë AL 168 A3
Maqueda E 46 D4
Mar P 38 E2
Mara I 64 C2
Marac F 26 E3
Maracalagonis I 64 E3
Marachkova BY 133 E4
Mărăcineni RO 160 D5
Mărăcineni RO 161 C9
Maradik SRB 158 C5
Maråker S 103 D13
Maranchón E 47 B8
Maranello I 66 C2
Marange-Silvange F 186 C1
Maranhão P 50 A4
Marano I 66 D3
Marano di Napoli I 60 B2
Marano sul Panaro I 66 D2
Marans F 28 C4
Maranville F 25 D12
Mărășești RO 153 F10
Mărașu RO 155 D1
Maratea I 60 D5
Marateca P 50 B2
Marathea GR 169 E6
Marathias GR 174 B4
Marathokampos GR 177 D8
Marathonas GR 175 C8
Marathopoli GR 174 E4
Maraussan F 34 D5
Maraye-en-Othe F 25 D10
Marazion GB 12 E4
Marazliyivka UA 154 E6
Marbach CH 70 D5
Marbach am Neckar D 27 C11
Marbäck S 91 D13
Marbella E 53 C7
Marboz F 31 C7
Marburg an der Lahn D 21 C11
Marby S 105 E16
Marça E 42 E5
Marcali H 149 C8
Marcaltő H 149 B8
Marčana HR 67 C8
Marcaria I 66 B2
Mărcăuți MD 153 A10
Marcellina I 62 C3
Marcelová SK 149 A10
Marcenais F 28 E5
Marcenat F 30 E2
March GB 11 F12
Marchamalo E 47 C6
Marchaux F 26 F5
Marche-en-Famenne B 19 D11
Marchegg A 77 F11
Marchena E 51 E9
Marchenoir F 24 E5
Marcheprime F 28 F4
Marchiennes F 19 D7
Marchin B 19 D11
Marchtrenk A 76 F6
Marciac F 33 C6
Marciana I 65 B2
Marciana Marina I 65 B2
Marcianise I 60 A2
Marciano della Chiana I 66 F4
Mārciena LV 135 C12
Marcigny F 30 C5
Marcilhac-sur-Célé F 33 A9
Marcilla E 32 F2
Marcillac F 28 E4
Marcillac-la-Croisille F 29 E10
Marcillac-Vallon F 33 B10
Marcillat-en-Combraille F 29 C11
Marcilly-en-Gault F 24 F6
Marcilly-en-Villette F 24 E7
Marcilly-le-Hayer F 25 D10
Marcilly-sur-Eure F 24 C5
Marcinkonys LT 137 E9
Marcinkowice PL 85 D10
Marcinkowice PL 144 D2
Marcinowice PL 81 E11
Marciszów PL 81 E10
Marck F 18 C4
Marckolsheim F 27 D8
Marco de Canaveses P 44 B4
Marcoing F 19 D7
Marcòn I 66 A5
Marcoux F 36 C4
Marcq-en-Barœul F 19 C7
Mărculești MD 153 B12
Mårdaklev S 87 A11
Mardarivka UA 154 B5
Mardeuil F 25 B10
Mårdsele S 107 B16
Mårdsjö S 106 E9
Mårdsjö S 107 C11
Mårdudden S 118 B6
Marebbe I 72 C4
Marennes F 28 D3
Maresfield GB 15 F9
Mareuil F 29 E6
Mareuil-sur-Arnon F 29 B10
Mareuil-sur-Ay F 25 B11
Mareuil-sur-Lay-Dissais F 28 B3
Marey-sur-Tille F 26 E3
Marga RO 159 B9
Margarites GR 178 E8
Mărgăritești RO 161 C9
Margariti GR 168 F3
Margate GB 15 E11
Mărgău RO 151 D10
Margecany SK 145 F3
Margerie-Hancourt F 25 C12
Margherita di Savoia I 60 A6
Marghita RO 151 C9
Margina RO 151 F9
Marginea RO 153 B7
Mărgineni RO 153 D9
Mărgineni RO 153 D9
Margionys LT 137 F9
Margone I 31 E11
Margonin PL 85 E12
Margraten NL 19 C12
Marguerittes F 35 C7
Margut F 19 E11
Marhaň SK 145 E3
María E 55 D8
Mariac F 30 F5
Mariager DK 86 B5
Maria Lankowitz A 73 B11
Maria Luggau A 73 C6
Marialva P 45 C6
Mariampole LV 133 D2
Mariana E 47 D8
Mariannelund S 92 D7
Mariano Comense I 69 B7
Marianopoli I 58 D4
Marianowo PL 85 D8
Mariánské Lázně CZ 75 C12
Mariapfarr A 73 B8
Maria Saal A 73 C9
Mariazell A 148 A4
Maribo DK 83 A10
Maribor SLO 148 C5
Marieberg S 92 A6
Marieby S 106 E7
Mariefred S 98 D8
Mariehamn FIN 99 B13
Marieholm S 87 D12
Marieholm S 91 E14
Mariembourg B 19 D10
Marienberg D 80 E4
Marienhafe D 17 A8
Marienhagen D 78 B6
Marienheide D 21 B9
Mariental D 79 B8
Mariestad S 91 B14
Marifjøra N 100 D6
Marigliano I 60 B2
Marignana F 37 G9
Marignane F 35 D9
Marigné-Laillé F 24 E3
Marigny F 23 B9
Marigny-le-Châtel F 25 D10
Marijampolė LT 136 D7
Marikaj AL 168 B2
Marikostinovo BG 169 B9
Marín E 38 D2
Marina di Alberese I 65 B4
Marina di Amendolara I 61 D7
Marina di Arbus I 64 D1
Marina di Camerota I 60 C4
Marina di Campo I 65 B2
Marina di Carrara I 69 E9
Marina di Castagneto Donoratico I 66 F2
Marina di Cecina I 66 F1
Marina di Chieuti I 63 D8
Marina di Gioiosa Ionica I 59 C9
Marina di Grosseto I 65 B3
Marina di Leuca I 61 D10
Marina di Massa I 69 E9
Marina di Novaglie I 61 D10

Marina di Palma I 58 E4
Marina di Pulsano I 61 C8
Marina di Ragusa I 59 F6
Marina di Ravenna I 66 C5
Marinaleda E 53 B7
Marina Palmense I 67 F8
Marina Romea I 66 C5
Marina Schiavonea I 61 D7
Marinella I 58 D2
Marineo I 58 D3
Marines E 48 E3
Marines F 24 B6
Maringues F 30 D3
Marinha das Ondas P 44 D3
Marinha Grande P 44 E3
Marinhas P 38 E2
Marinići HR 67 B9
Marinka BG 167 E8
Marinkainen FIN 123 C10
Māriņkalns LV 133 B1
Marino I 62 D3
Mar'insko RUS 132 D4
Mariotto I 61 A7
Mărișelu RO 152 C5
Maritsa GR 181 D8
Marizy F 30 B5
Märja EST 131 E13
Marjaliza E 46 E5
Märjamaa EST 131 D8
Marjaniemi FIN 119 D13
Marjokylä FIN 121 E14
Marjonieemi FIN 127 C14
Marjovaara FIN 125 E15
Marjusaari FIN 123 D12
Mark GB 13 C9
Mark S 107 B10
Markaryd S 87 C13
Markaz H 147 F10
Markby FIN 122 D9
Markdorf D 27 E11
Markebäck S 92 B5
Markelo NL 17 D7
Market Deeping GB 11 F11
Market Drayton GB 10 F7
Market Harborough GB 15 C7
Markethill GB 7 D9
Market Rasen GB 11 E11
Market Warsop GB 11 E9
Market Weighton GB 11 D10
Markgröningen D 27 C11
Markhus N 94 C4
Marki PL 139 F11
Markina-Xemein E 41 B7
Markinch GB 5 C10
Märkisch Buchholz D 80 B5
Markitta S 116 D7
Markivka UA 154 D5
Markkina FIN 116 B8
Markkleeberg D 79 D11
Markkula FIN 123 C12
Marklohe D 17 C12
Marknesse NL 16 C5
Markneukirchen D 75 B11
Markopoulo GR 175 D8
Markovac SRB 159 C7
Markovac SRB 159 E7
Markovac Našički HR 149 E10
Markovac Trojstveni HR 149 E7
Markowa PL 144 C5
Markranstädt D 79 D11
Marksuhl D 79 E7
Markt Allhau A 148 B6
Marktbergel D 75 D7
Markt Berolzheim D 75 D8
Markt Bibart D 75 C7
Marktbreit D 187 B9
Markt Erlbach D 75 D8
Markt Hartmannsdorf A 148 B5
Marktheidenfeld D 74 C6
Markt Indersdorf D 75 F9
Marktjärn S 103 A11
Marktl D 76 F3
Marktleugast D 75 B10
Marktoberdorf D 71 B11
Marktoffingen D 75 E7
Marktredwitz D 75 B11
Markt Rettenbach D 71 B10
Markt Sankt Martin A 149 A6
Markt Schwaben D 75 F10
Marktseft D 75 C7
Markt Wald D 71 A11
Markusevec HR 148 E6
Markušica HR 149 F11
Markušovce SK 145 F2
Markuszów PL 141 H6
Marl D 17 D10
Marl D 17 E8
Marlborough GB 13 C11
Marldon GB 13 E7
Marle F 19 E8
Marlengo I 72 C3
Marlenheim F 27 C8
Marlhes F 30 E5
Marlishausen D 79 E9
Marlow D 83 B13
Marlow GB 15 D7
Marly CH 31 B11
Marly F 19 D8
Marly F 26 B5
Marma S 99 B8
Marmagne F 25 F7
Marmagne F 30 B5
Marmande F 33 A6
Marmara GR 174 B5
Marmara TR 173 C8
Marmaracik TR 173 B8
Marmaraereğlisi TR 173 C8
Marmari GR 175 C9
Marmaris TR 181 C8
Marmaro GR 177 B7
Marmelar P 50 C4
Marmeleira P 44 F3
Marmelete P 50 E2
Marmirolo I 66 B2
Marmolejo E 53 A8
Marmoutier F 27 C7
Marnardal N 90 C2
Marnäs S 103 E10
Marnay F 26 F4
Marne D 82 C6
Marne-la-Vallée F 25 C8
Marnes N 108 B7
Marnheim D 21 E10
Marnitz D 83 D11
Maroldsweisach D 75 B8
Marolles-les-Braults F 23 D12
Maromme F 18 F3
Maroneia GR 171 C9
Maroslele H 150 E5
Marostica I 72 E4
Maroué F 22 D6
Marousi GR 175 C8
Marpingen D 21 F8
Marpissa GR 176 E5
Marple GB 11 E7
Marpod RO 152 F5
Marquartstein D 72 A5
Marquion F 19 D7
Marquise F 15 F12
Marquixanes F 33 E10
Marradi I 66 D4
Marrasjärvi FIN 117 E14
Marraskoski FIN 117 E14
Marrubiu I 64 D2
Marrum NL 16 B5
Mârșa RO 160 E4
Marsac-en-Livradois F 30 E4
Marsac-sur-Don F 23 E8
Marsaglia I 37 B10
Marsal F 26 C6
Marsala I 58 D1
Mârșani RO 160 E4
Marsannay-la-Côte F 26 F2
Marsanne F 35 A8
Marsberg D 17 F11
Marsciano I 62 B2
Marseillan F 35 D6
Marseille F 35 D9
Marseille-en-Beauvaisis F 18 E4
Marsico Nuovo I 60 C5
Marsico Vetere I 60 C5
Marsillargues F 35 C7
Marsjärv S 118 B8
Mårslet DK 86 C6
Mārsnēni LV 135 B11
Marssac-sur-Tarn F 33 C10
Märsta S 99 C9
Marstal DK 83 A9
Märstetten CH 27 E11
Marston GB 13 B12
Marstrand S 91 D10
Marstrup DK 86 E4
Märsylä FIN 123 C11
Marta I 62 B1
Mårtanberg S 103 E9
Martano I 61 C10
Martel F 29 F9
Martelange B 19 E12
Martellago I 66 A5
Martello I 71 D11
Mártély H 150 E5
Marten BG 161 F8
Martfeld D 17 C12
Martfű H 150 C5
Marthon F 29 D6
Martiago E 45 D8
Martignacco I 73 D7
Martigné-Briand F 23 F11
Martigné-Ferchaud F 23 E9
Martigné-sur-Mayenne F 23 D10
Martigny CH 31 C11
Martigny-le-Comte F 30 B5
Martigny-les-Bains F 26 D4
Martigny-les-Gerbonvaux F 26 D4
Martigues F 35 D9
Martiherrero E 46 C3
Martil MA 53 E6
Martim Longo P 50 E4
Martin SK 147 C7
Martina Franca I 61 B8
Martin Brod BIH 156 C5
Martinchel P 44 E4
Martinci SRB 158 C3
Martinci Čepinski HR 149 E10
Martín de la Jara E 53 B7
Martín del Río E 42 F2
Martín de Yeltes E 45 C8
Martinengo I 69 B8
Mărtinești RO 161 F11
Martinet E 33 F9
Martinfeld D 79 D7
Martinganca P 44 E3
Mărtiniș RO 152 E6
Martín Muñoz de las Posadas E 46 B3
Martinniemi FIN 119 D14
Martino GR 175 B7
Martinporra E 39 B8
Martinsberg A 77 F8
Martinšćica HR 67 C9
Martinsicuro I 62 B5
Martis I 64 B2
Martizay F 29 B8
Martley GB 13 A10
Martna EST 130 D7
Martock GB 13 D9
Martonvaara FIN 125 D12
Martorell E 43 E7
Martos E 53 A9
Martres-Tolosane F 33 D8
Mårtsbo S 103 E13
Martti FIN 115 D4
Marttila FIN 127 D8
Marttila FIN 127 D13
Marttisenjärvi FIN 124 C7
Marugán E 46 C4
Maruggio I 61 C9
Marum NL 16 B6
Marum S 99 C12
Mărunței RO 160 E4
Mārupe LV 135 C8
Maruszów PL 143 D12
Maruszów PL 144 B4
Marvão P 44 F6
Marvejols F 34 A5
Marville F 19 F11
Marxheim D 75 E8
Marxzell D 27 C9
Märy FIN 127 E9
Mar"yanivka UA 154 C6
Marykirk GB 5 B11
Marynychi UA 152 A6
Marypark GB 3 L10
Maryport GB 5 F10
Marywell GB 5 A11
Marzabotto I 66 D3
Marzahna D 79 B12
Marzahne D 79 A12
Marzamemi I 59 F7
Marzan F 23 E7
Mărzănești RO 161 F6
Marzling D 75 F10
Masa E 40 C4
Masainas I 64 E2
Masalavés E 48 F3
Masari GR 181 D8
Mas-Cabardès F 33 D10
Mascali I 59 D7
Mascalucia I 59 D7
Mascaraque E 46 E5
Mascarenhas P 38 E5
Maschito I 60 B5
Masclat F 29 F8
Mas de Barberans E 42 F4
Mas de las Matas E 42 F3
Masegosa E 47 C8
Masegoso E 55 B8
Masegoso de Tajuña E 47 C7
Maselheim D 71 A9
Masera I 68 A5
Maserada sul Piave I 72 E5
Masevaux F 27 E6
Masfjorden N 100 E2
Masham GB 11 C8
Masi N 113 E12
Maside E 38 D3
Masi Torello I 66 C4
Maskalyanyaty BY 133 E7
Maskaur S 109 E14
Masku FIN 126 D7
Maslenika HR 156 D4
Maslinica HR 156 F5
Mașloc RO 151 E7
Maslovare BIH 157 C8
Masłowice PL 143 D8
Masone I 37 B9
Masquefa E 43 E7
Massa I 69 E9
Massa Fiscaglia I 66 C5
Massafra I 61 B8
Massa Lombarda I 66 D4
Massa Lubrense I 60 B2
Massamagrell E 48 E4
Massa Marittimo I 65 A3
Massa Martana I 62 B3
Massarosa I 66 E1
Massat F 33 E8
Massay F 24 F6
Maßbach D 75 B7
Masseret F 29 D9
Masseube F 33 D7
Massford GB 7 D10
Massiac F 30 E3
Massiaru EST 131 F9
Massimino I 37 C8
Massing D 75 F12
Mas-St-Chély F 34 B5
Măstăcani RO 155 B2
Mastershausen D 185 D7
Masterud N 96 B7
Mastichari GR 177 F9
Mastrevik N 100 E1
Masua I 64 E1
Masugnsbyn S 116 D8
Masullas I 64 D2
Måsvik N 112 D2
Masyevichy BY 141 G9
Maszewo PL 81 B7
Maszewo PL 85 B13
Maszewo PL 85 D8
Maszewo Duże PL 139 E8
Matabuena E 46 B5
Matadepera E 43 D8
Mataguži MNE 163 E7
Matala GR 178 F8
Matalahti FIN 124 C8
Matalascañas E 51 E6
Matalebreras E 41 E7
Matallana de Valmadrigal E 39 D9
Matamala de Almazán E 41 E6
Matamorosa E 40 C3
Mataporquera E 40 C3
Matapozuelos E 39 F10
Matara FIN 125 D12
Mataragka GR 169 F7
Mataragka GR 174 B3
Mataraselkä FIN 117 C17
Mataró E 43 D8
Mataruge MNE 163 C7
Mataruška Banja SRB 158 F6
Mătăsari RO 159 D11
Mătăsaru RO 161 D6
Mätäsvaara FIN 125 D13
Matca RO 153 F11
Mateești RO 160 C3
Matei RO 152 D4
Matelica I 67 F7
Matera I 61 B7
Materija SLO 73 E9
Mateševo MNE 163 D8
Mátészalka H 145 H5
Mateuți MD 154 B3
Matfors S 103 B13
Matha F 28 D5
Mathay F 27 F6
Mathi I 68 C4
Matignon F 23 C7
Matigny F 18 E7
Matilda FIN 127 E8
Matinlompolo FIN 117 E12
Matino I 61 C10
Matīši LV 131 F10
Matkaniva FIN 119 F14
Matkavaara FIN 121 E12
Matku FIN 127 D10
Matkule LV 134 C5
Matlock GB 11 E8
Matosinhos P 44 B3
Matour F 30 C5
Mátraballa H 147 F10
Mátraderecske H 147 F10
Mátramindszent H 147 F9
Matrand N 96 B7
Mátraszele H 147 E9
Mátraszőlős H 147 F9
Mátraterenye H 147 E9
Mátraverebély H 147 F9
Matre N 94 C3
Matre N 100 E3
Matrei am Brenner A 72 B3
Matrei in Osttirol A 72 B6
Matsdal S 109 F10
Matsouki GR 174 B3
Matt CH 71 D8
Mattaincourt F 26 D5
Mattersburg A 149 A6
Mattighofen A 76 F4
Mattila S 119 C12
Mattilanmäki FIN 115 E4
Mattinata I 63 D10
Mattinen FIN 119 B13
Mattisudden S 116 E3
Mattmar S 105 E15
Mattsmyra S 103 D9
Måttsund S 118 C7
Matuizos LT 137 E10
Matulji HR 67 B9
Matúškovo SK 146 E5
Matyryna BY 133 F5
Maubert-Fontaine F 19 E9
Maubeuge F 19 D8
Maubourguet F 32 D6
Maubuisson F 28 E3
Mauchline GB 5 D8
Maud GB 3 K12
Mauerbach A 77 F10
Mauerkirchen A 76 F4
Mauerstetten D 71 B11
Maughold GBM 10 C3
Mauguio F 35 C7
Maukkula FIN 125 E15
Maula FIN 119 C13
Maulbronn D 27 C10
Mauléon F 28 B4
Mauléon-Barousse F 33 E7
Mauléon-d'Armagnac F 32 C5
Mauléon-Licharre F 32 D4
Maulévrier F 28 A4
Maum IRL 6 E3
Mauna FIN 116 B8
Maunu S 116 B8
Maunujärvi FIN 117 D14
Maunula FIN 119 D15
Maura N 95 B13
Maure-de-Bretagne F 23 E8
Maureillas-las-Illas F 34 F4
Măureni RO 159 C8
Maurens F 29 F6
Mauriac F 28 F5
Mauriac F 29 E10
Mauricemills IRL 8 C4
Maurik NL 183 B6
Maurnes N 110 C9
Mauron F 23 D7
Mauroux F 33 B8
Maurs F 29 F10
Maurset N 94 B6
Maurstad N 100 C2
Mauru FIN 119 B15
Maury F 34 E4
Mautern an der Donau A 77 F9
Mauterndorf A 73 B8
Mautern in Steiermark A 73 B10
Mauth D 76 E5
Mauthausen A 77 F7
Mauthen A 73 C7
Mauves F 30 E6
Mauvezin F 33 C7
Mauvoisin CH 31 C11
Mauzé-sur-le-Mignon F 28 C4
Mavranaioi GR 168 D5
Mavrochori GR 168 C5
Mavrodendri GR 169 D6
Mavrodin RO 160 E6
Mavrokklisi GR 171 B10
Mavromati GR 174 E4
Mavrommati GR 169 F6
Mavrommati GR 175 C7
Mavrothalassa GR 169 C10
Mavrovë AL 168 D2
Mavrovo NMK 163 F10
Mavrovouni GR 169 C7
Mavrovouni GR 169 E7
Maxent F 23 E7
Maxéville F 186 D1
Maxial P 44 F2
Maxieira P 44 E5
Măxineni RO 161 C11
Maxmo FIN 122 D8
Maxsain D 185 C8
Maxyakovskoye RUS 136 D5
Maybole GB 4 E7
Maydan UA 145 F7
Mayen D 21 D8
Mayenne F 23 D10
Mayet F 23 E12
Mayfield GB 15 E9
Mayobridge GB 7 D10
Mayorga E 39 D9
Mäyränperä FIN 119 F14
Mayres F 35 A7
Mayrhofen A 72 B4
Mäyry FIN 123 E10
Mayschoss D 21 C8
May's Corner GB 7 D10
Máza H 149 D10
Mazagón E 51 E6
Mazagran F 19 F10
Mažaičiai LT 134 F3
Mazaleón E 42 E4
Mazamet F 33 D10
Mazan F 35 B9
Mazara del Vallo I 58 D2
Mazarakia GR 168 F3
Mazarambroz E 46 E4
Mazarete E 47 C8
Mazarrón E 56 F2
Mazé F 23 F11
Mažeikiai LT 134 D4
Mažeiniai LT 135 E8
Mazères F 33 D9
Mazerolles F 32 D5
Mazeyrolles F 33 A8
Mazi TR 181 B7
Mazières-en-Gâtine F 28 B5
Mazirbe LV 130 F4
Mažonai LT 134 F4
Mazsalaca LV 131 F10
Mažučište NMK 169 B5
Mazzano I 66 A1
Mazzano Romano I 62 C2
Mazzarino I 58 E5
Mazzarrone I 59 E6
Mazzo di Valtellina I 69 A9
Mborje AL 168 C4
Mbrostar AL 168 C2
Mdiq MA 53 E6
Meadela P 38 E2
Mealhada P 44 D4
Mealsgate GB 5 F10
Meana Sardo I 64 D3
Meare GB 13 C9
Measham GB 11 F8
Meåstrand S 107 E11
Meaulne F 29 B11
Méaulte F 18 E6
Meaux F 25 C8
Meauzac F 33 B8
Mechelen B 19 B9
Mechelen NL 183 D7
Mechernich D 21 C7
Mechowo PL 85 C8
Mechterstädt D 79 E8
Mecidiye TR 172 C6
Mecidiye TR 173 C10
Mecidiye TR 177 B10
Měčín CZ 76 D4
Mecina-Bombarón E 55 F6
Męcinka PL 81 D10
Meckenbeuren D 71 B9
Meckenheim D 21 C8
Meckesheim D 187 C6
Meco E 46 C6
Mecseknádasd H 149 D10
Meda P 45 C6
Međa SRB 159 B6
Medåker S 97 D14
Međas BIH 157 D10
Meddersheim D 21 E9
Meddo NL 183 A9
Mede I 68 C6
Medebach D 21 B11
Međeđa BIH 158 F3
Medeikiai LT 135 D9
Medelås S 107 B14
Medelim P 45 D6
Medellín E 51 B8
Medemblik NL 16 C4
Medena-Selišta BIH 157 D6
Medeno Polje BIH 156 C5
Medenychi UA 145 E8
Međeš BIH 158 D3
Medesano I 66 C1
Medgidia RO 155 E2
Medgyesbodzás H 151 D6
Medgyesegyháza H 151 E7
Medhamn S 91 A14
Mediana E 41 F10
Mediaș RO 152 E4
Medicina I 66 D4
Medieșu Aurit RO 151 B11
Medinaceli E 47 B8
Medina de las Torres E 51 C7
Medina del Campo E 39 F10
Medina de Pomar E 40 C5
Medina de Rioseco E 39 E9
Medina-Sidonia E 52 D5
Medingėnai LT 134 E4
Medinilla E 45 D9
Medininkai LT 137 D12
Mediona E 43 E7
Médis F 28 D4
Medkovets BG 159 F11
Mede S 118 E5
Medlov CZ 77 C12
Medneva LV 133 B3
Medolla I 66 C3
Medousa GR 171 B8
Medovoye RUS 136 D1
Mędrzechów PL 143 F10
Medsėdžiai LT 134 D3
Medskog S 103 E12
Medskogsbygget S 102 B5
Medstugan S 105 D12
Međugorje BIH 157 F8
Međuhana SRB 164 C3
Medulin HR 67 C8
Međumajdan HR 156 B5
Medumi LV 135 E12
Meduno I 73 D6
Međurečje SRB 163 B9
Međuvođe BIH 157 B6
Medveđa SRB 159 E7
Medveđa SRB 159 F7
Medveđa SRB 164 D4
Medviđa HR 156 D4
Medvode SLO 73 D9
Medyka PL 144 D6
Medze LV 134 C2
Medzev SK 145 F2
Medzibrod SK 147 D8
Medzilaborce SK 145 E4
Meenaclady IRL 6 B6
Meenavean IRL 6 C5
Meer B 182 C5
Meerane D 79 E11
Meerapalu EST 132 E1
Meerbeck D 17 D12
Meerbusch D 17 F7
Meerhout B 183 C6
Meerkerk NL 182 B5
Meerle B 182 C5
Meerlo NL 183 B8
Meersburg D 27 E11
Meerssen NL 19 C12
Meetkerke B 182 C2
Meeuwen B 19 B12
Mefjordvær N 111 A13
Mega Dereio GR 171 B10
Megala Kalyvia GR 169 F6
Megali Panagia GR 169 D10
Megali Volvi GR 169 C9
Megalochori GR 169 E6
Megalo Chorio GR 174 B4
Megalo Chorio GR 181 D6
Megalo Livadi GR 175 E9
Megalopoli GR 174 E5
Megara GR 175 C7
Megardssætra N 105 C13
Megen NL 183 B7
Megève F 31 D10
Megyaszó H 145 G3
Mehadia RO 159 D9
Mehadica RO 159 C9
Mehamn N 113 A20
Mehedeby S 99 B8
Mehikoorma EST 132 E1
Méhkerék H 151 D7
Mehren D 21 D7
Mehring D 21 E7
Mehrstetten D 74 F6
Mehtäkylä FIN 119 F12
Mehun-sur-Yèvre F 25 F7
Meidrim GB 12 B6
Meigh GB 7 D10
Meigle GB 5 B10
Meijel NL 16 F5
Meikleour GB 5 B10
Meilen CH 27 F10
Meilhan F 32 C4
Meillac F 23 D8
Meillant F 29 B10
Meillerie F 31 C10
Meimoa P 45 D6
Meina I 68 B6
Meine D 79 B8
Meinersen D 79 B7
Meinerzhagen D 185 B8
Meiningen D 79 E7
Meira E 38 B5
Meiringen CH 70 D6
Meisdorf D 79 C9
Meise B 182 D4
Meisenheim D 21 E9
Meißen D 80 D4
Meitingen D 75 E8
Meix-devant-Virton B 19 E11
Mejlby DK 86 C6
Mejorada E 46 D3
Mejorada del Campo E 46 D6
Mejrup DK 86 C3
Meka Gruda BIH 157 F9
Mekinje SLO 73 D10
Mel I 72 D5
Melalahti FIN 121 F10
Melampes GR 178 E8
Melanthi GR 168 D5
Melay F 23 F10
Melay F 26 E4
Melazzo I 37 B8
Melbå N 111 C11
Melbourn GB 15 C9
Melbu N 110 C8
Melby GB 3 E13
Melchow D 84 E5
Meldal N 104 E7
Meldola I 66 D5
Meldorf D 82 B6
Mele I 37 C9
Melegnano I 69 C7
Melenci SRB 158 B5
Melendugno I 61 C10
Melfi I 60 B5
Melfjordbotn N 108 C6
Melgaço P 38 D3
Melgar de Arriba E 39 D9
Melgar de Fernamental E 40 D3
Melgar de Tera E 39 E7
Melgven F 22 E4
Melhus N 104 E8
Melia GR 169 E8
Meliana E 48 E4
Melick NL 20 B6
Melicucco I 59 C9
Mélida E 32 F2
Melide E 38 C4
Melides P 50 C2
Meligalas GR 174 E4
Meliki GR 169 C7
Melilli I 59 E7
Melinești RO 160 D3
Mélisey F 26 E6
Meliskerke NL 182 B3
Melissa GR 171 B7
Melissa I 61 E8
Melissano I 61 D10
Melissochori GR 175 C7
Melissopetra GR 168 D4
Melitaia GR 174 A5
Meliti GR 169 C6
Melito di Porto Salvo I 59 D8
Melivoia GR 169 E8
Melivoia GR 171 B7
Melk A 77 F8
Melkadalen N 111 D12
Melkefoss N 114 E7
Melksham GB 13 C10
Mellac F 22 E4
Mellajärvi FIN 119 B13
Mellakoski FIN 119 B12
Mellanfjärden S 103 C13
Mellansel S 107 E14
Mellansjö S 103 B10
Mellanström S 109 E15
Mellau A 71 C9
Mellbystrand S 87 B11
Melle B 19 B8
Melle D 17 D10
Melle F 28 C5
Mellen D 83 D11
Mellenbach-Glasbach D 79 E9
Mellendorf (Wedemark) D 78 A6
Mellensee D 80 B4
Mellerud S 91 B11
Mellerup DK 86 B6
Mellgård S 103 A9
Mellilä FIN 127 D8
Mellin D 79 A8
Mellingen D 79 E9
Mellösa S 93 A9
Mellrichstadt D 75 B7
Melmerby GB 5 F11
Melnbārži LV 135 B11
Melnica SRB 159 E7
Melnik BG 169 A9
Mělník CZ 77 B6
Mel'nikovo RUS 129 D12
Melnitsa BG 167 E7
Melnsils LV 130 F5
Melón E 38 D3
Meloy N 110 C9
Meløysund N 108 C6
Melrand F 22 E5
Melres P 44 B4
Melrose GB 5 D11
Mels CH 71 C8
Melsdorf D 83 B8
Melsungen D 78 D6
Melsvik N 112 C11
Meltaus FIN 117 E14
Meltham GB 11 D8
Melton GB 15 C11
Melton Mowbray GB 11 F10
Meltosjärvi FIN 117 E13
Melun F 25 C8
Melvaig GB 2 K5
Melvich GB 3 H9
Mélykút H 150 E3
Melzo I 69 C7
Memaliaj AL 168 D2
Membrey F 26 E4
Membrilla E 55 B6
Membrío E 45 E6
Mēmele LV 135 D8
Memleben D 79 D9
Memmelsdorf D 75 C8
Memmingen D 71 B10
Memmingerberg D 71 B10
Memsie GB 3 K12
Menaggio I 69 A7
Menai Bridge GB 10 E3
Menaldum NL 16 B5
Menars F 24 E5
Menasalbas E 46 E4
Menat F 30 C2
Menata I 66 C5
Mendavia E 32 F1
Mende F 34 A6
Menden (Sauerland) D 17 F9
Mendenitsa GR 175 B6
Menderes TR 177 C9
Mendig D 21 D8
Mendiga P 44 E3
Mendigorría E 32 E2
Menditte F 32 D4
Mendrisio CH 69 B6
Ménéac F 22 D7
Menemen TR 177 B9
Menen B 19 C7
Menesjärvi FIN 117 A16
Ménesplet F 29 E6
Ménessaire F 25 F11
Menet F 29 E11
Menetes GR 181 F6
Menetou-Salon F 25 F7
Menfi I 58 D2
Mengabril E 51 B8
Meņģele LV 135 C10
Mengen D 27 D11
Mengerskirchen D 21 C10
Mengeš SLO 73 D10
Mengíbar E 53 A9
Menidi GR 174 A3
Ménigoute F 28 C5
Ménil-la-Tour F 26 C4
Ménil-sur-Belvitte F 26 D6
Menin B 19 C7
Menin B 182 D2
Menkijärvi FIN 123 E11
Menkulas AL 168 C4
Mennecy F 25 C7
Mennetou-sur-Cher F 24 F6
Menou F 25 F9
Mens F 31 F8
Mensignac F 29 E7
Menslage D 17 C9
Mentana I 62 C3
Menteroda D 79 D8
Menteșe TR 181 B8
Menton F 37 D7
Méntrida E 46 D4
Menznau CH 70 C6
Méobecq F 29 B8
Meolo I 72 E5
Méounes-les-Montrieux F 35 D10
Meppel NL 16 C6
Meppen D 17 C8
Mequinenza E 42 E4
Mer F 24 E6
Mera RO 153 F9
Merag HR 67 C9
Meråker N 105 E11
Meråkervollen N 105 E11
Merano I 72 C3
Méracq F 32 C5
Merasjärvi S 116 C7
Merasjärvi S 117 C10
Merate I 69 B7
Merbes-le-Château B 19 D9
Mercadillo E 40 B5
Mercatale I 66 F5
Mercatello sul Metauro I 66 E5
Mercatino Conca I 66 E6
Mercato San Severino I 60 B3
Mercato Saraceno I 66 E5
Merćez SRB 163 C11
Merching D 71 A11
Merchtem B 19 C9
Mercœur F 29 E9
Mercogliano I 60 B3
Mercuès F 33 B8
Merdrignac F 22 D7
Mērdzene LV 133 C3
Mere B 19 C8
Mere GB 13 C10
Méreau F 24 F7
Merei RO 161 C9
Merelbeke B 19 C8
Meremäe EST 132 F2
Merenberg D 185 C9
Mereni MD 154 D4
Mereni RO 155 E2
Mereni RO 161 E7
Mérens-les-Vals F 33 E9
Merești RO 153 E6
Méréville F 24 D7
Merghindeal RO 152 F5
Mergozzo I 68 B5
Meria F 37 F10
Méribel-les-Allues F 31 E10
Meriç TR 171 B10
Merichas GR 175 E9
Merichleri BG 166 E4
Mérida E 51 B7
Meriden GB 13 A11
Merijärvi FIN 119 F12
Merikarvia FIN 126 B6
Meriläinen FIN 123 D12
Merimasku FIN 126 E6
Měřín CZ 77 D9
Mering D 71 A11
Merișani RO 160 D5
Mérk H 151 B9
Merkendorf A 148 C5
Merkendorf D 75 D8
Merkenes S 109 C11
Merkinė LT 137 E9
Merklín CZ 76 C4
Merklingen D 74 E6
Merksplas B 182 C5
Merlara I 66 B3
Merlevenez F 22 E5
Merlines F 29 D10
Mern DK 87 E10
Mērnieki LV 131 F8
Mernye H 149 C9
Merošina SRB 164 C4
Merrey F 26 D4
Mersch L 20 E6
Merseburg (Saale) D 79 D10
Mersinbeleni TR 177 D10
Mers-les-Bains F 18 D3
Mērsrags LV 134 B6
Mertajärvi S 116 B8
Mertert L 20 E6
Mertesdorf D 186 B2
Merthyr Tydfil GB 13 B8
Mertingen D 75 E8
Mertloch D 185 D7
Mértola P 50 D4
Mertzwiller F 186 D4
Méru F 18 F5
Mervans F 31 B7
Mervent F 28 B4
Merville F 18 C6
Merville F 33 C8
Méry-sur-Seine F 25 C10
Merzen D 17 D9
Merzig D 21 F7
Mesagne I 61 B9
Mesagros GR 175 D8
Mésanger F 23 F9
Mesão Frio P 44 B5
Mesaria GR 177 F6
Meschede D 17 F10
Meschers-sur-Gironde F 28 D4
Mešeišta NMK 168 B4
Meselefors S 107 C11
Mesenikolas GR 169 F6
Meseșenii de Jos RO 151 C10
Mesgrigny F 25 D10
Mesi GR 171 C8
Mesići BIH 157 E11
Mesihovina BIH 157 E7
Mesimeri GR 169 D9
Mesinge DK 86 E7
Meskla GR 178 E6
Meškuičiai LT 134 D6
Meslay-du-Maine F 23 E10
Mesocco CH 71 E8
Mesochora GR 168 F5
Mesochori GR 169 E7
Mesochori GR 181 E6
Mesola I 66 C5
Mesolongi GR 174 C3

Monforte da Beira P 45 E6
Monforte d'Alba I 37 B7
Monforte del Cid E 56 E3
Monforte de Lemos E 38 C4
Monforte de Moyuela E 42 E2
Monfortinho P 45 D7
Monghidoro I 66 D3
Mongrando I 68 B5
Mongstad N 100 E2
Monguelfo I 72 C5
Monheim D 75 E8
Moniaive GB 5 E9
Monieux F 35 B9
Monifieth GB 5 C11
Monilea IRL 7 E8
Mõniste EST 131 F13
Monistrol-d'Allier F 30 F4
Monistrol de Calders E 43 D8
Monistrol de Montserrat
E 43 D7
Monistrol-sur-Loire F 30 E5
Monivea IRL 6 F5
Mönkeberg D 83 B8
Mońki PL 140 D7
Monkokehampton GB 12 D6
Monléon-Magnoac F 33 D7
Monmouth GB 13 B9
Monnaie F 24 E4
Mönni FIN 125 E14
Monninkylä FIN 127 E14
Monok H 145 G3
Monolithos GR 181 D7
Monopoli I 61 B8
Monor H 150 C3
Monor RO 152 D5
Monostorapáti H 149 C9
Monostorpályi H 151 C8
Monóvar E 56 E3
Monpazier F 33 A7
Monreal E 32 E3
Monreal del Campo E 47 C10
Monreale I 58 C3
Monreith GB 4 F7
Monroy E 45 E8
Monroyo E 42 F3
Mons B 19 D8
Mons F 34 C4
Mons F 36 D5
Monsampolo del Tronto I 62 B5
Monsaraz P 51 C5
Monschau D 20 C6
Monsec F 29 E7
Monségur F 33 A6
Monselice I 66 B4
Monsempron-Libos F 33 B7
Monserrat E 48 F3
Monsheim D 187 B5
Mönsheim D 187 D6
Mønsted DK 86 C4
Monster NL 16 D2
Mönsterås S 89 A10
Monsummano Terme I 66 E2
Monta I 37 B7
Montabaur D 21 D9
Montaberner E 56 D4
Montady F 34 D5
Montagnac F 34 D5
Montagnana I 66 B3
Montagne F 28 F5
Montagney F 26 F4
Montagnol F 34 C5
Montagrier F 29 E6
Montaigu F 28 B3
Montaigu-de-Quercy F 33 B8
Montaigut F 30 C2
Montaigut-sur-Save F 33 C8
Montaione I 66 E2
Montalbán E 42 F2
Montalbán de Córdoba E 53 A7
Montalbano Elicona I 59 C7
Montalbano Jonico I 61 C7
Montalbo E 47 E7
Montalcino I 65 A4
Montale I 66 E3
Montalegre P 38 E4
Montalieu-Vercieu F 31 D7
Montalivet-les-Bains F 28 E3
Montallegro I 58 E3
Montalto delle Marche I 62 B5
Montalto di Castro I 65 C5
Montalto Marina I 65 C5
Montalto Uffugo I 60 E6
Montalvão P 44 E5
Montamarta E 39 E8
Montana BG 165 C7
Montana CH 31 C11
Montanejos E 48 D3
Montaner F 32 D5
Montano Antilia I 60 C4
Montans F 33 C9
Montaquila I 62 D6
Montargil P 44 F4
Montargis F 25 E8
Montastruc-la-Conseillère
F 33 C9
Montataire F 18 F5
Montauban F 33 B8
Montauban-de-Bretagne
F 23 D7
Montaudin F 23 D10
Montauriol F 33 A7
Montauroux F 36 D5
Montaut F 32 C4
Montaut F 32 D5
Montaut F 33 D9
Montayral F 33 B7
Montazzoli I 63 D6
Montbard F 25 E11
Montbarrey F 31 A8
Montbazens F 33 B10
Montbazin F 35 C6
Montbazon F 24 F4
Montbéliard F 27 E6
Montbenoît F 31 B9
Montbeton F 33 B8
Montblanc E 42 E6
Montboucher-sur-Jabron
F 35 A8
Montbozon F 26 F5
Montbrió del Camp E 42 E6
Montbrison F 30 D5
Montbron F 29 D7
Montbrun F 33 A9
Montbrun-les-Bains F 35 B9
Montcada i Reixac E 43 E8
Montcavrel F 15 F12
Montceau-les-Mines F 30 B5
Montcenis F 30 B5
Montchanin F 30 B5
Montcornet F 19 E9
Montcresson F 25 E8
Montcuq F 33 B8
Montcy-Notre-Dame F 19 E10
Montdardier F 35 C6
Mont-Dauphin F 36 B5
Mont-de-Marsan F 32 C5
Montdidier F 18 E6
Mont-Dore F 30 D2
Monteagudo E 41 E8
Monteagudo de las Salinas
E 47 E9
Monteagudo de las Vicarías
E 41 F7
Montealegre del Castillo
E 55 B10
Montebello Ionico I 59 D8
Montebello Vicentino I 66 B3
Montebelluna I 72 E5
Montebourg F 23 B9
Montebruno I 37 B10
Montecalvo in Foglia I 66 E6
Montecalvo Irpino I 60 A4
Monte-Carlo MC 37 D6
Montecarotto I 67 E7
Montecassiano I 67 F7
Monte Castello di Vibio I 62 B2
Montecastrilli I 62 B2
Montecatini Terme I 66 E2
Montecatini Val di Cecina
I 66 F2
Montecchio I 67 E6
Montecchio Emilia I 66 C1
Montecchio Maggiore I 66 A3
Montech F 33 C8
Montechiaro d'Asti I 37 A8
Montechiarugolo I 66 C1
Montecilfone I 63 D7
Montecorice I 60 C3
Montecosaro I 67 F8
Montecreale Valcellina I 73 D6
Montecreto I 66 D2
Monte da Pedra P 44 F5
Monte das Flores P 50 B4
Montederramo E 38 D5
Monte di Procida I 60 B2
Monte do Trigo P 50 C4
Montefalco I 62 B3
Montefalcone di Val Fortore
I 60 A4
Montefalcone nel Sannio
I 63 D7
Montefano I 67 F7
Montefelcino I 67 E6
Montefiascone I 62 B2
Montefiore dell'Aso I 62 A5
Montefiorino I 66 D2
Montefortino I 62 B4
Montefranco I 62 B3
Montefrío E 53 B8
Montegiordano I 61 C7
Montegiorgio I 67 F8
Monte Gordo P 50 E5
Montegranaro I 67 F8
Montegrotto Terme I 66 B4
Montehermoso E 45 D8
Monteiasi I 61 C8
Monteils F 33 B9
Monteiros P 44 A5
Montejaque E 53 C6
Montejícar E 53 A10
Montejo de la Sierra E 46 B5
Montelabbate I 67 E6
Montelanico I 62 D4
Montelavar P 50 B1
Montel-de-Gelat F 29 D11
Monteleone di Puglia I 60 A4
Monteleone di Spoleto I 62 B3
Monteleone d'Orvieto I 62 B2
Monteleone Rocca Doria I 64 C2
Montelepre I 58 C3
Montelibretti I 62 C3
Montélier F 31 F7
Montélimar F 35 A8
Montella I 60 B4
Montellano E 51 E8
Montels F 33 D8
Montelupo Fiorentino I 66 E3
Montelupone I 67 F8
Montemaggiore Belsito I 58 D4
Montemagno I 37 B8
Montemarciano I 67 E7
Montemayor E 53 A7
Montemayor de Pililla E 40 E3
Montembœuf F 29 D7
Montemesola I 61 B8
Montemiletto I 60 A3
Montemilone I 60 A5
Montemolín E 51 C7
Montemonaco I 62 B4
Montemor-o-Novo P 50 B3
Montemurlo I 66 E3
Montemurro I 60 C5
Montenay F 23 D10
Montendre F 28 E5
Montenegro de Cameros
E 40 D6
Montenero di Bisaccia I 63 D7
Montenerodomo I 63 C6
Monte Porzio I 67 E7
Monteprandone I 62 B5
Montepulciano I 62 A1
Monterblanc F 22 E6
Monterchi I 66 F5
Monte Real P 44 E3
Montereale I 62 B4
Montereau-fault-Yonne F 25 D8
Monte Redondo P 44 E3
Monterenzio I 66 D3
Monteriggioni I 66 F3
Monteroduni I 63 D6
Monte Romano I 62 C1
Monteroni d'Arbia I 66 F3
Monteroni di Lecce I 61 C10
Monterosso Almo I 59 E6
Monterosso Calabro I 59 B9
Monterotondo I 62 C3
Monterotondo Marittimo
I 66 F2
Monterrei E 38 E5
Monterroso E 38 C4
Monterrubio de la Serena
E 51 B9
Monterubbiano I 62 A5
Montesa E 56 D3
Monte San Biagio I 62 E4
Monte San Giovanni Campano
I 62 D5
Montesano Salentino I 61 D10
Montesano sulla Marcellana
I 60 C5
Monte San Savino I 66 F4
Monte Santa Maria Tiberina
I 66 F5
Monte Sant'Angelo I 63 D9
Monte San Vito I 67 E7
Montesarchio I 60 A3
Montescaglioso I 61 B7
Montesclaros E 46 D3
Montescudaio I 66 F2
Montese I 66 D2
Montesilvano I 63 B6
Montespertoli I 66 E3
Montesquieu F 33 B8
Montesquieu-Volvestre F 33 D8
Montesquiou F 33 C6
Montes Velhos P 50 D3
Monteux F 35 B8
Montevago I 58 D2
Montevarchi I 66 E4
Montevecchia I 64 D2
Monteverde I 60 A5
Montevil P 50 C2
Montfaucon F 23 F9
Montfaucon F 29 F9
Montfaucon-d'Argonne F 19 F11
Montfaucon-en-Velay F 30 E5
Montferran-Savès F 33 C7
Montferrat F 36 D4
Montferrier F 33 E9
Montfoort NL 182 A5
Montfort F 23 D8
Montfort F 32 D4
Montfort NL 183 C7
Montfort-en-Chalosse F 32 C4
Montfort-l'Amaury F 24 C6
Montfort-le-Gesnois F 24 D3
Montfort-sur-Risle F 18 F2
Montgai E 42 D5
Montgaillard F 33 D6
Montgaillard F 33 E9
Montgenèvre F 31 F10
Montgeron F 25 C7
Montgiscard F 33 D9
Montgivray F 29 B9
Montgomery GB 10 F5
Montguyon F 28 E5
Monthermé F 19 E10
Monthey CH 31 C10
Monthois F 19 F10
Monthureux-sur-Saône F 26 D4
Monti I 64 B3
Monticelli d'Ongina I 69 C8
Monticello F 37 F9
Montichiari I 66 B1
Monticiano I 65 A4
Montiel E 55 B7
Montier-en-Der F 25 D12
Montieri I 65 A4
Montiers-sur-Saulx F 26 C3
Montiglio I 68 C5
Montignac F 29 E8
Montignies-le-Tilleul B 19 D9
Montignoso I 66 D1
Montigny F 27 C6
Montigny-la-Resie F 25 E10
Montigny-le-Roi F 26 D3
Montigny-lès-Metz F 26 B5
Montigny-Mornay-Villeneuve-
sur-Vingeanne F 26 E3
Montigny-sur-Aube F 25 E12
Montijo E 51 B6
Montijo P 50 B2
Montilla E 53 A7
Montillana E 53 A9
Montivilliers F 23 A12
Montizón E 55 C6
Montjaux F 34 B4
Montjean F 23 D10
Montjovet I 68 B4
Montlaur F 34 D4
Montlieu-la-Garde F 28 E5
Mont-Louis F 33 E10
Montluçon F 29 C11
Montluel F 31 D7
Montmarault F 30 C2
Montmartin-sur-Mer F 23 C8
Montmédy F 19 E11
Montmélian F 31 D9
Montmelo E 43 D8
Montmeyran F 31 F6
Montmeyan F 36 D4
Montmirail F 24 D4
Montmirail F 25 C10
Montmirey-le-Château F 26 F4
Montmoreau-St-Cybard F 29 E6
Montmorillon F 29 C7
Montmorin F 35 B10
Montmorot F 31 B8
Montmort-Lucy F 25 C10
Montoir-de-Bretagne F 23 F7
Montoire-sur-le-Loir F 24 E4
Montoison F 30 F6
Montoito P 50 B4
Montola FIN 124 F8
Montón E 47 B10
Montone I 66 F5
Montopoli di Sabina I 62 C3
Montorio al Vomano I 62 B5
Montoro E 53 A8
Montory F 32 D4
Montournais F 28 B4
Montpelier IRL 8 C6
Montpellier F 35 C6
Montpeyroux F 34 A4
Montpezat F 33 B7
Montpézat F 33 D7
Montpezat-de-Quercy F 33 B8
Montpezat-sous-Bauzon F 30 F5
Montpon-Ménestérol F 29 E6
Montpont-en-Bresse F 31 B7
Mont-ras E 43 D10
Montréal F 25 E11
Montréal F 33 C6
Montréal F 33 D10
Montredon-Labessonnié
F 33 C10
Montregard F 30 E5
Montréjeau F 33 D7
Montrésor F 24 F5
Montresta I 64 C2
Montret F 31 B7
Montreuil F 15 G12
Montreuil-Bellay F 23 F11
Montreuil-Juigné F 23 E10
Montreux CH 31 C10
Montrevault F 23 F9
Montrevel-en-Bresse F 31 C7
Montrichard F 24 F5
Montricoux F 33 B9
Montriond F 31 C10
Mont-roig del Camp E 42 E5
Montrond F 31 B8
Montrond-les-Bains F 30 D5
Montrose GB 5 B12
Montroy E 48 F3
Monts F 24 F4
Montsalvy F 29 F10
Montsauche-les-Settons
F 25 F11
Montségur F 33 E9
Montseny E 43 D8
Montsoué F 32 C4
Mont-sous-Vaudrey F 31 B8
Monts-sur-Guesnes F 29 B6
Mont-St-Aignan F 18 F3
Mont-St-Jean F 25 F11
Mont-St-Martin F 19 E12
Mont-St-Vincent F 30 B5
Montsûrs F 23 D10
Montsuzain F 25 D11
Mõntu EST 130 F4
Montuïri E 57 B10
Montvalent F 29 F9
Montville F 18 E3
Montzen B 183 D7
Montzéville F 20 F4
Monza I 69 B7
Monzelfeld D 21 E8
Monzingen D 21 E9
Monzón E 42 D4
Monzón de Campos E 40 D3
Mook NL 183 B7
Moone IRL 7 G9
Moordorf (Südbrookmerland)
D 17 B8
Moorends GB 11 D10
Moorenweis D 75 F9
Moorfields GB 4 F4
Moorrege D 82 C7
Moorslede B 19 C7
Moorweg D 17 A9
Moos D 76 E3
Moosbach D 75 C11
Moosburg A 73 C9
Moosburg an der Isar D 75 F10
Moosinning D 75 F10
Mooste EST 131 E14
Mór H 149 B10
Mora E 46 E5
Mora P 50 B3
Mora S 97 B14
Mora S 102 D8
Móra d'Ebre E 42 E5
Mora de Rubielos E 48 D3
Moradillo de Roa E 40 E4
Morag PL 139 C8
Mórahalom H 150 E4
Moraice MNE 163 C7
Moraira E 56 D5
Morais P 39 E6
Moraïtika GR 168 E2
Morakovo MNE 163 D7
Moral de Calatrava E 54 B5
Moraleda de Zafayona E 53 B9
Moraleja E 45 D7
Moraleja del Vino E 39 F8
Moraleja de Sayago E 45 B9
Morales de Campos E 39 E9
Morales del Vino E 39 F8
Morales de Toro E 39 E9
Morales de Valverde E 39 E8
Moralina E 39 F7
Moräng S 118 D3
Morano Calabro I 60 D6
Morano sul Po I 68 C5
Morar GB 4 B5
Morărești RO 160 C5
Morasverdes E 45 C8
Morata de Jalón E 41 F9
Morata de Tajuña E 46 D6
Moratalla E 55 C9
Morava BG 166 C4
Morava MD 154 C4
Morava SLO 73 E10
Moravany CZ 77 B9
Moravany CZ 77 D11
Moravany SK 145 F4
Moravče SLO 73 E10
Moravice HR 67 B11
Moravița RO 159 C7
Moravka BG 166 C6
Morávka CZ 147 B7
Moravská Třebová CZ 77 C11
Moravské Budějovice CZ 77 D9
Moravské Lieskové SK 146 D5
MoravskýMoravskýx CZ 146 B4
Moravský Svätý Ján SK 77 E12
Morawica PL 143 E10
Morbach D 21 E8
Morbegno I 69 A8
Morbier F 31 B9
Mörbisch am See A 149 A7
Mörby S 99 C10
Mörbylånga S 89 B10
Morcenx F 32 B4
Morciano di Leuca I 61 D10
Morciano di Romagna I 66 E6
Morcone I 60 A3
Mordelles F 23 D8
Mordoğan TR 177 B8
Mordy PL 141 F7
More LV 135 B10
Moréac F 22 E6
Moreanes P 50 D4
Morebattle GB 5 D12
Morecambe GB 10 C6
Moreda E 39 B8
Moreda E 55 E6
Morée F 24 E5
Mörel CH 70 E6
Morella E 42 F3
Moreni RO 161 D7
Morenish GB 5 C8
Morentín E 32 E1
Moreruela de Tábara E 39 E8
Mores I 64 B2
Morestel F 31 D7
Moretonhampstead GB 13 D7
Moreton-in-Marsh GB 13 B11
Moret-sur-Loing F 25 D8
Moretta I 37 B7
Moreuil F 18 E5
Morez F 31 B9
Morfa Nefyn GB 10 F2
Morfasso I 69 D8
Mörfelden D 187 B6
Morfi GR 168 D5
Morfi GR 168 F3
Morfovouni GR 169 F6
Morgat F 22 D2
Morgedal N 95 D8
Morges CH 31 B10
Morgex I 31 D11
Morgongåva S 98 C7
Morhange F 26 C6
Mori I 69 B10
Moria GR 177 A8
Moricone I 62 C3
Morienval F 18 F6
Moriles E 53 B7
Morinë AL 163 E10
Morinë RKS 163 E9
Moringen D 78 C6
Morino I 62 D4
Moritzburg D 80 D5
Morjärv S 118 B9
Mork N 104 F3
Mørke DK 86 C6
Morkkaperä FIN 115 E1
Mørkøv DK 87 D9
Morkovice CZ 77 D12
Mörkret S 102 C4
Morlaàs F 32 D5
Morlaix F 22 C4
Morlanne F 32 C4
Morlanwelz B 19 D9
Mörlenbach D 21 E11
Morley F 26 C3
Morley GB 11 D8
Morley's Bridge IRL 8 E4
Mörlunda S 89 A9
Mormanno I 60 D6
Mormant F 25 C8
Mormoiron F 35 B9
Mornant F 30 D6
Mornas F 35 B8
Mornese I 37 B9
Moroeni RO 161 C6
Morolo I 62 D4
Morón de Almazán E 41 F7
Morón de la Frontera E 51 E9
Moros E 41 F8
Morosaglia F 37 G10
Morottaja FIN 115 E4
Morović SRB 158 C3
Morozova RUS 129 F14
Morozovo BG 166 D4
Morozzo I 37 C7
Morpeth GB 5 E13
Mørrevatnet N 104 D8
Morrfjord N 110 D8
Morriston GB 13 B7
Morrovalle I 67 F8
Mörrum S 89 C7
Morsbach D 21 C9
Morschen D 78 D6
Morshyn UA 145 E8
Mörsil S 105 E15
Morskoga S 97 C13
Morskogen N 95 B14
Morsum D 17 C12
Mørsvikbotn N 111 E10
Mortagne-au-Perche F 24 C4
Mortagne-sur-Gironde F 28 E4
Mortagne-sur-Sèvre F 28 A4
Mortágua P 44 D4
Mortain F 23 C10
Mortara I 68 C6
Morteau F 31 A10
Morteaux-Coulibœuf F 23 C11
Mörtebo S 103 E12
Mortegliano I 73 E7
Mortelle I 59 C8
Morteni RO 160 D6
Mortensnes N 112 C11
Mortensnes N 114 C6
Mortimer's Cross GB 13 A9
Morton GB 11 F11
Mortrée F 23 C12
Mörtschach A 73 C6
Mortsel B 19 B9
Mörtsjön S 106 D7
Mortsund N 110 D6
Morud DK 86 E6
Morunglav RO 160 E4
Morville GB 10 F7
Mor'ye RUS 129 E15
Moryń PL 84 E6
Morzeszczyn PL 138 C6
Morzine F 31 C10
Moșana MD 153 A11
Mosar BY 133 F2
Mosås S 92 A6
Mosätt S 102 B7
Mosbach D 21 F12
Mosbjerg DK 90 D7
Mosborough GB 11 E9
Mosby N 90 C2
Moscavide P 50 B1
Moščenica HR 149 F6
Moščenička Draga HR 67 B9
Moschopotamos GR 169 D7
Mosciano Sant'Angelo I 62 B5
Mościcha PL 140 C8
Moscovei MD 154 F2
Moscow GB 5 D8
Moseby DK 86 A5
Mosėdis LT 134 D3
Mosel D 79 E11
Möser D 79 B10
Mosina PL 81 B11
Mosjö S 107 E13
Mosjøen N 108 E5
Moskaret N 101 B12
Mosko BIH 162 D5
Moskorzew PL 143 E8
Moskosel S 109 E17
Moskuvaara FIN 115 C1
Moslavna Podravska HR 149 E9
Moșna RO 152 E4
Moșna RO 153 D11
Moșnița Nouă RO 159 B7
Moșoaia RO 160 D5
Moso in Passiria I 72 C3
Mosonmagyaróvár H 146 F4
Mosonszolnok H 146 F4
Mošovce SK 147 D7
Mosqueruela E 48 D4
Moss N 95 D13
Mossala FIN 126 E5
Mossat GB 3 L11
Mossbo S 103 D11
Mössingen D 27 D11
Mossley GB 4 F5
Mossley GB 11 D7
Moss-side GB 4 E4
Mosstakan S 96 C7
Most BG 166 F5
Most CZ 76 A5
Mostar BIH 157 F8
Mosteiro E 38 B5
Mosteiro P 44 E5
Mosteiro P 50 D4
Mostek CZ 77 B9
Moșteni RO 161 E7
Mosterhamn N 94 C2
Mostkowo PL 85 E8
Mostkowo PL 139 C9
Most na Soči SLO 73 D8
Móstoles E 46 D5
Mosty PL 141 G8
Mostys'ka UA 144 D7
Mosty u Jablunkova CZ 147 B7
Mosvik N 105 D10
Mosyr UA 144 A9
Moszczenica PL 143 C8
Mota del Cuervo E 47 F7
Mota del Marqués E 39 E9
Moțăieni RO 160 C6
Motala S 92 B6
Motarzyno PL 85 B12
Moțăței RO 159 E11
Moțca RO 153 C9
Motherwell GB 5 D9
Môtiers CH 31 B10
Motike BIH 156 D6
Motike BIH 157 C7
Motilla del Palancar E 47 E9
Motilleja E 47 F9
Motjärnshyttan S 97 C10
Motoșeni RO 153 E10
Motovun HR 67 B8
Motril E 53 C9
Motru RO 159 D10
Motta Montecorvino I 63 D8
Motta San Giovanni I 59 C8
Motta Visconti I 69 C6
Motten D 74 B6
Möttingen D 75 E8
Mottola I 61 B8
Möttönen FIN 123 D13
Mötz A 71 C11
Mou DK 86 B6
Moucha GR 174 A4
Mouchamps F 28 B3
Mouchan F 33 C6
Moudon CH 31 B10
Moudros GR 171 E8
Mougins F 36 D6
Mouhijärvi FIN 127 B9
Moularès F 33 B10
Moulay F 23 D10
Mouleydier F 29 F7
Mouliherne F 23 F12
Moulin-Neuf F 33 D9
Moulins F 30 C3
Moulins-Engilbert F 30 B4
Moulins-la-Marche F 24 C3
Moulis-en-Médoc F 28 E4
Moulismes F 29 C7
Moult F 23 B11
Moulton GB 15 C7
Moulton GB 15 C9
Mountbellew IRL 6 F6
Mount Bellew IRL 6 F6
Mountbenger GB 5 D10
Mountcharles IRL 6 C6
Mountcollins IRL 8 D4
Mount Hamilton GB 4 F2
Mountjoy GB 4 F2
Mountjoy GB 7 C9
Mountmellick IRL 7 F8
Mount Norris GB 7 D10
Mount Nugent IRL 7 E8
Mountrath IRL 7 F8
Mountshannon IRL 8 C6
Mountsorrel GB 11 F9
Moura P 50 C5
Mourão P 51 C5
Mourenx F 32 D4
Mouriès F 35 C8
Mouries GR 169 B8
Mouriki GR 175 C7
Mourisca do Vouga P 44 C4
Mouriscas P 44 E4
Mournies GR 178 E7
Mourujärvi FIN 121 B11
Mouscron B 19 C7
Moussac F 35 C7
Moussey F 27 D7
Moussoulens F 33 D10
Moussy F 25 F9
Moustéru F 22 C5
Moustey F 32 B4
Moustheni GR 170 C6
Moustiers-Ste-Marie F 36 D4
Mouthe F 31 B9
Mouthier-Haute-Pierre F 31 A9
Mouthiers-sur-Boëme F 29 D6
Mouthoumet F 34 E4
Moutier CH 27 F7
Moutier-d'Ahun F 29 C10
Moûtiers F 31 E10
Moutiers-les-Mauxfaits F 28 C3
Moutnice CZ 77 D11
Moutsouna GR 177 E6
Moux F 34 D4
Moux-en-Morvan F 25 F11
Mouy F 18 F5
Mouzaki GR 169 F6
Mouzaki GR 174 D4
Mouzay F 19 F11
Mouzon F 19 E11
Moviken S 103 C12
Movila RO 155 D1
Movila Miresii RO 155 C1
Movileni RO 153 C10
Movileni RO 153 F10
Movileni RO 160 E5
Movilița RO 153 F10
Movilița RO 161 D8
Moville IRL 4 E2
Movollen N 105 F11
Mowtie GB 5 B12
Moy GB 3 L8
Moy GB 7 D9
Moya E 47 E10
Moyard IRL 6 E2
Moyasta IRL 8 C3
Moycullen IRL 6 F4
Moy-de-l'Aisne F 19 E7
Moyenmoutier F 27 D6
Moyenneville F 18 D4
Moygashel GB 7 D9
Moyivka UA 154 A2
Möykkylänperä FIN 119 E13
Möykkyylänperä FIN 119 F17
Moylaw IRL 6 D4
Moylett IRL 7 E8
Moylough IRL 6 F5
Moymore IRL 8 C5
Moyne IRL 7 E7
Moyvalley IRL 7 F9
Moyvore IRL 7 E7
Mozac F 30 D3
Mozăceni RO 160 D6
Mozárbez E 45 C9
Mozelj SLO 73 E10
Mozelos P 44 C5
Mozgovo SRB 159 F8
Mozirje SLO 73 D10
Mozoncillo E 46 B4
Mozsgó H 149 D9
Mozyr' RUS 136 E3
Mračaj BIH 157 E7
Mrągowo PL 136 F3
Mrákov CZ 76 D3
Mrakovica BIH 157 B6
Mramor BIH 157 F8
Mramorak SRB 159 D6
Mratinje MNE 157 F10
Mrčajevci SRB 158 F6
Mrežičko NMK 169 B6
Mrkalji BIH 157 D10
Mrkonjić-Grad BIH 157 D7
Mrkopalj HR 67 B10
Mrmoš SRB 164 B3
Mrocza PL 85 D13
Mroczeń PL 142 D4
Mroczków PL 141 H3
Mroczno PL 139 D8
Mrozy PL 141 F5
Mścice PL 85 B10
Mściwojów PL 81 D10
Mšené Lázně CZ 76 B6
Mšeno CZ 77 B7
Mshinskaya RUS 132 C6
Mstów PL 143 E7
Mszana PL 147 B7
Mszana Dolna PL 144 D1
Mszczonów PL 141 G3
Muccia I 62 A4
Much D 21 C8
Muchalls GB 5 A12
Mucharz PL 147 B9
Mücheln (Geiseltal) D 79 D10
Muchow D 83 D11
Muchówka PL 144 D1
Much Wenlock GB 10 F6
Mucientes E 39 E10
Mücka D 81 D7
Mücke-Große-Eichen D 21 C12
Mücke-Nieder-Ohmen D
21 C12
Muckross IRL 8 D4
Múcsony H 145 G2
Mudanya TR 173 D10
Mudau D 187 B7
Müdelheim D 183 C9
Müden (Aller) D 79 A7
Müden (Örtze) D 83 E8
Mudersbach D 185 C8
Müdrets BG 166 E6
Muel E 41 F9
Muelas del Pan E 39 E8
Muff IRL 4 E2
Muga de Sayago E 39 F7
Mugardos E 38 B3
Muge P 44 F3
Mügeln D 80 C4
Mügeln D 80 D4
Mugeni RO 152 E6
Muggensturm D 187 D5
Muggia I 73 E8
Muğla TR 181 B8
Müglen BG 167 D8
Müglizh BG 166 D5
Mugron F 32 C4
Mühlacker D 27 C10
Mühlanger D 79 C12
Mühlbachl A 72 B3
Mühlberg D 79 E8
Mühlberg D 80 D4
Mühldorf A 73 C7
Mühldorf am Inn D 75 F12
Mühldorf bei Feldbach A 148 C5
Mühlen A 73 B10
Mühlenbeck D 84 E4
Mühlhausen D 21 F11
Mühlhausen D 75 D9
Mühlhausen (Thüringen)
D 79 D7
Mühltroff D 75 A10
Muhola FIN 123 D14
Muhos FIN 119 E15
Muhr am See D 75 D8
Muhur AL 163 F9
Muineachán IRL 7 D9
Muine Bheag IRL 9 C9
Muiños E 38 E4
Muirdrum GB 5 B11
Muirhead GB 5 C10
Muirkirk GB 5 D8
Muir of Ord GB 2 K8
Muizon F 19 F8
Mujdić BIH 157 D7
Mujejärvi FIN 125 C12
Mukacheve UA 145 G6
Mukařov CZ 77 C7
Mukhavyets BY 141 F9
Mukhovo BG 165 E8
Mukkala FIN 115 D5
Mukkavaara FIN 115 D4
Mula E 55 C10
Mulbarton GB 15 B11
Muleby DK 88 E7
Mulešići BIH 157 C9
Mulfingen D 74 D6
Mülheim an der Ruhr D 17 F7
Mülheim-Kärlich D 185 D7
Mulhouse F 27 E7
Muljava SLO 73 E10
Mullach Íde IRL 7 F10
Mullagh IRL 7 E9
Mullagh IRL 7 F9
Mullaghroe IRL 6 E6
Mullany's Cross IRL 6 D5
Mullartown GB 7 D11
Müllheim D 27 E8
Mullhyttan S 92 A5
Mullingar IRL 7 E8
Mullion GB 12 E4
Müllrose D 80 B6
Mullsjö S 91 D14
Mulrany IRL 6 E3
Mulsanne F 23 E12
Mulseryd S 91 D14
Multia FIN 123 F13
Multiperä FIN 121 C15
Mümliswil CH 27 F8
Munakka FIN 122 E9
Muñana E 45 C10
Munapirtti FIN 128 E6
Münchberg D 75 B10
Müncheberg D 80 A6
München D 75 F10
Münchenbernsdorf D 79 E10
Münchenbuchsee CH 31 A11
Münchhausen D 21 C11
Münchsteinach D 75 C8
Münchweiler an der Rodalb
D 186 C4
Münchwilen CH 27 F11
Mundaka E 41 B6
Munderkingen D 187 E8
Mundesley GB 15 B11
Mundford GB 15 B10
Mundheim N 94 B3
Mundolsheim F 27 C8
Munebrega E 41 F8
Munera E 55 A8

Mungia E 40 B6
Mungret IRL 8 C5
Muñico E 45 C10
Muniesa E 42 E2
Munilla E 41 D7
Munka-Ljungby S 87 C11
Munkbyn S 103 B11
Munkebakken N 114 D6
Munkebo DK 86 E7
Munkedal S 91 C10
Munken N 104 D6
Munkflohögen S 106 D7
Munkfors S 97 C10
Munklia N 111 D14
Munksund S 118 D7
Munktorp S 98 C6
Munkzwalm B 19 C8
Munne FIN 128 C7
Münnerstadt D 75 B7
Munningen D 75 E8
Muñogalindo E 46 C3
Munsala FIN 122 D8
Münsingen CH 31 B12
Münsingen D 74 F5
Münster A 72 B4
Münster CH 70 E6
Münster D 17 E9
Münster D 21 E11
Münster D 83 E8
Munster F 27 D7
Münsterdorf D 82 C7
Munstergeleen NL 183 D7
Münsterhausen D 75 F7
Münstermaifeld D 185 D7
Muntendam NL 17 B7
Munteni RO 153 F10
Munteni-Buzău RO 161 D9
Muntenii de Jos RO 153 D11
Münzenberg D 21 D11
Münzkirchen A 76 F5
Muodoslompolo S 117 C10
Muonio FIN 117 C11
Muonionalusta S 117 C11
Muotathal CH 71 D7
Muotkajärvi FIN 117 B10
Muotkavaara FIN 117 C12
Mur SRB 163 C9
Muradiye TR 173 D9
Muradiye TR 177 B9
Murakeresztúr H 149 D7
Muráň SK 147 D10
Muras E 38 B4
Murasson F 34 C4
Muraste EST 131 C8
Muraszemenye H 149 D7
Murat F 30 E2
Muratlar TR 181 B9
Muratli TR 173 B7
Murato F 37 F10
Murat-sur-Vèbre F 34 C4
Murau A 73 B9
Muravera I 64 E4
Murazzano I 37 C8
Murça P 38 F5
Murchante E 41 D8
Mŭrchevo BG 165 B7
Murchin D 84 C5
Murcia E 56 F2
Murczyn PL 138 E4
Mur-de-Barrez F 29 F11
Mûr-de-Bretagne F 22 D6
Mur-de-Sologne F 24 F6
Mureck A 148 C5
Mürefte TR 173 C7
Muret F 33 D8
Murgeni RO 153 E12
Murgenthal CH 27 F8
Murgești RO 161 C9
Murgia E 40 C6
Muri CH 27 F9
Muri CH 31 B11
Murias de Paredes E 39 C7
Muriedas E 40 B4
Murighiol RO 155 C4
Murillo de Río Leza E 32 F1
Murillo el Fruto E 32 F3
Murino MNE 163 D8
Murisengo I 68 C5
Murjāņi LV 135 B9
Murjek S 116 F5
Murley GB 7 D8
Murlo I 66 F3
Murmastiene LV 135 C13
Murnau am Staffelsee D 72 A3
Muro E 57 B11
Muro F 37 F9
Muro P 38 F2
Muro de Alcoy E 56 D4
Murol F 30 D2
Murole FIN 127 B10
Muro Lucano I 60 B4
Muron F 28 C4
Murony H 151 D7
Muros E 38 C1
Muros E 39 A7
Muros I 64 B2
Murovane UA 144 C9
Murów PL 142 E4
Murowana Goślina PL 81 A12
Murrë AL 168 A3
Murrhardt D 74 E6
Murronkylä FIN 119 E16
Murroogh IRL 6 F4
Mursalli TR 177 D10
Mûrs-Erigné F 23 F10
Murska Sobota SLO 148 C6
Mursko Središće HR 149 C6
Murtas E 55 F6
Murtede P 44 D4
Murten CH 31 B11
Murter HR 156 E4
Murtino NMK 169 B8
Murto FIN 119 E15
Murtolahti FIN 125 D9
Murtomäki FIN 124 B9
Murtovaara FIN 121 C13
Murumoen N 105 C16
Murvica HR 156 D3
Murviel-lès-Béziers F 34 D5
Mürzsteg A 148 A5
Murzynowo PL 81 A8
Mürzzuschlag A 148 A5
Muša LV 135 D8
Musbury GB 13 D8
Müschenbach D 185 C8
Musei I 64 E2
Muselievo BG 160 F5
Mushtisht RKS 163 E10
Musile di Piave I 72 E6
Muskö S 93 B12
Mussalo FIN 128 E6
Musselburgh GB 5 D10
Musselkanaal NL 17 C8
Mussidan F 29 E6
Mussomeli I 58 D4
Musson B 19 E12
Mussy-sur-Seine F 25 E12
Mustafakemalpaşa TR 173 D9
Müstair CH 71 D10
Mustamaa FIN 119 F17
Mustamaa FIN 123 D10
Mustasaari FIN 122 D7
Mustavaara FIN 121 D12
Mustavaara FIN 121 F12
Mustinlahti FIN 125 E10
Mustjala EST 130 E4
Mustla EST 131 E11
Mustola FIN 114 F4
Mustolanmäki FIN 125 C10
Mustolanmutka FIN 125 B10
Mustvee EST 131 D13
Muszaki PL 139 D10
Muszyna PL 145 E2
Muta SLO 73 C11
Mutala FIN 127 B10
Mutalahti FIN 125 F16
Mütevelli TR 177 B10
Muthill GB 5 C9
Mutilva Baja E 32 E2
Mutné SK 147 C8
Mutriku E 32 D1
Mutterstadt D 21 F10
Mutxamel E 56 E4
Mutzig F 27 C7
Mutzschen D 80 D3
Muuga EST 131 C13
Muukajärvi S 116 E10
Muuksi EST 131 B11
Muurame FIN 123 F15
Muurasjärvi FIN 123 C14
Muurikkala FIN 128 D8
Muurla FIN 127 E9
Muurola FIN 119 B14
Muurola FIN 128 D8
Muuruvesi FIN 125 D10
Muxía E 38 B1
Muzillac F 22 E7
Mužla SK 149 A11
Myahuny BY 137 C14
Myakishevo RUS 133 C5
Myaretskiya BY 133 F3
Myazhany BY 135 E13
Mybster GB 3 J10
Myckelgensjö S 107 D13
Myckle S 118 E5
Myedna BY 141 G9
Myggenäs S 91 C10
Myggsjö S 102 C8
Myhinpää FIN 124 F7
Myjava SK 146 D5
Mykanów PL 143 E7
Mykhal'cha UA 153 A7
Mykhaylivka UA 154 F5
Myki GR 171 B7
Myklebostad N 110 E9
Mykolayiv UA 145 D8
Mykolayivka UA 154 E4
Mykolayivka-Novorosiys'ka
UA 154 E5
Mykonos GR 176 E5
Mykulychyn UA 152 A5
Mykytychi UA 144 B9
Myllykoski FIN 128 D6
Myllykylä FIN 122 E8
Myllykylä FIN 127 E10
Myllykylä FIN 128 D7
Myllylahti FIN 121 D13
Myllymäki FIN 123 E12
Myloi GR 175 D6
Mylopotamos GR 178 C4
Mynämäki FIN 126 D7
Mynttilä FIN 128 C6
Myon F 31 A8
Myory BY 133 E3
Myra GR 169 F8
Myrås S 109 E14
Myre N 110 C9
Myre N 111 B10
Myresjö S 92 E5
Myrhaug N 101 A14
Myrheden S 118 D4
Myrhult S 92 B4
Myrina GR 171 E8
Myriokefala GR 178 E7
Myrkky FIN 122 F7
Myrland N 110 D5
Myrland N 110 D9
Myrland N 111 C10
Myrlandshaugen N 111 C13
Myrmoen N 101 A15
Myrne UA 155 B4
Myrnes N 112 C9
Myrnopillya UA 154 E4
Myrsini GR 174 D3
Myrsini GR 178 B3
Myrskylä FIN 127 D14
Myrties GR 177 F8
Myrtos GR 179 E10
Myrviken S 105 E16
Mysen N 95 C14
Myshall IRL 9 C9
Myślachowice PL 143 F7
Mysłakowice PL 81 E9
Myślenice PL 147 B9
Myślibórz PL 85 E7
Myślice PL 139 C8
Mysłowice PL 143 F7
Mysovka RUS 134 F2
Myssjö S 102 A7
Mystegna GR 177 A7
Mystras GR 174 E5
Myszków PL 143 E7
Myszyniec PL 139 D11
Mytikas GR 174 B2
Mytilini GR 177 A8
Mytilinioi GR 177 D8
Mýtina SK 147 E9
Mýto CZ 76 C5

N

Nå N 94 B5
Naaldwijk NL 16 E2
Naamankylä FIN 119 E17
Naamijoki FIN 117 E11
Naantali FIN 126 E7
Naapurinvaara FIN 121 F11
Naarden NL 183 A6
Näärinki FIN 128 B8
Naarn im Machlande A 77 F7
Naartijärvi S 119 C11
Naarva FIN 125 D16
Naas IRL 7 F9
Näätämö FIN 114 D6
Näätänmaa FIN 125 F10
Näätävaara FIN 121 E13
Nabburg D 75 D11
Nábrád H 145 G5
Na Cealla Beaga IRL 6 C6
Načeradec CZ 77 C7
Nacha BY 137 E10
Náchod CZ 77 B10
Nacina Ves SK 145 F4
Näckådalen S 102 D7
Nackel D 83 E13
Nackenheim D 185 E9
Näcksjö S 103 C12
Na Clocha Liathe IRL 7 F10
Nacpolsk PL 139 E9
Nad IRL 8 D5
Nadalj SRB 158 C4
Nadarzyce PL 85 D11
Nadarzyn PL 141 F3
Naddvik N 100 D7
Nadeş RO 152 E5
Nădlac RO 150 E6
Nădrag RO 159 B9
Nadrichne UA 154 E4
Nádudvar H 151 C7
Năeni RO 161 C8
Nærbø N 94 E3
Næroset N 101 E13
Nærsnes N 95 C13
Næsbjerg DK 86 D3
Næstved DK 87 E9
Näfels CH 27 F11
Nafferton GB 11 C11
Nafpaktos GR 174 C4
Nafplio GR 175 D6
Nagele NL 16 C5
Naggen S 103 B11
Naglarby S 97 B14
Na Gleannta IRL 6 C6
Nagli LV 133 C1
Nagłowice PL 143 E9
Nagold D 27 C10
Nagore E 32 E3
Nago-Torbole I 69 B10
Nagu FIN 126 E6
Nagyatád H 149 D8
Nagybajom H 149 D9
Nagybánhegyes H 151 E6
Nagybaracska H 149 D11
Nagybarca H 145 G2
Nagyberény H 149 C10
Nagyberki H 149 D10
Nagycenk H 149 A7
Nagycsécs H 145 H2
Nagycserkesz H 145 H4
Nagydobos H 145 G5
Nagydorog H 149 C11
Nagyecsed H 145 H5
Nagyfüged H 150 B5
Nagyhalász H 145 G4
Nagyharsány H 149 E10
Nagyhegyes H 151 B7
Nagyigmánd H 149 A10
Nagyiván H 151 C6
Nagykálló H 145 H4
Nagykanizsa H 149 D7
Nagykapornak H 149 C7
Nagykáta H 150 C4
Nagykereki H 151 C8
Nagykónyi H 149 C10
Nagykőrös H 150 C4
Nagykörű H 150 C5
Nagykovácsi H 149 A11
Nagylak H 150 E6
Nagylóc H 147 E9
Nagylók H 149 C11
Nagylózs H 149 A7
Nagymágocs H 150 D5
Nagymaros H 149 A11
Nagynyárád H 149 E11
Nagyoroszi H 147 F8
Nagyrécse H 149 C8
Nagyréde H 150 B4
Nagyszénás H 150 D6
Nagyszokoly H 149 C10
Nagytarcsa H 150 B3
Nagytőke H 150 D5
Nagyvarsány H 145 G5
Nagyvázsony H 149 C9
Nagyvisnyó H 145 G1
Naha EST 132 E1
Naharros E 47 D8
Nahe D 83 C8
Nahirne UA 155 C2
Nahrendorf D 83 D9
Naidăş RO 159 D8
Naila D 75 B10
Nailloux F 33 D9
Nailsworth GB 13 B10
Naimakka S 116 A7
Naintré F 29 B6
Naipköy TR 173 C7
Nairn GB 3 K9
Naives-Rosières F 26 C3
Naizin F 22 E6
Najac F 33 B9
Nájera E 40 D6
Näkkälä FIN 117 A11
Nakkerud N 95 B12
Nakkila FIN 126 C7
Náklo CZ 77 C12
Nakło PL 143 E8
Naklo SLO 73 D9
Nakło nad Notecią PL 85 D13
Nakomiady PL 136 E3
Nākotne LV 134 C6
Nakovo SRB 150 F6
Nakskov DK 83 A10
Nalbach D 186 C2
Nalbant RO 155 C3
Nalda E 41 D7
Nälden S 105 E16
Nałęczów PL 141 H6
Nálepkovo SK 145 F2
Näljänkä FIN 121 D11
Nalkki FIN 121 E10
Nalliers F 28 C3
Nalžovské Hory CZ 76 D5
Namborn D 21 E8
Nambroca E 46 E5
Namdalseid N 105 C10
Náměšť nad Oslavou CZ 77 D10
Náměšť na Hané CZ 77 C12
Námestovo SK 147 C8
Nämpnäs FIN 122 E6
Namsos N 105 C11
Namsskogan N 105 B14
Namsvatn N 105 B15
Namur B 19 D10
Namysłów PL 142 D4
Nana RO 161 E9
Nána SK 147 F7
Nançay F 24 F7
Nanclares de la Oca E 40 C6
Nancy F 26 C5
Nandrin B 183 D6
Nănești RO 161 B10
Nangis F 25 C9
Nannestad N 95 B13
Nanov RO 160 F6
Nans-les-Pins F 35 D10
Nant F 34 B5
Nanterre F 25 C7
Nantes F 23 F8
Nanteuil-le-Haudouin F 25 B8
Nantiat F 29 C8
Nantua F 31 C8
Nantwich GB 10 E6
Naousa GR 169 C7
Naousa GR 176 E5
Napajedla CZ 146 C5
Napiwoda PL 139 D9
Napkor H 145 H4
Napola I 58 D2
Napoli I 60 B2
Napp N 110 D5
Năpradea RO 151 C11
Náquera E 48 E4
När S 93 E13
Nåra N 100 D1
Nárai H 149 B7
Narberth GB 12 B5
Narbolia I 64 C2
Narbonne F 34 D5
Narbonne-Plage F 34 D5
Narborough GB 15 B10
Narbuvoll N 101 B14
Narcao I 64 E2
Narcy F 25 F9
Nardò I 61 C10
Narechenski Bani BG 165 F10
Narew PL 140 E9
Narewka PL 141 E9
Närhilä FIN 123 E16
Narin IRL 6 C6
Nārinciems LV 134 B5
Narkaus FIN 119 B16
Narken S 116 E9
Narlidere TR 177 C9
Narni I 62 B3
Naro I 58 E4
Narol PL 144 C7
Närpes FIN 122 F6
Narrosse F 32 C3
Narta HR 149 E7
Nartë AL 168 D1
Năruja RO 153 F9
Naruska FIN 115 D6
Naruszewo PL 139 E9
Narva EST 132 C3
Narva FIN 127 C10
Narva-Jõesuu EST 132 C3
Närvijoki FIN 122 E7
Narvik N 111 D13
Narzole I 37 B7
Narzym PL 139 D9
Näs FIN 99 B14
Näs N 90 A5
Näs S 93 E12
Näs S 97 B12
Näs S 102 A8
Näsåker S 107 E11
Năsăud RO 152 C4
Nasavrky CZ 77 C9
Näsberg S 103 C10
Nasbinals F 34 A5
Näs bruk S 98 B6
Näsby S 89 C10
Na Sceirí IRL 7 E10
Näset S 103 D9
Nashec RKS 163 E10
Našice HR 149 F10
Nasielsk PL 139 E10
Näske S 107 E15
Näsliden S 107 A16
Naso I 59 C6
Nassau D 21 D9
Nassereith A 71 C11
Nässja S 92 C5
Nässjö S 92 D5
Nässjö S 107 D10
Nassogne B 19 D11
Nästansjö S 107 B11
Nastätten D 185 D8
Nästeln S 102 A7
Nastola FIN 127 D14
Năsturelu RO 161 F6
Näsum S 88 C7
Nasutów PL 141 H6
Näsviken S 103 C12
Näsviken S 106 D9
Naszály H 149 A10
Natalinci SRB 159 E6
Nateby GB 11 C7
Naters CH 68 A4
Nattavaara S 116 E5
Nattavaara by S 116 E6
Nattheim D 75 E7
Nättraby S 89 C9
Naturno I 71 D11
Naucelle F 33 B10
Naucelles F 29 F10
Naudaskalns LV 133 B2
Nauders A 71 D11
Naudīte LV 134 C6
Nauen D 79 A12
Nauendorf D 79 C10
Nauheim D 21 E10
Naujac-sur-Mer F 28 E3
Naujamiestis LT 135 E8
Naujasodis Daugėliškis LT 135 F12
Naujoji Akmenė LT 134 D5
Naujoji Vilnia LT 137 D11
Naukšēni LV 131 F10
Naul IRL 7 E10
Naulaperä FIN 121 E10
Naulavaara FIN 125 C10
Naumburg (Hessen) D 17 F12
Naumburg (Saale) D 79 D10
Naundorf D 80 D3
Naundorf D 80 E4
Naunhof D 79 D12
Nauroth D 21 C9
Naurstad N 108 B8
Naustbukta N 105 B11
Naustdal N 100 C3
Nauste N 101 A8
Nautijaur S 109 C17
Nautsi RUS 114 E6
Nautsund N 100 D2
Nava E 39 B9
Navacepeda de Tormes
E 45 D10
Navaconcejo E 45 D9
Nava de Arévalo E 46 C3
Nava de la Asunción E 46 B4
Nava del Rey E 39 F9
Nava de Sotrobal E 45 C10
Navadrutsk BY 133 F2
Navafría E 46 B5
Navahermosa E 46 E4
Navajas E 48 E4
Naval E 42 C4
Navalagamella E 46 D4
Navalcaballo E 41 E6
Navalcán E 45 D10
Navalcarnero E 46 D4
Navalero E 40 E6
Navalmanzano E 46 B4
Navalmoral E 46 D3
Navalmoral de la Mata E 45 E9
Navalonguilla E 45 D10
Navalosa E 46 D3
Navalperal de Pinares E 46 C4
Navalpino E 46 F3
Navaluenga E 46 D3
Navalvillar de Ibor E 45 E10
Navalvillar de Pela E 45 F10
Navamorcuende E 46 D3
Navan IRL 7 E9
Navapolatsk BY 133 E5
Navarcles E 43 D7
Navardún E 32 E3
Navarredonda de la Rinconada
E 45 C8
Navarrenx F 32 D4
Navarrés E 48 F3
Navarrete E 41 D6
Navarrevisca E 46 D3
Navàs E 43 D7
Navascués E 32 E3
Navas de Estrena E 46 E3
Navas de Jorquera E 47 F9
Navas del Madroño E 45 E7
Navas del Rey E 46 D4
Navas de Oro E 46 B4
Navas de San Juan E 55 C6
Navasfrías E 45 D7
Navata E 43 C9
Navatalgordo E 46 D3
Nave I 69 B9
Nave P 50 E2
Nave de Haver P 45 C7
Nävekvarn S 93 B9
Navelli I 62 C5
Nåverdal N 101 A12
Näverede S 106 E8
Nave Redonda P 50 E3
Näverkärret S 97 C14
Näverrys FIN 119 C15
Naverstad S 91 B10
Navès E 43 D7
Naves F 29 E9
Navezuelas E 45 E10
Navia E 39 A6
Navilly F 31 B7
Navit N 112 D8
Năvodari RO 155 E3
Nävragöl S 89 C9
Nawojowa PL 145 D2
Naxos GR 176 E5
Nay-Bourdettes F 32 D5
Nazaré P 44 E2
Nazelles-Négron F 24 F4
Nazza D 79 D7
Ndroq AL 168 B2
Nea Agathoupoli GR 169 D8
Nea Alikarnassos GR 178 E9
Nea Anchialos GR 169 F8
Nea Apollonia GR 169 C9
Nea Artaki GR 175 B8
Nea Efesos GR 169 D7
Nea Epidavros GR 175 D7
Nea Figaleia GR 174 E4
Nea Filadelfeia GR 175 C8
Nea Fokaia GR 169 D9
Nea Ionia GR 169 F8
Nea Iraklitsa GR 171 C6
Nea Kallikrateia GR 169 D9
Nea Karvali GR 171 C6
Nea Karya GR 171 C7
Nea Kerdylia GR 169 C10
Nea Kios GR 175 D6
Nea Koroni GR 174 F4
Nea Lampsakos GR 175 C8
Neale IRL 6 E4
Nea Liosia GR 175 C8
Nea Madytos GR 169 C10
Nea Makri GR 175 C8
Nea Malgara GR 169 C8
Nea Mesimvria GR 169 C8
Nea Michaniona GR 169 D8
Nea Moudania GR 169 D9
Nea Olynthos GR 169 D9
Nea Pella GR 169 C8
Nea Peramos GR 171 C6
Nea Peramos GR 175 C7
Nea Plagia GR 169 D9
Neapoli GR 168 D5
Neapoli GR 178 B5
Neapoli GR 179 E10
Nea Poteidaia GR 169 D9
Nea Roda GR 170 D5
Nea Santa GR 169 C8
Nea Santa GR 171 B9
Nea Silata GR 169 D9
Nea Styra GR 175 C9
Neath GB 13 B7
Nea Tiryntha GR 175 D6
Nea Triglia GR 169 D9
Neaua RO 152 E5
Nea Vravrona GR 175 D9
Nea Vyssa GR 171 A11
Nea Zichni GR 169 B10
Nebel D 82 A4
Nébias F 33 E10
Nebljusi HR 156 C4
Nebra (Unstrut) D 79 D10
Nebreda E 40 E4
Nechanice CZ 77 B9
Neckarbischofsheim D 187 C6
Neckargemünd D 21 F11
Neckarsteinach D 21 F11
Neckarsulm D 21 F12
Neckartenzlingen D 27 C11
Necșești RO 160 E6
Necton GB 15 B10
Nečujam HR 156 F5
Neda E 38 B3
Nedansjö S 103 B12
Nedašov CZ 146 C6
Neddemin D 84 C4
Neded SK 146 E5
Nedelino BG 171 B8
Nedelišće HR 149 D6
Nederby DK 86 B4
Nederhögen S 102 B7
Nederhorst den Berg NL 183 A6
Neder Hvam DK 86 C4
Nederlangbroek NL 183 A6
Nedervetil FIN 123 C10
Neder Vindinge DK 87 E9
Nederweert NL 16 F5
Nedlitz D 79 B11
Nedožery-Brezany SK 147 D7
Nedrebø N 94 E4
Nedre Saxnäs S 109 F14
Nedre Soppero S 116 B7
Nedstrand N 94 D3
Nedvědice CZ 77 D10
Nedyalsko BG 167 E7
Nędza PL 142 F5
Neede NL 17 D7
Needham Market GB 15 C11
Neer NL 183 C8
Neerijnen NL 183 B6
Neermoor D 17 B8
Neeroeteren B 183 C7
Neerpelt B 19 B11
Neetze D 83 D9
Nefyn GB 10 F2
Negenborn D 78 C6
Negoi RO 160 F2
Negomir RO 159 D11
Negorci NMK 169 B7
Negoslavci HR 157 B11
Negotin SRB 159 E10
Negotino NMK 163 F10
Negotino NMK 169 B7
Negrar I 66 A2
Negrași RO 160 D6
Negredo E 47 B7
Negreira E 38 C2
Nègrepelisse F 33 B9
Negrești RO 153 D10
Negrești-Oaș RO 145 H7
Negri RO 153 D9
Negru Vodă RO 155 F2
Nehoiu RO 161 C8
Neiden N 114 D6
Neidin IRL 8 E3
Neitaskaite S 116 E8
Neitsuanto S 116 D5
Neittävä FIN 119 E17
Neive I 37 B8
Nejdek CZ 75 B12
Nekézseny H 145 G1
Nekla PL 81 B12
Neksø DK 89 E8
Nelas P 44 C5
Nellim FIN 114 F4
Nellingen D 74 E6
Nelson GB 11 D7
Nemaitonys LT 137 D9
Neman RUS 136 C5
Nemanjica NMK 164 F4
Nemanskoye RUS 136 C5
Nembro I 69 B8
Nemea GR 175 D6
Nemenčinė LT 137 D11
Nemesgulács H 149 C8
Nemesnádudvar H 150 E3
Nemesvámos H 149 B9
Nemesvid H 149 C8
Németkér H 149 C11
Nemėžis LT 137 D11
Nemours F 25 D8
Nemsdorf-Göhrendorf D 79 D10
Nemšová SK 146 D6
Nemunaitis LT 137 E9
Nemunėlio Radviliškis LT
135 D9
Nemyriv UA 144 C7
Nenagh IRL 8 C6
Nendaz CH 31 C11
Nenince SK 147 E8
Nenita GR 177 C7
Nennhausen D 79 A12
Nennslingen D 75 D9
Nenonpelto FIN 124 F8
Nentershausen D 21 D9
Nentershausen D 78 D6
Nenthead GB 5 F12
Nenzing A 71 C9
Neo Agioneri GR 169 C8
Neochoraki GR 175 C7
Neochori GR 169 B9
Neochori GR 169 F6
Neochori GR 171 B10
Neochori GR 174 A3
Neochori GR 174 C3
Neo Erasmio GR 171 C7
Neoi Epivates GR 169 C8
Neo Monastiri GR 169 F7
Neoneli I 64 C2
Neo Petritsi GR 169 B9
Neorić HR 156 E6
Neos Kafkasos GR 168 C5
Neos Marmaras GR 169 D10
Neos Mylotopos GR 169 C7
Neo Souli GR 169 B10
Neos Pagontas GR 175 B8
Neos Pyrgos GR 175 B7
Neos Skopos GR 169 B10
Néoules F 36 E4
Nepi I 62 C2
Nepomuk CZ 76 D5
Nérac F 33 B6
Neratovice CZ 77 B7
Nerău RO 150 F6
Neravai LT 137 E9
Nerchau D 79 D12
Nercillac F 28 D5
Nerdal N 101 A9
Nerde Gärdsjö S 103 E9
Néré F 28 D5
Nereju RO 153 F9
Neresheim D 75 E7
Neresnica SRB 159 E8
Neresnytsya UA 145 G8
Nereta LV 135 D10
Nereto I 62 B5
Nerezine HR 67 C9
Nerežišće HR 156 F6
Néris-les-Bains F 29 C11
Nerja E 53 C9
Nerkoo FIN 124 D8
Nerlia N 108 E7
Nerokouros GR 178 E7
Néronde F 30 D5
Nérondes F 30 B2
Neroth D 21 D7
Nerpio E 55 C8
Nersac F 28 D6
Nersingen D 75 F7
Nerskogen N 101 A11
Nerushay UA 155 B5
Nerva E 51 D6
Nervesa della Battaglia I 72 E5
Nervieux F 30 D5
Nes FO 2 A3
Nes N 95 D9
Nes N 96 A2
Nes N 110 D9
Nes N 111 D10
Nes NL 16 B5
Nesbyen N 101 E10
Neschwitz D 80 D6
Nesebŭr BG 167 D9
Neset N 112 C7
Nes Flaten N 94 C5
Nesgrenda N 90 B4
Nesheim N 94 D3
Nesje N 110 D6
Nesjegjerde N 100 A6
Nesland N 110 D5
Neslandsvatn N 90 B5
Nesle F 18 E6
Nesna N 108 D5
Nesovice CZ 77 D12
Nessa F 37 F9
Nesse D 17 A8
Nesseby N 114 C6
Nesselwang D 71 B11
Nesslau CH 27 F11
Nessodtangen N 95 C13
Nestani GR 175 D5
Nestby N 108 B9
Nesterov RUS 136 D6
Neston GB 10 E5
Nestorio GR 168 D5
Nestoyita UA 154 B4
Nesttun N 94 B2
Nesvady SK 146 F6
Nesvatnstemmen N 90 B3
Nesvik N 94 D4
Nethy Bridge GB 3 L9
Netolice CZ 76 D6
Netphen D 21 C10
Netra (Ringgau) D 79 D7
Netretić HR 148 E4
Netstal CH 71 C8
Nettancourt F 25 C12
Nettersheim D 21 D7
Nettetal D 16 F6
Nettuno I 62 E3
Netvořice CZ 77 C7
Neu-Anspach D 21 D11
Neuberend D 82 A7
Neuberg an der Mürz A 148 A5
Neubeuern D 72 A5
Neubiberg D 75 F10
Neubrandenburg D 84 C4
Neubruchhausen D 17 C11
Neubrunn D 187 B8
Neubukow D 83 B11
Neubulach D 27 C10
Neuburg am Rhein D 187 D5
Neuburg an der Donau D 75 E9
Neuburg-Steinhausen D 83 C11
Neuburxdorf D 80 D4
Neuchâtel CH 31 B10
Neu Darchau D 83 D9
Neudietendorf D 79 E8
Neudorf A 146 F2
Neudrossenfeld D 75 B10
Neuenbürg D 27 C10
Neuendettelsau D 75 D8
Neuenhagen Berlin D 80 A5
Neuenhaus D 17 D7
Neuenhof CH 27 F9
Neuenkirch CH 27 F9
Neuenkirchen D 17 A11
Neuenkirchen D 17 C11
Neuenkirchen D 17 D8
Neuenkirchen D 17 D9
Neuenkirchen D 82 B6
Neuenkirchen D 82 D7
Neuenkirchen D 84 A4
Neuenkirchen D 84 B4
Neuenkirchen (Oldenburg)
D 17 C10
Neuenkirchen-Seelscheid
D 21 C8
Neuenrade D 185 B8
Neuenstadt am Kocher D
27 B11
Neuenstein D 187 C8
Neuenwalde D 17 A11
Neuerburg D 20 D6
Neufahrn bei Freising D 75 F10
Neufahrn in Niederbayern
D 75 E11
Neufchâteau B 19 E11
Neufchâteau F 26 D4
Neufchâtel-en-Bray F 18 E3
Neufchâtel-Hardelot F 15 F12
Neufchâtel-sur-Aisne F 19 F9
Neufeld D 17 A12
Neufeld an der Leitha A 77 G10
Neuffen D 27 C11
Neufmanil F 184 E2
Neufra D 27 D11
Neugersdorf D 81 E7
Neuharlingersiel D 17 A9
Neuhaus A 73 A11
Neuhaus A 73 C10
Neuhaus (Oste) D 17 A12
Neuhaus am Inn D 76 F4
Neuhaus am Klausenbach
A 148 C6
Neuhaus am Rennweg D 75 A9
Neuhaus an der Pegnitz
D 75 C10
Neuhausen CH 27 E10
Neuhausen D 80 E4
Neuhausen D 187 D6
Neuhausen ob Eck D 27 E10
Neuhof D 74 B6
Neuhof an der Zenn D 75 D8
Neuhofen D 187 C5
Neuhofen an der Krems A 76 F6
Neuillé-Pont-Pierre F 24 E4
Neuilly F 25 F10
Neuilly-en-Thelle F 18 F5
Neuilly-le-Réal F 30 C3
Neuilly-l'Évêque F 26 E3
Neuilly-St-Front F 25 B9
Neu-Isenburg D 187 A6
Neukalen D 83 C13
Neu Kaliß D 83 D10
Neukirch D 80 D6
Neukirchen D 21 C12
Neukirchen D 80 E3
Neukirchen D 83 B10
Neukirchen D 86 F3
Neukirchen am Großvenediger
A 72 B5
Neukirchen an der Enknach
A 76 F4
Neukirchen an der Vöckla
A 76 F5
Neukirchen-Balbini D 75 D11
Neukirchen beim Heiligen Blut
D 76 D3
Neukirchen vorm Wald D 76 E4
Neukloster D 83 C11

Neulengbach A 77 F9
Neuler D 75 E7
Neulewin D 84 E6
Neulikko FIN 121 E10
Neulise F 30 D5
Neu Lübbenau D 80 B5
Neum BIH 162 D4
Neumagen D 185 E6
Neumark D 79 E11
Neumarkt am Wallersee A 73 A7
Neumarkt im Mühlkreis A 77 F6
Neumarkt in der Oberpfalz D 75 D9
Neumarkt in Steiermark A 73 B9
Neumarkt-Sankt Veit D 75 F12
Neu Mukran D 84 B5
Neumünster D 83 B7
Neunburg vorm Wald D 75 D11
Neundorf D 75 A11
Neung-sur-Beuvron F 24 E6
Neunkirch CH 27 E10
Neunkirchen A 148 A6
Neunkirchen D 21 C10
Neunkirchen D 21 F8
Neunkirchen am Brand D 75 C9
Neunkirchen am Sand D 75 C9
Neuötting D 75 F12
Neupetershain D 80 C6
Neupölla A 77 E8
Neureichenau D 76 E5
Neuruppin D 83 E13
Neuschönau D 76 E4
Neusiedl am See A 77 G11
Neusorg D 75 C10
Neuss D 21 B7
Neussargues-Moissac F 30 E2
Neustadt D 27 E9
Neustadt D 79 E10
Neustadt D 83 E12
Neustadt (Harz) D 79 C8
Neustadt (Hessen) D 21 C12
Neustadt (Wied) D 21 C8
Neustadt am Kulm D 75 C10
Neustadt am Rübenberge D 78 A5
Neustadt an der Aisch D 75 C8
Neustadt an der Donau D 75 E10
Neustadt an der Waldnaab D 75 C11
Neustadt an der Weinstraße D 21 F10
Neustadt bei Coburg D 75 B9
Neustadt-Glewe D 83 D11
Neustadt in Holstein D 83 B9
Neustadt in Sachsen D 80 D6
Neustift im Stubaital A 72 B3
Neustrelitz D 84 D4
Neutraubling D 75 E11
Neutrebbin D 80 A6
Neu-Ulm D 74 F7
Neuvéglise F 30 F2
Neuves-Maisons F 186 D1
Neuvic F 29 E6
Neuvic F 29 E10
Neuville-aux-Bois F 24 D7
Neuville-de-Poitou F 29 B6
Neuville-les-Dames F 31 C7
Neuville-lès-Dieppe F 18 E3
Neuville-sur-Saône F 30 D6
Neuvilly-en-Argonne F 26 B3
Neuvy-Grandchamp F 30 B4
Neuvy-le-Roi F 24 E4
Neuvy-Pailloux F 29 B9
Neuvy-St-Sépulchre F 29 B9
Neuvy-sur-Barangeon F 25 F7
Neuweiler D 27 C10
Neuwied D 21 D8
Neuwittenbek D 83 B8
Neu Wulmstorf D 83 D7
Neu Zauche D 80 C6
Neuzelle D 81 B7
Neu Zittau D 80 B5
Névache F 31 E10
Nevarėnai LT 134 D4
Neveja LV 130 F4
Neveklov CZ 77 C7
Nevel' RUS 133 D7
Nevele B 19 B8
Neverfjord N 113 C12
Nevernes N 108 F4
Neverness N 110 C9
Neveronys LT 137 D9
Nevers F 30 A3
Nevesinje BIH 157 F9
Nevestino BG 165 E6
Névez F 22 E4
Neviano I 61 C10
Néville F 18 E2
Nevlunghavn N 90 B6
Nevsha BG 167 C8
New Abbey GB 5 F9
New Aberdour GB 3 K12
New Alresford GB 13 C12
Newark-on-Trent GB 11 E10
Newbawn IRL 9 D9
Newbiggin-by-the-Sea GB 5 E13
Newbliss IRL 7 D8
Newborough GB 11 F11
Newbridge GB 13 B8
Newbridge IRL 7 F9
New Buildings GB 4 F2
Newburgh GB 3 L12
Newburgh GB 5 C10
Newbury GB 13 C12
Newby Bridge GB 10 C6
Newcastle GB 7 D11
Newcastle GB 13 A8
Newcastle IRL 7 F10
Newcastle IRL 7 F10
Newcastle Emlyn GB 12 A6
Newcastleton GB 5 E11
Newcastle-under-Lyme GB 11 E7
Newcastle upon Tyne GB 5 F13
Newcastle West IRL 8 D4
New Cumnock GB 5 E8
New Deer GB 3 K12
Newel D 21 E7
Newent GB 13 B10
New Galloway GB 5 E8
New Inn IRL 6 F6
New Inn IRL 7 E8
Newinn IRL 9 D7
New Kildimo IRL 8 C5
Newmarket GB 2 J4
Newmarket GB 15 C9
Newmarket IRL 8 D4
Newmarket IRL 9 D8
Newmarket-on-Fergus IRL 8 C5
Newmill GB 3 K11
New Milton GB 13 D11
Newnham GB 13 B10
New Pitsligo GB 3 K12
Newport GB 3 J10
Newport GB 11 F7
Newport GB 12 A5
Newport GB 13 B9
Newport GB 13 D12
Newport GB 15 D9
Newport IRL 6 E3
Newport IRL 8 C6
Newport-on-Tay GB 5 C11
Newport Pagnell GB 15 C7
Newport Trench GB 4 F3
New Quay GB 12 A6
Newquay GB 12 E4
New Radnor GB 13 A8
New Romney GB 15 F10
New Ross IRL 9 D9
Newry GB 7 D10
Newton GB 4 C6
Newton GB 10 D7
Newton Abbot GB 13 D7
Newton Aycliffe GB 5 F13
Newton Ferrers GB 12 E6
Newtonhill GB 5 A12
Newton-le-Willows GB 10 E6
Newton Mearns GB 5 D8
Newtonmore GB 5 A8
Newton Stewart GB 4 F8
Newtown GB 10 F5
Newtown GB 13 A9
Newtown IRL 6 F6
Newtown IRL 8 D5
Newtown IRL 8 D6
Newtown IRL 9 C8
Newtownabbey GB 4 F5
Newtownards GB 7 C11
Newtownbarry IRL 9 C9
Newtownbutler GB 7 D8
Newtown Crommelin GB 4 F4
Newtown Forbes IRL 7 E7
Newtown Mount Kennedy IRL 7 F10
Newtown St Boswells GB 5 D11
Newtownstewart GB 4 F2
Nexon F 29 D8
Neyland GB 12 B5
Nezamyslice CZ 77 D12
Nezavertailovca MD 154 D5
Nézsa H 147 F8
Nezvěstice CZ 76 C5
Nianfors S 103 C12
Niata GR 175 F6
Nibbiano I 37 B10
Nibe DK 86 B5
Nīca LV 134 D2
Nicastro I 59 B9
Nice F 37 D6
Nīcgale LV 135 D12
Nichelino I 37 A7
Nickelsdorf A 77 G12
Nicolae Bălcescu RO 153 B9
Nicolae Bălcescu RO 153 E9
Nicolae Bălcescu RO 155 D3
Nicolae Bălcescu RO 155 E2
Nicolae Bălcescu RO 160 D4
Nicolae Bălcescu RO 161 E9
Nicolae Titulescu RO 160 E5
Nicolaevca MD 154 B2
Nicolosi I 59 D7
Nicoreni MD 153 B11
Nicorești RO 153 F10
Nicosia I 58 D5
Nicotera I 59 B8
Nicșeni RO 153 B9
Niculești RO 161 D7
Niculițel RO 155 C2
Nida LT 134 F1
Nidau CH 27 F7
Nidda D 21 D12
Nidzica PL 139 D9
Niebla E 51 E6
Nieborów PL 141 F2
Niebüll D 82 A5
Niebylec PL 144 D4
Niechanowo PL 138 F4
Niechcice PL 143 D8
Niechłonin PL 139 D9
Niechlów PL 81 C10
Niechorze PL 85 B8
Niederaichbach D 75 E11
Niederanven L 20 E6
Niederau D 80 D5
Niederaula D 78 E6
Niederbipp CH 27 F8
Niederbrechen D 21 D10
Niederbreitbach D 185 C7
Niederbronn-les-Bains F 27 C8
Niederfinow D 84 E5
Niederfischbach D 185 C8
Niedergörsdorf D 80 C3
Niederkassel D 21 C8
Niederkirchen D 21 E9
Niederkrüchten D 20 B6
Niederndorf A 72 A5
Niederneisen D 21 D10
Niedernhall D 74 D6
Niedernhausen D 21 D10
Niederoderwitz D 81 E7
Nieder-Olm D 185 E9
Nieder-Rodenbach D 21 D12
Niederroßla D 79 D9
Niedersachswerfen D 79 C8
Niederselters D 21 D10
Niederstetten D 74 D6
Niederurnen CH 27 F11
Niederviehbach D 75 E11
Niederwerrn D 75 B7
Niederwörresbach D 186 B3
Niederzissen D 21 D8
Niedrzwica Duża PL 141 H6
Niedźwiada PL 141 G7
Niedźwiadna PL 139 C13
Niefern-Öschelbronn D 27 C10
Niegosław PL 85 E9
Niegosławice PL 81 C9
Niegowa PL 143 E7
Niegripp D 79 B10
Nieheim D 17 E12
Niekerk NL 16 B6
Niekłań Wielki PL 141 H3
Niekursko PL 85 D10
Niel B 182 C4
Nielisz PL 144 B7
Niemberg D 79 C11
Niemce PL 141 H7
Niemcza PL 81 E11
Niemegk D 79 B12
Niemelä FIN 113 C20
Niemelä FIN 115 E5
Niemelänkylä FIN 119 F12
Niemenkylä FIN 122 E7
Niemenkylä FIN 126 C6
Niemenpää FIN 119 B11
Niemis S 119 B11
Niemisel S 118 B7
Niemisjärvi FIN 123 F16
Niemisjärvi FIN 124 E8
Niemiskylä FIN 123 C17
Niemodlin PL 142 E4
Niemysłów PL 142 C6
Nienadówka PL 144 C5
Nienburg (Saale) D 79 C10
Nienburg (Weser) D 17 C12
Niepars D 84 B3
Niepołomice PL 143 F9
Nieporjt PL 139 F11
Nierstein D 21 E10
Niesa FIN 117 D11
Niesi FIN 117 D15
Niesky D 81 D7
Nieświń PL 141 H2
Nieszawa PL 138 E6
Nietsak S 116 D4
Nietulisko Duże PL 143 E11
Nieul F 29 D8
Nieuw-Amsterdam NL 17 C7
Nieuw-Bergen NL 16 E6
Nieuwegein NL 16 D4
Nieuwe-Niedorp NL 16 C3
Nieuwe Pekela NL 17 B7
Nieuwerkerk NL 16 E2
Nieuwerkerk aan de IJssel NL 16 E3
Nieuwerkerken B 19 C11
Nieuwe-Tonge NL 16 E2
Nieuw-Heeten NL 16 D6
Nieuwkoop NL 16 D3
Nieuw-Loosdrecht NL 183 A6
Nieuw-Milligen NL 183 A7
Nieuw-Namen NL 182 C4
Nieuwolda NL 17 B7
Nieuwpoort B 18 B6
Nieuwveen NL 182 A5
Nieuw-Vennep NL 16 D3
Nieuw-Vossemeer NL 182 B4
Nieuw-Weerdinge NL 17 C7
Nievern D 185 D8
Niewiglosz PL 141 G7
Niezabyszewo PL 85 B12
Nigrán E 38 D2
Nīgrande LV 134 D4
Nigrita GR 169 C10
Nigüelas E 53 C9
Niherne F 29 B9
Niinilahti FIN 123 E15
Niinimaa FIN 123 E10
Niinimäki FIN 125 F10
Niinisalo FIN 126 B8
Niinivaara FIN 125 D11
Niinivesi FIN 123 E16
Niirokumpu FIN 121 B11
Níjar E 55 F8
Nijemci HR 157 B11
Nijkerk NL 16 D4
Nijlen B 19 B10
Nijmegen NL 16 E5
Nijverdal NL 17 D6
Nikaia GR 169 F7
Nikaranperä FIN 123 E14
Nikel' RUS 114 E8
Niki GR 168 C5
Nikisiani GR 170 C6
Nikiti GR 169 D10
Nikkala S 119 C11
Nikkaluokta S 111 E17
Nikkaroinen FIN 127 C14
Nikkeby N 112 C6
Nikodin NMK 169 B6
Nikokleia GR 169 C9
Nikolaevo BG 165 C10
Nikolaevo BG 166 D5
Nikola-Kozlevo BG 161 F10
Nikolovo BG 161 F8
Nikolsdorf A 73 C6
Nikopol BG 160 F5
Nikopoli GR 174 A2
Nīkrāce LV 134 C3
Nikšić MNE 163 D6
Nikyup BG 166 C5
Nilivaara FIN 117 C14
Nilivaara S 116 D7
Nilsiä FIN 125 D10
Nilvange F 20 F6
Nim DK 86 D5
Nîmes F 35 C7
Nimigea RO 152 C4
Nimis I 73 D7
Nimisenkangas FIN 125 C11
Nimisjärvi FIN 119 E17
Nimtofte DK 86 C7
Nin HR 67 D11
Nina EST 131 D14
Nindorf D 82 B6
Ninemile Bar GB 5 E9
Ninemilehouse IRL 9 D8
Ninove B 19 C9
Niort F 28 C5
Nirza LV 133 D3
Niš SRB 164 C4
Nisa P 44 E5
Nisbet GB 5 D11
Niscemi I 58 E5
Niška Banja SRB 164 C5
Niskankorpi FIN 123 C13
Niskanpera FIN 119 B15
Nisko PL 144 B5
Niskos FIN 123 F10
Nismes B 19 D10
Nispen NL 16 F2
Nisporeni MD 154 C2
Nissafors S 91 E14
Nissan-lez-Enserune F 34 D5
Nissilä FIN 123 C17
Nissinvaara FIN 121 B13
Nissoria I 58 D5
Nissumby DK 86 B2
Nissum Seminarieby DK 86 B2
Nistelrode NL 16 E5
Nistorești RO 153 F9
Nītaure LV 135 B10
Nitra SK 146 E6
Nitrianske Hrnčiarovce SK 146 E6
Nitrianske Pravno SK 147 D7
Nitrianske Rudno SK 146 D6
Nitrianske Sučany SK 146 D6
Nitry F 25 E10
Nitta S 91 D13
Nittedal N 95 B13
Nittel D 20 E6
Nittenau D 75 D11
Nittendorf D 75 D10
Nittorp S 91 D14
Niukkala FIN 129 B12
Nivå DK 87 D11
Niva FIN 121 F14
Nivala FIN 123 C13
Nivankylä FIN 117 E15
Nivanpää FIN 117 E11
Nivelles B 19 C9
Nivenskoye RUS 136 D2
Nivillac F 23 E7
Nivillers F 18 F5
Nivnice CZ 146 D5
Nivolas-Vermelle F 31 D7
Nivyanin BG 165 C8
Niwiska PL 143 F12
Nižbor CZ 76 C6
Nižná SK 147 C9
Nižná Slaná SK 145 F1
Nižný Hrabovec SK 145 F4
Nižný Hrušov SK 145 F4
Nižný Šipov SK 145 F4
Nizza di Sicilia I 59 D7
Nizza Monferrato I 37 B8
Njavve S 109 C15
Njegovuđa MNE 163 C7
Një Maj AL 168 C3
Njetjavare S 116 E4
Njivice HR 67 B10
Njurundabommen S 103 B13
Njutånger S 103 C13
No DK 86 C2
Noailhac F 32 B5
Noailles F 18 F5
Noain E 32 E2
Noale I 66 A5
Noalejo E 53 A9
Noasca I 31 E11
Nöbbele S 89 B8
Nobber IRL 7 E9
Nobitz D 79 E11
Noblejas E 46 E6
Nočaj SRB 158 D4
Nocé F 24 D4
Nocera Inferiore I 60 B3
Nocera Terinese I 59 A9
Nocera Umbra I 62 A3
Noceto I 66 C1
Noci I 61 B8
Nociglia I 61 C10
Nociūnai LT 135 F8
Nocrich RO 152 F4
Nødebo DK 87 D10
Nødeland N 90 C2
Nödinge S 91 D11
Nodland N 94 F4
Nods F 26 F5
Noé F 33 D8
Noepoli I 61 C6
Noer D 83 B8
Nœux-les-Mines F 18 D6
Noez E 46 E4
Nofuentes E 40 C5
Nogales E 51 B6
Nogara I 66 B3
Nogaro F 32 C5
Nogent F 26 D3
Nogent-le-Bernard F 24 D3
Nogent-le-Roi F 24 C6
Nogent-le-Rotrou F 24 D4
Nogent-sur-Aube F 25 D11
Nogent-sur-Oise F 18 F5
Nogent-sur-Seine F 25 D10
Nogent-sur-Vernisson F 25 E8
Nogersund S 89 C7
Nógrád H 147 F8
Nógrádmegyer H 147 E9
Nógrádsáp H 147 F8
Nograles E 40 F6
Noguera de Albarracín E 47 D9
Noguères F 32 D4
Nogueruelas E 48 D3
Nohant-Vic F 29 B9
Nohfelden D 21 E8
Nohic F 33 C8
Noia E 38 C2
Noicattaro I 61 A7
Noidans-lès-Vesoul F 26 E5
Noilhan F 33 C7
Noirétable F 30 D4
Noirmoutier-en-l'Île F 28 A1
Noisseville F 26 B5
Noja E 40 B4
Nojorid RO 151 C8
Nokia FIN 127 C10
Nol S 91 D11
Nolay F 30 B6
Noli I 37 C8
Nolimo FIN 121 B11
Nolmyra S 99 B8
Nólsoy FO 2 A3
Nombela E 46 D4
Nomeland N 90 A2
Nomenj SLO 73 D9
Nomeny F 26 C5
Nomexy F 26 D5
Nomia GR 178 B5
Nonancourt F 24 C5
Nonantola I 66 C3
Nonaspe E 42 E4
None I 37 B7
Nonnenweier D 186 E4
Nonnweiler D 21 E7
Nontron F 29 D7
Nonza F 37 F10
Nõo EST 131 E13
Noordwijk aan Zee NL 182 A4
Noordwijk-Binnen NL 16 D2
Noordwijkerhout NL 16 D3
Noordwolde NL 16 C6
Noormarkku FIN 126 B6
Nootdorp NL 182 A4
Nopankylä FIN 122 E8
Noppikoski S 102 D8
Nor S 103 C11
Nora S 97 C13
Nora S 103 A12
Norager DK 86 B5
Noragugume I 64 C2
Norberg S 97 B14
Norcia I 62 B4
Nordagutu N 95 D10
Nordanå S 103 A13
Nordanås S 107 C14
Nordanås S 109 E16
Nordanås S 109 F11
Nordanede S 103 A11
Nordankäl S 107 D10
Nordannålden S 105 E16
Nordano S 98 B6
Nordborg DK 86 E5
Nordbotn N 112 D9
Nordby DK 86 D7
Nordby DK 86 E2
Norddeich D 17 A8
NorŠdepil FO 2 A3
Norddorf D 82 A4
Norddyrøy N 104 D5
Nordeide N 100 D3
Nordeidet N 112 D4
Norden D 17 A8
Nordendorf D 75 E8
Nordenham D 17 B10
Nordenskov DK 86 D3
Norderåsen S 106 E7
Norderney D 17 A8
Norderö S 105 E16
Norderstedt D 83 C8
Nordfjord N 114 B8
Nordfjordbotn N 111 B17
Nordfjordeid N 100 C3
Nordfold N 110 E9
Nordhalben D 75 B10
Nordhallen S 105 E13
Nordhastedt D 82 B6
Nordhausen D 79 D8
Nordheim D 27 B11
Nordholz D 17 A11
Nordhorn D 17 D8
Nordhuglo N 94 C3
Nordingrå S 103 A15
Nordkil N 111 D10
Nordkirchen D 17 E9
Nordkisa N 95 B14
Nordkjosbotn N 111 B18
Nordland N 110 E4
Nord-Leirvåg N 114 D7
Nordlenangen N 111 A19
Nordli N 105 C15
Nördlingen D 75 E7
Nordmaling S 107 D17
Nordmannvik N 112 D5
Nordmela N 111 B10
Nordnesøy N 108 C4
NorŠragøta FO 2 A3
Nordråk N 101 E12
Nordsand N 111 C12
Nordsinni N 101 E11
Nordsjö S 103 C12
Nordsjö S 107 D10
Nordsjona N 108 D5
NorŠskáli FO 2 A2
Nordskjør N 104 C8
Nordskot N 110 E8
Nordstemmen D 78 B6
Nord-Værnes N 108 C5
Nordvågen N 113 B17
Nordvik N 108 B9
Nordvik S 103 A14
Nordvika N 104 E4
Nordwalde D 17 D8
Nore S 103 C11
Noreikiškės LT 137 D8
Norem N 105 D10
Noreña E 39 B8
Noresund N 95 B11
Norg NL 17 B6
Norheimsund N 94 B4
Norinkylä FIN 122 E8
Norje S 88 C7
Norma I 62 D3
Norn S 97 B14
Nornäs S 102 D5
Noroy-le-Bourg F 26 E5
Norppa FIN 123 C11
Norra Åsum S 88 D6
Norra Blommaberg S 103 C9
Norra Bredåker S 118 C6
Norra bro S 92 A6
Norra Fjällnäs S 109 E10
Norra Holmnäs S 118 C3
Norråker S 106 C9
Norra Klagshamn S 87 D11
Norra Malånäs S 107 A15
Norra Prästholm S 118 C8
Norra Rödupp S 118 B9
Norra Skärvången S 105 D16
Norra Vallgrund FIN 122 D6
Norra Vi S 92 D6
Norrbäck S 103 B12
Norrbäck S 107 B13
Norrbo S 103 C12
Norrboda S 99 B10
Norrboda S 103 D9
Norrby FIN 122 C9
Norrby S 99 B11
Norrbyberg S 107 B14
Norrbyn S 122 C3
Norrbyskär S 122 C3
Nørre Aaby DK 86 E5
Nørre Alslev DK 84 A1
Nørreballe DK 83 A10
Nørre Bork DK 86 D2
Nørre Broby DK 86 E6
Nørre Felding DK 86 C3
Nørre Halne DK 86 A5
Nørre Kongerslev DK 86 B6
Nørre Nebel DK 86 D2
Norrent-Fontes F 18 C5
Nørre Snede DK 86 D4
Nørresundby DK 86 A5
Nørre Vejrup DK 86 D3
Nørre Vorupør DK 86 B2
Norrfällsviken S 107 F15
Norrfjärden S 103 B13
Norrfjärden S 118 D7
Norrfjärden S 122 C5
Norrflärke S 107 D14
Norrfors S 107 C14
Norrfors S 107 D15
Norrgårdssälen S 102 E6
Norr-Greningen S 106 E8
Norrhult-Klavreström S 89 A8
Norrköping S 93 B8
Norrlångträsk S 118 D5
Norr-Moflo S 107 E11
Norrnäs FIN 122 E6
Norrsjön S 106 B8
Norrskedika S 99 B10
Norrstig S 103 A14
Norrstrand S 109 E16
Norrsundet S 103 E13
Norrtälje S 99 C11
Norrtjärn S 103 E12
Norrvåge S 107 E15
Norrvik S 107 B13
Nors DK 86 A3
Norsholm S 92 B7
Norsjö S 107 B17
Nörten-Hardenberg D 78 C6
Northallerton GB 11 C9
Northam GB 12 C6
Northampton GB 15 C7
North Berwick GB 5 C11
Northborough GB 11 F11
North Cave GB 11 D10
North Dell GB 2 J4
North Duffield GB 11 D10
Northeim D 79 C6
North Ferriby GB 11 D10
North Grimston GB 11 C10
North Hykeham GB 11 E10
North Leigh GB 13 B12
North Shields GB 5 E14
North Somercotes GB 11 E12
North Sunderland GB 5 D13
North Tidworth GB 13 C11
Northton GB 2 K2
North Walsham GB 15 B11
Northwich GB 10 E6
Nortmoor D 17 B9
Norton GB 11 C10
Norton GB 15 C10
Norton Fitzwarren GB 13 C8
Nortorf D 83 B7
Nortrup D 17 C9
Nort-sur-Erdre F 23 F8
Norup DK 86 B6
Norvasalmi FIN 117 E15
Norwich GB 15 B11
Norwick GB 3 D15
Noșlac RO 152 E3
Nøss N 111 B10
Nossa Senhora da Boa Fé P 50 B3
Nossa Senhora da Graça de Póvoa e Meadas P 44 E5
Nossa Senhora da Graça do Divor P 50 B4
Nossa Senhora da Graça dos Degolados P 45 F6
Nossa Senhora das Neves P 50 C4
Nossa Senhora de Machede P 50 B4
Nossebro S 91 C12
Nossen D 80 D4
Nossendorf D 84 C3
Nossentiner Hütte D 83 C12
Noszlop H 149 B8
Noszvaj H 145 H1
Notaresco I 62 B5
Notia GR 169 B7
Nőtincs H 147 F8
Nötö FIN 126 F6
Noto I 59 F7
Notodden N 95 C10
Notre-Dame-de-Bellecombe F 31 D10
Notre-Dame-de-Gravenchon F 18 F2
Notre-Dame-de-Monts F 28 B1
Notre-Dame-d'Oé F 24 F4
Nötsch im Gailtal A 73 C8
Nottensdorf D 82 D7
Nottingham GB 11 F9
Nottuln D 17 E8
Notviken S 118 C8
Nouan-le-Fuzelier F 24 E7
Nouans-les-Fontaines F 24 F5
Nouart F 19 F11
Nõuni EST 131 E13
Nousiainen FIN 126 D7
Nousionmäki FIN 125 D10
Nousu FIN 115 D5
Nouvion F 18 D4
Nouzilly F 24 E4
Nouzonville F 19 E10
Nõva EST 130 C7
Nová H 149 C7
Nová Baňa SK 147 E7
Nova Breznica NMK 164 F3
Nova Bukovica HR 149 E9
Nová Bystřice CZ 77 D8
Nová Cerekev CZ 77 D8
Novachene BG 165 B10
Novachene BG 165 D8
Novaci NMK 168 B5
Novaci RO 160 C3
Nova Crnja SRB 158 B6
Nová Dedina SK 147 E7
Novadnieki LV 134 C4
Nová Dubnica SK 146 D6
Novafeltria I 66 E5
Nova Gorica SLO 73 E8
Nova Gradiška HR 157 B7
Nova Ivanivka UA 154 F4
Novaj H 145 H1
Novajidrány H 145 G3
Nova Kamena BG 161 F10
Nova Kasaba BIH 157 D11
Novaki HR 148 E5
Novakovo BG 166 F4
Nováky SK 147 D7
Novales E 40 B3
Novales E 41 D11
Nova Levante I 72 D4
Novalja HR 67 C10
Novallas E 41 E8
Nová Ľubovňa SK 145 E2
Nova Makhala BG 165 F9
Nova Nadezhda BG 166 E5
Nova Nekrasivka UA 155 C3
Nová Paka CZ 77 B9
Nova Pazova SRB 158 D5
Nova Pokrovka UA 155 B4
Novara I 68 C6
Novara di Sicilia I 59 C7
Nová Role CZ 75 B12
Nova Sela HR 157 F8
Nova Siri I 61 C7
Nova Siri Scalo I 61 C7
Novate Mezzola I 69 A7
Nova Topola BIH 157 B7
Nova Varoš SRB 163 C8
Nova Vas SLO 73 E9
Nová Včelnice CZ 77 D8
Nova Ves CZ 77 B8
Nová Ves nad Žitavou SK 146 E6
Nova Zagora BG 166 E6
Nové Hrady CZ 77 E7
Novelda E 56 E3
Novellara I 66 C2
Nové Město nad Metují CZ 77 B10
Nové Mesto nad Váhom SK 146 D5
Nové Město na Moravě CZ 77 C10
Nové Město pod Smrkem CZ 81 E8
Nove Misto UA 145 D6
Noventa di Piave I 72 E6
Noventa Vicentina I 66 B4
Novés E 46 D4
Noves F 35 C8
Nové Veselí CZ 77 C9
Nové Zámky SK 146 F6
Novgorodka RUS 133 B5
Novgrad BG 161 F7
Novi Banovci SRB 158 D5
Novi Bečej SRB 158 B5
Novi di Modena I 66 C2
Novi Dojran NMK 169 B8
Noviergas E 41 E7
Novi Grad BIH 157 B9
Novigrad HR 67 B8
Novigrad HR 156 D4
Novigrad Podravski HR 149 D7
Novi Iskŭr BG 165 D7
Novi Karlovci SRB 158 C5
Novi Khan BG 165 D8
Novi Kneževac SRB 150 E5
Novi Kozarci SRB 150 F6
Novi Ligure I 37 B9
Novillars F 26 F5
Noville B 182 D5
Novi Marof HR 149 D6
Novion-Porcien F 19 E9
Novi Pazar BG 167 C8
Novi Pazar SRB 163 C10
Novi Sad SRB 158 C4
Novi Šeher BIH 157 C9
Novi Slankamen SRB 158 C5
Novi Travnik BIH 157 D8
Novi Vinodolski HR 67 B10
Novo Beograd SRB 158 D5
Novoborysivka UA 154 C5
Novočići BIH 157 F9
Novo Delchevo BG 169 B9
Novokhovansk RUS 133 E7
Novo Korito SRB 159 F9
Novo Mesto SLO 73 E11
Novo Miloševo SRB 158 B5
Novomoskovskiy RUS 139 A9
Novomykolayivka UA 155 B5
Novo Orahovo SRB 150 F4
Novo Oryakhovo BG 167 D9
Novopetrivka UA 154 C5
Novorzhev RUS 133 B6
Novosamarka UA 154 B5
Novosedly CZ 77 E11
Novoselë AL 163 F10
Novoselë AL 168 C1
Novoselec HR 149 E7
Novoselets BG 166 E6
Novoselija BIH 157 C7
Novoselivka UA 154 E5
Novoselivka UA 154 D5
Novo Selo BG 159 E10
Novo Selo BG 161 F8
Novo Selo BG 165 E6
Novo Selo BG 166 F6
Novo Selo BIH 157 B8
Novo Selo BIH 157 B9
Novo Selo NMK 169 B8
Novo Selo SRB 159 F6
Novoselovo RUS 139 B9
Novoseltsi BG 167 C8
Novosel'ye RUS 132 E4
Novoselytsya UA 153 A8
Novoselytsya UA 154 A6
Novosil's'ke UA 155 C3
Novostroyevo RUS 136 E4
Novot SK 147 C8
Novo Virje HR 149 D8
Novovolyns'k UA 144 B9
Novoyavorivs'ke UA 144 D8
Novska HR 149 F7
Nový Bor CZ 81 E7
Nový Bydžov CZ 77 B8
Novy-Chevrières F 19 E9
Novy Dvor BY 137 F10
Nový Hrozenkov CZ 146 C6
Nový Jičín CZ 146 B5
Nový Knín CZ 76 C6
Nový Malín CZ 77 C12
Novy Pahost BY 133 F2
Nový Rychnov CZ 77 D8
Novyya Kruki BY 133 E3
Novyy Izborsk RUS 132 F2
Novyy Rozdil UA 145 E9
Nový Šivot SK 146 E4
Nowa Brzeźnica PL 143 D7
Nowa Cerekwia PL 142 F4
Nowa Chodorówka PL 140 C8
Nowa Dęba PL 143 F12
Nowa Karczma PL 138 B5
Nowa Ruda PL 81 E11
Nowa Sarzyna PL 144 C5
Nowa Słupia PL 143 E11
Nowa Sól PL 81 C9
Nowa Sucha PL 141 F2
Nowa Wieś Ełcka PL 140 C6
Nowa Wieś Lęborskie PL 85 A13
Nowa Wieś Wielka PL 138 E5
Nowa Wola PL 140 D9
Nowa Wola Gołębiowska PL 141 H4
Nowe PL 138 C6
Nowe Brusno PL 144 C7
Nowe Brzesko PL 143 F9
Nowe Czarnowo PL 84 D6
Nowe Miasteczko PL 81 C9
Nowe Miasto PL 139 E10
Nowe Miasto Lubawskie PL 139 D8
Nowe Miasto nad Pilicą PL 141 G3
Nowe Miasto nad Wartą PL 81 B12
Nowe Ostrowy PL 143 B7
Nowe Piekuty PL 141 E7
Nowe Skalmierzyce PL 142 C4
Nowe Warpno PL 84 C6
Nowinka PL 136 F6
Nowogard PL 85 C8
Nowogród PL 139 D12
Nowogród Bobrzański PL 81 C8
Nowogródek Pomorski PL 85 E8
Nowogrodziec PL 81 D8
Nowosady PL 141 E9
Nowosielce PL 145 D5
Nowosolna PL 143 C8
Nowotaniec PL 145 D5
Nowowola PL 140 D8
Nowy Bartków PL 141 F7
Nowy Duninów PL 139 E7
Nowy Dwór PL 138 D4
Nowy Dwór PL 140 C9
Nowy Dwór Gdański PL 138 B7
Nowy Dwór Mazowiecki PL 139 F10
Nowy Kawęczyn PL 141 G2
Nowy Korczyn PL 143 F10
Nowy Lubliniec PL 144 C7
Nowy Sącz PL 145 D2
Nowy Staw PL 138 B7
Nowy Targ PL 147 C10
Nowy Tomyśl PL 81 B10
Nowy Wiśnicz PL 144 D1
Nowy Żmigród PL 145 D4
Noyal-Muzillac F 22 E7
Noyalo F 22 E6
Noyal-Pontivy F 22 D6
Noyant F 23 E12

Orava EST 132 F1
Orava FIN 123 D10
Oravainen FIN 122 D8
Oravais FIN 122 D8
Oravala FIN 128 D6
Öravan S 107 B14
Oravankylä FIN 123 C15
Öravattnet S 106 E9
Oravi FIN 125 F11
Oravikoski FIN 124 E9
Oravisalo FIN 125 F13
Oravița RO 159 C8
Oravivaara FIN 121 E11
Oravská Polhora SK 147 B8
Oravské Veselé SK 147 C8
Oravský Podzámok SK 147 C8
Orba E 56 D4
Orbacém P 38 E2
Örbäck S 97 C15
Orbaden S 103 C11
Ørbæk DK 86 E7
Orbais-l'Abbaye F 25 C10
Orbara E 32 E3
Orbassano I 37 A7
Orbe CH 31 B10
Orbeasca RO 160 E6
Orbec F 24 B3
Orbeni RO 153 E10
Orbetello I 65 C4
Örbyhus S 99 B9
Orca P 44 D6
Orce E 55 D8
Orcera E 55 C7
Orchamps-Vennes F 26 F6
Orchies F 19 D7
Orchomenos GR 175 C6
Orchów PL 143 C7
Orchowo PL 138 E5
Orciano di Pesaro I 67 E6
Orcières F 36 B4
Orcival F 30 D2
Ordan-Larroque F 33 C6
Ordes E 38 B3
Ordizia E 32 D1
Ordona I 60 A5
Ordzhonikidze UA 154 C6
Orea E 47 C9
O Real E 38 B3
Örebäcken S 102 C4
Orebić HR 157 G7
Örebro S 97 D13
Ořechov CZ 77 D11
Öregcsertő H 150 D3
Öreglak H 149 C9
Öregrund S 99 B10
Orehoved DK 87 F9
Oreini GR 169 B10
Orekhovitsa BG 165 B9
Orellana de la Sierra E 51 A9
Orellana la Vieja E 51 A8
Ören TR 177 C10
Ören TR 181 B7
Orenhofen D 185 E6
Oreoi GR 175 B7
Orés E 32 F3
Oresh BG 166 B4
Oreshak BG 165 D10
Orestiada GR 171 B11
Öreström S 107 C16
Öretjändalen S 103 A10
Oreye B 19 C11
Orezu RO 161 D9
Orford GB 15 C12
Organi GR 171 B9
Organyà E 43 C6
Orgaz E 46 E5
Orgelet F 31 B8
Ørgenvika N 95 B11
Orgères-en-Beauce F 24 D6
Orgita EST 131 D8
Orgiva E 53 C10
Orgon F 35 C9
Orgosolo I 64 C3
Orhaneli TR 173 E10
Orhaniye TR 171 C10
Orhaniye TR 181 C8
Orhanlar TR 173 E8
Orhei MD 154 C3
Oria E 55 E8
Oria I 61 C9
O Rial E 38 D2
Origny-Ste-Benoîte F 19 E7
Orihuela E 56 E3
Orihuela del Tremedal E 47 C9
Orikhivka UA 154 F3
Orikum AL 168 D1
Orimattila FIN 127 D14
Oriniemi FIN 127 C9
Orio E 32 D1
Oriola P 50 C4
Oriolo I 61 C6
Oriolo Romano I 62 C2
Oripää FIN 126 D8
Orismala FIN 122 E8
Orissaare EST 130 D6
Oristà E 43 D8
Oristano I 64 D2
Oriston IRL 7 E9
Őriszentpéter H 149 C6
Oriv UA 145 E8
Oriveden asema FIN 127 B11
Orivesi FIN 127 B11
Orizare BG 167 D9
Orizari NMK 164 F5
Ørjavik N 104 F2
Ørje N 96 D6
Orkanger N 104 E7
Örkelljunga S 87 C12
Orkény H 150 C3
Orla PL 141 E8
Orlamünde D 79 E10
Orlat RO 152 F3
Orlea RO 160 F4
Orléans F 24 E6
Orlești RO 160 D4
Orlivka UA 155 C2
Orllan RKS 164 D3
Orlová CZ 146 B6
Orlov Dol BG 166 E6
Orlovets BG 166 C5
Orły PL 144 D6
Orlyak BG 161 F10
Orlyane BG 165 C10
Orma GR 169 C6
Ormanli TR 173 B9
Ormaryd S 92 D5
Ormea I 37 C7
Örményes H 150 C6
Örménykút H 150 D6
Ormos GR 176 D4
Ormos Panormou GR 176 D5
Ormos Prinou GR 171 C7
Ormož SLO 148 D6
Ormskirk GB 10 D6
Ormylia GR 169 D10
Ornaisons F 34 D4
Ornans F 26 F5
Ornäs S 97 A14
Örnäsudden S 109 E13
Ornavasso I 68 B5
Ornbau D 75 D8
Ornes N 105 B15
Ørnes N 108 C6
Orneta PL 139 B9
Ørnhøj DK 86 C3
Ornö S 93 A12
Ornontowice PL 142 F6
Örnsköldsvik S 107 E15
Orodel RO 159 E11
Orolik HR 157 B11
Orom SRB 150 F4
Oron-la-Ville CH 31 B10
Oronoz E 32 D2
Orońsko PL 141 H3
Oropa I 68 B4
Oropesa E 45 E10
Oropesa del Mar E 48 D5
Ororbia E 32 E2
Orosei I 64 C4
Orosháza H 150 D6
Oroslavje HR 148 E5
Oroszlány H 149 B10
Orpierre F 35 B10
Orreaga E 32 D3
Orrefors S 89 B9
Orrios E 42 F2
Orrmo S 102 C7
Orroli I 64 D3
Orrviken S 106 E6
Orsa S 102 D8
Orsara di Puglia I 60 A4
Orsay F 24 C7
Örsbäck S 107 D17
Orsennes F 29 C9
Örserum S 92 C5
Orsières CH 31 C11
Örsjö S 89 B9
Ørslev DK 87 E9
Ørsnes N 100 A5
Orsogna I 63 C6
Orsomarso I 60 D5
Orșova RO 159 D9
Ørsta N 100 B4
Ørsted DK 86 C6
Örsundsbro S 99 C8
Ortaca TR 181 C9
Ortacesus I 64 D3
Ortakent TR 177 E9
Ortaklar TR 177 D9
Ortaköy TR 173 B9
Ortala S 99 C11
Orta Nova I 60 A5
Orte I 62 C2
Orten N 100 A5
Ortenberg D 21 D12
Ortenberg D 27 D8
Ortenburg D 76 E4
Orth an der Donau A 77 F11
Orthez F 32 D4
Ortholmen S 102 B6
Orthovouni GR 168 E5
Ortigosa E 41 D6
Ortigueira E 38 A4
Ørting DK 86 D6
Ortisei I 72 C4
Orțișoara RO 151 F7
Ortnevik N 100 D4
Orton GB 10 C6
Ortona I 63 C6
Ortovera I 37 C8
Ortrand D 80 D5
Örträsk S 107 C15
Ortueri I 64 C2
Örtülüce TR 173 D7
Ørum DK 86 C5
Ørum DK 86 C7
Orune I 64 C3
Orusco E 47 D6
Orval F 29 B10
Orvalho P 44 D5
Orvault F 23 F8
Orvieto I 62 B2
Örviken S 118 E6
Orvinio I 62 C3
Oryakhovo BG 160 F3
Orzesze PL 142 F6
Orzinuovi I 69 C8
Orzyny PL 139 C11
Orzysz PL 136 F4
Os N 101 B14
Osa N 100 E6
Osa de Vega E 47 E7
Ošāni LV 135 D11
Osaonica SRB 163 C9
Osbaldwick GB 11 D9
Os Blancos E 38 D4
Osburg D 186 B2
Øsby DK 86 E5
Osby S 88 C5
Osbyholm S 87 D13
Oščadnica SK 147 C7
Oschatz D 80 D4
Oschersleben (Bode) D 79 B9
Oschiri I 64 B3
Ościsłowo PL 139 E9
Os Dices E 38 C2
Osdorf D 83 B8
Osečina SRB 158 E4
O Seixo E 38 E2
Oseja de Sajambre E 39 B9
Osek CZ 76 C5
Osek CZ 80 E5
Osen N 105 C9
Osen N 108 D6
Osenets BG 166 B6
Ošenieki LV 134 C4
Osera E 41 E10
Osești RO 153 D10
Oset N 101 D10
Osetno PL 81 C10
Ősi H 149 B10
Osica de Sus RO 160 E4
Osidda I 64 B3
Osie PL 138 C5
Osijciny PL 138 E6
Osieck PL 141 G4
Osieczna PL 81 C11
Osieczna PL 138 C5
Osiecznica PL 81 D8
Osiek PL 138 C5
Osiek PL 139 D7
Osiek PL 143 E11
Osiek PL 147 B8
Osiek Jasielski PL 145 D3
Osiek Mały PL 142 B6
Osiek nad Notecią PL 85 D12
Osielsko PL 138 D5
Osiglia I 37 C8
Osijek HR 149 E11
Osikovitsa BG 165 D9
Osilo I 64 B2
Osimo I 67 F7
Osina PL 85 C8
Osini I 64 D3
Osiny PL 141 H6
Osio Sotto I 69 B8
Osipaonica SRB 159 D7
Osjaków PL 142 D6
Oskar S 89 B9
Oskar-Fredriksborg S 99 D10
Oskarshamn S 93 E8
Oskarström S 87 B11
Oskava CZ 77 C12
Oskořínek CZ 77 B8
Osľany SK 146 D6
Oslättfors S 103 E12
Osli H 149 A8
Oslo N 95 C13
Osloß D 79 B8
Osma E 40 C5
Osma FIN 117 D15
Osmancali TR 177 B9
Osmancık TR 173 A7
Osmangazi TR 173 D11
Osmaniye TR 173 E10
Osmaniye TR 173 F10
Osmanki FIN 123 C16
Osmanli TR 173 A6
Os'mino RUS 132 C5
Ösmo S 93 B11
Osmolin PL 141 F1
Osmoloda UA 145 F9
Osnabrück D 17 D10
Osno Lubuskie PL 81 B7
Osny F 24 B7
Osoblaha CZ 142 F4
Osogna CH 69 A6
Osojnik HR 162 D5
Osoppo I 73 D7
Osor E 43 D9
Osor HR 67 C9
Oșorhei RO 151 C9
Osorno E 40 D3
Osowa PL 136 E6
Osowa Sień PL 81 C10
Osøyri N 94 B2
Ospitaletto I 69 B9
Oss NL 16 E5
Ossa GR 169 C9
Ossa de Montiel E 55 B7
Ossana I 69 A10
Osséja F 33 F9
Ossendrecht NL 182 C4
Ossès F 32 D3
Ossiach A 73 C8
Oßmannstedt D 79 D9
Ossun F 32 D5
Östa S 98 B7
Östanå S 88 C6
Östanfjärden S 119 C10
Östansjö S 92 A5
Östansjö S 109 E16
Östanskär S 103 A13
Östanvik S 103 D9
Oštarije HR 156 B3
Ostaszewo PL 138 B6
Ostavall S 103 B9
Ostbevern D 17 D9
Østbirk DK 86 D5
Östbjörka S 103 E9
Østby N 91 A9
Østby N 102 D4
Östby S 107 D13
Østed DK 87 D9
Ostellato I 66 C4
Osten D 17 A12
Ostend B 18 B6
Ostend B 182 C1
Ostenfeld (Husum) D 82 B6
Østengård DK 86 D4
Österäs S 107 E12
Øster Assels DK 86 B3
Øster Bjerregrav DK 86 C5
Øster Brønderslev DK 86 A6
Osterburg (Altmark) D 83 E11
Osterburken D 27 B11
Østerby D 82 B7
Østerby DK 86 A5
Österbybruk S 99 B9
Österbymo S 92 D6
Östeřede S 107 E11
Österfärnebo S 98 B7
Osterfeld D 79 D10
Österforse S 107 E12
Östergarn S 93 E13
Östergraninge S 107 F12
Österhankmo FIN 122 D7
Osterhever D 82 B5
Osterhofen D 76 E4
Øster Højst DK 86 E4
Osterholz-Scharmbeck D 17 B11
Øster Hornum DK 86 B5
Øster Hurup DK 86 B6
Østerild DK 86 A3
Øster Jølby DK 86 B3
Österjörn S 118 D4
Østerlars DK 89 E7
Øster Lindet DK 86 E4
Österlisa S 99 C11
Østermarie DK 89 E8
Östermark FIN 126 E8
Ostermiething A 76 F3
Ostermundigen CH 31 B11
Österноret S 107 C12
Östero FIN 122 D8
Osterode am Harz D 79 C7
Österrönfeld D 82 B7
Österskucku S 102 A8
Östersund S 106 E7
Östersundom FIN 127 E13
Øster Tørslev DK 86 B6
Øster Ulslev DK 83 A11
Östervåla S 98 B8
Øster Vedsted DK 86 E3
Østervrå DK 90 E7
Øster Vrøgum DK 86 D2
Osterwieck D 79 C8
Østese N 94 B4
Ostfildern D 187 D7
Östhammar S 99 B10
Ostheim vor der Rhön D 75 B7
Osthofen D 21 E10
Ostia I 62 D2
Ostiano I 66 B1
Ostiglia I 66 B3
Ostiz E 32 E2
Östloning S 103 A13
Östmark S 97 B8
Östmarkum S 107 E14
Östnor S 102 D7
Ostojićevo SRB 150 F5
Ostoros H 145 H1
Ostra I 67 E7
Ostra RO 153 C7
Östra Åliden S 118 D4
Ostrach D 27 E11
Östra Ed S 93 C9
Östra Frölunda S 91 E13
Östra Granberg S 118 C4
Östra Grevie S 87 E12
Östra Husby S 93 B9
Östra Ljungby S 87 C12
Östra Löa S 97 C13
Östra Lovsjön S 106 D7
Östra Ormsjö S 107 C10
Östra Ryd S 93 C8
Östra Skråmträsk S 118 E5
Östra Sönnarslöv S 88 D6
Östra Stugusjö S 103 A9
Ostrau D 79 C11
Ostrau D 80 D4
Ostrava CZ 146 B6
Östra Vemmerlöv S 88 D6
Ostravice CZ 146 B6
Östra Yttermark FIN 122 E6
Oštrelj BIH 156 D5
Ostren AL 168 B3
Ostřetín CZ 77 B10
Ostrhauderfehn D 17 B9
Ostricourt F 182 E2
Östringen D 21 F11
Ostritsa BG 166 B5
Ostritz D 81 D7
Ostróda PL 139 C8
Ostrołęka PL 140 D5
Ostromecko PL 138 D5
Ostroměř CZ 77 B9
Ostroróg PL 81 A10
Ostrov BG 160 F4
Ostrov CZ 76 B3
Ostrov RO 155 D2
Ostrov RO 161 E10
Ostrov RUS 133 B4
Ostrov SK 146 D5
Ostroveni RO 160 F3
Ostrovo BG 161 F9
Ostrov u Macochy CZ 77 D11
Ostrów PL 143 F12
Ostrówek PL 141 G7
Ostrówek PL 142 D6
Ostrowice PL 85 C9
Ostrowiec PL 85 B11
Ostrowiec Świętokrzyski PL 143 E11
Ostrowite PL 138 F5
Ostrowite PL 139 D7
Ostrów Lubelski PL 141 H7
Ostrów Mazowiecka PL 139 E12
Ostrowo PL 138 E5
Ostrów Wielkopolski PL 142 C4
Ostrowy nad Okszą PL 143 E7
Ostrožac BIH 156 C4
Ostrožac BIH 157 E8
Ostrożeń PL 141 G5
Østrup DK 86 B4
Ostrzeszów PL 142 D4
Ostuni I 61 B9
Ostvik S 118 E6
Ostwald F 186 D4
Osula EST 131 F13
Osuna E 53 B6
Ošupe LV 135 C13
Osvallen S 102 A4
Osvica BIH 157 C8
Oswaldkirk GB 11 C9
Oswestry GB 10 F5
Oświęcim PL 143 F7
Ota F 37 G9
Otaci MD 154 A1
Otalampi FIN 127 E12
Otaņķi LV 134 D2
Otanmäki FIN 120 F9
Otaslavice CZ 77 D12
Otava FIN 128 B7
Otavice HR 156 E5
Oteiza E 32 E2
Oțeleni RO 153 C10
Oțelu Roșu RO 159 B9
Otepää EST 131 E12
Oteren N 111 B18
Oterma FIN 120 E9
Otero de Bodas E 39 E7
Otervik N 105 A11
Oțeșani RO 160 C4
Oteševo NMK 168 C4
Otfinów PL 143 F10
Othem S 93 D13
Ötigheim D 27 C9
Ötisheim D 27 C10
Otišić HR 156 E5
Otívar E 53 C9
Otley GB 11 D8
Otley GB 15 C11
Otmuchów PL 77 B12
Otnes N 101 C14
Otočac HR 156 C3
Otok HR 157 B10
Otok HR 157 E6
Otoka BIH 156 C5
Otopeni RO 161 D8
Otorowo PL 81 A10
O Toural E 38 D2
Otovica NMK 164 F4
Otradnoye RUS 129 F14
Otranto I 61 C10
Otricoli I 62 C2
Otrokovice CZ 146 C5
Otta N 101 C11
Ottana I 64 C3
Ottaviano I 60 B2
Ottenby S 89 C10
Ottendorf-Okrilla D 80 D5
Ottenheim D 186 E4
Ottenhöfen im Schwarzwald D 27 C9
Ottenschlag A 77 F8
Ottensheim A 76 F6
Ottenstein D 78 C5
Otterbach D 186 C4
Otterbäcken S 91 B15
Otterberg D 21 E9
Otterburn GB 5 E12
Otter Ferry GB 4 C6
Otterfing D 72 A4
Otterlo NL 16 D5
Otterndorf D 17 A11
Ottersberg D 17 B12
Ottersøy N 105 B10
Otterstad S 91 B13
Ottersweier D 27 C9
Otterswick GB 3 D14
Otterup DK 86 D6
Otterwisch D 79 D12
Öttevény H 149 A9
Ottignies B 19 C10
Ottmarsheim F 27 E8
Ottobeuren D 71 B10
Ottobrunn D 75 F10
Öttömös H 150 E4
Ottone I 37 B10
Ottrau D 21 C12
Ottsjö S 105 E14
Ottsjön S 106 D7
Ottweiler D 21 F8
Otwock PL 141 F4
Otxandio E 41 B6
Otyń PL 81 C9
Otzing D 76 E3
Ouanne F 25 E9
Ouarville F 24 D6
Ouca P 44 C3
Oucques F 24 E5
Oud-Beijerland NL 16 E2
Ouddorp NL 182 B3
Oudehaske NL 16 C5
Oudemirdum NL 16 C5
Oudenaarde B 19 C8
Oudenbosch NL 16 E3
Oudenburg B 18 B7
Oudeschild NL 16 B3
Oude-Tonge NL 16 E2
Oudewater NL 182 A5
Oud-Gastel NL 16 E2
Oudon F 23 F9
Oud-Turnhout B 16 F3
Oud-Vossemeer NL 16 E2
Oudzele B 182 C2
Oued Laou MA 53 F6
Ouffet B 19 D11
Oughterard IRL 6 F4
Ougney F 26 F4
Ouguela P 45 F6
Ouistreham F 23 B11
Oulainen FIN 119 F13
Oulanka FIN 115 F5
Oulchy-le-Château F 25 B9
Oulder B 20 D6
Oullins F 30 D6
Oulton GB 15 C12
Oulu FIN 119 D14
Oulunsalo FIN 119 E14
Oulx I 31 E10
Oundle GB 15 C8
Oupeye B 19 C12
Ouranoupoli GR 170 D5
Oure DK 87 E7
Ourém P 44 E3
Ourense E 38 D4
Ourique P 50 D3
Ourol E 38 A4
Ouroux-en-Morvan F 25 F10
Ouroux-sur-Saône F 31 B6
Ourville-en-Caux F 18 E2
Oust F 33 E8
Outakoski FIN 113 D16
Outarville F 24 D7
Outeiro P 38 E2
Outeiro P 39 E6
Outeiro de Rei E 38 B4
Outeiro Seco P 38 E5
Outokumpu FIN 125 E12
Outomuro E 38 D4
Outreau F 15 F12
Outwell GB 11 F12
Ouveillan F 34 D4
Ouzouer-le-Marché F 24 E6
Ouzouer-sur-Loire F 25 E7
Ovada I 37 B9
Ovanåker S 103 D10
Ovanmo S 107 D10
Ovar P 44 C3
Ovaro I 73 D6
Ovča SRB 158 D6
Ovcha Mogila BG 166 C4
Ovcharovo BG 166 E6
Ovchepoltsi BG 165 E9
Ove DK 86 B5
Ovelgönne D 17 B10
Överammer S 107 E9
Överäng S 105 D14
Overås N 100 A8
Overath D 21 C8
Överberg S 102 B7
Overbister GB 3 G11
Øverbygd N 111 C17
Överbyn S 103 C12
Overdinkel NL 183 A10
Over Feldborg DK 86 C3
Øvergard N 111 B18
Overhalla N 105 B11
Överhogdal S 102 B8
Överhörnäs S 107 E15
Over Hornbæk DK 86 C5
Overijse B 19 C10
Överissjö S 107 C13
Over Jerstal DK 86 E4
Överkalix S 119 B9
Overlade DK 86 B4
Överlännäs S 107 E13
Överlida S 91 E12
Overloon NL 183 B7
Övermalax FIN 122 E7
Övermark FIN 122 E6
Övermorjärv S 118 B9
Övernäs S 109 D14
Överö FIN 99 B15
Overøye N 100 B6
Overpelt B 19 B11
Over Simmelkær DK 86 C3
Överstbyn S 118 B7
Övertänger S 103 E10
Overton GB 10 F6
Overton GB 13 C12
Övertorneå S 119 B11
Överturingen S 102 B8
Överum S 93 D8
Ovezande NL 16 F1
O Vicedo E 38 A4
Ovidiu RO 155 E3
Oviedo E 39 B8
Oviglio I 37 B8
Oviken S 105 E16
Ovindoli I 62 C5
Oviši LV 130 F3
Öv Långträsk S 109 E16
Ovodda I 64 C3
Övra S 107 D11
Øvre Alta N 113 D11
Øvre Årdal N 100 D7
Øvre Åstbru N 101 D13
Øvre Bredåker S 118 C6
Övre Flåsjön S 118 B7
Øvre Kildal N 112 D7
Övre-Konäs S 105 D14
Øvrella N 95 C10
Øvre Rendal N 101 C14
Övre Soppero S 116 B7
Övre Tväråsel S 118 C5
Ovria GR 174 C4
Övsjöbyn S 107 E9
Ovtrup DK 86 D2
Owen D 27 C11
Owingen D 27 E11
Owińska PL 81 A11
Owschlag D 82 B7
Öxabäck S 91 E12
Oxberg S 102 D7
Oxelösund S 93 B10
Oxenhope GB 11 D8
Oxentea MD 154 C4
Oxford GB 13 B12
Oxhalsö S 99 C11
Oxie S 87 D12
Oxkangar FIN 122 D8
Oxshott GB 15 E8
Oxted GB 15 E9
Oxton GB 5 D11
Oxylithos GR 175 B9
Øyangen N 104 E7
Øydegarden N 104 E4
Øyenkilen N 91 A8
Øyer N 101 D12
Øyeren N 96 B7
Øyjord N 108 B9
Oy-Mittelberg D 71 B10
Øynes N 108 B9
Øynes N 111 C11
Oyonnax F 31 C8
Øyslebø N 90 C2
Oyten D 17 B12
Øyvatnet N 111 C12
Oza E 38 B3
Ozaeta E 41 C7
Ozalj HR 148 E4
Ożarów PL 143 E12
Ożarów Mazowiecki PL 141 F3
Ožbalt SLO 148 C4
Özbaşı TR 177 D9
Özbek TR 177 C8
Ózd H 145 G1
Oždany SK 147 E9
Özdere TR 177 D9
Ożenna PL 145 E3
Ozersk RUS 136 E5
Ozieri I 64 B3
Ozimek PL 142 E5
Ozimica BIH 157 D9
Özlüce TR 181 B9
Ozoir-la-Ferrière F 25 C8
Ozolaine LV 131 F9
Ozoli LV 131 F9
Ozoli LV 134 B4
Ozoli LV 135 C12
Ozolmuiža LV 133 D2
Ozolnieki LV 134 C7
Ozora H 149 C10
Ozorków PL 143 C7
Ozun RO 153 F7
Ozzano dell'Emilia I 66 D3
Ozzano Monferrato I 68 C5

P

Pääaho FIN 121 D10
Pääjärvi FIN 123 E13
Paakinmäki FIN 121 F11
Paakkila FIN 125 E11
Paakkola FIN 119 C13
Paal B 183 C6
Paalasmaa FIN 125 D12
Paaso FIN 127 C15
Paasvere EST 131 C13
Paatela FIN 129 B9
Paattinen FIN 126 D7
Paatus FIN 113 D17
Paavola FIN 119 E14
Pabaiskas LT 135 F9
Paberže LT 137 D11
Pabianice PL 143 C7
Pabillonis I 64 D2
Pabiržė LT 135 D9
Pabneukirchen A 77 F7
Pabradė LT 137 D12
Pabu F 22 C5
Pacanów PL 143 F11
Paceco I 58 D2
Pacheia Ammos GR 179 E10
Pachino I 59 F7
Pachni GR 171 B7
Paciano I 62 A2
Pácin H 145 G4
Pačir SRB 150 F3
Pack A 73 C10
Pačlavice CZ 77 D12
Pacos de Ferreira P 38 F3
Pacov CZ 77 D8
Pacsa H 149 C8
Păcureți RO 161 C8
Pacyna PL 143 B8
Pacy-sur-Eure F 24 B5
Paczków PL 77 B12
Padasjoki FIN 127 C13
Padborg DK 82 A6
Padbury GB 14 D7
Padej SRB 150 F5
Pađene HR 156 D5
Paderborn D 17 E11
Paderne P 38 D3
Paderne P 50 E3
Paderne de Allariz E 38 D4
Padeș RO 159 C10
Padesh BG 165 F7
Padew Narodowa PL 143 F12
Padežine BIH 157 F8
Padiham GB 11 D7
Pădina RO 159 E11
Padina RO 161 D10
Padina SRB 159 C6
Padinska Skela SRB 158 D5
Padirac F 29 F9
Padise EST 131 C8
Padoby BY 133 F2
Padoux F 26 D6
Padova I 66 B4
Padria I 64 C2
Padrón E 38 C2
Padru I 64 B4
Padstow GB 12 D5
Padsvillye BY 133 F3
Padul E 53 B9
Padula I 60 C5
Paduli I 60 A3
Padure LV 134 C3
Păduréni RO 153 D12
Paesana I 37 B6
Paese I 72 E5
Pag HR 67 D11
Pagani I 60 B3
Paganica I 62 C4
Paganico I 65 B4
Pagėgiai LT 134 F3
Pagiriai LT 135 F8
Pagiriai LT 137 D11
Paglieta I 63 C6
Pagny-sur-Moselle F 26 C5
Pagondas GR 177 D8
Pagouria GR 171 B8
Pagramantis LT 134 F4
Paharova S 116 E8
Páhi H 150 D3
Pahkakoski FIN 119 D16
Pahkakumpu FIN 115 E3
Pahkakumpu FIN 121 C12
Pahkala FIN 119 F11
Pahkamäki FIN 123 D16
Pähl D 72 A3
Pahlen D 82 B6
Pahranichny BY 140 D9
Pahtaoja FIN 119 C14
Paião P 44 D3
Paide EST 131 D11
Paignton GB 13 E7
Paihola FIN 125 E13
Päijälä FIN 127 B12
Paikuse EST 131 E9
Pailhès F 33 D8
Paillet F 32 A5
Paimbœuf F 23 F7
Paimela FIN 127 C14
Paimio FIN 126 E8
Paimpol F 22 C5
Paimpont F 23 D7
Painswick GB 13 B10
Painten D 75 E10
Paipis FIN 127 E13
Paisley GB 5 D8
Paistu EST 131 E11
Paisua FIN 124 C9
Päivăjoki FIN 115 F2
Pajala S 117 D10
Pajares de la Lampreana E 39 E8
Pajarón E 47 E9
Pajęczno PL 143 D6
Pajukoski FIN 125 C11
Pajukoste FIN 113 C20
Pajūris LT 134 F4
Pajuskylä FIN 124 D7
Pajuvaara FIN 121 D14
Páka H 149 C7
Pakaa FIN 127 D14
Pakalnė LT 134 F2
Pakalniai LT 135 F10
Pakapė LT 134 E6
Pakarila FIN 123 E17
Pakisjärvi FIN 117 E12
Pakkala FIN 127 C11
Pakod H 149 C8
Pakość PL 138 E5
Pakosław PL 81 C12
Pakoštane HR 156 E4
Pákozd H 149 B11
Pakrac HR 149 F8
Pakruojis LT 134 E7
Paks H 149 C11
Paksuniemi S 116 C5
Pala EST 131 D14
Palacios del Sil E 39 C7
Palacios de Sanabria E 39 D6
Palaciosrubios E 45 B10
Palade EST 130 D5
Palafrugell E 43 D10
Palagianello I 61 B7
Palagiano I 61 B8
Palagonia I 59 E6
Palaia I 66 E2
Palaia Fokaia GR 175 D8
Palaikastro GR 179 E11
Palaiochora GR 169 C9
Palaiochora GR 178 E6
Palaiochori GR 169 D6
Palaiochori GR 169 D10
Palaiochori GR 175 C7
Palaiokastritsa GR 168 E2
Palaiokastro GR 177 D9
Palaiokipos GR 177 A7
Palaiokomi GR 170 C5
Palaiomonastiro GR 169 F6
Palaiopoli GR 176 D4
Palaiopyrgos GR 169 E6
Palaiopyrgos GR 169 E8
Palaiopyrgos GR 174 C4
Palaiovracha GR 174 B5
Palairos GR 174 B2
Palaiseau F 25 C7
Palamas GR 169 F7
Palamós E 43 D10
Palamuse EST 131 D13
Palanca RO 153 D8
Palanga LT 134 E2
Pålänge S 119 C9
Palanzano I 66 D1
Palárikovo SK 146 E6
Palas de Rei E 38 C4
Palata BY 133 E7
Palata I 63 D7
Pălatca RO 152 D4
Palau I 64 A3
Palavas-les-Flots F 35 C6
Palazzo Adriano I 58 D3
Palazzolo Acreide I 59 E6
Palazzolo sull'Oglio I 69 B8
Palazzo San Gervasio I 60 B6
Paldiski EST 131 C8
Pale BIH 157 E10
Päle LV 131 F9
Paleičiai LT 134 F2
Palena I 63 D6
Palencia E 40 D2
Palenciana E 53 B7
Palenzuela E 40 D3
Palermo AL 168 D2
Palermo I 58 C3
Paleśnica PL 144 D2
Palestrina I 62 D3
Palėvenėlė LT 135 E10
Palež BIH 158 E3
Palhaça P 44 C3
Pálháza H 145 G4
Palia Kavala GR 171 C6
Paliano I 62 D4
Palić SRB 150 E4
Palinges F 30 B5
Palinuro I 60 C4
Paliouri GR 169 E10
Paliouria GR 169 E6
Palis F 25 D10
Paliseul B 19 E11
Palivere EST 131 D7
Palizzi I 59 D9
Paljakka FIN 121 B14
Paljakka FIN 121 E11

Petreto-Bicchisano F 37 H9
Petriano I 67 E6
Petricani RO 153 C8
Petrich BG 169 B9
Petrijevci HR 149 E11
Petrila RO 160 C2
Petrinja HR 148 F6
Petriș RO 151 E9
Petritoli I 62 A5
Petrivka UA 154 D4
Petrivs'k UA 154 E3
Petrochori GR 174 B4
Petrodvorets RUS 129 F12
Pétrola E 55 B9
Petromäki FIN 125 E9
Petronà I 59 A10
Petroșani RO 160 C2
Petrota GR 166 F6
Petroussa GR 170 B6
Petrov CZ 146 D4
Petrova RO 152 B4
Petrovac MNE 163 E6
Petrovac SRB 159 E7
Petrovany SK 145 F3
Petrovaradin SRB 158 C4
Petrovec NMK 164 F4
Petrovice CZ 76 C6
Petrovice u Karvine CZ 147 B7
Petrovići BIH 157 D10
Petrovići MNE 162 D6
Petrovo BG 169 B9
Petrovo RUS 136 D1
Petrovo Selo SRB 159 D9
Petruma FIN 125 F11
Petru Rareș RO 152 C4
Petrușeni MD 153 B10
Petřvald CZ 146 B6
Petřvald CZ 146 B6
Petsakoi GR 174 C5
Petsmo FIN 122 D7
Petten NL 16 C3
Pettigo GB 7 C7
Pettineo I 58 D5
Petting D 73 A6
Pettneu am Arlberg A 71 C10
Pettorano sul Gizio I 62 D5
Petŭrch BG 165 D7
Petworth GB 15 F7
Peuerbach A 76 F5
Peujard F 28 E5
Peura FIN 119 B14
Peurajärvi FIN 119 B16
Peurasuvanto FIN 115 C1
Pevensey GB 15 F9
Peveragno I 37 C7
Pewsey GB 13 C11
Pewsum (Krummhörn) D 17 B8
Pexonne F 27 D6
Peymeinade F 36 D5
Peynier F 35 D10
Peypin F 35 D10
Peyrat-le-Château F 29 D9
Peyrehorade F 32 C3
Peyriac-Minervois F 34 D4
Peyrieu F 31 D8
Peyrins F 31 E7
Peyrolles-en-Provence F 35 C10
Peyruis F 35 B10
Pézenas F 34 D5
Pįzino PL 85 D8
Pezinok SK 146 E4
Pezuls F 29 F7
Pfaffenberg D 75 E11
Pfaffendorf D 80 B6
Pfaffenhausen D 71 A10
Pfaffenhofen an der Ilm D 75 E10
Pfaffenhofen an der Roth D 187 E9
Pfaffenhoffen F 27 C8
Pfäffikon CH 27 F10
Pfaffing D 75 F11
Pfalzfeld D 185 D8
Pfalzgrafenweiler D 27 C10
Pfarrkirchen D 76 F3
Pfarrweisach D 75 B8
Pfarrwerfen A 73 B7
Pfedelbach D 27 B11
Pflach A 71 B11
Pfons A 72 B3
Pförring D 75 E10
Pforzen D 71 B11
Pforzheim D 27 C10
Pfreimd D 75 D11
Pfronstetten D 27 D11
Pfronten D 71 B11
Pfullendorf D 27 E11
Pfullingen D 27 D11
Pfunds A 71 D11
Pfungstadt D 21 E11
Pfyn CH 27 E10
Phalsbourg F 27 C7
Philippeville B 19 D10
Philippine NL 182 C3
Philippsburg D 187 C5
Philippsreut D 76 E5
Piacenza I 69 C8
Piadena I 66 B1
Piana F 37 G9
Piana GR 174 D5
Piana Crixia I 37 C8
Piana degli Albanesi I 58 D3
Piancastagnaio I 62 B1
Piandimeleto I 66 E5
Piàn di Scò I 66 E4
Pianella I 62 C6
Pianello Val Tidone I 37 B10
Piano del Voglio I 66 D3
Pianoro I 66 D3
Pianosa I 65 B2
Pianotolli-Caldarello F 37 J10
Pians A 71 C11
Piansano I 62 B1
Pianu RO 152 F2
Pias P 50 C5
Piaseczno PL 85 D7
Piaseczno PL 141 F4
Piasek PL 84 E6
Piaski PL 81 C12
Piaski PL 141 H7
Piastów PL 141 F3
Piątek PL 143 B7
Piątnica Poduchowna PL 139 D13
Piatra RO 160 F6
Piatra Neamț RO 153 D8
Piatra Olt RO 160 E4
Piatra ḑoimului RO 153 D8
Piau-Engaly F 33 E6
Piazza al Serchio I 66 D1
Piazza Armerina I 58 E5
Piazza Brembana I 69 B8
Piazzatorre I 69 B8
Piazzola sul Brenta I 66 A4
Pibrac F 33 C8
Pićan HR 67 B9
Picar AL 168 D3
Picassent E 48 F4
Picauville F 23 B9
Picerno I 60 B5
Picher D 83 D10
Pichl bei Wels A 76 F5
Pickering GB 11 C10
Pico I 62 E5
Picón E 54 A4
Picoto P 44 B3
Picquigny F 18 E5
Pidbuzh UA 145 E7
Pidhorodtsi UA 145 E7
Pidlisne UA 153 A7
Piebalgas LV 135 C8
Piechcin PL 138 E5
Piechowice PL 81 E9
Piecki PL 139 C11
Piecnik PL 85 D10
Piedicorte-di-Gaggio F 37 G10
Piedicroce F 37 G10
Piedimonte Etneo I 59 D7
Piedimonte Matese I 60 A2
Piedimulera I 68 A5
Piedrabuena E 54 A4
Piedrafita de Babia E 39 C7
Piedrahita E 45 D10
Piedralaves E 46 D3
Piedras Albas E 45 E7
Piedras Blancas E 39 A8
Piedruja LV 133 E2
Piegaro I 62 B2
Piégut-Pluviers F 29 D7
Piehinki FIN 119 E12
Piekary Śląskie PL 143 F6
Piekielnik PL 147 C9
Piekoszów PL 143 E9
Pieksämäen mlk FIN 124 F8
Pieksämäki FIN 124 F8
Pielavesi FIN 123 D17
Pielești RO 160 E3
Pielgrzymka PL 81 D9
Pienava LV 134 C6
Pienijżnica PL 85 C11
Pienijżno PL 139 B9
Pieńkowo PL 85 B11
Piennes F 19 F12
Pieńsk PL 81 D8
Pienza I 62 A1
Piera E 43 D7
Pierowall GB 3 G11
Pierre-Buffière F 29 D8
Pierre-Châtel F 31 F8
Pierre-de-Bresse F 31 B7
Pierrefeu-du-Var F 36 E4
Pierrefitte-Nestalas F 32 E5
Pierrefitte-sur-Aire F 26 C3
Pierrefonds F 18 F6
Pierrefontaine-les-Varans F 26 F6
Pierrefort F 30 F2
Pierrelatte F 35 B8
Pierrepont F 19 F12
Pierres F 24 C6
Pierrevert F 35 C10
Piershil NL 182 B4
Piertinjaure S 109 C17
Pierzchnica PL 143 E10
Piesau D 75 A9
Pieścirogi PL 139 E10
Piesendorf A 73 B6
Pieski PL 81 B8
Piesport D 185 E6
Piešťany SK 146 D5
Pieszkowo PL 136 E2
Pieszyce PL 81 E11
Pietrabbondante I 63 D6
Pietracatella I 63 D7
Pietracorbara F 37 F10
Pietra-di-Verde F 37 G10
Pietragalla I 60 B5
Pietralba F 37 F10
Pietra Ligure I 37 C8
Pietralunga I 66 F5
Pietramelara I 60 A2
Pietramontecorvino I 63 D8
Pietraperzia I 58 E5
Pietraporzio I 36 C6
Pietrari RO 160 C4
Pietrasanta I 66 E1
Pietravairano I 60 A2
Pietroasa RO 151 D10
Pietroasele RO 161 C9
Pietroșani RO 161 F7
Pietrosella F 37 H9
Pietroșița RO 161 C6
Pietrowice Wielkie PL 142 F5
Pieve d'Alpago I 72 D5
Pieve del Cairo I 68 C6
Pieve di Bono I 69 B10
Pieve di Cadore I 72 D5
Pieve di Cento I 66 C3
Pieve di Soligo I 72 E5
Pieve di Teco I 37 C7
Pieve Fosciana I 66 D1
Pievepelago I 66 D2
Pieve Santo Stefano I 66 E5
Pieve Torina I 62 A4
Pieve Vergonte I 68 A5
Piffonds F 25 D9
Piges GR 174 E5
Pigi GR 169 E6
Pigi GR 177 A7
Piglio I 62 D4
Pigna I 37 D7
Pignans F 36 E4
Pignataro Interamna I 62 E5
Pignataro Maggiore I 60 A2
Pignola I 60 B5
Pihlajakoski FIN 127 B13
Pihlajalahti FIN 127 B10
Pihlajalahti FIN 129 B9
Pihlajavaara FIN 125 D16
Pihlajavesi FIN 123 F12
Pihlava FIN 126 B6
Pihtipudas FIN 123 D15
Piikkiö FIN 126 E8
Piilijärvi S 116 C6
Piiloperä FIN 121 B12
Piippola FIN 119 F15
Piipsjärvi FIN 119 F13
Piirsalu EST 131 C8
Piispa FIN 125 D11
Piispajärvi FIN 121 D13
Piittisjärvi FIN 119 B17
Pijnacker NL 16 D2
Pikkarala FIN 119 E15
Pikkula FIN 119 D17
Piktupėnai LT 134 F3
Pila I 66 C5
Piła PL 85 D11
Pilar de la Mola E 57 D8
Pilas E 51 E7
Pilawa PL 141 G5
Piława Górna PL 81 E11
Pilchowice PL 142 F6
Pilda LV 133 D3
Piles E 56 D4
Pilgrimstad S 103 A9
Pili GR 175 B8
Pilica PL 143 F8
Pilis H 150 C4
Piliscsaba H 149 A11
Pilisszántó H 149 A11
Pilisszentiván H 149 A11
Pilisvörösvár H 149 A11
Pill A 72 B4
Pilling GB 10 D6
Pilníkov CZ 77 A9
Pilpala FIN 127 D11
Pilsach D 75 D10
Pilskalns LV 135 B13
Pilsting D 75 E12
Piltene LV 134 B3
Pilträsk S 118 C4
Pilu RO 151 D7
Pilviškiai LT 136 D7
Pilzno PL 143 G11
Pimentel I 64 E3
Pimperne GB 13 D10
Pimpiö S 117 E10
Piña de Campos E 40 D3
Piña de Esgueva E 40 E3
Piñar E 53 B10
Pinarbași TR 171 E10
Pinarca TR 173 B9
Pinarejo E 47 E8
Pinarhisar TR 173 A8
Pinarköy TR 181 B7
Pinarlibelen TR 177 E10
Pinasca I 31 F11
Pincehely H 149 C10
Pinchbeck GB 11 F11
Pińczów PL 143 E10
Pindstrup DK 86 C6
Pineda de Cigüela E 47 D7
Pineda de la Sierra E 40 D5
Pineda de Mar E 43 D9
Pinela P 39 E6
Piñel de Abajo E 40 E3
Pinerolo I 31 F11
Pineto I 62 B6
Piney F 25 D11
Pinggau A 148 B6
Pinhal Novo P 50 B2
Pinhanços P 44 D5
Pinhão P 44 B5
Pinheiro P 50 C2
Pinheiro Grande P 44 F4
Pinhel P 45 C6
Pinhoe GB 13 D8
Pinilla de Molina E 47 C9
Pinilla de Toro E 39 E9
Pinkafeld A 148 B6
Pinneberg D 82 C7
Pinnow D 81 C7
Pino E 39 E7
Pino F 37 F10
Pino del Río E 39 C10
Pinofranqueado E 45 D8
Pinols F 30 E3
Piñor E 38 C3
Pinoso E 56 E2
Pinos-Puente E 53 B9
Pinsac F 29 F9
Pinsiö FIN 127 B9
Pinsoro E 41 D9
Pintamo FIN 121 D10
Pintano E 32 E3
Pinto E 46 D5
Pinwherry GB 4 E7
Pinzano al Tagliamento I 73 D6
Pinzio P 45 C6
Pinzolo I 69 A10
Piobbico I 66 E6
Piolenc F 35 B8
Pioltello I 69 C7
Piombino I 65 B3
Piombino Dese I 72 E4
Pionerskiy RUS 139 A9
Pionki PL 141 H4
Pionsat F 29 C11
Pioraco I 67 F6
Piornal E 45 D9
Piossasco I 31 F11
Piotrkowice PL 81 D11
Piotrków Kujawski PL 138 E5
Piotrków Trybunalski PL 143 D8
Piove di Sacco I 66 B5
Piovene Rocchette I 69 B11
Piperskärr S 93 D9
Pipirig RO 153 C8
Pipriac F 23 E8
Piqeras AL 168 D2
Pir RO 151 C9
Piraino I 59 C6
Piran SLO 67 A8
Pirčiupiai LT 137 E10
Pirdop BG 165 D9
Pirg AL 168 C4
Pirgovo BG 161 F7
Piriac-sur-Mer F 22 F6
Piricse H 151 B9
Pirin BG 169 A10
Pirinçi TR 173 B10
Pîrjolteni MD 154 C2
Pirkkala FIN 127 C10
Pîrlița MD 153 C11
Pîrlița MD 154 A2
Pirmasens D 21 F9
Pirna D 80 E5
Pirnmill GB 4 D6
Pirot SRB 164 C6
Pirovac HR 156 E4
Pirtó H 150 E3
Pirttijoki FIN 121 E9
Pirttikoski FIN 119 B18
Pirttikoski FIN 119 F12
Pirttikoski FIN 127 C10
Pirttimäki FIN 123 C17
Pirttimäki FIN 124 E7
Pirttimäki FIN 125 C10
Pirttinen FIN 123 D10
Pirttivaara FIN 121 D14
Pirttivuopio S 111 E17
Pisa FIN 119 B14
Pisa I 66 E1
Pisanets BG 161 F8
Pisarovina HR 148 E5
Pisarovo BG 165 C9
Pischelsdorf in der Steiermark A 148 B5
Pișchia RO 151 F7
Pisciotta I 60 C4
Pișcolt RO 151 B9
Piscu RO 155 B1
Piscu Vechi RO 159 F11
Pišece SLO 148 D5
Písečná CZ 77 B12
Písek CZ 76 D6
Písek CZ 147 B7
Pishcha UA 141 G9
Pishchana UA 154 A5
Pishchanka UA 154 A3
Pisisaare EST 131 D11
Piskokefalo GR 179 E11
Piškorevci HR 157 B9
Pisoderi GR 168 C5
Pisogne I 69 B9
Pissonas GR 175 B8
Pissos F 32 B4
Pistiana GR 168 F5
Pisticci I 61 C7
Pisto FIN 121 D13
Pistoia I 66 E2
Pisz PL 139 C12
Piszczac PL 141 G8
Pitagowan GB 5 B9
Pitäjänmäki FIN 123 C15
Pitarque E 42 F2
Piteå S 118 D6
Pitești RO 160 D5
Pithiviers F 25 D7
Pitigliano I 65 B5
Pitkäjärvi FIN 127 D9
Pitkälä FIN 129 B11
Pitkälahti FIN 124 E9
Pitkäsenkylä FIN 119 F12
Pitkyaranta RUS 129 B15
Pitlochry GB 5 B9
Pitomača HR 149 E8
Pitrags LV 130 F4
Pitres E 55 F6
Pîtres F 18 F3
Pitscottie GB 5 C11
Pitsinaiika GR 174 C4
Pitstone GB 15 D7
Pitsund S 118 D7
Pitt GB 13 C12
Pittem B 19 C7
Pitten A 148 A6
Pittentrail GB 3 K8
Pittenweem GB 5 C11
Pitvaros H 150 E6
Pivašiūnai LT 137 E9
Pivka SLO 73 E9
Pivnice SRB 158 C3
Piwniczna-Zdrój PL 145 E2
Pizarra E 53 C7
Pizzighettone I 69 C8
Pizzo I 59 B9
Pizzoferrato I 63 D6
Pizzoli I 62 C4
Pjedsted DK 86 D5
Pjelax FIN 122 F6
Pjenovac BIH 157 D10
Pjesker S 118 C3
Plaaz D 83 C12
Plabennec F 22 C3
Placencia de las Armas E 32 D1
Plachkovtsi BG 166 D4
Plācis LV 135 B9
Plaffeien CH 31 B11
Plagia GR 169 B8
Plaidt D 21 D8
Plăieșii de Jos RO 153 E8
Plaintel F 22 D6
Plaisance F 33 C6
Plaisance-du-Touch F 33 C8
Plaisir F 24 C6
Plaka GR 168 F5
Plaka GR 171 D8
Plaka GR 175 E6
Plaka GR 179 B7
Plakhtiyivka UA 154 E5
Plakias GR 178 E7
Plakovo BG 166 D5
Plana BIH 157 G9
Planá CZ 75 C12
Plana GR 169 D10
Planá nad Lužnicí CZ 77 D7
Plaňany CZ 77 B8
Plancher-Bas F 27 E6
Plancoët F 23 C7
Plancy-l'Abbaye F 25 C10
Plan-de-Baux F 31 F7
Plan-de-la-Tour F 36 E5
Plandište SRB 159 C7
Plan-d'Orgon F 35 C8
Planegg D 75 F9
Planès F 33 F10
Plāņi LV 131 F11
Plánice CZ 76 D4
Planina SLO 73 E9
Planina SLO 148 D4
Planina SRB 158 E3
Planinica SRB 159 F9
Planjane HR 156 E5
Plankenfels D 75 C9
Planos GR 174 D2
Plasencia E 45 D8
Plasencia del Monte E 41 D10
Plaški HR 156 B3
Plassen N 102 D4
Plášťovce SK 147 E7
Plasy CZ 76 C4
Plataies GR 175 C7
Platamona Lido I 64 B1
Platamonas GR 169 E8
Platamonas GR 171 B7
Platania I 59 A9
Platanias GR 175 A7
Platanistos GR 175 C10
Platanorrevma GR 169 D7
Platanos GR 174 D4
Platanos GR 175 A6
Platanos GR 178 E6
Platanos GR 178 E8
Platanovrysi GR 174 C4
Plătărești RO 161 E8
Plataria GR 168 F3
Plate D 83 C11
Plateliai LT 134 D3
Platerów PL 141 F7
Plati GR 171 A10
Platì I 59 C9
Platiana GR 174 D4
Platičevo SRB 158 D4
Platja d'Aro E 43 D10
Platja de Nules E 48 E4
Platone LV 134 C7
Plattling D 76 E3
Platy GR 169 C8
Platykampos GR 169 E8
Platys Gialos GR 176 E5
Platys Gialos GR 176 F4
Plau D 83 D12
Plaue D 79 E8
Plauen D 75 A11
Plav MNE 163 D8
Plavë RKS 163 E10
Plaveč SK 145 E2
Plavecký Štvrtok SK 77 F12
Plaviņas LV 135 C11
Plavna SRB 159 E9
Plavni UA 155 C3
Plavnica SK 145 E2
Plavno HR 156 D5
Plavy CZ 81 E8
Pławno PL 85 C10
Plaza E 40 B6
Plazac F 29 E8
Płazów PL 144 C7
Pleaux F 29 E10
Plech D 75 C9
Plecka Dąbrowa PL 143 B8
Pleine-Fougères F 23 C8
Pleikšņi LV 133 D2
Plélan-le-Grand F 23 D7
Plélo F 22 C6
Plémet F 22 D6
Plénée-Jugon F 23 D7
Pléneuf-Val-André F 22 C6
Plenița RO 159 E11
Plentzia E 40 B6
Plérin F 22 C6
Plescop F 22 E6
Pleșcuța RO 151 E9
Pleșeni MD 154 E2
Plešivec SK 145 F1
Plesná CZ 75 B11
Pleśna PL 144 D2
Pleșoiu RO 160 E4
Plessa D 80 D5
Plessé F 23 E8
Plestin-les-Grèves F 22 C4
Pleszew PL 142 C4
Pleternica HR 157 B8
Plettenberg D 21 B9
Pleubian F 22 C5
Pleudihen-sur-Rance F 23 C8
Pleumartin F 29 B7
Pleumeur-Bodou F 22 C4
Pleurs F 25 C10
Pleuven F 22 E3
Pleven BG 165 C10
Plevník-Drienové SK 147 C7
Pleyben F 22 D4
Pleyber-Christ F 22 C4
Pliego E 55 D10
Plienciems LV 134 B6
Plieśovce SK 147 E8
Pliezhausen D 187 D7
Plikati GR 168 D4
Plisa BY 133 F3
Pliska BG 167 C8
Plitvica HR 156 C4
Pljevlja MNE 163 C7
Pllanejë RKS 163 E10
Ploaghe I 64 B2
Plobannalec F 22 E3
Plobsheim F 186 E4
Ploče HR 157 F7
Ploce LV 134 C2
Plochingen D 187 D7
Pločica SRB 159 D6
Płociczno PL 136 E6
Płock PL 139 E8
Plodovoye RUS 129 D13
Ploegsteert B 182 D1
Ploemeur F 22 E5
Ploeren F 22 E6
Ploërmel F 23 E7
Plœuc-sur-Lié F 22 D6
Plogonnec F 22 D3
Plogshagen D 84 A4
Ploiești RO 161 D8
Plomari GR 177 B7
Plombières-les-Bains F 26 E5
Plomeur F 22 E3
Plomin HR 67 B9
Plomodiern F 22 D3
Plön D 83 B8
Plonéour-Lanvern F 22 E3
Plonévez-du-Faou F 22 D4
Plonevez-Porzay F 22 D3
Płońsk PL 139 E9
Plop MD 153 A11
Plopana RO 153 D10
Plopeni RO 161 C7
Plopi MD 154 B4
Plopii-Slăvitești RO 160 F5
Plopșoru RO 160 D2
Plopu RO 161 C8
Plosca RO 160 E6
Ploscoș RO 152 D3
Ploska UA 152 B6
Płoskinia PL 139 B8
Płośnica PL 139 D9
Plößberg D 75 C11
Płoty PL 85 C8
Plötzin D 79 B12
Plötzky D 79 B10
Plou E 42 F2
Plouagat F 22 C6
Plouaret F 22 C5
Plouarzel F 22 D2
Plouay F 22 E5
Ploubalay F 23 C7
Ploubazlanec F 22 C5
Ploubezre F 22 C5
Ploudalmézeau F 22 C2
Ploudiry F 22 D3
Plouescat F 22 C3
Plouézec F 22 C6
Ploufragan F 22 D6
Plougasnou F 22 C4
Plougastel-Daoulas F 22 D3
Plougonven F 22 C4
Plougonver F 22 D5
Plougrescant F 22 C5
Plouguenast F 22 D6
Plouguerneau F 22 C2
Plouguernével F 22 D5
Plouguiel F 22 C5
Plouguin F 22 C2
Plouha F 22 C6
Plouharnel F 22 E5
Plouhinec F 22 D3
Plouhinec F 22 E5
Plouigneau F 22 C4
Ploumagoar F 22 C5
Ploumilliau F 22 C4
Plounévez-Moëdec F 22 C5
Plounévez-Quintin F 22 D5
Plouray F 22 D5
Plouvorn F 22 C3
Plouyé F 22 D4
Plouzané F 22 D2
Plouzévédé F 22 C3
Plovdiv BG 165 E10
Plozévet F 22 E3
Pluck IRL 7 C7
Plüderhausen D 187 D8
Plugari RO 153 C10
Plumbridge GB 4 F2
Plumelec F 22 E6
Pluméliau F 22 E6
Plumergat F 22 E6
Plumlov CZ 77 D12
Pluneret F 22 E6
Plungė LT 134 E3
Pluszkiejmy PL 136 E5
Pluvigner F 22 E5
Plužine BIH 157 F9
Plužine MNE 157 F10
Płużnica PL 138 D6
Pluzunet F 22 C5
Plwmp GB 12 A6
Plymouth GB 12 E6
Plympton GB 12 E6
Plymstock GB 12 E6
Plytra GR 178 B4
Plyussa RUS 132 E5
Plyusy BY 133 E2
Plzeň CZ 76 C4
Pniewo PL 85 D11
Pniewo PL 139 E11
Pniewo PL 143 B8
Pniewy PL 81 A10
Pniewy PL 141 G3
Poarta Albă RO 155 E2
Pobedím SK 146 D5
Pobedino RUS 136 D6
Poběžovice CZ 75 C12
Pobiedno PL 145 D5
Pobiedziska PL 81 B12
Pobierowo PL 85 B7
Pobikry PL 141 E7
Pobladura del Valle E 39 D8
Poblete E 54 B5
Pobłocie PL 85 A13
Poboleda E 42 E5
Poboru RO 160 D5
Pobožje NMK 164 E3
Počátky CZ 77 D8
Poceirão P 50 B2
Pöchlarn A 77 F8
Pociems LV 131 F9
Počitelj BIH 157 F8
Pociumbeni MD 153 B10
Pöcking D 75 G9
Pocking D 76 F4
Pocklington GB 11 D10
Pocola RO 151 D9
Pocrnje BIH 157 F9
Pocsaj H 151 C8
Pócspetri H 145 H4
Poczesna PL 143 E7
Podareš NMK 169 A8
Podari RO 160 E3
Podayva BG 161 F9
Podbiel SK 147 C8
Podbořany CZ 76 B4
Podborov'ye RUS 132 F4
Podbožur MNE 163 D6
Podbrdo BIH 157 D7
Podbrdo SLO 73 D8
Podbrezová SK 147 D9
Podčetrtek SLO 148 D5
Poddjbice PL 143 C6
Poděbrady CZ 77 B8
Podedwórze PL 141 G8
Podegrodzie PL 145 D2
Podelzig D 81 B7
Podem BG 165 B10
Podeni RO 159 D10
Podenii Noi RO 161 C8
Podensac F 32 A5
Podenzana I 69 E8
Podenzano I 37 B11
Podersdorf am See A 77 G11
Podgajci Posavski HR 157 C10
Podgaje PL 85 D11
Podgora HR 157 F7
Podgorač HR 149 F10
Podgorac SRB 159 F8
Podgoria RO 161 C10
Podgorica MNE 163 E7
Podgorica SLO 73 D10
Podgorie AL 168 C4
Podgoritsa BG 167 C6
Podgórze PL 139 D13
Podgrab BIH 157 E10
Podgrad SLO 67 A9
Podgrade BIH 157 E8
Podhorod SK 145 F5
Podhum BIH 157 E7
Podil's'k UA 154 B5
Podivín CZ 77 E11
Podkova BG 171 B8
Podkowa Leśna PL 141 F3
Podkrajewo PL 139 D9
Podkrepa BG 166 F5
Podkum SLO 73 D11
Podlapača HR 156 C4
Podlehnik SLO 148 D5
Podles NMK 169 A6
Podlipoglav SLO 73 D10
Podmilečje BIH 157 D7
Podnanos SLO 73 E8
Podnovlje BIH 157 C9
Podochori GR 170 C6
Podogora GR 174 B3
Podoima MD 154 B3
Podoleni RO 153 D9
Podolí CZ 77 D11
Podolie SK 146 D5
Podolínec SK 145 E2
Podorozhnye UA 145 E9
Podosoje BIH 162 D5
Podrašnica BIH 157 D6
Podravske Sesvete HR 149 D8
Podromanija BIH 157 E10
Podsreda SLO 148 D5
Podstrana HR 156 F6
Podtabor SLO 73 E10
Podturen HR 149 D7
Podu Iloaiei RO 153 C10
Podujevë RKS 164 D3
Poduri RO 153 E9
Podu Turcului RO 153 E10
Podvelež BIH 157 F8
Podvrška SRB 159 D9
Podvysoká SK 147 C7
Podwilk PL 147 B9
Poederlee B 182 C5
Poeni RO 160 E6
Poenița MD 153 A11
Pofi I 62 D4
Pogăceaua RO 152 D4
Pogana RO 153 E11
Pogar BIH 157 D9
Poggendorf D 84 B4
Poggiardo I 61 C10
Poggibonsi I 66 F3
Poggio Berni I 66 D5
Poggio Bustone I 62 B3
Poggio Catino I 62 C3
Poggiodomo I 62 B3
Poggio Imperiale I 63 D8
Poggio-Mezzana F 37 G10
Poggio Mirteto I 62 C3
Poggio Moiano I 62 C3
Poggio Picenze I 62 C5
Poggio Renatico I 66 C4
Poggiorsini I 60 B6
Poggio Rusco I 66 C3
Pöggstall A 77 F8
Pogny F 25 C11
Pogoanele RO 161 D9
Pogoniani GR 168 E3
Pogorzela PL 81 C12
Pogorzelice PL 85 B13
Pogradec AL 168 C4
Pogrodzie PL 139 B8
Pohja FIN 127 C12
Pohja FIN 127 E10
Pohja-Lankila FIN 129 C11
Pohjasenvaara FIN 117 D11
Pohjaslahti FIN 119 B17
Pohjaslahti FIN 123 F12
Pohjavaara FIN 121 F11
Pohjois-Ii FIN 119 D14
Pohjoisjärvi FIN 123 F13
Pohorelá SK 147 D10
Pohořelice CZ 77 E11
Pohronská Polhora SK 147 D9
Pohronský Ruskov SK 147 F7
Poian RO 153 E8
Poiana RO 161 D7
Poiana Blenchii RO 152 C3
Poiana Câmpina RO 161 C7
Poiana Cristei RO 161 B9
Poiana Lacului RO 160 D5
Poiana Mare RO 159 F11
Poiana Mărului RO 160 B6
Poiana Sibiului RO 152 F3
Poiana Stampei RO 152 C6
Poiana Teiuliu RO 153 C7
Poiana Vadului RO 151 E10
Poibrene BG 165 E8
Pöide EST 130 D6
Poienari RO 153 D10
Poienarii Burchii RO 161 D8
Poienarii de Argeș RO 160 C5
Poienești RO 153 D11
Poieni RO 151 D10
Poienile de Sub Munte RO 152 B4
Poijula FIN 121 D10
Poikajärvi FIN 117 E15
Põikva EST 131 D10
Poinçon-lès-Larrey F 25 E11
Poing D 75 F10
Pointis-Inard F 33 D7
Poirino I 37 B7
Poiseux F 25 F9
Poissons F 26 D3
Poissy F 24 C7
Poitiers F 29 B6
Poix-de-Picardie F 18 E4
Poix-Terron F 19 E10
Pojan AL 168 C4
Pojanluoma FIN 122 E9
Pojatno HR 148 E5
Pojejena RO 159 D8
Pojo FIN 127 E10
Pojorâta RO 152 B6
Pókaszepetk H 149 C7
Poķi LV 134 C7
Pokka FIN 117 B15
Poklečani BIH 157 E7
Pokoj BIH 156 C4
Pokój PL 142 E4
Pokrówka PL 141 H8
Pokupsko HR 148 F5
Polac RKS 163 D10
Polača HR 156 D5
Polače HR 162 D3
Pola de Allande E 39 B6
Pola de Laviana E 39 B8
Pola de Lena E 39 B8
Pola de Siero E 39 B8
Pola de Somiedo E 39 B7
Polaincourt-et-Clairefontaine F 26 E5
Połajewo PL 85 E11
Polán E 46 E4
Polanica-Zdrój PL 77 B10
Połaniec PL 143 F11
Polanów PL 85 B11
Polatsk BY 133 F5
Polch D 21 D8
Polcirkeln S 116 E6
Połczyno PL 138 A5
Połczyn Zdrój PL 85 C10
Polegate GB 15 F9
Polena BG 165 F7
Poleñino E 41 E11
Polepy CZ 76 A6
Polesella I 66 C4
Polessk RUS 136 D3
Polgár H 145 H3
Polgárdi H 149 B10
Polgaste EST 131 F13
Polia I 59 B9
Poliçan AL 168 C3
Poliçan AL 168 D3
Police PL 84 C7
Police nad Metuj CZ 81 E10
Polichni GR 169 C8
Polichnitos GR 177 A7
Polička CZ 77 C10
Policoro I 61 C7
Policzna PL 141 H5
Polientes E 40 C4
Polignano a Mare I 61 B8
Poligny F 31 B8
Polikrayshte BG 166 C5
Polisot F 25 D11
Polistena I 59 C9
Politika GR 175 B8
Pölitz D 83 C8
Polizzi Generosa I 58 D5
Põljä FIN 124 D9
Poljana SRB 159 D7
Poljanak HR 156 C4
Poljana Pakračka HR 149 F7
Poljane SLO 73 D9
Poljčane SLO 148 D5
Polje BIH 157 C8
Poljica HR 156 D3
Poljice BIH 157 D10
Poljice-Popovo BIH 162 D5

Ravelsbach *A* 77 E9
Rävemåla *S* 89 B8
Ravenglass *GB* 10 C5
Ravenna *I* 66 D5
Ravensburg *D* 71 B9
Ravenstein *NL* 16 E5
Ravières *F* 25 E11
Ravijoki *FIN* 128 D8
Ravik *N* 108 B7
Rävlanda *S* 91 D12
Ravna Dubrava *SRB* 164 C5
Ravna Gora *HR* 67 B10
Ravna Reka *SRB* 159 E8
Ravne *SLO* 73 D11
Ravne na Koroškem *SLO* 73 C10
Ravnets *BG* 167 D8
Ravni *BIH* 157 F8
Ravnište *SRB* 164 C3
Ravnje *SRB* 158 D3
Ravnkilde *DK* 86 B5
Ravno *BIH* 157 E7
Ravno *BIH* 162 D4
Ravnogor *BG* 165 F9
Ravno Selo *SRB* 158 C4
Ravnshøj *DK* 90 E7
Ravnstrup *DK* 86 C4
Rävsön *S* 103 A15
Ravsted *DK* 86 E4
Rawa Mazowiecka *PL* 141 G2
Rawicz *PL* 81 C11
Rawmarsh *GB* 11 E9
Rawtenstall *GB* 11 D7
Raykovo *BG* 171 A7
Rayleigh *GB* 15 D10
Rayol-Canadel-sur-Mer *F* 36 E4
Räyrinki *FIN* 123 D11
Ražana *SRB* 158 E4
Ražanac *HR* 156 D3
Ražanj *SRB* 159 F8
Războieni *RO* 153 C9
Razboj *BIH* 157 B7
Razbojna *SRB* 164 C3
Razdelna *BG* 167 C9
Razdol *BG* 169 A9
Razdrto *SLO* 73 E9
Razès *F* 29 C8
Razgrad *BG* 160 F2
Razgrad *BG* 167 B7
Ražljevo *BIH* 157 C10
Razlog *BG* 165 F7
Razlovci *NMK* 165 F6
Ražňany *SK* 145 E3
Ráztočno *SK* 147 D7
Răzvad *RO* 161 D6
Reading *GB* 14 E7
Reaghstown *IRL* 7 E9
Real *P* 38 F3
Réalmont *F* 33 C10
Realmonte *I* 58 E3
Réalville *F* 33 B8
Rear Cross *IRL* 8 C6
Réaup *F* 33 B6
Reay *GB* 3 H9
Rebais *F* 25 C9
Rebbenesbotn *N* 112 C2
Rebecq *B* 19 C9
Rébénacq *F* 32 D5
Rebild *DK* 86 B5
Rebollosa de Jadraque *E* 47 B7
Reboly *RUS* 125 C15
Rebordelo *E* 38 B3
Rebordelo *P* 38 E5
Rebra *RO* 152 C4
Rebricea *RO* 153 D11
Rebrișoara *RO* 152 C4
Rebrovo *BG* 165 D7
Rebŭrkovo *BG* 165 C8
Reca *SK* 146 E4
Reçan *RKS* 163 E10
Recanati *I* 67 F8
Recaș *RO* 151 F8
Recco *I* 37 C10
Recea *MD* 153 B11
Recea *MD* 154 C3
Recea *RO* 151 B12
Recea *RO* 152 F5
Recea *RO* 160 D6
Recea-Cristur *RO* 152 C3
Recess *IRL* 6 F3
Recey-sur-Ource *F* 25 E12
Réchicourt-le-Château *F* 27 C6
Rechlin *D* 83 D13
Rechnitz *A* 149 B6
Recht *B* 20 D6
Rechtenbach *D* 74 C6
Reci *RO* 153 F7
Rečica *SLO* 73 D11
Rečice *BIH* 157 F8
Recke *D* 17 D9
Reckingen *CH* 70 E6
Recklinghausen *D* 17 E8
Recoaro Terme *I* 69 B11
Recoubeau-Jansac *F* 35 A9
Recsk *H* 147 F10
Recuerda *E* 40 F6
Recz *PL* 85 D9
Rjczno *PL* 141 H1
Reda *PL* 138 A5
Redalen *N* 101 E13
Redange *L* 20 E5
Redcar *GB* 11 B9
Redcastle *IRL* 4 E2
Redcross *IRL* 9 C10
Reddelich *D* 83 B11
Redditch *GB* 13 A11
Réde *H* 149 B9
Redea *RO* 160 E4
Redefin *D* 83 D10
Redhill *GB* 15 E8
Rédics *H* 149 C6
Réding *F* 27 C7
Redinha *P* 44 D3
Rediu *RO* 153 C11
Rediu *RO* 153 D9
Rediu *RO* 153 F11
Rediul Mare *MD* 153 A11
Rednitzhembach *D* 75 D9
Redon *F* 23 E7
Redondela *E* 38 D2
Redondelo *P* 38 E4
Redondo *P* 50 B4
Redován *E* 56 E3
Red Point *GB* 2 K5
Redruth *GB* 12 E4
Redsted *DK* 86 B3
Reduzum *NL* 16 B5
Rjdzikowo *PL* 85 B12
Rjdziny *PL* 143 E7
Reen *IRL* 8 E3
Reens *IRL* 8 C5
Reepham *GB* 15 B11
Rees *D* 16 E6
Reeßum *D* 17 B12
Reetz *D* 79 B11
Reetz *D* 83 D11
Reftele *S* 87 A13
Regalbuto *I* 59 D6
Regen *D* 76 E4
Regensburg *D* 75 D11
Regensdorf *CH* 27 F9
Regenstauf *D* 75 D11
Reggello *I* 66 E4
Reggio di Calabria *I* 59 C8
Reggiolo *I* 66 C2
Reggio nell'Emilia *I* 66 C2
Reghin *RO* 152 D5
Reghiu *RO* 153 F9
Regna *S* 92 B7
Regnitzlosau *D* 75 B11
Régny *F* 30 D5
Regöly *H* 149 C10
Regozero *RUS* 121 D17
Regstrup *DK* 87 D9
Reguengo *E* 38 D2
Reguengos de Monsaraz *P* 50 C4
Rehau *D* 75 B11
Rehburg (Rehburg-Loccum) *D* 17 D12
Rehden *D* 17 C10
Rehling *D* 75 F8
Rehlingen-Siersburg *D* 21 F7
Řehlovice *CZ* 80 E5
Rehmsdorf *D* 79 D11
Rehna *D* 83 C10
Rehula *FIN* 129 C9
Reibitz *D* 79 C11
Reichelsheim (Odenwald) *D* 187 B6
Reichenau an der Rax *A* 148 A5
Reichenbach *CH* 70 D5
Reichenbach *D* 79 E11
Reichenbach *D* 187 B6
Reichenberg *D* 74 C6
Reichenfels *A* 73 B10
Reichenthal *A* 76 E6
Reichertsheim *D* 75 F11
Reichia *GR* 178 B5
Reichling *D* 71 B11
Reichmannsdorf *D* 75 A9
Reicholzheim *D* 74 C6
Reichraming *A* 73 A9
Reichshoffen *F* 27 C8
Reichstett *F* 186 D4
Reiden *CH* 27 F8
Reigada *P* 45 C7
Reigate *GB* 15 E8
Reignac *F* 28 E4
Reignier *F* 31 C9
Reil *D* 21 D8
Reilingen *D* 187 C6
Reillanne *F* 35 C10
Reillo *E* 47 E9
Reims *F* 19 F9
Reina *E* 51 C8
Reinach *CH* 27 F8
Reinach *CH* 27 F9
Reinbek *D* 83 C8
Reinberg *D* 84 B4
Reine *N* 110 E5
Reinfeld (Holstein) *D* 83 C8
Reinheim *D* 21 E11
Reinosa *E* 40 C3
Reinøysund *N* 114 D8
Reinsfeld *D* 21 E7
Reinskard *N* 112 D4
Reinskloster *N* 104 D7
Reinstad *N* 111 C10
Reinsvik *N* 104 E3
Reinsvoll *N* 101 E13
Reipa *N* 108 C6
Reisbach *D* 75 E12
Reischach *D* 75 F12
Reisjärvi *FIN* 123 C13
Reiskirchen *D* 21 C11
Reiss *GB* 3 J10
Reitan *N* 100 B8
Reitan *N* 101 A14
Reitano *I* 58 D5
Reith bei Seefeld *A* 72 B3
Reit im Winkl *D* 72 A5
Reittiö *FIN* 125 D9
Reivyčiai *LT* 134 D4
Rejmyre *S* 92 B7
Rejowiec *PL* 141 H8
Rejsby *DK* 86 E3
Reka *HR* 149 D7
Rekava *LV* 133 B3
Rekavice *BIH* 157 C7
Reken *D* 17 E8
Rekijoki *FIN* 127 E9
Rekken *NL* 17 D7
Reklynets' *UA* 144 C9
Rekovac *SRB* 159 F7
Rekowo *PL* 85 B12
Rekvik *N* 111 A15
Rėkyva *LT* 134 E6
Relíquias *P* 50 D3
Relletti *FIN* 119 E13
Relleu *E* 56 D4
Rellingen *D* 83 C7
Rém *H* 150 E3
Remagen *D* 21 C8
Rémalard *F* 24 D4
Rembercourt-Sommaisne *F* 26 C3
Remda *D* 79 E9
Remels (Uplengen) *D* 17 B9
Remennikovo *RUS* 133 C5
Remeskylä *FIN* 123 C16
Remetea *RO* 151 D9
Remetea *RO* 152 D6
Remetea Chioarului *RO* 152 B3
Remetea Mare *RO* 151 F7
Remeți *RO* 145 H8
Remetinec *HR* 149 D6
Remetské Hámre *SK* 145 F5
Remich *L* 20 E6
Remicourt *B* 183 D6
Remiremont *F* 26 D6
Remmam *S* 107 D14
Remmen *S* 102 B8
Remmet *S* 102 B7
Remnes *N* 108 E4
Remolinos *E* 41 E9
Remouchamps *B* 183 E7
Remoulins *F* 35 C8
Remplin *D* 83 C13
Remptendorf *D* 75 A10
Remscheid *D* 21 B8
Remte *LV* 134 C5
Remungol *F* 22 E6
Rémuzat *F* 35 B9
Rena *E* 45 F9
Rena *N* 101 D14
Renaison *F* 30 C4
Renålandet *S* 106 D8
Renazé *F* 23 E9
Rencēni *LV* 131 F10
Renchen *D* 27 C9
Renda *LV* 134 B4
Rende *I* 60 E6
Rendsburg *D* 82 B7
Renedo *E* 39 E10
Renedo *E* 40 B4
Renedo de la Vega *E* 39 D10
Renens *CH* 31 B10
Renesse *NL* 16 E1
Renfrew *GB* 5 D8
Renginio *GR* 175 B6
Rengsdorf *D* 21 C8
Rengsjö *S* 103 D12
Renholmen *S* 118 D6
Reni *UA* 155 C2
Renko *FIN* 127 D11
Renkomäki *FIN* 127 D14
Renkum *NL* 183 B7
Renndal *N* 104 E5
Rennerod *D* 21 C10
Rennertshofen *D* 75 E9
Rennes *F* 23 D8
Rennes-les-Bains *F* 33 E10
Renningen *D* 27 C10
Rennweg *A* 73 B8
Renòn *I* 72 C3
Rens *DK* 86 F4
Rensjön *S* 111 D18
Reńska Wieś *PL* 142 F5
Renström *S* 118 E4
Renswoude *NL* 183 A7
Rentina *GR* 174 A4
Rentjärn *S* 107 A15
Rentweinsdorf *D* 75 B8
Renwez *F* 19 E10
Renzow *D* 83 C10
Repbäcken *S* 97 A13
Répcelak *H* 149 B8
Repedea *RO* 152 B4
Repino *RUS* 129 E12
Repki *PL* 141 F6
Replot *FIN* 122 D6
Repojoki *FIN* 117 B15
Repolka *RUS* 132 C6
Reposaari *FIN* 126 B5
Repparfjord *N* 113 C13
Reppelin *D* 83 B12
Reppen *N* 108 C6
Reppenstedt *D* 83 D8
Reps *AL* 163 F9
Repton *GB* 11 F8
Repvåg *N* 113 B16
Requejo *E* 39 D6
Requena *E* 47 F10
Réquista *F* 33 B11
Rerik *D* 83 B11
Resana *I* 72 E4
Resarö *S* 99 D10
Resavica *SRB* 159 E8
Resele *S* 107 E12
Resen *BG* 166 C5
Resen *NMK* 168 B5
Resenbro *DK* 86 C5
Resende *P* 44 B5
Rešetari *HR* 157 B7
Reșița *RO* 159 C8
Resko *PL* 85 C8
Resna *MNE* 163 E6
Resolven *GB* 13 B7
Respenda de la Peña *E* 39 C10
Resse (Wedemark) *D* 78 A6
Ressons-sur-Matz *F* 18 E6
Restelicë *RKS* 163 F10
Restinga *MA* 53 E6
Reston *GB* 5 D12
Resuttano *I* 58 D5
Retamal *E* 51 B8
Retford *GB* 11 E10
Rethel *F* 19 E9
Rethem (Aller) *D* 17 C12
Rethymno *GR* 178 E7
Retie *B* 16 F4
Retiers *F* 23 E9
Retje *SLO* 73 E10
Retortillo *E* 45 C8
Retortillo de Soria *E* 40 F6
Retournac *F* 30 E5
Rétság *H* 147 F8
Retuerta del Bullaque *E* 46 F4
Retunen *FIN* 125 E11
Retz *A* 77 E9
Reuden *D* 79 B11
Reuilly *F* 24 F7
Reurieth *D* 75 B8
Reus *E* 42 E6
Reusel *NL* 16 F4
Reut *D* 76 F3
Reute *D* 27 D8
Reuțel *MD* 153 B11
Reuterstadt Stavenhagen *D* 84 C3
Reutlingen *D* 27 D11
Reutte *A* 71 C11
Reutuaapa *FIN* 119 B15
Reuver *NL* 16 F6
Revel *F* 33 D10
Revello *I* 37 B6
Revest-du-Bion *F* 35 B10
Révfülöp *H* 149 C9
Revholmen *N* 91 A8
Reviga *RO* 161 D10
Revigny-sur-Ornain *F* 26 C2
Revilla de Collazos *E* 40 C3
Revilla del Campo *E* 40 D4
Revin *F* 19 E10
Revine-Lago *I* 72 E5
Řevnice *CZ* 76 C6
Řevničov *CZ* 76 B5
Revò *I* 72 D3
Revonlahti *FIN* 119 E13
Revsnes *N* 100 D6
Revsnes *N* 111 C11
Revsund *S* 103 A9
Revúca *SK* 147 D10
Rewal *PL* 85 B8
Rexbo *S* 103 E9
Reyrieux *F* 30 D6
Rezé *F* 23 F8
Rēzekne *LV* 133 C2
Rezi *H* 149 C8
Rezina *MD* 154 B3
Rēzna *LV* 133 D2
Rezovo *BG* 167 F10
Rezzato *I* 66 A1
Rezzo *I* 37 C7
Rezzoaglio *I* 37 B10
Rgotina *SRB* 159 E9
Rhade *D* 17 B12
Rhaunen *D* 21 E8
Rhayader *GB* 13 A7
Rheda-Wiedenbrück *D* 17 E10
Rhede *D* 17 E7
Rhede (Ems) *D* 17 B8
Rheden *NL* 183 A8
Rheinau *D* 27 C8
Rheinbach *D* 21 C7
Rheinberg *D* 17 E7
Rheinböllen *D* 185 E8
Rheinbreitbach *D* 21 C8
Rheinbrohl *D* 185 D7
Rheine *D* 17 D8
Rheinfelden (Baden) *D* 27 E8
Rheinsberg *D* 84 D3
Rheinstetten *D* 27 C9
Rheinzabern *D* 187 C5
Rhêmes-Notre-Dame *I* 31 D11
Rhêmes-St-Georges *I* 31 D11
Rhenen *NL* 16 E5
Rhens *D* 185 D8
Rhiconich *GB* 2 J7
Rhinau *F* 27 D8
Rhinow *D* 83 E12
Rhisnes *B* 182 D5
Rho *I* 69 B7
Rhode *IRL* 7 F8
Rhoden (Diemelstadt) *D* 17 F12
Rhoon *NL* 182 B4
Rhoose *GB* 13 C8
Rhosllanerchrugog *GB* 10 E5
Rhôs-on-Sea *GB* 10 E4
Rhossili *GB* 12 B6
Rhuddlan *GB* 10 E5
Rhydaman *GB* 12 B7
Rhyl *GB* 10 E5
Rhymney *GB* 13 B8
Riace *I* 59 C9
Riachos *P* 44 F3
Riaillé *F* 23 E9
Rialp *E* 33 F8
Riaño *E* 39 C10
Riano *I* 62 C3
Rians *F* 35 C10
Riantec *F* 22 E5
Rianxo *E* 38 C2
Riaz *CH* 31 B11
Riba *E* 40 B4
Ribadavia *E* 38 D3
Ribadelago *E* 39 D6
Riba de Mouro *P* 38 D3
Ribadeo *E* 38 A5
Riba de Saelices *E* 47 C8
Ribadesella *E* 39 B9
Ribaforada *E* 41 D8
Ribafrecha *E* 32 F1
Ribarci *SRB* 164 E6
Ribare *SRB* 164 C4
Ribari *SRB* 158 D3
Ribaritsa *BG* 165 D9
Riba-roja d'Ebre *E* 42 E4
Riba-roja de Turia *E* 48 E3
Ribbåsen *S* 102 D7
Ribchester *GB* 10 D6
Ribe *DK* 86 E3
Ribeauvillé *F* 27 D7
Ribécourt-Dreslincourt *F* 18 E6
Ribeira *E* 38 C2
Ribeira *P* 38 E3
Ribeira de Pena *P* 38 E4
Ribemont *F* 19 E7
Ribera *I* 58 E3
Ribérac *F* 29 E6
Ribera del Fresno *E* 51 B7
Ribesalbes *E* 48 D4
Ribes de Freser *E* 33 F10
Ribița *RO* 151 E10
Ribnica *BIH* 157 D9
Ribnica *SLO* 73 E10
Ribnica *SLO* 148 C4
Ribnica *SRB* 158 F4
Ribnik *HR* 148 E4
Rîbnița *MD* 154 B4
Ribnitz-Damgarten *D* 83 B12
Ribnovo *BG* 165 F8
Ribota *E* 40 F5
Ricadi *I* 59 B8
Říčany *CZ* 77 C7
Říčany *CZ* 77 D10
Riccia *I* 63 E7
Riccio *I* 66 F5
Riccione *I* 66 D6
Riccò del Golfo di Spezia *I* 69 E8
Richardménil *F* 26 C5
Richelieu *F* 29 A6
Richhill *GB* 7 D9
Richka *UA* 152 A5
Richmond *GB* 11 C8
Richvald *SK* 145 E3
Rickebo *S* 103 D11
Rickenbach *D* 27 E8
Rickinghall *GB* 15 C10
Rickling *D* 83 B8
Rickmansworth *GB* 15 D8
Ricla *E* 41 E9
Ricse *H* 145 G4
Ridasjärvi *FIN* 127 D13
Riddarhyttan *S* 97 C14
Ridderkerk *NL* 16 E3
Riddes *CH* 31 C11
Riđica *SRB* 150 F3
Rīdzene *LV* 135 B10
Riebiņi *LV* 135 D13
Riebnesluspen *S* 109 D13
Riec-sur-Belon *F* 22 E4
Ried *CH* 68 A5
Riede *D* 17 C11
Riedenburg *D* 75 E10
Rieder *D* 79 C9
Ried im Innkreis *A* 76 F4
Ried im Oberinntal *A* 71 C11
Ried im Zillertal *A* 72 B4
Ried in der Riedmark *A* 77 F7
Riedlingen *D* 71 A8
Riegelsberg *D* 21 F7
Riegersburg *A* 148 B5
Riego de la Vega *E* 39 D8
Riehe (Suthfeld) *D* 78 B5
Riehen *CH* 27 E8
Rielasingen-Worblingen *D* 27 E10
Riello *E* 39 C8
Rielves *E* 46 E4
Riemst *B* 19 C12
Rieneck *D* 187 A8
Rieni *RO* 151 D9
Rieponlahti *FIN* 124 E7
Riepsdorf *D* 83 B9
Riesa *D* 80 D4
Rieseby *D* 83 A7
Riesi *I* 58 E5
Riestedt *D* 79 D9
Rietavas *LT* 134 E3
Rietberg *D* 17 E10
Rieth *D* 84 C6
Riethoven *NL* 183 C6
Rieti *I* 62 C3
Rietschen *D* 81 D7
Rieumes *F* 33 D8
Rieupeyroux *F* 33 B10
Rieutort-de-Randon *F* 34 A5
Rieux *F* 23 E7
Rieux *F* 33 D8
Riez *F* 36 D4
Rifiano *I* 72 C3
Rīga *LV* 135 C8
Rigaio *GR* 169 F8
Rigaud *F* 36 D5
Riggisberg *CH* 31 B11
Rignac *F* 33 B10
Rignano Flaminio *I* 62 C2
Rignano Garganico *I* 63 D9
Rignano sull'Arno *I* 66 E3
Rigny-le-Ferron *F* 25 D10
Rigny-sur-Arroux *F* 30 B5
Rigny-Ussé *F* 24 F3
Rigside *GB* 5 D9
Rihtniemi *FIN* 126 C5
Riihimäki *FIN* 127 D12
Riihivaara *FIN* 125 C14
Riikonkumpu *FIN* 117 C14
Riipi *FIN* 117 D16
Riippi *FIN* 122 F7
Riisipere *EST* 131 C8
Riistavesi *FIN* 125 E10
Riitiala *FIN* 127 B8
Riječa *BIH* 157 E10
Riječani *BIH* 157 D9
Rijeka *BIH* 157 F11
Rijeka *HR* 67 B9
Rijeka Crnojevića *MNE* 163 E7
Rijen *NL* 16 E3
Rijkevorsel *B* 16 F3
Rijnsburg *NL* 16 D2
Rijsbergen *NL* 16 E3
Rijssel *F* 19 C7
Rijssen *NL* 17 D7
Rijswijk *NL* 16 D2
Rikava *LV* 133 C2
Riksgränsen *S* 111 D15
Rila *BG* 165 E7
Rilhac-Rancon *F* 29 D8
Rilland *NL* 182 C4
Rillé *F* 23 F12
Rillieux-la-Pape *F* 30 D6
Rillo *E* 42 F2
Rillo de Gallo *E* 47 C9
Rimavská Baňa *SK* 147 D9
Rimavská Seč *SK* 145 G1
Rimavská Sobota *SK* 147 E10
Rimavské Janovce *SK* 147 E10
Rimbach *D* 76 D3
Rimbach *D* 187 B6
Rimbo *S* 99 C10
Rimetea *RO* 152 E3
Rimforsa *S* 92 C7
Rimicāni *LV* 135 D12
Rimini *I* 66 D6
Rimjokk *S* 118 B5
Riminmäki *FIN* 127 D11
Rimóc *H* 147 E9
Rimogne *F* 184 E2
Rimont *F* 33 E8
Rimpar *D* 74 C6
Rimsbo *S* 103 D11
Rimšė *LT* 135 E12
Rimšēnai *LT* 135 F12
Rimske Toplice *SLO* 73 D11
Rimsting *D* 72 A5
Rinchnach *D* 76 E4
Rincón de la Victoria *E* 53 C8
Rincón de Soto *E* 41 D8
Rinda *LV* 134 A3
Rindal *N* 104 E6
Rindsholm *DK* 86 C4
Rineia *GR* 176 E5
Rinella *I* 59 B6
Ringarum *S* 93 C8
Ringaudai *LT* 137 D8
Ringe *D* 17 C7
Ringe *DK* 86 E6
Ringebu *N* 101 C12
Ringelia *N* 101 E12
Ringen *N* 95 B12
Ringford *GB* 5 F8
Ringhals *S* 87 A10
Ringkøbing *DK* 86 C2
Ringleben *D* 79 D9
Ringsend *GB* 4 E3
Ringsta *S* 106 E7
Ringsted *DK* 87 E9
Ringvattnet *S* 106 C8
Ringville *IRL* 9 D7
Ringwood *GB* 13 D11
Rinkaby *S* 88 D6
Rinkabyholm *S* 89 B10
Rinkenæs *DK* 86 F5
Rinkilä *FIN* 129 B10
Rinloan *GB* 5 A10
Rinn *S* 97 B9
Rinneen *IRL* 8 C4
Rinøyvåg *N* 111 D10
Rintala *FIN* 123 D10
Rinteln *D* 17 D12
Rio *GR* 174 C4
Rio Caldo *P* 38 E3
Rio de Mel *P* 44 C6
Rio de Moinhos *P* 50 B4
Rio de Moinhos *P* 50 C3
Rio de Moinhos *P* 50 D3
Rio de Onor *P* 39 E6
Rio di Pusteria *I* 72 C4
Riofrío *E* 46 C3
Riofrío de Aliste *E* 39 E7
Riogordo *E* 53 C8
Rioja *E* 55 F8
Riola Sardo *I* 64 D2
Riolobos *E* 45 E8
Riolo Terme *I* 66 D4
Riols *F* 34 C4
Riom *F* 30 D3
Riomaggiore *I* 69 E8
Rio Maior *P* 44 F3
Rio Marina *I* 65 B2
Riom-ès-Montagnes *F* 29 E11
Rion-des-Landes *F* 32 C4
Rionegro del Puente *E* 39 D7
Rio nell'Elba *I* 65 B2
Rionero in Vulture *I* 60 B5
Rionero Sannitico *I* 63 D6
Rions *F* 32 A5
Riorges *F* 30 C5
Ríos *E* 38 E5
Rioseco de Tapia *E* 39 C8
Rio Tinto *P* 44 B3
Rio Torto *P* 38 E5
Rioz *F* 26 F5
Ripač *BIH* 156 C4
Ripacandida *I* 60 B5
Ripalimosano *I* 63 D7
Ripanj *SRB* 158 D6
Riparbella *I* 66 F2
Ripatransone *I* 62 B5
Ripe *I* 67 E7
Ripi *I* 62 D4
Ripiceni *RO* 153 B10
Ripley *GB* 11 C8
Ripley *GB* 11 E9
Ripoll *E* 43 C8
Ripon *GB* 11 C8
Riposto *I* 59 D7
Rips *NL* 183 B7
Riquewihr *F* 27 D7
Risan *MNE* 163 D6
Risarven *S* 103 C10
Risbäck *S* 106 B9
Risberg *S* 102 D6
Risca *GB* 13 B8
Rișca *RO* 151 D11
Rîșcani *MD* 153 B11
Riscle *F* 32 C5
Risdal *N* 90 B3
Risede *S* 106 C8
Rish *BG* 167 D7
Risinge *S* 92 B7
Risliden *S* 107 B16
Risnabben *S* 118 D3
Risnes *N* 94 E5
Risør *N* 90 B5
Risøyhamn *N* 111 C10
Rissa *N* 104 D7
Rissna *S* 106 E8
Rissnaben *S* 118 D4
Riste *FIN* 126 C7
Risteli *FIN* 125 B12
Risti *EST* 131 D8
Ristiina *FIN* 128 B7
Ristijärvi *FIN* 121 F11
Ristilä *FIN* 121 B11
Ristilampi *FIN* 117 E17
Ristinen *FIN* 124 D7
Ristinkylä *FIN* 125 E12
Ristioja *FIN* 121 B13
Ristonmännikkö *FIN* 117 D16
Risträsk *S* 107 B12
Risudden *S* 119 B11
Risum-Lindholm *D* 82 A5
Rītausmas *LV* 135 D8
Rite *LV* 135 D10
Rīteri *LV* 135 C11
Ritini *GR* 169 D7
Ritola *FIN* 123 E11
Ritterhude *D* 17 B11
Rittersdorf *D* 185 D5
Rittersgrün *D* 75 B12
Riudarenes *E* 43 D9
Riudecols *E* 42 E5
Riudoms *E* 42 E6
Riutta *FIN* 123 C12
Riutula *FIN* 113 F18
Rīva *LV* 134 C2
Riva del Garda *I* 69 B10
Riva di Solto *I* 69 B9
Riva di Tures *I* 72 C5
Rivanazzano *I* 37 B10
Rivardo Ligure *I* 37 C9
Rivarolo Canavese *I* 68 C4
Rivarolo Mantovano *I* 66 B1
Rivas-Vaciamadrid *E* 46 D6
Rive-de-Gier *F* 30 D6
Rivedoux-Plage *F* 28 C3
Rivello *I* 60 C5
Riverchapel *IRL* 9 C10
Rivergaro *I* 37 B11
Rivero *E* 40 B3
Riverstown *IRL* 7 F7
Riverstown *IRL* 8 E6
Rivery *F* 18 E5
Rives *F* 31 E8
Rivesaltes *F* 34 E4
Rivière-sur-Tarn *F* 34 B5
Rivignano *I* 73 E7
Rivinperä *FIN* 119 F16
Rivodutri *I* 62 B3
Rivoli *I* 68 C4
Rivolta d'Adda *I* 69 C8
Rixensart *B* 19 C10
Rixheim *F* 27 E7
Rixö *S* 91 C9
Riza *GR* 175 C6
Rizes *GR* 174 E5
Rizia *GR* 171 A10
Rizomata *GR* 169 D7
Rizomylos *GR* 169 F8
Rizziconi *I* 59 C8
Rjånes *N* 100 B3
Rjukan *N* 95 C9
Rø *DK* 89 E7
Ro *I* 66 C4
Rö *S* 103 A14
Roa *E* 40 E4
Roa *N* 95 B13
Roade *GB* 15 C7
Roadside *GB* 3 H10
Roadside of Kinneff *GB* 5 B12
Roager *DK* 86 E3
Roaillan *F* 32 B5
Roald *N* 100 A4
Roan *N* 104 C8
Roanne *F* 30 C5
Roata de Jos *RO* 161 E7
Roath *GB* 13 C8
Röbäck *S* 122 C4
Robănești *RO* 160 E4
Robbio *I* 68 C6
Robeasca *RO* 161 C10
Robecco d'Oglio *I* 69 C9
Röbel *D* 83 D13
Robella *I* 68 C5
Robert-Espagne *F* 26 C3
Roberton *GB* 5 D9
Roberton *GB* 5 E11
Robertsfors *S* 118 F5
Robežnieki *LV* 133 E3
Robiac-Rochessadoule *F* 35 B7
Robilante *I* 37 C6
Robin Hood's Bay *GB* 11 C10
Robion *F* 35 C9
Robledo *E* 55 B8
Robledo de Chavela *E* 46 C4
Robledo del Mazo *E* 46 E3
Robledollano *E* 45 E9
Robles de la Valcueva *E* 39 C9
Robliza de Cojos *E* 45 C9
Robøle *N* 101 E11
Robregordo *E* 46 B5
Robres *E* 41 E11
Robres del Castillo *E* 32 F1
Roč *HR* 67 B9
Rocafort de Queralt *E* 43 E6
Rocamadour *F* 29 F9
Roca Vecchia *I* 61 C10
Roccabianca *I* 66 B1
Roccadaspide *I* 60 C4
Rocca d'Evandro *I* 62 E5
Rocca di Cambio *I* 62 C4
Rocca di Mezzo *I* 62 C5
Rocca di Neto *I* 61 E7
Rocca di Papa *I* 62 D3
Roccafranca *I* 69 C8
Roccagloriosa *I* 60 C4
Roccagorga *I* 62 D4
Rocca Grimalda *I* 37 B9
Rocca Imperiale *I* 61 C7
Roccalbegna *I* 65 B5
Roccalumera *I* 59 D7
Roccamandolfi *I* 63 D6
Roccamassima *I* 62 D3
Roccamena *I* 58 D3
Roccamonfina *I* 60 A1
Roccamontepiano *I* 62 C6
Roccanova *I* 60 C6
Roccapalumba *I* 58 D4
Rocca Pia *I* 62 D5
Roccaraso *I* 62 D6
Rocca San Casciano *I* 66 D4
Rocca San Giovanni *I* 63 C6
Roccasecca *I* 62 D5
Roccasecca dei Volsci *I* 62 E4
Rocca Sinibalda *I* 62 C3
Roccastrada *I* 65 A4
Roccavione *I* 37 C6
Roccella Ionica *I* 59 C9
Rocchetta Sant'Antonio *I* 60 A4
Rochdale *GB* 11 D7
Roche *GB* 12 E5
Rochechouart *F* 29 D7
Rochefort *B* 19 D11
Rochefort *F* 28 D4
Rochefort-en-Terre *F* 23 E7
Rochefort-Montagne *F* 30 D2
Rochefort-sur-Nenon *F* 26 F4
Rochehaut *B* 184 E3
Roche-la-Molière *F* 30 E5
Rochemaure *F* 35 A8
Roches-Bettaincourt *F* 26 D3
Rocheservière *F* 28 B2
Rochester *GB* 15 E12
Rochester *GB* 15 E10
Rochetaillée *F* 26 E3
Rochford *GB* 15 D10
Rochfortbridge *IRL* 7 F8
Rochin *F* 19 C7
Rochlitz *D* 79 D12
Rociana del Condado *E* 51 E6
Ročinj *SLO* 73 D8
Rociu *RO* 160 D6
Rockanje *NL* 182 B4
Rockchapel *IRL* 8 D4
Rockcliffe *GB* 5 F9
Rockcorry *IRL* 7 D8
Rockenhausen *D* 21 E9
Rockesholm *S* 97 C12
Rockhammar *S* 97 C13
Rockhill *IRL* 8 D5
Rockingham *GB* 11 F10
Rockmills *IRL* 8 D6
Rockneby *S* 89 B10
Röckingen *D* 79 D12
Rocourt-St-Martin *F* 25 B9
Rocroi *F* 19 E10
Roda de Bara *E* 43 E6
Roda de Ter *E* 43 D8
Rodalben *D* 21 F9
Rodaljice *HR* 156 D4
Rödåsel *S* 118 F3
Rodberg *N* 95 B9
Rødbergshamn *N* 111 B15
Rødby *DK* 83 A10
Rødbyhavn *DK* 83 A10
Rødding *DK* 86 B3
Rødding *DK* 86 C5
Rødding *DK* 86 E4
Rödeby *S* 89 C9
Rodeiro *E* 38 C4
Rødekro *DK* 86 E4
Rodel *GB* 2 K3
Rodellar *E* 32 F5
Rodelle *F* 34 A4
Roden *NL* 17 B6
Ródenas *E* 47 C10
Rodenkirchen (Stadland) *D* 17 B10
Rödental *D* 75 B9
Rodewald *D* 82 E6
Rodewisch *D* 75 A11
Rodez *F* 33 B11
Rodi Garganico *I* 63 D9
Roding *D* 75 D12
Rodingträsk *S* 107 C14
Rödjebro *S* 98 B8
Rødkærsbro *DK* 86 C4
Rodleben *D* 79 C11
Rødlia *N* 108 E7
Rödmyra *S* 103 C11
Rodna *RO* 152 C5
Rododafni *GR* 174 C5
Rodolivos *GR* 170 C5
Rödön *S* 105 E16
Rodopoli *GR* 169 B9
Rodopos *GR* 178 D6
Rodos *GR* 181 D8
Rødovre *DK* 87 D10
Rødsand *N* 111 B13
Rødsand *N* 114 D8
Rødseidet *N* 105 B11
Rödvattnet *S* 107 D13
Rødvig *DK* 87 E10
Roela *EST* 131 C13
Roermond *NL* 20 B5
Roeselare *B* 19 C7
Roești *RO* 160 D4
Roetgen *D* 20 C6
Röfors *S* 92 B5
Rofrano *I* 60 C4
Rogač *HR* 156 F5
Rogačica *SRB* 158 E4
Rogaška Slatina *SLO* 148 D5
Rogaszyce *PL* 142 D4
Rogate *GB* 15 E7
Rogatec *SLO* 148 D5
Rogatica *BIH* 157 E11
Rogätz *D* 79 B10
Roggel *NL* 16 F5
Roggenburg *D* 75 F7
Roggendorf *D* 83 C10
Roggentin *D* 84 D3
Roggiano Gravina *I* 60 D6
Roghudi *I* 59 C8
Rogienice Wielkie *PL* 139 D13
Rogil *P* 50 E2
Rogliano *F* 37 F10
Rogliano *I* 61 E6
Rognac *F* 35 D9

Sachsenberg (Lichtenfels) D 21 B11
Sachsenbrunn D 75 B8
Sachsenburg A 73 C7
Sachsenhagen D 17 D12
Sachsenhausen (Waldeck) D 17 F12
Sachsenheim D 27 C11
Sacile I 72 E5
Sacoşu Turcesc RO 159 B7
Sacović BIH 156 E6
Sacquenay F 26 E3
Sacramenia E 40 E4
Sacu RO 159 B9
Săcueni RO 151 C9
Săcuieu RO 151 D10
Sačurov SK 145 F4
Sada E 38 B3
Sádaba E 32 F3
Sadala EST 131 D13
Sadali I 64 D3
Saddell GB 4 D5
Sadina BG 166 C6
Sadki PL 85 D12
Sadkowice PL 141 G3
Sadkowo PL 85 C10
Sadlinki PL 138 C6
Sadova MD 154 C2
Sadova RO 152 B6
Sadova RO 160 F3
Sadove UA 154 E4
Sadovets BG 165 C9
Sadovo BG 165 E10
Sadowie PL 143 E11
Sadowne PL 139 E12
Sadská CZ 77 B7
Sadu RO 160 B4
Sädvaluspen S 109 D12
Sæbo N 94 B6
Sæbø N 100 B4
Sæbøvik N 94 C3
Sæby DK 87 D8
Sæby DK 90 E8
Sæd DK 86 F3
Saelices E 47 E7
Saelices de la Sal E 47 C8
Saelices del Rio E 39 C9
Saelices de Mayorga E 39 D9
Saerbeck D 17 D9
Særslev DK 86 D6
Sæter N 104 C8
Sætra N 104 E6
Sætre N 95 C13
Saeul L 20 E5
Sævareid N 94 B3
Safaalan TR 173 B9
Safara P 51 C5
Säffle S 91 A12
Saffré F 23 E8
Saffron Walden GB 15 C9
Sâg RO 151 C10
Sâg RO 159 B7
Sagama I 64 C2
Sagard D 84 A5
Sage D 17 C10
Săgeata RO 161 C9
Sågen S 97 B11
Sagiada GR 168 E3
Sağirlar TR 173 F9
Sağlamtaş TR 173 C7
Sågmyra S 103 E9
Sagna RO 153 D10
Sagone F 37 G9
Sagres P 50 E2
Sagstua N 95 B15
Sâgu RO 151 E7
Sagunto E 48 E4
Sagvåg N 94 C2
Ságvár H 149 C10
Sagy F 31 B7
Sahagún E 39 D9
Sahaidac MD 154 D3
Sahalahti FIN 127 C11
Sahankylä FIN 122 F8
Saharna Nouă MD 154 B3
Săhăteni RO 161 C8
Şahin TR 173 B6
Şahinli TR 172 D6
Sahl DK 86 C5
Sahrajärvi FIN 123 F14
Sahun E 33 E6
Sahune F 35 B9
Šahy SK 147 E7
Saiakopli EST 131 C12
Saighdinis GB 2 K2
Saija FIN 115 D5
Säijä FIN 127 C10
Saikari FIN 124 E7
Saillagouse F 33 F10
Saillans F 35 A9
Sail-sous-Couzan F 30 D4
Saimaanharju FIN 129 C9
Säimen FIN 125 F12
Sains-Richaumont F 19 E8
St Abbs GB 5 D12
St-Affrique F 34 C4
St-Agnan F 30 B4
St-Agnan-en-Vercors F 31 F7
St-Agnant F 28 D4
St-Agnant-de-Versillat F 29 C9
St Agnes GB 12 E4
St-Agrève F 30 E5
St-Aignan F 24 F5
St-Aignan-sur-Roë F 23 E9
St-Aigulin F 28 E5
St-Albain F 30 C6
St-Alban F 22 C6
St-Alban-Leysse F 31 D8
St Albans GB 15 D8
St-Alban-sur-Limagnole F 30 F3
St-Amand-en-Puisaye F 25 E9
St-Amand-les-Eaux F 19 D7
St-Amand-Longpré F 24 E5
St-Amand-Montrond F 29 B11
St-Amand-sur-Fion F 25 C12
St-Amans F 34 A5
St-Amans-des-Cots F 30 F2
St-Amans-Soult F 33 D10
St-Amant-de-Boixe F 29 D6
St-Amant-Roche-Savine F 30 D4
St-Amant-Tallende F 30 D3
St-Amarin F 27 E7
St-Ambroix F 35 B7
St-Amour F 31 C7
St-Andiol F 35 C8
St-André F 34 E4
St-André-de-Corcy F 31 D6
St-André-de-Cruzières F 35 B7
St-André-de-Cubzac F 28 F5
St-André-de-l'Eure F 24 C5
St-André-de-Sangonis F 34 C6
St-André-de-Valborgne F 35 B6
St-André-le-Gaz F 31 D8
St-André-les-Alpes F 36 D5
St-André-les-Vergers F 25 D11
St Andrews GB 5 C11
St-Angel F 29 D10
St Anne GBG 23 A7
St-Anthème F 30 D4
St-Antonin-Noble-Val F 33 B9
St-Août F 29 B9
St-Apollinaire F 26 F3
St-Arcons-d'Allier F 30 E4
St-Arnoult-en-Yvelines F 24 C6
St Asaph GB 10 E5
St-Astier F 29 E7
St-Astier F 29 F6
St Athan GB 13 C8
St-Auban F 36 D5
St-Auban-sur-l'Ouvèze F 35 B9
St-Aubin F 31 A7
St-Aubin-Château-Neuf F 25 E9
St-Aubin-d'Aubigné F 23 D8
St-Aubin-de-Blaye F 28 E4
St-Aubin-du-Cormier F 23 D9
St-Aubin-lès-Elbeuf F 18 F3
St-Aubin-sur-Mer F 23 B11
St-Aulaye F 29 E6
St Austell GB 12 E5
St-Avé F 22 E6
St-Avertin F 24 F4
St-Avold F 26 B6
St-Ay F 24 E6
St-Aygulf F 36 E5
St-Barthélemy-d'Agenais F 33 A6
St-Barthélemy-de-Vals F 30 E6
St-Bauzille-de-Putois F 35 C6
St-Béat F 33 E7
St-Beauzély F 34 B4
St Bees GB 10 C4
St-Benin-d'Azy F 30 A3
St-Benoît F 29 B6
St-Benoît F 33 D10
St-Benoît-du-Sault F 29 C8
St-Benoît-sur-Loire F 25 E7
St-Béron F 31 D8
St-Berthevin F 23 D10
St-Bertrand-de-Comminges F 33 D7
St-Blaise CH 31 A10
St-Blaise-la-Roche F 27 D7
St-Blin-Semilly F 26 D3
St-Boil F 30 B6
St-Bonnet-de-Bellac F 29 C7
St-Bonnet-de-Joux F 30 C5
St-Bonnet-en-Bresse F 31 B7
St-Bonnet-en-Champsaur F 36 B4
St-Bonnet-le-Château F 30 E5
St-Bonnet-le-Froid F 30 E5
St-Bonnet-sur-Gironde F 28 E4
St-Branchs F 24 F4
St Brelade GBJ 23 B7
St-Brevin-les-Pins F 23 F7
St-Briac-sur-Mer F 23 C7
St-Brice-en-Coglès F 23 D9
St Brides Major GB 13 C7
St-Brieuc F 22 C6
St-Bris-le-Vineux F 25 E10
St-Brisson F 25 F11
St-Broing-les-Moines F 25 E12
St Buryan GB 12 E3
St-Calais F 24 E4
St-Cannat F 35 C9
St-Céré F 29 F9
St-Cergue CH 31 C9
St-Cergues F 31 C9
St-Cernin F 29 E10
St-Chaffrey F 31 F10
St-Chamarand F 33 A8
St-Chamas F 35 C9
St-Chamond F 30 E6
St-Chaptes F 35 C7
St-Chef F 31 D7
St-Chély-d'Apcher F 30 F3
St-Chély-d'Aubrac F 34 A4
St-Chinian F 34 D4
St-Christol F 35 B9
St-Christol-lès-Alès F 35 B7
St-Christoly-Médoc F 28 E4
St-Christophe I 31 D11
St-Christophe-en-Bazelle F 24 F6
St-Christophe-en-Brionnais F 30 C5
St-Ciers-sur-Gironde F 28 E4
St-Cirq-Lapopie F 33 B9
St-Clair-du-Rhône F 30 E6
St-Clar F 33 C7
St-Claud F 29 D6
St-Claude F 31 C8
St Clears GB 12 B6
St-Clément F 25 D9
St-Clément F 26 C6
St-Clément F 29 E9
St Clement GBJ 23 B7
St-Clément-de-Rivière F 35 C6
St Columb Major GB 12 E5
St Combs GB 3 K13
St-Constant F 29 F10
St-Cosme-en-Vairais F 24 D3
St-Cricq-Chalosse F 32 C4
St-Cyprien F 29 F8
St-Cyprien F 33 B8
St-Cyprien F 34 E5
St-Cyr-sur-Loire F 24 F4
St-Cyr-sur-Mer F 35 D10
St Cyrus GB 5 B12
St David's GB 9 E12
St Day GB 12 E4
St-Denis F 25 C7
St-Denis-d'Anjou F 23 E11
St-Denis-de-Gastines F 23 D10
St-Denis-de-Jouhet F 29 B9
St-Denis-de-Pile F 28 F5
St-Denis-d'Oléron F 28 C3
St-Denis-en-Bugey F 31 D7
St-Denis-lès-Bourg F 31 C7
St Dennis GB 12 E5
St-Désert F 30 B6
St-Didier-en-Velay F 30 E5
St-Didier-sur-Chalaronne F 30 C6
St-Dié F 27 D6
St-Dier-d'Auvergne F 30 D3
St-Dizier F 25 C12
St-Dizier-Leyrenne F 29 C9
St-Dolay F 23 E7
St-Donat-sur-l'Herbasse F 31 E6
St-Doulchard F 25 F7
Ste-Adresse F 23 A12
Ste-Alvère F 29 F7
Ste-Bazeille F 33 A6
Ste-Cécile-les-Vignes F 35 B8
Ste-Croix CH 31 B10
Ste-Croix F 31 B7
Ste-Croix F 31 F7
Ste-Croix-Volvestre F 33 D8
Ste-Engrâce F 32 D4
Ste-Énimie F 34 B5
Ste-Eulalie d'Olt F 34 B4
Ste-Eulalie-en-Born F 32 B3
Ste-Feyre F 29 C9
Ste-Foy-de-Peyrolières F 33 D8
Ste-Foy-la-Grande F 29 F6
Ste-Foy-l'Argentière F 30 D5
Ste-Foy-lès-Lyon F 30 D6
Ste-Foy-Tarentaise F 31 D10
Ste-Geneviève F 18 F5
Ste-Geneviève-sur-Argence F 30 F2
St-Égrève F 31 E8
Ste-Hélène F 28 F4
Ste-Hermine F 28 B3
Ste-Livrade-sur-Lot F 33 B7
St-Élix-le-Château F 33 D8
St-Élix-Theux F 33 D6
Ste-Lizaigne F 29 A10
St-Éloy-les-Mines F 30 C2
Ste-Lucie-de-Tallano F 37 H10
Ste-Marguerite F 186 E2
Ste-Marie F 34 E5
Ste-Marie-aux-Mines F 27 D7
Ste-Maure-de-Peyriac F 33 B6
Ste-Maure-de-Touraine F 24 F4
Ste-Maxime F 36 E5
Ste-Menehould F 25 B12
Ste-Mère-Église F 23 B9
St-Émiland F 30 B5
St Endellion GB 12 D5
St Enoder GB 12 E5
Ste-Orse F 29 E8
Ste-Pazanne F 23 F8
Ste-Radegonde F 28 B5
St-Erme-Outre-et-Ramecourt F 19 E8
St Erth GB 12 E4
Saintes F 28 D4
Ste-Sabine F 25 F12
Ste-Savine F 25 D11
Ste-Sévère-sur-Indre F 29 C10
St-Esteben F 32 D3
St-Estèphe F 28 E4
St-Estève F 34 E4
Ste-Suzanne F 23 D11
St-Étienne F 30 E5
St-Étienne-de-Baïgorry F 32 D3
St-Étienne-de-Fontbellon F 35 A7
St-Étienne-de-Fursac F 29 C9
St-Étienne-de-Montluc F 23 F8
St-Étienne-de-St-Geoirs F 31 E7
St-Étienne-de-Tinée F 36 C5
St-Étienne-du-Bois F 31 C7
St-Étienne-du-Rouvray F 18 F3
St-Étienne-en-Dévoluy F 35 A10
St-Étienne-les-Orgues F 35 B10
St-Étienne-lès-Remiremont F 26 D6
St-Étienne-Vallée-Française F 35 B6
Ste-Tulle F 35 C10
Ste-Vertu F 25 E10
St-Fargeau F 25 E9
St-Félicien F 30 E6
St-Félix-Lauragais F 33 D9
St Fergus GB 3 K13
St-Ferme F 28 F6
Saintfield GB 7 D11
St Fillans GB 5 C8
St-Firmin F 26 D5
St-Firmin F 31 F9
St-Flavy F 25 D10
St-Florent F 37 F10
St-Florent-des-Bois F 28 B3
St-Florentin F 25 D10
St-Florent-le-Vieil F 23 F9
St-Florent-sur-Cher F 29 B10
St-Flour F 30 E3
St-Flovier F 29 B8
St-Fons F 30 D6
St-Fort-sur-Gironde F 28 E4
St-Frajou F 33 D7
St-François-Longchamp F 31 E9
St-Front-de-Pradoux F 29 E6
St-Fulgent F 28 B3
St-Galmier F 30 D5
St-Gaudens F 33 D7
St-Gaultier F 29 B8
St-Gein F 32 C5
St-Gély-du-Fesc F 35 C6
St-Genest-Malifaux F 30 E5
St-Geniez F 36 C4
St-Geniez-d'Olt F 34 B4
St-Genis-de-Saintonge F 28 E4
St-Genis-Laval F 30 D6
St-Genis-Pouilly F 31 C9
St-Genix-sur-Guiers F 31 D8
St-Genou F 29 B8
St-Geoire-en-Valdaine F 31 E8
St-Georges-Buttavent F 23 D10
St-Georges-d'Aurac F 30 E4
St-Georges-de-Commiers F 31 E8
St-Georges-de-Didonne F 28 D4
St-Georges-de-Luzençon F 34 B4
St-Georges-de-Mons F 30 D2
St-Georges-de-Reneins F 30 C6
St-Georges-des-Groseillers F 23 C10
St-Georges-d'Oléron F 28 D3
St-Georges-du-Vièvre F 18 F2
St-Georges-en-Couzan F 30 D4
St-Georges-lès-Baillargeaux F 29 B6
St-Georges-sur-Baulche F 25 E10
St-Georges-sur-Cher F 24 F5
St-Georges-sur-Loire F 23 F10
St-Geours-de-Maremne F 32 C3
St-Gérand-le-Puy F 30 C4
St-Germain-Chassenay F 30 B3
St-Germain-de-Calberte F 35 B6
St-Germain-de-la-Coudre F 24 D4
St-Germain-des-Fossés F 30 C3
St-Germain-d'Esteuil F 28 E4
St-Germain-du-Bel-Air F 33 A8
St-Germain-du-Bois F 31 B7
St-Germain-du-Corbéis F 23 D12
St-Germain-du-Plain F 31 B6
St-Germain-du-Puy F 25 F7
St-Germain-du-Teil F 34 B5
St-Germain-en-Laye F 24 C7
St-Germain-Laval F 30 D5
St-Germain-Lembron F 30 E3
St-Germain-les-Belles F 29 D8
St-Germain-les-Vergnes F 29 E9
St-Germain-l'Herm F 30 E4
St Germans GB 12 E6
St-Germé F 32 C5
St-Gervais F 28 B1
St-Gervais F 31 E7
St-Gervais-d'Auvergne F 30 C2
St-Gervais-la-Forêt F 24 E5
St-Gervais-les-Bains F 31 D10
St-Gervais-les-Trois-Clochers F 29 B6
St-Gervais-sur-Mare F 34 C5
St-Géry F 33 B9
St-Ghislain B 19 D8
St-Gildas-de-Rhuys F 22 E6
St-Gildas-des-Bois F 23 E7
St-Gilles F 35 C7
St-Gilles-Croix-de-Vie F 28 B2
St-Gingolph F 31 C10
St-Girons F 33 E8
St-Girons-Plage F 32 C3
St-Gobain F 19 E7
St-Guénolé F 22 E3
St-Guilhem-le-Désert F 35 C6
St-Haon-le-Châtel F 30 C4
St-Héand F 30 D5
St Helens GB 10 E6
St Helier GBJ 23 B7
St-Herblain F 23 F8
St-Hilaire F 33 D10
St-Hilaire-de-Brethmas F 35 B7
St-Hilaire-de-Riez F 28 B2
St-Hilaire-des-Loges F 28 C4
St-Hilaire-de-Villefranche F 28 D4
St-Hilaire-du-Harcouët F 23 C9
St-Hilaire-du-Rosier F 31 E7
St-Hilaire-Fontaine F 30 B4
St-Hilaire-le-Grand F 25 B11
St-Hilaire-St-Florent F 23 F11
St-Hippolyte F 27 D7
St-Hippolyte F 27 F6
St-Hippolyte-du-Fort F 35 C6
St-Honoré-les-Bains F 30 B4
St-Hostien F 30 E5
St-Hubert B 19 D11
St-Imier CH 27 F6
St-Ismier F 31 E8
St Ive GB 12 E6
St Ives GB 12 E4
St Ives GB 15 C8
St-Izaire F 34 C4
St-Jacques-de-la-Lande F 23 D8
St-James F 23 C9
St-Jean F 33 C8
St-Jean-Bonnefonds F 30 E5
St-Jean-Brévelay F 22 E6
St-Jean-d'Angély F 28 D4
St-Jean-d'Assé F 23 D12
St-Jean-de-Bournay F 31 D7
St-Jean-de-Braye F 24 E6
St-Jean-de-Daye F 23 B9
St-Jean-de-la-Ruelle F 24 E6
St-Jean-de-Losne F 26 F3
St-Jean-de-Luz F 32 D2
St-Jean-de-Marsacq F 32 C3
St-Jean-de-Maurejols-et-Avéjan F 35 B7
St-Jean-de-Maurienne F 31 E9
St-Jean-de-Monts F 28 B1
St-Jean-de-Sixt F 31 D9
St-Jean-de-Védas F 35 C6
St-Jean-d'Illac F 28 F4
St-Jean-du-Bruel F 34 B5
St-Jean-du-Falga F 33 D9
St-Jean-du-Gard F 35 B6
St-Jean-le-Centenier F 35 A8
St-Jean-Pied-de-Port F 32 D3
St-Jean-Poutge F 33 C6
St-Jean-sur-Erve F 23 D11
St-Jeoire F 31 C9
St-Jeure-d'Ay F 30 E6
St-Jeures F 30 E5
St-Joachim F 23 F7
St John GBJ 23 B7
St John's Chapel GB 5 F12
St John's Town of Dalry GB 5 E8
St-Jores F 23 B9
St-Jorioz F 31 D9
St-Jory F 33 C8
St-Jouan-des-Guérets F 23 C8
St-Jouin-Bruneval F 23 A12
St-Jouin-de-Marnes F 28 B5
St-Julien F 31 C7
St-Julien F 33 D8
St-Julien-Beychevelle F 28 E4
St-Julien-Boutières F 30 F5
St-Julien-Chapteuil F 30 E5
St-Julien-de-Concelles F 23 F9
St-Julien-de-Vouvantes F 23 E9
St-Julien-du-Sault F 25 D9
St-Julien-du-Verdon F 36 D5
St-Julien-en-Beauchêne F 35 A10
St-Julien-en-Born F 32 B3
St-Julien-en-Genevois F 31 C9
St-Julien-l'Ars F 29 B7
St-Junien F 29 D7
St-Just F 35 B8
St Just GB 12 E3
St-Just-en-Chaussée F 18 E5
St-Just-en-Chevalet F 30 D4
St-Just-Ibarre F 32 D3
St-Justin F 32 C5
St Just in Roseland GB 12 E4
St-Just-la-Pendue F 30 D5
St-Just-Luzac F 28 D3
St-Just-Sauvage F 25 C10
St-Just-St-Rambert F 30 E5
St Keverne GB 12 E4
St-Lambert-des-Levées F 23 F11
St-Lary-Soulan F 33 E6
St-Laurent F 36 C5
St-Laurent-Bretagne F 32 D5
St-Laurent-d'Aigouze F 35 C7
St-Laurent-de-Carnols F 35 B8
St-Laurent-de-Cerdans F 34 F4
St-Laurent-de-Chamousset F 30 D5
St-Laurent-de-la-Cabrerisse F 34 D4
St-Laurent-de-la-Salanque F 34 E4
St-Laurent-de-Neste F 33 D6
St-Laurent-des-Autels F 23 F9
St-Laurent-du-Pont F 31 E8
St-Laurent-du-Var F 37 D6
St-Laurent-en-Caux F 18 E2
St-Laurent-en-Grandvaux F 31 B8
St-Laurent-les-Bains F 35 A6
St-Laurent-Médoc F 28 E4
St-Laurent-Nouan F 24 E6
St-Laurent-sur-Gorre F 29 D7
St-Laurent-sur-Sèvre F 28 B4
St-Léger B 19 E12
St-Léger-des-Vignes F 30 B3
St-Léger-en-Yvelines F 24 C6
St-Léger-sous-Beuvray F 30 B5
St-Léonard F 27 D6
St-Léonard-de-Noblat F 29 D8
St Leonards GB 13 D11
St-Lizier F 33 D8
St-Lô F 23 B9
St-Lon-les-Mines F 32 C3
St-Loubès F 28 F5
St-Louis-lès-Bitche F 186 D3
St-Loup-Géanges F 30 B6
St-Loup-Lamairé F 28 B5
St-Loup-sur-Semouse F 26 E5
St-Lubin-des-Joncherets F 24 C5
St-Lunaire F 23 C7
St-Lupicin F 31 C8
St-Lyé F 25 D11
St-Lys F 33 C8
St-Macaire F 32 A5
St-Macaire-en-Mauges F 23 F10
St-Magne F 32 A4
St-Magne-de-Castillon F 28 F5
St-Maime F 35 C10
St-Maixent-l'École F 28 C5
St-Malo F 23 C7
St-Malo-de-la-Lande F 23 B8
St-Mamert-du-Gard F 35 C7
St-Marcel F 24 B5
St-Marcel F 29 B9
St-Marcel F 30 B6
St-Marcel-d'Ardèche F 35 B8
St-Marcel-lès-Annonay F 30 E6
St-Marcel-lès-Sauzet F 35 A8
St-Marcel-lès-Valence F 31 F6
St-Marcellin F 31 E7
St-Marc-sur-Seine F 25 E12
St-Mards-en-Othe F 25 D10
St Margaret's Hope GB 3 H11
St-Marsal F 34 E4
St-Mars-d'Outillé F 24 E3
St-Mars-du-Désert F 23 F9
St-Mars-la-Brière F 24 D3
St-Mars-la-Jaille F 23 E9
St-Martial F 35 B6
St-Martial-de-Nabirat F 29 F8
St-Martial-de-Valette F 29 D7
St-Martin F 35 C10
St Martin GBG 22 B6
St Martin GBJ 23 B7
St-Martin-Boulogne F 15 F12
St-Martin-d'Ablois F 25 B10
St-Martin-d'Arrossa F 32 D3
St-Martin-d'Auxigny F 25 F7
St-Martin-de-Belleville F 31 E10
St-Martin-de-Castillon F 35 C10
St-Martin-de-Crau F 35 C8
St-Martin-de-Landelles F 23 C9
St-Martin-de-Londres F 35 C6
St-Martin-d'Entraunes F 36 C5
St-Martin-de-Ré F 28 C3
St-Martin-des-Besaces F 23 B10
St-Martin-des-Champs F 22 C4
St-Martin-de-Seignanx F 32 C3
St-Martin-de-Valamas F 30 F5
St-Martin-de-Valgalgues F 35 B7
St-Martin-d'Hères F 31 E8
St-Martin-d'Oney F 32 C4
St-Martin-du-Mont F 31 C7
St-Martin-du-Var F 37 D6
St-Martin-en-Bresse F 31 B7
St-Martin-le-Beau F 24 F4
St-Martin-sur-Ouanne F 25 E9
St-Martin-Valmeroux F 29 E10
St-Martin-Vésubie F 37 C6
St-Martory F 33 D7
St Mary's GB 3 H11
St-Mathieu F 29 D7
St-Mathurin F 28 B2
St-Maur F 29 B9
St-Maurice CH 31 C10
St-Maurice-de-Lignon F 30 E5
St-Maurice-des-Lions F 29 D7
St-Maurice-la-Souterraine F 29 C8
St-Maurice-l'Exil F 30 E6
St-Maurice-Navacelles F 35 C6
St-Maurin F 33 B7
St Mawes GB 12 E4
St-Max F 26 C5
St-Maximin-la-Ste-Baume F 35 D10
St-Médard-en-Jalles F 28 F4
St-Méen-le-Grand F 23 D7
St-Méloir-des-Ondes F 23 C8
St-Memmie F 25 C11
St-Menoux F 30 B3
St Merryn GB 12 D5
St-Mesmin F 25 D10
St-Mesmin F 29 E8
St-Michel F 19 E9
St-Michel F 28 D6
St-Michel F 33 D6
St-Michel-Chef-Chef F 23 F7
St-Michel-de-Castelnau F 32 B5
St-Michel-de-Maurienne F 31 E9
St-Michel-en-l'Herm F 28 C3
St-Michel-sur-Meurthe F 27 D6
St-Mihiel F 26 C4
St Monans GB 5 C11
St-Montant F 35 B8
St-Nabord F 26 D6
St-Nauphary F 33 C8
St-Nazaire F 23 F7
St-Nazaire-le-Désert F 35 A9
St-Nectaire F 30 D2
St Neots GB 15 C8
St-Nicolas B 183 D7
St-Nicolas F 18 D6
St-Nicolas-d'Aliermont F 18 E3
St-Nicolas-de-la-Grave F 33 B8
St-Nicolas-de-Port F 26 C5
St-Nicolas-de-Redon F 23 E7
St-Nicolas-du-Pélem F 22 D5
St-Oedenrode NL 16 E4
St-Omer F 18 C5
St-Orens-de-Gameville F 33 C9
St-Ost F 33 D6
St Osyth GB 15 D11
St-Ouen F 18 D5
St-Ouen F 24 E5
St Ouen GBJ 23 B7
St-Ouen-des-Toits F 23 D10
St-Pair-sur-Mer F 23 C8
St-Palais F 32 D3
St-Palais-sur-Mer F 28 D3
St-Pal-de-Chalancon F 30 E4
St-Pal-de-Mons F 30 E5
St-Pantaléon F 30 B5
St-Pantaléon F 33 B8
St-Papoul F 33 D10
St-Pardoux-Isaac F 33 A6
St-Pardoux-la-Rivière F 29 E7
St-Parize-le-Châtel F 30 B3
St-Parres-lès-Vaudes F 25 D11
St-Paterne F 23 D12
St-Paterne-Racan F 24 E3
St-Paul F 36 B5
St-Paul-Cap-de-Joux F 33 C9
St-Paul-de-Fenouillet F 33 E11
St-Paul-de-Jarrat F 33 E9
St-Paul-en-Born F 32 B3
St-Paul-en-Forêt F 36 D5
St-Paul-et-Valmalle F 35 C6
St-Paulien F 30 E4
St-Paul-le-Jeune F 35 B7
St-Paul-lès-Dax F 32 C3
St-Paul-lès-Durance F 35 C10
St-Paul-Trois-Châteaux F 35 B8
St-Pé-de-Bigorre F 32 D5
St-Pée-sur-Nivelle F 32 D2
St-Péray F 30 F6
St-Père F 25 F10
St-Père-en-Retz F 23 F7
St Peter in the Wood GBG 22 B6
St Peter Port GBG 22 B6
St-Phal F 25 D10
St-Philbert-de-Bouaine F 28 B2
St-Philbert-de-Grand-Lieu F 28 A2
St-Pierre I 31 D11
St-Pierre-d'Albigny F 31 D9
St-Pierre-de-Chignac F 29 E7
St-Pierre-de-Côle F 29 E7
St-Pierre-de-la-Fage F 34 C5
St-Pierre-de-Maillé F 29 B7
St-Pierre-de-Plesguen F 23 D8
St-Pierre-des-Champs F 34 D4
St-Pierre-des-Corps F 24 F4
St-Pierre-des-Échaubrognes F 28 A4
St-Pierre-des-Landes F 23 D9
St-Pierre-des-Nids F 23 D11
St-Pierre-de-Trivisy F 33 C10
St-Pierre-d'Irube F 32 D3
St-Pierre-d'Oléron F 28 D3
St-Pierre-du-Chemin F 28 B4
St-Pierre-du-Mont F 32 C4
St-Pierre-Église F 23 A9
St-Pierre-en-Faucigny F 31 C9
St-Pierre-en-Port F 18 E1
St-Pierre-le-Moûtier F 30 B3
St-Pierre-lès-Elbeuf F 18 F3
St-Pierre-les-Nemours F 25 D8
St-Pierre-Montlimart F 23 F9
St-Pierre-Quiberon F 22 E5
St-Pierre-sur-Dives F 23 B11
St-Plancard F 33 D7
St-Pois F 23 C9
St-Poix F 23 E9
St-Pol-de-Léon F 22 C4
St-Pol-sur-Mer F 18 B5
St-Pol-sur-Ternoise F 18 D5
St-Pompont F 29 F8
St-Pons F 36 C5
St-Pons-de-Thomières F 34 D4
St-Porchaire F 28 D4
St-Pourçain-sur-Sioule F 30 C3
St-Prex CH 31 C9
St-Priest F 30 D6
St-Priest-de-Champs F 30 D2
St-Priest-Laprugne F 30 D4
St-Priest-Taurion F 29 D8
St-Privat F 29 E10
St-Privat-d'Allier F 30 F4
St-Prix F 30 C4
St-Projet F 33 B9
St-Puy F 33 C6
St-Quentin F 19 E7
St-Quentin-la-Poterie F 35 B7
St-Quirin F 27 C7
St-Rambert-d'Albon F 30 E6
St-Rambert-en-Bugey F 31 D7
St-Raphaël F 36 E5
St-Remèze F 35 B7
St-Rémy F 30 B6
St-Rémy-de-Provence F 35 C8
St-Remy-en-Bouzemont-St-Genest-et-Isson F 25 C12
St-Rémy-sur-Avre F 24 C5
St-Rémy-sur-Durolle F 30 D4
St-Renan F 22 D2
St-Révérien F 25 F10
St-Rhemy I 31 D11
St-Riquier F 18 D4
St-Romain-en-Gal F 30 D6
St-Romain-sur-Cher F 24 F5
St-Romans F 31 E7
St-Rome-de-Cernon F 34 B4
St-Rome-de-Tarn F 34 B4
St-Saëns F 18 E3
St Sampson GBG 22 B6
St-Saturnin-lès-Apt F 35 C9
St-Saud-Lacoussière F 29 D7
St-Saulge F 25 F10
St-Sauves-d'Auvergne F 29 D11
St-Sauveur F 22 D3
St-Sauveur F 26 E5
St-Sauveur-de-Montagut F 30 F6
St-Sauveur-en-Puisaye F 25 E9
St-Sauveur-Gouvernet F 35 B9
St-Sauveur-Lendelin F 23 B9
St-Sauveur-le-Vicomte F 23 B8
St-Sauveur-sur-Tinée F 36 C6
St-Sauvy F 33 C7
St-Savin F 28 E5
St-Savin F 29 B7
St-Savinien F 28 D4
St Saviour GBJ 23 B7
St-Sébastien-de-Morsent F 24 B5
St-Sébastien-sur-Loire F 23 F8
St-Seine-l'Abbaye F 25 F12
St-Sernin F 35 A7
St-Sernin-sur-Rance F 34 C4
St-Seurin-sur-l'Isle F 28 E5
St-Sever F 32 C4
St-Sever-Calvados F 23 C9
St-Siméon-de-Bressieux F 31 E7
St-Simon F 19 E7
St-Simon F 29 F11
St-Sorlin-d'Arves F 31 E9
St-Soupplets F 25 B8
St-Sulpice F 33 C9
St-Sulpice-Laurière F 29 C8
St-Sulpice-les-Champs F 29 D10
St-Sulpice-les-Feuilles F 29 C8
St-Sulpice-sur-Lèze F 33 D8
St-Sulpice-sur-Risle F 24 C4
St-Sylvain F 23 B11
St-Symphorien F 30 F4
St-Symphorien F 32 B5
St-Symphorien-de-Lay F 30 D5
St-Symphorien-sur-Coise F 30 D5
St Teath GB 12 D5
St-Thégonnec F 22 C4
St-Thibéry F 34 D5
St-Thiébault F 26 D4
St-Thurien F 22 E4
St-Trivier-de-Courtes F 31 C7
St-Trivier-sur-Moignans F 30 C6
St-Trojan-les-Bains F 28 D3
St-Tropez F 36 E5
St-Uze F 30 E6
St-Valérien F 25 D9
St-Valery-en-Caux F 18 E2
St-Valery-sur-Somme F 18 D4
St-Vallier F 30 B5
St-Vallier F 30 E6
St-Vallier-de-Thiey F 36 D5
St-Varent F 28 B5
St-Vaury F 29 C9
St-Victor F 30 E6
St-Victor-de-Cessieu F 31 D7
St-Victoret F 35 D9
St-Victor-la-Coste F 35 B8
St Vigeans GB 5 B11
St-Vigor-le-Grand F 23 B10
St-Vincent I 68 B4
St-Vincent-de-Connezac F 29 E6
St-Vincent-de-Paul F 32 C4
St-Vincent-les-Forts F 36 C4
St-Vit F 26 F4
St-Vite F 33 B7
St-Vith B 20 D6
St-Vivien-de-Médoc F 28 E3
St-Xandre F 28 C3
St-Yan F 30 C5
St-Ybars F 33 D8
St-Yorre F 30 C3
St-Yrieix-la-Perche F 29 D8
St-Yrieix-sur-Charente F 29 D6
St-Yvy F 22 E4
St-Zacharie F 35 D10
Sainville F 24 D6
Saissac F 33 D10
Saittarova S 116 D8
Saivomuotka S 116 B10
Saïx F 33 C10
Sajaniemi FIN 127 D11
Šahyajince SRB 164 E5
Šajkaš SRB 158 C5
Sajóbábony H 145 G2
Sajókaza H 145 G2
Sajókeresztúr H 145 G2
Sajólád H 145 G2
Sajószentpéter H 145 G2
Sajószöged H 145 H3
Sajóvámos H 145 G2
Säjvis S 119 C11
Saka LV 134 C2
Sakajärvi S 116 D5
Sakalishcha BY 133 E5
Sakaravaara FIN 121 E12
Šakiai LT 136 D7
Säkinmäki FIN 123 F16
Sakizköy TR 173 B7
Säkkilä FIN 121 B13
Sakshaug N 105 D10
Saksild DK 86 D6
Sakskøbing DK 83 A11
Saksun FO 2 A2
Saku EST 131 C9
Sakule SRB 158 C6
Säkylä FIN 126 C7
Šakyna LT 134 D6
Sala LV 134 C7
Sala LV 135 C11
Sala S 98 C7
Šaľa SK 146 E5
Salaca LV 131 F10
Sălacea RO 151 C9
Salacgrīva LV 131 F8
Sala Consilina I 60 C5
Salagnac F 29 E8
Salahmi FIN 124 C7
Salaise-sur-Sanne F 30 E6
Salakas LT 135 E12
Salakos GR 181 D7
Salakovac BIH 157 F8
Salamajärvi FIN 123 D13
Salamanca E 45 C9
Salamina GR 175 D7
Salandra I 61 B6
Salanki FIN 117 B13
Salantai LT 134 D3
Salar E 53 B8
Sălard RO 151 C9
Salardu E 33 E7
Salarli TR 172 B6
Salas E 39 B7
Salaš SRB 159 E9
Salas de los Infantes E 40 D5
Salash BG 164 B6
Salaspils LV 135 C8
Sălaşu de Sus RO 159 C10
Sălăţig RO 151 C11
Sălătrucel RO 160 C4
Sălătrucu RO 160 C5
Salaunes F 28 F4
Salberg S 107 D16
Salbertrand I 31 E10
Sălboda S 97 C8
Salbohed S 98 C6
Salbris F 24 F7
Salbu N 100 D2
Salcea RO 153 B8
Salching D 75 E12
Salcia RO 159 E10
Salcia RO 160 F5
Salcia RO 161 C8
Salcia Tudor RO 161 C10
Sălciile RO 161 D8
Šalčininkai LT 137 E11
Šalčininkėliai LT 137 E11
Sălciua RO 151 E11
Salcombe GB 13 E7
Sălcuţa MD 154 D4
Sălcuţa RO 160 E2
Saldaña E 39 C10
Saldón E 47 D10
Salduero E 40 E6
Saldus LV 134 C4
Sale GB 11 E7
Sale I 37 B9
Saleby S 91 C13
Salem D 27 E11
Salem D 83 C9
Salemi I 58 D2

Santiponce E 51 E7
Santisteban del Puerto E 55 C6
Santiuste de San Juan Bautista E 46 B3
Santiz E 45 B9
Sant Jaime Mediterráneo E 57 B13
Sant Jaume d'Enveja E 42 F5
Sant Joan de Labritja E 49 F8
Sant Joan de les Abadesses E 43 C8
Sant Joan de Vilatorrada E 43 D7
Sant Joan les Fonts E 43 C9
Sant Josep de sa Talaia E 57 D7
Sant Julià de Lòria AND 33 F9
Sant Llorenç de Morunys E 43 C7
Sant Llorenç des Cardassar E 57 B11
Sant Lluís E 57 B13
Sant Martí de Tous E 43 D7
Sant Martí Sarroca E 43 E7
Sant Mateu E 42 G4
Sant Miquel de Balansat E 57 C7
Santo Aleixo P 50 B5
Santo Aleixo da Restauração P 51 C5
Santo Amador P 51 C5
Santo André P 50 C2
Santo Antoniño E 38 C2
Santo António dos Cavaleiros P 50 B1
Santo Domingo de la Calzada E 40 D6
Santo Domingo de Silos E 40 E5
Santo Estêvão P 50 B2
Santo Estêvão P 50 E4
Santo Isidro de Pegões P 50 B2
Santok PL 85 E8
Santomera E 56 E2
Sant Omero I 62 B5
Santoña E 40 B5
Santo Pietro I 58 E6
Santo-Pietro-di-Tenda F 37 F10
Santo-Pietro-di-Venaco F 37 G10
Santo Stefano al Mare I 37 D7
Santo Stefano Belbo I 37 B8
Santo Stefano d'Aveto I 37 B10
Santo Stefano di Cadore I 72 C6
Santo Stefano di Camastra I 58 C5
Santo Stefano di Magra I 69 E8
Santo Stefano Quisquina I 58 D3
Santo Stino di Livenza I 73 E6
Santo Tirso P 38 F3
Santo Tomé E 55 C6
Santovenia E 39 E8
Santpedor E 43 D7
Sant Pere de Ribes E 43 E7
Sant Pere de Torelló E 43 C8
Sant Pere Pescador E 43 C10
Sant Pol de Mar E 43 D9
Santpoort NL 182 A5
Sant Privat d'en Bas E 43 C8
Sant Quintí de Mediona E 43 E7
Sant Quirze de Besora E 43 C8
Sant Sadurní d'Anoia E 43 E7
Santullano E 39 B8
Santu Lussurgiu I 64 C2
Santurtzi E 40 B5
Sant Vicenç dels Horts E 43 E8
Sant Vincenç de Castellet E 43 D7
San Venanzo I 62 B2
San Vendemiano I 72 E5
San Vero Milis I 64 C2
San Vicente de Alcántara E 45 F6
San Vicente de Arana E 32 E1
San Vicente de la Barquera E 40 B3
San Vicente de la Sonsierra E 40 C6
San Vicente del Raspeig E 56 E3
San Vicente de Palacio E 46 B3
San Vicente de Toranzo E 40 B4
San Vicenzo E 38 C2
San Vincenzo I 59 B7
San Vincenzo I 65 A3
San Vincenzo Valle Roveto I 62 D5
San Vitero E 39 E7
San Vito I 64 E4
San Vito al Tagliamento I 73 E6
San Vito Chietino I 63 C6
San Vito dei Normanni I 61 B9
San Vito di Cadore I 72 D5
San Vito lo Capo I 58 C2
San Vito Romano I 62 D3
San Vito sullo Ionio I 59 B9
San Vittoria in Matenano I 62 A4
Sanxenxo E 38 D2
Sanxhax AL 168 A2
Sanza I 60 C5
Sânzieni RO 153 E8
Sanzoles E 39 F8
São Barnabé P 50 E3
São Bartolomeu P 44 F5
São Bartolomeu da Serra P 50 C2
São Bartolomeu de Messines P 50 E3
São Bento do Cortiço P 50 B4
São Brás P 50 D4
São Brás de Alportel P 50 E4
São Brás do Regedouro P 50 C3
São Brissos P 50 C4
São Cosmado P 44 B5
São Domingos P 50 D2
São Facundo P 44 F4
São Francisco da Serra P 50 C2
São Geraldo P 50 B3
São Gregório P 50 B4
São Jacinto P 44 C3
São João da Madeira P 44 C4
São João da Pesqueira P 44 B6
São João da Venda P 50 E4
São João do Campo P 44 D4
São João dos Caldeireiros P 50 D4
São José da Lamarosa P 44 F4
São Lourenço de Mamporcão P 50 B4
São Luís P 50 D2
São Manços P 50 C4
São Marcos da Ataboeira P 50 D4
São Marcos da Serra P 50 E3
São Marcos do Campo P 50 C4
São Martinho da Cortiça P 44 D4
São Martinho das Amoreiras P 50 D3
São Martinho de Angueira P 39 E7
São Martinho do Porto P 44 E2
São Matias P 50 C4
São Miguel de Acha P 45 D6
São Miguel de Machede P 50 B4
São Miguel de Rio Torto P 44 F4
São Miguel do Outeiro P 44 C4
São Miguel do Pinheiro P 50 D4
Saône F 26 F5
São Pedro da Cadeira P 44 F2
São Pedro de Muel P 44 E2
São Pedro de Solis P 50 E4
São Pedro do Sul P 44 C4
Saorge F 37 D7
São Romão P 51 B5
São Romão do Sado P 50 C3
São Sebastião dos Carros P 50 D4
São Teotónio P 50 D2
Saou F 35 A9
São Vicente P 38 E5
São Vicente da Beira P 44 D5
Sáp H 151 C7
Sapanca TR 171 E10
Săpânța RO 145 H8
Sapareva Banya BG 165 E7
Saparevo BG 165 E7
Săpata RO 160 D5
Sapes GR 171 B9
Sapna BIH 157 C11
Sa Pobla E 57 B11
Săpoca RO 161 C9
Sapotskin BY 137 F8
Sappada I 73 C6
Sap'parjåkka N 113 D17
Sappee FIN 127 C11
Sappen N 112 D7
Sappetavan S 107 A13
Sappetsele S 107 A13
Sappisaasi S 116 C7
Sapri I 60 C5
Sapsalampi FIN 123 F11
Sapsoperä FIN 125 B11
Sara FIN 122 F9
Saraby N 113 C12
Saracena I 60 D6
Saračinec HR 148 D6
Sarafovo BG 167 D9
Saraiķi LV 134 C2
Säräisniemi FIN 119 F17
Saraiu RO 155 D2
Sarajärvi FIN 120 C9
Sarajärvi FIN 129 B11
Sarajevo BIH 157 E9
Saramo FIN 125 C12
Saramon F 33 C7
Saran F 24 E6
Sáránd H 151 C8
Sarandë AL 168 E3
Sarantaporo GR 169 D7
Sarantsi BG 165 D8
Sa Ràpita E 57 C10
Sarasău RO 145 H8
Sarata UA 154 E5
Sărata Galbenă MD 154 D2
Sărata-Monteoru RO 161 C9
Sărata Nouă MD 154 E2
Sărăteni MD 154 D2
Sărătenii Vechi MD 154 B3
Saray TR 173 B8
Sarayakpinar TR 167 F7
Saraylar TR 173 C8
Šarbanovac SRB 159 F9
Sărbeni RO 161 E6
Sárbogárd H 149 C11
Sarcelles F 25 C7
Sarconi I 60 C5
Sardara I 64 D2
Šardice CZ 77 E12
Sardinia GR 174 B3
Sardoal P 44 E4
Sare F 32 D2
S'Arenal E 49 E10
Šarengrad HR 158 C3
Sarentino I 72 C3
Särevere EST 131 D10
Sarezzo I 69 B9
Sargans CH 71 C8
Sariai LT 137 C13
Saribeyler TR 173 F8
Saricaali TR 171 C10
Sariçam TR 177 B9
Sarichioi RO 155 D3
Saridanişment TR 167 F7
Sariegos E 39 C8
Sarikemer TR 177 D9
Sariköy TR 173 D8
Sariñena E 42 D3
Šarišské Michaľany SK 145 E3
Sariyer TR 173 B11
Sarjankylä FIN 123 B14
Sarkad H 151 D7
Sarkadkeresztúr H 151 D7
Särkelä FIN 121 C12
Sárkeresztúr H 149 B11
Särkijärvi FIN 117 C11
Särkijärvi FIN 119 C15
Särkijärvi FIN 120 E9
Särkikorpi FIN 125 D12
Särkikylä FIN 123 D11
Särkilahti FIN 127 B14
Särkilahti FIN 129 B11
Särkiluoma FIN 121 B14
Särkimo FIN 122 D8
Särkisalmi FIN 129 B11
Särkisalo FIN 123 E16
Särkisalo FIN 127 E8
Şarköy TR 173 C7
Sarlat-la-Canéda F 29 F8
Sarliac-sur-l'Isle F 29 E7
Sărmaş RO 152 D6
Sărmăşag RO 151 C10
Sărmaşu RO 152 D4
Sármellék H 149 C8
Sarmijärvi FIN 114 F4
Sarmizegetusa RO 159 B10
Särna S 102 C5
Sarnadas do Ródão P 44 E5
Sarnaki PL 141 F7
Sarnano I 62 A4
Särnate LV 134 B2
Sarnen CH 70 D6
Sarniç TR 177 C9
Sarnico I 69 B8
Sarno I 60 B3
Sarnowa PL 81 C11
Särnstugan S 102 C5
Särö S 91 D10
Sarochyna BY 133 F5
Saronno I 69 B7
Sárosd H 149 B11
Sárospatak H 145 G4
Šarovce SK 147 E7
Sarow D 84 C4
Sarpsborg N 95 D14
Sarracín E 40 D4
Sarral E 42 E6
Sarralbe F 27 C7
Sarrance F 32 D4
Sarrancolin F 33 E6
Sarraquinhos P 38 E4
Sarras F 30 E6
Sarre GB 15 E11
Sarre I 31 D11
Sarreaus E 38 D4
Sarrebourg F 27 C7
Sarreguemines F 27 B7
Sárrétudvari H 151 C7
Sarre-Union F 27 C7
Sarria E 38 C5
Sarrià de Ter E 43 C9
Sarrians F 35 B8
Sarrión E 48 D3
Sarroca de Lleida E 42 E5
Sarròch I 64 E3
Sarród H 149 A7
Sarrola-Carcopino F 37 G9
Sarron F 32 C5
Sarry F 25 C11
Sarsina I 66 E5
Sarstedt D 78 B6
Sárszentágota H 149 C11
Sárszentlőrinc H 149 C11
Sart B 183 D7
Sartaguda E 32 F1
Sarteano I 62 B1
Sartène F 37 H9
Sarti GR 170 D5
Sartilly F 23 C9
Sartininkai LT 134 F3
Sarud H 150 B6
Şaru Dornei RO 152 C6
Şaruhanli TR 177 B10
Sarule I 64 C3
Sărulești RO 161 C9
Sărulești RO 161 E9
Sárvár H 149 B7
Sarvela FIN 122 F9
Sarvijoki FIN 122 E7
Sarvikumpu FIN 125 F12
Sarviluoma FIN 122 F8
Sarvinki FIN 125 E14
Sarvisé E 32 E5
Sarvisvaara S 116 E6
Sarvsjön S 102 A5
Sar"ya BY 133 E3
Sarzana I 69 E8
Sarzeau F 22 E6
Sarzedas P 44 E5
Sarzedo P 44 B5
Sasa NMK 164 E6
Sasalli TR 177 C8
Sasamón E 40 D3
Sasbach D 27 C9
Sasbachwalden D 186 D5
Sasca Montană RO 159 D8
Saschiz RO 152 E5
Săsciori RO 152 F3
Sascut RO 153 E10
Sásd H 149 D10
Sasina BIH 157 C6
Sasnava LT 137 D7
Sassali FIN 117 D15
Sassano I 60 C5
Sassari I 64 B2
Sassello I 37 C8
Sassen D 84 B4
Sassenage F 31 E8
Sassenberg D 17 E10
Sassenheim NL 16 D3
Sassetta I 65 A3
Sassnitz D 84 A5
Sassocorvaro I 66 E5
Sassoferrato I 67 F6
Sasso Marconi I 66 D3
Sassuolo I 66 C2
Sástago E 41 F11
Šaštín-Stráže SK 77 E12
Sas Van Gent NL 16 F1
Sáta H 145 G1
Satão P 44 C5
Satchinez RO 151 F7
Šateikiai LT 134 E3
Sätenäs villastad S 91 C12
Säter S 97 B14
Sätervallen S 102 A5
Sati LV 134 C5
Satiķi LV 134 C5
Sätila S 91 D11
Satillieu F 30 E6
Satkūnai LT 134 D7
Satnica Đakovačka HR 149 F10
Sätofta S 87 D13
Sátoraljaújhely H 145 G4
Satovcha BG 170 A5
Satow D 83 C11
Sätra brunn S 98 C6
Satriano di Lucania I 60 B5
Satrup D 82 A7
Sattajärvi FIN 119 B12
Sattajärvi S 117 D10
Sattanen FIN 117 D17
Satteins A 71 C9
Satteldorf D 75 D7
Satter S 116 E7
Sattledt A 76 F6
Satulung RO 151 B11
Satu Mare RO 151 B10
Saubusse F 32 C3
Saúca E 47 B7
Sauca MD 154 A1
Săuca RO 151 C9
Saucats F 32 A4
Săucești RO 153 D9
Sauclières F 34 C5
Sauda N 94 C4
Saue EST 131 C9
Sauerlach D 75 G10
Sauga EST 131 E8
Saugnacq-et-Muret F 32 B4
Saugos LT 134 F2
Saugues F 30 F4
Saujon F 28 D4
Sauk AL 168 B2
Sauka LV 135 D10
Šaukėnai LT 134 E5
Saukko FIN 125 C11
Saukkoaapa FIN 115 D2
Saukkojärvi FIN 119 B16
Saukkola FIN 127 E10
Saukkoriipi FIN 117 E12
Saukonkylä FIN 123 E11
Sauland N 95 C9
Saulce-sur-Rhône F 35 A8
Sauldorf D 27 E11
Saulepi EST 130 E7
Săulești RO 160 D2
Saulgau D 71 A9
Saulgrub D 71 B12
Saulheim D 21 E10
Şăulia RO 152 D4
Saulieu F 25 F11
Saulkalne LV 135 C8
Saulkrasti LV 135 B8
Sault F 35 B9
Sault-de-Navailles F 32 C4
Sault-lès-Rethel F 19 F9
Saulx F 26 E5
Saulxures-sur-Moselotte F 27 E6
Saulzais-le-Potier F 29 B11
Saumos F 28 F3
Saumur F 23 F11
Saunajärvi FIN 125 C13
Saunakylä FIN 123 D13
Saunavaara FIN 115 D3
Saundersfoot GB 12 B5
Saurat F 33 E9
Saurieši LV 135 C8
Sauris I 73 D6
Saursfjord N 110 E9
Sausnēja LV 135 C11
Sausset-les-Pins F 35 D9
Saussy F 26 F2
Sautens A 71 C11
Sautiņi LV 135 B8
Sautron F 23 F8
Sautso Kraftverk N 113 D12
Sauvagnon F 32 D5
Sauve F 35 C6
Sauveterre-de-Béarn F 32 D4
Sauveterre-de-Guyenne F 28 F5
Sauveterre-la-Lémance F 33 A8
Sauviat-sur-Vige F 29 D9
Sauvo FIN 126 E8
Sauxillanges F 30 D3
Sauzet F 33 B8
Sauzé-Vaussais F 29 C6
Sauzon F 22 F5
Sava I 61 C9
Sava SLO 73 D10
Săvădisla RO 151 D11
Savalia GR 174 D3
Savaloja FIN 119 E15
Sävar S 122 C5
Săvârşin RO 151 E9
Sävast S 118 C7
Savaştepe TR 173 F8
Säve S 91 D10
Savelli I 61 E7
Savenay F 23 F8
Săveni RO 153 B9
Săveni RO 161 D11
Saverdun F 33 D9
Saverna EST 131 E13
Saverne F 27 C7
Sävi FIN 126 B8
Säviä FIN 123 D17
Saviaho FIN 125 C10
Savières F 25 D10
Savigliano I 37 B7
Savignac-les-Églises F 29 E7
Savignano Irpino I 60 A4
Savignano sul Rubicone I 66 D5
Savigné-l'Évêque F 23 D12
Savigneux F 30 D5
Savigny-en-Sancerre F 25 F8
Savigny-lès-Beaune F 25 F12
Savigny-sur-Braye F 24 E4
Savijärvi FIN 125 C13
Savikylä FIN 125 C11
Savilahti FIN 129 C10
Savimäki FIN 124 C7
Savines-le-Lac F 36 B4
Săvinești RO 153 D8
Savino Selo SRB 158 B4
Saviranta FIN 121 F10
Saviselkä FIN 123 B16
Savitaipale FIN 128 C8
Sävja S 99 C9
Šavnik MNE 157 G11
Savognin CH 71 D9
Savoisy F 25 E11
Savona I 37 C8
Savonlinna FIN 129 B10
Savonranta FIN 125 F12
Savran' UA 154 A6
Sävsjö S 92 E5
Sävsjön S 97 C12
Savudrija HR 67 B7
Savukoski FIN 115 D4
Sawin PL 141 H8
Sawston GB 15 C9
Sax E 56 D3
Saxdalen S 97 B12
Saxen A 77 F7
Saxhyttan S 97 C11
Saxilby GB 11 E10
Saxmundham GB 15 C11
Saxnäs S 106 B8
Saxon CH 31 C11
Saxthorpe GB 15 B11
Saxvallen S 105 D12
Sayalonga E 53 C8
Sayatón E 47 D7
Sayda D 80 E4
Säynäjä FIN 121 B13
Säynätsalo FIN 123 F15
Säyneinen FIN 125 D10
Sázava CZ 77 C7
Sazli TR 171 E10
Sazli TR 177 D9
Sazoba TR 173 D7
Sazoba TR 177 B10
Scaër F 22 D4
Scăești RO 160 E3
Scafa I 62 C5
Scalasaig GB 4 C4
Scalby GB 11 C11
Scalea I 60 D5
Scaletta Zanclea I 59 C7
Scalloway GB 3 E14
Scandale I 61 E7
Scandiano I 66 C2
Scandicci I 66 E3
Scandriglia I 62 C3
Scanno I 62 D5
Scano di Montiferro I 64 C2
Scansano I 65 B4
Scânteia RO 153 D11
Scânteia RO 161 D10
Scânteiești RO 153 F12
Scanzano Jonico I 61 C7
Scapa GB 3 H11
Scarborough GB 11 C11
Scardovari I 66 C5
Scarinish GB 4 B3
Scario I 60 C4
Scărişoara RO 160 F5
Scarlino I 65 B3
Scarperia I 66 E3
Scartaglen IRL 8 D4
Scartaglin IRL 8 D4
Šćenica-Bobani BIH 162 D5
Scerni I 63 C7
Scey-sur-Saône-et-St-Albin F 26 E4
Schaafheim D 187 B7
Schaan FL 71 C9
Schaarsbergen NL 183 A7
Schaerbeek B 19 C9
Schaesberg NL 20 C6
Schaffhausen CH 27 E10
Schafflund D 82 A6
Schafstädt D 79 D10
Schafstedt D 82 B6
Schäftlarn D 75 G9
Schagen NL 16 C3
Schaijk NL 183 B7
Schalchen A 76 F4
Schalkau D 75 B9
Schalkhaar NL 183 A8
Schalksmühle D 17 F9
Schänis CH 27 F11
Schapen D 17 D9
Schaprode D 84 A4
Scharbeutz D 83 B9
Schardenberg A 76 E4
Schärding A 76 F4
Scharendijke NL 16 E1
Scharnebeck D 83 D9
Scharnitz A 72 B3
Scharnstein A 73 A8
Scharrel (Oldenburg) D 17 B9
Scharwoude NL 16 C4
Schashagen D 83 B9
Schattendorf A 149 A7
Schebheim D 75 C7
Scheemda NL 17 B7
Scheer D 27 D11
Scheeßel D 82 D6
Schefflenz D 21 F12
Scheggia e Pascelupo I 67 F6
Scheggino I 62 B3
Şcheia RO 153 B8
Şcheia RO 153 D11
Scheibbs A 77 F8
Scheiblingkirchen A 148 A6
Scheidegg D 71 B9
Scheifling A 73 B9
Scheinfeld D 75 C7
Schela RO 155 B1
Schela RO 160 C2
Schelklingen D 74 F6
Schellerten D 79 B7
Schemmerhofen D 71 A9
Schenefeld D 82 B6
Schenefeld D 83 C7
Schenkenfelden A 76 E6
Schenkenzell D 187 E5
Schenklengsfeld D 78 E6
Schermbeck D 17 E7
Schermen D 79 B10
Schermerhorn NL 16 C3
Scherpenheuvel B 19 C10
Scherpenzeel NL 16 D4
Scherwiller F 27 D7
Scherzingen CH 27 E11
Scheßlitz D 75 C9
Schiavi di Abruzzo I 63 D6
Schiedam NL 16 E2
Schieder-Schwalenberg D 17 E12
Schieren L 20 E6
Schierling D 75 E11
Schiermonnikoog NL 16 B6
Schiers CH 71 D9
Schiffdorf D 17 A11
Schifferstadt D 21 F10
Schifflange L 20 E6
Schiffweiler D 186 C3
Schijndel NL 16 E4
Schilde B 16 F3
Schillingen D 186 B2
Schillingsfürst D 75 D7
Schilpario I 69 A9
Schiltach D 27 D9
Schiltigheim F 27 C8
Schimatari GR 175 C8
Schinnen NL 183 D7
Schinos GR 174 B3
Schinveld NL 20 C5
Schio I 69 B11
Schipkau D 80 C5
Schipluiden NL 182 B4
Schirmeck F 27 D7
Schirmitz D 75 C11
Schitu RO 160 E5
Schitu RO 161 E7
Schitu Duca RO 153 C11
Schitu Golești RO 160 C6
Schkeuditz D 79 D11
Schkölen D 79 D10
Schköna D 79 C12
Schkopau D 79 D10
Schlabendorf D 80 C5
Schladen D 79 B8
Schlangen D 17 E11
Schlangenbad D 21 D10
Schleching D 72 A5
Schleiden D 20 C6
Schleife D 81 C7
Schleinbach A 77 F10
Schleitheim CH 27 E9
Schleiz D 79 E10
Schlema D 79 E12
Schlepzig D 80 B5
Schleswig D 82 A7
Schleusingen D 75 A8
Schlieben D 80 C4
Schliengen D 27 E8
Schlier D 71 B9
Schlierbach A 73 A9
Schlieren CH 27 F9
Schliersee D 72 A4
Schlitters A 72 B4
Schlitz D 78 E6
Schlossberg A 148 C4
Schloss Holte-Stukenbrock D 17 E11
Schlossvippach D 79 D9
Schlosswil CH 70 D5
Schlotheim D 79 D8
Schluchsee D 27 E9
Schlüchtern D 74 B6
Schlüsselfeld D 75 C8
Schmallenberg D 21 B10
Schmelz D 21 F7
Schmidgaden D 75 D11
Schmidmühlen D 75 D10
Schmiedeberg D 80 E5
Schmölln D 79 E11
Schmölln D 84 D6
Schnabelwaid D 75 C10
Schnackenburg D 83 D11
Schnaittach D 75 C9
Schneeberg D 79 E12
Schneidlingen D 79 C9
Schneizlreuth D 73 A6
Schnelldorf D 187 C9
Schnellmannshausen D 79 D7
Schneverdingen D 82 D7
Schnürpflingen D 187 E8
Schobüll D 82 A6
Schodnia PL 142 E5
Schoenberg B 20 D6
Scholen D 17 C11
Schollene D 83 E12
Schöllkrippen D 187 A7
Schöllnach D 76 E4
Schömberg D 27 D10
Schömberg D 187 D6
Schönaich D 187 D7
Schönau D 76 F3
Schönau im Schwarzwald D 27 E8
Schönbach A 77 F8
Schönberg D 83 C9
Schönberg D 84 E3
Schönberg (Holstein) D 83 B8
Schönberg am Kamp A 77 E9
Schönberg im Stubaital A 72 B3
Schönborn D 80 C5
Schondra D 74 B6
Schönebeck D 83 D12
Schönebeck (Elbe) D 79 B10
Schöneck D 75 B11
Schönecken D 20 D6
Schönenberg-Kübelberg D 186 C3
Schönermark D 84 D5
Schönewalde D 80 C4
Schönewörde D 79 A8
Schongau D 71 B11
Schönhausen D 79 A11
Schöningen D 79 B8
Schönkirchen D 83 B8
Schönow D 84 E5
Schönsee D 75 C12
Schöntal D 74 D6
Schönthal D 75 D12
Schönwalde D 80 C5
Schönwalde am Bungsberg D 83 B9
Schönwies A 71 C11
Schoondijke NL 16 F1
Schoonebeek NL 17 C7
Schoonhoven NL 16 E3
Schoorl NL 16 C3
Schopfheim D 27 E8
Schopfloch D 75 D7
Schöppenstedt D 79 B8
Schoppernau A 71 C10
Schöppingen D 17 D8
Schörfling am Attersee A 73 A8
Schorndorf D 74 E6
Schorndorf D 75 D12
Schortens D 17 A9
Schoten B 16 F2
Schotten D 21 D12
Schramberg D 27 D9
Schrecksbach D 21 C12
Schrems A 77 E8
Schrepkow D 83 E12
Schriesheim D 21 F11
Schrobenhausen D 75 E9
Schröder A 73 B9
Schrozberg D 74 D6
Schruns A 71 C9
Schübelbach CH 27 F10
Schuby D 82 A6
Schulenberg im Oberharz D 79 C7
Schull IRL 8 E3
Schulzendorf D 84 E6
Schüpfheim CH 70 D6
Schuttertal D 186 E4
Schutterwald D 186 E4
Schüttorf D 17 D8
Schwaan D 83 C12
Schwabach D 75 D9
Schwäbisch Gmünd D 74 E6
Schwäbisch Hall D 74 D6
Schwabmünchen D 71 A11
Schwabstedt D 82 B6
Schwafördern D 17 C11
Schwaigern D 27 B11
Schwalbach D 21 F7
Schwalmstadt-Treysa D 21 C12
Schwalmstadt-Ziegenhain D 21 C12
Schwanberg A 73 C11
Schwanden CH 71 C8
Schwandorf D 75 D11
Schwanebeck D 79 C9
Schwanenstadt A 76 F5
Schwanewede D 17 B11
Schwangau D 71 B11
Schwanstetten D 75 D9
Schwarme D 17 C12
Schwarmstedt D 82 E7
Schwarz D 83 D13
Schwarza D 79 E8
Schwarzach D 76 E3
Schwarzau im Gebirge A 148 A5
Schwarzenau A 77 E8
Schwarzenbach A 149 A6
Schwarzenbach am Wald D 75 B10
Schwarzenbek D 83 C8
Schwarzenberg D 79 E12
Schwarzenborn D 78 E5
Schwarzenburg CH 31 B11
Schwarzenfeld D 75 D11
Schwarzheide D 80 D5
Schwaz A 72 B4
Schwechat A 77 F10
Schwedeneck D 83 B8
Schwedt an der Oder D 84 D6
Schwegenheim D 187 C5
Schwei (Stadland) D 17 B10
Schweiburg D 17 B10
Schweich D 21 E7
Schweigen-Rechtenbach D 27 B8
Schweighouse-sur-Moder F 186 D4
Schweinfurt D 75 B7
Schweinitz D 80 C4
Schweinrich D 83 D13
Schwelm D 17 F8
Schwendau A 72 B4
Schwendi D 71 A9
Schwenningen D 27 D10
Schwepnitz D 80 D5
Schwerin D 83 C10
Schweringen D 17 C12
Schwerte D 17 F9
Schwichtenberg D 84 C5
Schwieberdingen D 27 C11
Schwiesau D 79 A9
Schwindegg D 75 F11
Schwinkendorf D 83 C13
Schwoich A 72 A5
Schwyz CH 71 C7
Sciacca I 58 D3
Sciara I 58 D4
Scicli I 59 F6
Sciez F 31 C9
Scigliano I 61 E6
Scilla I 59 C8
Ścinawa PL 81 D10
Scionzier F 31 C10
Scoarța RO 160 C2
Scobinți RO 153 C9
Scoglitti I 58 F5
Scolaticci I 59 C6
Scole GB 15 C11
Scone GB 5 C10
Sconser GB 2 L4
Scopello I 68 B5
Scoppito I 62 C4
Scorbé-Clairvaux F 29 B6
Scordia I 59 E6
Scornicești RO 160 D5
Scorrano I 61 C10
Scorțaru Nou RO 161 C11
Scorțeni MD 154 C3
Scorțeni RO 153 D9
Scorțeni RO 161 C7
Scorțoasa RO 161 C9
Scorton GB 11 C8
Scorzè I 66 A5
Scotch Corner GB 11 C8
Scotch Corner IRL 7 D9
Scotshouse IRL 7 D8
Scourie GB 2 J6
Scousburgh GB 3 F14
Scrabster GB 3 H9
Screeb IRL 6 F3
Screggan IRL 7 F7
Scremerston GB 5 D13
Scribbagh GB 6 D6
Scrioaștea RO 160 E5
Scriob IRL 6 F3
Sculeni MD 153 C11
Scundu RO 160 D4
Scunthorpe GB 11 D10
Scuol CH 71 D10
Scurcola Marsicana I 62 C4
Scurtu Mare RO 160 E6
Scutelnici RO 161 D9
Seaca RO 160 E5
Seaca RO 160 C6
Seaca de Pădure RO 160 E2
Seaford GB 15 F9
Seaham GB 5 F14
Seahouses GB 5 D13
Seamer GB 11 C11
Seapatrick GB 7 D10
Seara P 38 E2
Seascale GB 10 C5
Seaton GB 5 F9
Seaton GB 13 D8
Seaton Delaval GB 5 E13
Seaton Sluice GB 5 E14
Seaview GB 13 D12
Sebal P 44 D3
Sébazac-Concourès F 34 B4
Sebbersund DK 86 B5
Sebechleby SK 147 E7
Sebedražie SK 147 D7
Sebeș RO 152 F3
Šebetov CZ 77 C11
Sebezh RUS 133 D4
Sebiș RO 151 E9
Sebnitz D 80 E6
Seč CZ 77 C9
Sečanj SRB 159 C6
Seča Reka SRB 158 E4
Secăria RO 161 C7
Secaș RO 151 F8
Sece LV 135 C10
Secemin PL 143 E8
Seckach D 27 B11
Seckau A 73 B10
Seclin F 19 C7
Secondigny F 28 B5
Sečovce SK 145 F4
Sečovská Polianka SK 145 F4
Secu RO 160 E2
Secuieni RO 152 E5
Secuieni RO 153 D9
Secuieni RO 153 D10
Secusigiu RO 151 E6
Seda LT 134 D4
Seda LV 131 F11
Sedan F 19 E10
Sedano E 40 C4
Sedbergh GB 10 C6
Seddülbahir TR 171 D10
Seden DK 86 E6
Sēdere LV 135 E12
Séderon F 35 B10
Sedgefield GB 5 F14
Sedico I 72 D5
Sedilo I 64 C2
Sedini I 64 B2
Sedlarica HR 149 E8
Sedlčany CZ 77 C6
Sedlec Prčice CZ 77 C7
Sedlice CZ 76 D5
Sedlice SK 145 F3
Sedliská SK 145 F4
Sedlnice CZ 146 B6
Sedrina I 69 B8
Šeduva LT 134 E7
Sjdziejowice PL 143 C7
Sjdzin PL 138 E6
Sjdziszów PL 143 F9
Sjdziszów Małopolski PL 143 F12
See A 71 C10
See A 73 B7
Seebach D 79 E7
Seebach D 187 D5
Seebergen D 79 E8
Seeboden A 73 C8
Seebruck D 72 A5
Seeburg D 79 C7
Seedorf D 83 C9
Seefeld D 75 F9
Seefeld D 80 A5
Seefeld (Stadland) D 17 B10

Sissach CH 27 F8
Sisses GR 178 E8
Sissonne F 19 E8
Şiştarovăţ RO 151 E8
Sisteron F 35 B10
Sistranda N 104 D5
Sistrans A 72 B3
Sita Buzăului RO 161 B8
Sitaniec PL 144 B7
Siteia GR 179 E11
Sitges E 43 E7
Sitkówka-Nowiny PL 143 E10
Sitnica BIH 157 C7
Sitochori GR 169 C10
Sitovo BG 161 E10
Sitsyenyets BY 133 E6
Sittard NL 19 C12
Sittensen D 82 D7
Sittersdorf A 73 C10
Sittingbourne GB 15 E10
Sitzendorf an der Schmida A 77 E9
Sitzenroda D 80 D3
Siulaisiadar GB 2 J4
Siuntio FIN 127 E11
Siuro FIN 127 C9
Siurua FIN 119 D16
Siurunmaa FIN 115 D1
Sivac SRB 158 B3
Sivakka FIN 125 C13
Sivakkajoki FIN 119 B13
Sivakkavaara FIN 125 E11
Siverić HR 156 E5
Siverskiy RUS 132 C7
Sivertgården N 108 E7
Sivry B 19 D9
Sivry-sur-Meuse F 19 F11
Sixarby S 99 B9
Six-Fours-les-Plages F 35 D10
Sixmilebridge IRL 8 C5
Sixmilecross GB 7 C8
Six Road Ends GB 4 F5
Sixt-Fer-à-Cheval F 31 C10
Sizun F 22 D3
Sjemeć BIH 158 F3
Sjenica SRB 163 C9
Sjetlina BIH 157 E10
Sjoa N 101 C11
Sjøåsen N 105 C10
Sjöbo S 87 D13
Sjöbotten S 118 E6
Sjöbrånet S 107 C17
Sjøholt N 100 B5
Sjølund DK 86 E5
Sjömarken S 91 D12
Sjonbotn N 108 D6
Sjørring DK 86 B3
Sjørslev DK 86 C4
Sjørup DK 86 C4
Sjösa S 93 B10
Sjösäter S 99 B11
Sjötofta S 91 E13
Sjötorp S 91 B14
Sjoutnäset S 106 B7
Sjøvassbotn N 111 B17
Sjøvegan N 111 C14
Sjövik S 91 D11
Sjulsåsen S 106 C7
Sjulsmark S 118 C7
Sjunnen S 92 E6
Sjuntorp S 91 C11
Sjursvik N 111 B12
Skademark S 107 E16
Skælsør DK 87 E8
Skærbæk DK 86 E3
Skævinge DK 87 D10
Skaftung FIN 122 F6
Skagen DK 90 D8
Skagersvik S 91 B15
Skäggebyn S 91 A12
Skagshamn S 107 E16
Skaidi N 113 C13
Skaidiškės LT 137 D11
Skaill GB 3 H11
Skaista LV 133 E2
Skaistgiriai LT 135 E8
Skaistgirys LT 134 D6
Skaistkalne LV 135 D9
Skala GR 174 C2
Skala GR 175 B7
Skala GR 175 F6
Skala GR 177 E8
Skała PL 143 F8
Skala Eresou GR 177 A6
Skala Kallonis GR 177 A7
Skala Marion GR 171 C7
Skålan S 102 A7
Skaland N 111 B13
Skala Oropou GR 175 C8
Skålavik FO 2 B3
Skalbmierz PL 143 F9
Skåle N 105 C15
Skålevik N 90 C3
Skälgården S 103 A12
Skáli FO 2 A3
Skalica SK 146 D4
Skalice CZ 81 E7
Skalité SK 147 C7
Skalitsa BG 166 E6
Skallelv N 114 C8
Skällinge S 87 A10
Skallvik S 93 C9
Skalmodal S 108 F8
Skalmsjö S 107 D13
Skalná CZ 75 B11
Skålö S 97 A11
Skaloti GR 171 B6
Skals DK 86 B4
Skålsjön S 103 D10
Skalstugan S 105 D12
Skålsvik N 108 B7
Skålvallen S 103 C10
Skån S 103 B11
Skanderåsen S 102 A7
Skanderborg DK 86 C5
Skånes-Fagerhult S 87 C12
Skåne-Tranås S 88 D5
Skånevik N 94 C3
Skåningen N 112 C4
Skaņkalne LV 131 F10
Skänninge S 92 C6
Skanör med Falsterbo S 87 E11
Skansbacken S 97 B11
Skansen N 105 D9
Skansholm S 107 B10
Skansnäs S 107 A10
Skansnäs S 109 E13
Skansnäset S 106 C9
Skåpafors S 91 A11
Skape PL 81 B8
Skapiškis LT 135 E10
Skår N 94 D4
Skara S 91 C13
Skäran S 118 F6
Skarberget N 111 D11
Skärblacka S 92 B7
Skarda S 107 C15
Skardmodalen N 108 F7
Skardmunken N 111 A18
Skardstein N 111 B11
Skardsvåg N 113 A16
Skare N 94 C5
Skåre S 97 D9
Skärhamn S 91 D10
Skarkdalen S 102 A4
Skärkind S 92 C7
Skarnes N 96 B6
Skärplinge S 99 B9
Skarp Salling DK 86 B4
Skarrild DK 86 D3
Skärså S 103 D13
Skarsfjord N 112 D2
Skärsjövålen S 102 B5
Skarstad N 111 D11
Skärstad S 92 D4
Skarsvåg N 111 B15
Skarszewy PL 138 B5
Skårup DK 86 E7
Skarv N 112 C11
Skärvången S 105 D16
Skarvfjordhamn N 112 B11
Skarvsjöby S 107 B12
Skaryszew PL 141 H4
Skarżysko-Kamienna PL 141 H3
Skasenden N 96 B7
Skästra S 103 C11
Skatamark S 118 C7
Skatan S 103 B13
Skattkärr S 97 D10
Skattungbyn S 102 D8
Skatvik N 111 B14
Skaudvilė LT 134 F5
Skaugvoll N 108 C7
Skaulo S 116 D6
Škaune LV 133 D3
Skavdal N 111 B10
Skave DK 86 C3
Skavnakk N 112 C7
Skawina PL 143 G8
Skebobruk S 99 C11
Skebokvarn S 93 A9
Skeda udde S 92 C7
Šķēde LV 134 C4
Skede S 92 E6
Skedevi S 92 B7
Skedsmokorset N 95 B14
Skee S 91 B9
Skegness GB 11 E12
Skegrie S 87 E12
Skei N 100 C4
Skei N 105 A11
Skela SRB 158 D5
Skelby DK 87 E9
Skelde DK 82 A7
Skelhøje DK 86 C4
Skellefteå S 118 E5
Skelleftehamn S 118 E6
Skelmersdale GB 10 D6
Skelton GB 11 B10
Šķeltova LV 133 D2
Skelund DK 86 B6
Skelwick GB 3 G11
Skėmiai LT 134 E7
Skenderaj RKS 163 D10
Skender Vakuf BIH 157 D7
Skenfrith GB 13 B9
Skepasto GR 174 C5
Skjpe PL 139 E7
Skepplanda S 91 D11
Skeppshamn S 103 B14
Skeppshult S 87 A12
Skeppsmalen S 107 E16
Skerries IRL 7 E10
Skhidnytsya UA 145 E7
Ski N 95 C13
Skiathos GR 175 A7
Skibbereen IRL 8 E4
Skibbild DK 86 C3
Skibby DK 87 D9
Šķibe LV 134 C6
Skibinge DK 87 E10
Skibotn N 111 B19
Skidal' BY 140 C10
Skiemonys LT 135 F10
Skien N 90 A6
Šķieneri LV 135 B13
Skierbieszów PL 144 B7
Skierniewice PL 141 G2
Skiippagurra N 114 C4
Šķilbēni LV 133 B3
Skillebotn N 108 F3
Skillefjordnes N 113 C11
Skillingaryd S 92 E4
Skillinge S 88 E6
Skillvassbakk N 111 D10
Skinias GR 178 E9
Skinnarud N 101 E12
Skinnskatteberg S 97 C14
Skipmannvik N 109 B9
Skipness GB 4 D6
Skipsea GB 11 D11
Skipton GB 11 D7
Skiptvet N 95 D14
Skirlaugh GB 11 D11
Skitelv N 111 A17
Skiti GR 169 E8
Skivarp S 87 E13
Skive DK 86 B4
Skivjan RKS 163 E9
Skivsjön S 107 C16
Skiwy Duże PL 141 F7
Skjærhalden N 91 A9
Skjåholmen N 113 B12
Skjånes N 113 B18
Skjånes N 113 B21
Skjåvika N 108 E6
Skjeberg N 91 A9
Skjeggedal N 90 B3
Skjelelv N 111 C13
Skjellbreid N 105 C14
Skjelman N 111 A17
Skjelnes N 111 A18
Skjelstad N 105 D10
Skjelvik N 108 B7
Skjern DK 86 D3
Skjern N 105 C9
Skjerstad N 108 B9
Skjervøy N 112 C6
Skjød DK 86 C5
Skjold N 111 B17
Skjoldastraumen N 94 D3
Skjolden N 100 D7
Skjombotn N 111 D13
Skjøtningberg N 113 A19
Sklithro GR 169 E8
Skobelevo BG 166 D4
Skoby S 99 B10
Skočivir NMK 169 C6
Škocjan SLO 148 E4
Skoczów PL 147 B7
Skodborg DK 86 E4
Skodje N 100 A5
Skøelv N 111 B15
Škofja Loka SLO 73 D9
Škofljica SLO 73 E10
Skog S 103 D12
Skogaholm S 92 A6
Skoganvarri N 113 D15
Skoger N 95 C12
Skogfoss N 114 E7
Skoghall S 97 D9
Skogly N 114 E6
Skogmo N 105 B12
Skogn N 105 D10
Skogså S 118 C7
Skogsby S 89 B11
Skogsfjord N 112 C3
Skogshöjden S 91 C11
Skogstorp S 87 B10
Skogstorp S 98 D6
Skogstue N 112 D11
Skogum N 114 E6
Skoki PL 85 E12
Sköldinge S 93 A8
Skole UA 145 E8
Skollenborg N 95 C11
Sköllersta S 92 A6
Skoltenes N 110 C8
Skoltevatn N 114 E7
Skołyszyn PL 144 D3
Skomlin PL 142 D5
Skonseng N 108 D7
Skönvik S 103 E12
Skopelos GR 175 A8
Skopelos GR 177 A7
Skopi GR 179 E11
Skopje NMK 164 F3
Skopos GR 169 C6
Skopos GR 171 B7
Skopun FO 2 B3
Skórcz PL 138 C6
Skorica SRB 159 F8
Skorild N 104 E6
Skorogoszcz PL 142 E4
Skoroszyce PL 142 E3
Skorovatn N 105 B14
Skorped S 107 E13
Skorpetorp S 89 A10
Skørping DK 86 B5
Skorstad N 105 B10
Skórzec PL 141 F6
Skoteini GR 174 D5
Skotfoss N 90 A6
Skotina GR 169 D8
Skotoussa GR 169 B9
Skotselv N 95 C11
Skotterud N 96 C7
Skottsund S 103 B13
Skoura GR 175 E5
Skourta GR 175 C8
Skoutari GR 169 B10
Skoutari GR 178 B4
Skoutaros GR 171 F10
Skovby DK 86 C5
Skövde S 91 C14
Skoved S 107 E14
Skovlund DK 86 D3
Skovsgård DK 86 A4
Skra GR 169 B7
Skräddrabo S 103 D10
Skradin HR 156 E4
Skråmestø N 100 E1
Skranstad N 110 E9
Skravena BG 165 D8
Skrea S 87 B11
Skreia N 101 E13
Skriaudžiai LT 137 D8
Skrinyano BG 165 E6
Skřipov CZ 146 B5
Skrīveri LV 135 C10
Skröven S 116 E7
Skrøytnes N 114 E7
Skrudaliena LV 135 E13
Skrunda LV 134 C4
Skruv S 89 B8
Skrwilno PL 139 D8
Skrzatusz PL 85 D11
Skrzyńsko PL 141 H3
Skrzyszów PL 143 G11
Skucani BIH 157 E6
Skudeneshavn N 94 D2
Skuhrov nad Bělou CZ 77 B10
Skujene LV 135 B10
Skujetnieki LV 133 C2
Skuķi LV 133 E3
Skuldelev DK 87 D10
Skule S 107 E14
Skulerud N 95 C15
Skulgammen N 111 A17
Skulsfjord N 111 A16
Skulsk PL 138 F5
Skulte LV 135 B8
Skulte LV 135 C7
Skultorp S 91 C14
Skultuna S 98 C6
Skuodas LT 134 D3
Skurträsk S 107 C16
Skurup S 87 E13
Skuteč CZ 77 C9
Skutskär S 103 E13
Skutvik N 110 D9
Skutvik N 111 B16
Skwierzyna PL 81 A9
Skýcov SK 146 D6
Skydra GR 169 C7
Skyllberg S 92 B6
Skylnäs S 103 A9
Skyros GR 175 B10
Skyttmon S 106 E9
Skyttorp S 99 B9
Slabodka BY 133 E2
Słaboszów PL 143 F9
Sládkovičovo SK 146 E5
Slagavallen S 102 B5
Slagelse DK 87 E8
Slagnäs S 109 E15
Slaidburn GB 10 D7
Slaka S 92 C7
Slampe LV 134 C6
Slane IRL 7 E9
Slanec SK 145 F3
Slangerup DK 87 D10
Slănic RO 161 C7
Slănic Moldova RO 153 E8
Slano HR 162 D4
Slantsy RUS 132 C3
Slaný CZ 76 B6
Slap BIH 158 F3
Slap MNE 163 D7
Slap SLO 73 D8
Šlapaberžė LT 135 F7
Šlapanice CZ 77 D11
Släppträsk S 107 A15
Slate LV 135 D12
Slatina BIH 157 C7
Slatina BIH 157 C8
Slatina BIH 157 E8
Slatina BIH 157 E10
Slatina HR 149 E9
Slatina RO 153 C8
Slatina RO 160 E4
Slatina SRB 158 E4
Slatiňany CZ 77 C9
Slatina-Timiș RO 159 C9
Slatino NMK 168 B4
Slatinski Drenovac HR 149 E9
Slătioara RO 160 C3
Slătioara RO 160 E4
Slato BIH 157 F9
Slättberg S 102 D8
Slåttholmen N 110 D8
Slättmon S 103 A13
Slattum N 95 C13
Slava Cercheză RO 155 D3
Slava Rusă RO 155 D3
Slaveino BG 165 F10
Slavičín CZ 146 C5
Slavinja SRB 165 C6
Slavkov CZ 146 B5
Slavkovichi RUS 132 F5
Slavkov u Brna CZ 77 D11
Slavonice CZ 77 E8
Slavonski Brod HR 157 B9
Slavošovce SK 145 F1
Slavotin BG 165 B7
Slavovitsa BG 160 F4
Slavovitsa BG 165 E9
Slavsk RUS 136 C4
Slavs'ke UA 145 F7
Slavsko Polje HR 148 F5
Slavyani BG 165 C10
Slavyanovo BG 165 C10
Slavyanovo BG 166 C6
Slavyanovo BG 166 F5
Sława PL 81 C10
Sławatycze PL 141 G9
Sławięcin PL 85 C13
Sławków PL 143 F7
Sławno PL 85 B11
Sławoborze PL 85 C9
Sławsko PL 85 B11
Sleaford GB 11 F11
Sledmere GB 11 C10
Sleen NL 17 C7
Sleidinge B 182 C3
Sleights GB 11 C10
Slemmestad N 95 C12
Ślesin PL 138 D4
Ślesin PL 138 F5
Sletta N 112 C9
Slevik N 91 A8
Sliač SK 147 D8
Slidre N 101 D9
Sliedrecht NL 16 E3
Šlienava LT 137 D9
Sligachan GB 2 L4
Sligeach IRL 6 D6
Sligo IRL 6 D6
Slimminge DK 87 E9
Slimnic RO 152 F4
Slinfold GB 15 E8
Slipra N 105 D9
Slišane SRB 164 D4
Slite S 93 D13
Sliven BG 166 D6
Slivilești RO 159 D11
Slivnitsa BG 165 D7
Slivo Pole BG 161 F8
Śliwice PL 138 C5
Sllatinë e Madhe RKS 164 D3
Slobidka UA 154 B4
Slobozia MD 154 D5
Slobozia RO 160 D6
Slobozia RO 161 D10
Slobozia RO 161 F7
Slobozia Bradului RO 161 C10
Slobozia Ciorăști RO 161 B10
Slobozia Conachi RO 155 B1
Slobozia Mândra RO 160 F5
Slobozia Mare MD 155 B2
Slobozia Moară RO 161 D7
Slochteren NL 17 B7
Slöinge S 87 B11
Słomniki PL 143 F9
Słonowice PL 85 C9
Słońsk PL 81 A7
Slootdorp NL 16 C3
Slottsskogen S 99 C9
Slough GB 15 D7
Sloupnice CZ 77 C10
Sløvåg N 100 E2
Slovenj Gradec SLO 73 C11
Slovenska Bistrica SLO 148 D5
Slovenská Ľupča SK 147 D8
Slovenská Ves SK 145 E1
Slovenske Konjice SLO 148 D4
Slovenské Nové Mesto SK 145 G4
Slovenský Grob SK 146 E4
Slovinci HR 157 B6
Slovinky SK 145 F2
Sløvra N 110 D8
Slov"yanoserbka UA 154 D5
Słowik PL 143 C7
Słubice PL 81 B7
Słubice PL 139 F8
Sluderno I 71 D11
Sluis NL 19 B7
Sluiskil NL 16 F1
Šluknov CZ 81 D6
Slunj HR 156 B4
Słupca PL 142 B4
Słupcza PL 144 B4
Słupia PL 141 G1
Słupia PL 143 D9
Słupia PL 143 E8
Słupno PL 139 E8
Słupsk PL 85 B12
Slušovice CZ 146 C5
Slussfors S 109 F11
Słuszków PL 142 C5
Slyuda RUS 115 D8
Smailholm GB 5 D11
Smålandsstenar S 87 A12
Smalåsen N 105 A14
Smalfjord N 113 C21
Smalininkai LT 136 C6
Smalvos LT 135 E12
Smârdan RO 155 C1
Smârdan RO 155 C2
Smärde LV 134 C6
Smârdioasa RO 161 F6
Smardzewice PL 141 H2
Smardzewo PL 81 B9
Smardzko PL 85 C9
Smarhon' BY 137 E13
Šmarje pri Jelšah SLO 148 D5
Šmarjeta SLO 148 E4
Šmartno SLO 73 D10
Šmartno SLO 73 D11
Smarves F 29 B6
Smedby S 89 B10
Smederevo SRB 159 D6
Smederevska Palanka SRB 159 E6
Smedjebacken S 97 B13
Smedsbyn S 118 C8
Smedvik N 110 D6
Smeeni RO 161 C9
Smęgorzów PL 143 F11
Smelror N 114 C10
Smelteri LV 135 D13
Smętowo Graniczne PL 138 C6
Smidary CZ 77 B8
Smidstrup DK 86 D5
Smidstrup DK 87 C10
Śmigiel PL 81 B11
Smiľčić HR 156 D4
Smilde NL 17 C6
Smilets BG 165 E9
Smilevo NMK 168 B5
Smilgiai LT 135 D9
Smilgiai LT 135 E8
Smilgiai LT 137 D8
Smilgynai LT 134 E2
Smilovci SRB 165 C6
Śmiłowice PL 138 E7
Śmiłowo PL 85 D11
Smiltene LV 135 B11
Smiltynė LT 134 E2
Smilyan BG 171 A7
Smines N 110 C8
Smiřice CZ 77 B9
Smirnenski BG 159 F11
Smirnenski BG 161 F8
Smiugard N 101 D11
Smižany SK 145 F2
Smögen S 91 C9
Smokvica HR 162 D2
Smokvica NMK 169 B7
Smołdzino PL 85 A12
Smolenice SK 146 D4
Smolice PL 81 C12
Smolmark S 96 C7
Smolnica PL 84 E7
Smolník SK 145 F2
Smolyan BG 171 A7
Smolyanovtsi BG 165 C6
Smørfjord N 113 B15
Smulți RO 153 F11
Smyadovo BG 167 C8
Smygehamn S 87 E12
Smyków PL 143 D9
Snagov RO 161 D8
Snainton GB 11 C10
Snaith GB 11 D9
Snålroa N 102 E2
Snappertuna FIN 127 E10
Snaptun DK 86 D6
Snarby N 111 A18
Snåre FIN 123 C10
Snartemo N 94 F6
Snåsa N 105 C12
Snave Bridge IRL 8 E4
Snedsted DK 86 B3
Sneek NL 16 B5
Sneem IRL 8 E3
Snejbjerg DK 86 C3
Snēpele LV 134 C3
Snerta N 101 C15
Snertinge DK 87 D8
Snesslinge S 99 B10
Snesudden S 118 B4
Snettisham GB 11 F13
Śniadowo PL 139 D12
Snikere LV 134 D6
Snina SK 145 F5
Šnjegotina Velika BIH 157 C8
Snøde DK 87 E7
Snøfjord N 113 B14
Snogebæk DK 89 E8
Snoghøj DK 86 D5
Snoldelev DK 87 D10
Soajo P 38 E3
Șoarș RO 152 F5
Soave I 66 B3
Søberg N 110 C7
Soběslav CZ 77 D7
Sobienie-Jeziory PL 141 G4
Sobolew PL 141 G5
Sobota PL 143 B8
Soboth A 73 C11
Sobotín CZ 77 B12
Sobotište SK 146 D4
Sobotka CZ 77 B8
Sobótka PL 81 E11
Sobótka PL 142 C4
Sobótka PL 143 E12
Sobowidz PL 138 B6
Sobra HR 162 D4
Sobradelo E 39 D6
Sobradiel E 41 E9
Sobrado E 38 B3
Sobrado E 38 D3
Sobral da Adiça P 51 C5
Sobral de Monte Agraço P 50 A1
Sobrance SK 145 F5
Sobreira Formosa P 44 E5
Søby DK 86 F6
Soča SLO 73 D8
Sočanica RKS 163 C10
Soçanicë RKS 163 C10
Socchieve I 73 D6
Sočerga SLO 67 B8
Sochaczew PL 141 F2
Sochaux F 27 E6
Sochocin PL 139 E9
Sochos GR 169 C9
Socodor RO 151 D7
Socol RO 159 D7
Socond RO 151 B10
Socovos E 55 C9
Socuéllamos E 47 F7
Sodankylä FIN 117 D17
Söderåkra S 89 C10
Söderala S 103 D12
Söderås S 103 E9
Söderbärke S 97 B14
Söderboda S 99 B10
Söderby-Karl S 99 C11
Söderfors S 98 B8
Söderhamn S 103 D13
Söderköping S 93 C8
Söderkulla FIN 127 E13
Södersvik S 99 C11
Södertälje S 93 A11
Södra Åbyn S 118 E5
Södra Bränntäsk S 118 C4
Södra Drängsmark S 118 E5
Södra Harads S 118 B5
Södra Johannisberg S 109 F15
Södra Löten S 102 E4
Södra Sandby S 87 D12
Södra Sandträsk S 107 A16
Södra Sunderbyn S 118 C7
Södra Tresund S 107 B11
Södra Vallgrund FIN 122 D6
Södra Vi S 92 D7
Sodražica SLO 73 E10
Soerendonk NL 16 F5
Soest D 17 E10
Soest NL 16 D4
Soesterberg NL 183 A6
Sofades GR 169 F7
Sofia BG 165 D7
Sofia MD 153 B11
Sofiko GR 171 B11
Sofiko GR 175 D7
Sofporog RUS 121 C17
Șofrîncani MD 153 A10
Șofronea RO 151 E7
Sofronievo BG 160 F3
Søften DK 86 C6
Søftestad N 90 A4
Sofular TR 181 A9
Sögel D 17 C9
Sogndalsfjøra N 100 D6
Søgne N 90 C2
Soğucak TR 173 A8
Soğucak TR 173 F8
Soğucak TR 177 D9
Soğukoluk TR 181 A7
Söğüt TR 181 C8
Söğütalan TR 173 D10
Soham GB 15 C9
Sohatu RO 161 E9
Soheit-Tinlot B 19 D11
Sohland D 80 D6
Sohodol RO 151 E11
Sohren D 21 E8
Soidinkumpu FIN 121 B12
Soidinvaara FIN 121 F12
Soignies B 19 C9
Soikko FIN 119 C14
Șoimari RO 161 C8
Șoimi RO 151 D9
Șoimuș RO 151 F10
Soing F 26 E4
Soings-en-Sologne F 24 F6
Soini FIN 123 E12
Soinilansalmi FIN 125 F10
Soinlahti FIN 124 C8
Soissons F 19 F7
Soivio FIN 121 C13
Soizy-aux-Bois F 25 C10
Sójkowa PL 144 C5
Söjtör H 149 C7
Sokal' UA 144 C9
Söke TR 177 D9
Soklot FIN 122 C9
Sokna N 95 B11
Sokndal N 94 F4
Sokobanja SRB 159 F8
Sokojärvi FIN 125 D14
Sokolac BIH 157 E10
Sokolany PL 140 D8
Sokolce SK 146 F5
Sokolivka UA 154 A3
Sokółka PL 140 D9
Sokółki PL 136 E5
Sokolnice CZ 77 D11
Sokolniki PL 142 D5
Sokolov CZ 75 B12
Sokolovac HR 149 D7
Sokolovce SK 146 D5
Sokolovici BIH 157 E10
Sokolovo BG 166 C5
Sokolovo BG 167 C10
Sokolovo BIH 157 C6
Sokołów Małopolski PL 144 C5
Sokołów Podlaski PL 141 F6
Sokoły PL 140 E7
Sokorópátka H 149 B9
Sokyrnytsya UA 145 G7
Sól PL 144 B6
Soľ SK 145 F4
Sola N 94 E3
Solacolu RO 161 E9
Solana de los Barros E 51 B6
Solana del Pino E 54 C4
Solana de Rioalmar E 45 C11
Søland N 95 B10
Solarino I 59 E7
Solaro F 37 H10
Solberg N 101 E15
Solberg N 111 B14
Solberg S 107 D11
Solberg S 107 D13
Solberga S 92 D5
Solbjerg DK 86 C6
Solca RO 153 B7
Solčava SLO 73 D10
Solda I 71 D11
Șoldănești MD 154 B3
Șoldanu RO 161 E9
Søldatnes N 113 D14
Sölden A 71 D12
Soldeu AND 33 E9
Solec Kujawski PL 138 D5
Solec-Zdrój PL 143 F10
Solenzara F 37 H10
Solesino I 66 B4
Solesmes F 19 D7
Solesmes F 23 E11
Solești RO 153 D11
Soleto I 61 C10
Solf FIN 122 D7
Solférino F 32 B4
Solferino I 66 B2
Solfjellsjøen N 108 D4
Soliera I 66 C2
Solignano I 69 D8
Solihull GB 13 A11
Solin HR 156 E5
Solina PL 145 E5
Solingen D 21 B8
Solivella E 42 E6
Soljani HR 157 C10
Sölje S 97 D8
Sölkei FIN 128 C8
Söll A 72 A5
Sollacaro F 37 H9
Sollas GB 2 K2
Sollebrunn S 91 C12
Sollefteå S 107 E12
Sollenau A 77 G10
Sollenkroka S 99 D11
Sollentuna S 99 D9
Sóller E 49 E10
Sollerön S 102 E8
Søllested DK 83 A10
Söllichau D 79 C12
Solliès-Pont F 36 E4
Solliès-Toucas F 36 E4
Sollihøgda N 95 C12
Söllingen D 79 B8
Sollstedt D 79 D8
Solmaz TR 181 B9
Solms D 21 C10
Solnice CZ 77 B10
Solnik BG 167 D9
Solofra I 60 B3
Solojärvi FIN 113 F18
Solomiac F 33 C7
Solomos GR 175 D6
Solopaca I 60 A3
Solórzano E 40 B4
Solosancho E 46 C3
Sološnica SK 146 E4
Solothurn CH 27 F8
Solotvyna UA 145 H8
Soløy N 111 C14
Solre-le-Château F 19 D9
Solrød Strand DK 87 D10
Solsem N 105 A11
Solskjela N 104 E4
Solsnes N 100 A6
Solsona E 43 D7
Solsvik N 94 B1
Solt H 150 D3
Soltau D 83 E7
Soltendieck D 83 E9
Sol'tsy RUS 132 E7
Soltszentimre H 150 D3
Soltvadkert H 150 E3
Solumshamn S 103 A14
Solva GB 9 E12
Solvalla S 99 C10
Solvarbo S 97 B14
Sölvesborg S 88 C7
Solvorn N 100 D6
Solymár H 149 A11
Soma TR 177 A10
Somain F 19 D7
Somberek H 149 D11
Sombernon F 25 F12
Sombor SRB 150 F3
Sombreffe B 19 C10
Șomcuța Mare RO 151 B11
Somercotes GB 11 E9
Someren NL 16 F5
Somerniemi FIN 127 D10
Somero FIN 127 D10
Someronkylä FIN 119 F12
Somerovaara FIN 119 D16
Sõmerpalu EST 131 F13
Somerton GB 13 C9
Sõmeru EST 131 C12
Someș-Odorhei RO 151 C11
Somianka PL 139 E11
Sominy PL 85 B13
Somlóvásárhely H 149 B8
Sommacampagna I 66 B2
Somma Lombardo I 68 B6
Sommariva del Bosco I 37 B7
Sommarøy N 110 C9
Sommarøy N 111 A15
Sommarset N 109 A10
Sommatino I 58 E4
Somme-Leuze B 19 D11
Sommen S 92 C5
Sommepy-Tahure F 19 F10
Sömmerda D 79 D9
Sommerfeld D 84 E4
Sommersted DK 86 E4
Sommesous F 25 C11
Somme-Suippe F 25 B12
Sommevoire F 25 D12
Sommières F 35 C7
Sommières-du-Clain F 29 C6
Somogyapáti H 149 D9
Somogyjád H 149 D9
Somogyszob H 149 D8
Somogyudvarhely H 149 D8
Somogyvár H 149 C9
Somonino PL 138 B5
Somontín E 55 E8
Somotor SK 145 G4
Somova RO 155 C3
Somovit BG 160 F5
Sompa EST 131 C14
Sompolno PL 138 F6
Sompujärvi FIN 119 C14
Somzée B 19 D9
Son N 95 C13
Son NL 16 E4
Sona I 66 B2
Sona N 105 E10
Șona RO 152 E4
Sonceboz CH 27 F7
Soncillo E 40 C4
Soncino I 69 C8
Sonda EST 131 C13
Sondalo I 69 A9
Søndeled N 90 B5
Sønder Balling DK 86 B3
Sønder Bjerre DK 86 D5
Sønder Bjert DK 86 E5
Sønderborg DK 86 F5
Sønderby DK 87 D10
Sønder Dråby DK 86 B3
Sønder Felding DK 86 D3
Sønderho DK 86 E2
Sønderholm DK 86 A5
Sønder Hygum DK 86 E3
Sønder Nissum DK 86 C2
Sønder Omme DK 86 D3
Sønder Onsild DK 86 B5
Sønder Rubjerg DK 90 E6
Sondershausen D 79 D8
Sønderso DK 86 E6
Sønder Stenderup DK 86 E5
Sønder Vilstrup DK 86 E5
Sønder Vissing DK 86 C5
Sønder Vium DK 86 D2
Sondori LV 133 C2
Sondrio I 69 A8
Soneja E 48 E4
Songe N 90 B5
Songeons F 18 E4
Sonim P 38 E5
Sonka FIN 117 E14
Sonkajärvi FIN 124 C9
Sonkakoski FIN 124 C9
Sonkamuotka FIN 117 B10
Sonneberg D 75 B9
Sonneborn D 79 E8
Sonnefeld D 75 B9
Sonnewalde D 80 C5
Sonnino I 62 E4
Sonntag A 71 C9

Sonntagberg A 77 G7
Sonseca E 46 E5
Son Servera E 57 B11
Sońsk PL 139 E10
Sonstorp S 92 B7
Sonta SRB 157 A11
Sontheim an der Brenz D 75 E7
Sonthofen D 71 B10
Sontra D 78 D6
Soodla EST 131 C10
Söörmarkku FIN 126 B6
Soorts-Hossegor F 32 C3
Sopeira E 33 F7
Sopelana E 40 B6
Sopilja BIH 157 F9
Sopište NMK 164 F3
Soponya H 149 B10
Šoporňa SK 146 E5
Sopot BG 165 C9
Sopot BG 165 D10
Sopot PL 138 B6
Sopot RO 160 E3
Sopot SRB 158 D6
Sopotnica NMK 168 B5
Șopotu Nou RO 159 D8
Soppela FIN 115 E3
Sopron H 149 A7
Sopronkövesd H 149 A7
Sora I 62 D5
Soraga I 72 D4
Soragna I 66 C1
Söråker S 103 A14
Sörång S 103 D11
Sorano I 62 B1
Sørarnøy N 108 B6
Sør-Audnedal N 90 C1
Sorbas E 55 E8
Sorbie GB 5 F8
Sorbiers F 30 E5
Sörbo S 103 D11
Sörböle S 103 B13
Sorbolo I 66 C1
Sörby S 97 C9
Sörbygden S 103 A11
Sørbymagle DK 87 E8
Sörbyn S 118 B7
Sörbyn S 118 E4
Sorcy-St-Martin F 26 C4
Sord IRL 7 F10
Sørdal N 109 C10
Sorde-l'Abbaye F 32 C3
Sore F 32 B4
Sørebo N 100 D3
Sören S 118 C9
Søreng N 111 B19
Soresina I 69 C8
Sorèze F 33 D10
Sörfjärden S 103 B13
Sørfjord N 108 D5
Sørfjord N 111 C14
Sørfjorden N 111 C10
Sørfjordmoen N 109 A10
Sörflärke S 107 E13
Sörfors S 103 B13
Sörfors S 122 C4
Sörforsa S 103 C12
Sorge D 79 C8
Sorges F 29 E7
Sorgono I 64 C3
Sorgues F 35 B8
Sørheim N 100 D6
Soria E 41 E7
Soriano Calabro I 59 B9
Soriano nel Cimino I 62 C2
Sorihuela E 45 D9
Sorihuela del Gaudalimar E 55 C6
Sorisdale GB 4 B4
Sørkjosen N 112 D6
Sørkjosen N 112 D6
Sorkwity PL 136 F3
Sørland N 110 E4
Sørlenangen N 111 A19
Sørli N 105 C15
Sørli N 111 B14
Sörmark S 97 B8
Sörmjöle S 122 C4
Sørmo N 111 C16
Sorn GB 5 D8
Sornac F 29 D10
Sörnoret S 107 C12
Sorø DK 87 E9
Soroca MD 154 A2
Sorokino RUS 133 B7
Soroni GR 181 D7
Sorradile I 64 C2
Sørreisa N 111 B15
Sorrento I 60 B2
Sorring DK 86 C5
Sørrollnes N 111 C12
Sorsakoski FIN 124 F9
Sorsele S 109 E14
Sörsjön S 102 D5
Sorso I 64 B2
Sörstafors S 98 C6
Sørstraumen N 112 D8
Sort E 33 F8
Sortavala RUS 129 B14
Sortelha P 45 D6
Sortino I 59 E7
Sörtjärn S 102 B8
Sortland N 110 C9
Sør-Tverrfjord N 112 C8
Sõru EST 130 D5
Sørum N 101 E11
Sorumsand N 95 C14
Sorunda S 93 A11
Sorup D 82 A7
Sørvad DK 86 C3
Sørvær N 112 B8
Sörvåge S 107 E15
Sørvågen N 110 E5
Sørvágur FO 2 A2
Sörvattnet S 102 B4
Sørvik N 111 C13
Sörvik S 97 B13
Sørvika N 101 B15
Sörviken S 107 D9
Sorvilán E 55 F6
Sos F 33 B6
Sosandra GR 169 C7
Sösdala S 87 C13
Sos del Rey Católico E 32 E3
Sosedno RUS 132 E4
Soses E 42 D4
Soshe-Ostrivs'ke UA 154 C5
Sösjö S 103 A9
Sóskút H 149 B11
Sośnica PL 85 D10
Sośnie PL 142 D4
Sośno PL 138 D4
Sosnovka RUS 136 D3
Sosnovo RUS 129 D13
Sosnovyy Bor RUS 129 F11
Sosnowica PL 141 G8
Sosnowiec PL 143 F7
Sosnówka PL 141 G8
Soso FIN 119 E15
Sospel F 37 D6
Sossonniemi FIN 121 C14
Sost F 33 E7
Šoštanj SLO 73 D11
Sostis GR 171 B8
Sot N 96 C6
Șotânga RO 160 D6
Sotés E 41 D6
Sotiel Coronada E 51 D6
Sotillo de la Adrada E 46 D3
Sotillo del Rincón E 41 E6
Sotin HR 157 B11
Sotkajärvi FIN 119 E16
Sotkamo FIN 121 F11
Soto E 39 A7
Soto de la Vega E 39 D8
Soto del Real E 46 C5
Soto de Ribera E 39 B8
Soto en Cameros E 41 D7
Sotopalacios E 40 D4
Sotos E 47 D8
Sotoserrano E 45 D8
Soto y Amío E 39 C8
Sotres E 39 B10
Sotresgudo E 40 C3
Șotrile RO 161 C7
Sotrondio E 39 B8
Sotta F 37 H10
Sotteville-lès-Rouen F 18 F3
Sottomarina I 66 B5
Sottrum D 17 B12
Sottunga FIN 99 B15
Sotuélamos E 55 A7
Soual F 33 C10
Soubès F 34 C5
Soucy F 25 D9
Souda GR 178 E7
Soudan F 23 E9
Soueix F 33 E8
Souesmes F 24 F7
Soufflenheim F 27 C8
Soufli GR 171 B10
Sougia GR 178 E6
Souillac F 29 F8
Souilly F 26 B3
Souk el Had el Rharbia MA 52 E5
Souk-Khémis-des-Anjra MA 53 E5
Soukolojärvi S 119 B11
Souk Tleta Taghramet MA 53 E6
Soulac-sur-Mer F 28 D3
Soulaines-Dhuys F 25 D12
Soulatgé F 33 E11
Souli GR 175 D6
Soullans F 28 B2
Soulom F 32 E5
Soultz-Haut-Rhin F 27 E7
Soultz-sous-Forêts F 27 C8
Soumagne B 19 C12
Soumoulou F 32 D5
Souppes-sur-Loing F 25 D8
Souprosse F 32 C4
Sourdeval F 23 C10
Soure P 44 D3
Sournia F 33 E10
Souro Pires P 45 C6
Sourpi GR 175 A6
Sours F 24 D6
Sourzac F 29 E6
Sousceyrac F 29 F10
Sousel P 50 B4
Soustons F 32 C3
Southam GB 13 A12
Southampton GB 13 D12
South Anston GB 11 E9
South Bank GB 11 B9
Southborough GB 15 E9
South Cave GB 11 D10
South Chard GB 13 D9
Southend GB 4 E5
Southend-on-Sea GB 15 D10
Southery GB 11 F12
Southgate GB 15 D8
South Harting GB 15 F7
South Kelsey GB 11 E11
South Kirkby GB 11 D9
Southminster GB 15 D10
South Molton GB 13 C7
South Ockendon GB 15 D9
Southport GB 10 D5
South Queensferry GB 5 D10
South Shields GB 5 F14
Southwell GB 11 E10
Southwold GB 15 C12
South Woodham Ferrers GB 15 D10
Souto E 38 C4
Souto P 38 E2
Souto P 44 E4
Souto P 45 D7
Souto da Casa P 44 D5
Soutuperä FIN 123 B14
Souvala GR 175 D8
Souvigny F 30 B3
Șovarna RO 159 D10
Søvassli N 104 E6
Sovata RO 152 D6
Soveja RO 153 E9
Soverato I 59 B10
Soveria F 37 G10
Soveria Mannelli I 59 A9
Sovetsk RUS 136 C4
Sovetskiy RUS 129 D10
Sovići BIH 157 F7
Sovicille I 66 F3
Søvik N 100 A4
Søvind DK 86 D5
Sowno PL 85 B11
Sowno PL 85 D7
Soyaux F 29 D6
Soye F 26 F5
Soylu TR 173 B7
Soymy UA 145 F7
Soyons F 30 F6
Sozopol BG 167 E9
Spa B 19 D12
Spa IRL 8 D3
Spabrücken D 21 E9
Spačince SK 146 E5
Spačva HR 157 B10
Spadafora I 59 C7
Spaichingen D 27 D10
Spalding GB 11 F11
Spálené Poříčí CZ 76 C5
Spalt D 75 D8
Spangenberg D 78 D6
Spanish Point IRL 8 C4
Spantekow D 84 C5
Spanțov RO 161 E9
Sparanise I 60 A2
Sparbu N 105 D10
Spāre LV 134 B4
Sparreholm S 93 A9
Spartà I 59 C8
Sparti GR 174 E5
Sparto GR 174 B3
Spartylas GR 168 E2
Spasovo BG 155 F2
Spata GR 175 D8
Spay D 185 D8
Spean Bridge GB 4 B7
Specchia I 61 D10
Speen GB 13 C12
Speia MD 154 D4
Speicher D 21 E7
Speichersdorf D 75 C10
Spello I 62 B3
Spenge D 17 D10
Spennymoor GB 5 F13
Spentrup DK 86 B6
Spercheiada GR 174 B5
Sperlinga I 58 D5
Sperlonga I 62 E4
Spermezeu RO 152 C4
Spersboda S 99 C11
Spetalen N 95 D13
Spetses GR 175 E7
Spey Bay GB 3 K10
Speyer D 21 F10
Spezzano Albanese I 61 D6
Spiczyn PL 141 H7
Spiddal IRL 6 F4
Spielberg bei Knittelfeld A 73 B10
Spiere B 182 D2
Spiesen-Elversberg D 21 F8
Spiez CH 70 D5
Spigno Monferrato I 37 B8
Spigno Saturnia I 62 E5
Spiinigied'di N 113 E15
Spijk NL 17 B7
Spijkenisse NL 16 E2
Spikberg S 118 B5
Spilamberto I 66 C3
Spili GR 178 E8
Spilimbergo I 73 D6
Spilinga I 59 B8
Spillersboda S 99 C11
Spillum N 105 C11
Spilsby GB 11 E12
Spinazzola I 60 B6
Spincourt F 19 F12
Špindlerův Mlýn CZ 81 E9
Spinea I 66 B5
Spineni RO 160 D5
Spinetoli I 62 B5
Spink IRL 9 C8
Spinuș RO 151 C9
Špionica BIH 157 C10
Špišić-Bukovica HR 149 E8
Spiss A 71 D10
Spišská Belá SK 145 E1
Spišská Nová Ves SK 145 F2
Spišská Stará Ves SK 145 E1
Spišská Teplica SK 145 E1
Spišské Bystré SK 145 F1
Spišské Podhradie SK 145 F2
Spišské Vlachy SK 145 F2
Spišský Hrušov SK 145 F2
Spital am Pyhrn A 73 A9
Spital am Semmering A 148 A5
Spitsyno RUS 132 D2
Spittal GB 3 J10
Spittal an der Drau A 73 C7
Spittal of Glenshee GB 5 B10
Spitz A 77 F8
Spjald DK 86 C3
Spjelkavik N 100 B4
Spjutsbygd S 89 C9
Spjutsund FIN 127 E14
Split HR 156 E5
Splügen CH 71 D8
Spodnja Idrija SLO 73 D9
Spodnje Hoče SLO 148 C5
Spodsbjerg DK 87 F7
Spofforth GB 11 D9
Spoleto I 62 B3
Spoltore I 63 C6
Spondigna I 71 D11
Spontin B 19 D11
Spornitz D 83 D11
Spotorno I 37 C8
Spraitbach D 74 E6
Sprakensehl D 83 E9
Sprâncenata RO 160 E5
Sprängsviken S 103 A14
Spreenhagen D 80 B5
Spremberg D 80 C6
Sprendlingen D 185 E8
Spresiano I 72 E5
Spriana I 69 A8
Sprimont B 19 C12
Spring RO 152 F3
Springe D 78 B6
Springholm GB 5 E9
Springliden S 107 A16
Sproatley GB 11 D11
Sprockhövel D 17 F8
Sproge S 93 E12
Sprogī LV 135 D10
Sprova N 105 C10
Sprowston GB 15 B11
Sproxton GB 11 C9
Spunģēni LV 135 C11
Spuž MNE 163 D7
Spychowo PL 139 C11
Spydeberg N 95 C14
Spytihněv CZ 146 C5
Spytkowice PL 143 G7
Spytkowice PL 147 B9
Squillace I 59 B10
Squinzano I 61 C10
Sráid an Mhuilinn IRL 8 D4
Sraith Salach IRL 6 F3
Sranea IRL 6 D6
Srath an Urláir IRL 7 C7
Srbac BIH 157 B8
Srbobran SRB 158 B4
Srbovac RKS 163 D10
Srdevići BIH 157 E6
Srebrenica BIH 158 E3
Srebrenik BIH 157 C10
Srebŭrna BG 161 E10
Sredets BG 166 E5
Sredets BG 167 E8
Središče SLO 148 D6
Sredishte BG 161 F10
Srednje BIH 157 D9
Srednjevo SRB 159 D8
Sredno Gradishte BG 166 E4
Šrem PL 81 B12
Sremčica SRB 158 D5
Sremska Kamenica SRB 158 C4
Sremska Mitrovica SRB 158 D4
Sremski Karlovci SRB 158 C4
Srenica BIH 156 D6
Srnice BIH 157 C9
Srockowo PL 136 E4
Środa Śląska PL 81 D11
Środa Wielkopolska PL 81 B12
Srpska Crnja SRB 158 B6
Srpski Itebej SRB 159 B6
Srpski Miletić SRB 157 A11
Sta S 105 E13
Staatz A 77 E10
Stabbfors S 108 E8
Stabbursnes N 113 C14
Stabroek B 16 F2
Stabulnieki LV 135 D13
Staburags LV 135 C11
Staburnaäs S 107 B11
Staby DK 86 C2
Stachy CZ 76 D5
Stade D 17 A12
Staden B 18 C7
Stadl-Paura A 76 F5
Stadra S 97 C12
Stadsbygd N 104 E7
Stadskanaal NL 17 C7
Stadtallendorf D 21 C12
Stadtbergen D 75 F8
Stadthagen D 17 D12
Stadtilm D 79 E9
Stadtkyll D 21 D7
Stadtlauringen D 75 B7
Stadtlohn D 17 E7
Stadtroda D 79 E10
Stadtschlaining A 148 B6
Stadum D 82 A6
Stäfa CH 27 F10
Staffanstorp S 87 D12
Staffin GB 2 K4
Staffolo I 67 F7
Stafford GB 11 F7
Stahovica SLO 73 D10
Stai N 101 D14
Staicele LV 131 F9
Staig D 74 F6
Stainach A 73 A9
Staindrop GB 11 B8
Staines-upon-Thames GB 15 E7
Stainforth GB 11 C7
Stainforth GB 11 D9
Stainton GB 11 C11
Stainville F 26 C3
Stainz A 148 C4
Staìti I 59 D9
Stakčín SK 145 F5
Stakevtsi BG 164 B6
Stāķi LV 135 B13
Stakiai LT 134 F6
Stakkvik N 112 D4
Stakliškės LT 137 D9
Stakroge DK 86 D3
Stalać SRB 159 F7
Stalbe LV 135 B10
Stålbo S 98 B7
Stalbridge GB 13 D10
Stalden CH 68 A4
Staldzene LV 134 B3
Stalģenai LT 134 E3
Stalģene LV 135 C7
Stalham GB 15 B12
Stalheim N 100 E5
Stalidzāni LV 135 C13
Staliogargo N 113 B12
Stall A 73 C7
Stallarholmen S 98 D8
Ställberg S 97 C12
Ställdalen S 97 C12
Stallwang D 75 D12
Stalon S 107 B9
Stalowa Wola PL 144 B5
Stâlpeni RO 160 C5
Stâlpu RO 161 C9
Stamboliyski BG 165 E10
Stambulčić BIH 157 E10
Stamford GB 11 F11
Stamford Bridge GB 11 D10
Stamfordham GB 5 E13
Stammham D 75 E9
Stamna GR 174 B3
Stamovo BG 166 E5
Stams A 71 C11
Stamstik N 110 E9
Stamsund N 110 D6
Stânceni RO 152 D6
Stăncuța RO 155 D1
Standdaarbuiten NL 182 B5
Standish GB 10 D6
Stănești RO 159 C11
Stănești RO 161 F7
Stånga S 93 E12
Stângăceaua RO 160 D2
Stangnes N 111 B13
Stångviken S 105 D16
Stanhoe GB 15 B10
Stanhope GB 5 F12
Stănilești RO 154 D2
Stanin PL 141 G6
Stănișești RO 153 E10
Stanišić SRB 150 F3
Stanišinci SRB 163 B10
Stanisławów PL 141 F5
Stănița RO 153 C10
Štanjel SLO 73 E8
Staňkov CZ 76 C4
Stankovany SK 147 C8
Stanley GB 5 C10
Stanley GB 5 F13
Stanley GB 11 D9
Stannington GB 5 E13
Stanomino PL 85 C9
Stanos GR 169 C10
Stanos GR 174 B3
Stan'ovsti BG 165 D6
Stans CH 71 D6
Stansted Mountfitchet GB 15 D9
Stantër RKS 163 D10
Stanton GB 15 C10
Stanzach A 71 C11
Stanz im Mürztal A 148 B5
Stapar SRB 158 B3
Stapel D 83 D9
Stapelburg D 79 C8
Stapelfeld D 83 C8
Staphorst NL 16 C6
Staplehurst GB 15 E10
Stąporków PL 141 H3
Stara Błotnica PL 141 G3
Stará Bystrica SK 147 C7
Starachowice PL 143 D11
Stara Gradina HR 149 E9
Stará Huť CZ 76 C6
Stara Kamienica PL 81 E9
Stara Kamionka PL 140 D9
Stara Kiszewa PL 138 C5
Stara Kornica PL 141 F7
Stara Kul'na UA 154 B4
Stara Łubianka PL 85 D11
Stará Ľubovňa SK 145 E2
Stara Moravica SRB 150 F3
Stara Novalja HR 67 C10
Stara Pazova SRB 158 D5
Stara Ploščica HR 149 E7
Stara Reka BG 166 D6
Stara Rudnica PL 84 E6
Stara Sil' UA 145 E6
Stara Tsarychanka UA 154 E5
Stará Turá SK 146 D5
Stara vas-Bizeljsko SLO 148 E5
Stará Ves nad Ondřejnicí CZ 146 B6
Staravina NMK 169 B6
Stara Wieś PL 144 B6
Stara Zagora BG 166 E5
Stara Zhadova UA 153 A7
Starčevo SRB 158 D6
Starchiojd RO 161 C8
Starcross GB 13 D8
Stare Babice PL 141 F3
Stare-Bogaczowice PL 81 E10
Stare Budkowice PL 142 E5
Stařeč CZ 77 D9
Stare Czarnowo PL 85 D7
Stare Dąbrowa PL 85 D8
Stare Dolistowo PL 140 C7
Stare Hołowczyce PL 141 F7
Stare Kurowo PL 85 E9
Staré Město CZ 77 B12
Staré Město u Uherského Hradiště CZ 146 C4
Stare Miasto PL 142 B5
Stare Pole PL 139 B7
Stare Puchały PL 141 E7
Stare Selo UA 144 D9
Stare Strącze PL 81 C10
Stargard Szczeciński PL 85 D8
Star Huta SK 147 E8
Stari LV 135 B13
Stari Banovci SRB 158 D5
Staříč CZ 146 B6
Stari Dulići BIH 157 F10
Starigrad HR 67 C10
Starigrad HR 156 D3
Starigrad HR 156 F6
Stari Gradac HR 149 E8
Stari Kuty UA 152 A6
Stari Log SLO 73 E10
Stari Majdan BIH 156 C6
Stari Mikanovci HR 157 B10
Stari Trg SLO 67 B11
Stari Trg SLO 73 E9
Stari Troyany UA 155 B4
Starkenberg D 79 E11
Stärkesmark S 122 B3
Starnberg D 75 G9
Starogard PL 85 C9
Starogard Gdański PL 138 C6
Starognjevice BIH 158 E3
Starokozache UA 154 E5
Staro Oryakhovo BG 167 D9
Staropatitsa BG 159 F9
Staro Petrovo Selo HR 157 B8
Starosel BG 165 E10
Staro Selo BG 161 F9
Staro Selo BIH 157 D7
Staro Selo SRB 159 E7
Staroseltsi BG 165 B9
Starosiedle PL 81 C7
Starowa Góra PL 143 C7
Staroye Syalo BY 133 F7
Staro Zhelezare BG 165 E10
Starożreby PL 139 E8
Startforth GB 11 B8
Starup DK 86 E5
Stary Brus PL 141 H8
Stary Cykarzew PL 143 E7
Stary Dzierzgoń PL 139 C7
Stary Dzikowiec PL 144 C4
Stary Kisielin PL 81 C9
Stary Kobrzyniec PL 139 E7
Starý Kolín CZ 77 B8
Stary Majdan PL 144 C6
Starynovichy BY 133 F6
Stary Pahost BY 133 F3
Starý Plzenec CZ 76 C4
Stary Sącz PL 145 D2
StarýStarý SK 145 E1
Stary Szelków PL 139 E11
Stary Targ PL 139 C7
Stary Uścimów PL 141 H7
Staryy Sambir UA 145 E6
Stary Zamość PL 144 B7
Starzyno PL 138 A5
Staškov SK 147 C7
Staßfurt D 79 C10
Staszów PL 143 E11
Stathelle N 90 A6
Statland N 105 C10
Stätsås S 107 B11
Statzendorf A 77 F9
Stăuceni MD 154 C3
Stăuceni RO 153 B9
Stauchitz D 80 D4
Staufenberg D 21 C11
Staupitz D 80 C5
Štavalj SRB 163 C9
Stavang N 100 C2
Stavanger N 94 E3
Stavaträsk S 118 D4
Stavchany UA 153 A8
Stave N 111 B10
Staveley GB 11 E9
Stavelot B 20 D5
Stavenisse NL 16 E2
Stavern N 90 B7
Stavertsi BG 165 B9
Stavky UA 144 A9
Stavne UA 145 F6
Stavning DK 86 D2
Stavoren NL 16 C4
Stavre S 103 A9
Stavre S 105 E16
Stavreviken S 103 A13
Stavrodromi GR 174 D4
Stavros GR 169 C7
Stavros GR 169 C10
Stavros GR 169 F7
Stavros GR 174 C2
Stavroupoli GR 171 B7
Stavrove UA 154 B5
Stavsätra S 103 C10
Stavsnäs S 99 D11
Stavtrup DK 86 C6
Staw PL 85 E7
Stawiguda PL 139 C9
Stawiski PL 139 D13
Stawiszyn PL 142 C5
Steane N 95 D9
Stębark PL 139 C9
Steblevë AL 168 B3
Stebnyk UA 145 E8
Steccato I 61 F7
Štěchovice CZ 76 C6
Stechow D 79 A11
Steckborn CH 27 E10
Stedesdorf D 17 A9
Stedten D 79 D10
Steeg A 71 C10
Steenbergen NL 16 E2
Steenderen NL 183 A8
Steenvoorde F 18 C6
Steenwijk NL 16 C6
Steeton GB 11 D8
Stefanaconi I 59 B9
Ștefan cel Mare RO 153 D9
Ștefan cel Mare RO 153 D11
Ștefan cel Mare RO 153 E9
Ștefan cel Mare RO 155 E1
Ștefan cel Mare RO 160 D6
Ștefan cel Mare RO 160 F4
Ștefănești MD 154 E5
Ștefănești RO 153 B10
Ștefănești RO 160 D5
Ștefănești RO 161 D9
Ștefăneștii de Jos RO 161 D8
Stefani GR 175 C8
Štefanje HR 149 E7
Stefan Karadzha BG 167 C8
Stefan-Karadzhovo BG 167 E7
Štefanov SK 146 D4
Stefanovikeio GR 169 F8
Stefanovo BG 167 C9
Stefanovouno GR 169 E7
Ștefan Vodă MD 154 D5
Ștefan Vodă RO 161 E10
Ștefești RO 161 C7
Steffisburg CH 70 D5
Stegaurath D 75 C8
Stege DK 87 F10
Stegelitz D 79 B10
Stegersbach A 148 B6
Stegna PL 138 B7
Stegny PL 139 B8
Stehag S 87 D12
Ștei RO 151 D9
Steigen N 110 E8
Steigra D 79 D10
Steimbke D 17 C12
Stein D 75 D9
Stein NL 19 C12
Steinach D 75 B9
Steinach D 75 E12
Steinach D 186 E5
Steinach am Brenner A 72 B3
Stein am Rhein CH 27 E10
Steinau D 17 A11
Steinau an der Straße D 74 B5
Steinbach D 21 C11
Steinbach D 80 E4
Steinbach am Attersee A 73 A8
Steinbach am Wald D 75 B9
Steinbakk N 114 E7
Steinberg D 75 D11
Steinberg D 82 A7
Steine N 105 D11
Steine N 110 C7
Steinen D 27 E8
Steinfeld A 73 C7
Steinfeld D 186 C5
Steinfeld D 187 B8
Steinfeld (Oldenburg) D 17 C10
Steinfjord N 111 B13
Steinfort L 20 E5
Steinfurt D 17 D8
Steingaden D 71 B11
Steinhagen D 17 D10
Steinhagen D 84 B3
Steinheim D 17 E12
Steinheim N 111 B15
Steinheim am Albuch D 187 D9
Steinheim an der Murr D 187 D7
Steinhöring D 75 F11
Steinhorst D 83 E8
Steinigtwolmsdorf D 80 D6
Steinkirchen D 82 C7
Steinkjer N 105 C11
Steinland N 110 C9
Steinløysa N 100 A7
Steinsdorf D 81 B7
Steinsfeld D 75 D7
Steinshamn N 100 A5
Steinsholt N 95 D11
Steinskjærnes N 114 D7
Steinsland N 94 B2
Steinsvik N 100 C3
Steinwenden D 186 C4
Steinwiesen D 75 B9
Stejaru RO 155 D3
Stejaru RO 160 E5
Stekene B 19 B9
Stelle D 83 D8
Stellendam NL 16 E2
Stelnica RO 155 E1
Stelpe LV 135 C9
Stemland N 108 B9
Stemmen D 82 D7
Stemnes N 111 D13
Stemnitsa GR 174 D5
Stemshorn D 17 D10
Stenåsa S 89 B11
Stenay F 19 F11
Stenbacken S 111 D17
Stenbjerg DK 86 B2
Stenbo S 93 E8
Stendal D 79 A10
Stende LV 134 B5
Stenderup DK 86 D3
Steneset N 108 D4
Stengelse N 113 D11
Stenhammar S 91 B13
Stenhamra S 99 D9
Stenhousemuir GB 5 C9
Stenico I 69 A10
Steninge S 87 B11
Stenis S 102 E7
Stenkumla S 93 D12
Stenkyrka S 93 D13
Stenlille DK 87 D9
Stenløse DK 87 D10
Stennäs S 107 D14
Stenness GB 3 E13
Steno GR 174 D5
Steno GR 175 E5
Stensån S 103 B9
Stensele S 107 A12
Stensjö S 107 E10
Stensjön S 92 D5
Stenskär S 99 B10
Stenstorp S 91 C14
Stensträsk S 107 A17
Stenstrup DK 86 E6
Stensund S 109 D15
Stensund S 109 F13
Stensved DK 87 F10
Stenton GB 5 D11
Stenträsk S 118 B3
Stenudden S 109 C14
Stenum DK 90 E6
Stenungsund S 91 C10
Stenvad DK 86 C7
Stenzharychi UA 144 B9
Stepanci NMK 169 B6
Stepanivka UA 154 D5
Štěpánov CZ 77 C12
Stepen BIH 157 F10
Stepnica PL 84 C7
Stepojevac SRB 158 D5
Stepping DK 86 E4
Sterdyń-Osada PL 141 E6
Sterławki-Wielkie PL 136 E4
Sterna GR 171 A10
Sterna GR 175 D6
Sterna HR 67 B8
Šternberg D 83 C11
Šternberk CZ 146 B4
Sternes GR 178 D7
Stes-Maries-de-la-Mer F 35 D7
Stjszew PL 81 B11
Štětí CZ 76 B6
Stetten am kalten Markt D 27 D11
Steuerberg A 73 C9
Steutz D 79 C11
Stevenage GB 15 D8
Stevenston GB 4 D7
Stevensweert NL 183 C7
Stevnstrup DK 86 C5
Stewarton GB 4 D7
Stewartstown GB 7 C9
Steyerberg D 17 C12
Steyning GB 15 F8
Steyr A 76 F6
Steyregg A 76 F6
Stěžery CZ 77 B9
Stezherovo BG 166 C4
Stźyca PL 138 B4
Stźyca PL 141 G5
Stia I 66 E4
Stibb Cross GB 12 D6
Stickney GB 11 E12
Stidsvig S 87 C12
Stiege D 79 C8
Stiens NL 16 B5
Stienta I 66 C4
Stigen S 91 B11
Stigliano I 60 C6
Stignano I 59 C9
Stigsjö S 103 A14
Stigtomta S 93 B9
Stijena BIH 156 C5
Stikli LV 134 B4
Stilligarry GB 2 L2
Stilling DK 86 C5
Stillington GB 11 C9
Stillorgan IRL 7 F10
Stilo I 59 C9
Stilton GB 11 G11
Stimpfach D 75 D7
Stintino I 64 B1
Stio I 60 C4
Štip NMK 164 F5
Stirfaka GR 174 B5
Stiring-Wendel F 21 F7
Stirling GB 5 C9
Štitar HR 157 B10
Štitar SRB 158 D4
Štítina CZ 146 B6
Štítnik SK 145 F1
Štíty CZ 77 C11
Știubieni RO 153 B9
Știuca RO 159 B8
Štivan HR 67 C9
Stjær DK 86 C5
Stjärnfors S 97 C13
Stjärnhov S 93 A9
Stjärnorp S 92 B7
Stjørdalshalsen N 105 E9
Støa N 101 E14
Støa N 102 D4
Stobiecko Miejskie PL 143 D7
Stobreč HR 156 E6
Stoby S 87 C13
Stochov CZ 76 B5
Stocka S 103 C13
Stockach D 27 E11
Stockamöllan S 87 D12
Stockaryd S 88 A7
Stöcke S 122 C4
Stockelsdorf D 83 C9
Stockenboi A 73 C8
Stockerau A 77 F10
Stockheim D 75 B9
Stockholm S 99 D10
Stocking A 148 C5
Stockport GB 11 E7
Stocksfield GB 5 F13
Stockstadt am Rhein D 21 E10
Stockton-on-Tees GB 11 B9
Stockvik S 103 B13
Stoczek PL 139 E12
Stoczek Łukowski PL 141 G5
Stod CZ 76 C4
Stöde S 103 B12
Stoenești RO 160 C4
Stoenești RO 160 C6
Stoenești RO 160 E5
Stoenești RO 161 E7
Stoer GB 2 J6
Stoholm DK 86 C4
Stoianovca MD 154 E2
Stoicănești RO 160 E5
Stoilești RO 160 D4
Stoina RO 160 D3
Stojakovo NMK 169 B8
Stojdraga HR 148 E5
Stojnci SLO 148 D5
Stoke Ash GB 15 C11
Stoke-on-Trent GB 11 E7
Stokesay GB 13 A9
Stokesley GB 11 C9
Stokite BG 166 D4
Stokka N 108 E3
Stokkasjøen N 108 E4
Stokkdal N 111 D12
Stokke N 90 A7
Stokkemarke DK 83 A10
Stokkvågen N 108 D5
Stokmarknes N 110 C8
Štoky CZ 77 D9

Theix F 22 E6
Them DK 86 C5
Themar D 75 A8
The Mumbles GB 12 B6
Thenay F 29 B8
Thénezay F 28 B5
Thenon F 29 E8
Theologos GR 171 C7
Théoule-sur-Mer F 36 D5
The Pike IRL 9 D7
Therma GR 171 D9
Thermi GR 169 C9
Thermisia GR 175 E7
Thermo GR 174 B4
Thermopyles GR 175 B6
Thérouanne F 18 C5
The Sheddings GB 4 F4
Thespies GR 175 C7
Thesprotiko GR 168 F4
Thessaloniki GR 169 C8
The Stocks GB 15 E10
Thetford GB 15 C10
Theth AL 163 E8
Theux B 19 C12
Thèze F 32 D5
Thèze F 35 B10
Thiaucourt-Regniéville F 26 C4
Thiberville F 24 B3
Thibie F 25 C11
Thiéblemont-Farémont F 25 C12
Thiendorf D 80 D5
Thiene I 72 E3
Thierhaupten D 75 E8
Thierrens CH 31 B10
Thiers F 30 D4
Thiersee A 72 A5
Thiersheim D 75 B11
Thiesi I 64 B2
Thießow D 84 B5
Thiézac F 29 E11
Thimert-Gâtelles F 24 C5
Thin-le-Moutier F 19 E10
Thionville F 20 F6
Thiron Gardais F 24 D4
Thirsk GB 11 C9
Thisted DK 86 B3
Thisvi GR 175 C6
Thiva GR 175 C7
Thivars F 24 D5
Thiviers F 29 E7
Thizy F 30 C5
Thoirette F 31 C8
Thoiry F 24 C6
Thoissey F 30 C6
Tholen NL 16 E2
Tholey D 21 F8
Thomastown IRL 9 C8
Thommen B 20 D6
Thônes F 31 D9
Thonnance-lès-Joinville F 26 D3
Thonon-les-Bains F 31 C9
Thorame-Haute F 36 C5
Thoras F 30 F4
Thoré-la-Rochette F 24 E4
Thorenc F 36 D5
Thorigny-sur-Oreuse F 25 D9
Thörl A 73 A11
Thorn NL 19 B12
Thornaby-on-Tees GB 11 B9
Thornbury GB 13 B9
Thorne GB 11 D10
Thorney GB 11 F11
Thornhill GB 5 E9
Thorning DK 86 C4
Thornton GB 10 D5
Thorpe-le-Soken GB 15 D11
Thorpe Market GB 15 B11
Thorpeness GB 15 C12
Thorsager DK 86 C6
Thorshøj DK 90 E7
Thorsø DK 86 C5
Thouarcé F 23 F11
Thouaré-sur-Loire F 23 F9
Thouars F 28 B5
Thouria GR 174 E5
Thourotte F 18 F6
Thrapston GB 15 C7
Threshfield GB 11 C7
Thropton GB 5 E13
Thrumster GB 3 J10
Thuès-entre-Valls F 33 E10
Thueyts F 35 A7
Thuin B 19 D9
Thuine D 17 D9
Thuir F 34 E4
Thum D 80 E3
Thun CH 70 D5
Thundersley GB 15 D10
Thüngen D 74 C6
Thüngersheim D 74 C6
Thuré F 29 B6
Thuret F 30 D3
Thurey F 31 B7
Thüringen A 71 C9
Thurins F 30 D6
Thürkow D 83 C13
Thurlby GB 11 F11
Thurles IRL 9 C7
Thurnau D 75 B9
Thursby GB 5 F10
Thurso GB 3 H9
Thury-Harcourt F 23 C11
Thusis CH 71 D8
Thwaite GB 11 C7
Thyborøn DK 86 B2
Thyez F 31 C10
Thymiana GR 177 C7
Thyregod DK 86 D4
Thyrnau D 76 E5
Tia Mare RO 160 F5
Tiana I 64 C3
Țibana RO 153 D10
Țibănești RO 153 D10
Tibble S 99 D9
Tiberget S 102 D6
Tibi E 56 D3
Tibolddaróc H 145 H2
Tibro S 92 C4
Țibucani RO 153 C9
Tice BIH 156 D6
Ticehurst GB 15 E9
Ticha BG 167 D6
Tichá CZ 146 B6
Tichilești RO 155 C1
Tičići BIH 157 D9
Ticknall GB 11 F9
Țicleni RO 160 D2
Țicușu RO 152 F6
Ticvaniu Mare RO 159 C8
Tidaholm S 91 C14
Tidan S 91 B15
Tiddische D 79 A8
Tidenham GB 13 B9
Tidersrum S 92 D7
Tiebas E 32 E2
Tiedra E 39 E9
Tiefenbach D 75 D12
Tiefenbach D 76 E4
Tiefenbronn D 27 C10
Tiefencastel CH 71 D9
Tiefensee D 84 E5
Tiel NL 16 E4
Tielen B 182 C5
Tielt B 19 C7
Tiemassaari FIN 125 F10
Tienen B 19 C10
Tiengen D 27 E9
Tiercé F 23 E11
Tierga E 41 E8
Tierp S 99 B9
Tierzo E 47 C9
Țifești RO 153 F10
Țigănași RO 153 C10
Țigănești RO 160 F6
Țigare BIH 158 E3
Tighina MD 154 D4
Țighira MD 153 C11
Tighnabruaich GB 4 D6
Tignale I 69 B10
Tignes F 31 E10
Tigveni RO 160 C5
Tigy F 25 E7
Tiha Bârgăului RO 152 C5
Tihany H 149 C9
Tihemetsa EST 131 E10
Tihilä FIN 123 C16
Tihusniemi FIN 124 F9
Tiistenjoki FIN 123 E10
Tiitilänkylä FIN 123 E17
Tijesno HR 156 E4
Tijnje NL 16 B5
Tíjola E 55 E8
Tikkakoski FIN 123 F15
Tikkala FIN 123 F14
Tikkala FIN 125 F14
Tikkurila FIN 127 E13
Tikob DK 87 C10
Tilburg NL 16 E4
Tilbury GB 15 E9
Til-Châtel F 26 E3
Tildarg GB 4 F4
Tileagd RO 151 C9
Tilehurst GB 13 C12
Tilh F 32 C4
Tilișca RO 152 F3
Tillac F 33 D6
Tillberga S 98 C7
Tillicoultry GB 5 C9
Tillières-sur-Avre F 24 C5
Tilloy-et-Bellay F 25 B12
Tillyfourie GB 3 L11
Tilly-sur-Seulles F 23 B10
Tilvikai LT 134 E3
Tilža LV 133 C2
Tim DK 86 C2
Timahoe IRL 7 G8
Timár H 145 G3
Timau I 73 C7
Timelkam A 76 F5
Timiryazevo RUS 136 C4
Timișești RO 153 C9
Timișoara RO 151 F7
Timmele S 91 D13
Timmendorfer Strand D 83 C9
Timmernabben S 89 B10
Timmersdala S 91 B14
Timola FIN 125 F9
Timoleague IRL 8 E5
Timolin IRL 7 G9
Timoniemi FIN 121 F13
Timovaara FIN 125 D12
Timrå S 103 A13
Timring DK 86 C3
Timsgearraidh GB 2 J2
Tinahely IRL 9 C10
Tinajas E 47 D7
Tinalhas P 44 E5
Tinca RO 151 D8
Tinchebray F 23 C10
Tineo E 39 B7
Tingere LV 134 B5
Tinglev DK 86 F4
Tingsryd S 89 B7
Tingstad S 93 B8
Tingstäde S 93 D13
Tingvatn N 94 F6
Tingvoll N 100 A8
Tingwall GB 3 G10
Tinja BIH 157 C10
Tinjan HR 67 B8
Tinn N 95 C9
Tinnoset N 95 C10
Tinos GR 176 D5
Tiñosillos E 46 C3
Tinosu RO 161 D8
Tinqueux F 19 F8
Tintagel GB 12 D5
Tinténiac F 23 D8
Tintern Parva GB 13 B9
Tințești RO 161 C9
Tintigny B 19 E12
Tīnūži LV 135 C9
Tiobraid Árann IRL 8 D6
Tione di Trento I 69 A10
Tipasoja FIN 125 B11
Tipperary IRL 8 D6
Tiptree GB 15 D10
Tipu EST 131 E10
Tira MD 154 B2
Tiranë AL 168 B2
Tiranges F 30 E4
Tirano I 69 A9
Tiraspol MD 154 D5
Tiraspolul Nou MD 154 D5
Tire TR 177 C10
Tiream RO 151 B9
Tīreļi LV 134 C7
Tirgo E 40 C6
Tiriez E 55 B8
Tírig E 48 D5
Tiriolo I 59 B10
Tirkšliai LT 134 D4
Tîrnova MD 153 A11
Tirrenia I 66 E1
Tirro FIN 113 F18
Tirschenreuth D 75 C11
Tirstrup DK 86 C7
Tirteafuera E 54 B4
Tirza LV 135 B12
Tisău RO 161 C9
Tišća BIH 157 D10
Tishevitsa BG 165 C8
Tishono RUS 136 E2
Tišice CZ 77 B7
Tismana RO 159 C10
Tišnov CZ 77 D10
Tisovec SK 147 D9
Tistrup Stationsby DK 86 D3
Tisvilde DK 87 C10
Tiszaalpár H 150 D4
Tiszabecs H 145 G6
Tiszabezdéd H 145 G5
Tiszabő H 150 C5
Tiszabura H 150 C5
Tiszacsege H 151 B7
Tiszadada H 145 G3
Tiszaderzs H 150 B6
Tiszadob H 145 G3
Tiszaeszlár H 145 G3
Tiszaföldvár H 150 D5
Tiszafüred H 150 B6
Tiszagyenda H 150 C6
Tiszaigar H 150 B6
Tiszajenő H 150 C5
Tiszakanyár H 145 G4
Tiszakarád H 145 G4
Tiszakécske H 150 D5
Tiszakerecseny H 145 G5
Tiszakeszi H 151 B6
Tiszakürt H 150 D5
Tiszalök H 145 G3
Tiszalúc H 145 G3
Tiszanagyfalu H 145 G3
Tiszanána H 150 B6
Tiszaörs H 150 B6
Tiszapalkonya H 145 H3
Tiszapüspöki H 150 C5
Tiszaroff H 150 C5
Tiszasas H 150 D5
Tiszasüly H 150 C5
Tiszaszalka H 145 G5
Tiszaszentimre H 150 C6
Tiszasziget H 150 E5
Tiszatarján H 147 F12
Tiszatelek H 145 G4
Tiszatenyő H 150 C5
Tiszaug H 150 D5
Tiszaújváros H 145 H3
Tiszavárkony H 150 C5
Tiszavasvári H 145 H3
Titaguas E 47 E10
Titel SRB 158 C5
Țițești RO 160 C6
Tithorea GR 175 B6
Tito I 60 B5
Titova Korenica HR 156 C4
Titov Drvar BIH 156 D5
Titran N 104 D4
Tittelsnes N 94 C3
Titting D 75 E9
Tittmoning D 76 F3
Titu RO 161 D7
Titulcia E 46 D5
Tiukuvaara FIN 117 C13
Tiurajärvi FIN 117 C12
Tivat MNE 163 E6
Tivenys E 42 F5
Tiverton GB 13 D8
Tivissa E 42 E5
Tivoli I 62 D3
Tizzano F 37 H9
Tjæreborg DK 86 E3
Tjäkkjokk S 109 E15
Tjällmo S 92 B6
Tjåmotis S 109 C16
Tjappsåive S 109 E17
Tjärmyrberget S 106 C9
Tjärn S 107 D13
Tjärnäs S 98 A6
Tjärnberg S 107 A15
Tjärstad S 92 C7
Tjäruträsk S 118 B8
Tjautas S 116 D5
Tjeldnes N 111 D11
Tjeldstø N 100 E1
Tjelle N 100 A7
Tjentište BIH 157 F10
Tjöck FIN 122 F6
Tjøme N 90 A7
Tjønnefoss N 90 B4
Tjorhom N 94 E5
Tjörnarp S 87 D13
Tjøtta N 108 E3
Tjuda FIN 126 E8
Tjuvskjær N 111 C13
Tkon HR 156 E3
Tleń PL 138 C5
Tlmače SK 147 E7
Tłuchowo PL 139 E7
Tlumačov CZ 146 C5
Tłuszcz PL 139 F11
Toab GB 3 F14
Toaca RO 152 D5
Tóalmás H 150 C4
Toano I 66 D2
Tobar an Choire IRL 6 D5
Tobarra E 55 B9
Tobercurry IRL 6 D5
Tobermore GB 4 F3
Tobermory GB 4 B4
Tobo S 99 B9
Tobyn S 97 C8
Tocane-St-Apre F 29 E6
Tocco da Casauria I 62 C5
Tocha P 44 D3
Töcksfors S 96 C6
Tocón E 53 B9
Todal N 104 E5
Toddington GB 13 B11
Todi I 62 B2
Todireni RO 153 B10
Todirești RO 153 B8
Todirești RO 153 C9
Todirești RO 153 D10
Todmorden GB 11 D7
Todolella E 42 F3
Todorići BIH 157 D7
Todor-Ikonomovo BG 161 F10
Todorovo BG 161 F9
Todtmoos D 27 E8
Todtnau D 27 E8
Toén E 38 D4
Toft GB 3 E14
Toft N 108 F3
Tofta S 87 A10
Tofta S 93 D12
Tofte N 95 C13
Töftedal S 91 B10
Tofterup DK 86 D3
Toftir FO 2 A3
Toftlund DK 86 E4
Tofyeli BY 133 E5
Togher IRL 7 E10
Togher IRL 7 F7
Togher IRL 8 E4
Togston GB 5 E13
Tohmajärvi FIN 125 F14
Tohmo FIN 115 E2
Toholampi FIN 123 C12
Toija FIN 127 E9
Toijala FIN 127 C10
Toila EST 132 C2
Toirano I 37 C8
Toivakka FIN 119 B17
Toivakka FIN 123 F16
Toivala FIN 124 E9
Toivola FIN 128 C6
Tojaci NMK 169 B6
Töjby FIN 122 E6
Tök H 149 A11
Tokachka BG 171 B9
Tokaj H 145 G3
Tokarnia PL 143 E9
Tokarnia PL 147 B9
Tokod H 149 A11
Tököl H 149 B11
Tokrajärvi FIN 125 E15
Toksovo RUS 129 E14
Tolastadh Úr GB 2 J4
Tolbaños E 46 C3
Tolbert NL 16 B6
Tolcsva H 145 G3
Toledo E 46 E4
Tolentino I 67 F7
Tolfa I 62 C1
Tolga N 101 B14
Toliejai LT 135 F10
Tolja FIN 119 B17
Tolk D 82 A7
Tolkmicko PL 139 B8
Tollarp S 88 D5
Tollered S 91 D11
Tollesbury GB 15 D10
Tollo I 63 C6
Tølløse DK 87 D9
Töllsjö S 91 D12
Tolmachevo RUS 132 D6
Tolmezzo I 73 D7
Tolmin SLO 73 D8
Tolna H 149 D11
Tolnanémedi H 149 C10
Tolne DK 90 E7
Tolo GR 175 D6
Tolocănești MD 153 A11
Tolonen FIN 117 E14
Tolosa E 32 D1
Tolosa P 44 F5
Tolosenmäki FIN 125 F14
Tolox E 53 C7
Tolšići BIH 157 D10
Tolva E 42 C5
Tolva FIN 121 B12
Tolvayarvi RUS 125 F16
Tolve I 60 B6
Tomai MD 154 D2
Tomai MD 154 E3
Tomar P 44 E4
Tomares E 51 E7
Tomaševac SRB 158 C6
Tomaševo MNE 163 C8
Tomašica BIH 157 C6
Tomášikovo SK 146 E5
Tomášovce SK 147 E9
Tomaszów Lubelski PL 144 C7
Tomaszów Mazowiecki PL 141 G2
Tomatin GB 3 L9
Tombebœf F 33 A6
Tomelilla S 88 D5
Tomelloso E 47 F6
Tomești RO 151 E10
Tomești RO 151 F9
Tomești RO 153 C11
Tomice PL 147 B8
Tomiño E 38 E2
Tomintoul GB 3 L10
Tomislavgrad BIH 157 E7
Tømmerneset N 111 E10
Tommerup DK 86 E6
Tomnavoulin GB 3 L10
Tömörkény H 150 D5
Tompa H 150 E4
Tomra N 100 A5
Tomșani RO 161 D8
Tomșa E 43 D8
Tonara I 64 C3
Tonbridge GB 15 E9
Tondela P 44 C4
Tønder DK 86 F3
Tonezza del Cimone I 69 B11
Tongeren B 19 C11
Tongland GB 5 F8
Tongue GB 2 J8
Tönisvorst D 183 C8
Tonkopuro FIN 115 E4
Tonna GB 13 B7
Tonnay-Boutonne F 28 D4
Tonnay-Charente F 28 D4
Tonneins F 33 B6
Tonnerre F 25 E10
Tonnes N 108 C5
Tönning D 82 B5
Tønsberg N 95 D12
Tönsen S 103 D12
Tonstad N 94 E5
Tonsvik N 111 A17
Toombeola IRL 6 F3
Toomebridge GB 4 F4
Tootsi EST 131 D9
Topalu RO 155 D2
Topana RO 160 D5
Topares E 55 D8
Toparlar TR 181 C9
Topchii BG 161 F9
Töpchin D 80 B5
Topčic-Polje BIH 157 D8
Topcliffe GB 11 C9
Töpen D 75 B10
Topeno FIN 127 D11
Tophisar TR 173 D9
Topleț RO 159 D9
Topliceni RO 161 C10
Topli Do SRB 165 C6
Toplița RO 152 D6
Toplița RO 159 B10
Töplitz D 79 B12
Topojë AL 168 C1
Topola SRB 158 E6
Topolčani NMK 168 B5
Topoľčany SK 146 D6
Topoľčianky SK 146 E6
Topolia GR 178 E6
Topólka PL 138 E6
Topolnica SRB 159 E9
Topoľníky SK 146 F5
Topolog RO 155 D2
Topolovac HR 149 F6
Topolovățu Mare RO 151 F8
Topoloveni RO 160 D6
Topolovgrad BG 166 E6
Topolovnik SRB 159 D7
Topolovo BG 166 F4
Topolšica SLO 73 D11
Toponica SRB 158 F6
Toporec SK 145 E1
Toporivtsi UA 153 A8
Toporów PL 81 B8
Toporu RO 161 E7
Toporzyk PL 85 C10
Toppenstedt D 83 D8
Topraisar RO 155 E2
Topsham GB 13 D8
Topusko HR 156 B4
Torà E 43 D6
Toral de los Guzmanes E 39 D8
Toral de los Vados E 39 C6
Torano Castello I 60 E6
Torasalo FIN 125 F10
Toras-Sieppi FIN 117 C11
Torbali TR 177 C9
Torbjörntorp S 91 C14
Torbygget S 102 A4
Torchiara I 60 C4
Torchiarolo I 61 C10
Torcy F 30 B5
Torda SRB 158 B5
Tordas H 149 B11
Tordehumos E 39 E9
Tordera E 43 D9
Tordesillas E 39 E10
Tordesilos E 47 C9
Töre S 118 C9
Töreboda S 91 B15
Toreby DK 83 A11
Torekov S 87 C11
Torella del Sannio I 63 D7
Torellano E 56 E3
Torelló E 43 C8
Toreno E 39 C6
Torestorp S 91 E12
Torgau D 80 C3
Torgelow D 84 C6
Torgiano I 62 A2
Torhamn S 89 C9
Torhout B 19 B7
Tori EST 131 E9
Torigni-sur-Vire F 23 B10
Torija E 47 C6
Torino I 68 C4
Toritto I 61 B7
Torkanivka UA 154 A4
Torkovichi RUS 132 D7
Torla E 32 E5
Torma EST 131 D13
Tormac RO 159 B7
Törmänen FIN 113 E19
Törmänen FIN 115 A2
Törmänki FIN 117 E13
Törmänmäki FIN 121 E10
Törmäsenvaara FIN 121 C13
Törmäsjärvi FIN 119 B12
Tormestorp S 87 C13
Tormón E 47 D10
Tormore GB 4 D6
Tornadizos de Ávila E 46 C3
Tornaľa SK 145 F1
Tornavacas E 45 D9
Tornby DK 90 D6
Tornemark DK 87 E9
Tørnes N 100 A6
Tørnes N 111 D11
Tornesch D 82 C7
Tornetråsk S 111 D18
Tornimäe EST 130 D6
Tornio FIN 119 C12
Tornjoš SRB 150 F4
Torno I 69 B7
Tornos E 47 C10
Tornow D 84 D4
Toro E 39 E9
Torö S 93 B11
Törökbálint H 149 B11
Törökszentmiklós H 150 C5
Torony H 149 B7
Toros BG 165 C9
Toroshino RUS 132 F4
Torp FIN 99 B13
Torpa S 92 D6
Torphins GB 3 L11
Torpo N 101 E9
Torpoint GB 12 E6
Torpsbruk S 88 A7
Torpshammar S 103 B11
Torquay GB 13 E7
Torquemada E 40 D3
Torraiba de Calatrava E 54 A5
Torralba E 47 D8
Torralba I 64 B2
Torralba de Aragón E 41 E10
Torralba de El Burgo E 40 E6
Torralba de los Sisones E 47 C10
Torralba de Oropesa E 45 E10
Torrão P 50 C3
Torrböle S 107 D17
Torre-Alháquime E 51 F9
Torre Annunziata I 60 B2
Torrebaja E 47 D10
Torreblanca E 48 D5
Torreblascopedro E 53 A9
Torrebruna I 63 D7
Torrecaballeros E 46 C4
Torrecampo E 54 C3
Torre Canne I 61 B8
Torre-Cardela E 55 D6
Torrecilla de Alcañiz E 42 F3
Torrecilla de la Jara E 46 E3
Torrecilla de la Orden E 45 B10
Torrecilla del Rebollar E 42 F1
Torrecillas de la Tiesa E 45 E9
Torrecuso I 60 A3
Torre da Gadanha P 50 B3
Torre das Vargens P 44 F5
Torre de Coelheiros P 50 C4
Torre de Dona Chama P 38 E5
Torre de Embesora E 48 D4
Torredeita P 44 C4
Torre de Juan Abad E 55 B6
Torre del Bierzo E 39 C7
Torre del Burgo E 47 C6
Torre del Campo E 53 A9
Torre del Greco I 60 B2
Torre del Mar E 53 C8
Torredembarra E 43 E6
Torre de Miguel Sesmero E 51 B6
Torre de Moncorvo P 45 B6
Torre de'Passeri I 62 C5
Torre de Santa María E 45 F8
Torredonjimeno E 53 A9
Torre do Terrenho P 44 C6
Torrefarrera E 42 D5
Torregamones E 39 F7
Torregrossa E 42 D5
Torreiglesias E 46 B4
Torreira P 44 C3
Torrejoncillo E 45 E8
Torrejoncillo del Rey E 47 D7
Torrejón de Ardoz E 46 D6
Torrejón del Rey E 46 C6
Torrejón el Rubio E 45 E9
Torrelacarcel E 47 C10
Torrelaguna E 46 C5
Torrelapaja E 41 E8
Torrelavega E 40 B3
Torrellas E 41 E8
Torrelles de Foix E 43 E7
Torrelobatón E 39 E9
Torrelodones E 46 C5
Torremaggiore I 63 D8
Torremanzanas-La Torre de les Macanes E 56 D4
Torremayor E 51 B6
Torremegía E 51 B7
Torre Mileto I 63 D9
Torremocha E 45 F8
Torremocha de Jiloca E 47 C10
Torremolinos E 53 C7
Torrenostra E 48 D5
Torrent E 48 F4
Torrente del Cinca E 42 E4
Torrenueva E 55 B6
Torreorgaz E 45 F8
Torre Orsaia I 60 C4
Torre-Pacheco E 56 F3
Torre Pellice I 31 F11
Torreperogil E 55 C6
Torres E 53 A9
Torresandino E 40 E4
Torre San Giovanni I 61 D10
Torre Santa Susanna I 61 C9
Torres de Albánchez E 55 C7
Torres de Berrellén E 41 E9
Torres de la Alameda E 46 D6
Torres del Carrizal E 39 E8
Torresmenudas E 45 B9
Torres Novas P 44 F3
Torres Vedras P 44 F2
Torrevelilla E 42 F3
Torrevieja E 56 F3
Torrice I 62 D4
Torricella I 61 C9
Torricella in Sabina I 62 C3
Torricella Peligna I 63 C6
Torricella Sicura I 62 B5
Torricella Taverne CH 69 A6
Torrico E 45 E10
Torri del Benaco I 69 B10
Torridon GB 2 K5
Torriglia I 37 B10
Torrijas E 48 D3
Torrijo E 41 F8
Torrijo del Campo E 47 C10
Torrijos E 46 E4
Torrin GB 2 L4
Tørring DK 86 D4
Tørring N 105 C10
Torrita di Siena I 66 F4
Torroal P 50 C2
Torroella de Montgrí E 43 C10
Torrox E 53 C9
Torrubia del Campo E 47 E7
Torrubia de Soria E 41 E7
Tørrvika N 104 C7
Torsåker S 98 A6
Torsång S 97 B14
Torsås S 89 C10
Tørsbøl DK 86 F4
Torsbole S 107 E15
Torsborg S 102 A5
Torsby S 97 B9
Torsby S 97 C9
Torsebro S 88 C6
Torshälla S 98 D6
Tórshavn FO 2 A3
Torsholma FIN 126 E5
Torsken N 111 B13
Torslanda S 91 D10
Torsminde DK 86 C2
Torsö S 91 B14
Torsvåg N 112 C4
Törtel H 150 C4
Tortellà E 43 C9
Torteval GBG 22 B6
Torthorwald GB 5 E9
Tortinmäki FIN 126 D7
Tórtola de Henares E 47 C6
Tórtoles de Esgueva E 40 E3
Tortolì I 64 D4
Tortomanu RO 155 E2
Tortona I 37 B9
Tortora I 60 D5
Tortoreto I 62 B5
Tortorici I 59 C6
Tortosa E 42 F5
Tortozendo P 44 D5
Tortuera E 47 C9
Tortuna S 98 C7
Toruń PL 138 D6
Torun' UA 145 F8
Torup S 87 B12
Tõrva EST 131 E11
Tor Vaianica I 62 D2
Tõrvandi EST 131 E13
Torvenkylä FIN 119 F11
Torvik N 100 B3
Torvik N 104 F4
Torvikbukt N 104 F3
Tørvikbygd N 94 B4
Torvinen FIN 117 D17
Torvizcón E 55 F6
Torvsjö S 107 C12
Torysa SK 145 E2
Torzym PL 81 B8
Tosbotn N 108 F4
Toscolano-Maderno I 69 B10
Tossa E 43 D9
Tossåsen S 102 A5
Tossåsen S 102 A7
Tossavanlahti FIN 123 D16
Tosse F 32 C3
Tösse S 91 B12
Tossicia I 62 B5
Tosside GB 11 C7
Tõstamaa EST 131 E7
Tostedt D 82 D7
Tószeg H 150 C5
Toszek PL 142 F6
Totana E 55 D10
Totebo S 93 D8
Tôtes F 18 E3
Totești RO 159 B10
Tótkomlós H 150 E6
Totland GB 13 D11
Totnes GB 13 E7
Totra S 103 E13
Tótszerdahely H 149 D7
Tøttdal N 105 C10
Tottijärvi FIN 127 C9
Totton GB 13 D12
Tótvázsony H 149 B9
Touça P 45 B6
Toucy F 25 E9
Touffailles F 33 B8
Touget F 33 C7
Toul F 26 C4
Toulon F 35 D10
Toulon-sur-Allier F 30 B3
Toulon-sur-Arroux F 30 B5
Toulouges F 34 E4
Toulouse F 33 C8
Tounj HR 156 B3
Touques F 23 B12
Tourch F 22 D4
Tourcoing F 19 C7
Tourlaville F 23 A8
Tournai B 19 C7
Tournan-en-Brie F 25 C8
Tournay F 33 D6
Tournecoupe F 33 C7
Tournefeuille F 33 C8
Tournon-d'Agenais F 33 B7
Tournon-St-Martin F 29 B7
Tournon-sur-Rhône F 30 E6
Tournus F 30 B6
Tourny F 24 B6
Tourouvre F 24 C4
Tours F 24 F4
Tourteron F 19 E10
Tourtoirac F 29 E8
Toury F 24 D6
Tous E 48 F3
Tõusi EST 131 D7
Touvois F 28 B2
Toužim CZ 76 B3
Tovačov CZ 146 C4
Tovariševo SRB 158 C3
Tovarné SK 145 F4
Tovarnik HR 157 B11
Toven N 108 D5
Tovrljane SRB 164 C3
Towcester GB 14 C7
Tower IRL 8 E5
Toymskardlia N 106 A5
Töysä FIN 123 E11
Traar D 183 C9
Trabada E 38 B5
Trabanca E 45 B8
Trabazos E 39 E7
Traben D 21 E8
Trąbki PL 144 D1
Trąbki Wielkie PL 138 B6
Traboch A 73 B10
Trabotivište NMK 165 F6
Traby BY 137 E12
Trachili GR 175 B9
Tradate I 69 B6
Trädet S 91 D14
Trædal N 111 D14
Trafrask IRL 8 E3
Tragacete E 47 D9
Tragana GR 175 B7
Tragano GR 174 D3
Tragjas AL 168 D2
Tragwein A 77 F7
Traian RO 153 D10
Traian RO 155 C1
Traian RO 155 C2
Traian RO 160 E4
Traian RO 160 F6
Traian Vuia RO 151 F9
Traid E 47 C9
Traiguera E 42 F4
Train D 75 E10
Traînel F 25 D9
Traînou F 24 E7
Traisen A 77 F9
Traiskirchen A 77 F10
Traismauer A 77 F9
Traitsching D 75 D12
Trakai LT 137 D10
Trakovice SK 146 E5
Trakšėdžiai LT 134 F2
Tralee IRL 8 D3
Trá Lí IRL 8 D3
Tramacastilla E 47 D9
Tramagal P 44 F4
Tramariglio I 64 B1
Tramatza I 64 C2
Tramayes F 30 C6
Tramelan CH 27 F7
Trá Mhór IRL 9 D8
Tramonti di Sopra I 73 D6
Tramonti di Sotto I 73 D6
Tramore IRL 9 D8
Tramutola I 60 C5
Tranås S 92 C5
Tranbjerg DK 86 C6
Trancoso P 44 C6
Tranebjerg DK 86 D7
Tranemo S 91 E13
Trången S 105 D15
Trånghalla S 92 D4
Trångslet S 102 D6
Trångsviken S 105 E16
Trani I 61 A6
Trannes F 25 D12
Tranovalto GR 169 D6
Tranøy N 111 D10
Trans F 23 D8
Trans-en-Provence F 36 D4
Transtrand S 102 D5
Transtrand S 102 E5
Tranum DK 86 A4
Tranvik S 99 D11
Trapani I 58 C2
Trapene LV 135 B13
Traplice CZ 146 C4
Trappes F 24 C7
Trarbach D 185 E7
Traryd S 87 B13
Trasacco I 62 D5
Träskvik FIN 122 F7
Trasmiras E 38 D4
Trasobares E 41 E8
Tratalias I 64 E2
Traun A 76 F6
Traunreut D 73 A6
Traunstein A 77 F8
Traunstein D 73 A6
Traupis LT 135 E9
Trava SLO 73 E10
Trävad S 91 C13
Travagliato I 66 A1
Travanca do Mondego P 44 D4
Travassô P 44 C4
Travemünde D 83 C9
Travenbrück D 83 C8
Travers CH 31 B10
Traversetolo I 66 C1
Trávnica SK 146 E6
Travnik BIH 157 D8
Travo I 37 B11

Trawniki PL 141 H8
Trawsfynydd GB 10 F4
Trbovlje SLO 73 D11
Trbuk BIH 157 C9
Trebaseleghe I 72 E5
Trebatice SK 146 D5
Trebatsch D 80 B6
Trebbin D 80 B4
Třebechovice pod Orebem CZ 77 B9
Trebel D 83 E10
Treben D 79 D11
Třebenice CZ 76 B5
Trebenow D 84 D5
Trèbes F 33 D10
Trébeurden F 22 C4
Třebíč CZ 77 D9
Trebinje BIH 162 D5
Trebisacce I 61 D7
Trebišov SK 145 F4
Trebnje SLO 73 E11
Trebolle E 38 C4
Třeboň CZ 77 D7
Trebsen D 79 D12
Trebujena E 51 F7
Trebur D 21 E10
Trecastagni I 59 D7
Trecate I 68 C6
Trecchina I 60 C5
Trecenta I 66 B3
Tredegar GB 13 B8
Tredington GB 13 A11
Tredozio I 66 D4
Treehoo IRL 7 D8
Trefaldwyn GB 10 F5
Trefeglwys GB 10 F4
Treffen A 73 C8
Treffort-Cuisiat F 31 C7
Trefurt D 79 D7
Trefriw GB 10 E4
Trefynwy GB 13 B9
Tregaron GB 13 A7
Trégastel F 22 C4
Tregde N 90 C2
Tregnago I 66 A3
Tregony GB 12 E5
Trégueux F 22 D6
Tréguier F 22 C5
Trégunc F 22 E4
Tregynon GB 10 F5
Trehörna S 92 C5
Trehörningsjö S 107 D15
Treia D 82 A6
Treia I 67 F7
Treignac F 29 D9
Treigny F 25 E9
Treimani EST 131 F8
Treis D 185 D7
Trekanten S 89 B10
Treklyano BG 165 D6
Trélazé F 23 F11
Trelech GB 12 B6
Trélissac F 29 E7
Trelleborg S 87 E12
Trelleck GB 13 B9
Trélon F 19 D9
Tremadog GB 10 F3
Tremblay-les-Villages F 24 C5
Tremedal de Tormes E 45 B8
Tremelo B 19 C10
Trémentines F 23 F10
Tremês P 44 F3
Tréméven F 22 E4
Tremezzo I 69 B7
Trémolat F 29 F7
Třemošná CZ 76 C4
Trémouilles F 34 B4
Tremp E 42 C5
Trenance GB 12 E4
Trenčianska Turná SK 146 D6
Trenčianske Jastrabie SK 146 D6
Trenčianske Stankovce SK 146 D5
Trenčianske Teplice SK 146 D6
Trenčín SK 146 D6
Trendelburg D 21 A12
Trengereid N 94 B3
Trensacq F 32 B4
Trent D 84 A4
Trenta SLO 73 D8
Trentels F 33 B7
Trento I 69 A11
Tréon F 24 C5
Treorchy GB 13 B7
Trepča HR 148 F5
Treppeln D 81 B7
Trept F 31 D7
Trepuzzi I 61 C10
Trequanda I 66 F4
Tres Cantos E 46 C5
Trescléoux F 35 B10
Trescore Balneario I 69 B8
Tresenda I 69 A9
Tresfjord N 100 A6
Tresigallo I 66 C4
Tresjuncos E 47 E7
Treski EST 132 F2
Treskog S 97 C8
Trešnjevica SRB 158 F5
Tresnuraghes I 64 C2
Trespaderne E 40 C5
Tressait GB 5 B9
Třešť CZ 77 D8
Tretower GB 13 B8
Trets F 35 D10
Tretten N 101 D12
Treuchtlingen D 75 E8
Treuenbrietzen D 79 B12
Treungen N 90 A4
Trévé F 22 D6
Trevélez E 55 F6
Tréveray F 26 C3
Trèves F 34 B5
Trevi I 62 B3
Treviana E 40 C5
Trévières F 23 B10
Treviglio I 69 B8
Trevignano Romano I 62 C2
Trévillers F 27 F6
Treviño E 40 C6
Treviso I 72 E5
Trevllazër AL 168 C2
Trevões P 44 B6
Trévoux F 30 D6
Trézelles F 30 C4
Trezzo sull'Adda I 69 B8
Trgovište SRB 164 E5
Trhová Hradská SK 146 F5
Trhové Sviny CZ 77 E7
Trhovište SK 145 F4
Trhový Štěpánov CZ 77 C8
Triacastela E 38 C5
Triaize F 28 C3
Trianta GR 181 D8
Triantaros GR 176 D5
Tribalj HR 67 B10
Tribanj-Krušćica HR 156 D3
Tribehou F 23 B9
Tribsees D 83 B13
Tribunj HR 156 E4
Tricarico I 60 B6
Tricase I 61 D10
Tricesimo I 73 D7
Trichiana I 72 D5
Tricot F 18 E6
Trieben A 73 A9
Triebes D 79 E11
Trie-Château F 18 F4
Trier D 21 E7
Trierweiler D 186 B2
Trieste I 73 E8
Trie-sur-Baïse F 33 D6
Trieux F 20 F5
Trifeşti RO 153 C11
Trifeşti RO 153 D9
Triftern D 76 F4
Trigaches P 50 C4
Trigance F 36 D4
Triggiano I 61 A7
Triglitz D 83 D12
Trignac F 23 F7
Trigrad BG 165 F9
Triguères F 25 E8
Trigueros E 51 E6
Trigueros del Valle E 39 E10
Triigi EST 130 D5
Trikala GR 169 E6
Trikāta LV 131 F11
Trikeri GR 175 A7
Trilj HR 157 E6
Trillevallen S 105 E14
Trillick GB 7 D8
Trillo E 47 C7
Trilofo GR 174 E5
Trilofos GR 169 D8
Trilport F 25 C8
Trim IRL 7 E9
Trimdon GB 5 F14
Trimley St Mary GB 15 D11
Trimmis CH 71 D9
Trimsaran GB 12 B6
Trindade P 38 F5
Trindade P 50 D4
Třinec CZ 147 B7
Tring GB 15 D7
Trinità d'Agultu I 64 B2
Trinitapoli I 60 A6
Trino I 68 C5
Trins A 72 B3
Trinta P 45 C6
Trinwillershagen D 83 B13
Triollo E 39 C10
Triora I 37 D7
Tripkau D 83 D10
Tripoli GR 174 D5
Tripotama GR 174 D4
Tripotamos GR 169 C7
Trippstadt D 21 F9
Triptis D 79 E10
Tritenii de Jos RO 152 D4
Trittau D 83 C8
Trittenheim D 21 E7
Trivalea-Moşteni RO 160 E6
Trivento I 63 D7
Trivero I 68 B5
Trivigno I 60 B5
Trizac F 29 E11
Trnakovac HR 157 B7
Trnava CZ 146 C5
Trnava SK 146 E5
Trnava SRB 158 F5
Trnavá Hora SK 147 D7
Trnjani BIH 157 C6
Trnovci NMK 168 B5
Trnovec Bartolovečki HR 149 D6
Trnovec nad Váhom SK 146 E5
Trnovica BIH 157 F9
Trnovo BIH 157 E9
Tro N 108 E4
Troarn F 23 B11
Tröbitz D 80 C4
Trochtelfingen D 27 D11
Trödje S 103 E13
Troense DK 86 E7
Trofa P 38 F2
Trofaiach A 73 B11
Trofors N 108 E5
Trogir HR 156 E5
Trøgstad N 95 C14
Troia I 60 A4
Tróia P 50 C2
Troianul RO 160 F6
Troina I 59 D6
Troisdorf D 21 C8
Troisfontaines F 186 D3
Trois-Ponts B 19 D12
Troissereux F 18 F5
Trois-Vèvres F 30 B3
Troisvierges L 20 D6
Troiţsoe MD 154 D4
Trojane SLO 73 D10
Trojanów PL 141 G5
Troldhede DK 86 D3
Trollbukta N 113 C19
Trollhättan S 91 C11
Trollvik N 112 D6
Tromello I 69 C6
Tromsdalen N 111 A16
Tromsø N 111 A16
Tromvik N 111 A15
Tronco P 38 E5
Trondenes N 111 C12
Trondheim N 104 E8
Trones N 105 B13
Trongisvágur FO 2 B3
Tronnes N 108 C8
Trönninge S 87 B11
Trönningeby S 87 A10
Trönö S 103 D12
Trontano I 68 A5
Tronvik N 105 D9
Tronville-en-Barrois F 26 C3
Tronzano Vercellese I 68 C5
Troo F 24 E4
Troon GB 4 D7
Trooz B 183 D7
Tropaia GR 174 D4
Tropea I 59 B8
Trory GB 7 D7
Trosa S 93 B11
Troshan AL 163 F8
Trösken S 98 B7
Troškūnai LT 135 E9
Trošmarija HR 148 F4
Trossin D 79 C12
Trossingen D 27 D10
Tröstau D 75 B10
Trostberg D 75 F12
Trostyanets' UA 145 E9
Trostyanets' UA 153 A12
Troszyn PL 139 D12
Troubky CZ 146 C4
Troubsko CZ 77 D10
Troutbeck GB 10 C6
Trouville-sur-Mer F 23 B12
Trouy F 29 A10
Troviscal P 44 E4
Trowbridge GB 13 C10
Troyan BG 165 D10
Troyanovo BG 167 D8
Troyes F 25 D11
Troyits'ke UA 154 B6
Troyits'ke UA 154 D6
Troyon F 26 B3
Trpanj HR 157 F7
Trpejca NMK 168 C4
Trpezi MNE 163 D9
Trpinja HR 157 B10
Trsa MNE 157 F10
Trstená SK 147 C9
Trstené pri Hornáde SK 145 F3
Trstenik HR 162 D3
Trstenik SRB 163 B11
Trstice SK 146 E5
Trstín SK 146 D4
Trubar BIH 156 D5
Trubia E 39 B8
Truchas E 39 D7
Truchtersheim F 27 C8
Trud BG 165 E10
Trudovets BG 165 D8
Trudy BY 133 E6
Trujillanos E 51 B7
Trujillo E 45 F9
Trulben D 27 B8
Trŭn BG 165 D6
Trun CH 71 D7
Trun F 23 C12
Trŭnchovitsa BG 165 C11
Truro GB 12 E4
Truşeşti RO 153 B10
Trusetal D 79 E7
Trush AL 163 F7
Truskava LT 135 F8
Truskavets' UA 145 E8
Trŭstenik BG 161 F7
Trŭstenik BG 165 C9
Trustrup DK 87 C7
Trutnov CZ 81 E9
Try N 90 C2
Tryavna BG 166 D4
Trybusivka UA 154 A3
Tryfos GR 174 B3
Tryggelev DK 83 A9
Trygona GR 168 E5
Tryńcza PL 144 C6
Tryserum S 93 C9
Trysil N 102 D3
Tryškiai LT 134 D5
Trysunda S 107 E15
Tržac BIH 156 C4
Trzcianka PL 85 D10
Trzcianka PL 139 E12
Trzcianne PL 140 D7
Trzciel PL 81 B9
Trzebiatów PL 85 B8
Trzebiechów PL 81 B9
Trzebiel PL 81 C7
Trzebielino PL 85 B12
Trzebień PL 81 D9
Trzebieszów PL 141 G7
Trzebieszowice PL 77 B11
Trzebież PL 84 C7
Trzebinia PL 143 F7
Trzebiszewo PL 81 A8
Trzebnica PL 81 D12
Trzebnice PL 81 D10
Trzebownisko PL 144 C5
Trzeciewiec PL 138 D5
Trzemeszno PL 138 E4
Trzemeszno Lubuskie PL 81 B8
Trześcianka PL 140 E8
Trześniów PL 145 D4
Trzeszczany Pierwsze PL 144 B8
Tržič SLO 73 D9
Trzrciński-Zdrój PL 84 E7
Trzyciąż PL 143 F8
Trzydnik Duży PL 144 B5
Tsagkarada GR 169 F9
Tsakarisianos GR 174 C2
Tsalapitsa BG 165 E10
Tsamantas GR 168 E3
Tsaparevo BG 169 A9
Tsareva Livada BG 166 D4
Tsarev Brod BG 167 C8
Tsarevo BG 167 E9
Tsarimir BG 165 E10
Tsaritsani GR 169 E7
Tsar Kaloyan BG 161 F8
Tsar-Petrovo BG 159 F10
Tschagguns A 71 C9
Tschernitz D 81 C7
Tsebrykove UA 154 C6
Tselina BG 166 E4
Tsenovo BG 166 B5
Tserovo BG 165 C7
Tserovo BG 165 E9
Tsiistre EST 131 F14
Tsirguliina EST 131 F12
Tsivaras GR 178 E7
Tsooru EST 131 F13
Tsotili GR 168 D5
Tsoukalades GR 174 B2
Tsŭrvaritsa BG 165 E6
Tsvetino BG 165 F8
Tsyatsyerki BY 133 E2
Tua N 105 D9
Tuaim IRL 6 E5
Tuaim Beola IRL 6 F3
Tuam IRL 6 E5
Tuamgraney IRL 8 C5
Tubbercurry IRL 6 D5
Tubbergen NL 17 D7
Tubilla del Agua E 40 C4
Tübingen D 27 C11
Tubize B 19 C9
Tubre I 71 D10
Tučepi HR 157 F7
Tuchan F 34 E4
Tüchen D 83 D12
Tuchheim D 79 B11
Tuchola PL 138 C4
Tuchomie PL 85 B12
Tuchów PL 144 D3
Tuchowicz PL 141 G6
Tuckur FIN 122 D8
Tuczna PL 141 G8
Tuczno PL 85 D10
Tudela E 41 D8
Tudela de Duero E 40 E2
Tudora RO 153 B9
Tudor Vladimirescu RO 155 B1
Tudu EST 131 C13
Tudulinna EST 131 C14
Tudweiliog GB 10 F2
Tuejar E 47 E10
Tuenno I 72 D3
Tufeni RO 160 E5
Tufeşti RO 155 D1
Tuffé F 24 D4
Tufjord N 113 A12
Tuhkakylä FIN 125 B10
Tui E 38 D2
Tuili I 64 D2
Tuin NMK 168 A5
Tuiskula FIN 122 E8
Tūja LV 135 B8
Tukhkala RUS 121 C16
Tukhol'ka UA 145 F7
Tukums LV 134 C6
Tula I 64 B2
Tulach Mhór IRL 7 F8
Tulare SRB 164 D3
Tuławki PL 136 F2
Tulbing A 77 F10
Tulca RO 151 D8
Tulce PL 81 B12
Tulcea RO 155 C3
Tulčík SK 145 E3
Tulette F 35 B8
Tulgheş RO 153 D7
Tuli BIH 162 D5
Tuliszków PL 142 B5
Tulje BIH 162 D5
Tulka S 99 B11
Tulla IRL 8 C5
Tullaghan IRL 6 D6
Tullamore IRL 7 F8
Tulle F 29 E9
Tullebølle DK 87 F7
Tulleng N 111 A15
Tulleråsen S 105 E16
Tullingsås S 106 D9
Tullins F 31 E7
Tulln A 77 F10
Tullow IRL 9 C9
Tully GB 7 D7
Tully GB 7 D8
Tullyallen IRL 7 E10
Tullyvin IRL 7 D8
Tulnici RO 153 F9
Tulos RUS 125 C14
Tulovo BG 166 D5
Tułowice PL 139 F9
Tułowice PL 142 E4
Tulppio FIN 115 C6
Tulsk IRL 6 E6
Tulstrup DK 87 D10
Tulucești RO 155 B2
Tumba S 93 A11
Tumbo S 98 D6
Tume LV 134 C6
Tummel Bridge GB 5 B8
Tumšupe LV 135 B9
Tun S 91 C12
Tunadal S 103 B13
Tuna-Hästberg S 97 B13
Tunari RO 161 D8
Tunbridge Wells, Royal GB 15 E9
Tunga GB 2 J4
Tungozero RUS 121 C17
Tunnerstad S 92 C4
Tunnhovd N 95 B9
Tunnsjø-Røyrvika N 105 B14
Tunsjön S 107 E12
Tunstall GB 15 C11
Tuntenhausen D 72 A5
Tunvågen S 102 A8
Tuohikotti FIN 128 C7
Tuohikylä FIN 115 E5
Tuolluvaara S 116 C4
Tuomikylä FIN 122 E9
Tuomioja FIN 119 E14
Tuorila FIN 126 B6
Tuoro sul Trasimeno I 66 F5
Tuovilanlahti FIN 124 D8
Tupilaţi RO 153 C9
Tuplice PL 81 C7
Tuppurinmäki FIN 125 E10
Tura H 150 B4
Turanlar TR 177 D10
Turany SK 147 C8
Turawa PL 142 E5
Turba EST 131 C8
Turbe BIH 157 D8
Turbenthal CH 27 F10
Turburea RO 160 D3
Turceni RO 160 D2
Turcia E 39 C8
Turčianske Teplice SK 147 D7
Turcifal P 44 F2
Turcinești RO 160 C2
Turcoaia RO 155 C2
Turda RO 152 D3
Turdaş RO 151 F11
Turégano E 46 B4
Turek PL 142 B6
Tureni RO 152 D3
Turenki FIN 127 D12
Turew PL 81 B11
Turgeliai LT 137 E12
Türgovishte BG 167 C7
Turgut TR 181 B8
Turgutalp TR 177 A10
Turgutbey TR 173 B7
Turgutlu TR 177 C10
Turgutreis TR 177 F9
Türi EST 131 D10
Turi I 61 B8
Turia RO 153 E8
Turić BIH 157 C10
Turie SK 147 C7
Turija BIH 157 C9
Turija SRB 158 B4
Turija SRB 159 D8
Turís E 48 F3
Turiya BG 166 D4
Türje H 149 C8
Turka UA 145 E7
Türkeve H 150 C6
Türkgücü TR 173 B8
Türkheim D 71 A11
Turki LV 135 D12
Türkmenli TR 171 E10
Turkova BY 133 E4
Turkovići BIH 162 D4
Turku FIN 126 E7
Turlava LV 134 C3
Turleque E 46 E5
Turmantas LT 135 E12
Turmenti BIH 162 D5
Turna LV 131 F11
Tŭrnak BG 165 C9
Turňa nad Bodvou SK 145 F2
Turnau A 148 A4
Tŭrnava BG 165 B8
Turnberry GB 4 E7
Turners Hill GB 15 E8
Turnhout B 16 F3
Turnišče SLO 149 C6
Türnitz A 77 G9
Turnov CZ 81 E8
Turnu Măgurele RO 160 F5
Turnu Roşu RO 160 B4
Turnu Ruieni RO 159 C9
Turobin PL 144 B6
Turośl PL 139 C12
Turośl PL 139 D12
Turów PL 141 G7
Turowo PL 85 C11
Turquel P 44 F3
Turrach A 73 C8
Turre E 55 E9
Turri I 64 D2
Turriff GB 3 K12
Tursi I 61 C6
Turţ RO 145 H7
Turtel NMK 164 F5
Turtola FIN 117 E11
Turulung RO 145 H7
Turup DK 86 E5
Tur"ya-Bystra UA 145 F6
Tur"ya-Polyana UA 145 F6
Turyatka UA 153 A8
Tur"ye UA 145 E7
Tur"yi Remety UA 145 F6
Turynka UA 144 C9
Turza Wielka PL 139 D9
Turzovka SK 147 C7
Tusa I 58 D5
Tuscania I 62 C1
Tuse DK 87 D9
Tuset N 105 E10
Tušilović HR 148 F5
Tuşnad RO 153 E7
Tussenhausen D 71 A11
Tüßling D 75 F12
Tuszów Narodowy PL 143 F11
Tuszyma PL 143 F12
Tuszyn PL 143 C8
Tutbury GB 11 F8
Tutjunniemi FIN 125 F13
Tuţora RO 153 C11
Tutova RO 153 E11
Tutow D 84 C4
Tutrakan BG 161 E9
Tuttlingen D 27 E10
Tütüncü TR 173 D8
Tutzing D 72 A3
Tützpatz D 84 C4
Tuudi EST 130 D7
Tuukkala FIN 127 B16
Tuuliharju FIN 117 D13
Tuulimäki FIN 121 F11
Tuulos FIN 127 C12
Tuupovaara FIN 125 F15
Tuuri FIN 123 E11
Tuusjärvi FIN 125 E10
Tuusniemi FIN 125 E10
Tuusula FIN 127 E12
Tuv N 101 E8
Tuv N 108 B8
Tuvattnett S 106 D7
Tuve S 91 D10
Tuvnes N 104 D5
Tuvträsk S 107 B15
Tuxford GB 11 E10
Tuzburgazi TR 177 D9
Tuzculu TR 177 B8
Tŭzha BG 166 D4
Tuzi MNE 163 E7
Tužina SK 147 D7
Tuzla BIH 157 C10
Tuzla RO 155 E3
Tuzla TR 171 E10
Tužno HR 148 D6
Tuzora MD 154 C2
Tuzsér H 145 G5
Tvååker S 87 A10
Tvärålund S 107 C17
Tvärån S 118 C6
Tvärträsk S 107 A13
Tvardiţa MD 154 E3
Tvärsele S 106 B8
Tvärskog S 89 B10
Tvede DK 86 B6
Tvedestrand N 90 B4
Tveit N 90 C3
Tveit N 94 D4
Tverai LT 134 E4
Tverečius LT 135 F13
Tverråga N 108 D7
Tverråmo N 109 B10
Tverrelmo N 111 C18
Tversted DK 90 D7
Tving S 89 C8
Tvis DK 86 C3
Tvøroyri FO 2 B3
Tvorozhkovo RUS 132 E4
Tvrdošín SK 147 C9
Tvrdošovce SK 146 E6
Tvŭrditsa BG 166 D5
Twardogóra PL 142 D3
Twatt GB 3 G10
Tweedmouth GB 5 D12
Tweedsmuir GB 5 D10
Twello NL 16 D6
Twist D 17 C8
Twiste (Twistetal) D 17 F11
Twistringen D 17 C11
Two Mile Borris IRL 9 C7
Twomileborris IRL 9 C7
Two Mile Bridge IRL 7 F8
Tworóg PL 142 E6
Twyford GB 13 C12
Twyford GB 15 E7
Twyning GB 13 A10
Tyachiv UA 145 G8
Tychero GR 171 B10
Tychówko PL 85 C10
Tychowo PL 85 C10
Tychy PL 143 F6
Tyczyn PL 144 D5
Tydal N 105 E11
Tydavnet IRL 7 D8
Tyfors S 97 B11
Tygelsjö S 87 D11
Tyinkrysset N 101 D8
Tykocin PL 140 D7
Tylawa PL 145 E4
Tylissos GR 178 E9
Tyllinge S 93 C8
Tylmanowa PL 145 D1
Tylösand S 87 B11
Tylstrup DK 86 A5
Tymbark PL 144 D1
Tymień PL 85 B9
Tymowa PL 81 D10
Tympaki GR 178 E8
Tynderö S 103 B14
Tyndrum GB 4 C7
Týnec nad Labem CZ 77 B8
Týnec nad Sázavou CZ 77 C7
Tynemouth GB 5 E14
Tyngsjö S 97 B10
Tyniewicze Małe PL 141 E8
Týniště nad Orlicí CZ 77 B10
Tynkä FIN 119 F12
Týn nad Vltavou CZ 77 D6
Tynset N 101 B13
Typpö FIN 119 F12
Typpyrä FIN 117 E14
Tyrämäki FIN 121 D12
Tyrävaara FIN 121 D12
Tyrawa Wołoska PL 145 D5
Tyresö S 99 D10
Tyringe S 87 C13
Tyristrand N 95 B12
Tyrjänsaari FIN 125 E15
Tyrnävä FIN 119 E15
Tyrnavos GR 169 E7
Tyrrellspass IRL 7 F8
Tyrväntö FIN 127 C11
Tysnes N 111 D10
Tysse N 94 B3
Tysse N 100 D2
Tyssebotnen N 100 E3
Tyssedal N 94 B5
Tystberga S 93 B10
Tyszowce PL 144 B8
Tytuvėnai LT 134 E6
Tyukod H 145 H6
Tyulenovo BG 167 B11
Tywyn GB 10 F3
Tyykiluoto FIN 119 D14
Tzermiado GR 178 E9
Tzummarum NL 16 B5

U

Uachdar GB 2 L2
Uachtar Ard IRL 6 F4
Ub SRB 158 E5
Übach-Palenberg D 183 D8
Ubby DK 87 D8
Úbeda E 53 A10
Überherrn D 21 F7
Überlingen D 27 E11
Übersee D 72 A5
Ubli HR 162 D2
Ubli MNE 163 D6
Ubli MNE 163 D7
Ubrique E 53 C6
Ubstadt-Weiher D 21 F11
Ucciani F 37 G9
Uccle B 19 C9
Ucea RO 152 F5
Uceda E 46 C6
Ucel F 35 A7
Ucero E 40 E5
Ucha P 38 E2
Uchanie PL 144 B8
Uchaux F 35 B8
Uchizy F 30 B6
Uchte D 17 D11
Üchtelhausen D 75 B7
Uchtspringe D 79 A10
Uckange F 186 C1
Uckfield GB 15 F9
Uckro D 80 C5
Uclés E 47 E7
Üçpınar TR 177 B9
Uda RO 160 D5
Udanin PL 81 D10
Udavské SK 145 F4
Udbina HR 156 C4
Udby DK 87 D9
Uddebo S 91 E13
Uddeholm S 97 B10
Uddel NL 183 A7
Uddevalla S 91 C10
Uddheden S 97 C8
Uddington GB 5 D9
Uden NL 16 E5
Udenhout NL 16 E4
Udenisht AL 168 C4
Uderns A 72 B4
Üdersdorf D 21 D7
Udeşti RO 153 B8
Udiča SK 146 C6
Udine I 73 D7
Udorpie PL 85 B13
Üdruma EST 131 D8
Udrycze PL 144 B7
Uebigau D 80 C4
Ueckermünde D 84 C6
Uehlfeld D 75 C8
Uelsen D 17 D7
Uelzen D 83 E9
Uetendorf CH 31 B12
Uetersen D 82 C7
Uettingen D 74 C6
Uetze D 79 B7
Uffculme GB 13 D8
Uffenheim D 75 C7
Uffing am Staffelsee D 72 A3
Uftrungen D 79 C8
Ugāle LV 134 B4
Ugao SRB 163 C9
Ugarana E 40 B6
Uge DK 86 F4
Ugelbølle DK 86 C6
Ugento I 61 D10
Ugerløse DK 87 D9
Uggdal N 94 B2
Uggelheden S 102 E3
Uggelhuse DK 86 C6
Uggerby DK 90 D7
Uggerslev DK 86 D6
Uggiano la Chiesa I 61 C10
Ugijar E 55 F6
Ugine F 31 D9
Üğlen BG 165 C9
Uglev DK 86 B3
Ugljan HR 67 D11
Ugljane HR 157 E6
Ugljevik BIH 157 C11
Ugod H 149 B9
Uğurchin BG 165 C9
Uğurlu TR 171 D9
Uharte-Arakil E 32 E2
Uherské Hradiště CZ 146 C4
Uherský Brod CZ 146 C5
Uhingen D 74 E6
Uhldingen D 27 E11
Uhlířské Janovice CZ 77 C8
Uhlstädt D 79 E9
Uhniv UA 144 C8
Uhtna EST 131 C13
Uhyst D 81 D7
Uig GB 2 K4
Uimaharju FIN 125 E14
Uimila FIN 127 C15
Uitgeest NL 16 C3
Uithoorn NL 16 D3
Uithuizen NL 17 B7
Uivar RO 159 B6
Ujazd PL 141 G1
Ujazd PL 142 F5
Újezd CZ 77 C12
Újezd CZ 146 C5
Újfehértó H 151 B8
Újhartyán H 150 C3
Újkér H 149 B7
Újkígyós H 151 D7
Újléta H 151 C8
Újpetre H 149 E10
Ujście PL 85 D11
Ujsoły PL 147 C8
Újszalonta H 151 D7
Újszász H 150 C5
Újszentiván H 150 E5
Újszentmargita H 151 B7
Újszilvás H 150 C4
Újtikos H 145 H3
Újudvar H 149 C7
Ukhozhany UA 154 A5
Ukkola FIN 125 E14
Ukmergė LT 135 F9
Ukri LV 134 D6
Ula BY 133 F6
Ula TR 181 B8
Ulamiş TR 177 C8
Uland S 103 A14
Ulan-Majorat PL 141 G6
Ulanów PL 144 C5
Ulaş TR 173 B8
Ulassai I 64 D4
Ula Tirso I 64 C2
Ulbjerg DK 86 B4
Ulbroka LV 135 C8
Ulbster GB 3 J10
Ulcinj MNE 163 F7
Uldum DK 86 D5
Ulefoss N 95 D10
Uleila del Campo E 55 E8
Ülenurme EST 131 E13
Ulëz AL 163 F8
Ulfborg DK 86 C2
Ulft NL 16 E6
Ulhówek PL 144 C8
Ulič SK 145 F5
Ulicoten NL 182 C5
Ulieş RO 152 E6
Ulieşti RO 161 D6
Ulila EST 131 E12
Uljanik HR 149 E8
Uljma SRB 159 C7
Ullånger S 107 E14
Ullapool GB 2 K6
Ullared S 87 A11
Ullatti S 116 D7
Ullava FIN 123 C11
Ullbergsträsk S 107 A17
Ulldecona E 42 F4
Ulldemolins E 42 E5
Ullerslev DK 86 E7
Ullervad S 91 B14
Üllés H 150 E4
Ulleskelf GB 11 D9
Ullisjaur S 107 A10
Ullits DK 86 B4
Üllő H 150 C3
Ullsfjord N 111 A18
Ulm D 74 F6
Ulma RO 152 B6
Ulmbach D 74 B5
Ulme P 44 F4
Ulmen D 21 D7
Ulmeni RO 151 C11
Ulmeni RO 161 C9
Ulmeni RO 161 E9
Ulmi RO 161 D6
Ulmu RO 161 D10
Ulmu RO 161 E9
Ulog BIH 157 F9
Uløybukta N 112 D6
Ulricehamn S 91 D13
Ulrichsberg A 76 E5
Ulrichstein D 21 C12
Ulrika S 92 C6
Ulriksberg S 97 B12
Ulriksfors S 106 D9
Ulrum NL 16 B6
Ulsberg N 101 A11
Ulsta GB 3 D14
Ulsted DK 86 A6
Ulsteinvik N 100 B3
Ulstrup DK 86 C5
Ulstrup DK 87 D7
Ulsvåg N 111 D10
Ultrå S 107 E16
Uluabat TR 173 D9
Ulucak TR 177 B9
Ulucak TR 177 C9
Ulukonak TR 181 A7
Ulvåker S 91 C14
Ulvenhout NL 16 E3
Ulverston GB 10 C5
Ulvik N 100 E5
Ulvila FIN 126 C6
Ulvöhamn S 107 E15
Ulvsjön S 102 C7
Ulvsjön S 103 B11
Ulvvik S 103 A14
Ul'yanovka UA 154 A6
Ul'yanovo RUS 136 D5
Umag HR 67 B8
Umberleigh GB 12 D7
Umbertide I 66 F5
Umbrăreşti RO 153 F10
Umbriatico I 61 E7
Umbukta N 108 D8
Umčari SRB 158 D6
Umeå S 122 C4
Umfors S 108 E9
Umgransele S 107 B14
Umhausen A 71 C11
Umin Dol NMK 164 E4
Umka SRB 158 D5
Umkirch D 27 D8
Umljanović HR 156 E5
Ummeljoki FIN 128 D6
Ummern D 79 A7
Umnäs S 109 F11
Ümraniye TR 173 B11
Umurbey TR 172 D6
Umurga LV 135 A9
Uña E 47 D9
Uña de Quintana E 39 D7

Unaja FIN 126 C6
Únanov CZ 77 E10
Unapool GB 2 J6
Unari FIN 117 D15
Unbyn S 118 C7
Uncastillo E 32 F3
Undenäs S 92 B4
Undereidet N 112 D9
Underfossen N 113 C18
Undersåker S 105 E14
Undingen D 27 D11
Undløse DK 87 D9
Undva EST 130 D3
Undy GB 13 B9
Unelanperä FIN 120 F9
Ungerhausen D 71 A10
Ungheni MD 153 C11
Ungheni RO 152 E4
Ungheni RO 160 E5
Ungra RO 152 F6
Unguraș RO 152 C4
Ungureni RO 153 B9
Ungureni RO 153 D10
Ungurpils LV 131 F9
Unhais da Serra P 44 D5
Unhais-o-Velho P 44 D5
Unhošť CZ 76 B6
Uničov CZ 77 C12
Uniejów PL 142 C6
Unieux F 30 E5
Unín SK 146 D4
Unirea RO 152 E3
Unirea RO 155 C1
Unirea RO 155 F3
Unirea RO 159 B10
Unirea RO 159 E11
Unirea RO 161 E11
Unisław PL 138 D5
Unkel D 21 C8
Unken A 73 A6
Unlingen D 71 A9
Unna D 17 E9
Unnaryd S 87 B13
Unnau D 185 C8
Unntorp S 102 D7
Unset N 101 C14
Unsholtet N 101 A14
Unstad N 110 D6
Untamala FIN 122 D9
Untamala FIN 126 D6
Unțeni RO 153 B9
Unterägeri CH 27 F10
Unterammergau D 71 B12
Unterdießen D 71 B11
Untergriesbach D 76 E5
Unterhaching D 75 F10
Unterkulm CH 27 F9
Unterlüß D 83 E8
Untermaßfeld D 75 A7
Untermerzbach D 75 B8
Untermünkheim D 74 D6
Unterneukirchen D 75 F12
Unterpleichfeld D 75 C7
Unterreit D 75 F11
Unterschächen CH 71 D7
Unterschleißheim D 75 F10
Untersiemau D 75 B8
Untersteinach D 75 B10
Unterweißenbach A 77 F7
Unterwössen D 72 A5
Unverre F 24 D5
Upavon GB 13 C11
Upenieki LV 134 C5
Upenieki LV 135 D12
Upesgrīva LV 134 B6
Upgant-Schott D 17 A8
Úpice CZ 77 A10
Upinniemi FIN 127 E11
Uplyme GB 13 D9
Upninkai LT 137 C10
Upper Knockando GB 3 L10
Upperlands GB 4 F3
Upphärad S 91 C11
Uppingham GB 11 F10
Upplanda S 99 B9
Upplands-Väsby S 99 C9
Uppsala S 99 C9
Uppsälje S 97 A11
Uppsete N 100 E5
Uppsjö S 103 C12
Upton upon Severn GB 13 A10
Upyna LT 134 E5
Upyna LT 134 F4
Upytė LT 135 E8
Urafirth GB 3 E14
Urago d'Oglio I 69 B8
Uraiújfalu H 149 B7
Uras I 64 D2
Ura Vajgurore AL 168 C2
Uraz PL 81 D11
Urbach D 21 C9
Urbania I 66 E6
Urbar D 185 D8
Urbe I 37 C9
Urberach D 187 B6
Urbino I 66 E6
Urbisaglia I 67 F7
Urbise F 30 C4
Určice CZ 77 D12
Urda E 46 F5
Urdari RO 160 D2
Urdax-Urdazuli E 32 D2
Urdorf CH 27 F9
Urdos F 32 E4
Urduña E 40 C6
Ure N 110 D6
Urecheni RO 153 C9
Urechești RO 153 E10
Urechești RO 161 B10
Urë e Shtrenjtë AL 163 E8
Urepel F 32 D3
Ureterp NL 16 B6
Urga LV 131 F9
Úrhida H 149 B10
Úri H 150 C4
Uri I 64 B2
Uricani RO 159 C11
Uriménil F 26 D5
Uringe S 93 A11
Uriu RO 152 C4
Urjala FIN 127 C10
Urk NL 16 C5
Ürkmez TR 177 C8
Úrkút H 149 B9
Urla TR 177 C8
Urlați RO 161 D8
Urlingford IRL 9 C7
Urmeniș RO 152 D4
Urmince SK 146 D6
Urnäsch CH 27 F11
Urnieta E 32 D2
Üröm H 150 B3
Urovica SRB 159 E9
Urrea de Gaén E 42 E3
Urrea de Jalón E 41 E9
Urretxu E 32 D1
Urriés E 32 E3
Urros P 45 B6
Urroz E 32 E3
Urrugne F 32 D2
Ursberg D 71 A10
Ursensollen D 75 D10
Urshult S 89 B7
Ursviken S 118 E6
Urszulin PL 141 H8
Urt F 32 D3
Urtenen CH 31 A11
Urtimjaur S 116 E5
Urueña E 39 E9
Ururi I 63 D8
Urville Nacqueville F 23 A8
Urzędów PL 144 B5
Urzica RO 160 F4
Urziceni RO 151 B9
Urziceni RO 161 D9
Urzicuța RO 160 E3
Urzulei I 64 C4
Urzy F 30 A3
Usagre E 51 C7
Ušari BIH 157 C7
Ušće SRB 163 C10
Uschlag (Staufenberg) D 78 D6
Uście Gorlickie PL 145 D3
Uście Solne PL 143 F10
Uscio I 37 C10
Usedom D 84 C5
Usellus I 64 D2
Useras E 48 D4
Ushachy BY 133 F5
Uši LV 130 F5
Usingen D 21 D11
Usini I 64 B2
Usk GB 13 B9
Uskali FIN 125 F14
Uskedal N 94 C3
Üsküdar TR 173 B11
Üsküp TR 167 F8
Uslar D 78 C6
Usma LV 134 B4
Úsov CZ 77 C12
Uspenivka UA 154 E5
Usquert NL 17 B7
Ussana I 64 E3
Ussassai I 64 D3
Usseglio I 31 E11
Ussel F 29 D10
Ussel F 29 F9
Usson-du-Poitou F 29 C7
Usson-en-Forez F 30 E4
Ustaoset N 95 B8
Ustaritz F 32 D3
Ust'-Chorna UA 145 G8
Ust'-Dolyssy RUS 133 D7
Úštěk CZ 80 E6
Uster CH 27 F10
Ustibar BIH 163 B7
Ustica I 58 B3
Ustikotlina BIH 157 E10
Ústí nad Labem CZ 80 E6
Ústí nad Orlicí CZ 77 C10
Ustiprača BIH 157 E11
Ustirama BIH 157 E8
Ustka PL 85 A11
Ust'-Luga RUS 132 B3
Ustou F 33 E8
Ustovo BG 171 A7
Ustrem BG 167 E6
Ustroń PL 147 B7
Ustronie Morskie PL 85 B9
Ustrzyki Dolne PL 145 E6
Ustya UA 154 A5
Ustyluh UA 144 B9
Usurbil E 32 D1
Uszew PL 144 D2
Uszód H 149 C11
Utajärvi FIN 119 E16
Utåker N 94 C3
Utakleiv N 110 D6
Utanede S 103 A12
Utanen FIN 119 E16
Utansjö S 103 A14
Utanskog S 107 E14
Utarp D 17 A8
Utbjoa N 94 C3
Utebo E 41 E10
Utelle F 37 D6
Utena LT 135 F11
Utersum D 82 A4
Uthaug N 104 D7
Uthleben D 79 D8
Uthlede D 17 B11
Utiel E 47 E10
Utne N 94 B5
Utö S 93 B12
Utoropy UA 152 A6
Utrecht NL 16 D4
Utrera E 51 E8
Utrillas E 42 F2
Utrine SRB 150 F4
Utro N 104 C8
Utsjoki FIN 113 D18
Utskor N 110 C8
Uttendorf A 72 B6
Uttendorf A 76 F4
Uttenweiler D 71 A9
Utterbyn S 97 B9
Utterliden S 109 F17
Uttersberg S 97 C14
Uttersjö S 107 D14
Utterslev DK 87 F8
Utti FIN 128 D6
Utting am Ammersee D 71 A12
Uttoxeter GB 11 F8
Utula FIN 129 C9
Utvalnäs S 103 E13
Utvik N 100 C5
Utvorda N 105 B9
Utzedel D 84 C4
Uuemõisa EST 130 D7
Uukuniemi FIN 129 B13
Uulu EST 131 E9
Uura FIN 121 F10
Uurainen FIN 123 E14
Uuro FIN 122 F8
Uusikaarlepyy FIN 122 C9
Uusikartano FIN 126 D7
Uusikaupunki FIN 126 D5
Uusikylä FIN 123 D12
Uusikylä FIN 127 D15
Uusi-Värtsilä FIN 125 F14
Uva FIN 121 E11
Uvac BIH 158 F4
Uvåg N 110 C8
Úvaly CZ 77 B7
Uvanå S 97 B10
Uvdal N 95 B9
Üvecik TR 171 E10
Uvernet-Fours F 36 C5
Uv'jaråtto N 113 D12
Uxbridge GB 15 D8
Uxeau F 30 B5
Üxheim D 21 D7
Uyeasound GB 3 D15
Uza F 32 B3
Užava LV 134 B2
Uzdin SRB 158 C6
Uzel F 22 D6
Uzer F 35 A7
Uzerche F 29 E9
Uzès F 35 B7
Uzhhorod UA 145 F5
Uzhok UA 145 F6
Užice SRB 158 F4
Uzlovoye RUS 136 D5
Uznovë AL 168 C2
Užpaliai LT 135 E11
Uzrechcha BY 133 F3
Uzundzhovo BG 166 F5
Uzunköprü TR 172 B6
Uzunkuyu TR 177 C8
Užventis LT 134 E5

V

Vaadinselkä FIN 115 E5
Vaajakoski FIN 123 F15
Vaajasalmi FIN 124 E7
Vääkiö FIN 121 D12
Vaala FIN 119 E17
Vaalajärvi FIN 117 D16
Vaale D 82 C6
Vaalimaa FIN 128 D8
Vaals NL 20 C6
Vaarakylä FIN 121 C11
Vaarankylä FIN 121 F10
Vaaranniva FIN 121 D11
Vaaraperä FIN 121 C13
Vaaraslahti FIN 123 D17
Väärinmaja FIN 124 G2
Vaas F 24 E3
Vaasa FIN 122 D7
Vaassen NL 16 D5
Väätäiskylä FIN 123 E13
Väätsa EST 131 D10
Vaattojärvi FIN 117 D12
Vabalninkas LT 135 E9
Vabole LV 135 D12
Vabre F 33 C10
Vabres-l'Abbaye F 34 C4
Vác H 150 B3
Văcărești RO 161 D6
Vaccarizzo Albanese I 61 D6
Váchartyán H 150 B3
Vacheresse F 31 C10
Vachlia GR 174 D4
Väckelsång S 89 B7
Vacov CZ 76 D5
Vacqueyras F 35 B8
Vácrátót H 150 B3
Văculești RO 153 B8
Vad RO 152 C3
Vad S 97 B14
Vadakste LV 134 D5
Vadaktai LT 135 E7
Vădastra RO 160 F4
Vădăstrița RO 160 F4
Vaddas gruver N 112 D8
Vădeni RO 155 C1
Väderstad S 92 C5
Vad Foss N 90 B5
Vadheim N 100 D3
Vadla N 94 D4
Vadocondes E 40 E4
Vadokliai LT 135 F8
Vado Ligure I 37 C8
Vadskinn N 111 C11
Vadsø N 114 C7
Vadstena S 92 C5
Vadu Crișului RO 151 D10
Vadu lui Isac MD 155 B2
Vadu Izei RO 145 H8
Vadul lui Vodă MD 154 C4
Vadul Turcului MD 154 B3
Vadum DK 86 A5
Vadu Moldovei RO 153 C8
Vadu Moților RO 151 E10
Vadu Pașii RO 161 C9
Vaduz FL 71 C9
Vadžgirys LT 134 F5
Væggerløse DK 83 A11
Vafaiika GR 171 B7
Vafiochori GR 169 B8
Våg N 94 D2
Vågaholmen N 108 C5
Vågåmo N 101 C10
Vagan BIH 157 D6
Vågan N 111 B14
Vågdalen S 106 D9
Våge N 94 B3
Våge N 94 G6
Vaggatem N 114 E6
Vaggeryd S 92 E4
Vågholmane N 100 A4
Vagia GR 175 C7
Văgiulești RO 159 D11
Vaglia I 66 E3
Vaglio Basilicata I 60 B5
Vagli Sotto I 66 D1
Vagney F 26 D6
Vagnhärad S 93 B11
Vagnsunda S 99 C11
Vagos P 44 C3
Vågseidet N 100 E2
Vägsele S 107 B14
Vågsodden N 108 E3
Vágur FO 2 C3
Vähäjoki FIN 119 B14
Vähäkangas FIN 123 B13
Vähäkyrö FIN 122 D8
Vähäniva FIN 116 B9
Vahanka FIN 123 E13
Vahastu EST 131 D10
Vahenurme EST 131 D8
Vähikkälä FIN 127 D12
Vahojärvi FIN 127 B9
Váhovce SK 146 E5
Vahterpää FIN 127 E15
Vahto FIN 126 D7
Vaiamonte P 44 F6
Vaiano I 66 E3
Vaickūniškės LT 137 D10
Vaida EST 131 C9
Vaidava LV 135 B10
Vaideeni RO 160 C3
Vaidotai LT 137 D11
Vaiges F 23 D11
Vaiguva LT 134 E5
Väike-Maarja EST 131 C12
Väike-Pungerja EST 131 C14
Vaikijaur S 116 E3
Vaikko FIN 125 D11
Vailly-sur-Aisne F 19 F8
Vailly-sur-Sauldre F 25 F8
Vaimastvere EST 131 D12
Väimela EST 131 F14
Vaimõisa EST 131 D8
Vainikkala FIN 129 D9
Vaiņode LV 134 D3
Vainotiškiai LT 134 F7
Vainupea EST 131 B12
Vairano Patenora I 60 A2
Vairano Scalo I 60 A2
Väisälä FIN 121 E11
Vaison-la-Romaine F 35 B9
Vaïssac F 33 B9
Vaišvydava LT 137 D9
Vaivio FIN 125 E12
Vaivre-et-Montoille F 26 E5
Vaja H 145 H5
Vajangu EST 131 C12
Vajdácska H 145 G4
Våje N 90 B4
Våje N 110 D5
Vajkal AL 168 A3
Vajmat S 109 C18
Vajska SRB 157 B11
Vajszló H 149 E9
Vajta H 149 C11
Vakarel BG 165 D8
Vakern S 97 B11
Vakiflar TR 173 B8
Vaklino BG 155 F2
Vaksdal N 94 B3
Vaksevo BG 165 E6
Vaksince NMK 164 E4
Vál H 149 B11
Valada P 44 F3
Vålådalen S 105 E13
Valadares P 38 D3
Valajanaapa FIN 119 C15
Valajaskoski FIN 119 B14
Valaliky SK 145 F3
Valand N 90 C2
Valandovo NMK 169 B8
Vålånger S 103 A14
Valanida GR 169 E7
Valanjou F 23 F10
Valareña E 41 D9
Valåsjø N 101 B10
Valaská SK 147 D9
Valaská Belá SK 146 D6
Valašská Bystřice CZ 146 C6
Valašská Polanka CZ 146 C5
Valašské Klobouky CZ 146 C6
Valašské Meziříčí CZ 146 C5
Välax FIN 127 E14
Valberg F 36 C5
Valberg N 110 D6
Vålberg S 97 D9
Valbiska HR 67 B9
Valbo S 103 E13
Valbom P 44 B3
Valbona E 48 D3
Valbondione I 69 A9
Valbonë AL 163 E8
Valbonnais F 31 F8
Valbonne F 36 D6
Valbuena de Duero E 40 E3
Valča SK 147 C7
Valcabrère F 33 D7
Valcău de Jos RO 151 C10
Vâlcele RO 153 F7
Vâlcele RO 160 E5
Vâlcelele RO 161 C10
Vâlcelele RO 161 E10
Valdagno I 69 B11
Valdahon F 26 F5
Valdaora I 72 C5
Valddak N 113 C14
Valdealgorfa E 42 E3
Valdeblore F 37 C6
Valdecaballeros E 45 F10
Valdecañas de Tajo E 45 E9
Valdecarros E 45 C10
Valdecilla E 40 B4
Valdecuenca E 47 D10
Valdefuentes E 45 F8
Valdeganga E 47 F9
Valdeķl LV 134 C5
Valdelacasa E 45 C9
Valdelacasa de Tajo E 45 E10
Valdelamusa E 51 D6
Valdelinares E 48 D3
Valdemanco del Esteras E 54 B3
Valdemārpils LV 134 B5
Valdemarsvik S 93 C9
Valdemeca E 47 D9
Valdemorillo E 46 C4
Valdemoro E 46 D5
Valdemoro-Sierra E 47 D9
Valdenoches E 47 C6
Valdeobispo E 45 D8
Valdeolivas E 47 C8
Valdepeñas E 55 B6
Valdepeñas de Jaén E 53 A9
Valderas E 39 D9
Val-de-Reuil F 18 F3
Valderice I 58 C2
Valderiès F 33 B10
Valderøy N 100 A4
Valderrobres E 42 F4
Val de Santo Domingo E 46 D4
Valdestillas E 39 F10
Valdetormo E 42 F4
Valdetorres E 51 B7
Valdeverdeja E 45 E10
Valdevimbre E 39 D8
Valdgale LV 134 B5
Valdice CZ 77 B8
Valdidentro I 71 E10
Valdilecha E 47 D6
Val-d'Isère F 31 E10
Valdisotto I 71 E10
Valdivienne F 29 B7
Val-d'Izé F 23 D9
Valdobbiadene I 72 E4
Valdoie F 27 E6
Valdunquillo E 39 D9
Vale GBG 22 B6
Våle N 95 D12
Våle S 103 A8
Valea Adîncă MD 154 A3
Valea Argovei RO 161 E9
Valea Călugărească RO 161 D8
Valea Chioarului RO 151 C11
Valea Ciorii RO 161 D11
Valea Crișului RO 153 F7
Valea Danului RO 160 C5
Valea Doftanei RO 161 C7
Valea Dragului RO 161 E8
Valea Ierii RO 151 D11
Valea Largă RO 152 D4
Valea lui Mihai RO 151 B9
Valea Lungă RO 152 E4
Valea Lungă RO 161 C7
Valea Măcrișului RO 161 D9
Valea Mare MD 153 C11
Valea Mare RO 160 D3
Valea Mare RO 160 D6
Valea Mare RO 160 E4
Valea Mare-Pravăț RO 160 C6
Valea Mărului RO 153 F11
Valea Moldovei RO 153 C8
Valea Nucarilor RO 155 C3
Valea Râmnicului RO 161 C10
Valea Salciei RO 161 C9
Valea Sării RO 153 F9
Valea Seacă RO 153 C9
Valea Seacă RO 153 E10
Valea Stanciului RO 160 F3
Valea Teilor RO 155 C3
Valea Ursului RO 153 D10
Valea Viilor RO 152 E4
Valea Vinului RO 151 B11
Vale da Rosa P 50 E4
Vale das Mós P 44 F4
Vale de Açor P 44 F5
Vale de Açor P 50 D4
Vale de Cambra P 44 C4
Vale de Cavalos P 44 F3
Vale de Espinho P 45 D7
Vale de Estrela P 45 C6
Vale de Figueira P 44 F3
Vale de Lobo P 50 E3
Vale de Prazeres P 44 D6
Vale de Reis P 50 C3
Vale de Salgueiro P 38 E5
Vale de Santarém P 44 F3
Vale do Peso P 44 F5
Válega P 44 C3
Valeggio sul Mincio I 66 B2
Valen N 94 C3
Valença P 38 D2
Valença do Douro P 44 B5
Valençay F 24 F6
Valence F 30 F6
Valence F 33 B7
Valence-d'Albigeois F 33 B10
Valence-sur-Baïse F 33 C6
Valencia E 48 F4
Valencia de Alcántara E 45 F6
Valencia de Don Juan E 39 D8
Valencia de las Torres E 51 C7
Valencia del Mombuey E 51 C5
Valencia del Ventoso E 51 C7
Valenciennes F 19 D8
Văleni RO 153 D11
Văleni RO 160 E5
Vălenii de Munte RO 161 C8
Valensole F 35 C10
Valentano I 62 B1
Valentigney F 27 F6
Valenza I 37 A9
Valenzano I 61 A7
Valenzuela E 53 A8
Valenzuela de Calatrava E 54 B5
Våler N 95 D13
Våler N 101 E15
Valera de Arriba E 47 E8
Valernes F 35 B10
Vales Mortos P 50 D5
Valestrand N 94 A2
Valevåg N 94 C2
Valfabbrica I 66 F6
Valfarta E 42 D3
Valfroicourt F 26 D5
Valfurva I 71 E10
Valga EST 131 F12
Valgalciems LV 134 B5
Valgale LV 134 B4
Valgrisenche I 31 D11
Valgu EST 131 D9
Valguarnera Caropepe I 58 E5
Valgunde LV 134 C7
Valhelhas P 44 D6
Valhermoso E 47 C9
Vålhovd N 101 E12
Välijoki FIN 119 B15
Välikangas FIN 119 B16
Väli-Kannus FIN 123 C11
Valikardhë AL 168 A3
Välikylä FIN 123 C11
Valimi GR 174 C5
Välitalo FIN 117 C16
Văliug RO 159 C9
Väli-Viirre FIN 123 C11
Valjala EST 130 E4
Valjevo SRB 158 E4
Valjok N 113 D16
Valjunquera E 42 F4
Valka LV 131 F12
Valkeajärvi FIN 123 F12
Valkeakoski FIN 127 C11
Valkeakoski FIN 117 E11
Valkeala FIN 128 D6
Valkeiskylä FIN 124 C8
Valkeiskylä FIN 125 D10
Valkenburg NL 183 D7
Valkenswaard NL 16 F4
Valkininkai LT 137 E10
Valkla EST 131 C10
Valko FIN 127 E15
Valkó H 150 B4
Valla S 93 A8
Valla S 107 E10
Valladolid E 39 E10
Valladolises E 56 F2
Vállaj H 151 B9
Vallåkra S 87 D11
Vallargärdet S 97 D10
Vallata I 60 A4
Vallauris F 36 D6
Vallberga S 87 C12
Vallbo S 105 E14
Vallbona d'Anoia E 43 D7
Vallda S 91 E10
Valldal N 100 B6
Vall d'Alba E 48 D4
Valldemossa E 49 E10
Valle E 40 B3
Valle LV 135 C9
Valle N 90 A2
Valle N 90 B6
Valle N 108 B6
Valle Castellana I 62 B5
Vallecorsa I 62 E4
Valle de Abdalajís E 53 C7
Valle de la Serena E 51 B8
Valle de Matamoros E 51 C6
Valle de Santa Ana E 51 C6
Valle di Cadore I 72 D5
Valledolmo I 58 D4
Valledoria I 64 B2
Valleiry F 31 C8
Vallelunga Pratameno I 58 D4
Valle Mosso I 68 B5
Vallen S 107 D11
Vallen S 118 F6
Vallenca E 47 D10
Vallendar D 185 D8
Vallentuna S 99 C10
Valleräs S 102 E6
Valleraugue F 35 B6
Vallermosa I 64 E2
Vallerotonda I 62 D5
Vallersund N 104 D7
Vallervatnet N 105 B15
Vallet F 23 F9
Valley D 72 A4
Valley GB 10 E2
Vallfogona de Riucorb E 42 D6
Vallières F 29 D10
Vallioniemi FIN 121 B12
Vallmoll E 42 E6
Valløby DK 87 E10
Vallo della Lucania I 60 C4
Vallo di Nera I 62 B3
Valloire F 31 E9
Vallombrosa I 66 E4
Vallon-en-Sully F 29 B11
Vallon-Pont-d'Arc F 35 B7
Vallorbe CH 31 B9
Vallorcine F 31 C10
Vallouise F 31 F9
Vallrun S 105 D16
Valls E 42 E6
Vallsbo S 103 E12
Vallsjön S 103 A11
Vallsta S 103 C11
Vallstena S 93 D13
Vallvik S 103 D13
Valmadrera I 69 B7
Valmadrid E 41 F10
Valmen N 101 D15
Valmiera LV 131 F10
Valmiermuiža LV 131 F10
Valmojado E 46 D4
Valmont F 18 E2
Valmontone I 62 D3
Valmorel F 31 E9
Valmy F 25 B12
Valnes N 108 B7
Valognes F 23 A9
Valongo P 44 B4
Valongo P 44 F5
Válor E 55 F6
Valoria la Buena E 40 E2
Valøy N 105 B9
Valøy N 105 C11
Valpaços P 38 E5
Valpalmas E 41 D10
Valpelline I 31 D11
Valperga I 68 C4
Valpovo HR 149 E10
Valpperi FIN 126 D7
Valras-Plage F 34 D5
Valréas F 35 B8
Valros F 34 D5
Vals CH 71 D8
Valsavarenche I 31 D11
Vålse DK 87 F9
Valseca E 46 B4
Valsequillo E 51 C9
Valsgård DK 86 B5
Valsgarth GB 3 D15
Valshed S 103 E9
Valsinni I 61 C6
Valsjöbyn S 105 C16
Valsjön S 103 B11
Valška SRB 158 E6
Valskog S 97 D14
Vals-les-Bains F 35 A7
Valsøybotn N 104 E5
Välsta S 103 C13
Valstagna I 72 E4
Val-Suzon F 26 F2
Valtablado del Río E 47 C8
Valtero GR 169 B9
Valtesiniko GR 174 D5
Valtice CZ 77 E11
Valtiendas E 40 F4
Valtierra E 41 D8
Valtimo FIN 125 C11
Valtola FIN 128 C7
Valtopina I 62 A3
Valtos GR 171 A10
Valtotopi GR 169 C10
Valtournenche I 68 B4
Valtura HR 67 C8
Valu lui Traian RO 155 E2
Valun HR 67 C9
Väluste EST 131 E11
Valverde de Burguillos E 51 C6
Valverde de Júcar E 47 E8
Valverde de la Virgen E 39 C8
Valverde del Camino E 51 D6
Valverde de Leganés E 51 B6
Valverde del Fresno E 45 D7
Valverde de Llerena E 51 C8
Valverde del Majano E 46 C4
Valverde de Mérida E 51 B7
Valvika N 108 B8
Valvträsk S 118 B7
Valyra GR 174 E4
Vama RO 145 H7
Vama RO 153 B7
Vama Buzăului RO 161 B7
Vamberk CZ 77 B10
Vamdrup DK 86 E4
Våmhus S 102 D7
Vamlingbo S 93 F12
Vammala FIN 127 C8
Vammen DK 86 B5
Vamos GR 178 E7
Vámosmikola H 147 F7
Vámospércs H 151 B8
Vámosújfalu H 145 G3
Vampula FIN 126 C8
Vamvakofyto GR 169 B9
Vamvakou GR 169 F7
Vanaja FIN 127 D12
Vana-Koiola EST 131 F14
Vânători RO 152 E5
Vânători RO 153 C9
Vânători RO 153 F10
Vânători RO 155 B2
Vânători RO 159 E10
Vânătorii Mici RO 161 E7
Vânători-Neamț RO 153 C8
Vanault-les-Dames F 25 C12
Vana-Vigala EST 131 D8
Vana-Võidu EST 131 E11
Váncsod H 151 C8
Vanda FIN 127 E12
Vandel DK 86 D4
Vandellós E 42 E5
Vandenesse F 30 B4
Vandenesse-en-Auxois F 25 F12
Vandœvre-lès-Nancy F 186 D1
Vandoies I 72 C4
Vändra EST 131 D10
Vändträsk S 118 C6
Vandzene LV 134 B5
Vandžiogala LT 135 F7
Vāne LV 134 C5
Väne-Åsaka S 91 C11
Vänersborg S 91 C11
Vañes E 40 C3
Vang N 101 D9
Vånga S 92 B7
Vangaži LV 135 B9
Vänge S 93 E13
Vängel S 107 D10
Vangshamn N 111 B15
Vangshylla N 105 D10
Vangsnes N 100 D5
Vangsvik N 111 B14
Vanha-Kihlanki FIN 117 C10
Vanhakylä FIN 122 F7
Vänjaurbäck S 107 C15
Vänjaurträsk S 107 C15
Vânjuleț RO 159 E10
Vânju Mare RO 159 E10
Vannareid N 112 C4
Vännäs S 122 C3
Vännäsberget S 118 B9
Vännäsby S 122 C3
Vannavalen N 112 C4
Vånne N 90 B2
Vannes F 22 E6
Vannvåg N 112 C4
Vannvikan N 104 D8
Vänö FIN 126 F7
Vansbro S 97 A11
Vanse N 94 F5
Vänsjö S 103 C9
Vantaa FIN 127 E12
Vanttausjärvi FIN 119 B17
Vanttauskoski FIN 119 B17
Vanvey F 25 E12
Vanyarc H 147 F8
Vanzone I 68 B5
Vaour F 33 B9
Vápenná CZ 77 B12
Vaplan S 105 E16
Vaqueiros P 50 E4
Vara EST 131 D13
Vara S 91 C12
Vara del Rey E 47 F8
Varades F 23 F9
Vărădia RO 159 C8
Vărădia de Mureș RO 151 E9
Varages F 35 C10
Varaire F 33 B9
Varajärvi FIN 119 B13
Varajoki FIN 121 F14
Varakļāni LV 135 C13
Varallo I 68 B5
Varangerbotn N 114 C5
Varano de'Melegari I 69 D8
Varapayeva BY 133 F2
Varapodio I 59 C8
Vărăști RO 161 E8
Văratec RO 153 C8
Varaždin HR 149 D6
Varaždinske Toplice HR 149 D6
Varazze I 37 C9
Varberg S 87 A10
Vărbilău RO 161 C7
Varbla EST 130 E7
Varbó H 145 G2
Varbola EST 131 C8
Varces-Allières-et-Risset F 31 E8
Vârciorog RO 151 D9
Varda GR 174 C3
Vardali GR 174 A5
Varde DK 86 D2
Vardim BG 161 F6
Vardište BIH 158 F3
Vårdö FIN 99 B14
Vardø N 114 C10
Várdomb H 149 D11
Varejoki FIN 119 B13
Varekil S 91 C10
Varel D 17 B10
Varėna LT 137 E10
Varengeville-sur-Mer F 18 E2
Varenna I 69 A7
Varennes-en-Argonne F 19 F11
Varennes-St-Sauveur F 31 C7
Varennes-sur-Allier F 30 C3
Varennes-Vauzelles F 30 A3
Vareš BIH 157 D9
Varese I 69 B6
Varese Ligure I 37 C11
Varetz F 29 E8
Vârfu Câmpului RO 153 B8
Vârfuri RO 161 C7
Vârfurile RO 151 E10
Vårgårda S 91 C12
Vărgata RO 152 D5
Vârghiș RO 153 E7
Vargön S 91 C11
Vargträsk S 107 C15
Varhaug N 94 E3
Vari GR 175 D8
Vari GR 176 E4
Variaș RO 151 E6
Varik NL 183 B6
Variku EST 130 C7
Varilhes F 33 D9
Varimbombi GR 175 C8
Varín SK 147 C7
Väring S 91 B14
Variņi LV 135 B12
Variskylä FIN 121 F9
Varislahti FIN 125 E11
Varistaipale FIN 125 E11
Varjakka FIN 119 E14
Varjisträsk S 109 D18
Varkaliai LT 134 E3
Varkaus FIN 125 F9
Vārkava LV 135 D13
Varkhi BY 133 E7
Vârlezi RO 153 F11
Varlosen (Niemetal) D 78 D6
Vārme LV 134 C4
Värmlandsbro S 91 A13
Varna BG 167 C9
Varna I 72 C4
Varna SRB 158 D4
Värnamo S 88 A6
Värnäs S 97 B9
Varnavas GR 175 C8
Varnhem S 91 C14
Varniai LT 134 E4
Varnja EST 131 E14
Varnsdorf CZ 81 E7
Varntresken N 108 E7
Varnyany BY 137 D13
Väröbacka S 87 A10

Wielichowo PL 81 B10
Wieliczka PL 143 G9
Wieliczki PL 136 F6
Wielka Wieś PL 143 F8
Wielkie Oczy PL 144 C7
Wielki Klincz PL 138 B5
Wielopole Skrzyńskie PL 143 G12
Wielowieś PL 142 E6
Wielsbeke B 182 D2
Wieluń PL 142 D6
Wiemersdorf D 83 C7
Wien A 77 F10
Wienerbruck A 77 G8
Wiener Neustadt A 77 G10
Wieniawa PL 141 H3
Wieniec PL 138 E6
Wienrode D 79 C8
Wiepke D 79 A9
Wieprz PL 147 B8
Wieprz PL 147 B8
Wiercień Duży PL 141 F7
Wierden NL 17 D7
Wieren D 83 E9
Wieringerwerf NL 16 C4
Wiernsheim D 187 D6
Wieruszów PL 142 D5
Wierzawice PL 144 C5
Wierzbica PL 141 H4
Wierzbica PL 141 H8
Wierzbica Górna PL 142 D4
Wierzbijcin PL 85 C8
Wierzbinek PL 138 F6
Wierzbnik PL 142 E3
Wierzbno PL 139 F12
Wierzbowa PL 81 D9
Wierzchlas PL 142 D6
Wierzchosławice PL 138 E5
Wierzchosławice PL 143 F10
Wierzchowo PL 85 C11
Wierzchowo PL 85 D10
Wierzchucino PL 138 A5
Wies A 148 C4
Wiesa D 80 E3
Wiesau D 75 C11
Wiesbaden D 21 D10
Wieselburg A 77 F8
Wiesen A 149 A6
Wiesen CH 71 D9
Wiesen D 74 B5
Wiesenau D 81 B7
Wiesenburg D 79 B11
Wiesenfelden D 75 D12
Wiesensteig D 187 D8
Wiesent D 75 D11
Wiesenthau D 75 C9
Wiesentheid D 75 C7
Wiesloch D 21 F11
Wiesmath A 148 A6
Wiesmoor D 17 B9
Wieszowa PL 142 F6
Wietmarschen D 17 C8
Wietze D 78 A6
Wietzen D 17 C12
Wietzendorf D 83 E7
Wiewiórczyn PL 143 C7
Wigan GB 10 D6
Wiggensbach D 71 B10
Wigierska Górka PL 147 B8
Wigliniec PL 81 D8
Wigmore GB 13 A9
Wigorzewo PL 136 E4
Wigorzyno PL 85 C9
Wigrów PL 139 F13
Wigrzynice PL 81 B8
Wigrzynowo PL 139 F9
Wigston GB 11 F9
Wigton GB 5 F10
Wigtown GB 5 F8
Wijchen NL 16 E5
Wijewo PL 81 C10
Wijhe NL 183 A8
Wijk aan Zee NL 16 D3
Wijk bij Duurstede NL 16 E4
Wijk en Aalburg NL 183 B6
Wil CH 27 F11
Wilamowice PL 147 B8
Wilczjta PL 139 B8
Wilczogóra PL 138 F5
Wilczyn PL 138 F5
Wildalpen A 73 A10
Wildau D 80 B5
Wildberg D 27 C10
Wildberg D 83 E13
Wildberg D 84 C4
Wildeck-Richelsdorf D 79 E7
Wildendürnbach A 77 E10
Wildenfels D 79 E12
Wildeshausen D 17 C10
Wildflecken D 74 B6
Wildon A 148 C5
Wildpoldsried D 71 B10
Wildshut A 76 F3
Wilga PL 141 G4
Wilhelminadorp NL 183 C6
Wilhelmsburg A 77 F9
Wilhelmsburg D 84 C5
Wilhelmsdorf D 27 E11
Wilhelmshaven D 17 A10
Wilkau-Haßlau D 79 E12
Wilkinstown IRL 7 E9
Wilkołaz Pierwszy PL 144 A5
Wilków PL 141 H5
Wilków PL 142 D4
Wilkowice PL 147 B8
Wilkowo PL 81 B8
Willand GB 13 D8
Willebadessen D 17 E12
Willebroek B 19 B9
Willemstad NL 16 E2
Willich D 17 F7
Willingdon GB 15 F9
Willingen (Upland) D 17 F11
Willingshausen D 21 C12
Willisau CH 27 F9
Williton GB 13 C8
Willstätt D 27 C8
Wilmersdorf D 84 D5
Wilmslow GB 11 E7
Wilnis NL 182 A5
Wilnsdorf D 21 C10
Wilp NL 183 A8
Wilsdruff D 80 D5
Wilsickow D 84 D5
Wilster D 82 C6
Wilsum D 17 C7
Wiltersdorf A 77 E11
Wiltingen D 21 E7
Wilton GB 13 C11
Wiltz L 20 E5
Wimblington GB 11 F12
Wimborne Minster GB 13 D11
Wimereux F 15 F12
Wimmelburg D 79 C10
Wimmis CH 70 D5
Wimpassing A 148 A6
Wincanton GB 13 C10
Winchburgh GB 5 D10
Winchelsea GB 15 F10
Wincheringen D 186 B1
Winchester GB 13 C12
Wincrange L 20 D5
Winda PL 136 E3
Windach D 71 A12
Windeby D 83 B7
Windermere GB 10 C6
Windesheim D 21 E9
Windhagen D 21 C8
Windigsteig A 77 E8
Windischeschenbach D 75 C11
Windischgarsten A 73 A9
Windorf D 76 E4
Windsbach D 75 D8
Windsor GB 15 E7
Wingate GB 5 F14
Wingene B 19 B7
Wingen-sur-Moder F 27 C7
Winklarn D 75 D11
Winkleigh GB 13 D7
Winklern A 73 C6
Winklern bei Oberwölz A 73 B9
Winnenden D 27 C11
Winnert D 82 B6
Winnica PL 139 E10
Winningen D 79 C9
Winningen D 185 D8
Winnweiler D 186 B4
Winschoten NL 17 B8
Winsen (Aller) D 83 E7
Winsen (Luhe) D 83 D8
Winsford GB 10 E6
Wińsko PL 81 D11
Winslow GB 15 D7
Winssen NL 183 B7
Winston GB 11 B8
Winsum NL 16 B5
Winterberg D 21 B11
Winterbourne Abbas GB 13 D9
Winterfeld D 83 E10
Winterswijk NL 17 E7
Winterthur CH 27 E10
Winterton GB 11 D10
Winton GB 11 C7
Wintrich D 185 E6
Wintzenheim F 27 D7
Winwick GB 15 C8
Winzenburg D 78 C6
Winzer D 76 E4
Wipperdorf D 79 D8
Wipperfürth D 21 B8
Wippra Kurort D 79 C9
Wirdumer (Wirdum) D 17 B8
Wirges D 185 D8
Wirksworth GB 11 E8
Wirsberg D 75 B10
Wisbech GB 11 F12
Wischhafen D 17 A12
Wishaw GB 5 D9
Wiskitki PL 141 F2
Wisła PL 147 B7
Wiślica PL 143 F10
Wismar D 83 C10
Wiśniew PL 141 F6
Wiśniewo PL 139 D9
Wiśniowa PL 144 D1
Wiśniowa PL 144 D4
Wissant F 15 F12
Wissembourg F 27 B8
Wissen D 21 C9
Wissenkerke NL 16 E1
Wistedt D 82 D7
Wisznia Mała PL 81 D12
Wisznice PL 141 G8
Witaszyce PL 142 C4
Witham GB 15 D10
Witheridge GB 13 D7
Withernsea GB 11 D12
Witkowo PL 85 D8
Witkowo PL 138 F4
Witley GB 15 E7
Witmarsum NL 16 B4
Witney GB 13 B12
Witnica PL 84 E6
Witnica PL 85 E7
Witonia PL 143 B7
Witosław PL 85 D12
Witry-lès-Reims F 19 F9
Wittdün D 82 A4
Witten D 17 F8
Wittenbach CH 27 F11
Wittenberge D 83 E11
Wittenburg D 83 C10
Wittenförden D 83 C10
Wittenhagen D 84 B4
Wittenheim F 27 E7
Wittibreut D 76 F3
Wittichenau D 80 D6
Wittighausen D 74 C6
Wittingen D 83 E9
Wittlich D 21 E7
Wittmar D 79 B8
Wittmund D 17 A9
Wittstock D 83 D12
Witzenhausen D 78 D6
Witzin D 83 C11
Witzwort D 82 B5
Wiveliscombe GB 13 C8
Wivenhoe GB 15 D10
Wiżajny PL 136 E6
Wizernes F 18 C5
Wizna PL 140 D6
Władysławów PL 142 B5
Władysławowo PL 138 A5
Wleń PL 81 D9
Włocławek PL 138 E7
Włodawa PL 141 G9
Włodzienin PL 142 F4
Włodzimierzów PL 143 D8
Włostów PL 143 E11
Włoszakowice PL 81 C10
Włoszczowa PL 143 E8
Wöbbelin D 83 D11
Woburn GB 15 D7
Wodynie PL 141 F5
Wodzierady PL 143 C7
Wodzisław PL 143 E9
Wodzisław Śląski PL 142 F5
Woensdrecht NL 182 C4
Woerden NL 16 D3
Wœrth F 27 C8
Wohlen CH 27 F9
Wohlen CH 31 B11
Wohlmirstedt D 79 D9
Wohltorf D 83 C8
Wöhrden D 82 B6
Wohyń PL 141 G7
Woippy F 26 B5
Wojaszówka PL 144 D4
Wojcieszków PL 141 G6
Wojcieszów PL 81 E9
Wójcin PL 138 E5
Wojkowice PL 143 F7
Wójnicz PL 143 G10
Wojnowo PL 138 D4
Wojsławice PL 144 B8
Woking GB 15 E7
Wokingham GB 15 E7
Wola PL 138 E7
Wola Mołodycka PL 144 C6
Wola Mysłowska PL 141 G5
Wolanów PL 141 H3
Wola-Rjbkowska PL 141 G5
Wola Uhruska PL 141 H9
Wola Wierzbowska PL 139 E10
Wolbórz PL 141 H1
Wolbrom PL 143 F8
Wołczyn PL 142 D5
Woldegk D 84 D5
Woldendorp NL 17 B8
Wolfach D 27 D9
Wolfegg D 71 B9
Wolfen D 79 C11
Wolfenbüttel D 79 B8
Wolfenschiessen CH 71 D6
Wölfersheim D 21 D11
Wolfhagen D 17 F12
Wölfis D 79 E8
Wolfpassing A 77 F8
Wolfratshausen D 72 A3
Wolfsberg A 73 C10
Wolfsburg D 79 B8
Wolfstein D 21 E9
Wolfurt A 71 C9
Wolgast D 84 B5
Wolhusen CH 70 C6
Wolin PL 84 C7
Wólka PL 139 E7
Wólka PL 141 H7
Wólka Dobryńska PL 141 F8
Wolkersdorf A 77 F11
Wollbach D 75 B7
Wollerau CH 27 F10
Wolmirstedt D 79 B10
Wolnzach D 75 E10
Wołomin PL 139 F11
Woloskowola PL 141 H8
Wołów PL 81 D11
Wolpertshausen D 74 D6
Wolpertswende D 71 B9
Wolphaartsdijk NL 182 B3
Wölpinghausen D 17 D12
Wolsingham GB 5 F13
Wolsztyn PL 81 B10
Woltersdorf D 80 B4
Woltersdorf D 83 E10
Wolvega NL 16 C6
Wolverhampton GB 11 F7
Wombwell GB 11 D9
Wommelgem B 19 B10
Wommels NL 16 B5
Wonfurt D 75 B7
Wonsees D 75 C9
Woodbridge GB 15 C11
Woodcote GB 13 B12
Woodford IRL 6 F6
Woodhall Spa GB 11 E11
Woodland GB 5 F13
Woodley GB 15 E7
Woodstock GB 13 B12
Woodton GB 15 C11
Woodtown IRL 7 E9
Wool GB 13 D10
Wooler GB 5 D12
Wootton Bassett GB 13 B11
Worb CH 31 B12
Worbis D 79 D7
Worcester GB 13 A10
Wördern A 77 F10
Worfield GB 11 F7
Wörgl A 72 B5
Workington GB 5 F9
Worksop GB 11 E9
Workum NL 16 C4
Wörlitz D 79 C11
Wormeldange L 20 E6
Wormerveer NL 16 D3
Wormhout F 18 C5
Worms D 21 E10
Worpswede D 17 B11
Wörrstadt D 21 E10
Wörschach A 73 A9
Wortel B 182 C5
Wörth A 73 B6
Worth GB 15 E8
Wörth am Main D 187 B7
Wörth am Rhein D 27 B9
Worthing GB 15 F8
Woudenberg NL 183 A6
Woudrichem NL 16 E3
Woudsend NL 16 C5
Woustviller F 27 B7
Wouw NL 16 E2
Woźniki PL 143 E7
Wragby GB 11 E11
Wrangle GB 11 E12
Wrecsam GB 10 E6
Wrjczyca Wielka PL 143 E6
Wredenhagen D 83 D13
Wrelton GB 11 C10
Wremen D 17 A11
Wrestedt D 83 E9
Wrexham GB 10 E6
Wriedel D 83 D8
Wriezen D 84 E6
Wrist D 82 C7
Wróblew PL 142 C6
Wrocław PL 81 D12
Wrohm D 82 B6
Wronki PL 85 E10
Wronki PL 136 E5
Wrotnów PL 139 E13
Wrząielka PL 142 B6
Wrzelowiec PL 144 A4
Wrzeście PL 85 A12
Września PL 85 F13
Wrzosowo PL 85 B9
Wschowa PL 81 C10
Wulfen D 79 C10
Wulfersdorf D 83 D12
Wülfershausen an der Saale D 75 B7
Wulfsen D 83 D8
Wulften D 79 C7
Wulkau D 83 E12
Wullersdorf A 77 E10
Wundschuh A 148 C4
Wünnenberg D 17 E11
Wünsdorf D 80 B4
Wunsiedel D 75 B11
Wunstorf D 78 B5
Wuppertal D 17 F8
Wurmlingen D 27 D10
Würselen D 20 C6
Wurzbach D 75 B10
Würzburg D 74 C6
Wurzen D 79 D12
Wüstenrot D 27 B11
Wusterhausen D 83 E12
Wusterhusen D 84 B5
Wustermark D 79 A12
Wusterwitz D 79 B11
Wustrau-Altfriesack D 84 E3
Wustrow D 83 E10
Wustrow D 84 D3
Wustrow D 83 B12
Wutha D 79 E7
Wutöschingen D 27 E9
Wuustwezel B 16 F3
Wyczechy PL 85 C12
Wydminy PL 136 F5
Wye GB 15 E10
Wygoda PL 143 E7
Wygon PL 85 D9
Wyhl D 27 D8
Wyk auf Föhr D 82 A5
Wylatowo PL 138 E4
Wylye GB 13 C11
Wymondham GB 15 B11
Wyre Piddle GB 13 A10
Wyrozjby-Konaty PL 141 F6
Wyry PL 143 F6
Wyryki-Połód PL 141 G8
Wyrzysk PL 85 D12
Wyśmierzyce PL 141 G3
Wysoka PL 85 D12
Wysoka PL 85 E8
Wysoka Kamieńska PL 85 C7
Wysokie PL 136 F6
Wysokie PL 144 B6
Wysokie Mazowieckie PL 141 E7
Wysowa PL 145 E3
Wyszanów PL 142 D5
Wyszki PL 141 E7
Wyszków PL 139 E11
Wyszogród PL 139 F9
Wyszyny PL 85 E11
Wythall GB 13 A11
Wytyczno PL 141 H8

X

Xanceda E 38 B3
Xanten D 17 E6
Xanthi GR 171 B7
Xarrë AL 168 E3
Xátiva E 56 D3
Xeraco E 56 C4
Xeresa E 56 C4
Xermade E 38 B4
Xerta E 42 F5
Xertigny F 26 D5
Xifiani GR 169 C7
Xino Nero GR 169 C6
Xinzo de Limia E 38 D4
Xirivella E 48 F4
Xirochori GR 174 D4
Xirokampi GR 174 F5
Xirokampo GR 177 E8
Xiropotamos GR 170 B6
Xixón E 39 A8
Xonrupt-Longemer F 27 D6
Xove E 38 A4
Xunqueira de Ambía E 38 D4
Xylagani GR 171 C8
Xylokastro GR 175 C6
Xyloupoli GR 169 C9

Y

Yablanitsa BG 165 C9
Yablanovo BG 167 D7
Yabluniv UA 152 A5
Yabŭlchevo BG 167 D8
Yabŭlkovo BG 166 E4
Yağci TR 173 C7
Yağcilar TR 173 F9
Yağcili TR 173 F8
Yagoda BG 166 D5
Yakimovo BG 160 F2
Yakoruda BG 165 E8
Yakovo BG 169 A9
Yaliçiftlik TR 173 D10
Yalikavak TR 177 E9
Yaliköy TR 173 B9
Yalova TR 171 D10
Yambol BG 167 E7
Yamkino RUS 132 F5
Yamm RUS 132 E3
Yampil' UA 154 A2
Yangi TR 181 C9
Yanguas E 41 D7
Yanikağil TR 173 B8
Yaniskoski RUS 114 F5
Yankavichy BY 133 E5
Yankovo BG 167 C8
Yantarnyy RUS 139 A8
Yapildak TR 172 D6
Yaraş TR 181 B8
Yareva BY 135 F13
Yarlovo BG 165 E7
Yarm GB 11 B9
Yarmouth GB 13 D12
Yarnton GB 13 B12
Yarove UA 154 E4
Yarrow GB 5 D10
Yasen BG 165 C10
Yasen' UA 145 F9
Yasenkovo BG 167 B7
Yasenovets BG 161 F9
Yasinya UA 152 A4
Yas'ky UA 154 D6
Yasna Polyana BG 167 E9
Yasnoye RUS 134 F3
Yassiören TR 173 B10
Yasski RUS 132 F7
Yatağan TR 181 B8
Yate GB 13 B10
Yatova E 48 F3
Yatton GB 13 C9
Yavora UA 145 E7
Yavoriv UA 144 D7
Yavoriv UA 152 A5
Yaxley GB 11 F11
Yaylagöne TR 172 C6
Yazibaşl TR 177 C9
Yaziköy TR 181 C6
Yazna BY 133 F4
Yazvina BY 133 F7
Ybbs an der Donau A 77 F8
Ybbsitz A 77 G7
Ychoux F 32 B4
Ydby DK 86 B2
Ydes F 29 E10
Ydra GR 175 E7
Ydrefors S 92 D7
Y Drenewydd GB 10 F5
Yeadon GB 11 D8
Yealmpton GB 12 E7
Yebra E 47 D7
Yebra de Basa E 32 F5
Yecla E 56 D2
Yecla de Yeltes E 45 C8
Yedy BY 133 F2
Yémeda E 47 E9
Yemişendere TR 181 B9
Yenice TR 171 C10
Yenice TR 173 D7
Yenice TR 173 D9
Yenice TR 181 B8
Yeniçiftlik TR 173 B8
Yeniçiftlik TR 173 D7
Yeniçiftlik TR 177 C9
Yenifoça TR 177 B8
Yenihisar TR 177 E9
Yeniköy TR 172 D6
Yeniköy TR 173 B6
Yeniköy TR 173 E8
Yeniköy TR 177 B9
Yeniköy TR 177 B10
Yeniköy TR 177 C9
Yeniköy TR 177 D10
Yeniköy TR 177 E9
Yeniköy TR 181 B8
Yenimuhacirköy TR 172 C6
Yenişakran TR 177 B9
Yenne F 31 D8
Yeovil GB 13 D9
Yepes E 46 E5
Yerkesik TR 181 B8
Yerseke NL 16 F2
Yershovo RUS 132 F3
Yerville F 18 E2
Yesa E 32 E3
Yeşilsirt TR 173 B7
Yeşilyurt TR 181 B8
Yeste E 55 C8
Yevtodiya UA 154 B4
Yezyaryshcha BY 133 E7
Y Fenni GB 13 B8
Ygos-St-Saturnin F 32 C4
Ygrande F 30 B2
Ykspihlaja FIN 123 C10
Ylakiai LT 134 D3
Yläkŏngäs FIN 113 D17
Ylä-Luosta FIN 125 D11
Ylämaa FIN 129 D9
Ylämylly FIN 125 E13
Yläne FIN 126 D7
Ylä-Valtimo FIN 125 C11
Ylihärmä FIN 122 D9
Yli-li FIN 119 D15
Ylijärvi FIN 128 D8
Yli-Kärppä FIN 119 C15
Ylikiiminki FIN 119 D16
Yli-Körkkö FIN 119 B16
Ylikulma FIN 127 E9
Yli-Kurki FIN 121 D10
Ylikylä FIN 115 E2
Ylikylä FIN 117 E15
Ylikylä FIN 123 D12
Ylikylä FIN 123 E10
Ylikylä FIN 125 C12
Yli-Kyrö FIN 117 B12
Yli-Lesti FIN 123 D13
Yli-Liakka FIN 119 C12
Yli-Livo FIN 120 C9
Yli-Muonio FIN 117 B10
Yli-Nampa FIN 117 E16
Ylinenjärvi S 117 E10
Yli-Olhava FIN 119 C15
Ylipää FIN 119 E12
Ylipää FIN 119 E13
Ylipää FIN 119 E13
Ylipää FIN 119 E14
Ylipää FIN 119 E16
Ylipää FIN 119 F13
Ylipää FIN 123 C14
Ylipää FIN 123 D11
Yli-Paakkola FIN 119 B13
Yli-Siurua FIN 119 C17
Ylistaro FIN 122 E9
Yli-Tannila FIN 119 D16
Ylitornio FIN 119 B11
Yli-Utos FIN 120 E8
Yli-Valli FIN 123 F9
Ylivieska FIN 123 B13
Yli-Vuotto FIN 119 E17
Ylläsjärvi FIN 117 C12
Ylöjärvi FIN 127 B10
Ylönkyla FIN 127 E9
Ylvingen N 108 E3
Ymonville F 24 D6
Yngsjö S 88 D6
Yoğuntaş TR 167 F8
Yolageldi TR 173 A6
Yonkovo BG 161 F9
York GB 11 D9
Youghal IRL 9 E7
Yovkovo BG 155 F2
Yoxford GB 15 C12
Ypäjä FIN 127 D9
Ypäjänkylä FIN 127 D9
Ypati GR 174 B5
Yport F 18 E1
Yppäri FIN 119 F12
Ypsos GR 168 E2
Ypyä FIN 123 C13
Yrittäperä FIN 121 D10
Yrttivaara S 116 E7
Ysane S 88 C7
Ysbyty Ystwyth GB 13 A7
Yset N 101 A12
Ysselsteyn NL 183 C7
Yssingeaux F 30 E5
Ystad S 87 E13
Ystalyfera GB 13 B7
Ytre Arna N 94 B2
Ytre Årnes N 111 B15
Ytre Billefjord N 113 C15
Ytre Kjæs N 113 B16
Ytre Sandvik N 113 C15
Ytterån S 105 E16
Ytteräng S 105 D14
Ytterberg S 102 B7
Ytter-Busjö S 107 B15
Ytteresse FIN 123 C9
Ytterhogdal S 102 B8
Ytterjeppo FIN 122 D9
Yttermalung S 102 E6
Yttersta S 118 D6
Ytterträsk S 118 F4
Ytterturingen S 103 B9
Yttervik S 109 E10
Yttre Lansjärv S 116 E8
Yukaribey TR 177 A9
Yukarikizilca TR 177 C9
Yukhavichy BY 133 D5
Yuncler E 46 D5
Yuncos E 46 D5
Yundola BG 165 E8
Yunquera E 53 C7
Yunquera de Henares E 47 C6
Yuper BG 161 F8
Yuratsishki BY 137 E12
Yuravichy BY 133 E5
Yürücekler TR 173 E10
Yürük TR 173 C7
Yutz F 20 F6
Yuzhnyy RUS 136 D2
Yverdon CH 31 B10
Yvetot F 18 E2
Yvignac F 23 D7
Yvoir B 19 D10
Yvoire F 31 C9
Yvonand CH 31 B10
Yxnerum S 93 C8
Yxsjö S 107 C13
Yxsjöberg S 97 B12
Yxskaftkälen S 106 D8
Yzeure F 30 B3
Yzeures-sur-Creuse F 29 B7

Z

Zaamslag NL 182 C3
Zaandam NL 16 D3
Zaazyer"ye BY 133 F5
Zăbala RO 153 F8
Žabalj SRB 158 C5
Žabari SRB 159 E7
Zabeltitz-Treugeböhla D 80 D5
Žabia Wola PL 141 F3
Zabica BIH 162 D5
Zabiče SLO 67 A9
Zabiele PL 139 D12
Zabierzów PL 143 F8
Ząbki PL 141 F4
Ząbkowice Śląskie PL 81 E11
Zablaće SRB 158 D4
Zablaće SRB 158 F5
Zableće BIH 157 D6
Žabljak MNE 163 C7
Zabłudów PL 140 D8
Žabno HR 149 E7
Żabno PL 143 F10
Žabno PL 144 B6
Zabok HR 148 D5
Žabokreky SK 147 C7
Žabokreky nad Nitrou SK 146 D6
Zabolova LV 133 A2
Zabór PL 81 C9
Zabor"ye BY 133 E6
Żabów PL 85 D7
Żabowo PL 85 C8
Zăbrani RO 151 E8
Zabrđe BIH 157 C10
Zábřeh CZ 77 C11
Zăbriceni MD 153 A10
Zabrze PL 142 F6
Zabŭrdo BG 165 F10
Zabuzhzhya UA 141 H9
Zacharo GR 174 E4
Zaclău RO 155 C2
Žacléř CZ 81 E9
Zaczopki PL 141 F8
Zadar HR 156 D3
Zadunayivka UA 154 F4
Zádveřice CZ 146 C5
Zadzim PL 142 C6
Zadzyezhzha BY 133 E4
Zafarraya E 53 C8
Zafferana Etnea I 59 D7
Zafirovo BG 161 F9
Zafra E 51 C7
Zafra de Záncara E 47 E7
Zafrilla E 47 D9
Žaga SLO 73 D7
Żagań PL 81 C8
Zăgar RO 152 E5
Žagarė LT 134 D6
Zagarise I 59 A10
Zagkliveri GR 169 C9
Žaglav HR 67 E11
Zagnańsk PL 143 E10
Zagon RO 153 F8
Zagora GR 169 F9
Zagorë AL 163 E8
Zagorje SLO 73 E9
Zagorje ob Savi SLO 73 D10
Zagórów PL 142 B4
Zagortsi BG 167 E8
Zagórz PL 145 D5
Zagra E 53 B8
Zagra RO 152 C4
Zagrazhden BG 160 F5
Zagrazhden BG 166 F3
Zagreb HR 148 E5
Zagrodno PL 81 D9
Žagrović HR 156 D5
Žagubica SRB 159 E8
Zagvozd HR 157 F7
Zagyvarékas H 150 C5
Zahara E 51 F9
Zahara de los Atunes E 52 D5
Zahinos E 51 C6
Zahna D 79 C12
Zahnitkiv UA 154 A3
Záhony H 145 G5
Záhorská Ves SK 77 F11
Zahor"ye BY 133 F5
Zăicani MD 153 B10
Zaiceva LV 133 B2
Zaidín E 42 D4
Žaiginys LT 134 F6
Zaim MD 154 D4
Zajas NMK 168 A4
Zaječar SRB 159 F9
Zaječí CZ 77 E11
Zaječov CZ 76 C5
Zajezierze PL 85 C9
Zákamenné SK 147 C8
Zákány H 149 D7
Zákányszek H 150 E4
Zakharnichy BY 133 E5
Zakliczyn PL 144 D2
Zaklików PL 144 B5
Zaklopača BIH 157 D11
Zakoma BIH 157 E10
Zakopane PL 147 C9
Zakros GR 179 E11
Zakrzew PL 141 H4
Zakrzewo PL 85 D12
Zakrzewo PL 138 E6
Zakrzówek-Wieś PL 144 B5
Zákupy CZ 81 E7
Zakynthos GR 174 D2
Zalaapáti H 149 C8
Zalaegerszeg H 149 C7
Zalakaros H 149 C8
Zalakomár H 149 C8
Zalalövő H 149 C7
Zalamea de la Serena E 51 B8
Zalamea la Real E 51 D6
Zalaszántó H 149 C8
Zalaszentbalázs H 149 C7
Zalaszentgrót H 149 C8
Zalaszentiván H 149 C7
Zalău RO 151 C11
Zalavár H 149 C8
Zalavas LT 137 D13
Załazy PL 141 H5
Zaldibar E 41 B6
Žalec SLO 73 D11
Zalenieki LV 134 C7
Zalesie PL 85 E13
Zalesie PL 141 F8
Zalesie Śląskie PL 142 F5
Zalesje LV 133 D4
Zales'ye RUS 136 D4
Zaleszany PL 144 B4
Zalewo PL 139 C8
Zalha RO 152 C3
Zālīte LV 135 C8
Zalivnoye RUS 136 D2
Zall-Dardhë AL 163 F9
Żalno PL 138 C4
Zalogovac SRB 159 F7
Zaltbommel NL 16 E4
Załuski PL 139 E10
Zalužje BIH 158 E3
Zalužnica HR 156 C3
Zalve LV 135 D10
Zalyessye BY 133 F3
Zalyessye BY 137 E13
Zam RO 151 E9
Zamárdi H 149 C9
Zamarte PL 85 C12
Žamberk CZ 77 B10
Zambrana E 40 C6
Zâmbreasca RO 160 E6
Zambrów PL 140 E6
Zambujal de Cima P 50 C1
Zambujeira do Mar P 50 D2
Zamjcin PL 85 D8
Zamfirovo BG 165 C7
Zamogil'ye RUS 132 D2
Zámoly H 149 B10
Zamora E 39 E8
Zamość PL 139 D12
Zamość PL 144 B7
Zamoshsha BY 133 F2
Zamostea RO 153 B8
Zams A 71 C11
Zámutov SK 145 F4
Zandhoven B 19 B10
Žandov CZ 80 E6
Zandvliet B 16 F2
Zandvoort NL 16 D3
Zănești RO 153 D9
Zaniemyśl PL 81 B12
Zante LV 134 C5
Zaorejas E 47 C8
Zaovine SRB 158 F3
Zapałów PL 144 C6
Zaplanik BIH 162 D5
Zaplyus'ye RUS 132 E6
Zăpodeni RO 153 D11
Zapolice PL 142 C6
Zapolyarnyy RUS 114 E9
Zapol'ye RUS 132 E2
Zaporozhskoye RUS 129 D14
Zappeio GR 169 F7
Zapponeta I 60 A5
Zaprešić HR 148 E5
Zapruddzye BY 133 F3
Zapytiv UA 144 D9
Zaragoza E 41 E10
Zărand RO 151 E8
Zarańsko PL 85 C9
Zarasai LT 135 E12
Zaratamo E 40 B6
Zaratán E 39 E10
Zarautz E 32 D1
Zarcilla de Ramos E 55 D9
Zarjby PL 139 D11
Zarjby-Kościelne PL 139 E13
Zarechcha BY 133 E7
Žarėnai LT 134 E4
Zaricheve UA 145 F6
Żarki PL 143 E7
Żarki Wielkie PL 81 C7
Zărnești RO 160 B6
Zărnești RO 161 C9
Žarnovica SK 147 D7
Żarnów PL 141 H2
Żarnowiec PL 143 F8
Zaronava BY 133 F7
Zaros GR 178 E8
Žarošice CZ 77 D11
Żarów PL 81 E10
Zarpen D 83 C9
Zarra E 47 F10
Zarren B 182 C1
Zarrentin D 83 C9
Zarszyn PL 145 D5
Żary PL 81 C8
Zarza Capilla E 51 B9
Zarza de Alange E 51 B7
Zarza de Granadilla E 45 D8
Zarza de Tajo E 47 D6
Zarzadilla de Totana E 55 D9
Zarza la Mayor E 45 E7
Zarzecze PL 144 D6
Zarzuela del Monte E 46 C4
Zarzuela del Pinar E 40 F3
Zas E 38 B2
Zasa LV 135 D11
Zaskarki BY 133 F5
Žaškov SK 147 C8
Žasliai LT 137 D10
Zásmuky CZ 77 C8
Zasów PL 143 F11
Zastražišće HR 157 F6
Žatec CZ 76 B5
Zaton HR 156 E4
Zaton HR 162 D5
Zátor CZ 142 F4
Zator PL 143 G7
Zatory PL 139 E11
Zătreni RO 160 D3
Zatyshshya UA 154 C5
Zaube LV 135 C10
Zau de Câmpie RO 152 D4
Zavadka UA 145 E7
Závadka nad Hronom SK 147 D9
Zavala BIH 162 D4
Zavala HR 157 F6
Zavalje BIH 156 C4
Zavallya UA 153 A11
Zavallya UA 154 A6
Zavattarello I 37 B10

Závažná Poruba SK 147 C9
Zaventem B 19 C9
Zavet BG 161 F9
Zavidovići BIH 157 D9
Zavlaka SRB 158 E3
Zăvoaia RO 161 D10
Závod SK 77 E12
Zăvoi RO 159 B9
Zavoj SRB 165 C6
Zavutstsye BY 133 F4
Zavyachellye BY 133 F5
Zavydovychi UA 144 D8
Zawada PL 81 C9
Zawada PL 141 G1
Zawada PL 142 E4
Zawada PL 143 E7
Zawada PL 144 B7
Zawady PL 140 D7
Zawadzkie PL 142 E5
Zawichost PL 144 B4
Zawidów PL 81 D8
Zawidz Kościelny PL 139 E8
Zawiercie PL 143 F7
Zawoja PL 147 B9
Zawonia PL 81 D12
Zaytsevo RUS 132 F4
Žažina HR 148 E6
Zázrivá SK 147 C8
Žažvic HR 156 E4
Zbąszyn PL 81 B9
Zbąszynek PL 81 B9
Zbehy SK 146 E6
Zberoaia MD 153 D12
Zbiczno PL 139 D7
Zbiersk PL 142 C5
Zbiroh CZ 76 C5
Zblewo PL 138 C5
Zbludowice PL 143 F10
Zbójna PL 139 D12
Zbójno PL 139 D7
Zborov SK 145 E3
Zborovice CZ 146 C4
Zborov nad Bystricou SK 147 C7
Zbraslav CZ 77 D10
Zbraslavice CZ 77 C8
Zbrzeźnica PL 140 D6
Zbuczyn Poduchowny PL 141 F6
Ždala HR 149 D8
Ždánice CZ 77 D12
Žďár CZ 77 A8
Žďár nad Sázavou CZ 77 C9
Zdenci HR 149 E9
Ždiar SK 145 E1
Zdice CZ 76 C5
Zdihovo HR 67 B11
Zdíkov CZ 76 D5
Ždírec nad Doubravou CZ 77 C9
Zdounky CZ 146 C4
Ždralovac BIH 157 E6
Zdravets BG 167 C9
Zdravinje SRB 164 C3
Ždrelac HR 156 D3
Ždrelo SRB 159 E8
Zdunje NMK 164 F3
Zduńska Wola PL 143 C6
Zduny PL 81 C12
Zduny PL 141 F1
Zdynia PL 145 E3
Zdziarzec PL 143 F11
Zdziechowa PL 85 E13
Zdzieszowice PL 142 F5
Zdziłowice PL 144 B6
Zębowice PL 142 E5
Žebrák CZ 76 C5
Zebreira P 45 E6
Zebrene LV 134 C5
Zebrzydowa PL 81 D8
Zechlinerhütte D 84 D3
Zeddam NL 183 B8
Zeddiani I 64 D2
Zedelgem B 19 B7
Zederhaus A 73 B8
Žednik SRB 150 F4
Żędowice PL 142 E6
Zeebrugge B 19 B7
Zeeland NL 16 E5
Zeewolde NL 183 A7
Zegama E 32 E1
Żegiestów PL 145 E2
Žegljane NMK 164 E4
Żegocina PL 144 D1
Zehdenick D 84 E4
Zehna D 83 C12
Žehra SK 145 F2
Zehren D 80 D4
Zeilarn D 76 F3
Žeimelis LT 135 D8
Žeimiai LT 135 F8
Zeiselmauer A 77 F10
Zeiskam D 187 C5
Zeist NL 16 D4
Zeithain D 80 D4
Zeitlofs D 74 B6
Zeitz D 79 D11
Zejmen AL 163 F8
Żelazków PL 142 C5
Zele B 19 B9
Żelechlinek PL 141 G2
Żelechów PL 141 G5
Zelena UA 152 A5
Zelena UA 152 B5
Zelena UA 153 A9
Zeleneč SK 146 E5
Zeleni Jadar BIH 158 E3
Zelenikovo BG 166 E4
Zelenikovo NMK 164 F4
Zelenogorsk RUS 129 E12
Zelenogradsk RUS 136 D1
Zelenohirs'ke UA 154 B6
Želetava CZ 77 D9
Železná Ruda CZ 76 D4
Železné SK 147 D8
Železnice CZ 77 B8
Železniki SLO 73 D9
Železný Brod CZ 81 E8
Zelhem NL 16 D6
Želiezovce SK 147 E7
Zelina HR 148 E6
Zelinja BIH 157 C9
Želino NMK 164 F3
Želiv CZ 77 C8
Željuša BIH 157 F8
Żelków-Kolonia PL 141 F6
Zell D 75 B10
Zell (Mosel) D 21 D8
Zella-Mehlis D 79 E8
Zell am Harmersbach D 27 D9
Zell am Main D 187 B8
Zell am See A 73 B6
Zell am Ziller A 72 B4
Zell im Wiesental D 27 E8
Zellingen D 74 C6
Zell-Pfarre A 73 D9
Zelmeņi LV 134 D6
Želovce SK 147 E8
Zelów PL 143 D7
Zeltingen-Rachtig D 21 E8
Zeltiņi LV 135 B13
Zeltweg A 73 B10
Želva LT 135 F10
Zelzate B 19 B8
Žemaičių Naumiestis LT 134 F3
Žemberovce SK 147 E7
Zemblak AL 168 C4
Zembrów PL 141 E6
Zembrzyce PL 147 B9
Zemen BG 165 E6
Zemeno GR 175 C6
Zemeș RO 153 D8
Zemianska Oľča SK 146 F5
Zemīte LV 134 C5
Zemitz D 84 C5
Zemmer D 21 E7
Zemné SK 146 F6
Zemplénagárd H 145 G5
Zemplínske Hámre SK 145 F5
Zemst B 19 C9
Zemun SRB 158 D5
Zenica BIH 157 D8
Zennor GB 12 E3
Zentene LV 134 B5
Žepa BIH 157 E11
Žepče BIH 157 D9
Žeravice CZ 146 C4
Zerbst D 79 C11
Zerf D 21 E7
Zerind RO 151 D8
Żerków PL 142 B4
Zernez CH 71 D10
Zernien D 83 D9
Zernitz D 83 E12
Zero Branco I 72 E5
Zerpenschleuse D 84 E5
Zerrenthin D 84 D6
Zestoa E 32 D1
Žetale SLO 148 D5
Zetea RO 152 E6
Zetel D 17 B9
Zet'ovo BG 166 E4
Zeulenroda D 79 E10
Zeven D 17 B12
Zevenaar NL 16 E6
Zevenbergen NL 16 E3
Zevgolatio GR 175 D6
Zevio I 66 B3
Zeytinalani TR 181 C9
Zeytinbağı TR 173 D10
Zeytindağ TR 177 B9
Zeytineli TR 177 C8
Zeytinli TR 173 E6
Zeytinliova TR 177 B10
Zgierz PL 143 C7
Zgłobice PL 143 G10
Zgornje Bitnje SLO 73 D9
Zgornje Jezersko SLO 73 D9
Zgornji Duplek SLO 148 C5
Zgorzelec PL 81 D8
Zgropolci NMK 169 A6
Zgurița MD 153 A11
Zhabinka BY 141 F10
Zhabokrychka UA 154 A3
Zhdeniyevo UA 145 F7
Zhegër RKS 164 E3
Zheleznodorozhnyy RUS 136 E3
Zhelyazkovo BG 167 E8
Zhelyu Voyvoda BG 167 D6
Zheravna BG 167 D6
Zhilino RUS 136 D4
Zhitkovo RUS 129 D11
Zhitnitsa BG 167 C9
Zhitom AL 168 C2
Zhodzishki BY 137 D13
Zhorany UA 141 H9
Zhovka UA 144 C8
Zhovtantsi UA 144 D9
Zhovtneve UA 144 B9
Zhovtneve UA 155 B3
Zhovty Yar UA 154 F5
Zhuprany BY 137 E13
Zhur RKS 164 E2
Zhvyrka UA 144 C9
Zhydachiv UA 145 E9
Zhyrmuny BY 137 E11
Žiar nad Hronom SK 147 D7
Zibalai LT 137 C10
Zibello I 66 B1
Zibreira P 44 F3
Zicavo F 37 H10
Žichovice CZ 76 D5
Zickhusen D 83 C10
Zidani Most SLO 73 D11
Zidarovo BG 167 E8
Židikai LT 134 D4
Židlochovice CZ 77 D11
Ziduri RO 161 C10
Ziębice PL 81 E12
Ziedkalne LV 134 D6
Ziegelroda D 79 D9
Ziegendorf D 83 D11
Ziegenrück D 79 E10
Ziegra D 80 D4
Zieleniewo PL 85 B9
Zieleniewo PL 85 D9
Zielitz D 79 B10
Zielkowice PL 141 F2
Zielona PL 139 D8
Zielona Chocina PL 85 C12
Zielona Góra PL 81 C9
Zielona Góra PL 85 E11
Zielonka PL 139 F11
Zielonki PL 143 F8
Zieluń PL 139 D8
Ziemeri LV 131 F14
Ziemnice Wielkie PL 142 E4
Ziemupe LV 134 C2
Zierenberg D 17 F12
Zierikzee NL 16 E1
Ziersdorf A 77 E9
Zierzow D 83 D11
Ziesar D 79 B11
Žiežmariai LT 137 D9
Žigljen HR 67 C10
Zīguri LV 133 B3
Žihárec SK 146 E5
Žihle CZ 76 B4
Zilaiskalns LV 131 F10
Žilina SK 147 C7
Žilinai LT 137 E10
Zillis CH 71 D8
Ziltendorf D 81 B7
Zilupe LV 133 D4
Zimandu Nou RO 151 E7
Zimbor RO 151 C11
Zimmersrode (Neuental) D 21 B12
Zimnicea RO 160 F6
Zimnitsa BG 167 D7
Žindaičiai LT 134 F5
Zingst D 83 B13
Zinkgruvan S 92 B6
Zinnowitz D 84 B5
Ziras LV 134 B3
Zirc H 149 B9
Zirchow D 84 C6
Žiri SLO 73 D9
Zirndorf D 75 D8
Zîrnești MD 154 E2
Zirņi LV 134 C4
Ziros GR 179 E11
Žirovnice CZ 77 D8
Zistersdorf A 77 E11
Žitište SRB 158 C6
Žitkovac SRB 164 B4
Žitni Potok SRB 164 C4
Žitomislići BIH 157 F8
Žitorađa SRB 164 C4
Žitoše NMK 168 B5
Zitsa GR 168 E4
Zittau D 81 E7
Zitz D 79 B11
Živaja HR 157 B6
Živinice BIH 157 D10
Živogošće HR 157 F7
Žiželice CZ 77 B8
Zizers CH 71 D9
Zizurkil E 32 D1
Zlarin HR 156 E4
Zlata SRB 164 C4
Zlatar BG 167 C7
Zlatar HR 148 D6
Zlatar-Bistrica HR 148 D6
Zlataritsa BG 166 C5
Zlaté Hory CZ 142 F3
Zlaté Klasy SK 146 E4
Zlaté Moravce SK 146 E6
Zlaten Rog BG 159 E10
Zlatitsa BG 165 D9
Zlatna RO 151 E11
Zlatna Panega BG 165 C9
Zlatograd BG 171 B8
Zlatokop SRB 164 D4
Zławieś Wielka PL 138 D5
Žlebič SLO 73 E10
Žleby CZ 77 C8
Zlēkas LV 134 B3
Zletovo NMK 164 F5
Žlibinai LT 134 E4
Zlín CZ 146 C5
Zliv CZ 76 D6
Žljebovi BIH 157 D10
Zllakuqan RKS 164 D2
Złocieniec PL 85 C10
Złoczew PL 142 D6
Zlokuchene BG 165 E8
Zlonice CZ 76 B6
Złota PL 141 G2
Złota PL 143 F10
Złotniki Kujawskie PL 138 E5
Złotoryja PL 81 D9
Złotów PL 85 D12
Złoty Stok PL 77 B11
Zlozela BIH 157 D7
Žlutice CZ 76 B4
Zmajevac BIH 156 C5
Zmajevac HR 149 E11
Zmajevo SRB 158 C4
Zmeyovo BG 166 E5
Żmigród PL 81 D11
Zmijavci HR 157 F7
Žminj HR 67 B8
Żmudź PL 144 A8
Znamensk RUS 136 D3
Żnin PL 138 E4
Znojmo CZ 77 E10
Zoagli I 37 C10
Zöblitz D 80 E4
Zoelen NL 183 B6
Zoersel B 16 F3
Zoetermeer NL 16 D2
Zofingen CH 27 F8
Zogno I 69 B8
Zografou GR 175 D8
Zola Predosa I 66 C3
Zolder B 19 B11
Zoldo Alto I 72 D5
Żółkiewka-Osada PL 144 B6
Zölkow D 83 C11
Zollikofen CH 31 A11
Zollikon CH 27 F10
Zolotkovychi UA 144 D6
Żółtnica PL 85 C11
Żołynia PL 144 C5
Zomba H 149 D11
Zomergem B 19 B8
Zonhoven B 19 C11
Zoni GR 171 A10
Zoniana GR 178 E8
Zonnebeke B 18 C6
Zonza F 37 H10
Żórawina PL 81 E12
Zörbig D 79 C11
Zorita E 45 F9
Zorita del Maestrazgo E 42 F3
Zorleni RO 153 E11
Zorlențu Mare RO 159 C8
Zorneding D 75 F10
Zornheim D 21 E10
Zörnigal D 79 C12
Zornitsa BG 167 C9
Zornitsa BG 167 E7
Żory PL 142 F6
Zossen D 80 B4
Zottegem B 19 C8
Zoutkamp NL 16 B6
Zoutleeuw B 183 D6
Zovi Do BIH 157 F9
Zovka RUS 132 E4
Zreče SLO 148 D4
Zrenjanin SRB 158 C5
Zrin HR 156 B5
Zrinski Topolovac HR 149 D7
Zrmanja Vrelo HR 156 D5
Zrnovci NMK 164 F5
Zruč CZ 76 C4
Zruč nad Sázavou CZ 77 C8
Zsadány H 151 D7
Zsáka H 151 C7
Zsámbék H 149 A11
Zsámbok H 150 B4
Zsana H 150 E4
Zschaitz D 80 D4
Zscherben D 79 D10
Zschopau D 80 E4
Zschortau D 79 D11
Zsombó H 150 E4
Zuberec SK 147 C9
Zubia E 53 B9
Zubiaur E 40 B6
Zubići BIH 157 D8
Zubiena I 68 C5
Zubieta E 32 D1
Zubieta E 32 D2
Zubin Potok RKS 164 D2
Zubiri E 32 E2
Zubří CZ 146 C6
Zubrohlava SK 147 C9
Żubrów PL 81 B8
Žuć SRB 164 C3
Zucaina E 48 D4
Zuchwil CH 27 F8
Zudaire E 32 E1
Zudar D 84 B4
Zuera E 41 E10
Zufre E 51 D7
Zug CH 27 F10
Zuhatzu-Kuartango E 40 C6
Zuheros E 53 A8
Zuid-Beijerland NL 182 B4
Zuidhorn NL 16 B6
Zuidland NL 182 B4
Zuidlaren NL 17 B7
Zuidwolde NL 17 C6
Zuienkerke B 182 C2
Zújar E 55 D7
Żuków PL 141 F2
Żuków PL 141 G8
Żukowice PL 81 C9
Żukowo PL 138 B5
Žuljana HR 162 D3
Žulová CZ 77 B12
Zülpich D 21 C7
Zulte B 19 C7
Zumaia E 32 D1
Zumarraga E 32 D1
Zundert NL 16 F3
Zungri I 59 B8
Zunzarren E 32 E3
Zuoz CH 71 D9
Županja HR 157 B10
Zūras LV 134 B3
Zúrgena E 55 E8
Zürich CH 27 F10
Zurndorf A 77 G12
Zürnevo BG 161 F10
Żuromin PL 139 D8
Zurow D 83 C11
Zusmarshausen D 75 F8
Züsow D 83 C11
Züssow D 84 C5
Žuta Lokva HR 67 C11
Žutautai LT 134 E2
Zutendaal B 19 C12
Zutphen NL 16 D6
Žužemberk SLO 73 E10
Zveçan RKS 164 D2
Zvejniekciems LV 135 B8
Zverino BG 165 C8
Zvezdë AL 168 C4
Zvezdel BG 171 B8
Zvezdets BG 167 E8
Zvolen SK 147 D8
Zvolenská Slatina SK 147 D8
Zvonce SRB 164 D6
Zvoriștea RO 153 B8
Zvornik BIH 157 D11
Zwartemeer NL 17 C8
Zwartsluis NL 16 C6
Zweeloo NL 17 C7
Zweibrücken D 21 F8
Zweisimmen CH 31 B11
Zwenkau D 79 D11
Zwethau D 80 C4
Zwettl A 77 E8
Zwevegem B 19 C7
Zwevezele B 182 C2
Zwickau D 79 E12
Zwiefalten D 27 D11
Zwierzyn PL 85 E9
Zwierzyniec PL 144 B6
Zwiesel D 76 D4
Zwijndrecht B 19 B9
Zwijndrecht NL 16 E3
Zwinge D 79 C7
Zwingen CH 27 F8
Zwingenberg D 21 E11
Zwochau D 79 D11
Zwoleń PL 141 H5
Zwolle NL 16 C6
Zwönitz D 79 E12
Zwota D 75 B11
Zyabki BY 133 F4
Zyal'ki BY 133 E4
Zyalyonka BY 133 E5
Żychlin PL 143 B8
Żydowo PL 85 B11
Żydowo PL 85 F13
Žygaičiai LT 134 F4
Zygos GR 171 B6
Zygry PL 143 C6
Žyniai LT 134 F2
Żyraków PL 143 F11
Żyrardów PL 141 F2
Żyrzyn PL 141 H6
Żytkiejmy PL 136 E6
Żytniów PL 142 D6
Żytno PL 143 E8
Żywiec PL 147 B8
Żywocice PL 142 F4

Æ

Ærøskøbing DK 86 F6

Ø

Ødis DK 86 E4
Ødsted DK 86 D4
Øie N 105 B12
Økdal N 101 A12
Øksfjord N 112 C9
Øksnes N 110 C8
Øksneshamn N 110 D9
Ølen N 94 C3
Ølgod DK 86 D3
Ølholm DK 86 D5
Ølsted DK 86 D5
Ølsted DK 87 D10
Ølstykke DK 87 D10
Ønslev DK 83 A11
Øra N 112 C8
Ørbæk DK 86 E7
Ørgenvika N 95 B11
Ørjavik N 104 F2
Ørje N 96 D6
Ørnes N 108 C6
Ørnhøj DK 86 C3
Ørslev DK 87 E9
Ørsnes N 100 A5
Ørsta N 100 B4
Ørsted DK 86 C6
Ørting DK 86 D6
Ørum DK 86 C5
Ørum DK 86 C7
Øsby DK 86 E5
Østbirk DK 86 D5
Østby N 91 A9
Østby N 102 D4
Østengård DK 86 D4
Øster Assels DK 86 B3
Øster Bjerregrav DK 86 C5
Øster Brønderslev DK 86 A5
Østerby DK 86 A5
Øster Hornum DK 86 B5
Øster Hurup DK 86 B6
Øster Højst DK 86 E4
Østerild DK 86 A3
Øster Jølby DK 86 B3
Østerlars DK 89 E7
Øster Lindet DK 86 E4
Østermarie DK 89 E8
Øster Tørslev DK 86 B6
Øster Ulslev DK 83 A11
Øster Vedsted DK 86 E3
Østervrå DK 90 E7
Øster Vrøgum DK 86 D2
Østese N 94 B4
Østrup DK 86 B4
Øverbygd N 111 C17
Øvergard N 111 B18
Øvre Alta N 113 D11
Øvre Kildal N 112 D7
Øvrella N 95 C10
Øvre Rendal N 101 C14
Øvre Årdal N 100 D7
Øvre Åstbru N 101 D13
Øyangen N 104 E7
Øydegarden N 104 E4
Øyenkilen N 91 A8
Øyer N 101 D12
Øyeren N 96 B7
Øyjord N 108 B9
Øynes N 108 B9
Øynes N 111 C11
Øyslebø N 90 C2
Øyvatnet N 111 C12

Å

Å N 104 F7
Å N 110 E4
Å N 111 B12
Å N 111 C13
Åberget S 109 E18
Åbo S 103 C10
Åbodarna S 107 E14
Åbogen N 96 B7
Åbosjö S 107 D13
Åby S 89 A7
Åby S 93 B8
Åbyen DK 90 D7
Åbyggeby S 103 E13
Åbyn S 118 D6
Åbytorp S 92 A6
Ådalsliden S 107 E11
Ådum DK 86 D3
Åfarnes N 100 A7
Åfjord N 104 D8
Åfoss N 90 A6
Ågerup DK 87 D10
Ågotnes N 94 B2
Ågskaret N 108 C5
Åheim N 100 B3
Åhus S 88 D6
Åkarp S 87 D12
Åkerbränna S 107 D11
Åkerby S 99 B9
Åkerholmen S 118 C6
Åkersberga S 99 D10
Åkers styckebruk S 98 D8
Åkerstrømmen N 101 C14
Åknes N 110 C9
Åkran N 105 D12
Åkrehamn N 94 D2
Åkullsjön S 118 F5
Åkvisslan S 107 E13
Ål N 101 E9
Ålberga S 93 B9
Ålbo S 98 B7
Ålbæk DK 90 D7
Åle DK 86 D5
Åled S 87 B11
Ålem S 89 B10
Ålen N 101 A14
Ålesund N 100 B4
Ålgnäs S 103 D12
Ålgård N 94 E3
Ålhult S 92 D7
Ålloluokta S 109 B17
Ålmo N 104 E4
Ålsrode DK 87 C7
Ålstad N 110 E9
Ålund S 118 D6
Ålvik N 94 B4
Ålvund N 101 A9
Ålvundeid N 101 A9
Ålåsen S 106 D7
Åmdals Verk N 95 D8
Åminne FIN 122 E7
Åminne S 87 A14
Åmland N 94 F5
Åmli N 90 A3
Åmli N 90 B3
Åmmeberg S 92 B6
Åmot N 94 C7
Åmot N 95 B11
Åmot N 95 C8
Åmot N 95 C11
Åmot S 103 E11
Åmotfors S 96 C7
Åmsele S 107 B16
Åmsosen N 94 D3
Åmynnet S 107 E15
Åmål S 91 A12
Åmål S 91 B12
Åmøyhamn N 108 C5
Åna-Sira N 94 F4
Åndalsnes N 100 A7
Åneby N 95 B13
Ånes N 104 E4
Ånge S 103 A10
Ånge S 109 E14
Ångelsberg S 97 C15
Ångersjö S 102 C8
Ånn S 105 E13
Ånstad N 110 C8
Ånsvik N 109 B9
Ånäset S 118 F6
Årbostad N 111 C13
Årby DK 87 D8
Årbyn S 118 C8
Årdal N 100 C4
Årdalstangen N 100 D7
Åre S 105 E14
Årfor N 105 B11
Årgård N 105 C10
Århult S 89 A10
Årjäng S 96 D7
Årnes N 95 B14
Årnes N 104 F5
Årnes N 111 B15
Årnäs S 91 B14
Åros N 95 C12
Årosjåkk S 111 E17
Årre DK 86 D3
Årrenjarka S 109 C15
Årsandøy N 105 A12
Årsdale DK 89 E8
Årset N 105 A11
Årslev DK 86 E6
Årstein N 111 C14
Årsunda S 98 A7
Årvik N 100 B3
Årviksand N 112 C6
Årvågen N 104 E5
Åryd S 89 B7
Åryd S 89 C8
Årøybukta N 111 A19
Årøysund N 90 A7
Ås N 95 C13
Ås N 105 E11
Ås S 96 C7
Ås S 97 C12
Ås S 106 E7
Ås S 107 E11
Åsa N 95 B12
Åsa S 91 E11
Åsan N 105 B12
Åsarna S 102 A7
Åsby S 87 A10
Åse N 111 B10
Åsebyn S 96 D7
Åseda S 89 A8
Åsegg N 105 C9
Åsele S 107 C12
Åselet S 118 D4
Åsen N 105 D10
Åsen S 102 C7
Åsen S 102 D6
Åsen S 106 E7
Åsen S 109 E16
Åsenbruk S 91 B11
Åseral N 90 B1
Åshammar S 103 E12
Åskilje S 107 B13
Åskogen S 118 C7
Åsli N 101 E11
Åsljunga S 87 C12
Åsmansbo S 97 B13
Åsmarka N 101 D13
Åsskard N 104 E5
Åsta N 101 D14
Åstan N 104 E7
Åsteby S 97 B9
Åstorp S 87 C11
Åstrand S 97 B9
Återvänningen S 103 A13
Åtorp S 92 A4
Åträsk S 118 B7
Åträsk S 118 D5
Åttonträsk S 107 C14
Åtvidaberg S 92 C7
Åva FIN 126 E5
Åvestbo S 97 C14
Åvist FIN 122 D9

Ä

Äetsä FIN 126 C8
Ähtäri FIN 123 E12
Ähtärinranta FIN 123 E12
Äijäjoki FIN 116 B10
Äijälä FIN 123 E16
Äkäsjokisuu FIN 117 D11
Äkäslompolo FIN 117 C12
Älandsbro S 103 A14
Älgarås S 92 B4
Älgered S 103 B12
Älghult S 89 A9
Älmestad S 91 D13
Älmhult S 88 B6
Älmsta S 99 C11
Älta S 99 D10
Älvdalen S 102 D7
Älvho S 102 D8
Älvkarleby S 103 E13
Älvkarleö S 99 A8
Älvros S 102 B8
Älvsbyn S 118 C6
Älvsered S 87 A11
Älvängen S 91 D11
Ämmälänkylä FIN 123 E9
Ämmänsaari FIN 121 E12
Ämådalen S 102 D8
Äng S 92 D5
Änge S 105 E16
Ängebo S 103 C11
Ängelholm S 87 C11
Ängersjö S 122 C3
Ängesleva FIN 119 E15
Ängesträsk S 118 B8
Ängesån S 116 E8
Ängom S 103 B13
Äppelbo S 97 B11
Ärla S 98 D7
Ärnäs S 102 D5
Ärnäs S 102 E5
Ärtled S 103 E9
Ärtrik S 107 E11
Äsarp S 91 C14
Äsbacka S 103 D11
Äsköping S 92 A8
Ässjö S 103 B12
Ätran S 87 A11
Äyskoski FIN 123 D17
Äystö FIN 122 F7
Äänekoski FIN 123 E15

Ö

Öckerö S 91 D10
Ödeborg S 91 B10
Ödeshog S 92 C5
Ödkarby FIN 99 B13
Ödsmål S 91 C10
Ödåkra S 87 C11
Öja FIN 123 C9
Öja S 93 E12
Öjarn S 106 D8
Öje S 102 E6
Öjebyn S 118 D6
Öjeforsen S 103 B9
Öjingsvallen S 103 C8
Öjung S 103 C10
Öksajärvi S 116 C8
Öllölä FIN 125 F15
Ölmbrotorp S 97 D13
Ölme S 97 D11
Ölsboda S 92 A4
Ömossa FIN 122 F7
Önnestad S 88 C6
Önningby FIN 99 B14
Öratjärn S 103 C10
Öravan S 107 B14
Öravattnet S 106 E9
Örbyhus S 99 B9
Örbäck S 97 C15
Örebro S 97 D13
Örebäcken S 102 C4
Öregrund S 99 B10
Öreström S 107 C16
Öretjändalen S 103 A10
Örkelljunga S 87 C12
Örnsköldsvik S 107 E15
Örnäsudden S 109 E13
Örsbäck S 107 D17
Örserum S 92 C5
Örsjö S 89 B9
Örsundsbro S 99 C8
Örträsk S 107 C15
Örviken S 118 E6
Ösmo S 93 B11
Östa S 98 B7
Östanfjärden S 119 C10
Östansjö S 92 A5
Östansjö S 109 E16
Östanskär S 103 A13
Östanvik S 103 D9
Östanå S 88 C6
Östavall S 103 B9
Östbjörka S 103 E9
Östby S 107 D13
Österbybruk S 99 B9
Österbymo S 92 D6
Österede S 107 E11
Österforse S 107 E12
Österfärnebo S 98 B7
Östergarn S 93 E13
Östergraninge S 107 F12
Österhankmo FIN 122 D7
Österjörn S 118 D4
Österlisa S 99 C11
Östermark FIN 126 E8
Östernoret S 107 C12
Östero FIN 122 D8
Österskucku S 102 A8
Östersund S 106 E7
Östersundom FIN 127 E13
Östervåla S 98 B8
Österås S 107 E12
Östhammar S 99 B10
Östloning S 103 A13
Östmark S 97 B8
Östmarkum S 107 E14
Östnor S 102 D7
Östra Ed S 93 C9
Östra Frölunda S 91 E13
Östra Granberg S 118 C4
Östra Grevie S 87 E12
Östra Husby S 93 B9
Östra Ljungby S 87 C12
Östra Lovsjön S 106 D7
Östra Löa S 97 C13
Östra Ormsjö S 107 C10
Östra Ryd S 93 C8
Östra Skrämträsk S 118 E5
Östra Stugusjö S 103 A9
Östra Sönnarslöv S 88 D6
Östra Vemmerlöv S 88 E6
Östra Yttermark FIN 122 E6
Östra Åliden S 118 D4
Överammer S 107 E9
Överberg S 102 B7
Överbyn S 103 C12
Överhogdal S 102 B8
Överhörnäs S 107 E15
Överissjö S 107 C13
Överkalix S 119 B9
Överlida S 91 E12
Överlännäs S 107 E13
Övermalax FIN 122 E7
Övermark FIN 122 E6
Övermorjärv S 118 B9
Övernäs S 109 D14
Överstbyn S 118 B7
Övertorneå S 119 B11
Överturingen S 102 B8
Övertänger S 103 E10
Överum S 93 D8
Överäng S 105 D14
Överö FIN 99 B15
Öv Långträsk S 109 E16
Övra S 107 D11
Övre Bredåker S 118 C6
Övre Fläsjön S 118 B7
Övre-Konäs S 105 D14
Övre Soppero S 116 B7
Övre Tväråsel S 118 C5
Övsjöbyn S 107 E9
Öxabäck S 91 E12

i-SPY

Collins

Look around you and discover the world with i-SPY

i-SPY At the shops
What can you spot?

i-SPY Birds
What can you spot?

i-SPY Butterflies and moths
What can you spot?

i-SPY Creepy crawlies
What can you spot?

i-SPY Dogs
What can you spot?

i-SPY Garden birds
What can you spot?

i-SPY In the city
What can you spot?

i-SPY In the countryside
What can you spot?

i-SPY Wild flowers
What can you spot?

Spy it
up to 200 fun things to spot around you

Spot it
tick off what you see as you go

Score it
score points for each spot and receive
your super-spotter certificate and badge!

co.uk/i-SPY

f facebook.com/collins4parents

What can you spot?

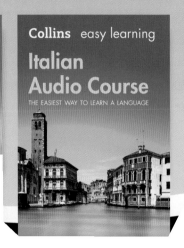
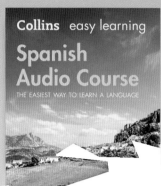

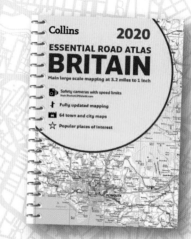
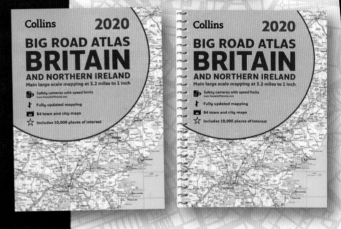
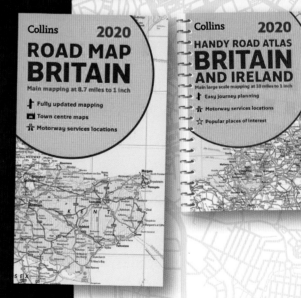